The United States Healthcare System

The United States Healthcare System

Overview, Driving Forces, and Outlook for the Future

Stephen L. Wagner

AUPHA

Health Administration Press, Chicago, Illinois

Association of University Programs in Health Administration, Washington, DC

Your board, staff, or clients may also benefit from this book's insight. For information on quantity discounts, contact the Health Administration Press Marketing Manager at (312) 424-9450.

This publication is intended to provide accurate and authoritative information in regard to the subject matter covered. It is sold, or otherwise provided, with the understanding that the publisher is not engaged in rendering professional services. If professional advice or other expert assistance is required, the services of a competent professional should be sought.

The statements and opinions contained in this book are strictly those of the author and do not represent the official positions of the American College of Healthcare Executives, the Foundation of the American College of Healthcare Executives, or the Association of University Programs in Health Administration.

25 24 23 22 21   5 4 3 2

Library of Congress Cataloging-in-Publication Data

Names: Wagner, Stephen L., 1951– author. | Association of University
  Programs in Health Administration, issuing body.
Title: The United States healthcare system : overview, driving forces, and
  outlook for the future / Stephen L. Wagner.
Description: Chicago, Illinois : Health Administration Press ; Washington,
  DC : Association of University Programs in Health Administration, [2021]
  | Includes bibliographical references and index. | Summary: "This book
  aims to provide a broad understanding of the healthcare system of the
  United States, with attention to its origins, development, and future"—
  Provided by publisher.
Identifiers: LCCN 2020001236 (print) | LCCN 2020001237 (ebook) | ISBN
  9781640551657 (hardcover ; alk. paper) | ISBN 9781640551664 (ebook) |
  ISBN 9781640551671 (xml) | ISBN 9781640551688 (mobi) | ISBN
  9781640551695 (epub)
Subjects: MESH: Delivery of Health Care | Health Policy | Quality of Health
  Care | Economics, Medical | Attitude to Health | Health Care Sector |
  United States
Classification: LCC RA412.2 (print) | LCC RA412.2 (ebook) | NLM W 84 AA1
  | DDC 368.38/200973—dc23
LC record available at https://lccn.loc.gov/2020001236
LC ebook record available at https://lccn.loc.gov/2020001237

Acquisitions editor: Janet Davis; Project manager: Michael Noren; Cover designer: James Slate; Layout: Integra

Found an error or a typo? We want to know! Please e-mail it to hapbooks@ache.org, mentioning the book's title and putting "Book Error" in the subject line.

For photocopying and copyright information, please contact Copyright Clearance Center at www.copyright.com or at (978) 750-8400.

Health Administration Press
A division of the Foundation of the American
  College of Healthcare Executives
300 S. Riverside Plaza, Suite 1900
Chicago, IL 60606-6698
(312) 424-2800

Association of University Programs
  in Health Administration
1730 M Street, NW
Suite 407
Washington, DC 20036
(202) 763-7283

Thanks to my family: Cindy, Matthew, Elizabeth, and Charles. Thanks especially to my wife, Cindy, for her support during this project and over the past 46 years of our lives together. Our son Matthew passed away in December 2019 after lifelong illnesses that began at birth. He inspired me to have a deep passion for healthcare and to work throughout my career to make our healthcare system better.

This book is also dedicated to the students who, I hope, will lead our healthcare system on a more equitable and sustainable path. It is my hope that this book provides insight and inspiration to develop the courage and the skills required to make the changes we need.

BRIEF CONTENTS

DETAILED CONTENTS

ACKNOWLEDGMENTS

I would like to acknowledge the assistance of Elizabeth A. Wagner, PhD, in the preparation of this manuscript. Her technical writing experience and her insight into teaching were greatly appreciated as this book was created.

Chapter 12 was written by Charles Stephen Wagner, a PhD candidate in the Department of Plant and Microbial Biology at the Plants for Human Health Institute at North Carolina State University. The focus of his research is the preclinical pharmacological characterization of botanicals and natural products related to metabolic, gastrointestinal, and infectious disease. He manages the Mobile Discovery citizen science program aimed at discovering novel antimicrobials from natural sources. Currently, he is finishing his doctoral thesis, entitled *Evidence Based Validation of Botanical Interventions from Scotland and Wales.*

PREFACE

This textbook has been written to guide the reader and the student of healthcare administration to develop a broad understanding of the healthcare system of the United States, with attention to its origins, its development, and its future.

The US healthcare system is incredibly complex, and it has been the subject of countless articles and books. Compared to many other works, this book focuses less on the data and specific details of the system's various elements and more on the system's history, its driving forces, and its overall direction. This approach has been taken in part because the data and details change constantly; furthermore, much of that information is covered in more specialized areas of the healthcare administration curriculum (e.g., finance, accounting, public health), where other textbooks can go into greater depth than this book can.

From my perspective, understanding the nature of the US healthcare system, knowing its history and transformation, and assessing its outlook for the years ahead is much more important than keeping up with the ever-shifting facts and figures. Take, for example, the rapidly increasing cost of our system. Does it really matter whether healthcare spending represents 17.9 percent of the country's gross domestic product or 18 percent? Probably not. What matters is that we understand the implications of an industry that consumes nearly 20 percent of the country's economy—in other words, one of every five dollars spent across the United States.

This book covers a broad range of topics. It looks at the development of the US healthcare system as a reflection of American beliefs and values; the various organizations, providers, and other entities that are involved in the delivery of care; healthcare economics and financing approaches; efforts to ensure quality and patient safety; and emerging technologies and directions for the future. The book also provides resources to help the reader dive more deeply into specific areas that may be of interest or assigned as part of coursework. By helping the reader locate the newest data and details at the time of the assignment or research, this book has an enduring usefulness.

Healthcare issues are often the subject of great controversy and competing viewpoints and priorities. Individuals interested in healthcare administration should consider their own positions carefully and independently, and they should avoid being overly biased by any one point of view. They should develop their own views based on a wide array of facts, stories, and evidence. Helping the reader do just that—to think deeply about these complex and often confusing issues—is a central goal of this book.

We must look at the impact our healthcare system has on people, and we must tell those people's stories, much as journalists do. Stories can highlight the importance of an issue more effectively than a simple collection of facts can. John Adams once said, "Facts are stubborn things," but people's minds can be even more stubborn (US National Archives 2019). To change people's minds, make the material relevant and personal.

This book is based on a variety of sources, including academic journals, government and other websites, newspapers, magazines, healthcare organizations, and advocacy groups. People interested in the US healthcare system and related issues need to understand that literally millions of pieces of information are available to them from a diverse range of sources. They should not be limited to a few select points of view or sources of information; rather, they should cast a wide net to gain the best insight and understanding into the system. Remember: Bias is everywhere. No source is immune from it, so read and think critically. Above all, keep an open mind.

A quote commonly attributed to Albert Einstein states, "It has become appallingly obvious that our technology has exceeded our humanity." Let's never forget why we learn and do what we do: We do it for the patients. As new generations of healthcare leaders and professionals become armed with a greater depth and breadth of knowledge, new solutions can be found to the intractable healthcare problems that our country has faced for more than a century. At the same time, however, managing the plethora of new technologies will be an ever-increasing challenge. We are probably inventing and developing new treatments for disease and injury faster than we can know how to appropriately use them and finance them. We have built a massive healthcare machine that focuses on treatment but not well-being; this book will explore the implications of that focus.

Moving from a healthcare system to a system of health must be a goal for the future. All stakeholders—patients, payers, providers, governments, and other institutions—need to work together to develop an optimum health and healthcare solution that will improve the lives of everyone in our country and do so at a cost the country can afford.

Once you stop learning, you start dying.
—Albert Einstein

Instructor Resources

This book's Instructor Resources include presentation PowerPoints, PowerPoints of the book's exhibits, answer guides to the in-book discussion questions, and essay/short-answer questions.

For the most up-to-date information about this book and its Instructor Resources, go to ache.org/HAP and search for the book's title, author name, or order code, 24101.

This book's Instructor Resources are available to instructors who adopt this book for use in their course. For access information, please email hapbooks@ache.org.

Reference

US National Archives. 2019. "Adams' Argument for the Defense: 3–4 December 1770." Accessed September 12. https://founders.archives.gov/documents/Adams/05-03-02-0001-0004-0016.

INTRODUCTION AND OVERVIEW OF THE UNITED STATES HEALTHCARE SYSTEM

> America's health care system is neither healthy, caring, nor a system.
> —Walter Cronkite

Learning Objectives

- Understand the general characteristics that differentiate the US healthcare system from the health systems of other countries.
- Evaluate the "conundrum" of cost, quality, and access.
- Understand the forces acting on the US healthcare system.
- Identify areas where the United States leads and where it lags other countries in healthcare.
- Recognize the major sources of concern about the US healthcare system.
- Understand the payment system used for healthcare in the United States.

Exhibit 1.1 presents the basis for the structure of this book. The aim of our healthcare system is to provide high-quality healthcare that leads to better health for our population. This effort requires optimizing the relationship between cost, equitable access, and quality of care in the context of what is best for patients. We also must consider the experience of the providers of care, who face tremendous pressure and high levels of stress (Bodenheimer and Sinsky 2014). This book will explore several specific areas that require the focus of our healthcare system, shown on the right-hand side of the exhibit.

We will begin our journey by considering some general aspects of our system, framed in the context of the Triple Aim. Developed by the Institute for Healthcare Improvement (IHI), the Triple Aim seeks to reduce per capita costs, improve the experience of care, and improve the health of populations (Berwick, Nolan, and Whittington 2008; IHI 2019). In pursuit of these aims, the US healthcare system must seek to balance the following:

1. *A per capita cost that is under control.* Overall costs, in absolute terms, will rise as our population grows. However, costs on a per person basis should rise more modestly or even decrease.

EXHIBIT 1.1
Areas of Focus
for This Book

The Aim of the Healthcare System

Issues That Require Our Attention

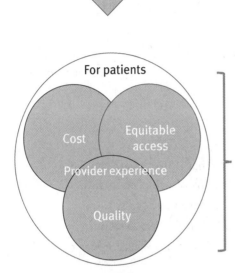

- Nature of our complex system
- Historical issues that have influenced the development of the system
- Beliefs and attitudes about health and healthcare
- Comparison with other developed countries
- Components of our healthcare system
- People and providers
- Patient care—the purpose of the system
- Financing a massive system
- Quality—easier said than done
- Medical and information technology
- The pharmaceutical industry
- Complementary and alternative medicine
- Politics/economics
- The future of the system

2. *Improved patient experience*. For healthcare organizations, a positive patient experience—reflecting both quality and satisfaction—provides a competitive advantage. It can also improve patients' compliance with medical advice—after all, if patients are satisfied with their provider, they are more likely to do what the provider says (Dias-Barbosa et al. 2012). Better healthcare outcomes require a focus on population health, as opposed to simply individual health.

3. *Access to healthcare that is fair and equitable.*

Healthcare is an excellent barometer of our society at large. Consider that there is virtually no aspect of our society's social problems, or the human enterprise in general, that does not wind up in the healthcare system (Andersen and Newman 1973). Most of us are born in a hospital, and many of us die there. The healthcare system is a place of great joy and sorrow, hope and despair; one only need visit an office waiting room or the local emergency room to see this reality. The importance of the healthcare system is hard to overstate, and recognizing the pivotal role that the system and its many components play is essential as we usher in a new era.

Many agree that a new paradigm of care delivery is needed (Cuckler et al. 2018) and that this new paradigm will require a mind-set in which the central goal of our healthcare system shifts from *healthcare* to *well-being*. This book will examine the current US system while also offering insights about the creation of this new paradigm of sustainable care. Meaningful and lasting change will require the full engagement of all stakeholders in the healthcare system.

Our task in this book is to help readers understand the integration between the aims of our healthcare system and the issues that require our focus to achieve the performance and outcomes we desire. As shown in exhibit 1.1, our healthcare system is struggling to balance cost, equitable access, and quality while also acting in the best interest of patients and improving provider experience. Attention to provider experience has increased in recent years because of the high levels of burnout and rising dissatisfaction seen in the healthcare professions. According to several surveys and reports, many physicians today would not encourage their children to follow them into the medical profession (Higgins 2017; Keeton et al. 2007; Shanafelt et al. 2012). Such findings do not bode well for recruiting the best and brightest to the field.

This book is divided into 14 chapters covering major areas of concern in the US healthcare system, and they seek to both foster understanding of the existing system and provide information to help us to move forward. Readers are encouraged, above all else, to think critically about the issues affecting our healthcare system; this critical thinking is, in many ways, more important than memorizing facts. Facts and figures within the healthcare system are changing constantly, but a thorough understanding of the system's drivers and their interrelationships will remain valuable to healthcare leaders well into our future. Having a diverse academic basis is an essential starting point.

As you read, think about the integration of the various issues and the ways each affects the others. Rarely can changes be made to one aspect of the healthcare system without affecting other parts of the system, often with unforeseen or even unwelcome consequences.

Understanding the Challenge Before Us

The cartoon in exhibit 1.2 reflects the feelings of many Americans as they try to make sense of the various aspects of the US healthcare system. The system is massive and complex, and keeping up with its ongoing changes requires continuous vigilance. The healthcare system is also highly politicized, especially with regard to financing and access, making future changes difficult to predict (Marmor and Wendt 2012).

The study of healthcare and the healthcare delivery system covers an enormous amount of information and opinion, touching virtually every aspect of human life. A thorough understanding of healthcare requires not only consideration of patient care and service but also cultural

competency. To serve our diverse society, cultural and language differ-ences must be respectfully acknowledged and adequately accounted for throughout the healthcare system. In addition, numerous complex social problems—such as unhealthy eating, addiction, gun violence, domestic violence, inadequate access to mental health care, and inadequate access to family planning and high-quality childcare—need to be considered, as indi-viduals and society commonly look to the healthcare system for solutions.

A quote commonly attributed to W. Somerset Maugham states that "there are three rules for writing a novel" but that "no one knows what they are" (Daigh 1979). The same applies to understanding our vast and com-plex healthcare system. We lack clear rules, and the landscape is changing at a rapid pace. Addressing every viewpoint and issue that will be of interest to students of the US healthcare system is impossible (Kisekka and Giboney 2018); nonetheless, this book tries to cover a wide scope. If we are to be effective as healthcare leaders, we need to have perspectives on the vari-ous aspects of the system, and we need to support those perspectives with research and facts.

Readers must develop a rigorous process for the analysis of issues and facts, and they should develop their own points of view based on that analysis. They should find and use diverse sources of information to stay informed of new developments, to expand their knowledge base, and to inform their thinking on complex and ever-changing issues. Critical thinking is probably the most important competency a leader in healthcare can possess. This book challenges the reader to think, ask questions, and seek facts. In many cases, it represents the starting point rather than the answer to the questions raised.

Healthcare leadership is a noble profession—one that requires a high level of commitment and dedication to balancing the needs of patients and the allocation of resources in a moral and just way. We are called upon to do what machines cannot do: to act ethically, competently, and with integrity and courage. As W. Edwards Deming (1982, 18) once said, "The transformation can only be accomplished by man, not by hardware (computers, gadgets, automation, new machinery). A company cannot buy its way into quality." We should keep these words in mind as we pursue a transformation in healthcare that, by many accounts, is certainly needed (Anderson 2006; Porter and Lee 2013).

General Characteristics That Distinguish the US Healthcare System

A comparison of the US healthcare system with the healthcare systems of other nations of the Organisation for Economic Co-operation and Development (OECD) highlights a number of ways in which the US system is unique (OECD 2013). By every measure, healthcare spending in the United States exceeds that of any other OECD country. Most of the other countries in the comparison provide universal coverage through a range of methods, using both private and public mechanisms. A more thorough comparison will be provided in chapter 4, but several distinguishing characteristics of the US system are listed in exhibit 1.3 and addressed in the sections that follow. Three areas that merit particular attention are division and fragmentation, technology, and the system's well-known problems and politicization.

Division and Fragmentation
In the opening of *A Tale of Two Cites*, Charles Dickens famously writes, "It was the best of times, it was the worst of times. . . ." We see this binary reflected in our healthcare system today. The United States offers some of the best treatment for serious disease and injury of any country in the world; however, for less serious conditions, preventative care, and more routine services, the United States is less effective than many other countries

EXHIBIT 1.3
Unique
Characteristics
of the US
Healthcare
System

- Highest cost of all Organisation for Economic Co-operation and Development countries
- Technological leader
- No system to provide universal coverage
- Highly fragmented delivery of care
- Many payer arrangements
- Major industries around performance, electronic systems, delivery system restructuring, and quality
- Lack of standardization, leading to inefficiencies and variation
- High administrative cost
- Leader in medical education and research
- Complex and sophisticated organizational structure and delivery models

(Heineman and Froemke 2012). An investigation into the reasons for these shortcomings will, in many instances, point clearly to the fragmented nature of US healthcare.

Indeed, the US healthcare "system" is not a single system but rather a hodgepodge of approaches, encompassing characteristics found in a number of other systems across the world. If you receive care through the US Department of Veterans Affairs, then you are in a system similar to the National Health System of the United Kingdom, which is owned and operated by the government and funded by taxes. If you have Medicare, your healthcare is a lot like Canada's, with private care delivery and a single-payer system funded by taxes and premiums. If you have Medicaid, then, well, who knows what you've got? The 50 states have 50 programs, with a combination of rules at the state and federal levels, funded by state and federal taxes. If you have employer-based coverage—something unique to the United States—then your care is funded privately. If you do not have any insurance, you have what is often called "self-pay–no-pay," which is funded privately (self-pay) or through charitable activities (no-pay). If you are extremely poor and do not qualify for Medicaid, then your only real option might be care in the emergency room, funded by everyone in society through cost shifting and subsidies (Lee 2004). Obviously, these descriptions are grossly oversimplified, but one can easily see how such a mix of options contributes to fragmentation, poor outcomes, injustice, and the incredible administrative costs of our system (Jiwani et al. 2014; Woolhandler, Campbell, and Himmelstein 2003).

One of the most significant features of the US healthcare system is its lack of a central process for governing it. The system is governed by a rather disorganized series of laws, policies, and rules at the local, state, and federal levels (Rice et al. 2013; Commonwealth Fund 2017)—an arrangement that produces complexity and confusion and certainly adds to the burden of administration, especially if an organization crosses state lines. In addition, many people have difficulty accessing US healthcare because of the cost, leading them to use the emergency room as a provider of last resort—which is both expensive and suboptimal (Carret, Fassa, and Kawachi 2007).

In the United States, access to healthcare is based on a system of third-party payment, in which insurers serve as intermediaries between finance and delivery. Such arrangements are seldom found in other countries, where single-payer systems are the norm (Rice et al. 2013). In the United States, a variety of payers offer a variety of plans, which makes the system cumbersome. One of the hopes of the Affordable Care Act, passed in 2010, was to make healthcare plans less diverse. Provisions of the law sought to ensure that plans covered similar things, so that people could better understand the coverage and make informed comparisons between different plans (Gaffney and McCormick 2017).

Technology

Scientific and technological advancement is another factor that sets the United States apart from other countries. Technology has made incredible progress across a wide variety of areas, and the United States has been a leader in the adoption of new equipment, procedures, pharmaceuticals, and other capabilities.

Numerous advances have helped make care more efficient and brought about significant improvements in people's health and well-being. Years ago, people would have surgery for peptic stomach ulcers; today, they buy over-the-counter medicine to reduce stomach acid to prevent the ulcers from occurring. Hip replacement was a major advance of the 1960s (American Association of Orthopedic Surgeons 2015), but the procedure remained somewhat rare until the late 1980s. Then, as technologies improved, the number of cases grew from an estimated 9,000 in 1984 to 138,700 in 2000 and to 310,800 in 2010 (Wolford, Palso, and Bercovitz 2015).

Such technological progress is life changing, and it is rightfully a source of pride. It does come with a cost, however. To paraphrase a famous line from the 1989 film *Field of Dreams*, "If we build it, they will use it." When new technologies become available, the US healthcare system is quick to adapt and begin using them, but it is often slow to develop policy to support those technologies. Additionally, we have often tended avoid tough societal questions about the direction of our healthcare system and the ways technology will fit into it (Starr 2011).

Well-Known Problems and Politicization

The US healthcare system is a constant source of debate, discussion, and concern. If you Google "US healthcare system," you will see more than 4 billion results (as of early 2020)—a powerful indication of how extensive and important the subject is. Discussion about the challenges of the US healthcare system is present even in our entertainment. In one episode of the animated series *The Simpsons*, the family travels to Denmark because Grandpa needs a medical procedure and Homer has learned that the healthcare system there is "free." The characters also discuss the issues of moral hazard and taxation (Polcino 2018).

In the United States, the fact that we spend nearly 1 of every 5 dollars of our economy on healthcare (amounting to 3.3 trillion spent in 2016) is practically common knowledge (Papanicolas, Woskie, and Jha 2018). This level of spending is significantly higher than that of any other country in the world, and yet most of us in the United States, whether we work in healthcare or not, have serious concerns about the value we get in return. If you bring up the topic at a social gathering, you will hear a variety of stories, some good and some bad, about people's experiences with the system.

To add to the complexity, healthcare has become a "hot button" political issue in the United States. In fact, one of several reasons the United States does not have a universal coverage system like those found in other countries is the prevalence of political messaging and corporate influence in the US government. Many US politicians and their followers do not consider healthcare a right or an entitlement, so the government's role in healthcare has been a constant source of political debate (Backman et al. 2008; Wilson 2018). As we will discuss later in the chapter, these political squabbles make reform extremely difficult.

Spread of Global Disease

Although the US system provides services for the people of the United States, it also must consider the global aspects of healthcare. Today, a person can travel almost anywhere in the world within 24 hours. The flow of goods and people from all over the world, the introduction of invasive species into our environment, and the effects of climate change are all leading to new challenges for healthcare delivery professionals, institutions, and policymakers. Many diseases seen in the United States today were, until a few years ago, found only in other parts of the world (Singh et al. 2017). The first US case of Ebola, for instance, occurred in 2015 (Lindblad, El Fiky, and Zajdowicz 2015). In light of these rapid changes, healthcare stakeholders must not only be able to recognize new ailments and issues but also know how to effectively treat and manage them (Fauci and Morens 2016; Paules et al. 2018).

In 2015, with subsequent reviews, the World Health Organization (WHO) identified the following infectious diseases that are likely to cause epidemics and that require serious research and development for vaccines and treatments (Luxton 2016; Mackey et al. 2014; WHO 2015; Medscape 2018; *Scientific American* 2018):

- Crimean-Congo hemorrhagic fever
- Ebola
- Filovirus diseases (e.g., Marburg)
- Highly pathogenic emerging coronaviruses relevant to humans (e.g., Middle East respiratory system coronavirus [MERS-CoV], severe acute respiratory syndrome [SARS])
- Lassa fever
- Nipah
- Rift Valley fever
- Chikungunya
- Severe fever with thrombocytopenia syndrome
- Zika

Information Technology

The internet has been—and will continue to be—a significant force for change. Although healthcare historically has been regarded as a local issue, advances in information technology have placed it in an increasingly global context (Hopkins et al. 2010). With a high-speed internet connection, services can now be provided by or to any person, virtually anywhere in the world (Weinstein et al. 2014).

In some ways, the internet is democratizing healthcare by providing a wealth of information and improved access to a greater number of people. A person seeking information about a medical condition need not rely completely on a health professional; much information can be accessed online. Significant concerns exist, however, about the quality of the information found online and its proper use (Cohen and Adams 2011; Ford et al. 2012).

Our improved ability to collect, analyze, and correlate health information, coupled with the development of artificial intelligence and the use of data analytics, offers the potential for healthcare advances that, in years past, we could have only dreamed of (Finlay 2014; Wu et al. 2016). With access to vast collections of information—often referred to as "big data"—we can analyze disease and health patterns like never before, enabling us to predict trends and even outbreaks of disease. By analyzing social media key words, we can identify the origins and status of outbreaks of infectious diseases such as the flu. Big data has been critical to the field of genomics and its applications in healthcare. These advances would have been impossible without the assistance of high-speed computers such as IBM's Watson; the human mind, or even any collection of humans, is incapable of such analytical work (Ferrucci et al. 2010; Wakeman 2011).

Physical Environment and Geography

The impact of our environment on our health and well-being has been well established (Roeder 2015). Pollution, for instance, can have a serious effect on people's health, as shown by a number of studies linking asthma in children to local air quality (Gauderman et al. 2015; Mabahwi, Leh, and Omar 2014). Safety concerns can also influence health. If you live in a neighborhood that lacks sufficient sidewalks and lighting, you might not feel comfortable going for a walk to get exercise, or letting your children play outside. In light of these and other issues, some have stated that a person's zip code is more predictive of health status than the person's genetic code (Graham 2016; Slade-Sawyer 2014).

Zip code will also affect a person's access to high-quality healthcare services, which will in turn influence health. For instance, if you live in rural Wyoming, 100 miles from the nearest town or doctor, your access to care is going to be limited, and the care you receive will likely not be as good as that provided in an urban downtown area with multiple major hospital organizations. The 1990s television show *Northern Exposure* reflected this situation. The story revolves around efforts to entice a young medical graduate from New York City to come to a rural Alaskan town to provide care. Although the show was a comedy, the situation is indicative of serious issues that exist around the distribution of medical services in the United States.

Legal Issues

The legal risks associated with practitioners' behaviors are an important factor in the rising cost of healthcare and the complexity of the US healthcare system. Relative to other nations, the United States is highly litigious; it has 13 times more lawyers per capita than Japan does (Obe 2016). Given the constant threat of malpractice lawsuits, practitioners purchase malpractice insurance, which significantly drives up costs.

The legal risks may also lead healthcare professionals to practice so-called defensive medicine, in which additional tests and services are ordered to minimize the risk of being sued (Jena et al. 2011; Anderson et al. 2004). Some tests and services are performed, at significant cost, primarily to prevent claims of omission, regardless of whether they will produce any meaningful benefit to the patient. In some instances, these extra services may produce data useful to the treatment of the patients, but these benefits still must be weighed against the additional costs and the potential for patient harm stemming from the procedures (Waxman et al. 2014).

The Conundrum

Can you see the conundrum in exhibit 1.1? We want high-quality care, we want access, and we want lower cost. As economists will acknowledge, having any two of these things is possible, but having all three at once is extremely difficult.

Some countries, for example, have chosen to pursue higher quality and lower cost while allowing reduction of access. Someone who needs a knee replacement in Scotland might get a perfectly good procedure at a reasonable cost, but they might have to wait for nine months to get it. By contrast, a similar patient in the United States might need wait for just a few weeks for the same procedure. The US system offers a high level of access, but our society pays dearly to build the necessary capacity.

Going forward, healthcare system managers have the task of optimizing the relationship between quality, access, and cost. Keeping quality high and at the same time preserving access and bending the cost curve will not be an easy task; it will require major reform to the delivery system and a greater emphasis on prevention and self-care.

Values, Attitudes, and Beliefs

Our healthcare system is heavily influenced by our society's beliefs about health and healthcare (Bunker 2001). We are constantly trying to balance social justice with market justice, and personal freedom with social responsibility, to name just two examples. Finding these balances will be difficult. To succeed, we need to commit to continuous learning and remain open to the new ideas and information that develop daily. The challenges we face require all of us to become lifelong learners, to be diligent in keeping up with the rapidly changing environment.

The diversity of our society its greatest strength; however, the many attitudes, beliefs, and values that come with such diversity present challenges to the healthcare system—a system that, at this point, does not always have the necessary level of cultural competence. *Cultural competence* in healthcare refers to the ability of providers and organizations to effectively deliver services that meet the social, cultural, and linguistic needs of patients (Health Policy Institute, Georgetown University 2004). Cultural competence is an essential aspect of providing competent care.

In a free market economy, we are constantly bombarded with marketing messages, some of which are not in the best interest of our health. Health literacy, therefore, is of paramount importance in helping people make proper lifestyle choices to support health status at the highest level possible. The ways we live, work, and play and our attitudes toward aging and prevention all affect the life choices we make, which in turn have consequences for our health status. These choices also have a lasting impact on our healthcare system.

A Large and Growing Problem: The Number of People with Chronic Medical Conditions

About half of US citizens have a chronic disease. Of the approximately $3 trillion the United States spends on healthcare, 86 percent goes toward chronic disease (Centers for Disease Control and Prevention [CDC] 2018). In 2014, the CDC (2014) reported that 9.4 percent of Americans had type II diabetes and another 33 percent were prediabetic. Such statistics have staggering implications, given that diabetes can lead to blindness, kidney failure, and other complications. Many people with heart disease also have diabetes (American Diabetes Association 2014). Type II diabetes is a severe health problem; however, it is also a relatively preventable and treatable condition.

The US healthcare system must become a system of health by better managing chronic disease. Improvement will require greater patient engagement. Patients must engage by helping to take care of themselves and by buying into practices that support wellness. We need to find ways to counterbalance the hamburger commercials that are often so seductive. Behavioral economics—the field focusing on cognitive, psychological, social, and cultural aspects of people's economic decision making—will play an important role in this effort (Cox 2017; Craig 2011; Sugden 2009).

A Perfect Storm

The popular book and movie *A Perfect Storm* (Junger 1997) is about a highly unusual meteorological storm that results from the confluence of several weather factors. The US healthcare system is experiencing a "perfect storm" of its own as a confluence of factors is producing a similarly unprecedented event, as illustrated in exhibit 1.4. Key factors in the storm include patient safety, cost of care, concerns about access and quality, huge demographic changes, rapid advances in technology and treatments, the digital

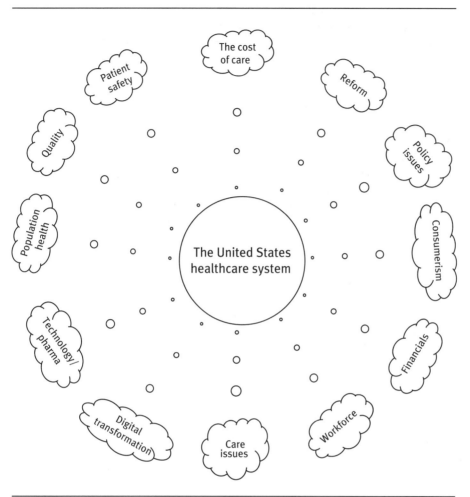

EXHIBIT 1.4
The Perfect Storm: Forces of Change Acting on the US Healthcare System

transformation, and data analytics. Workforce issues are also part of the storm. Today's workforce is unprecedented in that it consists of four generations at once. Each of these generations has its own cultural attitudes about work, creating significant challenges for management.

Generational differences in people's attitudes about healthcare are often striking. For example, members of the traditional generation (born prior to 1945) tend to be compliant and willing to follow instructions from the doctor or nurse. Baby boomers and younger people are less so, and they tend to have high expectations for anyone providing them service (Bowling, Rowe, and Mckee 2013). Perceptions and expectations associated with patients' age can contribute to differences in the way practitioners provide care (Wennberg 2011).

Exhibit 1.5 shows an expanded list of the pressures on the US healthcare system, bringing the perfect storm into greater detail.

EXHIBIT 1.5
Select Issues
That Will Have a
Major Impact on
Future Health
and Healthcare
Delivery in the
United States

Changes in Environmental and Demographic Factors	Operational Changes and Challenges
Aging population	Cybersecurity and the Internet of Things
Increasing diversity	Social media
Addressing end-of-life care	Artificial intelligence
Genomics	Big Data / data analytics
Shortage of certain healthcare workers (e.g., home health care workers)	Robotics in surgery
	Robotics in instruments of daily living
	Robotics in machine-assisted care
Effect of climate change on the nature and spread of disease	Precision medicine
	Culinary medicine
New emerging diseases	Telemedicine and virtual care
Zoonoses	Narrative medicine
Population expansion	Addressing end-of-life care
Pollution	Mini-hospitals
Environmental degradation	More nontraditional providers
Anthro-cultural forces	Consolidation and larger healthcare systems
Patient activation	More horizontal integration, funding
Continued political uncertainty	Organization and delivery are combined
Competing funding interests	

Major Obstacles to Reform

The resistance to change in the healthcare system is formidable (Gilley, Godek, and Gilley 2009; Gorman 2015; Kumar and Khiljee 2016). Reform efforts go back as far as the Roosevelt administration—not Franklin, but Theodore (Igel 2008)—and most have failed despite the overwhelming sense that change is necessary.

The US healthcare system's independent nature, its fragmentation, and its lack of centralization have made resistance to change a major issue. Entities with a vested interest in our system in its current state have been able to exert their influence and impede change (Kuratko, Covin, and Hornsby 2014). Additional obstacles stem from the large size of the country, its diversity, and various aspects of America's cultural identity. With so many different providers and components working independently of one another, it is difficult to change directions and even more difficult to stop the system from continuing on its course. As they say, "When the healthcare machine gets rolling, it is hard to stop."

One obstacle to reform is the fundamental disagreement about two common principles for equitable or reasonable distribution of healthcare services: market justice and social justice. Market justice theory states that healthcare is a product for purchase and therefore, like all other goods and services, is subject to the principles of economic theory. Supply and demand—which, in our context, may reflect a willingness to pay for a service—determine price and availability. Under market justice, the individual is responsible for the cost of their healthcare, the government should play a limited role, and the poor should be served through charitable means. The focus is clearly on the individual rather than on a collective responsibility for health. This theory accepts the notion that care will be rationed by the ability to pay (Karsten 1995; O'Laughlin 2016; Weinstein et al. 2017; Williams, Walker, and Egede 2016).

By contrast, social justice theory sees healthcare as a social good that should not be subject to strict economic principles. Under social justice, everyone should have access to care regardless of their ability to pay, and the government should intervene in situations where the market fails to provide adequate levels of service to people in need. Advocates of social justice believe that the government is better suited than the market is to determine how healthcare is distributed. Social justice theory, therefore, recognizes a shared responsibility for the health of the community and the factors beyond individuals' control (Braveman et al. 2011).

The disagreement between proponents of social justice and market justice can seem to be almost an insurmountable obstacle, both within our healthcare system and across the country itself. We must decide what kind of country and what kind of healthcare system we want to be part of.

Transitioning Toward Value

As an industry matures, most businesses undergo a transition, from a first curve to a second, shown in exhibit 1.6 (Morrison 1996). Each curve represents a paradigm—a distinct concept or, to put it more simply, a way of thinking about something or about what something is (Carraccio et al. 2002; Göktürk 2005). Paradigms are powerful tools, and they can be difficult to change.

The current US healthcare system is likely in the latter stages of the first curve, undergoing a painful transition to a new paradigm. Providers are still primarily paid for volume, based on what they do and how much of it they do, rather than on the quality, impact, or outcomes of what they do. A provider might say, "Well, we provided hundreds of services every day"—but if they were not necessary, high-quality services, then so what? In the second curve for healthcare, providers will be paid based on value (Ahmed et al. 2017; Gray 2017; Mandal et al. 2017; Porter 2010).

EXHIBIT 1.6
The Second
Curve and
Adoption of
Innovation

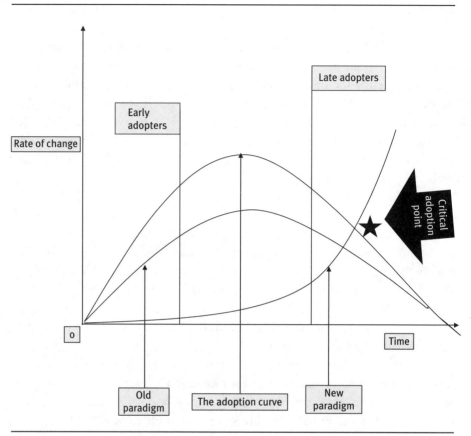

Source: Adapted from Morrison (1996).

Value is a function of cost and quality, and it can be expressed in an equation as follows:

$$Value = Cost/Quality$$

Imagine you are going to the grocery store to buy a can of peas. Why do you buy one can versus another can? Maybe one is less expensive? Maybe you perceive that one is better than another, or has a better value? You might even be willing to pay a little bit more for a can that you presume to be of higher quality. Cars offer another example. Some people drive expensive cars because they perceive that they are getting more quality for their money. In healthcare, paying providers for the value of their services rather than the quantity of their services will lead to better outcomes and better patient experience (Porter 2010).

As the US healthcare system transitions to the second curve, providers are beginning to be paid based not only on volume but also on quality, which is creating pressure and spurring change. Exhibit 1.6 shows the intersection of the first and second curves at the *critical adoption point*. This point occurs

The Old Paradigm	The New Paradigm
Volume of service	**Value** of service
Acute care (specialty-focused inpatient)	Primary care (outpatient-focused)
Treating illness	Preventive care
Fragmented care	Care on a continuum
Individual care	Population health
Generalized treatment for medical conditions	Precision medicine
Healthcare independent of social needs	Community well-being as part of healthcare
Independent organizations	Integrated delivery systems (e.g., accountable care organizations)

EXHIBIT 1.7
A New Paradigm of Healthcare

when strain is at its maximum in the system. It is a difficult and dangerous time for organizations; indeed, many businesses fail (Kotter 2009; Walston and Chou 2006). The challenge is to transition safely from the first curve to the second curve while working in both systems.

Exhibit 1.7 lists some key aspects of the paradigm shift affecting the fundamental nature of healthcare delivery in the United States. How does one make the necessary changes to transform to the new value-based paradigm of care and at the same time continue to be paid primarily by volume-based methodologies? Just imagine you are a provider caring for a patient. Are you being paid under a volume- or value-based system? Does the payment arrangement affect your behavior? This is the dilemma. We may like to think that provider behavior would be consistent regardless, but such thinking is simply naïve (Pracht, Langland-Orban, and Ryan 2018; van Dijk et al. 2013).

Missing the Second-Curve Paradigm Shift: The Kodak Story

History is replete with stories of missed paradigm shifts and their consequences. Consider, for instance, the record executive who rejected the Beatles in 1962, allegedly saying that "guitar groups are on the way out" and that the Beatles had "no future in show business" (*Telegraph* reporters 2012).

Consider the example of Kodak, once the leader in the production of cameras and film. Not long ago, people would go to the store to buy film for their cameras. Multiple types of film were available—fast speed or slow speed, daylight or nighttime, color or black and white. Shoppers would choose between multiple sizes of film, with various options for the number of pictures that could be taken on each roll. Film at that time was expensive, which helped make Kodak one of the most important companies in the United States—even part of the "Nifty 50" on Wall Street. For many years, Kodak was one of the safest, most stable investments that one could own. In 2012, however, the company went bankrupt after 131 years in business (De la Marced 2012; Mui 2012). So, what happened? Kodak failed to transition to the second curve.

Today, of course, most of us use digital cameras or our smart phones to take photographs. When was the last time you purchased a roll of film? Can you even find it in a store? We no longer think about the number of pictures we take, film size, choice between black and white or color, or other such matters. Kodak actually invented digital photography, but it lacked the insight to commit to the change. Instead, it remained fixated on film and cameras.

In a sense, Kodak forgot what business it was in. The company was managed by chemical engineers who had a great appreciation for the chemistry of photographic processes. However, customers were not actually enamored with film and cameras—they just wanted memories. If people go on vacation and get their picture taken by a waterfall, they are not doing so because of the film or the camera; they simply want a memory of the experience (Carl 2015). Kodak failed to realize that it was not in the film business but rather the picture-taking business, the memory business.

Kodak was a casualty of shifting paradigms in its industry. It remained on the first curve—film photography—until the curve went down to zero. Had Kodak moved on to the second curve—digital photography—at the right time, it would not be out of business.

Another important point to make is that, when an industry starts the second curve, that industry's knowledge base is small. In other words, everybody in that industry essentially starts over again in developing their business and their expertise. Entering the second curve is not an easy task, and organizations need time to gain proficiency. In the US healthcare system, we are going to need time to learn how to deliver care based on value rather than on quantity.

A Second Example: The Quartz Watch

Another example of a missed paradigm shift is the story of the quartz watch movement, often told by business and technology author Joel Barker (1993).

The quartz watch movement was invented by the Swiss, who are famous for their precision timepieces, in the 1960s. However, because the existing paradigm of what a high-quality watch should be was so strong within the community of Swiss watchmakers, they did not patent the quartz movement. The movement was displayed at a subsequent trade show, attracting significant interest from several Japanese companies. The Japanese quickly began producing watches with quartz movements, and the Swiss watch market soon collapsed—dropping from a 65 percent market share in 1968 to less than 10 percent in 1980 (Barker 1993). The story is yet another example showing how strong our paradigms can be and how those paradigms can cause smart people to overlook significant shifts in their industry.

We will discuss several paradigm shifts in healthcare over the course of this book. Is the healthcare field too comfortable with the status quo? Do we think that technology is the cure for all our problems? These and other questions need to be asked as we explore the complexities of the US system.

The Graying of America: US Census Projections

The American population is aging. As of 2017, people aged 65 or older represented 15.6 percent of the population (US Census Bureau 2017). The fastest-growing group of people in the country are those 85 or older. About 10,000 baby boomers turn 65 each day (Biegert 2016; Cohn and Taylor 2010).

The implications of this "Silver Tsunami" are significant for the healthcare system. Generally, the older we get, the more healthcare we use, and most Americans 65 or older rely on Medicare to fund their healthcare expenses. People are living much longer than in the past but often with failing health (Alemayehu and Warner 2004; Gawande 2014; Canadian Medical Association 2013). At the same time, the number of people working and funding Medicare relative to the number of people receiving Medicare benefits is shrinking (Centers for Medicare & Medicaid Services 2016).

Exhibit 1.8 shows projected changes in the US population between 1960 and 2060 across various age groups, clearly indicating the degree to which we are getting older as a society. By 2035, for the first time in history, people 65 or older are projected to outnumber children (US Census Bureau 2018b).

Equality Is a Healthcare Issue

While at a conference at St. Andrews College, I was speaking with a physician from Turkey. Noting that Turkey had increased its population's longevity dramatically—from about 45 years in 1960 to 78 years in 2016 (Countryeconomy.com 2018)—I asked: "What did you all do to jump-start such a magnificent improvement in life expectancy?" She answered, "We

EXHIBIT 1.8
Census Bureau
Projections

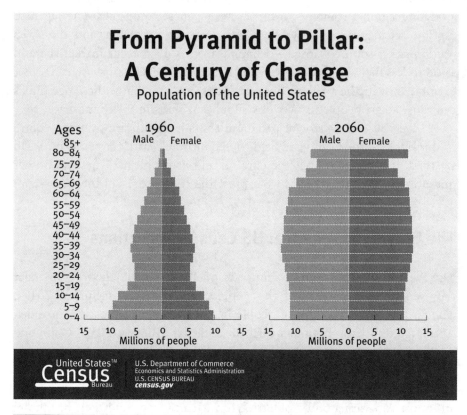

From Pyramid to Pillar:
A Century of Change
Population of the United States

Source: Reprinted from US Census Bureau (2018a).

taught women how to read." Her answer was a little surprising, but also not so surprising when you really think about it. Who are the primary caregivers in Turkey and many other societies? Who are the people who tend to make sure that the children have healthcare? Traditionally, those people have been women. So, perhaps we should not be surprised that empowering women would have such an enormous impact on an entire society.

In the United States, healthcare and health issues are too often regarded as a group of services that are provided to the population. This kind of thinking is incomplete and needs to change. As the story about the Turkish doctor makes clear, access to healthcare services is only one factor in health status; numerous other factors play a role as well, including the following (Healthy People 2018; WHO 2010):

- *Income and social status.* Higher income and social status are linked to better health. In any society, the greater the gap between the richest and poorest people, the greater the differences in health will be.

- *Education.* Low education levels are linked with poor health, more stress, and lower self-confidence.
- *Physical environment.* Safe water and clean air, healthy workplaces, safe houses and communities, and good roads all contribute to better health.
- *Employment and working conditions.* People who are employed are healthier, particularly if they have control over their working conditions.
- *Social support networks.* Strong support from families, friends, and communities is linked to better health.
- *Culture.* Customs, traditions, and the beliefs of family members and the community all affect health.
- *Genetics.* Inherited traits and hereditary diseases affect life span, healthiness, and the likelihood of developing certain illnesses.
- *Personal behavior and coping skills.* Eating a balanced diet, keeping active, not smoking, drinking only in moderation if at all, having access to mental health care, and effectively coping with life's stresses and challenges all affect health.
- *Biological sex.* People may be susceptible to different types of diseases at different ages depending on their biological sex.

To effectively manage illness and well-being, healthcare organizations must become more actively involved in their communities. They need to be concerned with such things as the following:

- Making sure that people have places where they can safely walk
- Making sure that neighborhoods have good lighting in the evening, so people are safe going outside
- Making sure that people have access to grocery stores that sell healthy, affordable food
- Making sure people have access to clean drinking water
- Making sure that people are able to read and understand basic facts about medicines, disease and illness, and their own bodies (i.e., healthcare literacy and accurate sex education)

In the United States, many of these concerns are treated as political issues, but they are undoubtedly healthcare issues—and the healthcare community needs to start taking responsibility for them. Health outcomes can be improved through a variety of approaches other than simply providing more healthcare services.

End-of-Life Care

With the aging of our population, the need to manage end-of-life care in a dignified and appropriate manner becomes increasingly important. In the quest to live as long as possible, people often engage in futile care during the last days, weeks, or months of their lives, rather than making the most of their remaining time with friends and family.

Unfortunately, death is inevitable, and the US healthcare system needs to develop better approaches for managing health and health resources at the end of life. This effort will require better education about end-of-life issues not only among health professionals but also across the public at large. Positive change will require new policies and approaches for the funding of alternative services such as hospice and palliative care. It will also require us to provide appropriate mental health care, counseling, and support services to patients and families at this important stage in life's journey (Bélanger et al. 2014; Prina 2017; Schneiderman 2011).

Physician Shortages

The United States is facing a physician shortage, and the situation is projected to worsen in the years ahead (Bodenheimer and Smith 2013; Dall et al. 2015; Edelman et al. 2013). The American Association of Medical Colleges (2015) estimates that the country will have a shortage of roughly 100,000 physicians by 2025. The shortage is particularly prevalent in primary care, but other specialties will feel the impact as well. According to McKibben and colleagues (2016), the average age of urologists in the United States is 55—which might be considered "getting up there" in terms of surgical careers—and shortages are likely to worsen as large numbers begin to retire. Increased use of advanced clinical professionals, such as physician assistants (PAs) and nurse practitioners (NPs), may offer some solutions to shortages (Bodenheimer and Smith 2013; Green, Savin, and Lu 2013). However, addressing issues of provider experience and attitudes toward the practice of medicine will likely have the most profound effect on the future supply of healthcare professionals.

The United States Leads the World in Many Ways

Luckily, the state of the US healthcare system is not all doom and gloom. Despite its many challenges and shortcomings, the system has many positive attributes. For instance, the United States is a global leader in medical technology—though, of course, we must reconcile the benefits of this technology with the cost. In addition, the United States remains a world leader in medical research, medical education and training, and advanced organizational development and processes.

The National Institutes of Health (NIH)—despite, regrettably, facing possible budget cuts and other problems due to political circumstances—funds and conducts a tremendous amount of research that helps advance healthcare in the United States and throughout the world (Gillum et al. 2011; Jacob and Lefgren 2011; NIH 2019). The NIH was responsible, for instance, for a breakthrough in the treatment of sickle cell anemia, a genetic disorder in which the individual does not have enough healthy red blood cells to carry sufficient oxygen throughout the body (Mayo Clinic 2019). The NIH pioneered a gene-based therapy that replaces the defective gene in the stem cell of the patient. The patient receives a bone marrow transplant with genetically modified stem cells that produce healthy red blood cells—leading to what appears to be a cure for the disease (*60 Minutes* 2019; NIH 2018).

Advances in healthcare technology are doing what once seemed unimaginable, with new treatments emerging for ailments previously considered untreatable (Kakkis et al. 2015). Take, for example, HIV. Not long ago, a diagnosis meant almost-certain death; now, HIV infection is regarded as a manageable chronic disease that can be treated via medication (Maartens, Celum, and Lewin 2014). Similarly, a hepatitis C infection at one time could only be treated with a series of drugs that had significant—nearly intolerable—side effects; now, most cases can be cured with oral medicine that has virtually no side effects (Webster, Klenerman, and Dusheiko 2015). Of course, these treatments described for HIV and hepatitis C are both very expensive; in the United States, they are only miracle cures for the people who can afford them.

Most people agree that change is needed in the US healthcare system. If you are reading this book, then you are responsible for helping make this change come about. So, what are we going to do? First, we need to ask two basic questions:

1. Is reform needed?
2. What is the purpose of reform?

To the first question, the answer is a resounding yes. The second question has many possible answers, but, for starters, we might say that the purpose of healthcare reform is to deliver healthcare to all our citizens in a cost-effective and high-quality way. As members of the healthcare community, we must learn as much as we can about the various elements of our system, broken as it is, so that we can design the best reforms possible.

Discussion Questions

1. What is the healthcare system's place in US society?
2. What challenges does the US healthcare system face?
3. What are some of the obstacles to healthcare reform?
4. What is or should be the goal for the US healthcare system?

References

Ahmed, F., N. Ahmed, T. W. R. Briggs, P. J. Pronovost, D. P. Shetty, A. K. Jha, and V. Govindarajan. 2017. "Can Reverse Innovation Catalyse Better Value Health Care?" *Lancet Global Health*. Published October. https://doi.org/10.1016/S2214-109X(17)30324-8.

Alemayehu, B., and K. E. Warner. 2004. "The Lifetime Distribution of Health Care Costs." *Health Services Research* 39 (3): 627–42. https://doi.org/10.1111/j.1475-6773.2004.00248.x.

American Association of Medical Colleges (AAMC). 2015. "New Physician Workforce Projections Show the Doctor Shortage Remains Significant." Published March 3. www.aamc.org/newsroom/newsreleases/426166/20150303.html.

American Association of Orthopedic Surgeons. 2015. "Total Hip Replacement." Reviewed August. https://orthoinfo.aaos.org/en/treatment/total-hip-replacement/.

American Diabetes Association. 2014. "Diagnosis and Classification of Diabetes Mellitus." *Diabetes Care*. Published January. https://doi.org/10.2337/dc14-S081.

Andersen, R., and J. F. Newman. 1973. "Societal and Individual Determinants of Medical Care Utilization in the United States." *Milbank Memorial Fund Quarterly, Health and Society* 51 (1): 95–124. https://doi.org/10.2307/3349613.

Anderson, G. 2006. "The Health Care Mess: How We Got Into It and What It Will Take to Get Out." *JAMA*. Published January 18. https://doi.org/10.1001/jama.295.3.331-b.

Anderson, G. F., P. S. Hussey, B. K. Frogner, and H. R. Waters. 2004. "Health Spending in the United States and the Rest of the Industrialized World." *Health Affairs* 24 (4): 903–14. https://doi.org/10.1377/hlthaff.24.4.903.

Backman, G., P. Hunt, R. Khosla, C. Jaramillo-Strouss, B. M. Fikre, C. Rumble, D. Pevalin, D. Acurio Páez, M. Armijos Pineda, A. Frisancho, D. Tarco, M. Motlagh, D. Farcasanu, and C. Vladescu. 2008. "Health Systems and the Right to Health: An Assessment of 194 Countries." *Lancet* 372 (9655): 2047–85. https://doi.org/10.1016/S0140-6736(08)61781-X.

Barker, J. A. 1993. *Paradigms: The Business of Discovering the Future*. New York: HarperBusiness.

Bélanger, E., C. Rodríguez, D. Groleau, F. Légaré, M. E. Macdonald, and R. March-and. 2014. "Initiating Decision-Making Conversations in Palliative Care: An Ethnographic Discourse Analysis." *BMC Palliative Care*. Published December 23. https://doi.org/10.1186/1472-684X-13-63.

Berwick, D. M., T. W. Nolan, and J. Whittington. 2008. "The Triple Aim: Care, Health, and Cost." *Health Affairs*. Published May 1. https://doi.org/10.1377/hlthaff.27.3.759.

Biegert, M. 2016. "10,000 Boomers Turning 65 Everyday." *Math Encounters Blog*. Published July 30. http://mathscinotes.com/2016/07/10000-boomers-turning-65-everyday/.

Bodenheimer, T., and C. Sinsky. 2014. "From Triple to Quadruple Aim: Care of the Patient Requires Care of the Provider." *Annals of Family Medicine* 12 (6): 573–76. https://doi.org/10.1370/afm.1713.

Bodenheimer, T. S., and M. D. Smith. 2013. "Primary Care: Proposed Solutions to the Physician Shortage Without Training More Physicians." *Health Affairs*. Published November 1. https://doi.org/10.1377/hlthaff.2013.0234.

Bowling, A., G. Rowe, and M. Mckee. 2013. "Patients' Experiences of Their Healthcare in Relation to Their Expectations and Satisfaction: A Population Survey." *Journal of the Royal Society of Medicine*. Published April 1. https://doi.org/10.1258/jrsm.2012.120147.

Braveman, P. A., S. Kumanyika, J. Fielding, T. LaVeist, L. N. Borrell, R. Manderscheid, and A. Troutman. 2011. "Health Disparities and Health Equity: The Issue Is Justice." *American Journal of Public Health* 101 (51): S149–55. https://doi.org/10.2105/AJPH.2010.300062.

Bunker, J. P. 2001. "The Role of Medical Care in Contributing to Health Improvements Within Societies." *International Journal of Epidemiology* 30 (6): 1260–63. https://doi.org/10.1093/ije/30.6.1260.

Canadian Medical Association. 2013. *Health and Health Care for an Aging Population. Policy Summary of The Canadian Medical Association*. Published December. www.cma.ca/sites/default/files/2018-11/CMA_Policy_Health_and_Health_Care_for_an_Aging-Population_PD14-03-e_0.pdf.

Carl, A. 2015. "What Kodak Can Teach Us About Avoiding Failure." *Device Magic*. Published February 6. www.devicemagic.com/blog/kodak-moment.

Carraccio, C., S. Wolfsthal, R. Englander, K. Ferentz, and C. Martin. 2002. "Shifting Paradigms: From Flexner to Competencies." Academic Medicine 77 (5): 361–67. https://doi.org/10.1097/00001888-200205000-00003.

Carret, M. L. V., A. G. Fassa, and I. Kawachi. 2007. "Demand for Emergency Health Service: Factors Associated with Inappropriate Use." *BMC Health Services Research*. Published August 18. https://doi.org/10.1186/1472-6963-7-131.

Centers for Disease Control and Prevention (CDC). 2018. "Health and Economic Costs of Chronic Disease." Accessed August 3. www.cdc.gov/chronicdisease/about/costs/index.htm.

————. 2014. *National Diabetes Statistics Report, 2014.* Accessed September 13. www.cdc.gov/diabetes/pdfs/data/2014-report-estimates-of-diabetes-and-its-burden-in-the-united-states.pdf.

Centers for Medicare & Medicaid Services (CMS). 2016. "National Health Expenditure Projections 2016–2025." Accessed September 13, 2019. www.cms.gov/Research-Statistics-Data-and-Systems/Statistics-Trends-and-Reports/NationalHealthExpendData/Downloads/proj2016.pdf.

Cohen, R. A., and P. F. Adams. 2011. "Use of the Internet for Health Information: United States, 2009." National Center for Health Statistics data brief. Published July. www.ncbi.nlm.nih.gov/pubmed/22142942.

Cohn, V., and P. Taylor. 2010. "Baby Boomers Approach 65—Glumly." Pew Research Center. Published December 20. www.pewsocialtrends.org/2010/12/20/baby-boomers-approach-65-glumly/.

Commonwealth Fund. 2017. *International Profiles of Health Care Systems.* Published May 31. www.commonwealthfund.org/publications/fund-reports/2017/may/international-profiles-health-care-systems.

Countryeconomy.com. 2018. "Turkey—Life Expectancy at Birth." Accessed August 3. https://countryeconomy.com/demography/life-expectancy/turkey.

Cox, L. A. Jr. 2017. "Misbehaving: The Making of Behavioral Economics by Richard Thaler." *Risk Analysis* 37 (9): 1796–98. https://doi.org/10.1111/risa.12871.

Craig, G. 2011. "How to Put 'Nudge' Principles to Work in the Health Service." Health Service Journal. Published January 4. www.hsj.co.uk/best-practice/how-to-put-nudge-principles-to-work-in-the-health-service/5022815.article.

Cuckler, G. A., A. M. Sisko, J. A. Poisal, S. P. Keehan, S. D. Smith, A. J. Madison, C. J. Wolfe, and J. C. Hardesty. 2018. "National Health Expenditure Projections, 2017–26: Despite Uncertainty, Fundamentals Primarily Drive Spending Growth." *Health Affairs.* Published February 14. https://doi.org/10.1377/hlthaff.2017.1655.

Daigh, R. 1979. *Maybe You Should Write a Book.* Englewood Cliffs, NJ: Prentice Hall.

Dall, T., T. West, R. Chakrabarti, and W. Iacobucci. 2015. *The Complexities of Physician Supply and Demand: Projections from 2013 to 2025.* Association of American Medical Colleges. Published March. www.aamc.org/download/426248/data/thecomplexitiesofphysiciansupplyanddemandprojectionsfrom2013to2.pdf.

De la Marced, M. J. 2012. "Eastman Kodak Files for Bankruptcy." *New York Times.* Published January 19. https://dealbook.nytimes.com/2012/01/19/eastman-kodak-files-for-bankruptcy/.

Deming, W. E. 1982. *Out of the Crisis.* Cambridge, MA: MIT Press.

Dias-Barbosa, C., M. M. Balp, K. Kulich, N. Germain, and D. Rofail. 2012. "A Literature Review to Explore the Link Between Treatment Satisfaction and Adherence, Compliance, and Persistence." *Patient Preference and Adherence* 2012 (6): 39–48. https://doi.org/10.2147/PPA.S24752.

Edelman, N., R. Goldsteen, K. Goldsteen, S. Yagudayev, F. Lima, and L. Chiu. 2013. "Institutions with Accredited Residencies in New York State with an Interest in Developing New Residencies or Expanding Existing Ones." *Academic Medicine* 88 (9): 1287–92. https://doi.org/10.1097/ACM.0b013e31829e581f.

Fauci, A. S., and D. M. Morens. 2016. "Zika Virus in the Americas—Yet Another Arbovirus Threat." *New England Journal of Medicine* 374: 601–4. https://doi.org/10.1056/NEJMp1600297.

Ferrucci, D., E. Brown, J. Chu-Carroll, J. Fan, D. Gondek, A. A. Kalyanpur, A. Lally, J. W. Murdock, E. Nyberg, J. Prager, N. Schlaefer, and C. Welty. 2010. "Building Watson: An Overview of the DeepQA Project." *AI Magazine* 31(3): 59–79. www.aaai.org/ojs/index.php/aimagazine/article/view/2303/2165.

Finlay, S. 2014. *Predictive Analytics, Data Mining and Big Data: Myths, Misconceptions and Methods.* New York: Palgrave Macmillan.

Ford, E., T. Huerta, R. Schilhavy, N. Menachemi, and V. U. Walls. 2012. "Effective US Health System Websites: Establishing Benchmarks and Standards for Effective Consumer Engagement." *Journal of Healthcare Management* 57 (1): 47–65. https://doi.org/10.1097/00115514-201201000-00009.

Gaffney, A., and D. McCormick. 2017. "The Affordable Care Act: Implications for Health-Care Equity." *Lancet* 389 (10077): 1442–52. https://doi.org/10.1016/S0140-6736(17)30786-9.

Gauderman, W. J., R. Urman, E. Avol, K. Berhane, R. McConnell, E. Rappaport, R. Chang, F. Lurman, and F. Gilliland. 2015. "Association of Improved Air Quality with Lung Development in Children." *New England Journal of Medicine* 372: 905–13. https://doi.org/10.1056/NEJMoa1414123.

Gawande, A. 2014. *Being Mortal: Medicine and What Matters in the End.* New York: Metropolitan Books.

Gilley, A., M. Godek, and J. W. Gilley. 2009. "Change, Resistance, and the Organizational Immune System." *SAM Advanced Management Journal* 74: 4–10.

Gillum, L. A., C. Gouveia, E. R. Dorsey, M. Pletcher, C. D. Mathers, C. E. McCulloch, and S. C. Johnston. 2011. "NIH Disease Funding Levels and Burden of Disease." *PLOS ONE.* Published February 24. https://doi.org/10.1371/journal.pone.0016837.

Göktürk, E. 2005. "What Is 'Paradigm'?" Department of Informatics, University of Oslo. Accessed September 13, 2019. http://citeseerx.ist.psu.edu/viewdoc/download?doi=10.1.1.697.4205&rep=rep1&type=pdf.

Gorman, D. 2015. "On the Barriers to Significant Innovation in and Reform of Healthcare." *Internal Medicine Journal* 45 (6): 597–99. https://doi.org/10.1111/imj.12775.

Graham, G. N. 2016. "Why Your ZIP Code Matters More Than Your Genetic Code: Promoting Healthy Outcomes from Mother to Child." *Breastfeeding Medicine.* Published August 11. https://doi.org/10.1089/bfm.2016.0113.

Gray, M. 2017. "Value Based Healthcare." *BMJ*. Published January 27. https://doi.org/10.1136/bmj.j437.

Green, L. V., S. Savin, and Y. Lu. 2013. "Primary Care Physician Shortages Could Be Eliminated Through Use of Teams, Nonphysicians, and Electronic Communication." *Health Affairs*. Published January. https://doi.org/10.1377/hlthaff.2012.1086.

Health Policy Institute, Georgetown University. 2004. "Cultural Competence in Health Care: Is It Important for People with Chronic Conditions?" Accessed October 4, 2018. https://hpi.georgetown.edu/agingsociety/pubhtml/cultural/cultural.html.

Healthy People. 2018. "Determinants of Health." Accessed August 3. www.healthypeople.gov/2020/about/foundation-health-measures/Determinants-of-Health.

Heineman, M., and S. Froemke (dirs.). 2012. *Escape Fire: The Fight to Rescue American Healthcare*. Santa Monica, CA: Lionsgate.

Higgins, S. L. 2017. "Mamas, Don't Let Your Babies Grow Up to Be Doctors." *Forbes*. Published January 6. www.forbes.com/sites/realspin/2017/01/06/mamas-dont-let-your-babies-grow-up-to-be-doctors/#7da79b564199.

Hopkins, L., R. Labonté, V. Runnels, and C. Packer. 2010. "Medical Tourism Today: What Is the State of Existing Knowledge?" *Journal of Public Health Policy* 31 (2): 185–98. https://doi.org/10.1057/jphp.2010.10.

Igel, L. H. 2008. "When Did Health Care Become a Campaign Issue?" *Society* 45 (6): 512–14. https://doi.org/10.1007/s12115-008-9151-z.

Institute for Healthcare Improvement (IHI). 2019. "The IHI Triple Aim." Accessed September 13. www.ihi.org/Engage/Initiatives/TripleAim/Pages/default.aspx.

Jacob, B. A., and L. Lefgren. 2011. "The Impact of Research Grant Funding on Scientific Productivity." *Journal of Public Economics* 95 (9–10): 1168–77. https://doi.org/10.1016/j.jpubeco.2011.05.005.

Jena, A. B., S. Seabury, D. Lakdawalla, and A. Chandra. 2011. "Malpractice Risk According to Physician Specialty." *New England Journal of Medicine* 365: 629–36. https://doi.org/10.1056/NEJMsa1012370.

Jiwani, A., D. Himmelstein, S. Woolhandler, and J. G. Kahn. 2014. "Billing and Insurance-Related Administrative Costs in United States' Health Care: Synthesis of Micro-Costing Evidence." *BMC Health Services Research*. Published November 13. https://doi.org/10.1186/s12913-014-0556-7.

Junger, S. 1997. *The Perfect Storm*. New York: W.W. Norton.

Kakkis, E. D., M. O'Donovan, G. Cox, M. Hayes, F. Goodsaid, P. K. Tandon, P. Furlong, S. Boynton, M. Bozic, M. Orfali, and M. Thornton. 2015. "Recommendations for the Development of Rare Disease Drugs Using the Accelerated Approval Pathway and for Qualifying Biomarkers as Primary Endpoints." *Orphanet Journal of Rare Diseases*. Published February 10. https://doi.org/10.1186/s13023-014-0195-4.

Karsten, S. G. 1995. "Health Care: Private Good vs. Public Good." *American Journal of Economics and Sociology* 54 (2): 129–44. https://doi.org/10.1111/j.1536-7150.1995.tb02684.x.

Keeton, K., D. Fenner, T. Johnson, and R. Hayward. 2007. "Predictors of Physician Career Satisfaction, Work–Life Balance, and Burnout." *Obstetrics & Gynecology* 109 (4): 949–55. https://doi.org/10.1097/01.AOG.0000258299.45979.37.

Kisekka, V., and J. S. Giboney. 2018. "The Effectiveness of Health Care Information Technologies: Evaluation of Trust, Security Beliefs, and Privacy as Determinants of Health Care Outcomes." *Journal of Medical Internet Research*. Published April. https://doi.org/10.2196/jmir.9014.

Kotter, J. P. 2009. "Leading Change: Why Transformation Efforts Fail." *IEEE Engineering Management Review*. Published September 15. https://doi.org/10.1109/EMR.2009.5235501.

Kumar, R. D. C., and N. Khiljee. 2016. "Leadership in Healthcare." *Anaesthesia and Intensive Care Medicine*. Published January 21. https://doi.org/10.1016/j.mpaic.2015.10.012.

Kuratko, D. F., J. G. Covin, and J. S. Hornsby. 2014. "Why Implementing Corporate Innovation Is So Difficult." *Business Horizons* 57 (5): 647–55. https://doi.org/10.1016/j.bushor.2014.05.007.

Lee, T. M. 2004. "An EMTALA Primer: The Impact of Changes in the Emergency Medicine Landscape on EMTALA Compliance and Enforcement." *Annals of Health Law* 13 (1): 145–78.

Lindblad, R., A. El Fiky, and T. Zajdowicz. 2015. "Ebola in the United States." *Journal of Allergy and Clinical Immunology* 135 (4): 868–71. https://doi.org/10.1016/j.jaci.2014.12.012.

Luxton, E. 2016. "Top 8 Emerging Diseases Likely to Cause Major Epidemics." World Economic Forum. Published April 7. www.weforum.org/agenda/2016/04/top-8-emerging-diseases-likely-to-cause-major-epidemics/.

Maartens, G., C. Celum, and S. R. Lewin. 2014. "HIV Infection: Epidemiology, Pathogenesis, Treatment, and Prevention." *Lancet* 384 (9939): 258–71. https://doi.org/10.1016/S0140-6736(14)60164-1.

Mabahwi, N. A. B., O. L. H. Leh, and D. Omar. 2014. "Human Health and Wellbeing: Human Health Effect of Air Pollution." *Procedia—Social and Behavioral Sciences* 153 (16): 221–29. https://doi.org/10.1016/j.sbspro.2014.10.056.

Mackey, T. K., B. A. Liang, R. Cuomo, R. Hafen, K. C. Brouwer, and D. E. Lee. 2014. "Emerging and Reemerging Neglected Tropical Diseases: A Review of Key Characteristics, Risk Factors, and the Policy and Innovation Environment." *Clinical Microbiology Reviews* 27 (4): 949–79. https://doi.org/10.1128/CMR.00045-14.

Mandal, A. K., G. K. Tagomori, R. V. Felix, and S. C. Howell. 2017. "Value-Based Contracting Innovated Medicare Advantage Healthcare Delivery and

Improved Survival." *American Journal of Managed Care.* Published January 10. www.ajmc.com/journals/issue/2017/2017-vol23-n2/value-based-contracting-innovated-medicare-advantage-healthcare-delivery-and-improved-survival.

Marmor, T., and C. Wendt. 2012. "Conceptual Frameworks for Comparing Healthcare Politics and Policy." *Health Policy* 107 (1): 11–20. https://doi.org/10.1016/j.healthpol.2012.06.003.

Mayo Clinic. 2019. "Sickle Cell Anemia." Accessed September 24. www.mayoclinic.org/diseases-conditions/sickle-cell-anemia/symptoms-causes/syc-20355876.

McKibben, M. J., E. W. Kirby, J. Langston, M. C. Raynor, M. E. Nielsen, A. B. Smith, E. M. Wallen, M. E. Woods, and R. S. Pruthi. 2016. "Projecting the Urology Workforce Over the Next 20 Years." *Urology* 98: 21–26. https://doi.org/10.1016/j.urology.2016.07.028.

Medscape. 2018. "Emerging and Reemerging Infectious Diseases." Accessed October 6. www.medscape.com/resource/infections.

Morrison, I. 1996. *The Second Curve: Managing the Velocity of Change.* New York: Ballantine.

Mui, C. 2012. "How Kodak Failed." *Forbes.* Published January 18. www.forbes.com/sites/chunkamui/2012/01/18/how-kodak-failed/.

National Institutes of Health (NIH). 2019. "Estimates of Funding for Various Research, Condition, and Disease Categories (RCDC)." Published April 19. https://report.nih.gov/categorical_spending.aspx.

————. 2018. "NIH Launches Initiative to Accelerate Genetic Therapies to Cure Sickle Cell Disease." Published September 13. www.nih.gov/news-events/news-releases/nih-launches-initiative-accelerate-genetic-therapies-cure-sickle-cell-disease.

O'Laughlin, B. 2016. "Pragmatism, Structural Reform and the Politics of Inequality in Global Public Health." *Development and Change* 47 (4): 686–711. https://doi.org/10.1111/dech.12251.

Obe, M. 2016. "Japanese Lawyers' Problem: Too Few Cases." Published April 3. www.wsj.com/articles/japanese-lawyers-problem-too-few-cases-1459671069.

Organisation for Economic Co-operation and Development (OECD). 2013. *Health at a Glance 2013: OECD Indicators.* Published November 21. https://doi.org/10.1787/health_glance-2013-en.

Papanicolas, I., L. R. Woskie, and A. K. Jha. 2018. "Health Care Spending in the United States and Other High-Income Countries." *JAMA* 319 (10): 1024–39. https://doi.org/10.1001/jama.2018.1150.

Paules, C. I., H. D. Marston, M. E. Bloom, and A. S. Fauci. 2018. "Tickborne Diseases—Confronting a Growing Threat." *New England Journal of Medicine* 379 (8): 701–3.https://doi.org/10.1056/NEJMp1807870.

Polcino, M. (dir.). 2018. *The Simpsons.* Season 29, episode 20, "Throw Grampa from the Dane." Aired May 13. 20th Century Fox Television.

Porter, M. E. 2010. "What Is Value in Health Care?" *New England Journal of Medicine* 363 (26): 2477–81. https://doi.org/10.1056/NEJMp1011024.

Porter, M. E., and T. H. Lee. 2013. "The Strategy That Will Fix Healthcare." *Harvard Business Review.* Published October. https://hbr.org/2013/10/the-strategy-that-will-fix-health-care.

Pracht, E. E., B. Langland-Orban, and J. L. Ryan. 2018. "The Probability of Hospitalizations for Mild-to-Moderate Injuries by Trauma Center Ownership Type." *Health Services Research* 53 (1): 35–48. https://doi.org/10.1111/1475-6773.12646.

Prina, L. L. 2017. "Foundation Funding for Palliative and End-of-Life Care." *Health Affairs.* Published July 1. https://doi.org/10.1377/hlthaff.2017.0653.

Rice, T., P. Rosenau, L. Unruh, A. J. Barnes, R. B. Saltman, and E. van Ginneken. 2013. "United States of America: Health System Review." *Health Systems in Transition* 15 (3): 1–431. www.euro.who.int/__data/assets/pdf_file/0019/215155/HiT-United-States-of-America.pdf.

Roeder, A. 2015. "Zip Code Better Predictor of Health than Genetic Code." Harvard T. H. Chan School of Public Health. Accessed September 16, 2019. www.hsph.harvard.edu/news/features/zip-code-better-predictor-of-health-than-genetic-code/.

Schneiderman, L. J. 2011. "Defining Medical Futility and Improving Medical Care." *Journal of Bioethical Inquiry.* Published March 20. https://doi.org/10.1007/s11673-011-9293-3.

Scientific American. 2018. "Social and Environmental Change Drives a World of Newly Emerged Infections." Published April 17. https://doi.org/10.1038/scientificamerican0518-42.

Shanafelt, T. D., S. Boone, L. Tan, L. N. Dyrbye, W. Sotile, D. Satele, C. P. West, J. Sloan, and M. R. Oreskovich. 2012. "Burnout and Satisfaction with Work–Life Balance Among US Physicians Relative to the General US Population." *Archives of Internal Medicine* 172 (18): 1377–85. https://doi.org/10.1001/archinternmed.2012.3199.

Singh, R. K., K. Dhama, Y. S. Malik, M. A. Ramakrishnan, K. Karthik, R. Khandia, R. Tiwari, A. Munjal, M. Saminathan, S. Sachan, P. A. Desingu, J. J. Kattoor, H. M. N. Iqbal, and S. K. Joshi. 2017. "Ebola Virus—Epidemiology, Diagnosis, and Control: Threat to Humans, Lessons Learnt, and Preparedness Plans." *Veterinary Quarterly* 37 (1): 98–135. https://doi.org/10.1080/01652176.2017.1309474.

60 Minutes. 2019. "Could Gene Therapy Cure Sickle Cell Anemia?" CBS, March 10. www.cbs.com/shows/60_minutes/video/kaxgqzPGVQulVXxP2ilWPqMZ-vWeraYeq/could-gene-therapy-cure-sickle-cell-anemia-/.

Slade-Sawyer, P. 2014. "Is Health Determined by Genetic Code or Zip Code? Measuring the Health of Groups and Improving Population Health." *North Carolina Medical Journal* 75 (6): 394–97. https://doi.org/10.18043/ncm.75.6.394.

Starr, P. 2011. *Remedy and Reaction: The Peculiar American Struggle over Health Care Reform*. New Haven, CT: Yale University Press. https://books.google.com/books?id=PNFLo4DWsJkC&pg=PA52.

Sugden, R. 2009. "On Nudging: A Review of *Nudge: Improving Decisions About Health, Wealth and Happiness* by Richard H. Thaler and Cass R. Sunstein." *International Journal of the Economics of Business* 16 (3): 365–73. https://doi.org/10.1080/13571510903227064.

Telegraph reporters. 2012. "Rejected Beatles Audition Tape Discovered." *Telegraph*. Published November 22. www.telegraph.co.uk/culture/music/the-beatles/9695499/Rejected-Beatles-audition-tape-discovered.html.

US Census Bureau. 2018a. "From Pyramid to Pillar: A Century of Change, Population of the U.S." Published March 13. www.census.gov/library/visualizations/2018/comm/century-of-change.html.

———. 2018b. "Older People Projected to Outnumber Children for First Time in U.S. History." Published March 13. www.census.gov/newsroom/press-releases/2018/cb18-41-population-projections.html.

———. 2017. "US Census Bureau QuickFacts." Accessed August 3, 2018. www.census.gov/quickfacts/fact/table/US/PST045217.

van Dijk, C. E., B. van den Berg, R. A. Verheij, P. Spreeuwenberg, P. P. Groenewegen, and D. H. de Bakker. 2013. "Moral Hazard and Supplier-Induced Demand: Empirical Evidence in General Practice." *Health Economics* 22 (3): 340–52. https://doi.org/10.1002/hec.2801.

Wakeman, N. 2011. "IBM's Watson Heads to Medical School." *Washington Technology*. Published February 17. http://washingtontechnology.com/articles/2011/02/17/ibm-watson-next-steps.aspx.

Walston, S. L., and A. F. Chou. 2006. "Healthcare Restructuring and Hierarchical Alignment: Why Do Staff and Managers Perceive Change Outcomes Differently?" *Medical Care* 44 (9): 879–89. https://doi.org/10.1097/01.mlr.0000220692.39762.bf.

Waxman, D. A., M. D. Greenberg, M. S. Ridgely, A. L. Kellermann, and P. Heaton. 2014. "The Effect of Malpractice Reform on Emergency Department Care." *New England Journal of Medicine* 371 (16): 1518–25. https://doi.org/10.1056/NEJMsa1313308.

Webster, D. P., P. Klenerman, and G. M. Dusheiko. 2015. "Hepatitis C." *Lancet* 385 (9973): 1124–35. https://doi.org/10.1016/S0140-6736(14)62401-6.

Weinstein, N. J., A. Geller, Y. Negussie, and A. Baciu. 2017. *Communities in Action: Pathways to Health Equity*. Washington, DC: National Academies Press. https://doi.org/10.17226/24624.

Weinstein, R. S., A. M. Lopez, B. A. Joseph, K. A. Erps, M. Holcomb, G. P. Barker, and E. A. Krupinski. 2014. "Telemedicine, Telehealth, and Mobile Health Applications That Work: Opportunities and Barriers."

American Journal of Medicine 127 (3): 183–87. https://doi.org/10.1016/j. amjmed.2013.09.032.

Wennberg, J. E. 2011. "Time to Tackle Unwarranted Variations in Practice." *BMJ.* Published March 17. https://doi.org/10.1136/bmj.d1513.

Williams, J. S., R. J. Walker, and L. E. Egede. 2016. "Achieving Equity in an Evolving Healthcare System: Opportunities and Challenges." *American Journal of the Medical Sciences* 351 (1): 33–43. https://doi.org/10.1016/j. amjms.2015.10.012.

Wilson, H. 2018. "State of the States 2017." *Journal of the American College of Cardiology* 71 (8): 949–50. https://doi.org/10.1016/j.jacc.2018.01.032.

Wolford, M. L., K. Palso, and A. Bercovitz. 2015. "Hospitalization for Total Hip Replacement Among Inpatients Aged 45 and Over: United States, 2000–2010." National Center for Health Statistics, Centers for Disease Control and Prevention. www.cdc.gov/nchs/data/databriefs/db186.pdf.

Woolhandler, S., T. Campbell, and D. U. Himmelstein. 2003. "Costs of Health Care Administration in the United States and Canada." *New England Journal of Medicine* 349 (8): 768–75. https://doi.org/10.1056/NEJMsa022033.

World Health Organization (WHO). 2015. "Blueprint for R&D Preparedness and Response to Public Health Emergencies Due to Highly Infectious Pathogens." Published December. www.who.int/blueprint/what/research-development/meeting-report-prioritization.pdf.

———. 2010. "The Determinants of Health." Accessed September 16, 2019. www. who.int/hia/evidence/doh/en/.

Wu, J., H. Li, S. Cheng, and Z. Lin. 2016. "The Promising Future of Healthcare Services: When Big Data Analytics Meets Wearable Technology." *Information & Management* 53 (8): 1020–33. https://doi.org/10.1016/j.im.2016.07.003.

HISTORY AND DEVELOPMENT OF THE US HEALTHCARE SYSTEM

Now, for the first time, we have not just the need but the will to get this job done. There is widespread support in the Congress and in the Nation for some form of comprehensive health insurance.
—Richard Nixon, 1974

Learning Objectives

- Understand that the modern healthcare system is a recent development.
- Recognize the significance of the rise of the physician and urbanization.
- Develop knowledge of key events and milestones in health and medical history.
- Create a list of the drivers of medical spending in the United States.
- Analyze past attempts to reform our healthcare system, and determine why they failed.
- Evaluate some of the key features of the Afforable Care Act in comparison to previous reform efforts.

The Modern Healthcare System Is a Recent Development

This chapter focuses on the history and development of the US healthcare system, describing key events and examining some of the reasons our system of care developed the way it did (see exhibit 2.1). It includes a time line of major milestones, making clear that healthcare has been an integral part of the human experience dating back to the earliest recorded history (Aceves-Avila, Medina, and Fraga 2001; Borchardt 2002; Finlayson 1893; Nutton 2004; Roberts and Manchester 2005). The first physician ever mentioned—Imhotep, dating back to 2600 BC in ancient Egypt (Hurry 1978)—was revered as a god, an indication of the special esteem and status that physicians would hold in society. However, despite these deep historic roots, the modern healthcare system is a relatively recent development. Until about the

EXHIBIT 2.1
Area of Focus
for This Chapter

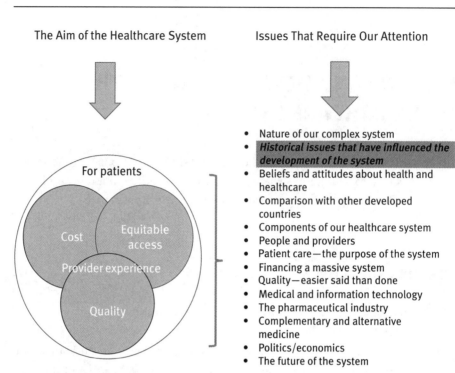

EXHIBIT 2.1
Area of Focus
for This Chapter

The Aim of the Healthcare System

Issues That Require Our Attention

For patients

Cost

Equitable access

Provider experience

Quality

- Nature of our complex system
- *Historical issues that have influenced the development of the system*
- Beliefs and attitudes about health and healthcare
- Comparison with other developed countries
- Components of our healthcare system
- People and providers
- Patient care—the purpose of the system
- Financing a massive system
- Quality—easier said than done
- Medical and information technology
- The pharmaceutical industry
- Complementary and alternative medicine
- Politics/economics
- The future of the system

last 100 years, medicine was largely unscientific; in many cases, providers had limited ability to change the course of disease (Cassedy 1991). Science and medicine have advanced side by side.

The practice of medicine and the US healthcare system developed simultaneously, both heavily influenced by the tremendous social and scientific changes of the eighteenth, nineteenth, and twentieth centuries. The history of medicine is an extensive topic and a field of study unto itself—too broad to cover in a single book chapter. However, a brief overview of key events can provide useful historical context and help us understand how our healthcare system got to where it is today.

Medicine in the 1700s and 1800s

In preindustrial times, American medicine had only primitive methods, primarily based on traditional cures and treatments. Healthcare was largely carried out in the home. Institutions that most closely resembled hospitals were known as pest houses (for infectious patients) and almshouses. Almshouses, also known as poorhouses, were places poor people could go to die to avoid dying on the street. These institutions were charitable in nature and often

Key Events and Milestones in Health and Medical History

Literally thousands of events and milestones could be included in this list. The following is just a sampling to provide background for the discussions later in this chapter.

2600 BC	Imhotep is a famous doctor and the first physician mentioned in recorded history. After his death, he is worshiped as a god (Hurry 1978).
1792–1750 BC	The Code of Hammurabi is written, setting forth laws to govern the practice of medicine (Johns 2000).
1500 BC	The Ebers Papyrus, the first known medical book, is written (Wreszinski 1913).
500 BC	Alcmaeon of Croton, in Italy, says that a body is healthy if it has the right balance of hot and cold, wet and dry. If the balance is upset, the body falls ill (Jones 1979).
460–370 BC	Hippocrates stresses careful observation and the importance of nutrition (Hippocrates 1868).
384–322 BC	Aristotle says the body is made up of the four humors or liquids: phlegm, blood, yellow bile, and black bile (Favreau 2012; Osborn 2018).
AD 130–200	The Roman doctor Galen creates writings that will become highly influential for centuries (Sarton 1954).
400s–1000s	While Western Europe experienced little scientific development during the Dark Ages, medical advances continued in the Middle East (Kaylin 2005; *Medical News Today* 2018).
1100s–1200s	Schools of medicine are founded in Europe. In the thirteenth century, barber-surgeons begin to work in towns. The church runs the only hospitals (Cobban 1999; Rashdall 1895).
1543	Andreas Vesalius publishes *The Fabric of the Human Body* (Garrison and Hast 2013).
1628	William Harvey publishes his discovery of how blood circulates in the body (Harvey 1968).
1751	Pennsylvania Hospital, the first public hospital in what is now the United States, is established by Benjamin Franklin and Thomas Bond (Benjamin Franklin Historical Society 2014).
1765	The University of Pennsylvania School of Medicine, America's first medical school, enrolls students in "anatomical lectures" and a course on "the theory and practice of physik" (McConaghy, Silberman, and Kalashnikova 2004).

(continued)

1796	Edward Jenner invents vaccination against smallpox (Winkelstein 1992).
1816	René Laennec invents the stethoscope (Roguin 2006).
1847	James Simpson uses chloroform as an anesthetic (Ball 1996).
1857	Elizabeth Blackwell becomes the first female physician in the United States (US National Library of Medicine 2015).
1860	Public hospitals emerge as a common feature of healthcare delivery (Risse 1990).
1861–1865	The Civil War, like all wars, has a significant impact on the treatment of injury and disease; it forces medical providers to address care issues that were seen in war and later generalizable to society at large.
1865	Joseph Lister develops antiseptic surgery (Bankston 2004).
1865	The first commercial ambulance service in the United States is established in Cincinnati, Ohio (Barkley 1990; Rosenstein 2018; America's Essential Hospitals 2018b).
1870s	Medical practice acts are passed; licensure of physicians becomes a state function (Stevens 1971).
1876	The American Association of Medical Colleges (AAMC) is founded (Coggeshall 1965).
1880	Louis Pasteur invents a cure for chicken cholera, the first animal vaccine (Debré 2000).
1884	Detroit's Harper Hospital Nursing School opens, helping usher in the profession of nursing (Schmeling 2002).
1893	Johns Hopkins School of Medicine opens (Johns Hopkins Medicine 2019).
1895	Wilhelm Conrad Röntgen discovers X-rays (Glasser 1933).
1904	The American Medical Association creates the Council on Medical Education (Hoffman 2008).
1910	The Abraham Flexner report on medical education is published, influencing the education and regulation of medical practitioners (Duffy 2011; Flexner 1910).
1914–1918	World War I spurs new developments in the treatment of injury and disease.
1928	Scottish scientist Alexander Fleming discovers penicillin and its use as an antibiotic (Ligon 2004).
1929	The first employer-sponsored health insurance plan (Blue Cross) is created by Baylor University Hospital and Dallas schoolteachers (Buchmueller and Monheit 2009).

(continued)

1931	The electron microscope is invented (Palucka 2002).
1937	The first blood bank is established at Cook County Hospital in Chicago (Eschner 2017; America's Essential Hospitals 2018c).
1939–1945	World War II further shapes treatment of injury and disease.
1940s	Healthcare costs begin to be tracked and studied.
1943	Willem Johan Kolff invents the first dialysis machine (Heiney 2003).
1945	Insurance becomes more commonplace (Murray 2007).
1946	The Hill-Burton Act is passed to increase funding and encourage spending on new hospitals (Perlstadt 1995).
1948	The World Health Organization (WHO) is founded (WHO 2019).
1948	Ethical principles for medical research are established as a result of the Nuremburg trials (Marrus 1997).
1950	Healthcare spending represents 4.6 percent of the US gross domestic product (GDP) (Fuchs 2012).
1951	Epidemiology studies identify health risks of cigarette smoking; Sir Richard Doll is the first to link smoking with lung cancer (Keating 2009).
1953	Jonas Salk develops a vaccine for polio (Koprowski 1960).
1953	Francis Crick and James Watson determine the structure of DNA (Dahm 2008).
1960	Healthcare spending represents 5 percent of the US GDP (Centers for Medicare & Medicaid Services [CMS] 2018b).
1965	Medicare and Medicaid are established (CMS 2019a).
1966–1982	Healthcare spending as a percentage of GDP grows from 5.7 percent to 10 percent (CMS 2018b).
1967	Christiaan Barnard performs the first heart transplant (Barnard 2011).
1970s	Smallpox is eradicated worldwide (Centers for Disease Control and Prevention [CDC] 2016).
1971	Paul Lauterbur invents magnetic resonance imaging (MRI) (Dawson 2013).
1973	The Health Maintenance Organization (HMO) Act is passed during the Nixon presidency (Dorsey 1975).
1980	Area safety-net hospitals are established, often representing the only healthcare organization in a community (America's Essential Hospitals 2018a).
1983–1992	Healthcare spending as a percentage of GDP grows from 10.1 to 13.1 (CMS 2018b).

(continued)

1984	Research groups led by Robert Gallo, Luc Montagnier, and Jay Levy identify a retrovirus as the cause of AIDS (Office of History, National Institutes of Health 2018).
1989	President George H. W. Bush signs the Omnibus Budget Reconciliation Act of 1989, enacting a physician payment schedule based on a resource-based relative value scale (RBRVS) (American Medical Association 2019b).
1990s	Research related to evidence-based medicine begins to be introduced into the literature (Kovner 2014).
1991	The first web servers outside the European Organization for Nuclear Research (CERN) are installed (O'Luanaigh 2012).
1993	The Clinton administration proposes sweeping healthcare reform that would have provided a "health care security card" to every citizen, entitling them to treatment and preventive services, including for pre-existing conditions (Clinton 1993; Moffitt 1993; Pear 1993).
1993–2002	Healthcare spending as a percentage of GDP grows from 13.4 percent to 14.9 percent (CMS 2018b).
1996	The Health Insurance Portability and Accountability Act (HIPAA) is passed as an amendment to the HMO Act (Atchinson and Fox 1997).
2000	The Institute of Medicine (IOM) releases its *To Err Is Human* report, drawing attention to issues of safety in healthcare (IOM 2000).
2001	The IOM releases *Crossing the Quality Chasm*, drawing attention to healthcare quality issues (IOM 2001).
2001	The 9/11 terrorist attack occurs.
2003	The human genome is sequenced (National Human Genome Research Institute 2019).
2003–2013	Healthcare spending as a percentage of GDP grows from 15.4 percent to 17.2 percent (CMS 2018b).
2005	Hurricane Katrina devastates the Gulf Coast, including New Orleans.
2008	The Institute for Healthcare Improvement puts forth the Triple Aim as a principle of healthcare management, emphasizing care, health, and cost (Berwick, Nolan, and Whittington 2008).
2008	Medicare Part D is enacted (Hargrave et al. 2007).

(continued)

2010	The Affordable Care Act (ACA) becomes law, though it would continue to be changed and challenged (Congress.gov 2019c; Harrington 2010).
2012	Consumer-directed health plans become more common (Bundorf 2012; Scandlen 2005).
2014	The Ebola crisis begins in West Africa (CDC 2019a).
2016	The Zika virus becomes a serious health threat (Meaney-Delman et al. 2016; CDC 2019b).
2017	Efforts are undertaken to repeal the ACA; major changes are implemented and planned (Friedmann, Andrews, and Humphreys 2017; Jost and Lazarus 2017; Obama 2017).
2017	Healthcare spending represents 17.9 percent of the GDP (CMS 2018b; Cuckler et al. 2018).
2019	Repeal of the ACA's individual mandate takes effect (Jost 2017).
2025	Healthcare spending in the United States is expected to reach 20 percent of the GDP (CMS 2019c; Cuckler et al. 2018; Keehan et al. 2017).

run by religious orders. Healing was not their goal. The people involved in healthcare had little scientific knowledge or training in patient care (Andrews 2011; Shryock 1956).

New York's Bellevue Hospital, which grew out of an almshouse in 1736, is often regarded as the oldest hospital in the United States (Burrows and Wallace 1998). However, two other hospitals existed in New Orleans during the early 1700s. Royal Hospital opened in in 1722, and Charity Hospital opened in 1736, at the same time as Bellevue. As the names implied, Charity Hospital focused on the care for the poor, and Royal Hospital primarily served people who had enough money to afford treatment (Salvaggio 1992). Pennsylvania Hospital was founded in Philadelphia in 1751.

During this time, healthcare was generally regarded as an activity of self-reliance. Interestingly, today we are in some ways seeing history repeat itself, with the increasing emphasis on self-care.

Medicine from the Late 1800s to Mid-1900s

The period from the late 1800s to the mid-1900s is marked by several key trends in US healthcare: the rise of the physician, urbanization, specialization in medicine, and institutionalization.

Rise of the Physician

The late nineteenth and early twentieth century saw American physicians begin to coalesce into a profession. Advances in science, medical education, and licensing helped establish the profession and move it forward, establishing criteria for being a physician. Education and training standards emerged, giving the public some assurance of physicians' qualifications. Physicians also began to gain professional sovereignty. They were able to control the demand for the services they provided because the patients generally did not know what services they needed and had to rely on the professional for guidance. This professional sovereignty is often thought to be a factor that contributed to escalating medical costs (Starr 1982).

In 1796, Edward Jenner created the first effective vaccine against smallpox (Stern and Markel 2005). Because of its great promise in preventing a serious and common disease at the time, President James Madison signed the Vaccine Act of 1813. The act encouraged the use of the smallpox vaccine and was the first federal law to deal with consumer protection and therapeutic substances.

Urbanization

The development of industry and the growth of major cities had a powerful impact on the US healthcare system. Prior to urbanization, physician house calls were the norm. However, as the country became more urban, physicians tended to settle in urban areas to avoid having to travel great distances to find people to treat. Physicians were able to become much more productive once they reduced their travel and had patients come to them (*Journal of Health Politics, Policy and Law* 2004; Starr 1982; Wailoo, Jost, and Schlesinger 2004). The demand for healthcare services was also influenced by the fact that many working families were unable to take care of one another as they had in the past because of the long hours spent working outside the home. At the same time, the entry of women into the workforce produced an opportunity for more physician services.

Specialization in Medicine

As scientific and medical knowledge grew and medical technologies became more sophisticated, the complete body of knowledge and skills for the practice of medicine became more than any one human being could possibly possess. As a result, specialization was inevitable. The earliest examples of medical specialization occurred in the 1830s, and the trend has continued ever since. In the 1950s, specialization became the predominant mode of practice in the United States (Weisz 2005). This characteristic distinguishes the US healthcare system from the systems of other nations, where primary care forms the foundation.

Institutionalization

Over time, with the institutionalization of healthcare, society began to expect that sick people could obtain medical care from a hospital to get well—a great departure from the days when most people who went to a hospital had no expectation of recovery. This changing mind-set allowed healthcare institutions and the medical profession to gain cultural authority. *Cultural authority* refers to an accumulation of public trust that leads to a sense of legitimacy, the granting of relative autonomy, and an ability to self-regulate (Pescosolido and Martin 2004). This trust was critical to the expansion of healthcare as a profession and the growth of hospitals and other medical and medically related institutions.

Medical practice acts passed by a number of states during the 1870s were another important development. They led to the upgrading of medical schools, and they relieved the intense competition by reducing the number of people who could practice medicine. The acts were just the beginning of the many reforms that would address medical education, the requirements of medical practice, and healthcare regulation (Sigerist 1935).

Exhibit 2.2 summarizes the key stages in the development of modern healthcare institutions, from almshouses to the modern system. Exhibit 2.3 illustrates the historical cycle of healthcare system development, which

Event	Time	Key Characteristics of the Period
Pesthouses and almshouses	1700s to mid-1800s	• Charitable social welfare • Primarily for the poor • Pesthouses used for isolating contagious diseases • Staffed by religious orders with little healing knowledge or training
Community hospitals	Beginning in the mid-1800s	• Privately owned • Supported by private donors
The emergence of medical practice in the hospital setting	Beginning in the late 1800s	• Advanced with medical discovery and technological progress • Introduction of new medical advances such as sterile technique laboratory and X-rays • Focused on treatment with an expectation of care
Proprietary hospitals	Beginning in the late 1800s	• Largely focused on more affluent patients with the ability to pay • Owned by physicians

EXHIBIT 2.2
Historical Development of Modern Healthcare Institutions

(continued)

EXHIBIT 2.2
Historical
Development
of Modern
Healthcare
Institutions
(continued)

Event	Time	Key Characteristics of the Period
The university-based medical center	Beginning in the early 1900s	• Formal affiliations with universities • Facilitation of research • Education provided and promoted • Addition of more well-trained professionals in ancillary healthcare services
The modern healthcare system	Late 1990s to the present	• Integration of a wide range of medical services • Common organization • Longitudinal care to wide demographic

essentially continues to this day. The cycle starts with medical and scientific research, which creates new knowledge. This new knowledge then enters practice through medical education, training, technological development, and licensing requirements. Institutional development occurs to support new practices and care models, with continued development of physician and medical services through the application of new technologies. The cycle has repeated itself throughout history, allowing care to improve and treatment options to proliferate.

EXHIBIT 2.3
Historical
Healthcare
Development
Cycle

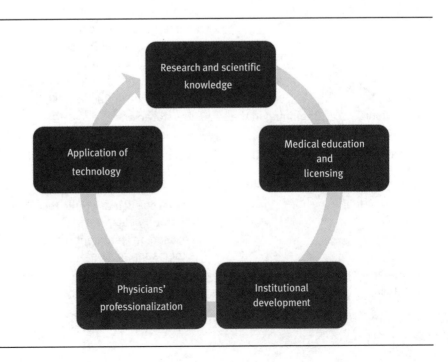

The US Healthcare System as We Know It

No Plan for a System: Humble Beginnings

To say that the current US healthcare system is the product of careful design and development would be misguided. Prior to World War II, healthcare delivery in the United States could hardly even be called a system; it was a patchwork of charitable institutions, providers with a wide range of education, and a focus on public health (Shryock 1947). The lack of modern tools and knowledge about the diagnosis and treatment of various medical conditions was a significant limitation. Healthcare was a cottage industry, with much of the care delivered at home.

Important Figures in the Development of the Modern System

The development of the modern US healthcare system was heavily influenced by Johns Hopkins University, Mayo Clinic, and the American Medical Association (AMA), as well as by William Osler, William Welch, the Mayo brothers, and Abraham Flexner (Bliss 1999; Fleming 1987; Hiatt and Stockton 2003; Johns Hopkins Medicine 2019; Mayo Clinic 2018). Certainly, these organizations and individuals are not the only important figures in the development of our healthcare system, but they are of particular interest to our discussion.

Prior to the contributions of these institutions and people, healthcare delivery in the United States was chaotic and unstandardized, and medical education was largely haphazard. Virtually anyone could enter the practice of medicine, and many did. According to census records, the United States had more than 62,000 physicians in 1870 (US Census Bureau 1872). These conditions began to change with the Flexner report of 1910, which, in many ways, was a key factor in the start of our modern system.

Johns Hopkins University

Johns Hopkins University was founded in Baltimore, Maryland, in 1876. The Johns Hopkins Hospital opened in 1889, followed four years later by the Johns Hopkins University School of Medicine. Relative to other medical schools that had existed up to that point, Johns Hopkins was unique in that it did the following (Johns Hopkins Medicine 2018):

- It established entrance requirements for medical students.
- It developed a medical school curriculum with an emphasis on the scientific method.
- It incorporated bedside teaching and laboratory research as part of the curriculum.
- It integrated the School of Medicine with the hospital through joint appointments of medical staff to the faculty.

Johns Hopkins was the first major medical school in the United States to admit women. It was also the first to use rubber gloves during surgery, to perform renal dialysis, and to perform cardiopulmonary resuscitation (CPR) (Johns Hopkins Medicine 2019). These practices were quickly adopted by the Mayo brothers. Much of the advancement in medical education and practice during this time depended on the work of individuals associated with Johns Hopkins. Notable among them were William Osler, Abraham Flexner, and William Welch.

William Osler

William Osler (July 12, 1849–December 29, 1919) was a Canadian physician and one of the four founding professors of Johns Hopkins Hospital. He is sometimes called the "Father of Modern Medicine." Osler created the first residency program for the training of physicians in specialty areas such as surgery, and he was the first to bring medical students to the bedside for clinical training. He also founded of the History of Medicine Society, which is part of the Royal Society of Medicine in London. In 1893, Osler played a key role in the creation of the Johns Hopkins School of Medicine and was one of its first professors of medicine (Bliss 1999).

Abraham Flexner

In 1904, the American Medical Association created the Council on Medical Education (CME) with the aim of restructuring American medical education and adopting standards for both classroom and clinical work. The CME asked the Carnegie Foundation for the Advancement of Teaching to survey the current state of US medical education. Abraham Flexner was approached to conduct the survey, and he produced a rather scathing report (King 1984).

Abraham Flexner (November 13, 1866–September 21, 1959) was not a physician, but he was educated in the natural sciences at Johns Hopkins University. An American educator, he was keenly interested in medical education in the United States and Canada. His report for the CME provided a framework for modern medical education and introduced a number of educational principles still in use today.

The Flexner report found that the United States had too many medical schools and that too many physicians were being trained as a result. The report called for a restructuring of medical education, the consolidation of medical institutions, and greater standardization of curricula to create a scientific paradigm of medical education and research. Homeopathy and many other complementary and alternative forms of medicine—some of which were widely practiced at that time—were strongly discouraged (Duffy 2011).

William Welch

William Welch (April 8, 1850–April 30, 1934) was a physician and founding professor at Johns Hopkins Hospital. He was the first dean of the Johns Hopkins University School of Medicine and the founder of the Johns Hopkins School of Hygiene and Public Health, the first school of public health in the United States. Welch promoted a more clinical approach to medical education, emphasizing bedside teaching and standardized clinical observation. He was also interested in laboratory analysis and research as part of the educational process, which Flexner also embraced.

The American Medical Association

The AMA was founded in 1847 with the goals of advancing science, supporting medical education, upholding medical ethics, and improving public health (AMA 2019a). In the early 1900s, the association provided background material that Flexner would use in building his report and providing a basis for medical licensing and accreditation of medical education. The AMA believed that promoting good medical education was in its best interest (Silverman 2011).

The Mayo Brothers and Mayo Clinic

William, James, and Charles Mayo founded Mayo Clinic in 1889, after joining the small for-profit practice started by their father, William Worrall Mayo, in Rochester, Minnesota. Mayo Clinic, from its beginning, focused on clinical excellence, research and the application of that research to patient care, the use of sterile technique (which had previously been neglected by many practitioners), clear organization, and collaborative group practice (National Library of Medicine 2016). Mayo Clinic pioneered many of the concepts we take for granted today (Mayo Clinic 2018). Despite its origins as a small family practice, Mayo Clinic today is a world-renowned destination for medical care.

A number of innovations and noteworthy characteristics have contributed to Mayo Clinic's success and influence. Unlike at most physician organizations, all of Mayo Clinic's physicians are salaried, which leads to less of an emphasis on volume of care and a greater focus on outcomes. Mayo Clinic was the first clinic to create a collaborative relationship with a hospital (St. Mary's Hospital) and to develop the concept of a multispecialty group practice; it did so because it recognized that no individual physician could possibly possess all the knowledge or skills needed for the expanding range of medical services. Mayo Clinic was also the first organization to develop a standardized medical record to be shared by multiple physicians.

Another important innovation was the effort to dissuade selective use of expensive services by pricing them the same as other, more conventional procedures. For instance, Mayo Clinic recognized that, because positron beam therapy for cancer treatment was significantly more expensive than the more traditional X-ray therapy, insurers were reluctant to pay for it. By pricing positron beam therapy the same as X-ray therapy, the clinic ensured that physicians' decisions to use one over the other would be based not on price but rather on what they viewed as the most beneficial option for the patient (Burns, Ewers, and Ewers 2018).

Mayo Clinic was one of the first healthcare organizations to integrate the application of evidence-based medicine by incorporating data that was collected and analyzed from its research. It also has a tradition of supporting and developing high levels of medical education (National Library of Medicine 2016).

Healthcare Spending

In tracing the major events and milestones in the development of the US healthcare system, we should note that, prior to 1940, healthcare spending was rarely a focus of study or discussion. Up to that time, the debate was mostly about access, and the literature tended to emphasize the advancement of medical science and patient care (US Department of Health, Education, and Welfare 1976). Only in the middle and late twentieth century did spending on healthcare begin to be treated as a major concern (Catlin and Cowan 2015). That spending continues to increase rapidly.

The Burden of Disease

The nature of mortality and morbidity from disease in the United States has changed dramatically in the past century, as the diseases and ailments that have been the focus of our healthcare system have shifted (Tippett 2014). Exhibit 2.4 shows the change in the top ten causes of death from 1900 to 2010. Overall death rates have dropped by 54 percent, from 1,719.1 deaths out of every 100,000 people in 1900 to 798.7 deaths out of every 100,000 in 2010, but the shifts in causes require the healthcare system to respond accordingly. One troubling current trend, for instance, is the growing number of opioid overdose-related deaths. Approximately 64,000 people died from drug overdoses in 2016 (Scholl et al. 2018). The opioid epidemic has become so severe that the overall longevity for Americans dropped from 2014 to 2016 (National Institute on Drug Abuse 2018; Stein 2017).

Infectious disease was a major killer before the discovery and development of antibiotics, and today it is reemerging as a serious threat (US Burden of Disease Collaborators 2013; WHO 2008). One particular disease event that had a lasting impact on our thinking about healthcare and disease was the Spanish flu outbreak of 1918. Some researchers have said the outbreak had origins in China, whereas others have traced it to a small town in Kansas. The first recorded case occurred in Fort Riley, Kansas (Crosby 1976).

EXHIBIT 2.4
Mortality and
Top Ten Causes
of Death in the
United States,
1900 and 2010

Mortality and Top 10 Causes of Death (rates per 100,000)

1900

2010

All Causes: 1,719.1

Mortality from all causes **declined 54%**
between 1900 and 2010.

Other, 620.1

Cancer, 64.0
Heart disease, 137.4
Senility, 50.2
Accidents, 72.3
Nephropathies, 88.6
Cerebrovascular disease, 106.9
Diphtheria, 40.3
Gastrointestinal infections,
142.7
Tuberculosis, 194.4

Pneumonia or influenza, 202.2

All Causes: 798.7

Suicide, 12.2

Other, 201.3

Diabetes, 22.3

Noninfectious
airways diseases,
44.6

Cancer, 185.9

Senility, 27.0

Heart disease, 192.9

Accidents, 38.2

Nephropathies, 16.3

Cerebrovascular disease, 41.8

Pneumonia or influenza, 16.2

Source: Adapted from Tippett (2014).

Although flu is a common occurrence each year in the United States, it is typically only deadly to the very young and the very old or infirm. In 1918, however, the flu mutated into something much more virulent. This deadlier flu acted unlike the usual flu, targeting the young and healthy. People between the ages of 20 and 35 seemed to be the most vulnerable (Taubenberger and Morens 2006).

From March 1918 to the spring of 1919, this flu strain spread rapidly around the globe. According to estimates, 50 million people died—as much as 5 percent of the world's population—and another 50 to 100 million were sickened (Ansart et al. 2009; Jordan 2019). The outbreak produced widespread fear and a huge public health response (see exhibit 2.5).

Why was the Spanish flu so important to the development of healthcare policy and delivery? First, it led to an increased emphasis on public health and health measurement (van Hartesveldt 2010). Second, the unsuccessful efforts to contain it represent an important learning opportunity. At the early stages of the outbreak, scientists and healthcare providers failed to recognize the seriousness of the situation. Their first response was to reassure the public and urge people not to panic. Of course, panic is never good, but the false sense of security that resulted from this reassurance contributed to the global spread of the disease. A related problem was that scientists

EXHIBIT 2.5
Advertisement
Urging the Use
of Masks During
the Spanish Flu
Outbreak

thought they understood the cause and origin of the outbreak but were actually mistaken, causing early actions against the disease to be unsuccessful. Complicating matters further was the fact that, because the United States had recently entered World War I, government officials felt they had to control the messaging around the epidemic. Unfortunately, their silence and lack of candor cost them their credibility and trust. The population believed rumors and braced for the worst possible outcomes, and the result was paralyzing fear (Barry 2009; Jordan 1927).

The lesson here is painfully obvious. Healthcare providers, organizations, the scientific community, and policymakers need to respect the nature of disease and be truthful with the public about what they know and do not know.

Major Advances in Healthcare Delivery

Providing care for the sick and dying has been part of the human experience since the dawn of humankind. Over time, the scope of healthcare expanded to include the prevention and curing of disease. For many years, we had little, if any, scientific support for the remedies and treatments in use, but we have now progressed to the point that our healthcare is highly complex and evidence based. Given the rapid changes and the ever-expanding body of knowledge, no individual can possibly understand the full range of treatment options for all types of conditions. However, with the advent of big data and artificial intelligence, we can better manage these massive amounts of information and apply them to the delivery of healthcare and the prevention of human disease.

Scholars can debate the most important advances in healthcare delivery over the past 200 years, and no list can be considered complete or definitive. However, the advances described in this section, most would agree, have had a significant impact on not only human health but also the course of human history.

World War II

World War II serves as a useful demarcation point for describing the history of the US healthcare system. After the war, insurance became much more commonplace, which caused people to have greater interest in and access to medical services. Also in the years following the war, the Hill-Burton Act fueled facility development, and technological development and medical discovery were occurring at a rapid pace. The war itself led to many medical innovations, including new procedures, surgical techniques, and medications (Morrisey 2014; Numbers 1979; Starr 1982).

Prior to the devastation of World War II, Europe had been a leader in healthcare delivery research and education, with a number of well-established institutions (Kesternich et al. 2014; Lindemann 2010). When Europe reemerged from the conflict, it had to create new healthcare systems, and these systems were significantly different from what had developed in the United States (Blank 1988). From the beginning, these European systems considered healthcare a right, not a privilege, and market approaches were deemphasized. The organization and funding of healthcare services were treated as collective responsibilities of the government and the people—a stark contrast from the approach of the United States.

Early Forms of Health Insurance

Insurance is one of the primary mechanisms for financing healthcare in the United States. It is one of the reasons healthcare has flourished in this country, though some would also say it has also been a major cost driver. Insurance will be addressed in greater depth in chapter 8, but for the purposes of this chapter's historical overview, we need to briefly examine several early stages in its development.

Sick Funds

Sick funds were established to provide compensation to workers who became ill or injured on the job. Workers' compensation for illness or injury probably existed in some limited form as far back as the Civil War, though it became much more prevalent in the early 1900s. Between 1910 and 1915, 32 states enacted some form of workers' compensation (Numbers 1979; Starr 1982).

Blue Cross

The first true insurance began in 1929 at Baylor University Hospital in Dallas, Texas. Around the start of the Great Depression, the hospital faced serious financial hardship, with decreases in revenue, occupancy, and charitable giving, along with a 400 percent increase in charitable care. The administrator of the hospital, Justin Kimball, enrolled Dallas public schoolteachers in what was then called the Baylor Plan. The plan only covered hospital services, in large part because the AMA opposed any form of health insurance (Morrisey 2014). For $0.50 a month, Kimball promised up to 21 days of care in Baylor University Hospital. By 1933, this concept had spread, and some 26 plans—called "hospital service plans"—were in operation (Cunningham and Cunningham 1997). The plans that grew out of Kimball's model became known as Blue Cross plans.

Blue Shield

The first medical service plan to cover physician services was established in 1939 in California, paving the way for the development of Blue Shield plans. The plans offered free choice of physician and were endorsed by the AMA. They were indemnity plans, helping to establish the long-held tradition of providing reimbursement to the patient, who in turn was responsible for paying the physician (Cunningham and Cunningham 1997; Morrisey 2014).

Commercial Insurance

Commercial insurance began to offer hospital coverage in 1934. Like the Blue Cross plans, these plans initially did not cover physician services, though surgical coverage began in 1938 (Morrisey 2014). The commercial insurance plans were also indemnity-style plans, in which patients would receive reimbursement and then be responsible to the provider. Many physicians at the time were skeptical about direct contracts with insurers and had concerns about the complication of payment arrangements; such concerns remain prevalent today (Murray 2007).

Medicare and Medicaid

In 1965, Medicare and Medicaid were enacted through amendments, Title XVIII and Title XIX, to the Social Security Act. These programs brought tremendous benefits to two groups of citizens whose access to healthcare services had often been limited because of their inability to pay. Medicare was intended to cover the elderly (age 65 or older), and Medicaid covered the poor (as defined by federal poverty definitions).

Prepaid Group Plans

Like Blue Cross plans, prepaid group plans date back to the time of the Great Depression. Some of the earliest examples were established in California, Minnesota, and Washington. The plans faced significant opposition, however. Notably, after founding the Kaiser Foundation health plan in California in 1933, Sidney Garfield was charged with unprofessional conduct, and the board of medical examiners suspended his license—though the action was later overturned by the courts. Another notable example involved the Group Health Cooperative in Washington, DC, established in 1937. The AMA sought to restrict members from engaging in the plan, but the US Supreme Court ruled in 1943 that the AMA's actions violated the Sherman Antitrust Act (Morrisey 2014). Over time, these plans continued their growth.

The Expansion of Insurance

Since its earliest forms, health insurance has undergone tremendous expansion and significant innovations. Newer types of insurance products that have become available include the following:

- Health maintenance organizations (HMOs)
- Managed care plans
- Narrow network plans (NNPs)
- Preferred provider organizations (PPOs)
- Point of service (POS) plans
- High-deductible health plans (HDHPs), or consumer-directed health plans (CDHPs)—currently being widely used
- Conventional insurance—representing only a small percentage of health insurance coverage today

Often, the distinctions between these plans are not as easy to determine as simple definitions might indicate. Terms such as "managed care" can have broad interpretations and different meanings from one instance to another (Morrisey 2014; Murray 2007; Stevens 2008).

Three primary forces drove the growing need for health insurance in the United States:

1. Advances in technology led to more treatments becoming available, and those treatments were expensive.
2. People's desire for medical treatment increased as they became aware of new services that were available to help people.
3. People became concerned with unpredictable medical needs and costs. A fundamental aspect of health insurance is the need protect against unknown but low-probability risks with severe consequences.

The History of Healthcare Reform Efforts in the United States, from the 1880s to the Present

The United States has had a long history of trying to address the deep-rooted challenges in its healthcare system. Exhibit 2.6 presents a time line of some of the more important laws and initiatives aimed at bringing about healthcare reform over the past century and a half.

The Progressive Era

Up until the late 1800s, various efforts had been made to create voluntary sick funds, but the government took little meaningful action, opting instead to leave such matters to the states and to private interests. Things began to change during the Progressive Era, which lasted from about 1883 until 1912. The Progressive Era was a time of social awakening, with greater attention paid to the plight of the working class. The progressive tradition that exists today had its roots during this period.

    During the Progressive Era, President Theodore Roosevelt was supportive of health insurance, because he believed that a strong country and a healthy workforce required adequate healthcare (Murray 2007). According to Bauman (1992), the United States was on the verge of having a national health insurance program around this time—the first of many attempts to move the country in that direction.

EXHIBIT 2.6
Time Line of Major Reform Efforts in US Healthcare

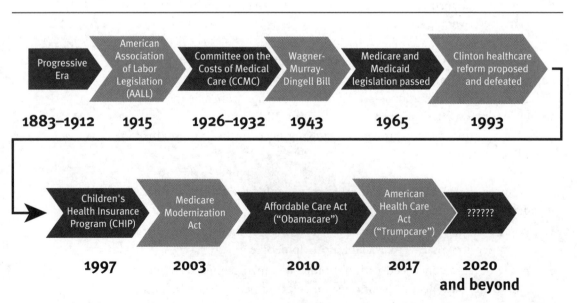

The American Association of Labor Legislation

The American Association of Labor Legislation (AALL) was founded in 1905 by a group of economists. In 1915, the AALL drafted a model bill that provided for physician and nurse services, sick pay, hospital benefits, maternity benefits, and a $50 death and funeral expense for workers in the United States who earned less than $1,200 per year (McVeigh and Wolfer 2004). The bill called for the cost to be shared by workers, employers, and states. Some of the features of this bill resembled the financing structure we use today (Gee 2012). Although this legislation never passed, it represented a major step forward in the progressive view of healthcare and social welfare (Moss 1996).

The Committee on the Costs of Medical Care

The Committee on the Costs of Medical Care (CCMC) was established in the late 1920s to research potential economic solutions and to propose an organizational structure for healthcare coverage in the United States. It was created out of concerns about the costs of healthcare, although those costs, as a share of GDP, were only a fraction of what they are today. Notably, the CCMC focused on physician and medical services, possibly because hospital services had not yet advanced to the point that they represented a large share of healthcare costs.

The committee met for five years and recommended the following six principles for healthcare coverage (CCMC 1932):

1. Safeguarding quality of service and personal relationships between physicians and patients
2. Providing for people's real medical needs
3. Providing service on financial terms that allow a majority of people access to services through individual and collective resources
4. Shifting the emphasis from cure to prevention
5. Allowing for the selection of competent practitioners
6. Providing adequate payment to practitioners and agencies

The CCMC did not win support from any major political or organizational group; even progressives opposed it. The AMA denounced the report as socialist and anti-American (*Journal of the American Medical Association* 1932). Although the CCMC's recommendations were not fully adopted, certain elements were later included in the Social Security Act of 1935 or considered in the development of other health insurance programs such as Blue Shield (Starr 1982). The CCMC was disbanded after producing some 15 reports (Gore 2013).

The Wagner-Murray-Dingell Bill

The Wagner-Murray-Dingell Bill was introduced to Congress in 1943. Drafted by the Social Security Board and sponsored by Robert F. Wagner and James E. Murray in the Senate (S. 1161) and John Dingell in the House of Representatives (H.R. 2861), the bill called for broad improvements to Social Security—notably, the inclusion of medical care. Organized labor was supportive of the bill, but the AMA and its closely linked National Physicians' Committee for the Extension of Medical Services were opposed (Corning 1969). The bill died in committee. Nonetheless, it initiated a serious debate that, decades later, would culminate in the passage of the Medicare and Medicaid amendments to the Social Security Act.

The Hospital Survey and Construction Act

By the end of World War II, many US hospitals were becoming obsolete, and authorities became concerned that the country lacked a sufficient number of hospital beds. An appropriate number of hospital beds at the time was considered to be 4.5 beds for every 1,000 people (Nickell 2018). These concerns led Congress to pass the Hospital Survey and Construction Act (Pub. L. No. 79-725, supplanted by Pub. L. No. 93-641) in 1946. The law, commonly known as the Hill-Burton Act, was passed even though the AMA, the American Hospital Association (AHA), and others opposed federal legislation concerning healthcare.

The Hill-Burton Act—described by the *Maryland Law Review* (1979, 316) as "the federal government's first federal health care initiative"—provided substantial subsidies for the building of hospitals and nursing homes over the subsequent two decades. By 1975, it had funded more than one-third of the hospitals in the United States (Schumann 2016).

Communities that received Hill-Burton funds had to commit to three specific requirements:

1. They were required offer care on a nondiscriminatory basis.
2. They were required offer a reasonable amount of free care over the next 20 years to residents of the area who could not afford to pay. This provision was revised in 1975 and became Title XVI of the Public Health Services Act, making the 20-year commitment permanent. Today, about 200 hospitals in the United States still fall under this requirement (Health Resources and Services Administration 2018; Thomas 2006).
3. They had to prove economic viability. Hill-Burton funding required matching funds from state and local government (Perlstadt 1995).

Hill-Burton was a significant event in the history of our healthcare system because it dramatically increased the availability of medical services provided by hospitals.

Legislation Establishing Medicare and Medicaid

The legislation creating Medicare and Medicaid as Title XVIII and Title XIX of the Social Security Act represented a landmark moment in the development of the US healthcare system. The bipartisan legislation was the culmination of decades of efforts to improve access to and the financing of healthcare for older adults and the poor. It passed the House of Representatives by a vote of 315 to 115 and the Senate by margin of 68 to 21. President Lyndon B. Johnson signed it into law on July 30, 1965 (Corning 1969; Morrisey 2014; Stevens 2008).

Medicare and Medicaid remain a major source of healthcare financing in the United States, and they will be discussed in depth in chapter 8. From a historical perspective, however, we should look at the creation of Medicare and Medicaid as part of a continued effort to develop national health insurance. The landslide election of Johnson in 1964 led to a strong Democratic majority in Congress, and Democrats wanted a program for providing healthcare to seniors. Advocates wanted universal coverage, but the legislation would ultimately reflect a substantial compromise. The three-pronged bill included Medicare Part A, to cover hospital and some nursing home expenses for people 65 years of age or older; a voluntary ambulatory service benefit, now known as Medicare Part B; and Medicaid to cover people with low income. Medicare Part A would be funded through payroll taxes, Medicare Part B through premiums, and Medicaid through a federal and state matching formula.

Employee Retirement Income Security Act of 1974

The Employee Retirement Income Security Act (ERISA) of 1974 is a federal law that sets minimum standards for most voluntarily established pension and health plans in private industry. Its aim is to protect the individuals enrolled in these plans (Morrisey 2014). The law was created in response to the closing of the Studebaker Corporation, an automobile manufacturer, which left the organization's pension plan unfunded and the workforce without benefits.

Although not specifically a healthcare law, ERISA was an important insurance regulation with significant healthcare implications. The law includes several provisions related to "welfare plans," meaning health insurance plans, that are relevant to our discussion:

- It places self-insured health plans under ERISA regulation rather than regulation by state insurance laws.
- It requires self-insured health plans to provide plan information to participants.
- It imposes fiduciary standards on the plans.
- It allows uniform operation of a multistate corporation's health plan across states (previously, such corporations often had variable regulation and rate structures).

ERISA placed two traditional insurance company functions—insurance risk and processing of claims—on the employer company. It ushered in a change in the health insurance industry by creating the need for administrative services specific to ERISA plans and the need for reinsurance for smaller plans (US Department of Labor 2018). ERISA changed the dynamics of state insurance regulations, and these regulations proliferated in the years following its passage. One reason cited by Morrisey (2014) is that large employers, which had often opposed such regulation, were no longer affected by it.

The Clinton Administration's Attempts at Reform

On September 22, 1993, President Bill Clinton proposed a bill that would provide a "health care security card" to every citizen, which would irrevocably entitle that individual to medical treatment and preventive services, including for pre-existing conditions (Clinton 1993). Features of the plan included the following (Moffitt 1993; Pear 1993):

- The plan required that every citizen and every permanent resident of the United States be enrolled in a qualified health plan either individually or through a business.
- All businesses with more than 5,000 full-time employees would be required to offer health insurance. Subsidies would be provided to help offset the cost to individuals, including 100 percent subsidies for people with low incomes.
- All states would establish regional health alliances, which everyone would be required to join, and the alliances would purchase insurance for the residents.
- The alliances could set fees for doctors charged on a fee-for-service basis.
- The federal government would provide funding for the administration of the plan.
- The federal government would also fund insolvent state programs, world programs, and long-term care programs.
- The plan specified necessary services that would have to be covered.
- The plan created a national health board to oversee the quality of healthcare services.
- The plan included malpractice and antitrust reform, as well as fraud prevention measures in a prescription drug benefit for Medicare.

The Clinton plan faced stiff opposition from conservatives, libertarians, medical organizations, and the insurance industry. One of the most effective strategies for swaying public opinion against the plan was a commercial produced by the insurance industry. It showed two individuals, "Harry and Louise," sitting at the kitchen table discussing the government takeover of healthcare, and it played on the fears of government control, loss of choice, and increasing costs (C-SPAN 1994). The proposal was never brought to a vote in Congress (Gottschalk 2000). However, some provisions of the Clinton plan are similar to those that were ultimately passed as part of the Affordable Care Act of 2010.

The Children's Health Insurance Program

The 105th Congress passed Children's Health Insurance Plan (CHIP) in 1997, during the Clinton administration. It arose out of the failed Clinton healthcare reform efforts and was included in the Balanced Budget Act of 1997 (Congress.gov 2019b). CHIP provides benefits to children, although those benefits may vary by state and by the type of CHIP program; states have flexibility to design their own programs within federal guidelines (CMS 2018a). CHIP represented another step, albeit a piecemeal one, to expand access to and financial support for healthcare services (Clinton 1997).

The Medicare Prescription Drug, Improvement, and Modernization Act

The Medicare Prescription Drug, Improvement, and Modernization Act (Pub. L. No. 108-173, 117)—often called the Medicare Modernization Act (MMA)—was enacted in 2003, and it brought about some of the most significant changes to Medicare since the program was established (Congress.gov 2019a). The most notable provision of the MMA was the creation of a prescription drug benefit called Medicare Part D. Prescription drugs had become a more significant part of the healthcare environment, and new and expensive drugs were placing greater financial burdens on the elderly. The law also prohibited the federal government from negotiating with drug companies and prevented the government from establishing a formulary.

Medicare Part D began in 2006 as a voluntary benefit available only through HMOs and insurance companies. The complex financing of Medicare Part D originally included a gap known as the "donut hole." Beneficiaries enrolled in Medicare Part D would pay an annual premium as well as a percentage of the drug's cost until total drug costs reached a certain limit. After reaching that initial limit, the donut hole would begin, and the beneficiary would have to pay more of the cost of the drug, until costs reached the upper limit of the donut hole. In 2019, the donut hole began when costs reached $3,820 and ended when out-of-pocket costs reached $5,100 (Bunis 2019; CMS 2019b). The donut hole was subsequently closed by the ACA, as of 2020.

The Proliferation of Managed Care and New Plan Designs

Beginning in the 1980s and continuing to the present, insurance companies and other organizations have developed several models to provide more efficient and effective healthcare. Managed care models likely developed in part as a result of a 1983 change made by Congress in the way Medicare paid hospitals. With that change, hospitals were no longer paid on a cost-plus basis but rather on a prospective basis, and they received a fixed price for their services based on the diagnosis of the patient (Morrisey 2014). Under this system, patients were classified into diagnosis-related groups (DRGs) that had specified levels of payment. Managed care typically takes three general forms—the HMO, the POS plan, or the PPO—which will be examined in greater detail in chapter 8.

Another type of plan that has become increasingly popular is the consumer-directed health plan. A CDHP pairs a high-deductible health plan with a health savings account (HSA) or health reimbursement account (HRA) (BlueCross BlueShield of Illinois 2018). Because the high-deductible plan requires the patient or responsible party to pay a significant deductible, the HSA or HRA allows for tax-advantaged savings by an individual (HAS) or tax-deductible contributions by a company (HRA) to be used to help meet these expenses. These tax-advantaged saving account models are only allowed for high-deductible plans (Newhouse 2004; Rowe et al. 2008).

The growing popularity of high-deductible plans is likely attributable to increasing health insurance premiums and a desire on the part of companies to share a larger percentage of healthcare costs with employees. Interest in these plans was also stimulated by the "Cadillac provision" of the ACA, which imposed a tax on high-benefit plans (French et al. 2016).

The Affordable Care Act

The Patient Protection and Affordable Care Act of 2010 (Pub. L. No. 111-148) represented the most sweeping effort to reform healthcare since the founding of Medicare and Medicaid in 1965. Attempts at establishing a more universal system of care had been going on for more than a century, and Barack Obama's victory in the 2008 presidential election, along with Democratic control of both houses of Congress, presented a unique opportunity to pass major legislation (Manchikanti et al. 2017).

The ACA, sometimes called "Obamacare," faced stiff opposition from conservative politicians and industry groups, and no Republican votes were cast in favor of the bill. Nonetheless, it passed on a strictly partisan basis and was signed into law in March of 2010.

Major provisions of the ACA include the following (Congress.gov 2019c; French et al. 2016):

- Insurance coverage was increased through expansions of Medicaid and CHIP.
- Individuals and businesses were mandated to buy and provide coverage for their employees; the government provided subsidies to assist in this effort.

- The act created a federal health insurance exchange and encouraged states to develop their own exchanges in the hopes of increasing competition among insurance carriers and offering greater choice to consumers.
- The law included a popular and long-sought provision requiring guaranteed issue of insurance and a measure preventing exclusion on the basis of pre-existing conditions. Insurers were required to issue coverage without regard to the individual's health status. This provision was essentially a *quid pro quo* for the individual mandate, because having all people in the insurance pool would create actuarially predictable community ratings.
- Another popular feature was the extension of coverage to dependents up to the age of 26. The limit had been age 23 prior to the ACA.
- Plans were no longer allowed to establish a lifetime limit on benefits or to rescind coverage based on usage. Policies could only be canceled for nonpayment of premiums.
- The act standardized insurance plans by requiring all policies to provide ten specified areas of healthcare service.
- The ACA laid out four benefit categories—bronze, silver, gold, and platinum—which established some coinsurance and copay levels. Deductibles and waiting periods were also limited.
- The law required certain preventive services be covered by all plans at 100 percent.
- The law provided a framework for the development of accountable care organizations, which would provide more longitudinal, outcomes-based care for specified populations of patients (Bennett 2012).
- The ACA also included several taxes and fees to help pay the costs of its provisions (Kaiser Family Foundation 2013).

In the years since its passage, the ACA has remained controversial. Efforts to repeal, replace, or amend the law have been ongoing, and political forces have been marshaled on all sides (Butler 2016). In 2012, the Supreme Court struck down the ACA provision requiring states to expand Medicaid or lose federal funds for the program, but it upheld the individual mandate, which opponents had sought to have declared unconstitutional. Critics had argued that requiring citizens to purchase health insurance was an unprecedented overreach by the federal government.

American Health Care Act of 2017

The debate over healthcare reform continued in the presidency of Donald Trump. The American Health Care Act (AHCA) of 2017 (H.R. 1628), sometimes called "Trumpcare," was a failed attempt to repeal and replace the ACA. The AHCA passed the House of Representatives by a narrow partisan margin but did not pass the Senate (Fabian 2017a, 2017b). Subsequent efforts to significantly alter the ACA came before the Senate—the Better Care Reconciliation Act of 2017, the Obamacare Repeal Reconciliation Act of 2017, and the Health Care Freedom Act of 2017—but were rejected (Kaiser Family Foundation 2019). These efforts sought to repeal ACA provisions such as the individual mandate, the employer mandate, and several of the taxes. They also sought to repeal the provisions that allowed an expansion of Medicaid enrollment. The Congressional Budget Office estimated that the AHCA would leave 23 million people uninsured by 2026 (Ku et al. 2017; Kurtzleben 2017; Reuters 2017).

Having failed to pass a full repeal of the ACA, Republicans in Congress instead incorporated changes to the ACA into a sweeping tax reform bill, the Tax Cuts and Jobs Act (TCJA) of 2017. The TCJA included a repeal of the ACA's individual mandate, effective January 1, 2019 (Kaplan and Rappeport 2017; Long 2017; Pear and Kaplan 2017).

In October 2017, Trump issued an executive order "promoting healthcare choice and competition" (White House 2017). On the same day, a separate decision refused to provide a key ACA healthcare subsidy, which had the effect of increasing ACA premiums. Between the repeal of some ACA provisions and the lack of enforcement for others, many of the promises of the ACA were no longer fulfilled. Uncertainty was widespread, and consumers faced rising costs.

The Present Challenge

Healthcare has long been a controversial issue in the United States, with consistent tension between the concepts of social justice and market justice and ongoing debates between conservative, libertarian, and liberal viewpoints, each with competing interests. Given these circumstances, one can easily see why major reform to our healthcare system has been so difficult. Unfortunately, these aspects of our system are unlikely to change any time soon. Nonetheless, we can gain a valuable perspective on why the US system is so complex, and we can begin to isolate the problems that make our system so difficult to understand, manage, and change. Cost, quality, and access have been consistent themes throughout the history of our healthcare system, and we must continue to focus on those areas as we work to improve the system for our patients.

Discussion Questions

1. What was the focus of the US healthcare system in the early twentieth century?
2. Describe some of the earliest forms of health insurance in the United States.

3. What were some of the most significant developments in healthcare around the world prior to the 1900s? How did these developments affect healthcare delivery in the United States?

4. What was the importance of the Abraham Flexner report?

5. Why was World War II a watershed moment for the US healthcare system?

6. What were the most significant developments in US healthcare during the middle and late twentieth century?

7. What are some of the reasons that enacting meaningful reform of the US healthcare system has been so difficult?

8. In what ways have healthcare challenges and medical needs changed over time?

References

Aceves-Avila, F. J., F. Medina, and A. Fraga. 2001. "Herbal Therapies in Rheumatology: The Persistence of Ancient Medical Practices." *Clinical and Experimental Rheumatology* 19 (2): 177–83. https://pdfs.semanticscholar.org/c5ea/6559b830527836fe3642bbf16551089153b2.pdf.

American Medical Association (AMA). 2019a. "AMA History." Accessed October 1. www.ama-assn.org/about/ama-history/ama-history.

———. 2019b. "RBRVS Overview." Accessed September 25. www.ama-assn.org/about/rvs-update-committee-ruc/rbrvs-overview.

America's Essential Hospitals. 2018a. "Establishing the Safety Net Hospital: 1980–2005." Accessed August 6. https://essentialhospitals.org/about-americas-essential-hospitals/history-of-public-hospitals-in-the-united-states/establishing-the-safety-net-hospital-1980-2005/.

———. 2018b. "First Hospital Ambulance Service." Accessed August 5. https://essentialhospitals.org/about-americas-essential-hospitals/history-of-public-hospitals-in-the-united-states/first-hospital-ambulance-service/.

———. 2018c. "First Hospital Blood Bank." Accessed August 5. https://essentialhospitals.org/about-americas-essential-hospitals/history-of-public-hospitals-in-the-united-states/first-hospital-blood-bank/.

Andrews, J. 2011. "History of Medicine: Health, Medicine and Disease in the Eighteenth Century." *Journal for Eighteenth-Century Studies* 34 (4): 503–15. https://doi.org/10.1111/j.1754-0208.2011.00448.x.

Ansart, S., C. Pelat, P.-Y. Boelle, F. Carrat, A. Flahault, and A.-J. Valleron. 2009. "Mortality Burden of the 1918–1919 Influenza Pandemic in Europe." *Influenza and Other Respiratory Viruses* 3 (3): 99–106. https://doi.org/10.1111/j.1750-2659.2009.00080.x

Atchinson, B. K., and D. M. Fox. 1997. "From the Field: The Politics of the Health Insurance Portability and Accountability Act." *Health Affairs* 16 (3): 146–50. www.healthaffairs.org/doi/full/10.1377/hlthaff.16.3.146.

Ball, C. 1996. "James Young Simpson, 1811–1870." *Anaesthesia and Intensive Care* 24 (6): 639. https://doi.org/10.1177/0310057X9602400601.

Bankston, J. 2004. *Joseph Lister and the Story of Antiseptics (Uncharted, Unexplored, and Unexplained)*. Bear, DE: Mitchell Lane.

Barkley, K. T. 1990. *The Ambulance: The Story of Emergency Transportation of Sick and Wounded Through the Centuries*. New York: Load N Go Press.

Barnard, M. 2011. *Defining Moments*. Cape Town, South Africa: Random House Struik.

Barry, J. M. 2009. "Pandemics: Avoiding the Mistakes of 1918." *Nature* 459: 324–25. https://doi.org/10.1038/459324a.

Bauman, H. 1992. "Verging on National Health Insurance Since 1910." In *Changing to National Health Care: Ethical and Policy Issues (Ethics in a Changing World)*, edited by R. P. Heufner and M. P. Battin, 29–49. Salt Lake City, UT: University of Utah Press.

Benjamin Franklin Historical Society. 2014. "Pennsylvania Hospital." Accessed March 1, 2019. www.benjamin-franklin-history.org/pennsylvania-hospital/.

Bennett, A. R. 2012. "Accountable Care Organizations: Principles and Implications for Hospital Administrators." *Journal of Healthcare Management* 57 (4): 244–54. https://doi.org/10.1097/00115514-201207000-00005.

Berwick, D. M., T. W. Nolan, and J. Whittington. 2008. "The Triple Aim: Care, Health, and Cost." *Health Affairs*. Published May 1. https://doi.org/10.1377/hlthaff.27.3.759.

Blank, R. H. 1988. *Rationing Medicine*. New York: Columbia University Press.

Bliss, M. 1999. *William Osler: A Life in Medicine*. New York: Oxford University Press.

BlueCross BlueShield of Illinois. 2018. "What Is a CDHP and How Does It Work?" Accessed October 11. https://connect.bcbsil.com/my-coverage-explained/b/weblog/posts/what-is-a-cdhp-and-how-does-it-work.

Borchardt, J. K. 2002. "The Beginnings of Drug Therapy: Ancient Mesopotamian Medicine." *Drug News and Perspectives* 15 (3): 187. https://doi.org/10.1358/dnp.2002.15.3.840015.

Buchmueller, T. C., and A. C. Monheit. 2009. "Employer-Sponsored Health Insurance and the Promise of Health Insurance Reform." National Bureau of Economic Research working paper no. 14839. Published April. www.nber.org/papers/w14839.

Bundorf, M. K. 2012. "Consumer Directed Health Plans." Robert Wood Johnson Foundation. Published October 1. www.rwjf.org/en/library/research/2012/10/consumer-directed-health-plans.html.

Bunis, D. 2019. "Understanding Medicare's Options." AARP. Updated September 23. www.aarp.org/health/medicare-insurance/info-01-2011/understanding_medicare_the_plans.html.

Burns, K., E. Ewers, and C. L. Ewers (dirs.). 2018. *The Mayo Clinic: Faith–Hope–Science*. Arlington, VA: Public Broadcasting Service.

Burrows, E. G., and M. Wallace. 1998. *Gotham: A History of New York City to 1898*. New York: Oxford University Press.

Butler, S. M. 2016. "The Future of the Affordable Care Act: Reassessment and Revision." *Journal of the American Medical Association* 316 (5): 495–97. https://doi.org/10.1001/jama.2016.9881.

Cassedy, J. H. 1991. *Medicine in America: A Short History*. Baltimore, MD: Johns Hopkins University Press.

Catlin, A. C., and A. C. Cowan. 2015. *History of Health Spending in the United States, 1960–2013*. Centers for Medicare & Medicaid Services. Published November 19. www.cms.gov/Research-Statistics-Data-and-Systems/Statistics-Trends-and-Reports/NationalHealthExpendData/Downloads/HistoricalNHEPaper.pdf.

Centers for Disease Control and Prevention (CDC). 2019a. "2014–2016 Ebola Outbreak in West Africa." Reviewed March 8. www.cdc.gov/vhf/ebola/history/2014-2016-outbreak/index.html.

———. 2019b. "Zika Virus." Reviewed June 4. www.cdc.gov/zika/index.html.

———. 2016. "History of Smallpox." Reviewed August 30. www.cdc.gov/smallpox/history/history.html.

Centers for Medicare & Medicaid Services (CMS). 2019a. "History." Updated August 5. www.cms.gov/About-CMS/Agency-information/History/.

———. 2019b. "Costs in the Coverage Gap." Accessed October 3. www.medicare.gov/drug-coverage-part-d/costs-for-medicare-drug-coverage/costs-in-the-coverage-gap.

———. 2019c. "National Health Expenditure Projections 2018–2027." Accessed September 25. www.cms.gov/Research-Statistics-Data-and-Systems/Statistics-Trends-and-Reports/NationalHealthExpendData/Downloads/ForecastSummary.pdf.

———. 2018a. "Children's Health Insurance Program (CHIP)." Accessed August 7. www.medicaid.gov/CHIP/index.html.

———. 2018b. "National Health Expenditure Data: Historical." Updated December 11. www.cms.gov/Research-Statistics-Data-and-Systems/Statistics-Trends-and-Reports/NationalHealthExpendData/NationalHealthAccountsHistorical.html.

Clinton, B. 1993. "September 22, 1993: Address on Health Care Reform." Miller Center. Accessed September 25, 2019. https://millercenter.org/the-presidency/presidential-speeches/september-22-1993-address-health-care-reform.

Clinton, H. R. 1997. "Our Chance for Healthier Children." *New York Times*. Published August 5. www.nytimes.com/1997/08/05/opinion/our-chance-for-healthier-children.html.

Cobban, A. B. 1999. *English University Life in the Middle Ages*. Columbus, OH: Ohio State University Press.

Coggeshall, L. T. 1965. *Planning for Medical Progress Through Education*. Evanston, IL: Association of Medical Colleges.

Committee on the Costs of Medical Care (CCMC). 1932. *Medical Care for the American People: The Final Report of the Committee on the Costs of Medical Care*. Chicago, IL: University of Chicago Press.

Congress.gov. 2019a. "H.R.1—Medicare Prescription Drug, Improvement, and Modernization Act of 2003." Accessed September 25. www.congress.gov/bill/108th-congress/house-bill/1?q=%7B%22search%22%3A%5B%22cite%3APL108-173%22%5D%7D&s=1&r=1.

———. 2019b. "H.R.2015—Balanced Budget Act of 1997." Accessed September 25. www.congress.gov/bill/105th-congress/house-bill/2015?q=%7B%22search%22%3A%5B%22Pain-Capable+Unborn+Child+Protection+Act%22%5D%7D&r=28.

———. 2019c. "H.R.3590—Patient Protection and Affordable Care Act." Accessed September 26. www.congress.gov/bill/111th-congress/house-bill/3590.

Corning, P. A. 1969. *The Evolution of Medicare: From Idea to Law*. Social Security Administration. Accesed September 25, 2019. www.ssa.gov/history/corning.html.

Crosby, A. W. 1976. *Epidemic and Peace, 1918*. Westport, CT: Greenwood Press.

C-SPAN. 1994. "'Harry and Louise' Health Care Advertisements." Published July 10. www.c-span.org/video/?58575-1/harry-louise-health-care-advertisements.

Cuckler, G. A., A. M. Sisko, J. A. Poisal, S. P. Keehan, S. D. Smith, A. J. Madison, C. J. Wolfe, and J. C. Hardesty. 2018. "National Health Expenditure Projections, 2017–26: Despite Uncertainty, Fundamentals Primarily Drive Spending Growth." *Health Affairs*. Published February 14. https://doi.org/10.1377/hlthaff.2017.1655.

Cunningham, R. III, and R. M. Cunningham Jr. 1997. *The Blues: A History of the Blue Cross and Blue Shield System*. DeKalb, IL: Northern Illinois University Press.

Dahm, R. 2008. "Discovering DNA: Friedrich Miescher and the Early Years of Nucleic Acid Research." *Human Genetics*, 122 (6): 565–81. https://doi.org/10.1007/s00439-007-0433-0.

Dawson, M. J. 2013. *Paul Lauterbur and the Invention of MRI*. Cambridge, MA: MIT Press.

Debré, P. 2000. *Louis Pasteur*. Baltimore, MD: Johns Hopkins University Press.

Dorsey, J. L. 1975. "The Health Maintenance Organization Act of 1973 (P.L. 93-222) and Prepaid Group Practice Plans." *Medical Care* 13 (1): 1–9. https://doi.org/10.1097/00005650-197501000-00001.

Duffy, T. P. 2011. "The Flexner Report—100 Years Later." *Yale Journal of Biology and Medicine* 84: 269–76. https://pdfs.semanticscholar.org/7bed/aff87f8e8b9af9591e4e166a0cfc245d9b28.pdf.

Eschner, K. 2017. "The First-Ever Blood Bank Opened 80 Years Ago Today." *Smithsonian*. Published March 15. www.smithsonianmag.com/smart-news/first-ever-blood-bank-opened-80-years-ago-today-180962486/.

Fabian, J. 2017a. "Ryan Heads to WH to Brief Trump on Health-care Bill." *The Hill*. Published March 24. http://thehill.com/policy/healthcare/325639-ryan-heads-to-wh-to-brief-trump-on-healthcare-bill.

———. 2017b. "White House: Lawmakers Will Vote Friday on Healthcare Plan." *The Hill*. Published March 23. http://thehill.com/homenews/house/325511-white-house-lawmakers-will-vote-friday-on-healthcare-plan.

Favreau, A.-M. 2012. "Physiognomy." *The Encyclopedia of Ancient History*. Wiley Online Library. Published October 26. https://doi.org/10.1002/9781444338386.wbeah21258.

Finlayson, J. 1893. "Ancient Egyptian Medicine." *British Medical Journal* 1: 748. https://doi.org/10.1136/bmj.1.1684.748.

Fleming, D. 1987. *William H. Welch and the Rise of Modern Medicine*. Baltimore, MD: Johns Hopkins University Press.

Flexner, A. 1910. *Medical Education in the United States and Canada*. Report to the Carnegie Foundation for the Advancement of Teaching. Accessed September 25, 2019. http://archive.carnegiefoundation.org/pdfs/elibrary/Carnegie_Flexner_Report.pdf.

French, M. T., J. Homer, G. Gumus, and L. Hickling. 2016. "Key Provisions of the Patient Protection and Affordable Care Act (ACA): A Systematic Review and Presentation of Early Research Findings." *Health Services Research* 51 (5): 1735–71. https://doi.org/10.1111/1475-6773.12511.

Friedmann, P. D., C. M. Andrews, and K. Humphreys. 2017. "How ACA Repeal Would Worsen the Opioid Epidemic." *New England Journal of Medicine*. Published March 9. https://doi.org/10.1056/NEJMp1700834.

Fuchs, V. R. 2012. "Major Trends in the U.S. Health Economy Since 1950." *New England Journal of Medicine* 366 (11): 973–77. https://doi.org/10.1056/NEJMp1200478.

Garrison, D. H., and M. H. Hast (trans.). 2013. *The Fabric of the Human Body: An Annotated Translation of the 1543 and 1555 Editions*. Basel, Switzerland: Karger.

Gee, J. 2012. "Twilight of Consensus: The American Association for Labor Legislation and Academic Public Policy Research." *Penn History Review*. Published September 6. http://repository.upenn.edu/phr/vol19/iss2/4.

Glasser, O. 1933. *Wilhelm Conrad Röntgen and the Early History of the Roentgen Rays*. London: John Bale, Sons, and Danielsson.

Gore, T. B. 2013. "A Forgotten Landmark Medical Study from 1932 by the Committee on the Cost of Medical Care." *Proceedings (Baylor University. Medical Center)* 26 (2): 142–43. www.ncbi.nlm.nih.gov/pmc/articles/PMC3603728/.

Gottschalk, M. 2000. *The Shadow Welfare State: Labor, Business, and the Politics of Health-Care in the United States*. Ithaca, NY: ILR Press.

Hargrave, E., J. Hoadley, K. Merrelli, and J. Cubanski. 2007. "Medicare Part D 2008 Data Spotlight: Specialty Tiers." Kaiser Family Foundation. Published

November 30. www.kff.org/medicare/issue-brief/medicare-part-d-data-spotlight-specialty-tiers/.

Harrington, S. E. 2010. "U.S. Health-Care Reform: The Patient Protection and Affordable Care Act." *Journal of Risk and Insurance* 77 (3), 703–8.

Harvey, W. 1968. *The Circulation of the Blood and Other Writings*, translated by K. J. Franklin. London: Orion.

Health Resources and Services Administration (HRSA). 2018. "Hill-Burton Free and Reduced-Cost Health Care." Reviewed April. www.hrsa.gov/get-health-care/affordable/hill-burton/index.html.

Heiney, P. 2003. *The Nuts and Bolts of Life: Willem Kolff and the Invention of the Kidney Machine*. Charleston, SC: History Press.

Hiatt, M. D., and C. G. Stockton. 2003. "The Impact of the Flexner Report on the Fate of Medical Schools in North America After 1909." *Journal of American Physicians and Surgeons* 8 (2): 37–40. www.jpands.org/vol8no2/hiatt.pdf.

Hippocrates. 1868. *Hippocrates Collected Works I*, translated by W. H. S. Jones. Cambridge, MA: Harvard University Press. https://daedalus.umkc.edu/hippocrates/HippocratesLoeb1/index.html.

Hoffman, B. 2008. "Health Care Reform and Social Movements in the United States." *American Journal of Public Health* 98 (Suppl. 1): S69–S79. https://doi.org/10.2105/AJPH.98.Supplement_1.S69.

Hurry, J. B. 1978. *Imhotep*, 2nd ed. New York: AMS Press.

Institute of Medicine. 2001. *Crossing the Quality Chasm: A New Health System for the 21st Century*. Washington, DC: National Academies Press. https://doi.org/10.17226/10027.

———. 2000. *To Err Is Human: Building a Safer Health System*. Washington, DC: National Academies Press. https://doi.org/10.17226/9728.

Johns, C. H. W. (trans.). 2000. *The Oldest Code of Laws in the World: The Code of Laws Promulgated by Hammurabi, King of Babylon, B.C. 2285–2242*. Clark, NJ: Lawbook Exchange Ltd.

Johns Hopkins Medicine. 2019. "History of the Johns Hopkins Hospital." Accessed September 25. www.hopkinsmedicine.org/medicine/education/hstrainingprogram/overview/hx_jhh.html.

———. 2018. "The History of Johns Hopkins Medicine." Accessed September 28. www.hopkinsmedicine.org/about/history/index.html.

Jones, W. H. S. 1979. *Philosophy and Medicine in Ancient Greece*. New York: Arno Press.

Jordan, D. 2019. "The Deadliest Flu: The Complete Story of the Discovery and Reconstruction of the 1918 Pandemic Virus." Centers for Disease Control and Prevention. Reviewed June 11. www.cdc.gov/flu/pandemic-resources/reconstruction-1918-virus.html.

Jordan, E. O. 1927. *Epidemic Influenza: A Survey*. Chicago: American Medical Association.

Jost, T. S. 2017. "Mandate Repeal Provision Ends Health Care Calm." *Health Affairs*. Published December 11. https://doi.org/10.1377/hlthaff.2017.1551.

Jost, T. S., and S. Lazarus. 2017. "Trump's Executive Order on Health Care—Can It Undermine the ACA if Congress Fails to Act?" *New England Journal of Medicine* 376: 1201–3. https://doi.org/10.1056/NEJMp1701340.

Journal of Health Politics, Policy and Law. 2004. "Précis of Paul Starr's *The Social Transformation of American Medicine.*" *Journal of Health Politics, Policy and Law* 29 (4–5): 575–620. https://doi.org/10.1215/03616878-29-4-5-575.

Journal of the American Medical Association. 1932. "The Committee on the Costs of Medical Care." *Journal of the American Medical Association* 99 (23): 1950–52. https://doi.org/10.1001/jama.1932.02740750052015.

Kaiser Family Foundation. 2019. "Compare Proposals to Replace the Affordable Care Act." Accessed September 27. www.kff.org/interactive/proposals-to-replace-the-affordable-care-act/.

———. 2013. "Summary of the Affordable Care Act." Published April 25. www.kff.org/health-reform/fact-sheet/summary-of-the-affordable-care-act/.

Kaplan, T., and A. Rappeport. 2017. "House Passes Tax Bill, as Does Senate Panel." *New York Times.* Published November 16. www.nytimes.com/2017/11/16/us/politics/house-tax-overhaul-bill.html.

Kaylin, J. 2005. "From the Middle East, in the Middle Ages." *Yale Medicine Magazine.* Accessed February 6, 2020. https://medicine.yale.edu/news/yale-medicine-magazine/from-the-middle-east-in-the-middle-ages/.

Keating, C. 2009. *Smoking Kills: The Revolutionary Life of Richard Doll.* Oxford, UK: Signal Books.

Keehan, S. P., D. A. Stone, J. A. Poisal, G. A. Cuckler, A. M. Sisko, S. D. Smith, A. J. Madison, C. J. Wolfe, and J. M. Lizonitz. 2017. "National Health Expenditure Projections, 2016–25: Price Increases, Aging Push Sector to 20 Percent of Economy." *Health Affairs* 36 (3): 553–63. https://doi.org/10.1377/hlthaff.2016.1627.

Kesternich, I., B. Siflinger, J. P. Smith, and J. K. Winter. 2014. "The Effects of World War II on Economic and Health Outcomes Across Europe." *Review of Economics and Statistics* 96 (1): 103–18. https://doi.org/10.1162/REST_a_00353.

King, L. S. 1984. "Medicine in the USA: Historical Vignettes—The Flexner Report of 1910." *Journal of the American Medical Association* 251 (8): 1079–86. https://doi.org/10.1001/jama.251.8.1079.

Koprowski, H. 1960. "Historical Aspects of the Development of Live Virus Vaccine in Poliomyelitis." *British Medical Journal* 2 (5192): 85–91. www.ncbi.nlm.nih.gov/pmc/articles/PMC2096806/pdf/brmedj03032-0023.pdf.

Kovner, A. R. 2014. "Evidence-Based Management: Implications for Nonprofit Organizations." *Nonprofit Management and Leadership* 24 (3): 417–24. https://doi.org/10.1002/nml.21097.

Ku, L., E. Steinmetz, E. Brantley, N. Holla, and B. Bruen. 2017. "The American Health Care Act: Economic and Employment Consequences for States."

Commonwealth Fund. Published June 14. www.commonwealthfund.org/publications/issue-briefs/2017/jun/ahca-economic-and-employment-consequences.

Kurtzleben, D. 2017. "GOP Health Plan Would Leave 23 Million More Uninsured, Budget Office Says." NPR. Published May 24. www.npr.org/2017/05/24/529902300/cbo-republicans-ahca-would-leave-23-million-more-uninsured.

Ligon, B. L. 2004. "Penicillin: Its Discovery and Early Development." *Seminars in Pediatric Infectious Diseases* 15 (1): 52–57.

Lindemann, M. 2010. *Medicine and Society in Early Modern Europe.* Cambridge, UK: Cambridge University Press.

Long, H. 2017. "The Final GOP Tax Bill Is Complete. Here's What Is in It." *Washington Post.* Published December 15. www.washingtonpost.com/news/wonk/wp/2017/12/15/the-final-gop-tax-bill-is-complete-heres-what-is-in-it/?noredirect=on&utm_term=.686d2a9c0534.

Manchikanti, L., S. Helm Ii, R. M. Benyamin, and J. A. Hirsch. 2017. "Evolution of US Health Care Reform." *Pain Physician* 20 (3): 107–10. www.ncbi.nlm.nih.gov/pubmed/28339426.

Marrus, M. R. 1997. "The Nuremberg Trial: Fifty Years After." *American Scholar* 66 (4): 563–70. www.jstor.org/stable/41212687?seq=1#page_scan_tab_contents.

Maryland Law Review. 1979. "The Hill-Burton Act, 1946–1980: Asynchrony in the Delivery of Health Care to the Poor." *Maryland Law Review* 39 (2): 316–75. https://digitalcommons.law.umaryland.edu/mlr/vol39/iss2/5/.

Mayo Clinic. 2018. "History of Surgery at Mayo Clinic." Accessed September 27. www.mayoclinic.org/departments-centers/surgery/overview/history.

McConaghy, M., M. Silberman, and I. Kalashnikova. 2004. "Penn in the 18th Century: School of Medicine." Penn University Archives and Records Center. Accessed October 11, 2018. https://archives.upenn.edu/exhibits/penn-history/18th-century/medical-school.

McVeigh, F. J., and L. Wolfer. 2004. *Brief History of Social Problems: A Critical Thinking Approach.* Lanham, MD: University Press of America.

Meaney-Delman, D., S. L. Hills, C. Williams, R. R. Galang, P. Iyengar, A. K. Hennenfent, I. B. Rabe, A. Panella, T. Oduyebo, M. A. Honein, S. Zaki, N. Lindsey, J. A. Lehman, N. Kwit, J. Bertolli, S. Ellington, I. Igbinosa, A. A. Minta, E. E. Petersen, P. Mead, S. A. Rasmussen, and D. J. Jamieson. 2016. "Zika Virus Infection Among U.S. Pregnant Travelers—August 2015–February 2016." *Morbidity and Mortality Weekly Report* 65 (8): 211–14. https://doi.org/10.15585/mmwr.mm6508e1.

Medical News Today. 2018. "What Was Medieval and Renaissance Medicine?" Published October 31. www.medicalnewstoday.com/articles/323533.php.

Moffitt, R. 1993. "A Guide to the Clinton Health Plan." Heritage Foundation. Published November 19. www.heritage.org/research/reports/1993/11/a-guide-to-the-clinton-health-plan.

Morrisey, M. A. 2014. *Health Insurance,* 2nd ed. Chicago: Health Administration Press.

Moss, D. A. 1996. *Socializing Security: Progressive-Era Economists and the Origins of American Social Policy.* Cambridge, MA: Harvard University Press.

Murray, J. E. 2007. *Origins of American Health Insurance: A History of Industrial Sickness Funds.* New Haven, CT: Yale University Press.

National Human Genome Research Institute. 2019. "Human Genome Project FAQ." Accessed September 26. www.genome.gov/human-genome-project/Completion-FAQ.

National Institute on Drug Abuse. 2018. "Overdose Death Rates." Accessed October 8. www.drugabuse.gov/related-topics/trends-statistics/overdose-death-rates.

National Library of Medicine. 2016. "The Origins and Evolution of the Mayo Clinic." Published June 14. https://circulatingnow.nlm.nih.gov/2016/06/14/the-origins-and-evolution-of-the-mayo-clinic/.

Newhouse, J. P. 2004. "Consumer-Directed Health Plans and the RAND Health Insurance Experiment." *Health Affairs* 23 (6): 107–13. https://doi.org/10.1377/hlthaff.23.6.107.

Nickell, F. 2018. "The Hill-Burton Act." NPR. Published May 29. www.krcu.org/post/hill-burton-act#stream/0.

Numbers, R. L. 1979. "The Third-Party: Health Insurance in America." In *The Therapeutic Revolution: Essays in the History of Medicine,* edited by M. J. Vogel and C. E. Rosenberg, 177–200. Philadelphia, PA: University of Pennsylvania Press.

Nutton, V. 2004. *Ancient Medicine.* London: Routledge. https://doi.org/10.4324/9780203490914.

Obama, B. H. 2017. "Repealing the ACA Without a Replacement—The Risks to American Health Care." *New England Journal of Medicine* 376: 297–99. https://doi.org/10.1056/NEJMp1616577.

Office of History, National Institutes of Health. 2018. "In Their Own Words. . . NIH Researchers Recall the Early Years of AIDS." Accessed August 7. https://history.nih.gov/NIHInOwnWords/docs/page_04.html.

O'Luanaigh, C. 2012. "This Month in 1991: The Web Spreads Beyond CERN." CERN. Published December 20. https://home.cern/news/news/computing/month-1991-web-spreads-beyond-cern.

Osborn, D. K. 2018. "Aristotle." GreekMedicine.net. Accessed August 6. www.greekmedicine.net/whos_who/Aristotle.html.

Palucka, T. 2002. "Overview of Electron Microscopy." Dibner Institute for the History of Science and Technology. Updated December 10. http://authors.library.caltech.edu/5456/1/hrst.mit.edu/hrs/materials/public/ElectronMicroscope/EM_HistOverview.htm.

Pear, R. 1993. "Clinton's Health Plan: The Overview; Congress Is Given the Clinton Plan for Health Care." *New York Times.* Published October 28. www.nytimes.com/1993/10/28/us/clinton-s-health-plan-overview-congress-given-clinton-proposal-for-health-care.html.

Pear, R., and T. Kaplan. 2017. "G.O.P. Health Bill Clears 2 House Panels After Marathon Sessions." *New York Times*. Published March 9. www.nytimes.com/2017/03/09/us/politics/health-bill-clears-house-panel-in-pre-dawn-hours.html.

Perlstadt, H. 1995. "The Development of the Hill-Burton Legislation: Interests, Issues and Compromises." *Journal of Health and Social Policy* 6(3): 77–96. https://doi.org/10.1300/J045v06n03_05.

Pescosolido, B. A., and J. K. Martin. 2004. "Cultural Authority and the Sovereignty of American Medicine: The Role of Networks, Class, and Community." *Journal of Health Politics, Policy and Law* 29 (4–5): 735–56. https://doi.org/10.1215/03616878-29-4-5-735.

Rashdall, H. 1895. *The Universities of Europe in the Middle Ages*. Oxford, UK: Clarendon Press. https://archive.org/details/universitieseur00unkngoog/page/n11.

Reuters. 2017. "House Passes New GOP Bill to Repeal Obamacare." *Fortune*. Published May 4. http://fortune.com/2017/05/04/ahca-health-care-bill-vote/.

Risse, G. B. 1990. *Mending Bodies, Saving Souls: A History of Hospitals*. New York: Oxford University Press.

Roberts, C., and K. Manchester. 2005. *The Archaeology of Disease*, 3rd ed. Stroud, UK: History Press.

Roguin, A. 2006. "Rene Theophile Hyacinthe Laënnec (1781–1826): The Man Behind the Stethoscope." *Clinical Medicine & Research* 4 (3): 230–35. www.ncbi.nlm.nih.gov/pmc/articles/PMC1570491/.

Rosenstein, B. 2018. "First Ambulance Service." OhioWins. Accessed October 11. http://ohiowins.com/first-ambulance-service/.

Rowe, J. W., T. Brown-Stevenson, R. L. Downey, and J. P. Newhouse. 2008. "The Effect of Consumer-Directed Health Plans on the Use of Preventive and Chronic Illness Services." *Health Affairs* 27 (1): 113–20. https://doi.org/10.1377/hlthaff.27.1.113.

Salvaggio, J. 1992. *New Orleans' Charity Hospital: A Story of Physicians, Politics, and Poverty*. Baton Rouge, LA: Louisiana State University Press.

Sarton, G. 1954. *Galen of Pergamon*. Lawrence, KS: University of Kansas Press.

Scandlen, G. 2005. "Consumer-Driven Health Care: Just a Tweak or a Revolution?" *Health Affairs* 24 (6): 1554–58. https://doi.org/10.1377/hlthaff.24.6.1554.

Schmeling, K. 2002. "Missionaries of Health: Detroit's Harper Hospital School of Nursing." *Michigan History* 86: 28–38.

Scholl, L., P. Seth, M. Kariisa, N. Wilson, and G. Baldwin. 2018. "Drug and Opioid-Involved Overdose Deaths—United States, 2013–2017." *Morbidity and Mortality Weekly Report* 67 (5152): 1419–27. https://doi.org/10.15585/mmwr.mm6751521e1.

Schumann, J. H. 2016. "A Bygone Era: When Bipartisanship Led to Health Care Transformation." NPR. Published October 2. www.npr.org/sections/

health-shots/2016/10/02/495775518/a-bygone-era-when-bipartisanship-led-to-health-care-transformation.

Shryock, R. H. 1956. "The History and Sociology of Science." *Items* 10 (2): 13–28. https://issuu.com/ssrcitemsissues/docs/items_vol10_no2_1956.

———. 1947. "The American Physician in 1846 and in 1946: A Study in Professional Contrasts." *Journal of the American Medical Association* 134 (5): 417–24. https://doi.org/10.1001/jama.1947.02880220001001.

Sigerist, H. 1935. "The History of Medical Licensure." *Journal of the American Medical Association* 104 (13): 1057–60. https://doi.org/10.1001/jama.1935.02760130007002.

Silverman, B. D. 2011. "William Henry Welch (1850–1934): The Road to Johns Hopkins." *Baylor University Medical Center Proceedings* 24 (3): 236–42. https://doi.org/10.1080/08998280.2011.11928722.

Starr, P. 1982. *The Social Transformation of American Medicine.* New York: Basic Books.

Stein, Rob. 2017. "Life Expectancy Drops Again as Opioid Deaths Surge in U.S." NPR. Published December 21. www.npr.org/sections/health-shots/2017/12/21/572080314/life-expectancy-drops-again-as-opioid-deaths-surge-in-u-s.

Stern, A. M., and H. Markel. 2005. "The History of Vaccines and Immunization: Familiar Patterns, New Challenges." *Health Affairs.* Published May 1. https://doi.org/10.1377/hlthaff.24.3.611.

Stevens, R. A. 2008. "History and Health Policy in the United States: The Making of a Health Care Industry, 1948–2008." *Social History of Medicine* 21 (3): 461–83. https://doi.org/10.1093/shm/hkn063.

———. 1971. *American Medicine and the Public Interest.* New Haven, CT: Yale University Press.

Taubenberger, J. K., and D. M. Morens. 2006. "1918 Influenza: The Mother of All Pandemics." *Emerging Infectious Diseases* 12 (1): 15–22. https://doi.org/10.3201/eid1201.050979.

Thomas, K. K. 2006. "The Hill-Burton Act and Civil Rights: Expanding Hospital Care for Black Southerners, 1939–1960." *Journal of Southern History* 72 (4): 823–70. www.questia.com/library/journal/1G1-155039477/the-hill-burton-act-and-civil-rights-expanding-hospital.

Tippett, R. 2014. "Mortality and Cause of Death, 1900 v. 2010." Carolina Demography. Published June 16. http://demography.cpc.unc.edu/2014/06/16/mortality-and-cause-of-death-1900-v-2010/.

US Burden of Disease Collaborators. 2013. "The State of US Health, 1990–2010: Burden of Diseases, Injuries, and Risk Factors." *Journal of the American Medical Association* 310 (6): 591–606. https://doi.org/10.1001/jama.2013.13805.

US Census Bureau. 1872. *1870 Census: Volume 1. The Statistics of the Population of the United States.* Accessed September 26, 2019. www2.census.gov/library/publications/decennial/1870/population/1870a-63.pdf?#.

US Department of Health, Education, and Welfare. 1976. *200 Years of American Medicine (1776–1976)*. US National Library of Medicine. Accessed September 26, 2019. www.nlm.nih.gov/hmd/pdf/200years.pdf.

US Department of Labor. 2018. "Health Plans & Benefits: ERISA." Accesed October 11. www.dol.gov/general/topic/health-plans/erisa.

US National Library of Medicine. 2015. "Dr. Elizabeth Blackwell." Updated June 3. https://cfmedicine.nlm.nih.gov/physicians/biography_35.html.

van Hartesveldt, F. R. 2010. "The Doctors and the 'Flu': The British Medical Profession's Response to the Influenza Pandemic of 1918–19." *International Social Science Review* 85 (1): 28–39. www.jstor.org/stable/41887429.

Wailoo, K., T. S. Jost, and M. Schlesinger. 2004. "Professional Sovereignty in a Changing Health Care System: Reflections on Paul Starr's *The Social Transformation of Medicine*." *Journal of Health Politics, Policy and Law* 29 (4): 557–68. https://doi.org/10.1215/03616878-29-4-5-557.

Weisz, G. 2005. *Divide and Conquer: A Comparative History of Medical Specialization*. New York: Oxford University Press.

White House. 2017. "Promoting Healthcare Choice and Competition Across the United States." Published October 13. www.whitehouse.gov/articles/promoting-healthcare-choice-competition-across-united-states/.

Winkelstein, W. Jr. 1992. "Not Just a Country Doctor: Edward Jenner, Scientist." *Epidemiology Review* 14: 1–15. https://doi.org/10.1093/oxfordjournals.epirev.a036081.

World Health Organization (WHO). 2019. "About WHO." Accessed September 26. www.who.int/about/who-we-are/en/.

———. 2008. *The Global Burden of Disease: 2004 Update*. Accessed September 26, 2019. www.who.int/healthinfo/global_burden_disease/2004_report_update/en/.

Wreszinski, W. 1913. *Der Papyrus Ebers*. Leipzig, Germany: Hinrichs.

AMERICAN BELIEFS, VALUES, AND ATTITUDES ABOUT HEALTH AND HEALTHCARE

Man is what he believes.

—Anton Chekhov

Learning Objectives

- Evaluate the question "What is health?"
- Recognize the various determinants of health.
- Appreciate the importance of cultural competence in healthcare delivery.
- Analyze how expectations for the healthcare system influence cost, quality, and access.
- Weigh key aspects of market justice versus social justice as the concepts apply to healthcare.

Of the many factors that influence the US healthcare system, perhaps none are more important than American beliefs and attitudes about health and healthcare (see exhibit 3.1). Our culture and beliefs—often rooted in imperfect knowledge—are among the most powerful forces we must address as we seek to bring about improvements in the system (Andersen and Newman 1973; Siddiqui, Salmon, and Omer 2013).

Although humorous, the cartoon in exhibit 3.2 illustrates a serious challenge facing healthcare today: Our understanding of the science of health, the information that is available to us, and our beliefs and attitudes about healthcare are all changing rapidly. Such changes affect the public at large, as well as healthcare professionals specifically. For instance, for many years, practitioners would routinely advise patients to avoid foods with cholesterol, based on the belief that dietary cholesterol was harmful. However, our knowledge of the issue has become more advanced through research studies, and we now recognize that the effects of cholesterol are more complicated than previously thought. Researchers began questioning previous dietary advice years ago, but widespread dissemination of their findings is just beginning (Cleveland Clinic 2018; Fernandez 2012; Havard University T. H. Chan School of Public Health 2018). Establishing a new belief system for cholesterol-containing foods will likely take years.

EXHIBIT 3.1
Area of Focus
for This Chapter

The Aim of the Healthcare System

Issues That Require Our Attention

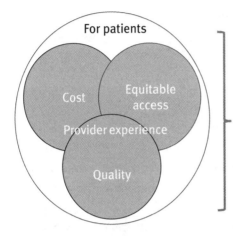

For patients

Cost

Equitable access

Provider experience

Quality

- Nature of our complex system
- Historical issues that have influenced the development of the system
- *Beliefs and attitudes about health and healthcare*
- Comparison with other developed countries
- Components of our healthcare system
- People and providers
- Patient care—the purpose of the system
- Financing a massive system
- Quality—easier said than done
- Medical and information technology
- The pharmaceutical industry
- Complementary and alternative medicine
- Politics/economics
- The future of the system

What Is Health?

The word *health* can be defined in different ways and understood through different models. In the broadest and simplest terms, health is the absence of disease or illness. Other definitions may be more detailed or sophisticated. The Society for Academic Emergency Medicine (1992), for instance, defines *health* as "a state of physical and mental well-being that facilitates the

EXHIBIT 3.2
Doctors in the
1950s

Source: WUMO © 2018 Wulffmorgenthanler. Reprinted with permission of ANDREWS MCMEEL SYNDICATION. All rights reserved.

achievement of individual and societal goals." Other sources may define the term specifically as a return to an illness- or disease-free state following a spell of illness (Emson 1987; Scully 2004; Tikkinen et al. 2012).

The World Health Organization (WHO) offers one of the broadest definitions of *health*: It is "a state of complete physical, mental and social well-being and not merely the absence of disease" (WHO 2019a). This definition reflects WHO's expansive thinking about what makes a person healthy. Such a broad definition can be justified based on the impact associated with numerous determinants of health.

Psychosocial models of health consider community and population well-being in the context of positive relationships, support networks for life's stresses, self-esteem, and responsibility. Other models focus on the use of preventive healthcare to avoid disease and promote health. The biomedical model of health and healthcare focuses on clinical diagnosis and the use of medical interventions to cure and relieve symptoms of disease and discomfort.

The biomedical model is the one that most closely reflects the traditional approach of the US system. Consider Medicare, for instance. Initially, the program was strictly intended to pay for the treatment of disease, and it covered no preventive services. Such an approach made sense in 1965, when Medicare was established. At that point, people age 65 or older were significantly underserved and undertreated, and few people appreciated the need for preventive efforts.

Illness and Disease

The terms *illness* and *disease*, though closely related, have some important distinctions. An illness is identified by people's perception and evaluation of how they are feeling. Generally, people are considered ill when they find that the condition interferes with their capacity to perform activities of daily living (ADLs) (Scully 2004). ADLs are things that most people do on a daily basis as they go about their lives—things most of us take for granted. Examples include bathing, dressing, eating, socializing, and walking (MedicineNet 2018).

Disease, on the other hand, is based on professional evaluation and diagnosis (Huber et al. 2011). For example, I may feel ill because I have a headache, but a disease (e.g., migraines) must be determined by a physician's diagnosis. That diagnosis, in turn, will enable the disease to be treated.

The tripartite, or epidemiological, model of disease focuses on three primary components (Centers for Disease Control and Prevention 2011):

1. *Agent.* The agent may be an infectious agent, such as a virus or bacteria, or a causative agent, such as use of an addictive drug or environmental exposure to a noxious substance.

2. *Host.* The host is the receptor of the agent—for the purposes of our discussion, it is the human. The host may come into contact with the agent either directly or through an intermediary. A mode of transmission to the host is called a vector—for instance, a mosquito might serve as a vector if it carries an infectious agent that causes West Nile virus or malaria in the host.

3. *Environment.* The environment provides the necessary conditions for the illness or disease to express itself. A number of environmental factors can increase a host's susceptibility to disease agents. For example, unsanitary conditions or close living arrangements can increase the likelihood of the spread of tuberculosis. Other environmental factors affecting the spread of disease may include access to healthcare or the availability of clean water.

What Determines Our Health?

Logically, if we are to develop optimal strategies for addressing health issues, then we need to think about what determines health status. As shown in chapter 2, US healthcare policy has traditionally focused to a large extent on access to care and on financing care. Such a focus, however, overlooks a wide range of issues—some independent of healthcare, per se—that can have both direct and indirect impacts on health. Often, the answer to a major problem in healthcare lies outside the walls of the institution or practice.

Although *healthcare* and *medical care* are sometimes treated as synonyms, *healthcare* has a much broader meaning, encompassing numerous factors beyond medical services or activities. A broad view that takes into account the various determinants of health is essential for any effective healthcare administrator. This section will examine these determinants in some detail.

Exhibit 3.3 shows some of the major categories of factors that influence our health status. We all start with our own genetic predisposition to disease, with variances that can make us more or less susceptible to certain disease states. I recall, many years ago, a student in a genetics class asking the professor, "How does one ensure that they will be healthy throughout their life?" The professor responded, "Pick your parents and your grandparents well." Of course, the response had an element of humor, but it also resonated in a deeper sense: Our health status is strongly influenced by our genetic makeup, which is determined before we are born—very little can be done about it.

Genetics provides a playbook for how disease may express itself in our lives. Often, a person will have a propensity for a certain malady; however, that malady might never manifest itself if the individual does not create conditions for it to occur. Consider heart disease, for example. Some people

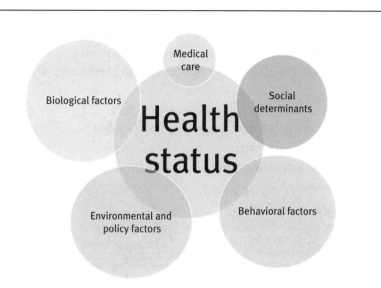

EXHIBIT 3.3
Major Factors
Determining
Health Status

might have a genetic predisposition toward heart disease but, through careful diet and lifestyle adjustments, prevent it from actually occurring. On the other hand, some people's predispositions might be so strong that, despite their best efforts, they develop the disease anyway (Slade-Sawyer 2014).

Environmental factors play a significant role in how our genes are expressed, and they can have a direct influence on the development of disease. For example, childhood asthma is often associated with small-particle air pollution, and some forms of cancer have been specifically associated with exposure to asbestos. Certain chemicals released into our environment through improper waste disposal can also cause disease (Mabahwi, Leh, and Omar 2014).

Medical care—for instance, seeing a physician when one has a disease or an illness, or having access to prescription drugs for treatment—is not the most important factor in determining our health, but it certainly is a critical one. McGinnis and colleagues (2002) have estimated that medical care contributes only about 10 to 15 percent to a person's health status, but if someone experiences a medical crisis such as a heart attack, the other factors relating to health status are no substitute for medical care. In such circumstances, medical care is indispensable (Schroeder 2007).

Social determinants are extremely important to health status as well. If social or economic factors limit people's access to an adequate diet, or if a neighborhood's safety concerns prevent people from going outside and exercising, overall health status will be negatively affected. Environmental situations that are conducive to violence and pollution are a significant health risk as well (Magnan 2017).

Beyond our genetics, our behaviors have some of the most significant effects on health status (Braveman and Gottlieb 2014; Rosenberg 2014). Risky behaviors that have a significant impact on morbidity and mortality from injury and disease include the following (Committee on Health and Behavior 2001):

- Smoking
- Substance abuse (alcohol or drugs, legal or illicit)
- Lack of physical exercise
- Poor eating behaviors / lack of balanced nutrition
- Improper use of motor vehicles
- Unsafe sex
- Obesity

Research comparing the various health risks suggests that obesity may be a more significant problem than the rest—even more significant than smoking (Sturm and Wells 2002).

Exhibit 3.4 provides an additional look at the determinants of health. Societal issues such as crime, housing, family relationships, culture, and behavior all have a significant impact, as do health regulations and policies affecting access, environmental protection, funding for services, and research (*New England Journal of Medicine* 2017). Biology includes genetics, sex, age, and the biology of disease itself—factors over which we generally have little control.

Intertwined with these various biological, social, and behavioral factors are our attitudes and beliefs about health and healthcare, which can be

EXHIBIT 3.4
Determinants of Health

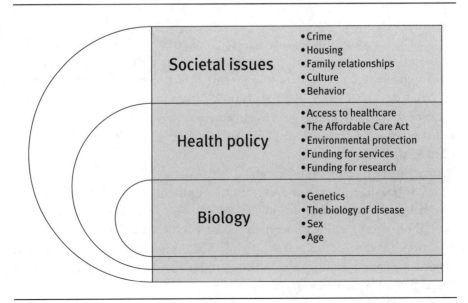

influenced by a variety of factors (see exhibit 3.5). Often, these attitudes and beliefs are influenced by religion (Green and Elliott 2010; Hummer et al. 2004; Miller and Thoresen 2003). For example, some people may believe they have little control over their destiny and are entirely in the hands of a higher power; as a result, they may take a less active role in managing their health behaviors. Our attitudes and beliefs may also be shaped by the language we use and the ways we discuss and represent our healthcare concerns—both verbally and nonverbally. From an early age, our manner of interacting with family members and other attributes of the family structure affect the way we think about health (National Institutes of Health 2016).

Attitudes and beliefs about health and healthcare may be influenced by age and generation, by biological sex and gender expression, and by race and ethnicity. Women, for instance, tend to seek healthcare services more often than men (Uchino et al. 2012). Some Native American cultures use traditional healers as part of the healthcare armamentarium (Goodkind et al. 2010; Portman and Garrett 2006)—sometimes in combination with modern medicine to achieve optimal results while also reflecting the belief system of the patient (Glanz, Rimer, and Viswanath 2008; Nutton 2004).

Socioeconomic status influences not only people's access to healthcare but also their beliefs and attitudes concerning health. Where health-related education is lacking, people may develop their way of thinking based on what they hear from others in their neighborhood or community, or from erroneous sources (Glanz, Rimer, and Viswanath 2008; Graham 2016).

Religious beliefs

Language

Nonverbal communication

Attitudes toward health practices

Family interaction

Food preferences

Age

Gender expression and biological sex

Race or ethnicity

Sexual orientation

Socioeconomic status

Community, neighborhood, and environment

Education

Experience with the healthcare system or providers

EXHIBIT 3.5
Factors
Affecting Our
Attitudes and
Beliefs About
Health and
Healthcare

Finally, our beliefs and attitudes about healthcare can be strongly influenced by our own personal experiences with the healthcare system and providers. If we have had good experiences in the past, we are likely to have a more positive attitude; obviously, the converse is true if our experiences have been negative. Our attitudes may influence our choices to seek care at the appropriate time, which can have a meaningful effect on our health outcomes (Cooper et al. 2003; Harder et al. 2016).

Why Is the American Healthcare System So Different from Those of Other Countries?

This question has already been addressed somewhat in previous chapters. We know that the current US healthcare system developed not through careful planning but rather through a series of efforts to build onto a system that dates back centuries. Furthermore, we have acknowledged many of the significant cultural differences that exist between the United States and other countries. Still, is there a deeper philosophical underpinning that has caused our system to be the way it is? The answer to this question might lie in two fundamental beliefs that date back to the country's beginning: manifest destiny and American exceptionalism (Brown 1980; Hidalgo 2003; Hietala 1985).

Manifest Destiny

According to the doctrine of manifest destiny, American people and institutions have special qualities that can benefit all people and therefore have a destiny to spread their influence. During the nineteenth century, proponents used this belief to encourage American expansion into the western territories, without regard to the consequences.

What does manifest destiny have do with healthcare? First, the idea that Americans are somehow endowed with special virtues creates a resistance to change and an unwillingness to learn from other countries. In the United States, the idea that "we know best" is unfortunately pervasive. Second, the focus on expansion suggests a notion that the United States has no limits on its capabilities or its resources—which, of course, is untrue. Similar observations have been postulated by economists such as Lester Thurow (1993, 1996) and written about by others, although rarely applied to healthcare (DeVoto 1998; Kaplan 2017).

American Exceptionalism

The ideology of American exceptionalism lacks a formal definition, but it represents a fundamental aspect of the American psyche. It is rooted in the idea that America is unique in its ideals of personal freedom and democracy.

The emphasis on personal freedom pervades many issues relating to healthcare and healthcare policy. Consider the controversy over the Affordable Care Act's individual mandate, discussed in chapter 2. The requirement for individuals to purchase health insurance was considered by many to be a violation of personal freedom, and the provision was strongly resisted and ultimately repealed. Americans' focus on personal freedom is often accompanied by a deeply rooted suspicion of government, which dates to the founding of the country and is embodied in the US Constitution.

Throughout the history of the US healthcare system, attempts at major reform have encountered resistance from people who insist that they should not be required to participate in a healthcare system and that a healthcare system should not be imposed upon them by the government. This issue of "personal choice" is always of paramount importance to discussions of healthcare reform or system design in the United States, and all healthcare administrators must acknowledge it (Hietala 1985; McDougall 1997).

Cultural Competence

In the United States, we are privileged to have a highly diverse society. Research shows that diversity makes the country more innovative, more thoughtful, and more diligent (Phillips 2014). Diversity also contributes to a broad range of thoughts and attitudes about health and healthcare. Although this diversity is ultimately a good thing, it does pose challenges in the delivery of healthcare services across a broad population. Often, providers are unaware of cultural variations in beliefs about illness and treatment, and this unawareness can become an enormous hindrance to the delivery of effective care. Cultural competence, therefore, is critical (Olsen et al. 2006).

Definitions and Scholarship

Culture refers to integrated patterns of human behavior. It includes the language, thoughts, communications, actions, customs, beliefs, values, and institutions of racial, ethnic, religious, and social groups. *Competence* refers to the capacity to function effectively as an individual or as an organization within various contexts. Cultural and linguistic competence, therefore, consists of a set of congruent behaviors, attitudes, and policies that come together in a system or agency, or among professionals, to enable effective work in cross-cultural situations presented by consumers and their communities. Cultural competence underscores the ability to meet others where they are and effectively engage with people of diverse backgrounds.

Sally Haslanger (2000, 2015, 2016), a noted philosopher and linguist, argues that the social context of diversity is based on several assumptions related directly to individuals' physical attributes but that natural attributes do not always describe identity correctly. Cultural competence, therefore, requires us to spend time getting to know others and treating them with compassion. Doing so will create greater opportunities for transparency, disclosure, and collaboration.

A significant amount of research and scholarship supports the business imperative of understanding and exhibiting cultural competence in organizations. However, little scholarly literature presents specific delivery models for enriching environments toward cultural competence. As a result, organizations must navigate a number of complexities and challenges as they seek to leverage diverse talent for the ultimate purpose of achieving transformational sustainability. Successful delivery models identify, foster, and share best practices to promote awareness and understanding through systematic transparency, disclosure, and cultural engagement (Padela, Gunter, and Killawi 2011; National Committee for Quality Assurance and Eli Lilly & Company 2007; Rousseau, Gill, and Haycock 2003).

The Influence of Culture and Language

Culture and language influence people's belief systems concerning health, healing, and wellness; the ways illness, disease, and their causes are perceived, both by the patient/consumer and the provider; the behaviors of patients/consumers who are seeking healthcare; and people's attitudes toward healthcare providers. If providers look at the world only through their own limited cultural perspective, the delivery of services may suffer, and access for patients from other cultures may be compromised.

The growth of minority racial and ethnic communities and linguistic groups, each with its own cultural traits and health profiles, presents a positive challenge to the US healthcare system. Providers and patients both bring their learned patterns of language and culture, and gaps must be transcended to achieve equal access and quality healthcare.

Two Stories

The following are two stories that illustrate some of the challenges associated with cultural competence in healthcare delivery.

A Cultural Misunderstanding

A young mother of Guatemalan ancestry is accompanying her 19-month-old son on his biweekly rehabilitation visit at the local children's hospital, where the child is relearning how to walk. During the appointment, the mother visits the gift shop. Upon returning, she is distressed to find her child's shoes in a cubbyhole, instead of on his feet. The child's shoes had been removed in two previous visits, and both times the mother explicitly told the physical therapist she wanted her son wearing shoes.

The physical therapist, who is focused on the boy's balance and physical control, explains that going barefoot is ideal for this type of therapy. The mother, on the other hand, is concerned about parasites on the ground, a common danger in rural Guatemala, and worries that others might view her negatively if her child is seen not wearing shoes. The physical therapist feels that the parent is refusing standard therapy practices for the child's healthy development, while the mother feels that the therapist is ignorant about environmental dangers and social stigma (Olsen et al. 2006). If the therapist had clearly communicated his reasoning and been aware of possible cultural misunderstandings, interactions with the mother would be improved, and the boy's rehabilitation process would go more smoothly.

These types of situations can cause discomfort and occasionally are explosive; other times, they go unrecognized as anything more than a simple lack of connection. Regardless, when they play out, disappointing outcomes are too often the result. For the diverse, complex, fast-paced organizations of the US healthcare system, the handling of cultural differences and misunderstandings can determine whether teammates remain engaged and whether patients feel respected (Foxx et al. 2013). Healthcare administrators therefore need to watch vigilantly for potential misunderstandings and help providers and staff manage them effectively.

Communication Issues with People with Disabilities

WM, a 26-year-old male with severe developmental disabilities, was being hospitalized for removal of a large kidney stone. Because of his disabilities, WM was not able to speak in a way that anyone except the people closest to him could understand. The procedure to remove the kidney stone was successful, but WM went into shock after surgery and needed blood. His bed was tilted to keep blood flowing to the brain, and he was given medications to support his blood pressure.

WM was anemic, but this condition was not discovered on the preoperative exam because the resident physician did not want to upset WM by taking blood. The resident also did not know how to overcome WM's fears and did not recognize that WM required careful preop care. The source of the anemia was not discovered until three weeks later, when WM began vomiting blood because of severe gastroesophageal reflux disease and esophageal erosion.

The problems did not end there. WM received severe third-degree burns from magnetic resonance imaging, requiring excision. The burns occurred because the technician did not remove WM's T-shirt, which was concealing electrocardiogram pads on his chest, and WM was unable to inform the technician or read the warnings posted around the radiology department.

As this story shows, people with disabilities are frequently burdened with challenges beyond the deficits directly associated with their disabilities. Their health, independence, and well-being can be compromised by suboptimal access to needed services, by errors and misunderstandings, by inconsistent or fragmented care, and by a lack of prevention and early intervention. Similar issues affect other vulnerable groups, and the general population as well. Such failures on the part of organizations, staff, and providers are not deliberate, but they are a common occurrence in the current US healthcare system—a system that tends to focus more on delivering services and receiving payment for those services than on developing and maintaining a clear understanding of patients' true needs.

Culturally competent interactions can be enhanced by taking into account individuals' communication preferences. If you ask patients, they (or, by proxy, their caregivers) are likely to make requests similar to the following:

- "Please talk to me, even if I'm using an interpreter or personal assistant. Encourage me to express my own opinion, even when parents or friends feel they can speak for me."
- "Please use a normal tone of voice. If I cannot hear or understand you, I'll let you know."
- "Please speak in simple, clear sentences. Simple language does not mean childish language. If necessary, use signs or gestures to help me understand."
- "Please take the time to explain procedures to me. Things are not as scary when I know what is going to happen."
- "Explain to me why you are prescribing medication and how it will help me."
- "Please be patient if I have a speech or language disability. I may need a little more time to respond to your question. Don't try to finish my sentences for me."

Funding Is Not the Only Answer

Much of the literature and many interventions in healthcare have focused on funding. Funding alone, however, is not the complete answer. If a person is unable to access care because of issues with provider availability, cultural competence, provider education, patient and caregiver knowledge, or communication skills, additional funding by itself is not likely solve the problem. The patient- and family-centered care model enables patients and their families to have more choice and to participate more in their care decisions, but many communities have not been given access to this model. For many minority racial and ethnic groups, as well as for people with disabilities, care remains completely dependent on a delegated model of care. As healthcare administrators, we have a duty to change that.

Best Corporate Practice: Kaiser Permanente

Kaiser Permanente is a large healthcare organization that has successfully integrated inclusion and social consciousness into its business model and manner of operation. The organization sees cultural competence as a quality-of-care issue, and it trains its workforce in relevant and meaningful ways.

Kaiser Permanente tries to demonstrate its commitment to cultural competence through action, not just words. For example, the organization manages a program that brings farmers markets into low-income and income-diverse communities, recognizing that healthy eating is critical to good health. Often, the program targets communities regarded as "food deserts"—areas that lack grocery stores or markets and where the stores that do exist sell mostly high-calorie, low-nutrition foods. The initiative helps the organization serve its customers and attract new ones.

Kaiser Permanente has also opened clinical care modules designed specifically to provide culturally competent care to three patient populations: the Chinese American community in San Francisco, the African American community in West Los Angeles, and the Latino community in East Los Angeles. The success of these modules has encouraged the organization to open other similar practices.

Kaiser Permanente emphasizes cultural competence across a number of population health strategies:

- It prints and posts all signs in multiple languages, specific to the population being served.
- It ensures that physicians and other staff members are multilingual.
- It provides extensive cultural training to staff, helping to ensure that everyone in the clinic understands cultural factors and considerations that may have an impact on patients' care.
- It identifies diseases and conditions that are unique to or frequently associated with the targeted communities.
- It provides clinicians with an overview of the epidemiological and other factors that often characterize cultural groups; the overview addresses ethnicity, country of origin, sexual orientation, and gender identity, among other areas.

Kaiser Permanente's Institute for Culturally Competent Care coordinates the organization's efforts nationally by consolidating research, funding, and oversight of projects related to cultural competence (Boult, Karm, and Groves 2008; Davino-Ramaya et al. 2012; Tang et al. 2011).

We as healthcare administrators can learn a lot from Kaiser Permanente's model, but the most important thing is to recognize that cultural competence is not an "extra." Rather, it is an essential aspect of patient care in the United States in the twenty-first century. An old car commercial once had the tagline, "Lead, follow, or get out of the way." If you are not open to diversity in terms of race, ethnicity, disability, sexual orientation, gender identity, nationality, language, and citizenship status, and if you are not willing to learn with an open mind about people who are different from you, then you should truly get out of the way—and find another field. Cultural competence is a necessity for healthcare administrators in the United States and, really, for anyone who wants to work in a healthcare setting.

Americans' Expectations for Their Healthcare System

The tremendous advances in biomedical research and technology have led Americans to rely increasingly on the healthcare system for their health and well-being and to have high—sometimes unrealistic—expectations about the system's ability to cure disease and treat injuries (Weinfurt 2004).

Doyle and colleagues (2001), for instance, surveyed patients who had advanced ovarian cancer and were receiving chemotherapy. Even though the chemotherapy was intended to be palliative in nature, 42 percent of the patients thought the treatment would cure them. Americans' high expectations are also reflected in the rising costs of medical care and the increasing numbers of pharmaceuticals being developed to treat serious illnesses such as cancer and diabetes (Bishop 2018; Papanicolas, Woskie, and Jha 2018).

Often, we see television commercials for over-the-counter medications intended to treat ailments that are largely related to the individual's eating behavior. In one such commercial, a well-known television personality states that he can eat whatever he likes because the medication prevents the heartburn that would normally result. Of course, this message ignores the fact that unhealthy eating is still unhealthy, even without the symptoms of heartburn. Research on the topic is limited, but one must question the true health effects of this pervasive belief that the healthcare system will magically solve all our problems.

What Do Americans Believe About Our Healthcare System?

Do Americans believe our healthcare system is in need of reform? If so, in what ways? According to a 2017 Gallup poll, 71 percent of Americans felt that the US healthcare system is either in crisis or has major problems (Jones and Saad 2017). This number has been consistently high since 2008 (see exhibit 3.6), peaking at 74 percent in 2011. The past decade has seen tremendous political energy expended on the issue of healthcare, yet little has changed in the public's perception of the system. The problem is not a matter

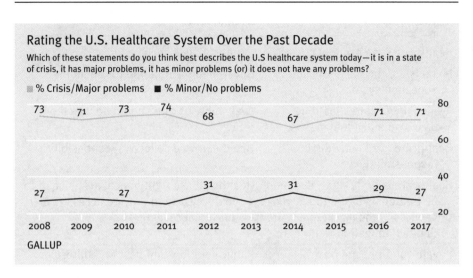

EXHIBIT 3.6
Beliefs About the US Healthcare System

Rating the U.S. Healthcare System Over the Past Decade

Which of these statements do you think best describes the U.S healthcare system today—it is in a state of crisis, it has major problems, it has minor problems (or) it does not have any problems?

% Crisis/Major problems   % Minor/No problems

Source: The Gallup Poll: Public Opinion 2017 by Rowman & Littlefield Publishers. Reproduced with permission.

of getting people to recognize the need for change but rather determining the kind of change we wish to implement. A key concern involves the competing concepts of market justice and social justice.

Market Justice Versus Social Justice

As noted in chapter 1, the tension between market justice and social justice has a powerful effect on people's attitudes and beliefs about healthcare, and it contributes to many of the challenges we face in reforming our system.

From the formation of the United States until the middle of the twentieth century, Americans seemed satisfied leaving healthcare to compete alongside other goods and services in the marketplace. With an emphasis on market justice, the system favored individualism, personal choice, volunteer behavior, personal effort, and consideration of one's self-interest. People were able choose what goods and services to buy, including healthcare, and resources were allocated based on those decisions.

Concerns about social justice grew more prevalent during the mid-1900s. Budetti (2008) suggests that the rise of health insurance may have awakened ideas about social justice as it relates to healthcare. In contrast to market justice, social justice takes more of a collective approach. Resources are allocated based on need rather than on ability or economic wherewithal to obtain needed services.

Debates between the market justice and social justice perspectives have been ongoing since the early healthcare reform initiatives more than 100 years ago (Karsten 1995). Exhibit 3.7 provides a comparison of some of the key characteristics of the two approaches. As the exhibit makes clear,

EXHIBIT 3.7
Characteristics
of Market
Justice and
Social Justice in
Healthcare

Market Justice	Social Justice
Healthcare is an economic good.	Healthcare is a social good.
Markets are the most efficient allocation system.	Government is required for equitable allocation.
Availability of care should be based on individual means.	Availability of care should be based on need.
Healthcare is an individual responsibility.	Healthcare is a collective responsibility.
Healthcare is not a right; it should be treated as other goods and services in the marketplace are (limited obligation to others).	Healthcare is a right; mechanisms need to be developed to provide access to all (universal coverage).
Private solutions are best.	Public solutions are best for addressing social problems
Rationing should occur on an economic basis.	Rationing should occur on a planned basis.
The individual is paramount.	Community should supersede the individual.

the two approaches reflect deeply rooted beliefs and principles that, in many instances, are diametrically opposite from one another. As a result, compromise can be difficult. Within the healthcare field, however, the prevailing belief is that healthcare should be as accessible as possible to all people.

Does Our State Federal Structure Affect These Attitudes?

Part of our difficulty in reaching consensus on healthcare and healthcare coverage stems from deeply rooted ideas about the role of government and about which government institutions should be in charge of key issues.

Americans have long demonstrated a certain amount of skepticism toward the government (Pew Research Center 1998). According to a 2015 survey, just 19 percent of Americans believed they "can trust the government always or most of the time," which was among the lowest levels in the past 50 years, and only 20 percent would describe government programs as being "well-run" (Pew Research Center 2015). Nonetheless, another study indicates that more than half of American believe that healthcare coverage is a responsibility of government (Kiley 2018). These seemingly contradictory findings may help explain the divisions that have hindered efforts to reform the healthcare system and move toward a universal system of coverage.

Healthcare reform efforts are further complicated by Americans' differing attitudes toward the federal and state governments. In a 2016 Gallup poll, 55 percent of respondents indicated a preference for state government power, whereas 37 percent favored federal government power (McCarthy 2016). Respondents to a similar survey during the 1930s slightly favored federal power, but a preference for state power became apparent by the 1980s. These preferences largely fall along party lines, with Republicans favoring state power (78 percent) and Democrats favoring federal power (62 percent) (McCarthy 2016). Such findings are consistent with Republicans' historical opposition to many federal reform efforts.

The US Preventive Services Task Force

The US Preventive Services Task Force (USPSTF), created in 1984, is an independent group of national experts dedicated to applying evidence-based medicine to important medical issues and providing recommendations based on research (USPSTF 2017). In this role, it has had a significant influence on the attitudes and beliefs of patients and providers, and it aims to keep those beliefs in line with current research findings. In 2018, for instance, the USPSTF issued a new recommendation concerning prostate cancer screenings for men between the ages of 55 and 69, based on evidence that only 13 lives are saved for every 100,000 screenings in that group. The new recommendation states that patients should make an individual decision about prostate cancer screening with their provider (USPSTF 2018).

The Antivaccination Movement

A particularly important example of how beliefs and attitudes affect modern healthcare delivery is the case of the antivaccination movement. Since the time of Edward Jenner, vaccinations have been responsible for saving countless lives and preventing widespread disease and suffering (Riedel 2005; College of Physicians of Philadelphia 2019; Bloch et al. 1985; Jit et al. 2015). They have been one of the miracles of medicine and one of the greatest inventions of modern times (Schlenoff 2013).

In 1998, the *Lancet* published a small case-series (based on a group of 12 children) by a gastroenterologist named Andrew Wakefield in which the author strongly suggested that the measles, mumps, and rubella (MMR) vaccine may predispose children to behavioral regression and pervasive developmental disorder, often referred to as autism. Wakefield and his study, however, were found to be fraudulent, and Wakefield was discredited and delisted from the British Medical Registry for his fraud, misconduct, and unethical behavior (Deer 2011; *New York Times* 2011). He was found to have engaged in numerous unethical practices, including overtreatment of patients and performance of unnecessary procedures, in addition to having financial conflicts of interest (Bone and Rose 2009; Boseley 2010).

The *Lancet* published a retraction of the article (see exhibit 3.8), but its impact remains. The widespread reporting of the study initiated the antivaccination movement that continues today.

EXHIBIT 3.8
The Retraction
That Appeared
in the *Lancet* in
2010

Early report

Ileal-lymphoid-nodular hyperplasia, non-specific colitis, and pervasive developmental disorder in children

A J Wakefield, S H Murch, A Anthony, J Linnell, D M Casson, M Malik, M Berelowitz, A P Dhillon, M A Thomson, P Harvey, A Valentine, S E Davies, J A Walker-Smith

Summary

Background We investigated a consecutive series of children with chronic enterocolitis and regressive developmental disorder.

Methods 12 children (mean age 6 years [range 3–10], 11 boys) were referred to a paediatric gastroenterology unit with a history of normal development followed by loss of acquired skills, including language, together with diarrhoea and abdominal pain. Children underwent gastroenterological, neurological, and developmental assessment and review of developmental records. Ileocolonoscopy and biopsy sampling, magnetic-resonance imaging (MRI), electroencephalography (EEG), and lumbar puncture were done under sedation. Barium follow-through radiography was done where possible. Biochemical, haematological, and immunological profiles were examined.

Findings Onset of behavioural symptoms was associated, by the parents, with measles, mumps, and rubella vaccination in eight of the 12 children, with measles infection in one child, and otitis media in another. All 12 children had intestinal abnormalities, ranging from lymphoid nodular hyperplasia to aphthoid ulceration. Histology showed patchy chronic inflammation in the colon in 11 children and reactive ileal lymphoid hyperplasia in seven, but no granulomas. Behavioural disorders included autism (nine), disintegrative psychosis (one), and possible postviral or vaccinal encephalitis (two). There were no focal neurological abnormalities and MRI and EEG tests were normal. Abnormal laboratory results were significantly raised urinary methylmalonic acid compared with age-matched controls (p=0·003), low haemoglobin in four children, and a low serum IgA in four children.

Interpretation We identified associated gastrointestinal disease and developmental regression in a group of previously normal children, which was generally associated in time with possible environmental triggers.

Lancet 1998; **351:** 637–41
See Commentary page

Inflammatory Bowel Disease Study Group, University Departments of Medicine and Histopathology (A J Wakefield FRCS, A Anthony MB, J Linnell PhD, A P Dhillon MRCPath, S E Davies MRCPath) **and the University Departments of Paediatric Gastroenterology** (S H Murch MB, D M Casson MRCP, M Malik MRCP, M A Thomson FRCP, J A Walker-Smith FRCP,), **Child and Adolescent Psychiatry** (M Berelowitz FRCPsych), **Neurology** (P Harvey FRCP), **and Radiology** (A Valentine FRCR), **Royal Free Hospital and School of Medicine, London NW3 2QG, UK**

Correspondence to: Dr A J Wakefield

Introduction

We saw several children who, after a period of apparent normality, lost acquired skills, including communication. They all had gastrointestinal symptoms, including abdominal pain, diarrhoea, and bloating and, in some cases, food intolerance. We describe the clinical findings, and gastrointestinal features of these children.

Patients and methods

12 children, consecutively referred to the department of paediatric gastroenterology with a history of a pervasive developmental disorder with loss of acquired skills and intestinal symptoms (diarrhoea, abdominal pain, bloating and food intolerance) were investigated. All children were admitted to the ward for 1 week, accompanied by their parents.

Clinical investigations

We took histories, including details of immunisations and exposure to infectious diseases, and assessed the children. In 11 cases the history was obtained by the senior clinician (JW-S). Neurological and psychiatric assessments were done by consultant staff (PH, MB) with HMS-4 criteria.[1] Developmental histories included a review of prospective developmental records from parents, health visitors, and general practitioners. Four children did not undergo psychiatric assessment in hospital; all had been assessed professionally elsewhere, so these assessments were used as the basis for their behavioural diagnosis.

After bowel preparation, ileocolonoscopy was performed by SHM or MAT under sedation with midazolam and pethidine. Paired frozen and formalin-fixed mucosal biopsy samples were taken from the terminal ileum; ascending, transverse, descending, and sigmoid colons, and from the rectum. The procedure was recorded by video or still images, and were compared with images of the previous seven consecutive paediatric colonoscopies (four normal colonoscopies and three on children with ulcerative colitis), in which the physician reported normal appearances in the terminal ileum. Barium follow-through radiography was possible in some cases.

Also under sedation, cerebral magnetic-resonance imaging (MRI), electroencephalography (EEG) including visual, brain stem auditory, and sensory evoked potentials (where compliance made these possible), and lumbar puncture were done.

Laboratory investigations

Thyroid function, serum long-chain fatty acids, and cerebrospinal-fluid lactate were measured to exclude known causes of childhood neurodegenerative disease. Urinary methylmalonic acid was measured in random urine samples from eight of the 12 children and 14 age-matched and sex-matched normal controls, by a modification of a technique described previously.[2] Chromatograms were scanned digitally on computer, to analyse the methylmalonic-acid zones from cases and controls. Urinary methylmalonic-acid concentrations in patients and controls were compared by a two-sample *t* test. Urinary creatinine was estimated by routine spectrophotometric assay.

Children were screened for antiendomyseal antibodies and boys were screened for fragile-X if this had not been done

Source: Editors of the *Lancet* (2010).

Members of the antivaccination movement base their position largely on beliefs rather than facts (Begley 2009), and beliefs are hard to change. Despite new studies that do not link the MMR vaccine with autism, the fear remains for some people (Eskola et al. 2015; Honda, Shimizu, and Rutter 2005; Siddiqui, Salmon, and Omer 2013). To paraphrase an old saying, "Don't confuse me with the facts, this is what I believe." Not surprisingly, these beliefs are related to the lack of trust that many people have in the healthcare system (Gilkey et al. 2014; Offit and Coffin 2003; Siddiqui, Salmon, and Omer 2013).

This situation illustrates the serious damage that dishonest and greedy behavior within the healthcare system can cause to our society. Measles cases, along with the associated misery, have increased since the antivaccination movement began (Calvert, Ashton, and Garnett 2013; Flaherty 2011). The World Health Organization (2019b) now ranks vaccine hesitancy as one of the top ten threats to global health.

Medicalization

Purdy (2001) writes: "It can be appropriate to use medical means to prevent suffering and enhance well-being even if the source of the problem is not a disease." This quote epitomizes the social concept of medicalization, a critically important issue in our discussion of attitudes, values, beliefs, and expectations concerning the US healthcare system.

Medicalization is the act of defining a nonmedical problem in medical terms, usually as an illness or disorder, and using medical interventions to treat it (Conrad 2007). Medicalization in and of itself is not necessarily bad, though it is related to misdiagnosis and overtreatment (van Dijk et al. 2016). When considering the issue of medicalization, we need to recognize the wide variation in what is normal in human health and behavior, as well as in our perceptions of what is normal (Conrad 2013; Frawley 2015).

Some argue that medicalization and the increased number of conditions that receive a medical diagnosis are indeed bad and can do serious harm by contributing to "diagnostic inflation." For example, as psychiatry has expanded the boundaries of various diagnoses, people could potentially be labeled with a mild mental disorder and treated with medication, even though they are simply experiencing difficult emotions that are perfectly normal within their circumstances and range of experience. These patients may require counseling or other forms of therapy to help address their emotions and improve their quality of life, but the emotions are not necessarily symptoms of an illness. This blurring of boundaries for diagnosis has contributed to a crisis of confidence in the medical profession. Great advances have been made in neurobiology, but studies suggest that the diagnosis of mental health conditions is often based more on provider opinion than on scientific support (Frances 2013).

Because the US healthcare system is geared toward diagnosis and treatment, management of the conditions created by medicalization has become a significant source of revenue. Birrer and Tokuda (2017) posit that the following factors have helped drive the trend toward medicalization:

- *Obsession with wellness.* Americans are inundated with images of the "perfect body," advice about how to stay healthy, and advertisements for health products. Against this influx of messages, people may have a tendency to view any minor deviation as abnormal (Birrer and Tokuda 2017).
- *Pharmaceutical industry.* The pharmaceutical industry stands to benefit from medicalization by selling products to treat these newly identified conditions (Birrer and Tokuda 2017).
- *Statistical saturation.* The more we examine the increasing volumes of data that are available, the more possibilities exist for finding deviations and outlying data that support a new finding. In many instances, data can be manipulated or presented in a manner that exaggerates or downplays certain aspects (Birrer and Tokuda 2017). Often, we fail to follow a common statistical parameter—such as a number needed to treat or test (NNT) or number needed to harm (NNH)—when undertaking data analysis (Brownlee 2007; Brownlee et al. 2017).
- *The role of the media and the internet.* Coverage of medical issues is extensive across all forms of media. According to the Pew Research Center (2013), 59 percent of Americans obtain medical information from the internet.
- *Research saturation.* The PubMed database includes citations for more than 30,000 journals (US National Library of Medicine 2018). Researchers are under tremendous academic pressure to publish studies, which may push them to seek out new areas in which to focus their work (Birrer and Tokuda 2017).
- *Litigation.* Medicalization can be encouraged during litigation through the use of expert witnesses who have a vested interest in promoting dubious diagnoses (Birrer and Tokuda 2017).

The potential corrupting influence of medicalization is significant. Preventing its negative effects will require a vigilant medical community and an enlightened public willing to recognize that medicine is an imperfect science (Birrer and Tokuda 2017; Parens 2011; Sholl 2017).

Summary

The United States has a great diversity of beliefs, attitudes, and values. With regard to healthcare, Americans' beliefs tend to be polarized into two points of view: one prioritizing market justice and the other prioritizing social justice. The tension between these two perspectives has persisted throughout history, serving as a major obstacle in our efforts to reform the healthcare system.

Americans overwhelmingly agree that our healthcare system is either in crisis or has major problems, yet we have been unable to implement meaningful reforms that satisfy the needs of these two divergent groups. One wonders if such a solution is even possible. Will we continue to see a series of back-and-forth reform efforts that satisfy either only market justice needs or only social justice concerns (Hensch 2017; Pollack 2010)? Healthcare administrators should play a role in finding balance and compromise between these two viewpoints, while continuing to advocate for patients.

Discussion Questions

1. What are some of the most significant determinants of health in the United States?
2. What are some of the common attitudes and beliefs that Americans hold about health and healthcare?
3. How does the state/federal structure affect Americans' attitudes about healthcare?
4. How have the concepts of manifest destiny and American exceptionalism influenced efforts to reform the US healthcare system?
5. How do other industries, such as the food industry, affect healthcare attitudes?
6. How does the American social environment affect healthcare attitudes?

References

Andersen, R. M., and J. F. Newman. 1973. "Societal and Individual Determinants of Medical Care Utilisation in the United States." *Milbank Memorial Fund Quarterly* 51 (1): 95–124. https://doi.org/10.1111/j.1468-0009.2005.00428.x.

Begley, S. 2009. "Autism: How Childhood Vaccines Became Villains." *Newsweek*. Published February 20. www.newsweek.com/autism-how-childhood-vaccines-became-villains-82273.

Birrer, R. B., and Y. Tokuda. 2017. "Medicalization: A Historical Perspective." *Journal of General and Family Medicine* 18 (2): 48–51. https://doi.org/10.1002/jgf2.22.

Bishop, S. 2018. "Policy Prescriptions for High Drug Costs: Experts Weigh In." *Commonwealth Fund Blog*. Published April 3. www.commonwealthfund.org/publications/blog/2018/mar/policy-prescriptions-for-high-drug-costs.

Bloch, A. B., W. A. Orenstein, H. C. Stetler, S. G. Wassilak, R. W. Amler, K. J. Bart, C. D. Kirby, and A. R. Hinman. 1985. "Health Impact of Measles Vaccination in the United States." *Pediatrics* 76 (4): 524–32. www.ncbi.nlm.nih. gov/pubmed/3931045.

Bone, J., and D. Rose. 2009. "MMR Scare Doctor Andrew Wakefield Makes Fortune in US." *Times*(London). Published February 14. www.thetimes.co.uk/article/mmr-scare-doctor-andrew-wakefield-makes-fortune-in-us-tg36fdn7k5g.

Boseley, S. 2010. "Andrew Wakefield Found 'Irresponsible' by GMC over MMR Vaccine Scare." *Guardian*. Published January 28. www.theguardian.com/society/2010/jan/28/andrew-wakefield-mmr-vaccine.

Boult, C., L. Karm, and C. Groves. 2008. "Improving Chronic Care: The 'Guided Care' Model." *Permanente Journal* 12 (1): 50–54. www.ncbi.nlm.nih.gov/pmc/articles/PMC3042340/.

Braveman, P., and L. Gottlieb. 2014. "The Social Determinants of Health: It's Time to Consider the Causes of the Causes." *Public Health Reports* 129 (1, Suppl. 2): 19–31. https://doi.org/10.1177/00333549141291S206.

Brown, C. H. 1980. *Agents of Manifest Destiny: The Lives and Times of the Filibusters*. Durham, NC: University of North Carolina Press.

Brownlee, S. 2007. *Overtreated: Why Too Much Medicine Is Making Us Sicker and Poorer*. New York: Bloomsbury Press.

Brownlee, S., K. Chalkidou, J. Doust, A. G. Elshaug, P. Glasziou, I. Heath, S. Nagpal, V. Saini, D. Srivastava, K. Chalmers, and D. Korenstein. 2017. "Evidence for Overuse of Medical Services around the World." *Lancet* 390 (10090): 156–68. https://doi.org/10.1016/S0140-6736(16)32585-5.

Budetti, P. P. 2008. "Market Justice and US Health Care." *Journey of the American Medical Assocation* 299 (1): 92–94. https://doi.org/10.1001/jama.2007.27.

Calvert, N., J. R. Ashton, and E. Garnett. 2013. "Mumps Outbreak in Private Schools: Public Health Lessons for the Post-Wakefield Era." *Lancet* 381 (9878): 1625–26. https://doi.org/10.1016/S0140-6736(13)60953-8.

Centers for Disease Control and Prevention. 2011. *Principles of Epidemiology in Public Health Practice: An Introduction to Applied Epidemiology and Biostatistics*. Updated November. www.cdc.gov/csels/dsepd/ss1978/index. html.

Cleveland Clinic. 2018. "Why You Should No Longer Worry About Cholesterol in Food." Published February 19. https://health.clevelandclinic.org/why-you-should-no-longer-worry-about-cholesterol-in-food/.

College of Physicians of Philadelphia. 2019. "History of Vaccines." Accessed September 25. www.historyofvaccines.org/.

Committee on Health and Behavior. 2001. *Health and Behavior: The Interplay of Biological, Behavioral, and Societal Influences: Consensus Report*. Washington, DC: National Academies Press.

Conrad, P. 2013. "Medicalization: Changing Contours, Characteristics, and Contexts." In *Medical Sociology on the Move*, edited by W. C. Cockerham, 195–214. Dordrecht, Netherlands: Springer. https://doi.org/10.1007/978-94-007-6193-3_10.

———. 2007. *The Medicalization of Society: On the Transformation of Human Conditions*. Baltimore, MD: Johns Hopkins Univeristy Press.

Cooper, L. A., D. L. Roter, R. L., Johnson, D. E. Ford, D. M. Steinwachs, and N. R. Powe. 2003. "Patient-Centered Communication, Ratings of Care, and Concordance of Patient and Physician Race." *Annals of Internal Medicine* 139 (11): 907–15. https://doi.org/10.7326/0003-4819-139-11-200312020-00009.

Davino-Ramaya, C., L. K. Krause, C. W. Robbins, J. S. Harris, M. Koster, W. Chan, and G. I. Tom. 2012. "Transparency Matters: Kaiser Permanente's National Guideline Program Methodological Processes." *Permanente Journal* 16 (1): 55–62. https://doi.org/10.7812/tpp/11-134.

Deer, B. 2011. "How the Case Against the MMR Vaccine Was Fixed." *BMJ* 342 (7788): 77–82. https://doi.org/10.1136/bmj.c5347.

DeVoto, B. 1998. *Across the Wide Missouri*. New York: Mariner Books.

Doyle, C., M. Crump, M. Pintilie, and A. M. Oza. 2001. "Does Palliative Chemotherapy Palliate? Evaluation of Expectations, Outcomes, and Costs in Women Receiving Chemotherapy for Advanced Ovarian Cancer." *Journal of Clinical Oncology* 19 (5): 1266–74. https://doi.org/10.1200/JCO.2001.19.5.1266.

Editors of the *Lancet*. 2010. "Retraction—Ileal-Lymphoid-Nodular Hyperplasia, Non-specific Colitis, and Pervasive Developmental Disorder in Children." *Lancet* 375 (9713): 445. https://doi.org/10.1016/S0140-6736(10)60175-4.

Emson, H. E. 1987. "Health, Disease and Illness: Matters for Definition." *Canadian Medical Association Journal/Journal de l'Association Medicale Canadienne* 136 (8): 811–13. www.ncbi.nlm.nih.gov/pmc/articles/PMC1492114/.

Eskola, J., P. Duclos, M. Schuster, N. E. MacDonald, and the SAGE Working Group on Vaccine Hesitancy. 2015. "How to Deal with Vaccine Hesitancy?" *Vaccine* 33 (34): 4215–17. https://doi.org/10.1016/j.vaccine.2015.04.043.

Fernandez, M. L. 2012. "Rethinking Dietary Cholesterol." *Current Opinion in Clinical Nutrition and Metabolic Care* 15 (2): 117–21. https://doi.org/10.1097/MCO.0b013e32834d2259.

Flaherty, D. K. 2011. "The Vaccine-Autism Connection: A Public Health Crisis Caused by Unethical Medical Practices and Fraudulent Science." *Annals of Pharmacotherapy* 45 (10): 1302–4. https://doi.org/10.1345/aph.1Q318.

Foxx, L., T. Redden, J. E. Taylor, and S. Wagner. 2013. "Cultural Competence at Carolinas HealthCare System." Carolinas HealthCare System. Accessed September 25, 2019. www.carolinashealthcare.org/documents/diversity-inclusion/CulturalCompetenceFINAL032814.pdf.

Frances, A. 2013. "The Past, Present and Future of Psychiatric Diagnosis." *World Psychiatry* 12 (2): 111–12. https://doi.org/10.1002/wps.20027.

Frawley, A. 2015. "Medicalization of Social Problems." In *Handbook of the Philosophy of Medicine*, edited by T. Schramme and S. Edwards, 1–18. Dordrecht, Netherlands: Springer. https://doi.org/10.1007/978-94-017-8706-2_74-1.

Gilkey, M. B., B. E. Magnus, P. L. Reiter, A. L. McRee, A. F. Dempsey, and N. T. Brewer. 2014. "The Vaccination Confidence Scale: A Brief Measure of Parents' Vaccination Beliefs." *Vaccine* 32 (47): 6259–65. https://doi.org/10.1016/j.vaccine.2014.09.007.

Glanz, K., B. K. Rimer, and K. Viswanath (eds.). 2008. *Health Behavior and Health Education: Theory, Research, and Practice*, 4th ed. San Francisco: Jossey-Bass.

Goodkind, J. R., K. Ross-Toledo, S. John, J. L. Hall, L. Ross, L. Freeland, E. Coletta, T. Becenti-Fundark, C. Poola, R. Begay-Roanhorse, and C. Lee. 2010. "Promoting Healing and Restoring Trust: Policy Recommendations for Improving Behavioral Health Care for American Indian/Alaska Native Adolescents." *American Journal of Community Psychology* 46 (3–4): 386–94. https://doi.org/10.1007/s10464-010-9347-4.

Graham, G. N. 2016. "Why Your ZIP Code Matters More than Your Genetic Code: Promoting Healthy Outcomes from Mother to Child." *Breastfeeding Medicine* 11 (8): 396–97. https://doi.org/10.1089/bfm.2016.0113.

Green, M., and M. Elliott. 2010. "Religion, Health, and Psychological Well-Being." *Journal of Religion and Health* 49 (2): 149–63. https://doi.org/10.1007/s10943-009-9242-1.

Harder, V. S., J. Krulewitz, C. Jones, R. C. Wasserman, and J. S. Shaw. 2016. "Effects of Patient-Centered Medical Home Transformation on Child Patient Experience." *Journal of the American Board of Family Medicine* 29 (1): 60–68. https://doi.org/10.3122/jabfm.2016.01.150066.

Harvard University, T. H. Chan School of Public Health. 2018. "Cholesterol." Accessed September 25, 2019. www.hsph.harvard.edu/nutritionsource/what-should-you-eat/fats-and-cholesterol/cholesterol/.

Haslanger, S. 2016. "What Is a (Social) Structural Explanation?" *Philosophical Studies* 173 (1): 113–30. https://doi.org/10.1007/s11098-014-0434-5.

———. 2015. "Distinguished Lecture: Social Structure, Narrative and Explanation." *Canadian Journal of Philosophy* 45 (1): 1–15. https://doi.org/10.1080/00455091.2015.1019176.

———. 2000. "Gender and Race: (What) Are They? (What) Do We Want Them to Be?" *Noûs* 34 (1): 31–55. https://doi.org/10.1111/0029-4624.00201.

Hensch, M. 2017. "Freedom Caucus Still Opposes GOP Healthcare Plan." *The Hill*. Published March 17. http://thehill.com/policy/healthcare/health-reform-implementation/324479-freedom-caucus-still-opposes-gop-health-plan.

Hidalgo, D. R. 2003. "Manifest Destiny." In *Dictionary of American History*. Accessed September 25, 2019. www.encyclopedia.com/doc/1G2-3401802517.html.

Hietala, T. R. 1985. *Manifest Design: Anxious Aggrandizement in Late Jacksonian America*. Ithaca, NY: Cornell University Press.

Honda, H., Y. Shimizu, and M. Rutter. 2005. "No Effect of MMR Withdrawal on the Incidence of Autism: A Total Population Study." *Journal of Child Psychology and Psychiatry and Allied Disciplines* 46 (6): 572–79. https://doi.org/10.1111/j.1469-7610.2005.01425.x.

Huber, M., J. A. Knottnerus, L. Green, H. Van Der Horst, A. R. Jadad, D. Kromhout, B. Leonard, K. Lorig, M. I. Loureiro, J. W. M. van der Meer, P. Schnabel, R. Smith, C. van Weel, and H. Smid. 2011. "How Should We Define Health?" *BMJ* 343: d4163. https://doi.org/10.1136/bmj.d4163.

Hummer, R. A., C. G. Ellison, R. G. Rogers, B. E. Moulton, and R. R. Romero. 2004. "Religious Involvement and Adult Mortality in the United States: Review and Perspective." *Southern Medical Journal* 97 (12): 1223–30. https://doi.org/10.1097/01.SMJ.0000146547.03382.94.

Jit, M., R. Hutubessy, M. E. Png, N. Sundaram, J. Audimulam, S. Salim, and J. Yoong. 2015. "The Broader Economic Impact of Vaccination: Reviewing and Appraising the Strength of Evidence." *BMC Medicine* 13 (1): 209. https://doi.org/10.1186/s12916-015-0446-9.

Jones, J., and L. Saad. 2017. "Americans Still Hold Dim View of U.S. Healthcare System." Gallup. Published December 11. http://news.gallup.com/poll/223403/americans-hold-dim-view-healthcare-system.aspx.

Kaplan, R. D. 2017. *Earning the Rockies: How Geogrpahy Shapes America's Role in the World*. New York: Random House.

Karsten, S. G. 1995. "Health Care: Private Good vs. Public Good." *American Journal of Economics and Sociology* 54 (2): 129–44. https://doi.org/10.1111/j.1536-7150.1995.tb02684.x.

Kiley, J. 2018. "Most Continue to Say Ensuring Health Care Coverage Is Government's Responsibility." Pew Research Center. Published October 3. www.pewresearch.org/fact-tank/2018/10/03/most-continue-to-say-ensuring-health-care-coverage-is-governments-responsibility/.

Mabahwi, N. A. B., O. L. H. Leh, and D. Omar. 2014. "Human Health and Wellbeing: Human Health Effect of Air Pollution." *Procedia: Social and Behavioral Sciences* 153: 221–29. https://doi.org/10.1016/j.sbspro.2014.10.056.

Magnan, S. 2017. "Social Determinants of Health 101 for Health Care: Five Plus Five." National Academy of Medicine. Published October 9. https://nam.edu/social-determinants-of-health-101-for-health-care-five-plus-five/.

McCarthy, J. 2016. "Majority in U.S. Prefer State over Federal Government Power." Gallup. Published July 11. https://news.gallup.com/poll/193595/majority-prefer-state-federal-government-power.aspx.

McDougall, W. A. 1997. *Promised Land, Crusader State: The American Encounter with the World Since 1776*. Boston: Houghton Mifflin.

McGinnis, J. M., P. Williams-Russo, and J. R. Knickman. 2002. "The Case for More Active Policy Attention to Health Promotion." *Health Affairs* 21 (2): 78–93. www.healthaffairs.org/doi/pdf/10.1377/hlthaff.21.2.78.

MedicineNet. 2018. "Definition of ADLs (Activities of Daily Living)." Reviewed December 4. www.medicinenet.com/script/main/art.asp?articlekey=2152.

Miller, W. R., and C. E. Thoresen. 2003. "Spirituality, Religion, and Health: An Emerging Research Field." *American Psychologist* 51 (8): 24–35. https://doi.org/10.1037/0003-066X.58.1.24.

National Committee for Quality Assurance and Eli Lilly & Company. 2007. "Multicultural Health Care: A Quality Improvement Guide." Accessed September 25, 2019. http://fliphtml5.com/vzpf/naoo/basic.

National Institutes of Health. 2016. "What Causes Obesity and Overweight?" Reviewed December 1. www.nichd.nih.gov/health/topics/obesity/conditioninfo/cause.

New England Journal of Medicine. 2017. "What Are the Social Determinants of Health?" *NEJM Catalyst.* Published December 1. https://catalyst.nejm.org/social-determinants-of-health/.

New York Times. 2011. "Study Linking Vaccine to Autism Is Called Fraud." January 6. https://query.nytimes.com/gst/fullpage.html?res=9C02E7DC1E3BF935A35752C0A9679D8B63.

Nutton, V. 2004. *Ancient Medicine.* London: Routledge.

Offit, P. A., and S. E. Coffin. 2003. "Communicating Science to the Public: MMR Vaccine and Autism." *Vaccine* 22 (1): 1–6. https://doi.org/10.1586/14760584.2.1.1.

Olsen, L., J. Bhattacharya, A. Scharf, and C. Tomorrow. 2006. "Cultural Competency: What It Is and Why It Matters." Lucile Packard Foundation for Children's Health. Published December 7. https://buildinitiative.org/Portals/0/Uploads/Documents/Cultural%20Competency%20-%20What%20It%20Is%20and%20Why%20It%20Matters.pdf.

Padela, A., K. Gunter, and A. Killawi. 2011. "Meeting the Healthcare Needs of American Muslims: Challenges and Strategies for Healthcare Settings." Institute for Social Policy. Published June. www.ispu.org/wp-content/uploads/2016/09/620_ISPU_Report_Aasim-Padela_final.pdf.

Papanicolas, I., L. R. Woskie, and A. K. Jha. 2018. "Health Care Spending in the United States and Other High-Income Countries." *JAMA* 319 (10): 1024–39. https://doi.org/10.1001/jama.2018.1150.

Parens, E. 2011. "On Good and Bad Forms of Medicalization." *Bioethics* 27 (1): 28–35. https://doi.org/10.1111/j.1467-8519.2011.01885.x.

Pew Research Center. 2015. "Beyond Distrust: How Americans View Their Government." Published November 23. www.people-press.org/2015/11/23/beyond-distrust-how-americans-view-their-government/.

———. 2013. "The Internet and Health." Published February 12. www.pewinternet.org/2013/02/12/the-internet-and-health/.

———. 1998. "How Americans View Government." Published March 10. www.people-press.org/1998/03/10/how-americans-view-government/.

Phillips, K. W. 2014. "How Diversity Makes Us Smarter." *Scientific American.* Published October 1. www.scientificamerican.com/article/how-diversity-makes-us-smarter/.

Pollack, H. 2010. "All Together Now: We Need Comprehensive Reform." *Washington Post.* Published February 18. http://views.washingtonpost.com/healthcarerx/panelists/2010/02/altogether-now-we-need-comprehensive-reform-if-we-really-want-to-cover-everybody.html.

Portman, T. A. A., and M. T. Garrett. 2006. "Native American Healing Traditions." *International Journal of Disability, Development and Education* 53 (4): 453–69. https://doi.org/10.1080/10349120601008647.

Purdy, L. 2001. "Medicalization, Medical Necessity, and Feminist Medicine." *Bioethics* 15 (3): 248–61. https://doi.org/10.1111/1467-8519.00235.

Riedel, S. 2005. "Edward Jenner and the History of Smallpox and Vaccination." *Baylor University Medical Center Proceedings* 18 (1): 21–25. https://doi.org/10.1080/08998280.2005.11928028.

Rosenberg, M. 2014. "Health Geography I: Social Justice, Idealist Theory, Health and Health Care." *Progress in Human Geography* 38 (3): 466–75. https://doi.org/10.1177/0309132513498339.

Rousseau, G. S., M. Gill, and D. B. Haycock (eds.). 2003. *Framing and Imagining Disease in Cultural History.* Basingstoke, UK: Palgrave Macmillan.

Schlenoff, D. 2013. "What Are the 10 Greatest Inventions of Our Time?" *Scientific American.* Published November 1. www.scientificamerican.com/article/inventions-what-are-the-10-greatest-of-our-time/?page=2.

Schroeder, S. A. 2007. "We Can Do Better—Improving the Health of the American People." *New England Journal of Medicine* 357: 1221–28. https://doi.org/10.1056/NEJMsa073350.

Scully, J. L. 2004. "What Is a Disease?" *EMBO Reports* 5 (7): 650–53. https://doi.org/10.1038/sj.embor.7400195.

Sholl, J. 2017. "The Muddle of Medicalization: Pathologizing or Medicalizing?" *Theoretical Medicine and Bioethics* 38(4): 265–78. https://doi.org/10.1007/s11017-017-9414-z.

Siddiqui, M., D. A. Salmon, and S. B. Omer. 2013. "Epidemiology of Vaccine Hesitancy in the United States." *Human Vaccines and Immunotherapeutics* 9 (12): 2643–48. https://doi.org/10.4161/hv.27243.

Slade-Sawyer, P. 2014. "Is Health Determined by Genetic Code or Zip Code? Measuring the Health of Groups and Improving Population Health." *North Carolina Medical Journal* 75 (6): 394–97. https://doi.org/10.18043/ncm.75.6.394.

Society for Academic Emergency Medicine. 1992. "An Ethical Foundation for Health Care: An Emergency Medicine Perspective." *Annals of Emergency Medicine* 21 (11): 1381–87. https://doi.org/10.1016/s0196-0644(05)81906-7.

Sturm, R., and K. B. Wells. 2002. *The Health Risks of Obesity.* Santa Monica, CA: RAND Corporation. Accessed September 25, 2019. www.rand.org/pubs/research_briefs/RB4549.html.

Tang, G., O. Lanza, F. Marinely Rodriguez, and A. Chang. 2011. "The Kaiser Permanente Clinician Cultural and Linguistic Assessment Initiative: Research and Development in Patient-Provider Language Concordance." *American Journal of Public Health* 101 (2): 205–8. https://doi.org/10.2105/AJPH.2009.177055.

Thurow, L. C. 1996. *The Future of Capitalism: How Today's Economic Forces Shape Tomorrow's World.* New York: William Morrow.

———. 1993. *Head to Head: The Coming Economic Battle Among Japan, Europe, and America.* New York: Warner Books.

Tikkinen, K. A. O., J. S. Leinonen, G. H. Guyatt, S. Ebrahim, and T. L. N. Järvinen. 2012. "What Is a Disease? Perspectives of the Public, Health Professionals and Legislators." *BMJ Open* 2 (6): e001632. https://doi.org/10.1136/bmjopen-2012-001632.

Uchino, B. N., R. M. Cawthon, T. W. Smith, K. C. Light, J. McKenzie, M. Carlisle, H. Gunn, W. Birmingham, and K. Bowen. 2012. "Social Relationships and Health: Is Feeling Positive, Negative, or Both (Ambivalent) About Your Social Ties Related to Telomeres?" *Health Psychology* 31 (6): 789–96. https://doi.org/10.1037/a0026836.

US National Library of Medicine. 2018. "List of All Journals Cited in PubMed." Accessed September 25, 2019. www.nlm.nih.gov/bsd/serfile_addedinfo.html.

US Preventive Services Task Force (USPSTF). 2018. "Prostate Cancer: Screening." Published May. www.uspreventiveservicestaskforce.org/Page/Document/UpdateSummaryFinal/prostate-cancer-screening1.

———. 2017. *Shared Decisionmaking About Screening and Chemoprevention.* Accessed September 25, 2019. www.uspreventiveservicestaskforce.org/Page/Name/shared-decisionmaking-about-screening-and-chemoprevention.

van Dijk, W., M. J. Faber, M. A. C. Tanke, P. P. T. Jeurissen, and G. P. Westert. 2016. "Medicalisation and Overdiagnosis: What Society Does to Medicine." *Kerman University of Medical Sciences* 5 (11): 619–22. https://doi.org/10.15171/ijhpm.2016.121.

Weinfurt, K. P. 2004. "Discursive Versus Information-Processing Perspectives on a Bioethical Problem." *Theory & Psychology* 14 (2): 191–203. https://doi.org/10.1177/0959354304042016.

World Health Organization (WHO). 2019a. "Constitution." Accessed October 4. www.who.int/about/who-we-are/constitution.

———. 2019b. "Ten Threats to Global Health in 2019." Accessed September 25. www.who.int/emergencies/ten-threats-to-global-health-in-2019.

4

COMPARING THE US HEALTHCARE SYSTEM WITH THOSE OF OTHER DEVELOPED COUNTRIES

> Families represent the basic building blocks of our society, and primary care a foundational piece of any healthcare system.
> —Tony Tan, former president of Singapore

Learning Objectives

- Understand what a healthcare system is and what it comprises.
- Analyze the variation in healthcare outcomes in the United States relative to other similar countries.
- Recognize some of the important factors that affect health expenditures in the United States.
- Consider why spending does not equal positive outcomes.
- Examine the importance of health behaviors on outcomes.
- Understand why global health is important to the United States.

This chapter, as highlighted in exhibit 4.1, will examine how the US healthcare system compares to the systems of other countries in terms of cost, quality, and access. It will also look at the ways other countries organize their systems and the ways they finance care. We will consider what might be learned from these other countries and what ideas might be applicable to the United States.

Healthcare Systems vs. Health Systems

The phrases *healthcare system* and *health system* have many definitions. The Dartmouth College Center of Excellence defines a health system as "an organization that consists of either at least one hospital plus at least one group of physicians or more than one group of physicians. For the purposes of this definition, the group of physicians must include at least three primary care physicians" (Agency for Healthcare Research and Quality [AHRQ] 2017).

EXHIBIT 4.1
Area of Focus
for This Chapter

The Aim of the Healthcare System

Issues That Require Our Attention

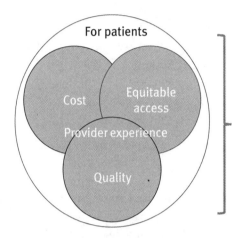

For patients

Cost

Equitable access

Provider experience

Quality

- Nature of our complex system
- Historical issues that have influenced the development of the system
- Beliefs and attitudes about health and healthcare
- *Comparison with other developed countries*
- Components of our healthcare system
- People and providers
- Patient care—the purpose of the system
- Financing a massive system
- Quality—easier said than done
- Medical and information technology
- The pharmaceutical industry
- Complementary and alternative medicine
- Politics/economics
- The future of the system

The National Bureau of Economic Research (NBER) Center of Excellence defines health systems in terms of "three types of arrangements between two or more health care provider organizations: (1) organizations with common ownership, (2) contractually integrated organizations (e.g., accountable care organizations), and (3) informal care systems, such as common referral arrangements" (AHRQ 2017). These systems include organizations that are combined horizontally (e.g., hospital systems) or vertically (e.g., a multihospital system that also owns physician practices and post-acute care facilities).

The RAND Center of Excellence defines a health system as "two or more health care organizations affiliated with each other through shared ownership or a contracting relationship for payment and service delivery" (AHRQ 2017).

The AHRQ's Compendium of US Health Systems defines a health system as "an organization that includes at least one hospital and at least one group of physicians that provides comprehensive care (including primary and specialty care) who are connected with each other and with the hospital through common ownership or joint management" (AHRQ 2017). In this definition, forms of joint management include foundation models but do not include providers' joint participation in an accountable care organization. The AHRQ Compendium definition also includes additional details about what constitutes a "group" of physicians as part of a healthcare system (AHRQ 2016).

The World Health Organization (WHO 2007a) defines a health system as follows:

> A health system consists of all organizations, people, and actions whose primary intent is to promote, restore, or maintain health. This includes efforts to influence determinants of health as well as more direct health-improving activities. A health system is therefore more than the pyramid of publicly owned facilities that deliver personal health services. It includes, for example, a mother caring for a sick child at home; private providers; behaviour change programmes; vector-control campaigns; health insurance organizations; occupational health and safety legislation. It includes inter-sectoral action by health staff, for example, encouraging the ministry of education to promote female education, a well-known determinant of better health.

With the exception of WHO's, all of these definitions—which, notably, are from organizations in the United States—focus on the organizational structure and components of a healthcare system and how each of these components should be defined. By contrast, the WHO definition focuses more on the human element of health systems. WHO (2019) even goes on to add other important performance characteristics to characterize what makes a good system:

> A good health system delivers quality services to all people, when and where they need them. The exact configuration of services varies from country to country, but in all cases requires a robust financing mechanism; a well-trained and adequately paid workforce; reliable information on which to base decisions and policies; well-maintained facilities and logistics to deliver quality medicines and technologies.

The contrast in these definitions, essentially, highlights the difference between a true *health* system and a mere *healthcare* system. Health involves so much more than simply organizing the delivery of components that provide healthcare services, and a true health system must attend to the numerous determinants of health outside of healthcare, as discussed in previous chapters.

A key factor that will determine how our healthcare system addresses *health* versus *healthcare* is the way the system is paid for the work it does. If our healthcare system is paid primarily on a fee-for-service basis (i.e., receiving payment based on each service provided), it is unlikely to evolve into a system that looks beyond healthcare and strives to be a true *health* system serving patients' total well-being. As the old saying goes, "In this world, you get what you pay for" (Vonnegut [1963] 1998, 128).

Examples of Healthcare Systems Around the World

Based on WHO data and other authors' analyses, we can estimate that approximately 40 to 50 countries in the world have organized healthcare delivery systems (Docteur and Oxley 2003; Mossialos et al. 2016; Rosenau 2012; Tandon et al. 2019; Thomson et al. 2013). Many other countries are simply too poor, too rural, or too disorganized to have meaningfully developed systems. Our discussion in this chapter will focus primarily on a select group of 36 countries that have developed or developing economies and belong to the Organisation for Economic Co-operation and Development (OECD). Data from OECD nations is often used for benchmarking in the United States (OECD 2017, 2019a).

No country has found the perfect healthcare delivery system. However, as we will see, most countries with developed economies and democratic political systems have found ways to finance and deliver healthcare at a substantially high level to most, if not all, of their populations. Universal coverage is the norm; in fact, the United States is the only OECD country that does not have some form of universal coverage. The other OECD countries have been able to strike a balance that the United States has failed to strike—the balance between cost, quality, and access. Importantly, these countries also regard healthcare as a basic right, not a merit-based good.

The world's healthcare systems have been the subject of extensive study and vast amounts of literature, and a comprehensive review of each would require a course all its own. This chapter will simply present concise overviews of several national healthcare systems that, in many ways, perform better than that of the United States. Exhibit 4.2 provides additional details about these systems (Mossialos et al. 2016).

Germany
Germany has universal coverage provided through a multipayer process that involves two types of health insurance—one government run and the other privately run. All people below a certain income level are required to participate in compulsory insurance plans known as "sick funds." People above a prescribed income level may choose to stay in a sick fund (which most do) or opt to purchase a private insurance plan (Mossialos et al. 2016). The sick

EXHIBIT 4.2 Various Healthcare Systems Throughout the World

	Healthcare System Public/Private Financing Role				Benefit Structure	
Country	Government Role	System Ownership	Public Financing	Private Insurance Benefits	Cost Sharing	Low-Income Protection
Australia	Universal public medical insurance administered on a regional basis	Public and private	General tax revenue and specific income tax earmarks	Approximately 50% buy complementary private insurance to supplement government coverage for select services	Cost sharing only on out-of-pocket pharmaceutical costs, which is capped based on income and total expenditures each year	Reduced cost sharing on out-of-pocket pharmaceutical costs
Canada	Universal public medical insurance administered on a regional basis	Public and private; most providers are private	Provincial and federal tax revenue	Greater than 60% buy complementary private insurance to supplement government coverage for select services	No cost sharing	No cost sharing for publicly covered services; coverage and cost sharing for low-income people vary by region
France	Statutory health insurance (SHI), incorporated into a single national exchange	Public and private	General tax revenue, earmarked taxes, employer/ employee income and payroll taxes earmarked for health coverage	Most citizens receive or buy statutory insurance coverage; limited use of complementary private insurance	Limits on deductibles of €50 for consultations and other services	Low-income people, chronically ill people, people with disabilities, and children are exempt from deductibles

(continued)

EXHIBIT 4.2 Various Healthcare Systems Throughout the World *(continued)*

| Country | Healthcare System Public/Private Financing Role | | | Benefit Structure | | |
	Government Role	System Ownership	Public Financing	Private Insurance Benefits	Cost Sharing	Low-Income Protection
Germany	Statutory health insurance with a total of 124 competing "sick funds"; SHI insurers participate in a national exchange; high-income earners may opt out permanently and buy private coverage	Public and private	Employer/ employee earmarked payroll taxes, general tax revenue	About 10% of German citizens opt out of SHI and buy substitute coverage	Out-of-pocket costs limited to 2% of household income and 1% for chronically ill people	Children and adolescents under 18 years of age are exempt from out-of-pocket costs
Italy	Ministry of Health structured into 12 directorates that oversee specific areas of healthcare (e.g., healthcare planning, levels of care, ethics of the system, human resources, information systems, pharmaceuticals and medical devices) and supervise the main institutions	Largely private	Federal corporate taxes and portions of the value-added tax are allocated to the regions; regions can provide additional funding	15% of citizens have private insurance	Government accounts for approximately 78% of total healthcare spending	Exemptions for low-income older adults and children; pregnant women; and people with chronic diseases, disabilities, and rare diseases
Japan	Statutory health insurance with more than 3,400 noncompeting insurance providers; national government sets provider fees, subsidizes local governments' insurers and providers, and supervises insurers and providers	Public and private	General tax revenue and contributions to insurance	Most of the population has coverage for cash benefits in case of sickness, which are often purchased as part of a life insurance package; a limited amount of supplemental and complementary insurance is independent of life insurance	Some limitations on cost sharing based upon age and income	Low-income monthly out-of-pocket ceilings and reduced cost sharing for young children, older people, chronically ill people, people with serious mental illness, and those with disabilities; those on social assistance receive tax-funded health services

Country	Description	Public/Private	Financing	Private insurance	Cost-sharing	Additional notes
New Zealand	National healthcare system responsible for planning and purchasing healthcare services executed through geographically defined district health boards	Public	General tax revenue	About a third buy complementary and supplemental coverage	Few limitations on cost sharing and some reduction in fees after 12 doctor visits per year; no drug copayments after 20 prescriptions per year per family	No primary care consulting charges for children under age 13; low-income subsidies and subsidies for some chronic conditions in high-need groups; Maori and Pacific Islanders receive certain additional benefits
Singapore	Medisave, a mandatory savings program for routine expenses; Medishield, catastrophic health insurance; Medifund, a government-endowed fund that subsidizes healthcare for people with low income and large medical bills; government-regulated private insurance; central planning and financing of infrastructure; some direct provision through public hospitals and clinics	Public and private	General tax revenue	Medisave-approved integrated shield plans to supplement Medishield coverage; employer-provided private medical insurance	No cost-sharing limitations	Low-income populations are subsidized (asset based and means tested); Medifund provides coverage for low-income individuals

(continued)

EXHIBIT 4.2 Various Healthcare Systems Throughout the World *(continued)*

	Healthcare System Public/Private Financing Role					Benefit Structure	
Country	Government Role	System Ownership	Public Financing	Private Insurance Benefits		Cost Sharing	Low-Income Protection
Taiwan	National Health Insurance (NHI)	Public and private	Government, employers, and employees	Universal coverage under the NHI		Some sharing based on the ability to pay	Six major categories of coverage, with subsidies for low-income patients
United Kingdom	National Health Service (NHS)	Publicly owned with emerging private sector	General tax revenue with employer contributions	Approximately 10% buy supplementary coverage		Cost sharing applies to prescription drugs and medical appliances	Low-income individuals are exempt from cost sharing, as are the elderly, children, pregnant women and new mothers, and some disabled and chronically ill people
United States	Medicare (government-sponsored insurance) for people 65 or older or with certain conditions; Medicaid (government-sponsored insurance) for low-income individuals and for some without employer coverage; state-level insurance exchanges and a federal exchange under the Affordable Care Act; a significant number of people are uninsured	Public and private	Medicare: payroll taxes, premiums, and federal tax revenue; Medicaid: federal and state tax revenue; private insurance: primarily through shared employer/employee expenses	About 65% have employer-sponsored or private individual health insurance; supplementary Medicare insurance may cover copays, deductibles, and uncovered services		As of 2018, private insurance plans had a $6,650 yearly out-of-pocket maximum for individuals and a $13,300 maximum for families; deductibles and coinsurances also apply to Medicare	Private insurance plans are limited to the deductibles described under cost sharing

Source: Adapted from Mossialos et al. (2016).

funds are usually paid through joint funding by employer and employee contributions. Services are mandated across a wide range of benefits, and providers are paid based on prenegotiated rates that were agreed upon by provider associations at the federal state level. The 16 federal states of Germany are analogous to the 50 states of America (German Health Insurance System 2019).

Canada

Canada uses a federally sponsored system, known as Medicare, in which roles and responsibilities are shared between the federal and all provincial governments (Government of Canada 2016). Canadian Medicare is a publicly funded, single-payer system that provides basic services, physician services, hospital benefits, and access to community and private clinics. Minimal fees may apply, and, in some instances, provinces may charge premiums to their citizens. Pharmaceutical prices are set by government price controls. Some Canadians opt to have additional private insurance, because some services they desire may not be covered under Canadian Medicare. Most providers in the Canadian system are private—unlike in the United Kingdom, where most providers work for the government.

Physician billing in each province is set through negotiations between the provincial government and the province's medical association. Much like in the United States, physicians may opt out of the publicly funded system, but those who participate in the Canadian Medicare system may not charge more than the established fee, even to patients not covered by the program (Government of Canada 2016).

Proponents of healthcare reform in the United States sometimes point to the Canadian system to illustrate the potential for cost-effective care under a single-payer system. Opponents, however, sometimes point to the number of Canadians who travel to the United States for care, often because the care is delayed in their own country or because superior quality is available in the United States (Fraser Institute 2018; Picard 2017).

France

France's national healthcare system consists of both private and public physician and hospital providers. The country's social security system includes not only healthcare but also social welfare benefits, including those for injuries at work, family allowances, unemployment insurance, old age pensions, and disability and death (Republic of France 2019). France has the distinction of spending the most of any European country on social benefits—approaching 30 percent of its gross domestic product (GDP) (OECD 2018). Healthcare accounts for approximately one third of this social benefit cost.

Healthcare is funded through the French social security system and managed by a network of local, regional, and national institutions, organized based on risk (Republic of France 2019). The system is administered by representatives of employers and employees under the supervision of the ministries in charge of social security (the Ministry for Solidarity and Health and the Ministry of Economy and Finance). Each of the social security organizations operates according to a budget and refunds patients for care at the rate of 100 percent in the case of long-term or costly illness. Some of the social security organizations allow private insurance.

The United Kingdom

The United Kingdom consists of four countries: England, Scotland, Wales, and Northern Ireland. Each has a separate but jointly operated public healthcare system called the National Health Service (NHS). All healthcare services are provided by a government-owned and government-funded system. Some cost sharing is applied to prescription drugs; however, the elderly, children, pregnant women, new mothers, people with disabilities, and the chronically ill are exempt from these fees (NHS 2019). Private-sector insurance options have emerged to pay for some services not provided by the NHS, including complementary and alternative medicine. The NHS was created in 1948, following the ravages of World War II, at a time when little, if any, organized healthcare was in place.

The NHS is another example commonly cited, both positively and negatively, in the debate over healthcare reform in the United States. Proponents highlight lower costs and universal access, whereas opponents point to long waits and provider dissatisfaction (Schütte, Acevedo, and Flahault 2018).

Japan

Japan has a mixture of private and public physician, hospital, and clinic providers. The public health insurance program is universal and covers most citizens and residents of Japan. A monthly premium is charged on a sliding scale based on income, and the plan pays for services in any of the public or private settings.

The statutory insurance system has more than 3,400 noncompeting public, quasi-public, and employer-based insurers (Mossialos et al. 2016). It covers up to 70 percent of the cost of medical services and pharmaceuticals, with the patient responsible for the balance up to certain income-based limits. Although most healthcare expenditures in Japan are by the government, supplementary private insurance is available to cover the national health plan coinsurance (Matsuda 2019).

Singapore

Singapore has a publicly financed universal healthcare system as well as a private healthcare system. The public system is controlled by the Ministry of Health. Healthcare in Singapore is highly efficient, and its level of healthcare spending as a percentage of GDP is one of the lowest in the world (World Bank 2019a). Healthcare is funded through a system of compulsory savings from payroll deductions, contributions by employers, and government subsidies (Liu and Haseltine 2019).

Singapore uses a mandatory medical savings program known as Medisave to help citizens pay for routine healthcare services. Medifund is a government fund to assist people with low income who have difficulty with medical expenses. MediShield is a catastrophic insurance program that pays for serious illness and injuries. Many citizens also purchase supplemental insurance for services not covered by the government programs (Liu and Haseltine 2019).

Price controls and supply regulations are important features of the Singaporean system. Patients have free choice of providers within the public or private system (Liu and Haseltine 2019).

New Zealand

New Zealand has a complex national system of providers and institutions that are operated through geographically defined district health boards. These boards are responsible for planning, purchasing, and providing health services for their districts. Funding is provided through general tax revenues, and supplemental insurance can be purchased to provide faster access and to cover elective surgeries, private hospital services, and cost sharing from the government-subsidized plan.

Physicians are mostly private, and hospitals are mostly public. Hospitals are paid on a global budget, which includes physician fees. Special provisions are made for people with serious or chronic illnesses that require more than 12 doctor visits per year, and drug copayments are eliminated after 12 prescriptions per year per family. No consultation charges are applied for indigenous people, children under the age of 13, low-income individuals, and some high-risk groups (New Zealand Ministry of Health 2017).

Australia

Australia has a national system known as Medicare, with a separate pharmaceutical benefit. A private health system exists as well. Australian Medicare covers all legal permanent residents for public hospital care. The system is funded through an income tax as well as general revenue, nongovernment organizations, and individual payments. An interesting feature of Australian healthcare is its use of a comparative cost-effectiveness system in determining subsidies for pharmaceuticals (Government of Western Australia Department of Health 2019).

Taiwan

Taiwan has a compulsory single-payer social insurance plan known as the national health insurance (NHI). The NHI covers virtually the entire Taiwanese population and pays for most of the healthcare provided in the country. It is financed through a combination of payroll taxes, government subsidies, and individual payments. Physicians and clinics are almost all private, and hospitals are predominantly public not-for-profit, though some private hospitals do exist. Hospitals are paid on a global budgeting system. Physicians are paid on a fee-for-service basis (Cheng 2019).

Italy

Italy's national healthcare system, known as *Servizio Sanitario Nazionale* (National Health Service), is regionally based and organized at the national, regional, and local levels (Mossialos et al. 2016). Responsibility for healthcare is shared by the national government and the 19 regions and 2 autonomous provinces by direction of the Italian constitution. Italy's central government controls the distribution of tax revenue (from corporate taxes and the value-added tax) for publicly financed healthcare. It defines the "essential benefits" package to be offered to all residents in every region.

The regions and autonomous provinces are responsible for the organization and delivery of health services through local health units. Each region has flexibility in determining the organization of its system with management at the local level (Mossialos et al. 2016).

Approximately 78 percent of total healthcare spending in Italy is publicly financed, with the balance being privately funded (Mossialos et al. 2016). Roughly 15 percent of Italian citizens carry some form of private insurance. Anecdotal evidence suggests that the percentage of private funding is increasing (per discussion with faculty members at the University of Milan, November 8, 2018).

Approaches to Comparing and Ranking Healthcare Systems

Three of the most widely referenced organizations that provide rankings and comparative information for healthcare systems are WHO, the Commonwealth Fund (CWF), and Bloomberg. Schütte, Acevedo, and Flahault (2018) carefully examined the methodology, comparability, and transparency of the data and criteria used by these three sources and found that WHO had the most complex process.

The WHO performance rankings took into account five indicators across three goals—health, responsiveness, and financial fairness—in addition to GDP and educational attainment. WHO's health and responsiveness components were composite indexes, with separate indicators for level of health and equity of distribution (Schütte, Acevedo, and Flahault 2018; Murray and Frenk 1999). The CWF used 80 indicators across five domains: (1) Quality, (2) Access, (3) Efficiency, (4) Equity, and (5) Healthy Lives. Bloomberg used three: (1) life expectancy, (2) cost as measured by share of GDP per capita, and (3) absolute cost per capita (Schütte, Acevedo, and Flahault 2018).

Based on these criteria, WHO ranked the United States thirty-seventh out of 191 countries in overall efficiency (Tandon et al. 2019). The CWF ranked the United States last out of 11 countries in its list. The other 10 countries in the CWF rankings—the United Kingdom, Australia, the Netherlands, New Zealand, Norway, Switzerland, Sweden, Germany, Canada, and France—were selected because they were considered the most similar to the United States (Schneider et al. 2017). The Bloomberg report, which focused on the efficiency of healthcare systems, ranked the United States forty-fourth out of 191 countries (Bloomberg 2014).

Regardless of the measurement or methodology being used, these reports clearly show that the US healthcare system does not rank well among its peers, or among the community of nations in general. International rankings and comparisons will be explored in greater detail later in the chapter.

The US Healthcare System, by the Numbers

The US healthcare system has been the subject of numerous articles and reports, and massive amounts of data are available. Two of the most prominent sources of these data are the Centers for Medicare & Medicaid Services (CMS) and the OECD. CMS primarily collects data pertaining to the US healthcare system, whereas the OECD collects data on 191 countries, including the United States.

Researchers and authors in healthcare rely heavily on CMS and OECD data for their work. Data collection represents a primary focus of both organizations' missions, and the information is generally considered accurate and unbiased, to the extent possible. The data collection efforts by CMS and OECD are well funded and far exceed the capabilities of individuals or most other organizations. Of course, information about the healthcare system changes constantly, so readers should always consider the time frame when assessing data's importance.

With the wealth of information that has been collected and made available, it is now common knowledge that the United States spends more on healthcare than any other country—whether costs are measured on an absolute basis, as a percentage of GDP, or on a per capita basis (Advisory Board 2017). The numbers are examined in greater detail in the pages ahead.

The Facts About Healthcare Expenditures in the United States

CMS (2019) reports the following data for 2017:

- National healthcare expenditures (NHE) were $3.5 trillion, or $10,739 per person—an increase of 3.9 percent from the previous year. They accounted for 17.9 percent of the GDP.
- Medicare spending grew 4.2 percent to $705.9 billion, or 20 percent of total NHE.
- Medicaid spending grew 2.9 percent to $581.9 billion, or 17 percent of total NHE.
- Private health insurance spending grew 4.2 percent to $1,183.9 billion, or 34 percent of total NHE.
- Out-of-pocket spending grew 2.6 percent to $365.5 billion, or 10 percent of total NHE.
- Hospital expenditures grew 4.6 percent to $1,142.6 billion; this rate was slower than the 5.6 percent growth recorded in 2016.
- Physician and clinical services expenditures grew 4.2 percent to $694.3 billion, slower than the 5.6 percent growth in 2016.
- Prescription drug spending increased 0.4 percent to $333.4 billion, slower than the 2.3 percent growth in 2016.
- The largest shares of total health spending were by the federal government (28.1 percent) and individual households (28.0 percent). Private business accounted for 19.9 percent of total healthcare spending, state and local governments accounted for 17.1 percent, and other private revenues accounted for 6.8 percent.

As noted, these data represent a snapshot of a particular point in time; the figures will vary as the environment, health strategies, and other factors change.

Projected Healthcare Expenditures for the United States (through 2027)

CMS (2018) reports that, under current law, national health spending is projected to grow at an average rate of 5.5 percent per year between 2018 and 2027, reaching nearly $6.0 trillion by 2027. Although this projected growth rate is more modest than the 7.3 percent rate observed from 1990 to 2007, it is more rapid than the 4.2 percent rate experienced from 2008 to 2016.

CMS (2018) projects health spending to grow 0.8 percent faster than GDP over the 2018–2027 period; as a result, health expenditures as a percentage of GDP are expected to rise from 17.9 percent in 2017 to 19.4 percent in 2027. Projected national health spending and enrollment growth over the next decade are largely driven by fundamental economic and demographic factors, including changes in projected income growth, increases in prices for medical goods and services, and enrollment shifts from private health insurance to Medicare.

Increases in spending for Medicare (7.4 percent per year) and Medicaid (5.5 percent per year) are substantial contributors to the rate of NHE growth for the projection period (CMS 2018). Both trends reflect the impact of an aging population, albeit in different ways. For Medicare, the primary driver is projected enrollment growth; for Medicaid, it is an increasing projected share of aged and disabled enrollees. The insured share of the population is expected to remain around 90 percent throughout the projection period.

Health Expenditures by Age Group and Gender

According to CMS (2019), personal healthcare (PHC) spending per person for the 65 or older population was $19,098 in 2014—more than five times higher than PHC spending per child ($3,749) and approximately three times the spending per working-age person ($7,153).

In 2014, children accounted for about 24 percent of the population and 11 percent of total PHC spending. The working-age group represented most of the population (61 percent) and spending (54 percent). Older adults were the smallest population group (nearly 15 percent of the population) and accounted for approximately 34 percent of all spending.

Per person spending for females ($8,811) was 21 percent higher than for males ($7,272) (CMS 2019). Spending for male children (up to age 18) was 9 percent more than for females. In the working-age and elderly groups, however, per person spending for females was higher than for males (26 percent more and 7 percent more, respectively).

State of Residence and Health Expenditures

In 2014, per capita PHC spending ranged from a low of $5,982 in Utah to a high of $11,064 in Alaska. The figure for Utah was about 26 percent lower than the national average ($8,045), whereas the figure for Alaska was 38 percent higher. These two states have ranked the lowest and highest in per capita PHC spending since 2012 (CMS 2019).

The spread between the states with the highest and the lowest per capita PHC spending stayed relatively stable from 2009 to 2014. The highest per capita spending levels were 80 to 90 percent higher per year than the lowest (CMS 2019).

Healthcare spending by region shows considerable variation. In 2014, the New England and Mideast regions had the highest levels of total per capita PHC spending, with $10,119 and $9,370, respectively (26 and 16 percent higher than the national average). In contrast, the Rocky Mountain and Southwest regions had the lowest levels, with $6,814 and $6,978 (roughly 15 percent lower than the national average) (CMS 2019).

From 2010 to 2014, average growth in per capita PHC spending was highest in Alaska, at 4.8 percent per year, and lowest in Arizona, at 1.9 percent per year. Average growth nationally was 3.1 percent (CMS 2019).

Medicare expenditures per beneficiary in 2014 were highest in New Jersey ($12,614) and lowest in Montana ($8,238). Medicaid expenditures per enrollee were highest in North Dakota ($12,413) and lowest in Illinois ($4,959) (CMS 2019).

Spending Does Not Equal Positive Outcomes

The impressive amount of money spent on healthcare in the United States generally has not translated to superior health outcomes. As noted in our discussion of health system rankings, the United States consistently ranks behind a number of countries that have significantly lower levels of spending—a finding that sparks serious concern about our healthcare system and its need for change.

Exhibit 4.3 shows the results of a survey, conducted by the Gallup organization, in which people were asked whether the US healthcare system is in a "state of crisis," has "major problems," has "minor problems," or "does not have any problems" (Jones and Saad 2017). In 2017, 71 percent of Americans indicated that our system is in a state of crisis or has major problems, whereas 27 percent said it only had minor problems or no problems. The remaining 2 percent either did not know or had no opinion. These findings are consistent with previous years. Since the survey data set was begun in 2008, the crisis and major problems responses have dominated, ranging from a low of 67 percent in 2014 to a high of 74 percent in 2011.

How Does the United States Compare?

Healthcare data for the United States and other countries can be presented and compared in virtually an endless number of ways, given the wealth of information available. Readers are encouraged to make their own

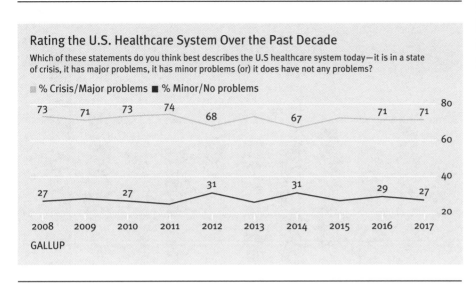

EXHIBIT 4.3
Rating the US
Healthcare
System

Source: The Gallup Poll: Public Opinion 2017 by Rowman & Littlefield Publishers. Reproduced with permission.

comparisons using the information available online through the OECD (www.oecd.org), the Dartmouth Atlas (www.dartmouthatlas.org), the Kaiser Family Foundation (www.kff.org), CMS (www.cms.gov), the Commonwealth Fund (www.cwf.org), the Robert Wood Johnson Foundation (www.rwjf.org), the Centers for Disease Control and Prevention (www.cdc.gov), and the World Health Organization (www.who.org).

The following sections will review some of the most significant variations in financial operations and outcomes, to help illustrate the differences between countries.

Spending Compared with Other Wealthy Countries

When considering the level of healthcare spending in the United States, the healthcare spending of other Western nations of comparable wealth provides a suitable basis for comparison, given that wealth is generally an important determinant of healthcare spending. As shown in exhibit 4.4, the United States spends significantly more on healthcare than any other country, including those Western countries with higher GDP per capita (Sawyer and Cox 2018).

In 2016, the United States spent 17.3 percent of its GDP on healthcare, significantly higher than the comparable country average of 10.6 percent (Sawyer and Cox 2018). The division of spending between the public sector and the private sector is also worth noting. In the United States, the public sector spent 8.5 percent of the GDP on healthcare, but the private sector spent an even larger amount—about 8.8 percent. The comparable

EXHIBIT 4.4
Health
Expenditures
as a Percentage
of GDP for the
United States
and Comparable
Western
Nations

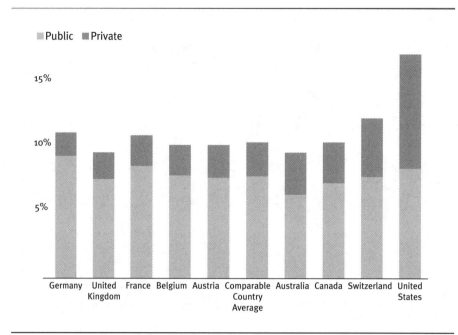

Source: Kaiser Family Foundation analysis of data from OECD (2017), "OECD Health Data: Health Expenditure and Financing: Health Expenditure Indicators," OECD Health Statistics (database). Reprinted from Sawyer and Cox (2018).

country average had public sector spending at 7.9 percent of GDP but private sector spending at just 2.7 percent. These findings indicate that other countries emphasize healthcare spending as a responsibility of the public sector more so than the United States does (Sawyer and Cox 2018).

Some simple calculations can help illustrate why healthcare costs are such a significant issue in the United States. In 2019, the United States had approximately $20.5 trillion in GDP (World Bank 2019b). If the United States spends 6.7 percent more of its GDP on healthcare than the comparable country average (17.3 − 10.6 = 6.7), it is using an extra $1.3 trillion that could otherwise be directed toward other important yet underfunded priorities such as public education and safe infrastructure. Considering that CMS (2019) expects spending on healthcare to grow at an average rate of 5.5 percent per year from 2018 to 2027, reaching nearly $6 trillion by 2027, the calculations become even more concerning.

International comparisons of healthcare spending on a per capita basis present similar findings. According to OECD (2019b) data, the United States spends more than $10,000 per year per person on healthcare, compared to an OECD average of approximately $4,000. In other words, the United States is spending two-and-a-half times more per capita than the typical OECD nation.

Outcomes Compared with Other Countries

Given the extraordinarily high level of healthcare spending in the United States, the relatively poor performance of the US healthcare system is a topic of great concern. Life expectancy for men and women in the United States—78.6 years—is only average. Men at the age of 65 in the United States live an additional 18.1 years, on average, whereas women at age 65 live an additional 20.6 years—both figures are lower than those found in many other OECD countries, particularly the wealthier Western nations (OECD 2019b). According to the OECD (2019b), the United States ranks thirty-third in infant mortality, with 5.8 deaths per 100,000 live births (OECD 2019b). The country also has a high suicide rate, at 13.9 deaths per 100,000 people.

Not all the news is bad, however. The United States has fewer cancer deaths (185.4 per 100,000 people in 2016) than many other wealthy Western nations. Success in this area can be attributed in part to advances in cancer treatment, which is related to the amount of medical research done in the United States (Miller et al. 2016).

Other important measures provide insights into overall performance and quality. Two widely used utilization measures are hospital length of stay (LOS) and the number of nuclear magnetic resonance imaging scans (MRIs) done. The average hospital LOS in the United States, at about five days per admission, ranks among the lowest in the OECD, reflecting a concerted effort by hospital managers to improve in this area (OECD 2019b). The utilization pattern for MRIs shows a different trend, however. The US rate of 111 MRI exams per 1,000 inhabitants in 2017 ranked high—although not the highest—among OECD countries (OECD 2019b).

The inconsistent performance of the United States on these measures highlights the complexity of healthcare and helps explain why healthcare costs vary so much from one country to the next. Although the US healthcare system today spends less time caring for patients (low LOS), it spends more money on diagnostic exams and other technologically driven procedures and treatments (high MRI rate). Of course, the healthcare cost dilemma has no easy answer, and these utilization measures represent just one part of the puzzle. Students of healthcare should carefully consider all the potential factors that may be involved.

Health Behaviors Compared with Other Countries

When comparing the United States with other countries, we also need to consider health behaviors, which have a tremendous influence on outcomes and health status. According to the OECD (2019b), 71 percent of the American population is considered overweight or obese. The US rate of tobacco use—with 10.5 percent of Americans over the age of 15 smoking daily—is lower than that of most OECD countries. Alcohol consumption the United States—at 8.9 liters per person over the age of 15 per year—is close to the OECD average (OECD 2019b). Antismoking campaigns, messages and penalties related to drunk driving, and other health education efforts have likely influenced these and other metrics (Hall 2006; Stewart, Cutler, and Rosen 2009; Sturm et al. 2013).

Pricing Variation

Another reason for the high level of healthcare spending in the United States is the pricing of products and services in the healthcare system (Anderson et al. 2003). Most countries control prices, but the United States generally does not (Benhamou 2017). Exhibit 4.5 shows the price variation between the United States and the United Kingdom for a number of frequently provided services and prescribed medications. The prices in the exhibit vary

EXHIBIT 4.5
Price Variation for Select Procedures and Drugs in the United States and the United Kingdom

Name of Drug or Procedure (year data available)	Pricing in United States	Pricing in United Kingdom	Difference Between US and UK Prices
Angioplasty (2015)	$31,620	$7,264	$24,356
Bypass surgery (2015)	$78,318	$24,059	$54,259
Hip replacement (2014)	$29,067	$16,335	$12,732
Appendectomy (2014)	$15,930	$8,009	$7,921
Colonoscopy (2014)	$1,301	$3,059	−$1,758
Magnetic resonance imaging (2014)	$1,119	$788	$331
Harvoni, four-week supply, 28 tablets (2014)	$32,114	$22,554	$9,560
Avastin, 400 mg vial (2014)	$3,930	$470	$3,460
Humira, prefilled syringes, 28-day supply (2014)	$2,669	$1,362	$1,307
Xarelto, 20 mg 30 capsules, 30-day supply (2014)	$292	$126	$166

Notes: Harvoni is used for the treatment of hepatitis C. If administered correctly, it can cure the infection in 12 weeks in 99 percent of cases. Avastin is used for the treatment of cancer. Humira is used to treat several autoimmune diseases, such as severe psoriasis and psoriatic arthritis. Xarelto is used to prevent blood clotting in patients with a risk of an embolism that could result in a stroke.

Source: Data from International Federation of Health Plans (2015); Sawyer and Cox (2018).

dramatically, and all of the US prices except for one (colonoscopies) are significantly higher than the corresponding prices in the United Kingdom (International Federation of Health Plans 2015; Sawyer and Cox 2018). In the case of the cancer drug Avastin, the US price is more than eight times the UK price. Papanicolas, Woskie, and Jha (2018) have concluded that higher prices for drugs and services are a major driver of US healthcare expenditures. This issue has been widely discussed in the United States for many years (*PBS NewsHour* 2011).

European countries generally regulate pricing through three primary means:

1. Product price control, the most commonly used method for establishing prices, is primarily accomplished through negotiation with manufacturers and providers. In some cases, prices are simply set at a desired level by a government authority (Nguyen et al. 2015).
2. Reference pricing is a process by which the patient shares in the cost of the product or service (usually pharmaceuticals). The insurer or plan covers a low-cost option in a therapeutic cluster of similar treatment options, and participants who choose a higher-cost option must pay the difference (Ess, Schneeweiss, and Szucs 2003). In external reference pricing, countries use a similar process in establishing drug prices through comparison with other countries (Rémuzat et al. 2015).
3. Profit control, which is mainly used in the United Kingdom, can be done when regulators have difficulty capping the use of products and services, as in the case of healthcare. One of the primary means for profit control involves the use of a global budget that cannot be exceeded. If services expand beyond the budgeted amount, profit margins are reduced or eliminated (Ess, Schneeweiss, and Szucs 2003; Schön 2016).

Regulation of pricing has long been controversial, especially in the United States. The primary argument against price control is that it will reduce the incentive for innovation and new product development—areas in which the United States has traditionally excelled. Golec, Vernon, and colleagues have found some evidence suggesting that price controls would reduce research and development of pharmaceuticals, thereby decreasing the development of new drugs (Golec and Vernon 2006; Vernon, Goldberg, and Golec 2009). Such a trend would also result in a reduction in employment in the pharmaceutical industry (Frank 2001; Winegarde 2017). Other researchers disagree, however, pointing out that research and development are only one of the causes of high pharmaceutical costs. They cite pricing policies, patent protection, pharmacy benefit managers, and protection of profits for manufacturers as additional factors (Scott 2019; Lakdawalla et al. 2009).

In considering price controls, we should also note that the price people are willing to pay is often related to the income level of the country where they reside. Even though low-income countries may pay a lower price for a product or service, it still may represent a larger portion of a typical person's overall income (Young, Soussi, and Toumi 2017).

Why Is Global Health Important to the United States?

Extensive international travel and commerce have brought the world closer together, requiring us all to think more globally about health (Office of Disease Prevention and Health Promotion 2019). Global health risks such as infectious diseases, foodborne illnesses, contaminated pharmaceuticals, and defective or unsafe medical products can have a serious impact on the United States, regardless of their place of origin.

Today, we can travel to virtually anywhere on the planet within a 24-hour period—which is well within the incubation period of many emerging and reemerging infectious diseases. Ebola, West Nile virus, and Zika virus, for instance, all originated elsewhere but have posed health threats to the United States just the same (Fauci and Morens 2016; Singh et al. 2017). According to an Institute of Medicine report, new diseases have emerged at a rate of one or more per year since the 1970s (Smolinski, Hamburg, and Lederberg 2003). We also face the risk of unsafe drugs flooding into the country. Fentanyl, for example, has contributed to the opioid crisis in the United States, with devastating effects (Sanger-Katz 2018).

By rapidly identifying and controlling infectious diseases in other countries and by monitoring the importation of pharmaceuticals and other medical products, we can take a proactive approach to global health risks and help to ensure safer care and better health. Investment in these activities will pay significant dividends not only for the United States but also for the entire world.

Issues of health and healthcare rank high on the world agenda. Countries throughout the world recognize the urgency of strengthening health systems to meet the needs of ever-growing populations and to address emerging health threats and challenges (WHO 2007b). The Alliance for Health Policy and Systems Research (2004)—a collaboration between the Global Forum for Health Research and WHO—has called for more research regarding health policies and systems, and it recommends the following criteria for prioritizing health problems:

- Magnitude of the problem
- Avoidance of duplication

- Feasibility
- Focused applicability of the research results
- Addition of new knowledge
- Political acceptability
- Ethical acceptability
- Urgency

The struggle with cost, quality, and access is not unique to the United States. In many ways, the United States and other countries share similar concerns about healthcare system development and reform—even though the focus and the magnitude of reform efforts may be vastly different. The United States must be willing to take a collaborative approach and engage in strengthening the global health system.

Summary of Important Differences Between the United States and Other Countries

This extended comparison of the US healthcare system with the systems of other countries leaves a lot to digest. Nonetheless, some of the most notable distinctions of the US system can be summarized as follows:

- Highest costs of all OECD countries
- Technological leader
- No system to provide universal coverage
- Highly fragmented delivery of care
- Many payer arrangements
- Major issues surrounding performance, electronic systems, delivery system restructuring, and quality
- Lack of standardization, leading to inefficiencies and variation
- High administrative costs
- Leader in medical education and research
- Highly complex organizational structures and delivery models
- Cultural differences

Meanwhile, the health systems of most other OECD countries are distinguished from that of the United States by the following fundamental principles (Himmelstein et al. 2014; Jiwani et al. 2014; Woolhandler, Campbell, and Himmelstein 2003):

- Coverage mandated either through private sources, government sources, or some combination

- Insurance companies or funds, mostly nonprofit, that are required to accept everyone
- Regulation of prices and acceptance of a standard set of fixed prices for the various services provided through the system
- Administrative costs significantly lower than in the United States

These principles have not been completely lost on the United States. In fact, if you look closely at the complex system of coverages in the United States, you can find certain approaches and characteristics that recall these other systems. The Veterans Health Administration within the US Department of Veterans Affairs, for instance, functions similarly to the National Health Service of the United Kingdom. The US Medicare system resembles the healthcare system in Taiwan, and the US reliance on healthcare coverage through employers resembles the German system. Interestingly, we have adopted so many healthcare coverage models to varying degrees, yet we have not found one that fits the country as a whole. (Lorenzoni, Belloni, and Sassi 2014; OECD 2016).

Discussion Questions

1. How does the United States compare with other countries on various outcome metrics?
2. What are the key differences between the US healthcare system and the systems of other Organisation for Economic Co-operation and Development countries?
3. What are the key differences in the organizational and institutional structures of healthcare systems in various countries?
4. How is healthcare funded in the countries described in this chapter?
5. How do the various countries regulate healthcare?

References

Advisory Board. 2017. "CMS: US Health Care Spending to Reach Nearly 20% of GDP by 2025." Daily Briefing. Published February 16. www.advisory.com/daily-briefing/2017/02/16/spending-growth.

Agency for Healthcare Research and Quality (AHRQ). 2017. "Defining Health Systems." Reviewed September. www.ahrq.gov/chsp/chsp-reports/resources-for-understanding-health-systems/defining-health-systems.html.

———. 2016. "Compendium of U.S. Health Systems, 2016." Reviewed May 2019. www.ahrq.gov/chsp/compendium/index.html.

Alliance for Health Policy and Systems Research. 2004. *Strengthening Health Systems: The Role and Promise of Policy and Systems Research.* Accessed October 18, 2019. www.who.int/alliance-hpsr/resources/Strengthening_complet.pdf.

Anderson, G. F., U. E. Reinhardt, P. S. Hussey, and V. Petrosyan. 2003. "It's the Prices, Stupid: Why the United States Is So Different from Other Countries." *Health Affairs* 22 (3): 89–105. https://doi.org/10.1377/hlthaff.22.3.89.

Benhamou, E. 2017. "Drug Pricing Trends in the EU Versus in the US." Results Healthcare. Published June 30. https://resultshealthcare.com/insight/drug-pricing-trends-eu-versus-us/.

Bloomberg. 2014. "Best (and Worst): Most Efficient Health Care 2014, Countries." Accessed September 29, 2019. www.bloomberg.com/graphics/best-and-worst/#most-efficient-health-care-2014-countries.

Centers for Medicare & Medicaid Services (CMS). 2019. "NHE Fact Sheet." Revised April 26. www.cms.gov/research-statistics-data-and-systems/statistics-trends-and-reports/nationalhealthexpenddata/nhe-fact-sheet.html.

———. 2018. "National Health Expenditure Projections 2018–2027." Accessed October 14, 2019. www.cms.gov/Research-Statistics-Data-and-Systems/Statistics-Trends-and-Reports/NationalHealthExpendData/Downloads/ForecastSummary.pdf.

Cheng, T.-M. 2019. "The Taiwan Health Care System." International Health Care System Profiles. Accessed September 29. https://international.commonwealthfund.org/countries/taiwan/.

Docteur, E., and H. Oxley. 2003. "Health-Care Systems: Lessons from the Reform Experience." Organisation for Economic Co-operation and Development Health Working Papers. Published December. www.oecd.org/dataoecd/5/53/22364122.pdf.

Ess, S. M., S. Schneeweiss, and T. D. Szucs. 2003. "European Healthcare Policies for Controlling Drug Expenditure." *PharmacoEconomics* 21 (2): 89–103. www.ncbi.nlm.nih.gov/pubmed/12515571.

Fauci, A. S., and D. M. Morens. 2016. "Zika Virus in the Americas—Yet Another Arbovirus Threat." *New England Journal of Medicine* 374 (7): 601–4. https://doi.org/10.1056/NEJMp1600297.

Frank, R. G. 2001. "Prescription Drug Prices: Why Do Some Pay More than Others Do?" *Health Affairs* 20 (2): 115–28. https://doi.org/10.1377/hlthaff.20.2.115.

Fraser Institute. 2018. "Timely Health Care—There's an App for That!" *Fraser Forum.* Published August 31. www.fraserinstitute.org/blogs/timely-health-care-there-s-an-app-for-that.

German Health Insurance System. 2019. "German Health Care System Guide." Accessed September 29. www.germanyhis.com/.

Golec, J. H., and J. A. Vernon. 2006. "European Pharmaceutical Price Regulation, Firm Profitability, and R&D Spending." National Bureau of Economic Research. Published November. https://doi.org/10.3386/w12676.

Government of Canada. 2016. "Canada's Health Care System." Updated August 22. www.canada.ca/en/health-canada/services/canada-health-care-system.html.

Government of Western Australia Department of Health. 2019. "Overview of the Australian Health System." Accessed September 29. https://ww2.health.wa.gov.au/Careers/International-applicants/International-medical-graduates/Overview-of-the-Australian-health-system.

Hall, C. 2006. "Obesity 'Worse than Drinking or Smoking.'" *Telegraph* (London). Published December 13. www.telegraph.co.uk/news/uknews/1536750/Obesity-worse-than-drinking-or-smoking.html.

Himmelstein, D. U., M. Jun, R. Busse, K. Chevreul, A. Geissler, P. Jeurissen, S. Thomson, M. A. Vinet, and S. Woolhandler. 2014. "A Comparison of Hospital Administrative Costs in Eight Nations: US Costs Exceed All Others by Far." *Health Affairs* 33 (9): 1586–94. https://doi.org/10.1377/hlthaff.2013.1327.

International Federation of Health Plans (IFHP). 2015. *International Federation of Health Plans 2015 Comparative Price Report Variation in Medical and Hospital Prices by Country.* London: IFHP.

Jiwani, A., D. Himmelstein, S. Woolhandler, and J. G. Kahn. 2014. "Billing and Insurance-Related Administrative Costs in United States' Health Care: Synthesis of Micro-costing Evidence." *BMC Health Services Research* 14 (1): 556. https://doi.org/10.1186/s12913-014-0556-7.

Jones, J., and L. Saad. 2017. "Americans Still Hold Dim View of U.S. Healthcare System." Gallup. Published December 11. http://news.gallup.com/poll/223403/americans-hold-dim-view-healthcare-system.aspx.

Lakdawalla, D. N., D. P. Goldman, P.-C. Michaud, N. Sood, R. Lempert, Z. Cong, H. de Vries, and I. Gutierrez. 2009. "U.S. Pharmaceutical Policy in a Global Marketplace." *Health Affairs* 28 (1): w138–50. https://doi.org/10.1377/hlthaff.28.1.w138.

Liu, C., and W. Haseltine. 2019. "The Singaporean Health Care System." Commonwealth Fund. Accessed September 29. https://international.commonwealthfund.org/countries/singapore/.

Lorenzoni, L., A. Belloni, and F. Sassi. 2014. "Health-Care Expenditure and Health Policy in the USA Versus Other High-Spending OECD Countries." *Lancet* 384 (9937): 83–92. https://doi.org/10.1016/S0140-6736(14)60571-7.

Matsuda, R. 2019. "The Japanese Health Care System." International Health Care System Profiles. Accessed September 29. https://international.commonwealthfund.org/countries/japan/.

Miller, K. D., R. L. Siegel, C. C. Lin, A. B. Mariotto, J. L. Kramer, J. H. Rowland, K. D. Stein, R. Alteri, and A. Jemal. 2016. "Cancer Treatment and Survivorship Statistics, 2016." *CA: A Cancer Journal for Clinicians* 66 (4): 271–89. https://doi.org/10.3322/caac.21349.

Mossialos, E., M. Wenzl, R. Osborn, and D. Sarnak (eds.). 2016. *2015 International Profiles of Health Care.* Commonwealth Fund. Published January. www.commonwealthfund.org/sites/default/files/documents/___media_files_publications_fund_report_2016_jan_1857_mossialos_intl_profiles_2015_v7.pdf.

Murray, C., and J. Frenk. 1999. "A WHO Framework for Health System Performance Assessment." Accessed September 29, 2019. www.who.int/healthinfo/paper06.pdf.

National Health Service (NHS). 2019. "Free NHS Prescriptions." Accessed October 14. www.nhsbsa.nhs.uk/help-nhs-prescription-costs/free-nhs-prescriptions.

New Zealand Ministry of Health. 2017. "Overview of the Health System." Updated March 30. www.health.govt.nz/new-zealand-health-system/overview-health-system.

Nguyen, T. A., R. Knight, E. E. Roughead, G. Brooks, and A. Mant. 2015. "Policy Options for Pharmaceutical Pricing and Purchasing: Issues for Low- and Middle-Income Countries." *Health Policy and Planning* 30 (2): 267280. https://doi.org/10.1093/heapol/czt105.

Office of Disease Prevention and Health Promotion. 2019. "Global Health." Healthy People 2020. Accessed September 29. www.healthypeople.gov/2020/topics-objectives/topic/global-health.

Organisation for Economic Co-operation and Development (OECD). 2019a. "List of OECD Member Countries—Ratification of the Convention on the OECD." Accessed September 29. www.oecd.org/about/membersandpartners/list-oecd-member-countries.htm.

———. 2019b. "OECD Health Statistics 2019." Published July 2. www.oecd.org/els/health-systems/health-data.htm.

———. 2018. "Social Spending." Accessed October 16, 2019. https://data.oecd.org/socialexp/social-spending.htm.

———. 2017. *Health at a Glance 2017: OECD Indicators.* Paris: OECD. https://doi.org/10.1787/health_glance-2017-en.

———. 2016. *Universal Health Coverage and Health Outcomes.* Published July 22. www.oecd.org/els/health-systems/Universal-Health-Coverage-and-Health-Outcomes-OECD-G7-Health-Ministerial-2016.pdf.

Papanicolas, I., L. R. Woskie, and A. K. Jha. 2018. "Health Care Spending in the United States and Other High-Income Countries." *JAMA* 319 (10): 1024–39. https://doi.org/10.1001/jama.2018.1150.

PBS NewsHour. 2011. "Why Does Health Care Cost So Much in the United States?" Published November 25. www.pbs.org/newshour/health/why-does-healthcare-cost-so-much.

Picard, A. 2017. "The Real Challenge to Canada's Health System Is Not Wait Times." *Globe and Mail* (Toronto). Published April 14. www.theglobeandmail.com/opinion/canada-must-address-the-problem-of-long-waits-for-medical-care/article34056251/.

Rémuzat, C., D. Urbinati, O. Mzoughi, E. El Hammi, W. Belgaied, and M. Toumi. 2015. "Overview of External Reference Pricing Systems in Europe." *Journal of Market Access & Health Policy* 3 (1): 27675. https://doi.org/10.3402/jmahp.v3.27675.

Republic of France. 2019. "The French Social Security System for Salaried Workers." Accessed September 29. www.cleiss.fr/docs/regimes/regime_france/an_index.html.

Rosenau, P. 2012. "Comparative Healthcare Systems: Policy Challenges and Economic Perspectives." Policy Studies Organization. Published July 30. www.ipsonet.org/proceedings/2012/07/30/comparative-healthcare-systems-policy-challenges-and-economic-perspectives/.

Sanger-Katz, M. 2018. "Bleak New Estimates in Drug Epidemic: A Record 72,000 Overdose Deaths in 2017." *New York Times.* Published August 15. www.nytimes.com/2018/08/15/upshot/opioids-overdose-deaths-rising-fentanyl.html.

Sawyer, B., and C. Cox. 2018. "How Does Health Spending in the U.S. Compare to Other Countries?" Peterson-Kaiser Health System Tracker. Published December 7. www.healthsystemtracker.org/chart-collection/health-spending-u-s-compare-countries/#item-start.

Schneider, E. C., D. O. Sarnak, D. Squires, A. Shah, and M. M. Doty. 2017. "Mirror, Mirror 2017: International Comparison Reflects Flaws and Opportunities for Better U.S. Health Care." Commonwealth Fund. Published July 14. www.commonwealthfund.org/publications/fund-reports/2017/jul/mirror-mirror-2017-international-comparison-reflects-flaws-and.

Schön, P. 2016. "The Welfare Inquiry—Limiting Profits in the Swedish Welfare Sector." European Commission. Flash Report 2016/09. Published December. https://ec.europa.eu/social/BlobServlet?docId=16819&langId=en.

Schütte, S., P. N. M. Acevedo, and A. Flahault. 2018. "Health Systems Around the World—A Comparison of Existing Health System Rankings." *Journal of Global Health* 8 (1). https://doi.org/10.7189/jogh.08.010407.

Scott, D. 2019. "Pharmaceutical CEOs Testify in Congress: 8 Ideas for Reducing Drug Prices." Vox. Updated February 26. www.vox.com/policy-and-politics/2019/1/14/18176707/congress-drug-prices-hearing-pharmaceutical-ceos.

Singh, R. K., K. Dhama, Y. S. Malik, M. A. Ramakrishnan, K. Karthik, R. Khandia, R. Tiwari, A. Munjal, M. Saminathan, S. Sachan, P. A. Desingu, J. J. Kattoor, H. M. N. Iqbal, and S. K. Joshi. 2017. "Ebola Virus—Epidemiology, Diagnosis, and Control: Threat to Humans, Lessons Learnt, and Preparedness Plans—An Update on Its 40 Year's Journey." *Veterinary Quarterly* 37 (1): 98–135. https://doi.org/10.1080/01652176.2017.1309474.

Smolinski, M. S., M. A. Hamburg, and J. Lederberg (eds.). 2003. *Microbial Threats to Health: Emergence, Detection, and Response.* Washington, DC: National Academies Press.

Stewart, S. T., D. M. Cutler, and A. B. Rosen. 2009. "Forecasting the Effects of Obesity and Smoking on U.S. Life Expectancy." *New England Journal of Medicine* 361 (23): 2252–60. https://doi.org/10.1056/NEJMsa0900459.

Sturm, R., R. An, J. Maroba, and D. Patel. 2013. "The Effects of Obesity, Smoking, and Excessive Alcohol Intake on Healthcare Expenditure in a Comprehensive Medical Scheme." *South African Medical Journal/Suid-Afrikaanse Tydskrif Vir Geneeskunde* 103 (11): 840–44. www.ncbi.nlm.nih.gov/pubmed/24148168.

Tandon, A., C. J. Murray, J. A. Lauer, and D. B. Evans. 2019. "Measuring Overall Health System Performance For 191 Countries." World Health Organization. DPE Discussion Paper Series No. 30. Accessed September 29. www.who.int/healthinfo/paper30.pdf.

Thomson, S., R. Osborn, D. Squires, and M. Jun (eds.). 2013. *International Profiles of Health Care Systems, 2013.* Commonwealth Fund. Published November 14. www.commonwealthfund.org/sites/default/files/documents/___media_files_publications_fund_report_2013_nov_1717_thomson_intl_profiles_hlt_care_sys_2013_v2.pdf.

Vernon, J. A., R. Goldberg, and J. Golec. 2009. "Economic Evaluation and Cost-Effectiveness Thresholds: Signals to Firms and Implications for R&D Investment and Innovation." *PharmacoEconomics* 27 (10): 797–806. https://doi.org/10.2165/11313750-000000000-00000.

Vonnegut, K. (1963) 1998. *Cat's Cradle.* New York: Dial Press Trade Paperbacks.

Winegarde, W. 2017. "Price Controls Will Reduce Innovation and Health Outcomes." *Forbes.* Published October 12. www.forbes.com/sites/econostats/2017/10/12/price-controls-will-reduce-innovation-and-health-outcomes/#1f102e7163a6.

Woolhandler, S., T. Campbell, and D. U. Himmelstein. 2003. "Costs of Health Care Administration in the United States and Canada." *New England Journal of Medicine* 349 (8): 768–75. https://doi.org/10.1056/NEJMsa022033.

World Bank. 2019a. "Current Health Expenditure (% of GDP)." Accessed October 16. https://data.worldbank.org/indicator/SH.XPD.CHEX.GD.ZS.

———. 2019b. "GDP (Current US$)." Accessed October 15. https://data.worldbank.org/indicator/ny.gdp.mktp.cd.

World Health Organization (WHO). 2019. "Health Systems." Accessed September 29. www.who.int/topics/health_systems/en/.

———. 2007a. *Everybody's Business: Strengthening Health Systems to Improve Health Outcomes: WHO's Framework for Action.* Accessed September 29, 2019. www.who.int/healthsystems/strategy/everybodys_business.pdf.

———. 2007b. *The World Health Report 2007: A Safer Future: Global Public Health Security in the 21st Century.* Accessed September 29, 2019. www.who.int/whr/2007/en/.

Young, K. E., I. Soussi, and M. Toumi. 2017. "The Perverse Impact of External Reference Pricing (ERP): A Comparison of Orphan Drugs Affordability in 12 European Countries: A Call for Policy Change." *Journal of Market Access & Health Policy* 5 (1): 1369817. https://doi.org/10.1080/20016689.2017.1369817.

5

COMPONENTS OF THE US HEALTHCARE SYSTEM

> Any intelligent fool can make things bigger and more complex . . . . It takes a touch of genius and a lot of courage to move in the opposite direction.
>
> —E. F. Schumacher

Learning Objectives

- Gain familiarity with the many components of the US healthcare system.
- Analyze some of the unique challenges and distinctive characteristics associated with the various components.
- Recognize several criteria that differentiate primary care from specialty care.
- Compare the care needs of people at varying stages of life.
- Analyze the pros and cons of integration.
- Understand the key features of an accountable care organization.

The US healthcare system, as we have seen, is both enormous and highly complex. It represents almost 20 percent of our economy and plays a literal "life-or-death" role in our lives. This chapter will examine the major components of that system, the ways the various entities are categorized, and the essential roles that each component plays (see exhibit 5.1).

Broadly speaking, the components of the US healthcare system include hospitals, long-term care facilities, and rehabilitation facilities; noninstitutional providers such as physicians, pharmacists, physical therapists, nurse practitioners, and physician assistants; the pharmaceutical industry, including pharmacy benefit managers and drug stores; the biotech industry; the medical device industry; and complementary and alternative medicine. This chapter will focus primarily on the components of the system involved in the organization, funding, and delivery of care (see exhibit 5.2).

The components that organize, deliver, and fund healthcare often have not worked together well, and for that reason, many reform efforts have

EXHIBIT 5.1
Area of Focus
for This Chapter

The Aim of the Healthcare System

Issues That Require Our Attention

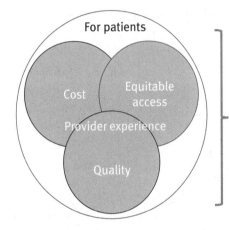

For patients

Cost

Equitable access

Provider experience

Quality

- Nature of our complex system
- Historical issues that have influenced the development of the system
- Beliefs and attitudes about health and healthcare
- Comparison with other developed countries
- *Components of our healthcare system*
- People and providers
- Patient care—the purpose of the system
- Financing a massive system
- Quality—easier said than done
- Medical and information technology
- The pharmaceutical industry
- Complementary and alternative medicine
- Politics/economics
- The future of the system

sought to streamline them. However, integrating organization, delivery of care, and funding has proved difficult (Bennett 2012; Bodenheimer 2008). Is the complexity of our healthcare system making it increasingly difficult, if not impossible, to produce the results we seek? This question needs to be carefully considered as we discuss the organization of our healthcare system and the ways we might reorganize it to more effectively produce quality health outcomes at a reasonable cost.

EXHIBIT 5.2
Fundamental
Components of
a Healthcare
System

Organization | Funding

Delivery

A lot of the complexity of the US healthcare system comes from its fragmentation. The observation that people in healthcare work in "silos" has been repeated to the point of becoming cliché, but, unfortunately, it remains all too true. We are only just beginning to organize the system in a way that breaks down the silos and allows various components to work together to achieve better cost, quality, and access for patients (Berwick and Hackbarth 2012; Kannampallil et al. 2011; Starr 1982; Weberg 2012).

New models of organizational structure and governance are emerging as the healthcare delivery landscape changes. In the broadest sense, healthcare delivery is divided into inpatient and outpatient services. Both inpatient and outpatient services may be used for acute illness (i.e., requiring immediate attention, typically for a shorter duration) or chronic illness or injury (i.e., requiring longer-term treatment or rehabilitation, potentially extending for the life of the patient) (Medline Plus 2019; Bernell and Howard 2016; O'Halloran, Miller, and Britt 2004).

Hospitals and Inpatient Services

Hospitals, according to most definitions, are institutions that provide medical and surgical treatment and nursing care for sick or injured people. They are often thought of as institutions that provide a high level of care, receiving referrals from doctors and other practitioners. Hospitals are available 24/7, making them a unique and vital component of the healthcare system (Hensher, Price, and Adomakoh 2006).

The World Health Organization (WHO 2019a) describes hospitals as follows: "Hospitals complement and amplify the effectiveness of many other parts of the health system, providing continuous availability of services for acute and complex conditions. Hospitals concentrate scarce resources within well-planned referral networks to respond efficiently to population health needs."

Characteristics of US Hospitals

Hospitals in the United States have evolved from the pest houses and almshouses of the 1700s and 1800s into the modern institutions at the center of medical care today. Hospitals must be constructed and operated under a variety of laws and rules that are established by the federal government, state health regulations, city ordinances, and Joint Commission standards (Facility Guidelines Institute 2018). The Joint Commission accredits all hospitals in the United States. Hospitals also must comply with fire and sanitation codes at the state and local levels.

The following are some of the specific characteristics of US hospitals:

- An institution must have at least six beds to be considered a hospital.
- The institution must be licensed by the state.
- The institution must have an organized physician staff, and it must provide continuous nursing services supervised by a registered nurse (RN).
- The institution must have a separately organized medical staff. The physicians must have an organization within the hospital that makes the rules related to medical care, allowing physicians the privilege to practice in the hospital and providing disciplinary actions when appropriate.
- The administrative structure and the medical staff structure report to the board of directors of the hospital (an interesting and important distinction between hospitals and many organizations in the nonmedical world).
- The hospital must have a medical record for each patient.
- The hospital must have pharmacy services that are supervised by a registered pharmacist.
- The hospital must provide food service that meets the nutritional needs of patients.
- In most cases, the hospital must have emergency services available.

Every state licenses hospitals and has specific definitions, regulations, and requirements. Medical administrators should read and understand the rules for their state (Finch 1994a; Hensher, Price, and Adomakoh 2006). Generally, each state's department of health and human services will make the key rules and regulations available on its website; Medicare and the US Department of Health and Human Services offer resources with a more national perspective.

Categorization of Hospitals by Tax Status

Hospitals can be categorized in a number of ways. One of the more frequently used distinctions is based on the hospital's tax status—not for profit (tax exempt) or for profit (not tax exempt). Not-for-profit and for-profit hospitals have substantially different ownership arrangements. Not-for-profit community hospitals are owned, for all intents and purposes, by the public of a municipality. They may also be owned by not-for-profit organizations, if those organizations qualify for tax-exempt status. By contrast, for-profit hospitals are primarily owned by shareholders, with the goal of making a profit from the facility's operations (Coyne et al. 2009; Eskoz and Peddecord 1985; American Hospital Association [AHA] 2018b).

Not-for-Profit Hospitals

A not-for-profit (or nonprofit) facility does not seek to make a profit for the benefit of its owners; instead, it invests any surpluses into the community it serves. The label "not for profit" does not imply that the hospital does not generate revenue greater than its expenses; rather, it simply designates that the income does not inure to the benefit of individuals or other organizations (Cheney 2017; Davis 2011).

Not-for-profit hospitals in the United States qualify for special treatment under Internal Revenue Code section 501(c)(3), which is applied to organizations that serve a charitable mission for the community. To qualify as a charitable organization, a hospital must "be organized and operated exclusively for exempt purposes set forth in section 501(c)(3), and none of its earnings may inure to any private shareholder or individual. In addition, it may not be an action organization, i.e., it may not attempt to influence legislation as a substantial part of its activities, and it may not participate in any campaign activity for or against political candidates" (Internal Revenue Service [IRS] 2019b).

Nonprofit hospitals must also comply with four additional IRS requirements (IRS 2019a):

- Section 501(r)(3) requires hospital organizations to "conduct a community health needs assessment (CHNA) every three years and to adopt an implementation strategy to meet the community health needs identified through the CHNA."
- Section 501(r)(4) requires hospital organizations to "establish a written financial assistance policy (FAP) and a written emergency medical care policy" for care provided by the hospital facility, including all such care provided in the hospital facility by "a substantially-related entity."
- A hospital organization meets the requirements of section 501(r)(5) only if "the hospital facility (and any substantially-related entity) limits the amount charged for any emergency or other medically necessary care it provides to a FAP-eligible individual to not more than the amount generally billed (AGB) to individuals who have insurance covering such care."
- Section 501(r)(6) requires hospital organizations to "make reasonable efforts to determine whether an individual is eligible for assistance under the hospital organization's financial assistance policy (FAP) before engaging in extraordinary collection actions (ECAs) against that individual."

The Affordable Care Act (ACA) of 2010 ushered in new requirements for nonprofit hospitals to demonstrate "community benefit." These requirements reflected a 2003 Tenth Circuit court ruling that "an organization cannot satisfy the community-benefit requirement based solely on the fact that it offers health-care services to all in the community in exchange for a fee" (Becker, Cerny, and Timmerman 2011; Case Briefs 2003). The growing emphasis on demonstrating community benefit also stemmed in part from the overall size to which the tax exemption had grown: A study by the Congressional Committee on Taxation found that the tax-exempt benefit to nonprofit hospitals had amounted to $24.6 billion in 2011 (Rosenbaum et al. 2015). The new ACA requirements for community benefit have led some hospitals to consider giving up their tax-exempt status (Becker, Cerny, and Timmerman 2011).

The rules and regulations around tax-exempt status are extensive and complex, and leaders must be vigilant in complying with all state and federal requirements if they hope to maintain that status. Nonprofit hospital organizations that expand into other areas of healthcare may find that portions of their operations no longer qualify (Young et al. 2013).

For-Profit Hospitals

As the name implies, for-profit hospitals are operated to produce income for individuals, partners, or shareholders of a corporation. Because they do not qualify as 501(c)(3) charitable organizations, they do not receive tax-exempt status. They are privately funded and are subject to income taxes, just as any other corporation or taxable entity is. For-profit hospitals are subject to the operational rules and regulations at the state and federal levels that govern all hospitals. Examples of for-profit hospital organizations include Tenet Healthcare, HCA Healthcare (formerly Hospital Corporation of America), Community Health Systems, and Cancer Treatment Centers of America.

The effect of a profit motive on the quality of medical care and organizational performance has long been the subject of debate. Some studies have found that for-profit hospitals have higher costs and mortality (Herrera et al. 2014), but other studies have been less conclusive. Most likely, the debate will continue to be fueled largely by people's differing beliefs about the role of hospitals in our society (Devereaux et al. 2004; Gray 1986). One could certainly argue that, if the practices of for-profit hospitals deviated too much from those of their not-for-profit counterparts, then they would have difficulty attracting patients, funding, and qualified practitioners—but without clear evidence, we cannot make that assumption. Nevertheless, most for-profit hospitals are accredited by The Joint Commission, meaning they have met the same standards as their not-for-profit counterparts.

Specific concerns have surrounded physician-owned hospitals—notably, the belief that some might selectively take patients who have potential for better outcomes and better sources of funding. The Medicare Modernization Act of 2003 imposed a two-year moratorium in which additional physician-owned hospitals were not allowed to be constructed or receive government funding, such as through Medicare and Medicaid (Shute 2018; CMS 2004). The moratorium expired without resolution of the issue, and the addition of new hospitals in that category was banned under the ACA. Debate is now resurfacing about whether physician-owned hospitals should be allowed, with some people questioning the validity of many of the cost and quality concerns (Shute 2018). Hopefully, solid evidence from well-conducted studies will emerge to resolve this debate.

Hospitals in the United States, by the Numbers

In 2017, the United States had 5,534 total registered hospitals, 4,840 of which were community hospitals (AHA 2018b). Of the community hospitals, almost 20 percent were state or government owned, approximately 59 percent were not-for-profit, and a little over 21 percent were for-profit. Exhibit 5.3 shows a more detailed breakdown of the numbers.

Total number of all US registered hospitals	5,534	**EXHIBIT 5.3** US Hospitals, by the Numbers
Number of US community hospitals	4,840	
Number of nongovernment not-for-profit community hospitals	2,849	
Number of investor-owned (for-profit) community hospitals	1,035	
Number of state and local government community hospitals	956	
Number of federal government hospitals	209	
Number of nonfederal psychiatric hospitals	397	
Number of nonfederal long-term care hospitals	78	
Number of hospital units of institutions (prison hospitals, college infirmaries, etc.)	10	
Total staffed beds in all US registered hospitals	894,574	
Staffed beds in community hospitals	780,272	
Total admissions in all US registered hospitals	35,158,934	
Admissions in community hospitals	33,424,253	
Total expenses for all US registered hospitals	$991,531,841,000	
Expenses for community hospitals	$902,891,035,000	
Number of rural community hospitals	1,825	
Number of urban community hospitals	3,015	
Number of community hospitals in a system	3,231	
Number of community hospitals in a network	1,689	

Source: Data from AHA (2018b).

Other Ways Hospitals Are Classified

Public

Public hospitals in the United States may be owned by the federal, state, or local governments. Some federal hospitals are specific to particular groups, such as Native Americans, members of the military, and veterans. Two major federal systems—the Veterans Health Administration and the Indian Health Service—will be discussed in a separate section later in the chapter. State-run hospitals in the United States are primarily psychiatric hospitals, long-term care facilities, and hospitals for people with developmental disabilities. The number of state-run hospitals has decreased as better alternatives have become available, on both an outpatient and an inpatient basis. Public hospitals overall have high utilization rates. They serve several population groups that have traditionally been associated with high utilization and longer lengths of stay, including the poor, the elderly, and people with disabilities (AHA 2018a).

Multi-Unit Affiliation (Hospital Chains)

Hospitals have seen a trend toward multi-unit affiliation not unlike that seen in the banking industry. Three or four decades ago, most banks were small community banks; today, Bank of America provides primary banking services for more than 24 million people all across the country (Szmigiera 2019).

More than half of all US hospitals are now chain affiliated (AHA 2018a). The push toward consolidation comes from a need to integrate services so that a broad spectrum of services can be provided, economies of scale can be gained, market power can be increased, capital can be accessed, and efficiency of capital assets (e.g., real estate) can be maximized. Consider, for instance, the 2018 merger of Aetna and CVS, which enabled the insurer to offer preferred access and payments to subscribers who use the primary care services at CVS locations. Exhibit 5.4 lists several other notable healthcare mergers.

Mergers and acquisitions are helping to create large healthcare organizations through both vertical and horizontal integration. Examples of vertical integration might include two or more hospitals merging to form a single organization, or two or more group practices merging to become one. Examples of horizontal integration might include a hospital and long-term care facility merging together, a pharmaceutical company and a hospital coming together, or a hospital and a physician group practice forming a single organization. Exhibits 5.5 and 5.6 list some of the largest not-for-profit and for-profit hospital systems in the United States.

Rural and Urban Hospitals

Hospitals may also be classified by size, usually in terms of the number of beds licensed to operate, or by geographic location, either rural or urban.

- American Healthcare and Griffin/American Healthcare REIT merge.
- University of Pennsylvania rebrands Princeton affiliate as Penn Medicine.
- CVS Health and Aetna merge.[a]
- UnitedHealth's Optum buys 300 medical clinics from DaVita Medical Group.
- Advocate and Aurora Health Care merge.
- Advisory Board and UnitedHealth's Optum merge.
- Steward Health Care and Iasis Healthcare merge.
- Beth Israel Deaconess Medical Center and Lahey Health merge.
- Carolinas Healthcare System and University of North Carolina Health Care merge.[b]
- Dignity Health and Catholic Health Initiatives merge.
- Partners Healthcare and Care New England Health System merge.
- Providence St. Joseph Health and Ascension Health merge.
- A new healthcare venture is initiated by Berkshire Hathaway, JP Morgan, and Amazon.

EXHIBIT 5.4
A Sampling of Major Healthcare Mergers and Acquisitions

[a] The antitrust division of the Department of Justice (DOJ) challenged this merger because of concerns that it would concentrate too much market power in the combined organization. As of October 2018, the DOJ has settled with the parties and approved the merger subject to the devesting of Aetna's Medicare Part D pharmacy business, which Aetna has sold.

[b] This merger was called off due to concerns over governance issues.

Sources: Sanborn (2018b); LaPointe (2018).

Large Not-for-Profit Hospital Systems and Their Headquarters Locations

EXHIBIT 5.5
Large Not-for-Profit Hospital Systems

Ascension Health (St. Louis, MO)
Kaiser Permanente (Oakland, CA)
Catholic Health Initiatives (Englewood, CO)
Sutter Health (Sacramento, CA)
Northwell Health (Great Neck, NY)
Baylor Scott & White Health (Dallas, TX)
SSM Health Care (St. Louis, MO)
Mercy Health (Cincinnati, OH)
Adventist Health (Roseville, CA)
UnityPoint Health (Des Moines, IA)
Mercy (Chesterfield, MO)

Trinity Health (Livonia, MI)
Dignity Health (San Francisco)
Adventist Health System (Winter Park, FL)
Providence Health and Services (Renton, WA)
Banner Health (Phoenix, AZ)
CHRISTUS Health (Irving, TX)
Intermountain Health Care (Salt Lake City, UT)
New York-Presbyterian Healthcare System (New York City)
UPMC (Pittsburgh, PA)
Hospital Sisters Health System (Springfield, IL)
Texas Health Resources (Arlington, TX)

(continued)

EXHIBIT 5.5
Large Not-for-
Profit Hospital
Systems
(continued)

Large Not-for-Profit Hospital Systems and Their Headquarters Locations

Aurora Health Care (Milwaukee, WI)	Franciscan Alliance (Mishawaka, IN)
Baptist Memorial Health Care (Memphis, TN)	Carolinas HealthCare System (Charlotte, NC)
Saint Joseph Health (Orange, CA)	Mayo Clinic Health System (Rochester, MN)
Bon Secours Health System (Marriottsville, MD)	Novant Health (Winston-Salem, NC)
Sentara Healthcare (Norfolk, VA)	
East Texas Medical Center Regional Healthcare System (Tyler, TX)	

Sources: *Becker's Hospital Review* (2015b); Alight (2019).

Geographic location is a particularly useful distinction because of the unique needs and concerns associated with rural and urban settings.

Rural hospitals have faced significant stresses for many years (Mullner et al. 1989). They often have a disproportionate number of poor and elderly patients, have difficulty keeping up with demographic changes, cannot afford to purchase the special equipment they need, or are unable to attract the specialty medical staff their communities demand. Urban hospitals in inner-city areas may also treat a disproportionate number of poor and elderly

EXHIBIT 5.6
Large For-
Profit Hospital
Systems

Name	Number of Facilities as of 2015
Community Health Systems (Franklin, TN)	188
HCA Healthcare (Nashville, TN)	166
Tenet Healthcare (Dallas, TX)	74
LifePoint Health (Brentwood, TN)	56
Prime Healthcare Services (Ontario, CA)	32
Universal Health Services (King of Prussia, PA)	28
IASIS Healthcare (Franklin, TN)	18
Ardent Health Services (Nashville, TN)	12
Capella Healthcare (Franklin, TN)	9
Steward Health Care System (Boston)	9

Source: *Becker's Hospital Review* (2015a).

patients, making their economic plight more difficult (AHA 2018a). Often, rural hospitals affiliate with larger hospitals in metropolitan areas to provide shared services.

Teaching Hospitals and Academic Medical Centers

Teaching hospitals provide American Medical Association–approved graduate medical education programs for physicians and education for other medical professionals. They often serve as the receptor sites for clinical experience during the training of nurses, respiratory therapists, nurse practitioners, physician assistants, physical therapists, occupational therapists, speech pathologists, and other clinical specialists. They are sometimes referred to as *academic medical centers* and are usually members of the Council of Teaching Hospitals. In addition to providing education and training, they serve as important locations for clinical research and offer a broad range of services, often tertiary in nature.

Religiously Affiliated Hospitals

Hospitals in the United States have had a long tradition of being sponsored and operated by religious organizations. One often sees names such as Baptist Medical Center, Jewish Hospital, Methodist Hospital, or Sisters of Charity Hospital. The Catholic hospital system is the largest private healthcare system in the country. In most cases, hospitals sponsored by religious organizations serve the community at large, and with a few notable—and sometimes arguably unconstitutional—exceptions, they provide all the services of other hospitals in the community.

Private groups such as the Shriners have established networks of hospitals to provide care at reduced or no cost to patients, primarily children; such networks may be supported through charitable donations from the public and other private fundraising activities. St. Jude's Hospital in Memphis, Tennessee, is another example of a private, charitably funded organization that provides reduced-cost or free care to children with cancer. St. Jude's is also a major research center for rare forms of childhood cancer.

Often, hospitals have been originally sponsored by religious orders and then sold or transferred to nonreligious entities, with their original names maintained. Therefore, a religious name does not necessarily mean that the organization is presently sponsored or operated by a religious entity.

Osteopathic Hospitals

Hospitals may be categorized as either osteopathic or allopathic, reflecting the differences between osteopathic and allopathic medical training. In general, osteopathic training emphasizes holistic care and the use of spinal and other manual adjustments more than the more conventional allopathic training does. At one time, osteopathic doctors (DOs) and allopathic or medical doctors (MDs) received significantly different training, and DOs often were not allowed to practice at allopathic hospitals. These differences have diminished over time, and now DOs will often seek residencies and fellowships in allopathic postgraduate training programs. Today, DOs and MDs, as well as their namesake hospitals, go through the same licensing and accreditation requirements.

Specialty Hospitals

Specialty hospitals typically provide a narrow range of specialized services geared toward a specific patient group or disease category. They may focus on such areas as rehabilitation and spinal cord injuries, cardiovascular services, orthopedic services, women's health, children's hospital services, or oncology. Often, specialty hospitals function within the organizational structure of large integrated delivery systems; they may even be housed within another hospital facility—a concept known as the "hospital within a hospital" (Healthcare Cost and Utilization Project [HCUP] 2018; Shactman 2005). A few specialty hospitals are still physician owned; however, as noted previously, creation of new physician-owned hospitals is prohibited under the ACA (Shute 2018).

Downsizing and Minihospitals

With advances in medicine, many services and procedures that were once performed only in hospitals can now be done safely and effectively on an outpatient basis. Examples include cardiac catheterization, angioplasty, and other minimally invasive surgeries of various types. The expanding scope of outpatient services has also followed changes in reimbursement. Services that previously were only reimbursed in hospital settings can now be paid for in outpatient environments as well—and in some cases, outpatient reimbursement is favored. This shift of services out of hospitals and into outpatient settings has led some hospitals to either reconfigure or downsize (Greenwald et al. 2006).

The downsizing of hospitals because of reduced patient demand has had a dramatic effect in rural areas. Many rural hospitals have been unable to provide advanced services requiring major investments in equipment and professional personnel because of their smaller population base. Patients in rural areas often must go to larger medical centers in urban areas for treatment.

Many rural hospitals were built in the 1940s and 1950s, using financing under the Hill-Burton Act, and are beginning to become obsolete because of age. Many rural communities, therefore, are facing a quandary of how to fulfill people's needs while also replacing an aging hospital with a more appropriate facility (Sanborn 2018a).

A number of concepts and approaches have been used to address this issue, one of the most important of which is the "minihospital." People in rural areas need access to emergency medical care and other healthcare services that are most appropriately provided in the community. However, given the smaller populations, they generally do not need a large number of hospital beds. A minihospital, therefore, can have only a small number of beds but still meet the needs of the community by providing care that is needed locally and ensuring access to more advanced care when needed. Minihospitals typically provide emergency services on-site and have sophisticated transport mechanisms—such as helicopters, fixed-wing aircraft, and ambulances—to transport patients to other affiliated medical centers for more advanced care.

Another response to the downsizing challenge has been the creation of the swing bed. Swing beds can be used for acute care, or they can be turned into long-term care beds, either on a permanent or temporary basis. The use of swing beds enables local communities to use their facilities more fully while also meeting the needs of an aging population.

Some rural hospitals receive special government funding to allow them to operate in communities that would otherwise have insufficient healthcare resources. Designated as critical access hospitals (CAHs), these facilities represent the only local source of medical care in their community, and they receive reimbursement based on their operating costs. According to The Joint Commission (2019), the United States has about 1,350 CAHs. Under guidelines by the Centers for Medicare & Medicaid Services (CMS 2013), hospitals must meet strict criteria to be eligible for this designation:

- Be in a State that has established a State Medicare Rural Hospital Flexibility Program;
- Be designated by the State as a CAH;
- Be in a rural area or an area that is treated as rural;
- Be located either more than 35 miles from the nearest hospital or CAH or more than 15 miles in areas with mountainous terrain or only secondary roads; OR prior to January 1, 2006, were certified as a CAH based on State designation as a "necessary provider" of health care services to residents in the area;
- Maintain no more than 25 inpatient beds that can be used for either inpatient or swing-bed services;
- Maintain an annual average length of stay of 96 hours or less per patient for acute inpatient care (excluding swing-bed services and beds that are within distinct part units);
- Demonstrate compliance with the CAH CoPs found at 42 CFR Part 485 subpart F; and
- Furnish 24-hour emergency care services 7 days a week

Rural hospitals have also expanded their use of telemedicine and telemonitoring to improve access to specialty services (e.g., cardiology, pulmonary medicine) that might not be routinely available in the community. The expansion of telemedicine services was one of the chief recommendations made by the Bipartisan Policy Center (2018) for the improvement of rural healthcare.

The Bipartisan Policy Center (2018) also offered three more recommendations based on its extensive study of healthcare in rural areas:

1. Public policy needs to recognize that a "one-size-fits-all" approach will not solve the problems of rural healthcare. Services need to be "rightsized" to match the needs of the community.
2. Funding mechanisms should reflect the unique challenges facing rural areas.
3. Efforts to build and support the primary care workforce should include not just physicians but also community health workers, case managers, home health workers, and others.

Important Hospital Metrics

Hospitals and healthcare systems have literally hundreds of metrics to choose from when measuring performance and outcomes. Organizations typically select specific metrics depending on the intended use. Some metrics may be used in reporting to outside agencies, some may be used by management for internal purposes, and others may be used by the board for governance purposes (AHA 2018a; McGlynn, McDonald, and Cassel 2015). These data are often used by other entities to make comparisons across hospitals.

Utilization Measures

Some of the more commonly used metrics for measuring hospital utilization include the following:

- *Average length of stay* is calculated by dividing the total days of care by the total number of discharges. Days of care are the cumulative total of inpatient days over a specified time. Discharges are the number of overnight patients a hospital serves in a given time.
- *Inpatient days* are determined by counting the number of nights spent by patients.
- *Average daily census* is defined as the average number of hospital beds occupied daily over a specified period. This census provides a measure of the number of patients receiving care each day.
- *Occupancy rate* is the percentage of a hospital's capacity that is being used. It is determined by dividing capacity used by total capacity.

Occupancy rate measures the efficiency of the use of the hospital's assets. For example, a 20 percent occupancy rate would be considered quite low, and it would be a matter of great concern for any organization. A hospital with that occupancy rate would likely need to find ways to reduce the capacity of the hospital or find new sources of patients to utilize the facilities. Conversely, a hospital with a high occupancy rate might consider increasing the number of available beds.

- *Capacity* is defined as the number of beds that are in service and staffed. One important note is that a hospital may be licensed to have more beds than it operates. For example, a hospital may be licensed to have 500 beds but, for various reasons (e.g., reduced patient load, staffing concerns), only operate 400 of them.

- *Clinical-staff-to-bed ratio* measures the number of clinical staff members on duty to serve patients. It is determined by dividing the number of clinical staff, such as nurses, by the number of beds that are occupied during any given time frame.

All of these measures may be taken on a daily, weekly, monthly, or yearly basis.

Outcome Measures

Important measures that reflect outcomes within the organization include the number of medication errors, patient waiting times, the number of patients leaving the emergency department (ED) without being seen, hospital-acquired infections (also called *nosocomial infections*), and sentinel events. Sentinel events are unexpected events that cause mortality or serious harm to a patient; they are usually preventable and should never happen.

Public Health Measures

Public health measures include data on childhood immunizations, educational programs, immunizations for the flu, the number of ED patients seen who do not have a primary care doctor, and premature births.

Utilization Patterns

Older adults and children under the age of one are typically high utilizers of hospital care. Women, on average, tend to use more hospital services than men, in part because of childbirth. African Americans tend to have higher utilization rates than many other groups (Agarwal, Mazurenko, and Menachemi 2017; Centers for Disease Control and Prevention 2018; Freeman et al. 2008; Lucas, Barr-Anderson, and Kington 2003; Zayas et al. 2016). Other groups with high utilization of hospital services include beneficiaries of Medicare (older adults and people with disabilities) and Medicaid (people with low incomes, often with disabilities, chronic conditions, or diseases in more serious stages) (HCUP 2018).

Poor people who lack access to healthcare often wait until they are seriously ill to seek treatment, at which point they go to the emergency room. Such individuals often are admitted to the hospital for conditions that might have been treatable on an outpatient basis had they received care at an earlier stage. The costs and inefficiencies associated with such preventable ED visits and hospital stays are a good argument for universal access and universal healthcare coverage (David et al. 2015).

Outpatient Services

The term *outpatient services*, like *inpatient services*, simply describes the location where the services are provided; it tells us little about the service itself. The term applies to any healthcare services that do not involve an overnight stay in a hospital or other institution (Shi and Singh 2010). Outpatient services are sometimes referred to as *ambulatory care*; for most purposes, the terms are synonymous. Blood tests, colonoscopies, chemotherapy, biopsies, ultrasound imaging, radiation treatments, and radiological diagnostic tests are all examples of common outpatient procedures (White and Griffith 2019).

In the past, outpatient services were typically limited to such services as physical exams, laboratory procedures, X-rays, and very minor surgical procedures. Over time, however, advances in technology and the skills of the medical profession have made outpatient services much more sophisticated. Procedures that once were offered only on an inpatient basis are now done routinely as outpatient services. Cardiac catheterization is one such example. Lumpectomies for breast cancer diagnosis and treatment are now also done on an outpatient basis in many cases.

Outpatient services are generally regarded as less costly than inpatient services to deliver. As a result, reimbursement schemes from private and government payers have begun to favor outpatient services when technology allows for their safe and effective application. Patients and providers often prefer the outpatient environment as well. These factors have been instrumental in fueling the growth of the outpatient components of the healthcare system (Hussey et al. 2014; Kaplan 2012).

Typically, outpatient services are provided in physician offices, outpatient departments of hospitals, ambulatory surgery centers, emergency rooms, urgent care centers, laboratory services centers, radiology centers, community health centers, and mobile hospitals. Outpatient services can even be provided in patients' homes, particularly in the case of home health, hospice, and palliative care services. Outpatient services can also be provided via telemedicine, an area that is rapidly gaining importance in the overall healthcare armamentarium (AHA 2017, 2018c; Burke and Hall 2015; Zanaboni and Wootton 2012).

Outpatient services have become increasingly important for hospital organizations. Nearly 50 percent of total hospital revenue is now derived from such services (AHA 2018b).

Primary Care

When we think of outpatient services, we often think of primary care. A fundamental area of healthcare delivery, primary care is what most people need most of the time to meet their common medical needs. The Institute of Medicine (IOM) defines *primary care* as "the provision of integrated, accessible health care services by clinicians who are accountable for addressing a large majority of personal health care needs, developing a sustained partnership with patients, and practicing in the context of family and community" (Yordy and Vanselow 1994). Primary care often serves as patients' entry point into the healthcare system, and it plays an important role in helping them sort out their medical needs (WHO 2008, 2019b).

Many countries have healthcare systems that are built on a primary care base. Until recently, however, the US healthcare system has placed relatively little emphasis on primary care. If the US healthcare system is to improve in a meaningful way, it will likely need to be reengineered with a greater primary care focus.

According to the World Health Organization (2019b), primary care has three essential aspects:

- Meeting people's health needs throughout their lives
- Addressing the broader determinants of health through multisectoral policy and action
- Empowering individuals, families, and communities to take charge of their own health

Similarly, the IOM stresses that the primary care be integrated, comprehensive, coordinated, and continuous; it further emphasizes accessibility and accountability as two essential attributes (Yordy and Vanselow 1994).

Primary care is important to the healthcare system for a number of reasons. Typically, primary care will provide a more longitudinal view of the patient than episodic care does. Many patients have known their family physician, internist, or other primary care provider for many years and are comfortable visiting that provider before they go elsewhere. Furthermore, health education and counseling on preventive measures are becoming increasingly important in our efforts to improve people's health status, and most preventive services, including early diagnostics, are done in primary care settings. Given the number of health problems in the United States stemming from preventable causes, interventions by primary care providers will be critical for bringing about improvement.

Primary Care Settings

The following sections will examine major categories of primary care settings.

Medical Practices

Medical practices can take a wide range of forms, from a small solo practice, to a medium-sized group practice, to an organized practice with hundreds or even thousands of providers. Medical practices have grown larger and more complex over time, offering a wider range of services and specialty care to their patients. This progressive development is illustrated in exhibit 5.7. Medical practices today are a common feature of integrated healthcare delivery systems, hospital organizations, and accountable care organizations (ACOs). In fact, an entity must include a medical practice if it is to be considered an ACO (CMS 2019a).

Specialized outpatient clinics, a type of medical practice, provide specialty services in such areas as pain management, mental health, urology, cardiology, or neurologic care. Virtually any care that can be delivered on an outpatient basis could be the focus of a specialty clinic. Specialty clinics may be part of a group practice, they may exist within integrated delivery systems or hospitals, or they may stand alone (Wagner 2017).

Community Health Centers

The community health center (CHC) model emerged in the 1960s as part of the "War on Poverty" under President Lyndon B. Johnson. The concept combined the resources of local communities with federal funds to establish

EXHIBIT 5.7
Medical Practice
Taxonomy

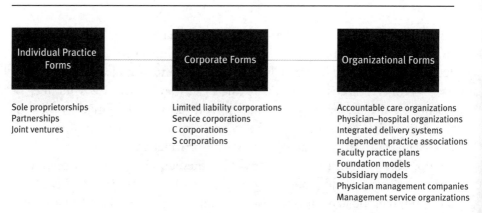

Individual Practice Forms	Corporate Forms	Organizational Forms
Sole proprietorships	Limited liability corporations	Accountable care organizations
Partnerships	Service corporations	Physician–hospital organizations
Joint ventures	C corporations	Integrated delivery systems
	S corporations	Independent practice associations
		Faculty practice plans
		Foundation models
		Subsidiary models
		Physician management companies
		Management service organizations

neighborhood clinics in both rural and urban areas throughout the United States. The CHC model was championed by H. Jack Geiger and patterned after neighborhood clinics he had observed in South Africa. Geiger was also a founder of Physicians for Human Rights and an activist for healthcare issues for the poor (National Association of Community Health Centers 2019).

CHCs in the United States often provide primary care to underserved communities, with federal and state support helping to cover costs. The centers can be especially important for rural communities where the population base is not large enough to support thriving practices. Often, elderly or poor members of those communities have great difficulty accessing care that requires transportation or knowledge of where appropriate care is available.

According to the National Association of Community Health Centers (2019), CHCs serve as the primary medical home for more than 28 million people in 11,000 rural and urban communities across the United States; hence, they need continued support.

Urgent Care Centers

Urgent care centers are outpatient facilities designed to provide services to patients who have illnesses or injuries that are not life-threatening but that require immediate attention. Patients can receive services at an urgent care center when they are unable to wait for an appointment with their primary care physician. In many cases, urgent care visits can replace trips to the hospital emergency room and provide the necessary services at a lower cost (Weinick, Burns, and Mehrotra 2010).

Pharmacies

Pharmacies can provide a variety of important services for patients. In addition to dispensing prescription medications and information about safety and drug interactions, some pharmacies offer basic medical services such as flu immunizations and blood pressure checks (Shi and Singh 2010). In a number of European countries, such as France, pharmacies act as an important entry point for primary care, and all registered pharmacists are trained as emergency medical technicians.

A brief story, based on actual events, can help illustrate the value of this approach. A young American tourist was visiting France and ate a traditional French crêpe, unaware that she was allergic to one of the ingredients, buckwheat. Soon after, she began to experience an allergic reaction. She and a friend went into a pharmacy, hoping to get something to counteract the allergic reaction. The pharmacist looked at the woman, realized immediately that she was going into anaphylactic shock, and administered first aid. An ambulance then took the woman to the hospital, where she was treated and had a full recovery.

In this story, the pharmacy's role as an entry point for care allowed for quick assessment and treatment, thereby avoiding more serious consequences. Furthermore, the large number of pharmacy locations in French cities equates to a large number of entry points, offering expanded access to care for people throughout the community. When pharmacies serve multiple functions, they can fulfill important primary care needs and help keep healthcare costs lower. The delivery of primary care services at US pharmacies is likely to increase as patient acceptance grows and licensing expands.

Home Health Care

Home health care, as the name implies, provides services to patients within their own homes. This type of service may be appropriate for people with disabilities, the chronically ill, older adults, and people recovering from illnesses or injuries who require monitoring. The healthcare professionals providing these services may be nurses, occupational therapists, speech therapists, or physical therapists; often, case managers and social workers will be involved, depending on the patient's status (Murray 2007; Canadian Medical Association 2013). Hospice and palliative care may also be provided at home; this category of services will be discussed later in the chapter.

A host of outpatient services have been developed to provide care not just where people live but also where they work or go to school. Examples include employer-based or school-based health clinics. Such clinics aim to bring care as close to the patient as possible, reducing inconvenience to the patient and thereby improving access (White and Griffith 2019).

Hospital Emergency Departments

Most of us are familiar with hospital emergency departments, or emergency rooms (ERs). They offer a broad range of services and are well-equipped to deal with various injuries and illnesses, including those of a serious nature. Hospital ERs offer these services 24 hours a day, seven days a week, and are staffed by specially trained providers. These providers are supported by all the services available within the hospital, including clinical, laboratory, radiology, and social services, and as well as administrative services.

For patients who require extended treatment or who are too sick or injured to go home, the ER may serve as a gateway to a hospital stay. Other patients may only require diagnosis and the initiation of treatment at the ER, which can then be followed up by care in other outpatient settings (Pines et al. 2015). Unfortunately, the current US system inadvertently causes many people—particularly those who do not have a primary care provider or insurance and who often delay visits to a primary care practice because of the inability to pay—to use the ER as a primary care source, which leads to high costs (Robert Wood Johnson Foundation 2013).·

Some communities that do not have full-service hospitals have begun using freestanding ERs to provide the necessary emergency services. These freestanding ERs are often affiliated with larger medical centers or hospitals, so patients who require extended care can be transferred to other facilities for continued treatment. The use of freestanding ERs reduces the need for hospital beds and services that are costly and difficult to maintain in many smaller communities (Gutierrez et al. 2016).

Ambulatory Long-Term Care Services

A variety of long-term care services may be provided to older adults, people with disabilities, or others on an outpatient basis. These services are adjunct to those provided to patients in their home environments or other settings. Adult day programs, for instance, may allow patients to socialize and engage in various activities—including occupational therapy or physical therapy— that improve their quality of life. These services are independent from nursing home care and other long-term care settings, which will be discussed later in the chapter.

Outpatient Public Health Services

Public health services provided on an outpatient basis include immunization, health screenings such as blood pressure checks, prenatal care, and other preventive care. These services are usually managed by the local health department and supported by tax dollars and charitable contributions. Because the services at public health clinics are typically provided free of charge, they are often the only primary care services available to people with limited resources (American Public Health Association 2019; CDC Foundation 2019).

Many hospitals and healthcare organizations also offer public health services to help satisfy their charitable missions and community benefit requirements. Atrium Health (2019), a large healthcare system based in Charlotte, North Carolina, provides one excellent example. Each year, the system presents "Heart of a Champion Day," which offers free health screenings and health education for student athletes. The program aims to identify high-risk disorders in student athletes, educate student athletes and their parents about injury prevention, provide at-risk student athletes with treatment plans, ensure that previous injuries have been treated properly, discuss referral options recommended for further evaluation, and provide resources to establish a primary care physician. Each participating student athlete receives the following, free of charge (Atrium Health 2019):

- Review of medical history
- General sports screening for North and South Carolina
- Electrocardiogram (EKG)

- Echocardiogram (ECHO) if needed
- Orthopedic screening (musculoskeletal exam)
- Vision exam
- Access to a registered dietician

In 2018, the Atrium Health (2019) program served 1,587 high school student athletes and engaged the services of more than 350 volunteer providers from many specialties—a powerful demonstration of how the medical community can be engaged to provide important public health services and avoid preventable tragedies (Atrium Health 2019). We should note, however, that such charitable programs would probably not be needed if universal healthcare were available.

End-of-Life and Long-Term Care

As we go through life, our medical needs change. Most of us will experience services across the continuum of healthcare shown in exhibit 5.8. We receive care before we are born, and we are typically born with medical assistance. We receive childhood interventions, such as immunizations and preventive

EXHIBIT 5.8
The Continuum of Healthcare

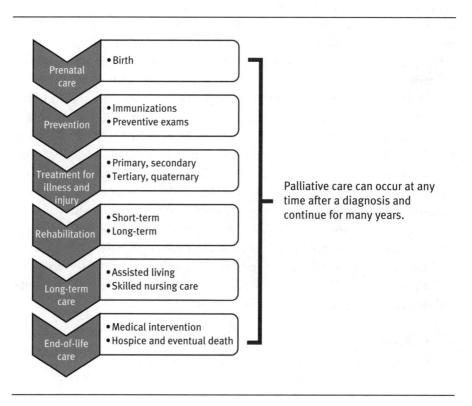

exams, to ensure proper development. Throughout our lives, we continue to need various levels of medical care—from minor primary care services to more serious tertiary and quaternary services, such as organ transplants. Often, an illness may leave us in need of rehabilitation services, in some cases leading to long-term care. As we age, most of us will need some assistance with activities of daily living (ADLs), such as eating, bathing, getting dressed, toileting, transferring, and continence (CMS 2018a). Some of us will need skilled nursing help to maintain the optimum level of function possible during the later years of our lives.

Of course, one of the certainties of life is death, and issues of end-of-life care eventually become a concern. Some question the wisdom of spending large sums of money on intensive care for people who are in their final stages of life and have no hope of recovery (Schneiderman 2011). On the other hand, who can question a well-intentioned desire to help a person's loved ones live as long as possible? The questions surrounding end-of-life care have no easy answers, but the data about the costs of such care can help us make better choices.

Cubanski and colleagues (2016) reviewed data from the National Center for Health Statistics (2016) and found that, of the 2.6 million people who died in the United States in 2014, 80 percent were Medicare patients and 55 percent were over the age of 80. Medicare in 2014 spent about 13.5 percent of its total budget on people in the last year of their lives (down from 18.6 percent in 2000). For the patients on Medicare who died in 2014, Medicare spent about $34,000 each—about three times what it spent on the average beneficiary. Of that $34,000, just over $3,300 was spent on hospice. These figures suggest that efforts are being made to reduce the use of unnecessary care but that hospice use likely needs to be increased in many cases.

Modern healthcare has increasingly come to recognize the importance of the continuum of healthcare as it develops new solutions for the healthcare system and considers needed reform and reengineering (Bélanger et al. 2014; Caulley, Gillick, and Lehmann 2018).

Promoting Function and Independence

We often think about aging in terms of two stages of our older years: the earlier years, when we are relatively healthy and active, and the later years, when our physical and mental abilities begin to change. During these later years, we will likely need assistance to ensure the best quality of life possible for the remainder of our lives.

The central aim of long-term care is to promote as much function and independence for the patient as possible. Long-term care is not delivered with a "one-size-fits-all" approach; services are delivered in accordance with a plan based on a needs assessment of the individual. Long-term care patients often need therapeutic care, nursing care, rehabilitative services, and social support, and such services can be informal or formal in nature. A person might receive, for instance, "meals on wheels" deliveries or visits from volunteers who provide support and social interaction. Ideally, the various types of care are well coordinated and provide for the patient's total needs.

Some retirement communities, known as *continuing care retirement communities* (CCRCs), seek to attend to patients' total needs by offering a continuum of services that can be varied to match each individual's present stage. Residents can begin with assisted living, where they live a virtually independent life at the facility, possibly with occasional monitoring and other nonmedical services; patients in this category usually need little if any help with ADLs. As the residents' needs change, they can move to higher levels of care and support, up to and including skilled nursing care.

The next several sections will discuss components of long-term care and some of the facilities that offer long-term services beyond residential support (White 2014; Sloane, Zimmerman, and D'Souza 2014).

Community-Based Services

Community-based services include adult daycare centers, home health care agencies, transportation services, respite care, and meal support programs. The US Department of Housing and Urban Development (2019) offers supportive housing services for seniors with low and moderate income; often these programs offer some assistance with meals and ADLs. Board and care homes are typically small, privately operated facilities that provide personal care and meals. They generally have 24-hour staffing but do not provide nursing and medical care. These facilities usually receive no federal or state funding.

Skilled Nursing Facilities

Skilled nursing facilities (SNFs), or nursing homes, offer 24-hour supervised, comprehensive, long-term care to chronically ill and elderly people who are no longer able to live at their home or in a less restrictive environment. These facilities provide housing, medical care (including regular evaluations and attention by physicians), therapeutic services, and personal care, which may include occupational therapy, physical therapy, recreational therapy, and careful attention to nutritional needs. SNFs must be licensed by the state and certified to receive Medicare and Medicaid funding. Requirements and regulations for all long-term care facilities, including SNFs, may vary from state to state.

Residents of SNFs usually stay for the long term. Occasionally, however, a person's admission might be episodic in nature, resulting from a temporary illness or injury that leaves the individual unable to live in a home environment but not suited to an acute care facility such as a hospital.

Long-Term Acute Care Hospitals

Long-term acute care hospitals (LTACHs) are highly specialized hospitals for the treatment of patients needing extended hospitalization (more than 25 days) and intensive care for serious illness or injury. They were developed as a result of the Medicare, Medicaid, and SCHIP Balanced Budget Refinement Act of 1999 (US Congress 1999). Though the conditions and technologies have changed, LTACHs are in some ways reminiscent of the early-1900s sanatoriums that treated people who had tuberculosis or other chronic diseases and required lengthy hospital stays. Today, patients at LTACHs tend to have greater disease and injury severity than those at SNFs. Many LTACH residents, for instance, require mechanical ventilation to breathe, often in connection with spinal cord injuries. These more complex needs are reflected in the cost: LTACHs are more expensive than SNFs (Makam et al. 2018).

LTACHs can be nonprofit or for profit, and they usually follow one of two models:

1. Hospital-within-hospital LTACHs are physically located inside of an acute care hospital and function as a separate unit of the hospital.
2. Freestanding LTACHs are separate facilities and operate as stand-alone entities.

LTACHs also can be associated with a healthcare system.

Intermediate Care Facilities for Individuals with Intellectual Disability

Intermediate care facilities for individuals with intellectual disability (ICF/IDs) are specialized long-term care facilities that provide comprehensive, individualized, and rehabilitative services to individuals with developmental disabilities (CMS 2019b). They are intended to promote functional status and independence for people requiring active treatment. Most are funded by the Medicaid program.

ICF/IDs provide specialized and generic training, treatment, health, and nutritional services, while also ensuring patient protection, behavioral support, and positive environments. They are required to have evaluations and individualized program plans (IPPs) constructed by an interdisciplinary team for each patient. Each facility must have a governing body of management, be licensed and surveyed by the state, and be certified by Medicaid to receive payment (CMS 2019b).

Long-Term Care Administration

Unlike acute care hospitals, most nursing homes and long-term care facilities require administrators to be licensed by the state. This licensure requires an intensive course of study and the completion of an examination (National Association of Long Term Care Administrator Boards 2019).

Hospice and Palliative Care

In some instances, hospice and palliative care may be preferable to traditional healthcare services at the end of a person's life. Hospice and palliative care both offer comprehensive services for the terminally ill, though the types of services differ. Palliative care can begin at the time of diagnosis and is intended to make the patient feel better; it can be concomitant with treatment for the condition and may go on for years. It often involves pain management, cognitive behavioral therapy, and spiritual counseling.

Hospice, on the other hand, begins after treatment of the condition has been discontinued and the patient is not expected to survive for more than six months. During hospice, specially trained professionals and caregivers provide care of a holistic nature, attending to physical, emotional, social, and spiritual needs. Specific services may include physical care, counseling, drugs, therapy, assistance with ADLs, and the use of equipment and supplies for the terminal illness or related conditions. This care is usually given in the home, though inpatient hospice facilities are available for more debilitated patients (CMS 2019c; Prina 2017). Whether inpatient or outpatient, hospice enables people who are facing death in the near term to spend time with family.

Palliative care and hospice are different, but they are not mutually exclusive. Often, hospice patients receive palliative care to maximize their comfort and help them live their last days to the fullest (Kelley and Morrison 2015; Medline Plus 2018; Prina 2017).

Special Healthcare Systems in the United States

The federal government of the United States operates two separate healthcare systems targeted at specific population groups: the Veterans Health Administration (VHA) and the Indian Health Service (IHS).

The Veterans Health Administration

The VHA is part of the US Department of Veterans Affairs (VA). The mission of the VA (2018a) is "To fulfill President Lincoln's promise 'To care for him who shall have borne the battle, and for his widow, and his orphan' by serving and honoring the men and women who are America's veterans." The

VHA, the largest integrated healthcare system in the United States, provides care at 1,255 healthcare facilities, which includes 170 medical centers and 1,074 outpatient clinics (VHA 2019). The system serves approximately 9 million enrolled veterans each year.

VA healthcare coverage is available for veterans; for family members of certain veterans who became disabled or died in combat; and, in certain cases, for veterans' children who have spina bifida (VHA 2019). Veterans enrolled in VA healthcare do not need to take additional coverage, and their out-of-pocket costs were not changed by the Affordable Care Act (VA 2018b).

The Indian Health Service

The IHS provides a variety of health services to federally recognized tribes of Native Americans and Alaskan Natives. According to its website, "The IHS is the principal federal health care provider and health advocate for Indian people, and its goal is to raise their health status to the highest possible level" (IHS 2019). The IHS serves approximately 2.6 million American Indians and Alaska Natives belonging to 573 federally recognized tribes in 37 states.

Integration and Modern Structural Forms

The components of the US healthcare system continue to evolve as a result of reform efforts and other changes in the landscape, and a number of emerging structural forms and concepts merit discussion here. They include integrated delivery systems, accountable care organizations, clinically integrated networks, and patient-centered medical homes.

Integrated Delivery Systems

Although a detailed discussion of integrated delivery systems (IDSs) is beyond the scope of this book, a brief overview is relevant to anyone with an interest in healthcare delivery or administration. Enthoven (2009) defines an IDS as "an organized, coordinated, and collaborative network that links various healthcare providers to provide a coordinated, vertical continuum of services to a particular patient population or community."

An IDS can be vertically integrated, horizontally integrated, or both. In vertical integration, organizations providing similar services are joined together by merger, acquisition, or other affiliation agreements. In horizontal integration, organizations providing different services are joined together. Ultimately, the IDS becomes a larger organization capable of providing a wide variety of services to its patients. In some cases, IDSs may include an insurance arm, thereby becoming involved in the financing as well as the provision of services.

All structural forms have their pros and cons, and certainly IDSs are no exception. Potential pros include the following:

- Integration may create economies of scale and improve cost-effectiveness.
- The scope of service can be broadened.
- Integration can enable greater access to capital, because of the larger financial base.
- More specialty staff with greater expertise can be hired.
- Competition may be eroded, given the generally low level of antitrust activity in healthcare in recent decades. (This point could be a pro or con depending on who you are.)

Cons include the following:

- Friction with physicians is common. Many physicians work better independently than they do in large integrated organizations.
- Decisions need to be made differently in large integrated practices. Members coming from smaller organizations may not be accustomed to the process.
- Seamless integration of information systems is necessary but often hard to achieve.
- Changes in work flow may be resisted by stakeholders, and standardizing processes to reduce variation can be difficult.
- Changes in policies must be reconciled, which can be difficult and costly. Various government regulations may require enhancement of the benefit packages (e.g., pension, health benefits) of the acquiring organization to comply with nondiscrimination rules (IRS 2019c).

A 2013 review article by Hwang and colleagues looked at 21 studies comparing IDS performance to the performance of other organizational forms. The review found that the clear majority of IDSs showed an improvement in the quality of care provided to patients; however, only one study showed an increase in cost savings, and none showed a decrease in utilization (Hwang et al. 2013).

Accountable Care Organizations

A central feature of the ACA, accountable care organizations (ACOs) represent one of the most important recent developments in the structure of healthcare organizations. An ACO is a group of providers who share responsibility for a population of patients with regard to the quality, cost, and coordination of their care. Whereas IDSs are a broad category of organizations, ACOs are more specific. All ACOs are probably IDSs, but not all IDSs are ACOs (Jacobs 2015).

In many ways, ACOs are more defined by what they do than by how they are structured. The goal of an ACO is to provide coordinated care, and the goal of coordinated care is to ensure that patients get the right care at the right time, while avoiding unnecessary duplication of services and preventing medical errors (Bennett 2012; CMS 2019a). Specifically, ACOs aim to

- improve population health,
- improve patient experience, and
- reduce total cost.

These goals are similar to concept of the Triple Aim, which has been discussed in other chapters of this book.

An ACO can be any combination of group practices, networks of practices, hospitals, or hospital-employed physicians and providers. All ACOs must include physicians in their membership. ACOs can be joint ventures, with the proviso that they must be able to receive and distribute payments. All the members of the organization do not have to be a single entity; they can be bound together by contract. ACOs work with various insurers to achieve improved health outcomes.

Most of the arrangements with the payers and the ACO involve incentives for reducing cost, so that the ACO receives monetary payments if agreed-upon targets are met. A central aspect of the ACO is to provide better preventive care, and, therefore, primary care physicians and providers are central to the ACO concept (Berwick 2011; CMS 2019a).

The formation of ACOs is encouraged under the Medicare Shared Savings Program (MSSP), which was established under section 3022 of the ACA. A key reform initiative in the Medicare delivery system, the MSSP was created to facilitate coordination and cooperation among providers to improve the quality of care for Medicare fee-for-service beneficiaries and to reduce unnecessary costs. The program aims to improve beneficiary outcomes and increase value of care by providing better care of individuals, providing better health for populations, and lowering growth in expenditures. Eligible providers, hospitals, and suppliers can participate in the MSSP by creating or participating in an ACO. The MSSP rewards ACOs that reduce their growth in healthcare costs while meeting performance standards on quality of care (CMS 2018b).

By the start of 2018, approximately 650 ACOs had been established in the United States (McWilliams et al. 2018).

Clinically Integrated Networks

Structuring organizations that include the full continuum of services needed by patients is a difficult endeavor. One approach to this challenge has been the creation of clinically integrated networks. Although the concept of clinical integration is sometimes vague, the AHA (2019) provides some clarity: "Clinical integration is needed to facilitate the coordination of patient care across conditions, providers, settings, and time in order to achieve care that is safe, timely, effective, efficient, equitable and patient-focused." The organization adds: "To achieve clinical integration we need to promote changes in provider culture, redesign payment methods and incentives, and modernize federal laws."

In most cases, clinical integration is achieved through contracts and other agreements between groups of healthcare providers and institutions, enabling them to provide care to a common group of patients in a more coordinated and consistent way. These agreements, in effect, create a virtual organization that can provide care seamlessly to the patients (*Becker's Hospital Review* 2012). Specific elements that need to be achieved for effective clinical integration include the following:

- Collaborative leadership
- Complaint resolution legal structure
- Culture change
- Value-based compensation
- High performance
- Clinical programs and disease programs
- Clinical metrics
- Technology infrastructure
- Disease registries
- Patient portal to enable engagement
- Governance body
- Payer strategy
- Aligned physicians/incentives
- Program infrastructure
- Network physician leadership and support
- Care protocols
- Population health management
- Health information exchange

- Patient longitudinal record
- Contract and payment administration

Patient-Centered Medical Homes

The patient-centered medical home (PCMH), a concept first introduced by Edward H. Wagner (1998), is focused on prevention and early intervention for patient care, which is especially important for the chronically ill. The PCMH provides the patient with a single location that serves as a starting point for all medical concerns, thereby offering greater continuity of care and expert guidance to the healthcare delivery system. Any physician practice can become a PCMH by adhering to certain principles and standards set forth by the National Committee for Quality Assurance (2019).

The six basic requirements for becoming a PCMH are as follows (Philip, Govier, and Pantely 2019):

1. *Team-based care.* All members of the practice must be engaged in partnerships with patients, families, and caregivers to provide for the patient's needs.
2. *Know and manage patients.* The practice must collect data and adhere to standards for population health management.
3. *Patient-centered access and continuity.* The practice must be able to provide needed care 24 hours a day.
4. *Care management and support.* The practice must support evidence-based guidelines for prevention and for acute and chronic care management.
5. *Care coordination and care transitions.* The practice must track and coordinate test referrals and care transitions.
6. *Performance measurement and quality improvement.* The practice must use data and experience for continuous improvement.

Creating an effective PCMH, like so many things in the healthcare world, is all about mind-set. It requires a deep understanding of what the organization wishes to accomplish, why the organization is doing it, and how the model can best be implemented. Ironically, in creating such a complex organization, we must always seek to simplify. If we do not take adequate time to think through the various concerns, we risk "bolting on" processes, procedures, and entities to the point that our systems become incredibly difficult and complex. In fact, the payment system used in US healthcare inadvertently encourages this lack of thinking through, because it leads practices to focus on "billable" activities, leaving little time for planning and process improvement.

Consider waiting time, for instance. Our scheduling structure has been largely dictated by our payment system, with practices determining what number of patients they need to see in a given period to make the budget work. As a result, patients might be scheduled for a 15-minute appointment even though, realistically, their concerns cannot possibly be addressed in such a short time. Then, as visits run long, waiting times increase. With modern data analytics, we should be able to match appointment times with patients' specified needs and demographic characteristics, ensuring that, for instance, patients who are older or have more complex needs receive more time than patients with more straightforward concerns. To an extent, many organizations already engage in this type of scheduling, but the typical 15-, 30-, and 45-minute options simply do not allow the flexibility to accommodate the variety of patients the typical practice sees while running an efficient schedule that stays on time.

With regard to wait times and numerous other issues, we need to think deeply about our problems and work to design novel solutions. We should also look to use technology to truly change the way we do things—not just to do the same things faster or marginally better. Paying for outcome, as opposed to paying for individual services, will improve many such problems because organizations will be able to better address patient needs without being confined by a services limitation (e.g., seeing a set number of patients every day) (Ewing 2013; Fleming et al. 2017; Jackson and Williams 2015; Sinaiko et al. 2017).

Sinaiko and colleagues (2017) analyzed studies of patient outcomes in PCMHs. Although the PCMH initiatives studied were generally not associated with significant changes in most outcomes, the initiatives were associated with the following:

- A reduction in the use of specialty visits
- An increase in cervical cancer screening
- A reduction in total spending
- An increase in breast cancer screening among higher-morbidity patients

These associations were significant. Sinaiko and colleagues (2017) concluded that "Identification of the components of PCMHs likely to improve outcomes is critical to decisions about investing resources in primary care."

Other Major Components of the Healthcare System

Pharmaceutical, insurance, and managed care companies are also important components of the US healthcare system, and they will be addressed specifically in chapters 8 and 11. As shown in exhibit 5.9, some of the largest US

Name	Industry Segment	Location
McKesson Corporation	Drug stores, pharmacy benefit managers (PBMs), and distributors	California
UnitedHealth Group, Inc.	Payers	Minnesota
CVS Health Corporation	Drug stores, PBMs, and distributors	Rhode Island
Amerisource Bergen Corporation	Drug stores, PBMs, and distributors	Pennsylvania
Cardinal Health Inc.	Drug stores, PBMs, and distributors	Ohio
Walgreens Boots Alliance, Inc.	Drug stores, PBMs, and distributors	Illinois
Express Scripts Holding	Drug stores, PBMs, and distributors	Missouri
Anthem Inc.	Drug stores, PBMs, and distributors	Indiana
Johnson & Johnson	Pharmaceuticals	New Jersey
Aetna Inc.	Payers	Connecticut
Humana Inc.	Payers	Kentucky
Pfizer Inc.	Pharmaceuticals	New York
HCA Holdings Inc.	Providers	Tennessee
Centene Corporation	Payers	Missouri
Merck & Co, Inc.	Pharmaceuticals	New Jersey
Cigna Corporation	Payers	Connecticut
Rite Aid Corporation	Drug stores	Pennsylvania
Gilead Sciences, Inc.	Biotechnology	California
Medtronic PLC	Medical devices	Dublin, Ireland
AbbVie Inc.	Biotechnology	Illinois

EXHIBIT 5.9
The Largest Healthcare Companies by Revenue (2016)

Note: PLC = public limited company.
Source: Visnji (2019).

healthcare companies are payers and pharmaceutical firms. Traditionally, such companies have been stand-alone entities, but as exhibit 5.10 illustrates, they are rapidly becoming part of a more aligned and integrated system of healthcare delivery.

EXHIBIT 5.10

Taxonomy of Healthcare Organization Integration

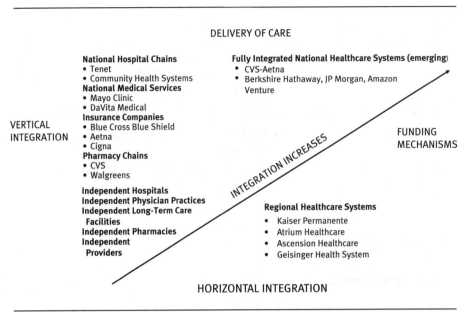

DELIVERY OF CARE

National Hospital Chains
• Tenet
• Community Health Systems
National Medical Services
• Mayo Clinic
• DaVita Medical
Insurance Companies
• Blue Cross Blue Shield
• Aetna
• Cigna
Pharmacy Chains
• CVS
• Walgreens

Fully Integrated National Healthcare Systems (emerging)
• CVS-Aetna
• Berkshire Hathaway, JP Morgan, Amazon Venture

VERTICAL INTEGRATION

FUNDING MECHANISMS

INTEGRATION INCREASES

Independent Hospitals
Independent Physician Practices
Independent Long-Term Care Facilities
Independent Pharmacies
Independent Providers

Regional Healthcare Systems
• Kaiser Permanente
• Atrium Healthcare
• Ascension Healthcare
• Geisinger Health System

HORIZONTAL INTEGRATION

Organization Governance

Simply put, organization governance is the system by which healthcare organizations are directed and controlled (Finch 1994b). For corporations—which is what most modern healthcare organizations are—governance is the responsibility of the board of directors (Arnwine 2002).

Mission, vision, and values are fundamental concepts of organization governance, as shown in exhibit 5.11. Essentially, the mission represents the organization's reason for existing, the vision expresses its aspirations for the future, and the values determine how the organization will achieve its mission and vision. The mission, vision, and values should be well known by every person within the organization, and they should be reflected in every decision made. For example, if a healthcare organization has a mission of caring for all citizens in the community regardless of their ability to pay, requiring payment at the time of service or denying care to patients unable to pay would be inappropriate. The mission, vision, and values are also key elements in determining the organization's strategic plan and the way the organization will develop and execute its plans; that development and execution, in turn, will determine the organization's operations and the way it will be managed.

Exhibit 5.12 illustrates the relationships between the components of the governance process. The board of directors links the external stakeholders with the CEO and senior management. Management is then responsible for leading the organization and its employees and for executing the strategic plan—within the context of the mission, vision, and values—to produce the

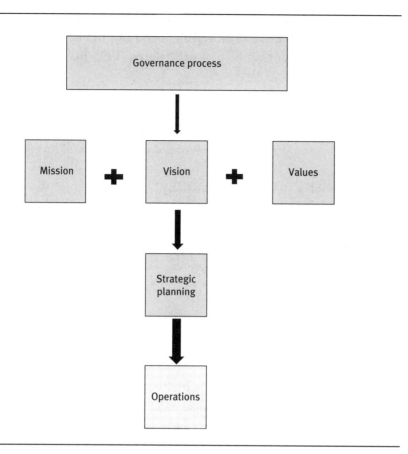

EXHIBIT 5.11
Mission, Vision, and Values

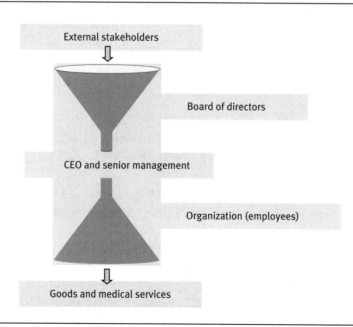

EXHIBIT 5.12
Components of the Governance Process

intended goods and services. These relationships place critical checks and balances on the influence of all stakeholders, and the integrity of the organization requires that they be honored (Biggs 2011; Jha and Epstein 2010; Kovner and Lemak 2015).

The understanding of and adherence to the norms of proper governance are essential for the ethical function of any organization, and they enable our society to function in a sophisticated manner. The reader is encouraged to seek additional information on governance through the following resources:

- Board Source (www.boardsource.org)
- The Corporate Directors Forum (www.directorsforum.com)
- The American College of Healthcare Executives (www.ache.org)
- The Governance Institute (www.governanceinstitute.com)
- The National Association of Corporate Boards (www.nacdonline.org)

Discussion Questions

1. Is our healthcare system too complex to produce the results we want?
2. What trends are apparent in the healthcare institutional landscape today?
3. Describe the various institutional forms in the US healthcare system.
4. Looking to the future, how large will healthcare organizations become?
5. What similarities or parallels exist between the US healthcare system and the financial services industry?
6. How do you think our healthcare institutional structures will evolve in the future?

References

Agarwal, R., O. Mazurenko, and N. Menachemi. 2017. "High-Deductible Health Plans Reduce Health Care Cost and Utilization, Including Use of Needed Preventive Services." *Health Affairs* 36 (10): 1762–68. https://doi.org/10.1377/hlthaff.2017.0610.

Alight. 2019. "Healthcare Fast Facts—Largest Hospital Systems in America." Accessed October 24. https://ideas.alight.com/consumer-healthcare-education/healthcare-fast-facts-top-30-largest-hospital-systems-in-america.

American Hospital Association (AHA). 2019. "Clinical Integration." Accessed October 1. www.aha.org/websites/2012-09-12-clinical-integration.

———. 2018a. *AHA Hospital Statistics, 2018 Edition.* Chicago: American Hospital Association. www.aha.org/statistics/2016-12-27-aha-hospital-statistics-2018-edition.

———. 2018b. "Fast Facts on US Hospitals." Accessed October 1, 2019. www.aha. org/system/files/2018-02/2018-aha-hospital-fast-facts.pdf.

———. 2018c. *Rural Chartbook*. www.aha.org/ensuringaccess.

———. 2017. "Emerging Strategies to Ensure Access to Health Care Services." Published November 16. www.aha.org/system/files/2018-06/task-force-emergency-medical-center.pdf.

American Public Health Association (APHA). 2019. "What Is Public Health?" Accessed September 30. www.apha.org/what-is-public-health.

Arnwine, D. L. 2002. "Effective Governance: The Roles and Responsibilities of Board Members." *Baylor University Medical Center Proceedings* 15: 19–22. www. ncbi.nlm.nih.gov/pmc/articles/PMC1276331/pdf/bumc0015-0019.pdf.

Atrium Health. 2019. "Health Screenings for Student Athletes." Accessed September 30. https://atriumhealth.org/medical-services/specialty-care/heart-care/ heart-of-a-champion.

Becker, S., M. Cerny, and A. Timmerman. 2011. "Hospital Tax-Exempt Status: Considerations Regarding Maintaining Exempt Status." *Becker's Hospital Review*. Published May 10. www.beckershospitalreview.com/hospital-management-administration/hospital-tax-exempt-status-considerations-regarding-maintaining-exempt-status.html.

Becker's Hospital Review. 2015a. "10 Largest For-Profit Hospital Systems." Published June 30. www.beckershospitalreview.com/lists/10-largest-for-profit-hospital-systems-2015.html.

———. 2015b. "20 Largest Nonprofit Hospital Systems." Published December 21. www.beckershospitalreview.com/lists/20-largest-nonprofit-hospital-systems-2015.html.

———. 2012. "The 7 Components of a Clinical Integration Network." Published October 19. www.beckershospitalreview.com/hospital-physician-relationships/the-7-components-of-a-clinical-integration-network.html.

Bélanger, E., C. Rodríguez, D. Groleau, F. Légaré, M. E. Macdonald, and R. Marchand. 2014. "Initiating Decision-Making Conversations in Palliative Care: An Ethnographic Discourse Analysis." *BMC Palliative Care* 13: 63. https://doi. org/10.1186/1472-684X-13-63.

Bennett, A. R. 2012. "Accountable Care Organizations: Principles and Implications for Hospital Administrators." *Journal of Healthcare Management* 57 (4): 244–54. https://doi.org/10.1097/00115514-201207000-00005.

Bernell, S., and S. W. Howard. 2016. "Use Your Words Carefully: What Is a Chronic Disease?" *Frontiers in Public Health* 4: 159. https://doi.org/10.3389/ fpubh.2016.00159.

Berwick, D. M. 2011. "Making Good on ACOs' Promise—The Final Rule for the Medicare Shared Savings Program." *New England Journal of Medicine* 365 (19): 1753–56. https://doi.org/10.1056/NEJMp1111671.

Berwick, D. M., and A. D. Hackbarth. 2012. "Eliminating Waste in US Health Care." *JAMA* 307 (14): 1513–16. https://doi.org/10.1001/jama.2012.362.

Biggs, E. 2011. *Healthcare Governance: A Guide for Effective Boards.* Chicago: Health Administration Press.

Bipartisan Policy Center. 2018. *Reinventing Rural Health Care: A Case Study of Seven Upper Midwest States.* Published January. https://bipartisanpolicy.org/wp-content/uploads/2018/01/BPC-Health-Reinventing-Rural-Health-Care-1.pdf.

Bodenheimer, T. 2008. "Coordinating Care—A Perilous Journey Through the Health Care System." *New England Journal of Medicine* 358 (10): 1064–71. https://doi.org/10.1056/NEJMhpr0706165.

Burke, B. L., and R. W. Hall. 2015. "Telemedicine: Pediatric Applications." *Pediatrics* 136 (1): e293–308. https://doi.org/10.1542/peds.2015-1517.

Canadian Medical Association. 2013. "Health and Health Care for an Aging Population." Published December. www.cma.ca/sites/default/files/2018-11/CMA_Policy_Health_and_Health_Care_for_an_Aging-Population_PD14-03-e_0.pdf.

Case Briefs. 2003. *IHC Health Plans, Inc. v. Commissioner of Internal Revenue (I).* Accessed September 30, 2019. www.casebriefs.com/blog/law/health-law/health-law-keyed-to-furrow/the-structure-of-the-health-care-enterprise/ihc-health-plans-inc-v-commissioner-of-internal-revenue-i/.

Caulley, L., M. R. Gillick, and L. S. Lehmann. 2018. "Substitute Decision Making in End-of-Life Care." *New England Journal of Medicine* 378 (24): 2339–41. https://doi.org/10.1056/NEJMclde1800817.

CDC Foundation. 2019. "What Is Public Health?" Accessed September 30. www.cdcfoundation.org/what-public-health.

Centers for Disease Control and Prevention (CDC). 2018. "Hospital Utilization (in Non-Federal Short-Stay Hospitals)." Accessed October 27. www.cdc.gov/nchs/fastats/hospital.htm.

Centers for Medicare & Medicaid Services (CMS). 2019a. "Accountable Care Organizations (ACOs): General Information." Updated September 24. https://innovation.cms.gov/initiatives/aco/.

———. 2019b. "Intermediate Care Facilities for Individuals with Intellectual Disability." Accessed October 1. www.medicaid.gov/medicaid/ltss/institutional/icfid/index.html.

———. 2019c. *Medicare Hospice Benefits.* Revised February. www.medicare.gov/Pubs/pdf/02154-Medicare-Hospice-Benefits.PDF.

———. 2018a. "Activities of Daily Living (ADLs)." Accessed September 30, 2019. www.cms.gov/research-statistics-data-and-systems/research/mcbs/downloads/2008_appendix_b.pdf.

———. 2018b. *Medicare Shared Savings Program: Accountable Care Organization (ACO) 2018 Quality Measures: Narrative Specifications Document.* Published January 20. www.cms.gov/Medicare/Medicare-Fee-for-Service-Payment/sharedsavingsprogram/Downloads/2018-reporting-year-narrative-specifications.pdf.

———. 2013. "Critical Access Hospitals." Updated April 9. www.cms.gov/medicare/provider-enrollment-and-certification/certificationandcomplianc/cahs.html.

———. 2004. "CMS Issues Guidance for Exceptions to Specialty Hospital Moratorium." Published March 19. www.cms.gov/newsroom/press-releases/cms-issues-guidance-exceptions-specialty-hospital-moratorium.

Cheney, C. 2017. "Top 5 Differences Between NFPs and For-Profit Hospitals." HealthLeaders. Published June 20. www.healthleadersmedia.com/finance/top-5-differences-between-nfps-and-profit-hospitals.

Coyne, J. S., M. T. Richards, R. Short, K. Shultz, and S. G. Singh. 2009. "Hospital Cost and Efficiency: Do Hospital Size and Ownership Type Really Matter?" *Journal of Healthcare Management* 54 (3): 163–75. https://doi.org/10.1097/00115514-200905000-00005.

Cubanski, J., T. Neuman, S. Griffin, and A. Damico. 2016. "Medicare Spending at the End of Life—Findings." Kaiser Family Foundation. Published July 14. www.kff.org/report-section/medicare-spending-at-the-end-of-life-findings/.

David, G., C. Gunnarsson, P. A. Saynisch, R. Chawla, and S. Nigam. 2015. "Do Patient-Centered Medical Homes Reduce Emergency Department Visits?" *Health Services Research* 50 (2): 418–39. https://doi.org/10.1111/1475-6773.12218.

Davis, C. 2011. "Nonprofit Hospitals and Community Benefit." Issue Brief. National Health Law Network. Published July. https://healthjusticenetwork.files.wordpress.com/2011/07/nhelp_community_benefit.pdf.

Devereaux, P., D. Heels-Ansdell, C. Lacchetti, T. Haines, K. E. Burns, D. J. Cook, N. Ravindran, S. D. Walter, H. McDonald, S. B. Stone, R. Patel, M. Bhandari, H. J. Schünemann, P. T.-L. Choi, A. M. Bayoumi, J. N. Lavis, T. Sullivan, G. Stoddart, and G. H. Guyatt. 2004. "Payments for Care at Private For-Profit and Private Not-for-Profit Hospitals: A Systematic Review and Meta-Analysis." *Canadian Medical Association Journal* 170 (12): 1817–24. https://doi.org/10.1503/cmaj.1040722.

Enthoven, A. C. 2009. "Integrated Delivery Systems: The Cure for Fragmentation." *American Journal of Managed Care* 15 (10 Suppl.): S284–90. www.ncbi.nlm.nih.gov/pubmed/20088632.

Eskoz, R., and K. M. Peddecord. 1985. "The Relationship of Hospital Ownership and Service Composition to Hospital Charges." *Health Care Financing Review* 6 (3): 51–58. www.ncbi.nlm.nih.gov/pmc/articles/PMC4191480/.

Ewing, M. 2013. "The Patient-Centered Medical Home Solution to the Cost-Quality Conundrum. *Journal of Healthcare Management* 58 (4): 258–66. https://doi.org/10.1097/00115514-201307000-00005.

Facility Guidelines Institute. 2018. *Guidelines for Design and Construction of Hospitals and Outpatient Facilities*. Chicago: American Society for Healthcare Engineering. www.fgiguidelines.org/guidelines/2018-fgi-guidelines/#.

Finch, J. 1994a. "Hospitals: Definition and Classification." In *Speller's Law Relating to Hospitals*, 7th ed., by John Finch, 1–17. Boston: Springer. https://doi.org/10.1007/978-1-4899-7122-7_1.

———. 1994b. "Voluntary Hospitals." In *Speller's Law Relating to Hospitals*, 7th ed., by John Finch, 73–81. Boston: Springer. https://doi.org/10.1007/978-1-4899-7122-7_3.

Fleming, N. S., B. da Graca, G. O. Ogola, S. D. Culler, J. Austin, P. McConnell, R. McCorkle, P. Aponte, M. Massey, and C. Fullerton. 2017. "Costs of Transforming Established Primary Care Practices to Patient-Centered Medical Homes (PCMHs)." *Journal of the American Board of Family Medicine* 30 (4): 460–71. https://doi.org/10.3122/jabfm.2017.04.170039.

Freeman, J. D., S. Kadiyala, J. F. Bell, and D. P. Martin. 2008. "The Causal Effect of Health Insurance on Utilization and Outcomes in Adults." *Medical Care* 46 (10): 1023–32. https://doi.org/10.1097/MLR.0b013e318185c913.

Gray, B. H. (ed.). 1986. *For-Profit Enterprise in Health Care*. Washington, DC: National Academies Press.

Greenwald, L., J. Cromwell, W. Adamache, S. Bernard, E. Drozd, E. Root, and K. Devers. 2006. "Specialty Versus Community Hospitals: Referrals, Quality, and Community Benefits." *Health Affairs* 25 (1): 106–18. https://doi.org/10.1377/hlthaff.25.1.106.

Gutierrez, C., R. A. Lindor, O. Baker, D. Cutler, and J. D. Schuur. 2016. "State Regulation of Freestanding Emergency Departments Varies Widely, Affecting Location, Growth, and Services Provided." *Health Affairs* 35 (10): 1857–66. https://doi.org/10.1377/hlthaff.2016.0412.

Healthcare Cost and Utilization Project (HCUP). 2018. "Healthcare Cost and Utilization Project (HCUP) Statistical Briefs." Accessed September 30, 2019. www.ncbi.nlm.nih.gov/pubmed/21413206.

Hensher, M., M. Price, and S. Adomakoh. 2006. "Referral Hospitals." In *Disease Control Priorities in Developing Countries*, edited by J. G. Jamison, 1229–43. Geneva: World Bank.

Herrera, C. A., G. Rada, L. Kuhn-Barrientos, and X. Barrios. 2014. "Does Ownership Matter? An Overview of Systematic Reviews of the Performance of Private For-Profit, Private Not-for-Profit and Public Healthcare Providers." *PLOS ONE* 9 (12): e93456. https://doi.org/10.1371/journal.pone.0093456.

Hussey, P. S., E. C. Schneider, R. S. Rudin, D. S. Fox, J. Lai, and C. E. Pollack. 2014. "Continuity and the Costs of Care for Chronic Disease." *JAMA Internal Medicine* 174 (5): 742–48. https://doi.org/10.1001/jamainternmed.2014.245.

Hwang, W., J. Chang, M. LaClair, and H. Paz. 2013. "Effects of Integrated Delivery System on Cost to Quality." *American Journal of Managed Care* 19 (5): e175–84. www.pcpcc.org/sites/default/files/resources/Effects of Integrated Delivery System on Cost and Quality.pdf.

Indian Health Service (IHS). 2019. "About IHS." Accessed October 29. www.ihs. gov/aboutihs/.

Internal Revenue Service (IRS). 2019a. "Community Health Needs Assessment for Charitable Hospital Organizations—Section 501(r)(3)." Updated September 20. www.irs.gov/charities-non-profits/community-health-needs-assessment-for-charitable-hospital-organizations-section-501r3.

———. 2019b. "Exemption Requirements—501(c)(3) Organizations." Reviewed August 7. www.irs.gov/charities-non-profits/charitable-organizations/exemption-requirements-501c3-organizations.

———. 2019c. "Publication 15-B (2019): Employer's Tax Guide to Fringe Benefits." Accessed October 1. www.irs.gov/publications/p15b.

Jackson, G. L., and J. W. Williams. 2015. "Does PCMH 'Work'? The Need to Use Implementation Science to Make Sense of Conflicting Results." *JAMA Internal Medicine* 175 (8): 1369–70. https://doi.org/10.1001/jamainternmed.2015.2067.

Jacobs, L. 2015. "A Truly Integrated Health Care System." *Hospitals & Health Networks* 89 (9): 12.

Jha, A., and A. Epstein. 2010. "Hospital Governance and the Quality of Care." *Health Affairs* 29 (1): 182–87. https://doi.org/10.1377/hlthaff.2009.0297.

The Joint Commission. 2019. "Facts About Critical Access Hospital Accreditation." Published September 24. www.jointcommission.org/facts_about_critical_access_hospital_accreditation/.

Kannampallil, T. G., G. F. Schauer, T. Cohen, and V. L. Patel. 2011. "Considering Complexity in Healthcare Systems." *Journal of Biomedical Informatics* 44 (6): 943–47. https://doi.org/10.1016/j.jbi.2011.06.006.

Kaplan, G. S. 2012. "Waste Not: The Management Imperative for Healthcare." *Journal of Healthcare Management* 57 (3): 160–66. https://doi.org/10.1097/00115514-201205000-00005.

Kelley, A. S., and R. S. Morrison. 2015. "Palliative Care for the Seriously Ill." *New England Journal of Medicine* 373 (8): 747–55. https://doi.org/10.1056/NEJMra1404684.

Kovner, A. R., and C. H. Lemak. 2015. "Managing and Governing Health Care Organizations." In *Jonas and Kovner's Health Care Delivery in the United States*, 11th ed., edited by J. R. Knickman and A. R. Kovner, 297–310. New York: Springer.

LaPointe, J. 2018. "6 Major Hospital Merger Deals Making Headlines in 2018." RevCycle Intelligence. Published January 4. https://revcycleintelligence.com/news/6-major-hospital-merger-deals-making-headlines-in-2018.

Lucas, J. W., D. J. Barr-Anderson, and R. S. Kington. 2003. "Health Status, Health Insurance, and Health Care Utilization Patterns of Immigrant Black Men." *American Journal of Public Health* 93 (10): 1740–47. https://doi.org/10.2105/AJPH.93.10.1740.

Makam, A. N., O. K. Nguyen, L. Xuan, M. E. Miller, J. S. Goodwin, and E. A. Halm. 2018. "Factors Associated with Variation in Long-Term Acute Care Hospital vs. Skilled Nursing Facility Use Among Hospitalized Older Adults." *JAMA Internal Medicine* 178 (3): 399–405. https://doi.org/10.1001/jamainternmed.2017.8467.

McGlynn, E. A., K. M. McDonald, and C. K. Cassel. 2015. "Measurement Is Essential for Improving Diagnosis and Reducing Diagnostic Error: A Report from the Institute of Medicine." *JAMA* 314 (23): 2501–2. https://doi.org/10.1001/jama.2015.13453.

McWilliams, J. M., L. A. Hatfield, B. E. Landon, P. Hamed, and M. E. Chernew. 2018. "Medicare Spending After 3 Years of the Medicare Shared Savings Program." *New England Journal of Medicine* 379 (12): 1139–49. https://doi.org/10.1056/NEJMsa1803388.

Medline Plus. 2019. "Acute vs. Chronic Conditions." Reviewed February 7. https://medlineplus.gov/ency/imagepages/18126.htm.

———. 2018. "What Is Palliative Care?" Reviewed January 14. https://medlineplus.gov/ency/patientinstructions/000536.htm.

Mullner, R. M., R. J. Rydman, D. G. Whiteis, and R. F. Rich. 1989. "Rural Community Hospitals and Factors Correlated with Their Risk of Closing." *Public Health Reports* 104 (4): 315–25. www.ncbi.nlm.nih.gov/pmc/articles/PMC1579948/.

Murray, J. E. 2007. *Origins of American Health Insurance: A History of Industrial Sickness Funds.* New Haven, CT: Yale University Press.

National Association of Community Health Centers. 2019. "About Health Centers." Accessed October 31. www.nachc.org/about-our-health-centers/.

National Association of Long Term Care Administrator Boards. 2019. "State Licensure Requirements." Accessed October 1. www.nabweb.org/state-licensure-requirements.

National Center for Health Statistics. 2016. "Deaths: Final Data for 2014." *National Vital Statistics Reports* 65 (4). Published June 30. www.cdc.gov/nchs/data/nvsr/nvsr65/nvsr65_04.pdf.

National Committee for Quality Assurance (NCQA). 2019. "Patient-Centered Medical Home (PCMH)." Accessed October 1. www.ncqa.org/programs/health-care-providers-practices/patient-centered-medical-home-pcmh/.

O'Halloran, J., G. C. Miller, and H. Britt. 2004. "Defining Chronic Conditions for Primary Care with ICPC-2." *Family Practice* 21 (4): 381–86. https://doi.org/10.1093/fampra/cmh407.

Philip, S., D. Govier, and S. Pantely. 2019. "Patient-Centered Medical Home: Developing the Business Case from a Practice Perspective." National Committee for Quality Assurance. Published June. www.ncqa.org/wp-content/uploads/2019/06/06142019_WhitePaper_Milliman_BusinessCasePCMH_Final.pdf.

Pines, J. M., V. Keyes, M. Van Hasselt, and N. McCall. 2015. "Emergency Department and Inpatient Hospital Use by Medicare Beneficiaries in Patient-Centered Medical Homes." *Annals of Emergency Medicine* 65 (6): 652–60. https://doi.org/10.1016/j.annemergmed.2015.01.002.

Prina, L. L. 2017. "Foundation Funding for Palliative and End-of-Life Care." *Health Affairs* 36 (7): 1340–42. https://doi.org/10.1377/hlthaff.2017.0653.

Robert Wood Johnson Foundation. 2013. "Low-Income Patients Say ER Is Better than Primary Care." Published July 9. www.rwjf.org/en/library/articles-and-news/2013/07/low-income-patients-say-er-is-better-than-primary-care.html.

Rosenbaum, S., D. A. Kindig, J. Bao, M. K. Byrnes, and C. O'Laughlin. 2015. "The Value of the Nonprofit Hospital Tax Exemption Was $24.6 Billion in 2011." *Health Affairs* 34 (7): 1225–33. https://doi.org/10.1377/hlthaff.2014.1424.

Sanborn, B. J. 2018a. "AHA Urges More Funding and Fewer Limitations for Rural Health Care Program." *Healthcare Finance.* Published July 19. www.healthcarefinancenews.com/news/aha-urges-more-funding-and-fewer-limitations-rural-health-care-program.

———. 2018b. "Merger and Acquisition Activity Has Record-Breaking First Quarter in 2018." *Healthcare Finance News.* Published March 29. www.healthcarefinancenews.com/news/merger-and-acquisition-activity-has-record-breaking-first-quarter-2018.

Schneiderman, L. J. 2011. "Defining Medical Futility and Improving Medical Care." *Journal of Bioethical Inquiry* 8: 123. https://doi.org/10.1007/s11673-011-9293-3.

Shactman, D. 2005. "Specialty Hospitals, Ambulatory Surgery Centers, and General Hospitals: Charting a Wise Public Policy Course." *Health Affairs* 24 (3): 868–73. https://doi.org/10.1377/hlthaff.24.3.868.

Shi, L., and D. A. Singh. 2010. *Essentials of the U.S. Health Care System*, 2nd ed. Sudbury, MA: Jones & Bartlett.

Shute, D. 2018. "Is It Time to Lift the Ban on Physician-Owned Hospitals?" *Medical Economics.* Published May 16. www.medicaleconomics.com/business/it-time-lift-ban-physician-owned-hospitals.

Sinaiko, A. D., M. B. Landrum, D. J. Meyers, S. Alidina, D. D. Maeng, M. W. Friedberg, L. M. Kern, A. M. Edwards, S. Peterson Flieger, P. R. Houck, P. Peele, R. J. Reid, K. McGraves-Lloyd, K. Finison, and M. B. Rosenthal. 2017. "Synthesis of Research on Patient-Centered Medical Homes Brings Systematic Differences into Relief." *Health Affairs* 36 (3): 500–508. https://doi.org/10.1377/hlthaff.2016.1235.

Sloane, P., S. Zimmerman, and M. D'Souza. 2014. "What Will Long-Term Care Be Like in 2040?" *North Carolina Medical Journal* 75 (5): 326–30. www.ncmedicaljournal.com/content/75/5/326.full.pdf.

Starr, P. 1982. *The Social Transformation of American Medicine*. New York: Basic Books.

Szmigiera, M. 2019. "Bank of America: Statistics & Facts." Statista. Published August 28. www.statista.com/topics/1245/bank-of-america/.

US Congress. 1999. "H.R. 3426—Medicare, Medicaid, and SCHIP Balanced Budget Refinement Act of 1999." Accessed October 1, 2019. www.congress.gov/bill/106th-congress/house-bill/3426.

US Department of Housing and Urban Development. 2019. "Information for Senior Citizens." Accessed October 1. www.hud.gov/topics/information_for_senior_citizens.

US Department of Veterans Affairs (VA). 2018a. "About VA." Updated April 1. www.va.gov/landing2_about.htm.

———. 2018b. "VA, Affordable Care Act and You." Accessed October 1. www.va.gov/health/aca/.

Veterans Health Administration (VHA). 2019. "Veterans Health Administration." Accessed October 29. www.va.gov/health/.

Visnji, M. 2019. "Top 20 U.S. Healthcare Companies by 2016 Revenues." *Revenues and Profits*. Published January 31. https://revenuesandprofits.com/top-20-u-s-healthcare-companies-by-2016-revenues/.

Wagner, E. H. 1998. "Chronic Disease Management: What Will It Take to Improve Care for Chronic Illness?" *Effective Clinical Practice* 1 (1): 2–4. https://ecp.acponline.org/augsep98/cdm.pdf.

Wagner, S. L. 2017. *Fundamentals of Medical Practice Management*. Chicago: Health Administration Press.

Weberg, D. 2012. "Complexity Leadership: A Healthcare Imperative." *Nursing Forum* 47 (4): 268–77. https://doi.org/10.1111/j.1744-6198.2012.00276.x.

Weinick, R. M., R. M. Burns, and A. Mehrotra. 2010. "Many Emergency Department Visits Could Be Managed at Urgent Care Centers and Retail Clinics." *Health Affairs* 29 (9): 1630–36. https://doi.org/10.1377/hlthaff.2009.0748.

White, H. K. 2014. "Long-Term Care in North Carolina." *North Carolina Medical Journal* 75 (5): 320–25. http://classic.ncmedicaljournal.com/wp-content/uploads/2014/03/NCMJ_75-5.pdf.

White, K. R., and J. R. Griffith. 2019. *The Well-Managed Healthcare Organization*, 9th ed. Chicago: Health Administration Press.

World Health Organization (WHO). 2019a. "Hospitals." Accessed October 1. www.who.int/hospitals/en/.

———. 2019b. "Primary Health Care." Accessed October 1. www.who.int/topics/primary_health_care/en/.

———. 2008. *The World Health Report 2008: Primary Health Care, Now More than Ever*. Accessed October 1, 2019. www.who.int/whr/2008/en/index.html.

Yordy, K., and N. Vanselow. 1994. *Defining Primary Care: An Interim Report*. Institute of Medicine. Accessed October 31, 2019. www.ncbi.nlm.nih.gov/books/NBK231308/.

Young, G. J., C.-H. Chou, J. Alexander, S.-Y. D. Lee, and E. Raver. 2013. "Provision of Community Benefits by Tax-Exempt U.S. Hospitals." *New England Journal of Medicine* 368 (16): 1519–27. https://doi.org/10.1056/NEJMsa1210239.

Zanaboni, P., and R. Wootton. 2012. "Adoption of Telemedicine: From Pilot Stage to Routine Delivery." *BMC Medical Informatics and Decision Making* 12: 1. https://doi.org/10.1186/1472-6947-12-1.

Zayas, C. E., Z. He, J. Yuan, M. Maldonado-Molina, W. Hogan, F. Modave, Y. Guo, and J. Bian. 2016. "Examining Healthcare Utilization Patterns of Elderly Middle-Aged Adults in the United States." *Proceedings of the International Florida AI Research Society Conference* 2016: 361–66. www.ncbi.nlm.nih.gov/pubmed/27430035.

PEOPLE AND PROVIDERS OF HEALTHCARE

> Bring your whole self to work; not only your knowledge and expertise, but also your values. Stay true to who you are, and have the courage of your convictions. If you do, you will become an authentic and courageous leader—something intensely needed at this time in healthcare. And you will have the power to change your workplace and the community around you.
>
> —Mary Brainerd, president and CEO of HealthPartners, Bloomington, Minnesota

Learning Objectives

- Recognize the wide range of positions held by workers in healthcare.
- Compare the various dimensions of medical practice.
- Understand the roles of physician assistants, nurse practitioners, and certified nurse specialists (i.e., advanced practice professionals) in our healthcare system.
- Evaluate the challenges facing modern nursing.
- Explain what healthcare administrators do.
- Analyze the reasons for conflict between clinical and administrative personnel in the healthcare system.

This chapter will provide a broad overview of who works in healthcare and what jobs they do (see exhibit 6.1). As noted in previous chapters, healthcare represents a major part of the US economy and employs a great number of people (see exhibit 6.2); in fact, it ranks as the largest employment sector in the country (Thompson 2018). Healthcare occupations account for one out of every eight jobs in the United States, and that proportion is expected to grow in the years ahead (Kaiser Family Foundation 2018; US Bureau of Labor Statistics [BLS] 2017b). The BLS (2017a) estimates that, by 2026, about one-third of all new jobs (totaling nearly 4 million) will be in the healthcare and social assistance sector. About 39 percent of the people employed in healthcare work in hospitals; another 26 percent work in the offices of medical professionals (Torpey 2014).

EXHIBIT 6.1
Area of Focus
for This Chapter

The Aim of the Healthcare System

Issues That Require Our Attention

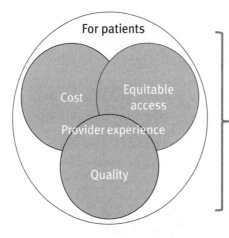

- Nature of our complex system
- Historical issues that have influenced the development of the system
- Beliefs and attitudes about health and healthcare
- Comparison with other developed countries
- Components of our healthcare system
- *People and providers*
- Patient care—the purpose of the system
- Financing a massive system
- Quality—easier said than done
- Medical and information technology
- The pharmaceutical industry
- Complementary and alternative medicine
- Politics/economics
- The future of the system

EXHIBIT 6.1
Area of Focus
for This Chapter

    The healthcare workforce comprises hundreds of job classifications and titles. This chapter will not attempt to name them all, but it will examine a number of important categories. A key distinction is between the clinical and nonclinical areas of the healthcare workforce. Clinical positions are those that provide direct or indirect care to patients. Examples of clinical staff include physicians, nurses, dentists, pharmacists, and laboratory technicians. Nonclinical positions support the clinical staff and the organization. Non-clinical workers include people involved in accounting, engineering, architecture, maintenance, business services, and administrative support (BLS 2019; Fayer and Watson 2015; Torpey 2014). Some positions may straddle the line

EXHIBIT 6.2
Total Healthcare
Employment
in the United
States

Total healthcare employment in the United States, as of 2017:	13,090,150
Percentage of US workforce:	9.1 percent

Note: Healthcare employment includes the following occupations from the US Bureau of Labor Statistics standard occupational classification system: medical and health services managers, healthcare practitioners and technical occupations, healthcare support occupations, and community health workers. Does not include pharmaceutical or medical manufacturing.

Source: Data from US Bureau of Labor Statistics (2017b).

between clinical and nonclinical work. For instance, a social worker might have to address a patient's clinical needs (e.g., by providing counseling) while also attending to nonclinical matters (e.g., financial assistance).

All healthcare administrators should become familiar with the wide range of positions and job categories present in healthcare. You don't know what you don't know, and a surprising number of administrators lack knowledge of this diversity of functions. The sections of this chapter will examine various healthcare positions in terms of work setting and type of service, though the list is by no means all-inclusive. The pharmaceutical industry will be addressed separately in chapter 11.

Physicians

Physicians play an essential role in the US healthcare system. This section will provide an overview of what physicians do; the ways they are educated, trained, and licensed; the various dimensions of medical practice; and some key issues affecting physicians in the United States.

What Do Physicians Do?

Physicians, along with other nonphysician providers, care for patients in a variety of ways, most notably the following:

- Diagnosing the patient's condition
- Assessing the patient's health status
- Prescribing and performing treatment

It has been said that the most expensive instrument in healthcare is the doctor's pen. Although amusing, the statement has a lot of truth: All diagnostic and surgical procedures and all office and hospital assessments—in fact, all care in general—are either done personally by the provider or performed based on the provider's orders.

Physicians work in medical practices of various types, and the nature and identity of each medical practice depend largely on the physicians who practice there. The physicians are the practice's primary producers of services and also its primary governance body; they are held accountable for the performance of the practice in a personal way. Often, physician practices represent the first line of care delivery for patients, offering longitudinal care that sustains health and well-being—especially in primary care settings. Given that medical practices are a fundamental component of the healthcare delivery system, physicians are a key to meaningful reform (World Health Organization [WHO] 2008; Laugesen 2016).

Total number of physicians in the United States:	968,743
Primary care physicians	467,447
Specialty physicians	501,296

Source: Data from US Bureau of Labor Statistics (2017b).

Exhibit 6.3 shows the total number of physicians licensed in the United States as of 2016, broken down between specialists and primary care providers. Note that the number of specialists is larger than the primary care base—which is unique to the United States and may not be in the best interests of patients and the overall healthcare system.

Education and Training to Become a Physician

All physicians are required to complete medical school. Schools of allopathic medicine grant doctor of medicine (MD) degrees, whereas schools of osteopathic medicine grant doctor of osteopathic medicine (DO) degrees. In general, allopathic training is more conventional, whereas osteopathic training places greater emphasis on holistic care and the use of spinal and other manual adjustments. The differences in training between MD and DO programs, however, have diminished over time.

According to the Association of American Medical Colleges (AAMC 2019a), the United States in 2019 had 154 accredited medical schools (granting MD degrees), nearly 400 major teaching hospitals and health systems (including 51 US Department of Veterans Affairs medical centers), and more than 80 academic societies. These organizations accounted for more than 128,000 faculty members, 83,000 medical students, and 110,000 resident physicians. According to the American Association of Colleges of Osteopathic Medicine (2019), the United States in 2019 had 36 colleges of osteopathic medicine (granting DO degrees).

Residencies and Fellowships

After completing medical school, graduates are required to complete residency training in the area of medicine that they have chosen to practice. Some may continue beyond residency and receive more specific training through a fellowship in a specialty area such as cardiac surgery. Some states may require successful completion of a residency and/or fellowship as a condition for licensing and staff privileges at hospitals. Physicians need hospital privileges so they can admit patients to the hospital and perform certain services, such as surgery.

Residencies and fellowships provide practitioners with valuable experience, and practitioner experience is widely recognized a key factor influencing the quality of care received by patients. Research has repeatedly shown that outcomes are highly correlated with the number of procedures that a practitioner has performed (Murray and Teasdale 2005; Sowden et al. 1997; Wagner 1994).

The Accreditation Council for Graduate Medical Education

The Accreditation Council for Graduate Medical Education (ACGME 2019), a private 501(c)(3) not-for-profit organization, sets standards for US graduate medical education programs (i.e., residencies and fellowships) and the institutions that sponsor such programs. Accreditation provides assurance that each program meets these rigorous standards. ACGME accreditation is achieved through a voluntary process of evaluation and review. However, most hospitals and government agencies require ACGME accreditation if a physician's education and training are to be recognized for purposes of licensing and hospital appointment. In this way, ACGME accreditation is analogous to the accreditation of hospitals and other healthcare organizations by The Joint Commission.

The ACGME accreditation process is overseen by review committees of volunteer specialty experts. These experts set accreditation standards for the recognized area of specialty and provide peer evaluation of residency and fellowship programs and sponsoring institutions (ACGME 2019). Each of the ACGME's recognized areas of specialty also contains several subspecialties. For example, within the family medicine specialty, one might further specialize in gerontology, the care of the elderly. In a specialty surgical area such as urology, one might focus on urological oncology. The broad range of specialties and subspecialties reflects the rapid expansion of knowledge and treatment options in healthcare delivery, and it enables a single individual to provide competent care across a variety of modalities for any given area of medicine.

One of the newer approaches to specialization is the "transitional year" residency, which allows participants to experience various specialties as they prepare to transition into medical practice. Transitional year residencies are intended to provide fundamental skills training and to offer broad exposure to the basic areas of medicine. Such programs are often cosponsored by multiple departments within a medical training facility, such as pediatrics and internal medicine (Elnicki et al. 2017).

Licensing for Physicians

All 50 states require physicians and medical providers to have a license. The licensing of medical providers is carried out under the auspices of a medical examining board or board of nursing. These boards have the right to grant licenses to practice medicine but also the responsibility to investigate and discipline providers in cases of inappropriate conduct. The licenses issued by these boards provide a general right and privilege to practice medicine, but

EXHIBIT 6.4

Partial List of Medical Specialties

Allergy and immunology	Neurology	Plastic surgery
Anesthesiology	Neurosurgery	Preventive medicine
Cardiology	Obstetrics	Primary care
Dermatology	Oncology	Psychiatry
Emergency medicine	Orthopedic surgery	Radiation oncology
Genetics	Otolaryngology	Radiology
Gerontology	Palliative care and hospice	Surgery
Gynecology	Pathology	Thoracic surgery
Hematology	Pediatrics and its specialties	Urology
Internal medicine		

Source: American Board of Medical Specialties (2019).

they usually do not grant specific privileges to practice particular medical specialties. Such specialized privileges are often managed by the hospital where the provider practices.

Many medical specialties are recognized by special board certification. Such certification indicates that a practitioner has received training in a specific area of medicine from an ACGME-accredited program. Exhibit 6.4 provides a partial list of medical specialties recognized by the American Board of Medical Specialties.

The Dimensions of Medical Practice

Medical practices can take a variety of forms, ranging from small sole proprietorships to large multispecialty medical practices. Today, many medical practices—whether solo practices or multispecialty entities—operate within larger healthcare organizations such as integrated delivery systems or accountable care organizations.

Single-specialty medical practices are those that focus on a single aspect of medicine, such as general surgery, family practice, orthopedics, cardiology, or internal medicine. Multispecialty medical practices contain several medical specialties. Multispecialty practices are highly integrated under a common governance and management structure, and they generally have a highly developed corporate system for managing finances and dealing with regulatory agencies. Such practices are much more complex than solo or small practices. In recent decades, medical practices have grown larger (Kane 2015). Exhibit 6.5 shows the distribution of physicians (at both single-specialty and multispecialty practices) by size of practice.

One emerging type of entity is the concierge medical practice, which, as the name implies, provides a very high level of service, including unlimited access, to a select clientele in exchange for substantial fees (*Concierge Medicine Today* 2019). Such practices are often appealing to patients and providers, though they raise a number of issues and ethical concerns (Shwartz 2017; Dauber and Newlin 2017).

	Physicians at Single-Specialty Practices (n = 1,452)	Physicians at Multispecialty Practices (n = 836)
In a practice with 1 physician	1.5%	0.3%
In a practice with 2–4 physicians	42.0%	13.8%
In a practice with 5–10 physicians	31.7%	20.8%
In a practice with 11–24 physicians	13.7%	17.2%
In a practice with 25–49 physicians	6.7%	11.1%
In a practice with 50+ physicians	4.5%	36.9%

EXHIBIT 6.5
Distribution of Single- and Multispecialty Physicians by Practice Size (2014)

Source: Data from Kane (2015).

Physician Burnout and Shortages

Burnout is a critical concern facing physicians in the United States, as well as in other countries (Rotenstein et al. 2018). Burnout is commonly assessed using the Maslach Burnout Inventory, which identifies depersonalization, emotional exhaustion, and lack of a sense of personal accomplishment as the primary characteristics of burnout (Maslach, Jackson, and Leiter 2015). Researchers using various forms of the measure have found significant levels of burnout among physicians, raising concerns about the health and well-being of the workforce (Rotenstein et al. 2018). Physician burnout can also negatively affect patient care. It can lead to serious disruptions in the workplace, cause patient complaints and dissatisfaction, and even raise the risk of malpractice claims (Hickson, Clayton, et al. 1992, 1994, 1995; Hickson, Federspiel, et al. 2002; Hickson and Entman 2008, 2010).

One approach to addressing the burnout problem has focused on creating more meaning in the physician's work by providing more time to interact with patients. Most physicians enter the profession because they want to help people, but this aspect of the job can often seem at odds with the hectic, production-oriented nature of our modern healthcare system (Chopra, Sotile, and Sotile 2004; Eisenstein 2018; Southwick and Southwick 2018). Other approaches seek to address the sheer volume of work, the long hours, and the stresses of care responsibility that contribute to burnout. The use of advanced practice professionals (discussed at length in the next section) can provide physicians with relief from certain responsibilities, such as call (Conroy 2018). Some researchers feel that burnout needs to be better understood before it can be fully addressed (Schwenk and Gold 2018).

A related problem involves the number of physicians who are available to take on this substantial workload. The AAMC projects a shortage of between 42,600 and 121,300 physicians by the end of 2030 (AAMC 2019b; Dall et al. 2019).

EXHIBIT 6.6	Number of nurse practitioners: 166,280
Nurse	Number of physician assistants: 109,220
Practitioners	Total: 275,500
and Physician	
Assistants, by	*Source:* Data from US Bureau of Labor Statistics (2017b).
the Numbers	
(2017)	

Advanced Practice Professionals

Advanced practice professionals (APPs)—including nurse practitioners, physician assistants, and clinical nurse specialists—are a growing category of medical service provider. Increasingly, APPs are taking on care delivery responsibilities previously performed by physicians, thereby enabling physicians to focus more on complex care that requires their expertise. Because of this role, APPs are sometimes called "physician extenders," though that term is not preferred. The number of nurse practitioners and physician assistants in the United States as of 2017 is shown in exhibit 6.6.

Nurse Practitioners

What Do Nurse Practitioners Do?

Nurse practitioners (NPs) are medical providers who have been licensed to diagnose and treat illness and disease in collaboration with a licensed physician. They typically work in physician offices, hospitals, and clinics, and they can prescribe medication for patients in all 50 states. In some special cases (e.g., in rural communities with limited providers), NPs can practice more independently and perform additional responsibilities, as defined by state regulations.

Education to Become a Nurse Practitioner

Several steps are required to become an NP:

- Earning a nursing undergraduate degree, usually a bachelor's in nursing (BSN)
- Passing the National Council Licensure Examination (NCLEX-RN) and becoming a registered nurse; the NCLEX-RN assesses application, critical thinking, and judgment and ensures that candidates are qualified to safely practice as entry-level nurses (National Council of State Boards of Nursing [NCSBN] 2019a)

- Completing a graduate degree in nursing, usually a master's in nursing (MSN)
- Fulfilling the requirements to receive an advanced practice nursing license in the state(s) where one intends to practice
- Completing additional training or certification

Because *nurse practitioner* is a general designation, an NP may wish to obtain a certification or do a fellowship with a specific focus, such as cardiology, urology, surgery, or obstetrics/gynecology.

Licensing for Nurse Practitioners

Each state's board of nursing sets the requirements for NP licensing. The requirements include the following:

- Any additional training or experience required to perform certain duties, such as working independently
- The ability to prescribe medication
- Any state-specific requirements

Although rules from state to state are often similar, any state-specific requirements must be understood. Some regulatory bodies favor moving toward a requirement that NPs complete a doctoral-level education to maintain their credentials to practice.

Physician Assistants

What Do Physician Assistants Do?

Physician assistants (PAs), like NPs, are medical providers licensed to diagnose and treat illness and disease in collaboration with a licensed physician. About 38.3 percent of PAs work in hospitals, and 45.5 percent work in outpatient offices and clinics (American Academy of PAs [AAPA] 2018). The remainder work in urgent care centers, schools, and colleges and universities. Most PAs work in surgical subspecialties or in primary care. PAs can prescribe medication for patients in all 50 states.

Education to Become a Physician Assistant

The education of PAs follows a different path from that of NPs. PAs are trained at the master's level in programs that cover three academic years over 27 months. A bachelor's-level degree—typically in biology, chemistry, or an equivalent—is required for acceptance into one of 255 PA programs across the United States (AAPA 2018, 2019). As part of their training, candidates must complete 2,000 hours of clinical rotations.

Licensing for Physician Assistants

The PA licensing requirements for virtually every state include graduating from an accredited PA program, passing a certification exam, and maintaining certification by completing 100 hours of continuing medical education every two years. PAs are required to recertify every 10 years (AAPA 2018).

Clinical Nurse Specialists

What Do Clinical Nurse Specialists Do?

Clinical nurse specialists (CNSs) are clinicians with advanced training in a specialized area of nursing. CNSs are often used in such areas as psychiatry, pediatrics, gerontology, obstetrics, and gynecology, and their roles vary based on their specialty. The roles may also be determined by setting (e.g., emergency room or critical care), by disease focus (e.g., diabetes, cancer), or by a specified problem area (e.g., pain management, wound care, stress management) (National Association of Clinical Nurse Specialists [NACNS] 2019). Unlike NPs and PAs, CNSs are not allowed to prescribe medications in any state. Other rules regarding CNS practice—for instance, rules about independent authority, ranging from no supervision, to a requirement for a collaborative agreement with a physician, to direct supervision—vary from state to state (NACNS 2016). Although the specialty has existed for many decades, the use of CNSs—like the use of other APPs—has recently become much more broadly accepted in various areas of patient care.

Education and Licensing for Clinical Nurse Specialists

Despite efforts to unify state requirements for licensing and practice of CNSs, differences from state to state remain. Fellowship programs are now being developed to allow PAs, NPs, and CNSs to gain specialty training in areas such as cardiology, urology, emergency medicine, pulmonary medicine, and internal medicine. These fellowships typically last for one year and involve rigorous clinical training in a hospital or outpatient setting. Programs at Vanderbilt University Medical Center and Seattle Children's Hospital serve as examples (Seattle Children's Hospital 2019; Vanderbilt Health 2019; Windey and Cullen 2018).

Nurses

For many years, nurses in the United States were not licensed, and their role in the healthcare system was mostly limited to private-duty nursing. The nursing profession saw significant activity during the Civil War, but it truly came into its own after World War I. During that conflict, demonstrations of nurses' value and expertise led to growing public recognition of the profession, essentially creating the image of the professional nurse (D'Antonio 1993). Today, nurses play important roles in virtually every healthcare setting.

What Do Nurses Do?

Nurses provide a broad range of services to patients and to the healthcare system in general. The duties performed by nurses vary widely. Some might provide community-based health services such as inoculations, whereas others serve as operating room assistants in a hospital (*Nurse Journal* 2018). Typical duties performed by a registered nurse include the following (American Nurses Association 2019b):

- Performing physical exams, taking health histories, and making critical decisions about the patient
- Providing health promotion, counseling, and education
- Administering medications and other individual interventions
- Coordinating care in collaboration with a wide array of healthcare professionals

Just as doctors take the Hippocratic oath, many nurses take the Nightingale pledge (see exhibit 6.7), named for English reformer Florence Nightingale, the founder of modern nursing. Written in 1893 by a committee led by Lystra Gretter at Farrand Training School for Nurses in Detroit, Michigan, the pledge expresses a commitment to the profession and to patients (Munson 1949). However, as the nursing profession has evolved, some feel that the pledge needs to be updated, given that nursing responsibilities today go well beyond assisting the physician (Moffa 2010).

EXHIBIT 6.7
The Florence Nightingale Pledge

THE FLORENCE NIGHTINGALE PLEDGE

I SOLEMNLY PLEDGE MYSELF BEFORE GOD AND IN THE PRESENCE OF THIS ASSEMBLY TO PASS MY LIFE IN PURITY AND TO PRACTICE MY PROFESSION FAITHFULLY. I WILL ABSTAIN FROM WHATEVER IS DELETERIOUS AND MISCHIEVOUS, AND WILL NOT TAKE OR KNOWINGLY ADMINISTER ANY HARMFUL DRUG.

I WILL DO ALL IN MY POWER TO MAINTAIN AND ELEVATE THE STANDARD OF MY PROFESSION, AND WILL HOLD IN CONFIDENCE ALL PERSONAL MATTERS COMMITTED TO MY KEEPING, AND ALL FAMILY AFFAIRS COMING TO MY KNOWLEDGE IN THE PRACTICE OF MY CALLING.

WITH LOYALTY WILL I ENDEAVOR TO AID THE PHYSICIAN IN HIS WORK, AND DEVOTE MYSELF TO THE WELFARE OF THOSE COMMITTED TO MY CARE.

Nurses today represent the largest group of medical professionals. In 2019, the United States had 4,095,518 registered nurses (RNs) and 919,445 practical nurses (PNs), also known as licensed practical nurses (NCSBN 2019b). RNs and PNs may perform many of the same functions, though RNs have more demanding educational requirements and greater responsibility.

Education and Training to Become a Nurse

For many years, nursing education was disorganized and nonstandard. One of the earliest steps toward a developed curriculum was the 1839 publication of *The Nurse's Guide: Containing a Series of Instructions to Females Who Wish to Engage in the Important Business of Nursing Mother and Child in the Lying-In Chamber* by Joseph Warrington (1839). In 1873, three nurses' educational programs—the New York Training School at Bellevue Hospital, the Connecticut Training School at the State Hospital (later renamed New Haven Hospital), and the Boston Training School at Massachusetts General Hospital—began operations. These programs became known as the "Nightingale schools" because they were based on ideas advanced by Florence Nightingale (Penn Nursing 2019).

Today, nursing curriculums are rigorous and standardized, and they can lead to associate's, bachelor's, master's, or doctorate degrees (American Association of Colleges of Nursing 2019). Additional programs are available for the APP categories discussed earlier in this chapter. The foundation of the nursing curriculum is the five-step "Nursing Process" (American Nurses Association 2019a):

1. *Assessment.* Nurses perform a physiological, economic, social, and lifestyle-based assessment for each patient.
2. *Diagnosis.* Nurses develop a diagnosis for each patient by considering the individual's physical symptoms and behavior.
3. *Outcomes/planning.* Nurses set and monitor realistic goals for their patients.
4. *Implementation.* Nurses provide consistent care to their patients and document all patients' progress.
5. *Evaluation.* Nurses monitor each patient, providing an opportunity to evaluate the effectiveness of the care and make necessary adjustments.

Licensing for Nurses

Nurses are licensed at the state level under the jurisdiction of each state's board of nursing. The board grants licenses, investigates complaints, and takes disciplinary action against licensed nurses, up to and including the revocation of the nurse's license to practice. The scope of practice varies by state and by qualification; it may also vary by institution, depending on policies and practices (NCSBN 2019b).

Shortages, Burnout, and Other Issues Facing Nursing

The nursing profession faces several challenges and areas of concern, many of which are similar to the issues facing physicians. With the aging of the US population, general population growth, and the retirement of existing professionals, demand for medical services is expected to increase significantly in the years ahead. According to a BLS report, the United States will likely need about one million additional nurses by the year 2022 (Oslund 2016).

Nursing shortages exist not simply because of the number of nurses but also because of nurses' uneven distribution. Many localities experience shortages, whereas other localities seem to have an oversupply. Some regional shortages may be attributed to cost of living or other factors that make certain areas unattractive for nurses (Lee and Anders 2018; Haddad and Toney-Butler 2019). Obviously, pay needs to be fair and reflective of the area's cost of living. Depending on the geographic location and the nursing specialty, nurse turnover ranges from 8.8 percent to 37 percent per year (Haddad and Toney-Butler 2019). Much of this turnover can be attributed to burnout. Nursing is a stressful, high-impact profession, and nurses often report needing to work overtime.

The US nursing profession is still largely female, and female nurses often pause or end their careers when raising children. This tendency is in large part a reflection of the inequitable distribution of parental responsibility in US society and the pervasive lack of affordable, high-quality childcare. If the US healthcare system wants to seriously address the nursing shortage, it should support policies that encourage gender equality (e.g., the Equal Rights Amendment) and support working mothers (e.g., programs that provide better access to childcare and family-leave options for parents of all genders). This issue affects not only nurses but most professional groups throughout the healthcare system.

Healthcare settings are hazardous working environments, and nurses regularly face injury risks and the potential for exposure to blood-borne pathogens and common diseases. Of particular concern is the alarming increase in the amount of violence in US healthcare settings. Studies have shown that nurses are more likely to be targeted by physical and emotional abuse than other healthcare professionals. According to a Medscape poll, 71 percent of nurses indicate that they have been harassed by patients; only 47 percent of physicians report similar harassment (Frelick 2018). Harassment in many instances may include persistent unwanted communications and inappropriate social media contact.

Dentists, Dental Hygienists, and Dental Assistants

Dental care is important for patients' overall health. The American Dental Association (ADA 2019a) represents more than 163,000 dentists across a number of recognized specialties. Like other areas of healthcare, dentistry is changing rapidly as new processes and technologies emerge. In addition to providing basic dental care, dentists will often spot medical issues such as oral cancer and refer patients to physicians for further evaluation and treatment; thus, dentists are important partners to other professionals in the healthcare system.

Education and Licensing for Dentists

Dentists must undergo a rigorous postbaccalaureate education at an accredited dental school, where they receive either a doctor of dental surgery (DDS) degree or a doctor of dental medicine (DMD) degree (Commission on Dental Accreditation 2019). All 50 states license dentists. Licensure is based on education, a written examination, a clinical examination, and the fulfillment of other requirements established by the dental examining board in each state. Some states have additional licensing requirements for practitioners wishing to engage in certain specialties (ADA 2019d).

What Do Dental Hygienists and Dental Assistants Do?

Dental hygienists and dental assistants practice as part of the dental care team. Dental hygienists typically work independently, focusing on oral exams (including radiological exams), oral hygiene (including the cleaning of teeth), the education of patients, documentation, and other duties as specified by the practice (ADA 2019c). Dental assistants typically work closely with either the dentist or the hygienist, functioning much as an operating room assistant would in a surgical suite (ADA 2019b). Both occupations require graduation from an accredited training program and licensing by the state of practice. Additional examinations and other requirements may be imposed by individual states (ADA 2019d).

Executive and Administrative Staff

Numerous positions in healthcare have responsibilities in the areas of business and administration. Such positions include executive roles; administrative staff positions; and jobs specializing in accounting, finance, and other fields.

What Do Executives Do?

Healthcare executives oversee organizational planning, ensure that strategies are implemented, and direct the managers and other individuals engaged in the day-to-day work of healthcare. Above all else, executives must be effective leaders who inspire and motivate their followers. Without followers, leaders can accomplish little. Top executives—especially in large, multidimensional organizations—must surround themselves with competent followers who have the necessary expertise and to whom authority can be safely delegated.

Depending on an organization's size, the executive staff may consist of a number of individuals responsible for various organizational segments. Most organizations, however, have one senior executive who is responsible to a governing body, such as a board of directors. This senior executive is responsible for the overall operational success of the organization and the fulfillment of the organization's mission and vision (Porter and Teisberg 2006; Trapp 2018).

Education and Training for Executive Staff

Virtually all executive staff positions in healthcare organizations require at least a bachelor's degree in healthcare administration, business administration, finance, or another related field of business or healthcare. Most often, healthcare executives have advanced degrees, such as a master's in healthcare administration or an advanced degree in a certain clinical area. Today, medical doctors often move into the executive ranks of healthcare organizations. Doctorates in healthcare administration are also becoming increasingly common (American College of Healthcare Executives [ACHE] 2019c). After receiving a degree, many executives begin or advance their careers by pursuing a fellowship to gain practical, hands-on experience in a healthcare organization (ACHE 2019b).

The first master's in healthcare administration (MHA) program was started in 1935 by Michael M. Davis at the University of Chicago. Davis had a PhD in sociology and innovative ideas about hospital administration. A formidable advocate for new methods of delivering and paying for medical care, Davis participated in the formation of the Social Security system (University of Chicago School of Social Service Administration 2018, 2019). Davis espoused the critical need for healthcare administrators to possess business skills, yet he also believed that new professionals must balance these business skills with a sense of social justice. Davis astutely recognized that escalating medical technology would require more competent management.

Nursing Home and Long-Term Care Administrators

A special category of healthcare executive that merits discussion here is the long-term care administrator. These executives lead and manage nursing homes and other long-term care facilities with the goal of optimizing services and ensuring residents' safety. Each state has its own requirements for obtaining a nursing home administrator (NHA), resource center for accessible living (RCAL), or home and community-based service (HCBS) license, as well as its own requirements for being an administrator in training (AIT) and for continuing education once a license is granted. The requirements for licensing, complaint investigation, and discipline are handled by the nursing home examining board in each state. The National Association of Long Term Care Administrator Boards (2019) and the American College of Health Care Administrators (2019) provide excellent resources related to long-term care administration, education, and development services.

Administrative and Business Office Staff

Most positions in the business areas of healthcare organizations require college degrees at the baccalaureate level or above. Special training in a particular skill set is often required as well. Many staff members focus on such areas as accounting, finance, business office management, billing, coding, insurance, or patient experience. One of the most important functions of a healthcare organization's accountants and accounting leadership is to maintain compliance with reporting and standard accounting practices as required by the Financial Accounting Standards Board (FASB 2019).

Various specialty societies offer certifications and fellowships in key competency areas of healthcare business. The American College of Healthcare Executives (ACHE) is a professional society consisting of more than 48,000 executives who lead hospitals, healthcare systems, and other healthcare organizations. The organization offers a credential called the Fellow of the American College of Healthcare Executives (FACHE) to signify mastery of the core body of knowledge needed for effective healthcare management. ACHE has 77 chapters across the country that provide networking, education, and career development (ACHE 2019a). Other organizations that support various business specialists in healthcare include the following:

- The Medical Group Management Association (MGMA)
- The Healthcare Information and Management Systems Society (HIMSS)
- The Healthcare Financial Management Association (HFMA)
- The American Health Information Management Association (AHIMA)
- The Society for Human Resource Management (SHRM)
- The American Academy of Professional Coders (AAPC)
- The American Institute of Certified Public Accountants (AICPA)

With the exception of long-term care administrators and certified public accountants, most administrative positions in healthcare do not require a license. However, many organizations require certifications and fellowships for certain positions, especially those at the management level; some such requirements may also be dictated by state regulations. Organizations have a responsibility to ensure that all workers are properly licensed or have the necessary certifications, registrations, or other credentials for their duties.

Data Analytics and Information Technologists

The advancement of data analysis and information technology (IT) science ranks among the most significant developments in healthcare administration in the past several decades. Professionals in these areas have a meaningful impact not only on the management of the organization's operations but also on the care received by patients. IT represents the operational backbone of most medical organizations. It provides platforms for medical records documentation, appointment scheduling, billing, and collection of revenue. It is essential for managing financial, human, and physical resources. Exhibit 6.8 illustrates

EXHIBIT 6.8
Partial List of Information Technology Jobs in Healthcare

Chief technology officer (CTO)	Desktop support specialist	Associate developer
IT director	Help desk technician	Computer programmer
IT manager	IT support manager	Developer
Management information systems director	IT support specialist	Java developer
Technical operations officer	IT systems administrator	Junior software engineer
Computer and information systems manager	Senior support specialist	Programmer (several levels)
Computer network architect	Senior system administrator	Programmer analyst
Computer systems analyst	Support specialist	Senior applications engineer
Computer systems manager	Systems administrator	Senior programmer analyst
IT analyst	Technical support engineer	Senior software engineer
Network administrator	Technical support specialist	Senior system architect
Network architect	Data center support specialist	Senior system designer
Network engineer	Data quality manager	Senior systems software engineer
Network systems administrator	Database administrator	Software architect
Senior network architect	Senior database administrator	Software developer
Senior network engineer	Application support analyst	Software engineer
Senior network system administrator	Systems analyst	Software quality assurance analyst
Telecommunications specialist	Systems designer	System architect
Customer support administrator	Chief information officer (CIO)	Systems software engineer
Customer support specialist	Information security	Front-end developer
	Security specialist	Senior web administrator
	Senior security specialist	Senior web developer
	Application developer	Web administrator
	Applications engineer	Web developer
		Webmaster

Source: Adapted from Doyle (2019).

the increasing variety of positions in the IT areas of healthcare organizations; many of these positions are newly emerging and not yet widely known.

Artificial intelligence has become an important feature in the analysis of healthcare data and the delivery of healthcare services. With the ability to correlate data from millions of records, we can better predict how patients will respond to various treatment options. Supercomputers allow clinical researchers and practitioners to apply the ever-increasing body of knowledge to the care of patients—and to do so in a more precise way. This trend will likely continue as technology improves and our ability to apply new technologies to healthcare delivery is better understood (Ashley 2015; Timmerman 2013). Robotics is another growing field that will affect the future healthcare workforce and delivery of care (Qureshi and Syed 2014); it will be discussed further in chapter 14.

Struggles Between Medicine and Management

Struggles and conflicts between administration (i.e., the business side of healthcare) and clinicians (i.e., the patient care side of healthcare) have existed since the beginning of organized medicine (Hunter 1992; Kirkpatrick et al. 2016). Surely, many experienced clinicians have heard hospital administrators say something to the effect of "You take care of patients, and I'll run the hospital." Obviously, such a comment reflects a dismal lack of appreciation for the need of administrators to work together with physicians and other clinicians to better serve patients. Ultimately, *all* aspects of any healthcare operation are about taking care of patients. Fortunately, healthcare administrators today are beginning to place a greater emphasis on developing closer working relationships with clinical staff.

A quote sometimes attributed to the president of the Catholic Hospital System states simply, "No money, no mission." In other words, for an organization to maintain operations and fulfill its mission, it needs to make financial ends meet. Many physicians, however, are so focused on patient care that they tend to overlook this need. Physicians often have little training in management and the "money" side of operations yet are still asked to participate in important business decisions, creating situations where differing perspectives and lack of understanding lead to conflict. Disagreements can be further complicated by poor communication, lack of clarity, faulty decision making, concerns about loss of physician autonomy, and competition for resources within the organization (Adler, Kwon, and Heckscher 2008; Ashworth et al. 2013; Meyer et al. 2014; Numerato, Salvatore, and Fattore 2012).

Interprofessional education (IPE) and interprofessional practice (IPP) have emerged as effective means of addressing healthcare workplace conflict. According to the Institute of Medicine (IOM 2015), IPE/IPP "occurs when learners of two or more health and/or social care professions engage in learning with, from, and about each other to improve collaboration and the delivery of care." IPE/IPP can provide a framework to enable clinical staff of

EXHIBIT 6.9
Interprofessional
Education
Process

Source: Adapted from WHO (2010).

various dimensions and administrative staff to work together in a more collaborative fashion to meet the goals of the organization and provide better care for patients.

Exhibit 6.9 illustrates the process of IPE/IPP. Applying interprofessional education to a fragmented system can help create a "collaborative-ready practice," which provides the basis for a truly collaborative practice and, ultimately, better outcomes for the people served by the organization (IOM 2015; WHO 2010).

The concept of IPE/IPP has been around for many years but has recently gained new traction in healthcare organizations and educational settings. Many medical schools and teaching hospitals now incorporate principles of IPE/IPP into their curricula (WHO 2010). Continued application of IPE/IPP to the healthcare field will likely lead to better working relationships, better working environments, and better patient outcomes (Brashers, Owen, and Haizlip 2015).

Discussion Questions

1. What are the main categories of people who work in healthcare?
2. How do we ensure that the individuals working in healthcare are qualified for their positions?
3. How do professionals keep up with the rapidly changing healthcare environment?
4. How do we manage and regulate the boundaries of provider services?
5. How can the issue of burnout be addressed in healthcare settings?

References

Accreditation Council for Graduate Medical Education (ACGME). 2019. "The ACGME for Residents and Fellows." Accessed October 4. www.acgme.org/Residents-and-Fellows/The-ACGME-for-Residents-and-Fellows.

Adler, P. S., S.-W. Kwon, and C. Heckscher. 2008. "Professional Work: The Emergence of Collaborative Community." *Organization Science* 19 (2): 359–76. https://doi.org/10.1287/orsc.1070.0293.

American Academy of PAs (AAPA). 2019. "Become a PA." Accessed October 4. www.aapa.org/career-central/become-a-pa/.

———. 2018. "What Is a PA?" Accessed October 4, 2019. www.aapa.org/wp-content/uploads/2018/03/What-is-a-PA-Infographic-Legal-Size_3.22_FINAL.pdf.

American Association of Colleges of Nursing (AACN). 2019. "Baccalaureate Education." Accessed October 4. www.aacnnursing.org/Nursing-Education-Programs/Baccalaureate-Education.

American Association of Colleges of Osteopathic Medicine. 2019. "U.S. Colleges of Osteopathic Medicine." Accessed November 5. www.aacom.org/become-a-doctor/u-s-colleges-of-osteopathic-medicine.

American Board of Medical Specialties. 2019. "Specialty and Subspecialty Certificates." Accessed October 4. www.abms.org/member-boards/specialty-subspecialty-certificates/.

American College of Health Care Administrators (ACHCA). 2019. "Education." Accessed October 4. https://achca.memberclicks.net/education.

American College of Healthcare Executives (ACHE). 2019a. "About ACHE." Accessed October 4. www.ache.org/aboutache.cfm.

———. 2019b. " Postgraduate Fellowships." Accessed October 4. www.ache.org/postgrad/default.aspx.

———. 2019c. "Which Degree Should I Pursue?" Accessed October 4. www.ache.org/carsvcs/whichdegree.cfm.

American Dental Association (ADA). 2019a. "About the ADA." Accessed November 5. www.ada.org/en/about-the-ada.

———. 2019b. "Dental Assistant." Accessed October 4. www.ada.org/en/education-careers/careers-in-dentistry/dental-team-careers/dental-assistant.

———. 2019c. "Dental Hygienist." Accessed October 4. www.ada.org/en/education-careers/careers-in-dentistry/dental-team-careers/dental-hygienist.

———. 2019d. "Licensure Overview." Accessed October 4. www.ada.org/en/education-careers/licensure.

American Nurses Association. 2019a. "The Nursing Process." Accessed October 4. www.nursingworld.org/practice-policy/workforce/what-is-nursing/the-nursing-process/.

————. 2019b. "What Is Nursing?" Accessed October 4. www.nursingworld.org/practice-policy/workforce/what-is-nursing/.

Ashley, E. A. 2015. "The Precision Medicine Initiative: A New National Effort." *JAMA* 313 (21): 2119–20. https://doi.org/10.1001/jama.2015.3595.

Ashworth, R., E. Ferlie, G. Hammerschmid, M. J. Moon, and T. Reay. 2013. "Theorizing Contemporary Public Management: International and Comparative Perspectives." *British Journal of Management* 24: S1–17. https://doi.org/10.1111/1467-8551.12035.

Association of American Medical Colleges (AAMC). 2019a. "Data and Reports." Accessed October 4. www.aamc.org/data.

————. 2019b. "New Research Shows Increasing Physician Shortages in Both Primary and Specialty Care." Published April 23. https://news.aamc.org/press-releases/article/workforce_report_shortage_04112018/.

Brashers, V., J. Owen, and J. Haizlip. 2015. "Interprofessional Education and Practice Guide No. 2: Developing and Implementing a Center for Interprofessional Education." *Journal of Interprofessional Care* 29 (2): 95–99. https://doi.org/10.3109/13561820.2014.962130.

Chopra, S. S., W. M. Sotile, and M. O. Sotile. 2004. "Physician Burnout." *JAMA* 291 (5): 633. https://doi.org/10.1001/jama.291.5.633.

Commission on Dental Accreditation. 2019. "Commission on Dental Accreditation." Accessed October 5. www.ada.org/en/coda.

Concierge Medicine Today. 2019. "What Is Concierge Medicine?" Accessed October 5. https://conciergemedicinetoday.org/what-is-concierge-medicine-concierge-medicine-definition-concierge-medicine-defined/.

Conroy, S. 2018. "How PAs Help Practices in Rural Areas During the Holidays." *Physicians Practice.* Published December 3. www.physicianspractice.com/career/how-pas-help-practices-rural-areas-during-holidays.

Dall, T., R. Reynolds, K. Jones, R. Chakrabarti, and W. Iacobucci. 2019. *2019 Update: The Complexities of Physician Supply and Demand: Projections from 2017 to 2032.* Association of American Medical Colleges. Published April. https://aamc-black.global.ssl.fastly.net/production/media/filer_public/31/13/3113ee5c-a038-4c16-89af-294a69826650/2019_update_-_the_complexities_of_physician_supply_and_demand_-_projections_from_2017-2032.pdf.

D'Antonio, P. 1993. "The Legacy of Domesticity: Nursing in Early Nineteenth-Century." *American Nursing History Review* 1: 229–46.

Dauber, M. S., and J. Newlin. 2017. "The Real Problem with Concierge Medicine." Published July 13. *Becker's Hospital Review.* www.beckershospitalreview.com/quality/the-real-problem-with-concierge-medicine.html.

Doyle, A. 2019. "IT Jobs: Career Options, Job Titles, and Descriptions." Balance Careers. Updated September 13. www.thebalancecareers.com/list-of-information-technology-it-job-titles-2061498.

Eisenstein, L. 2018. "To Fight Burnout, Organize." *New England Journal of Medicine* 379 (6): 509–11. https://doi.org/10.1056/NEJMp1803771.

Elnicki, D. M., M. K. Aiyer, M. L. Cannarozzi, A. Carbo, P. R. Chelminski, S. G. Chheda, S. M. Chudgar, H. E. Harrell, L. C. Hood, M. Horn, K. Johl, G. C. Kane, D. B. McNeill, M. D. Muntz, A. G. Pereira, E. Stewart, H. Tarantino, and T. R. Vu. 2017. "An Entrustable Professional Activity (EPA)-Based Framework to Prepare Fourth-Year Medical Students for Internal Medicine Careers." *Journal of General Internal Medicine* 32 (11): 1255–60. https://doi.org/10.1007/s11606-017-4089-8.

Fayer, S., and A. Watson. 2015. *Employment and Wages in Healthcare Occupations.* US Bureau of Labor Statistics. Published December. www.bls.gov/spotlight/2015/employment-and-wages-in-healthcare-occupations/pdf/employment-and-wages-in-healthcare-occupations.pdf.

Financial Accounting Standards Board (FASB). 2019. "Standards." Accessed October 5. www.fasb.org/jsp/FASB/Page/LandingPage&cid=1175805317350.

Frelick, M. 2018. "Harassment from Patients Prevalent, Poll Shows." MedScape. Published February 1. www.medscape.com/viewarticle/892006.

Haddad, L. M., and T. J. Toney-Butler. 2019. "Nursing Shortage." StatPearls. Published January 19. www.ncbi.nlm.nih.gov/pubmed/29630227.

Hickson, G. B., E. W. Clayton, S. S. Entman, C. S. Miller, P. B. Githens, K. Whetten Goldstein, and F. Sloan. 1995. "Malpractice, Patient Satisfaction, and Physician-Patient Communication—Reply." *JAMA* 274 (1): 23–24. https://doi.org/10.1001/jama.1995.03530010036019.

———. 1994. "Obstetricians' Prior Malpractice Experience and Patients' Satisfaction with Care." *JAMA* 272 (20): 1583–87. https://doi.org/10.1001/jama.1994.03520200039032.

Hickson, G. B., E. W. Clayton, P. B. Githens, and F. A. Sloan. 1992. "Factors That Prompted Families to File Medical Malpractice Claims Following Perinatal Injuries." *JAMA* 267 (10): 1359–63. https://doi.org/10.1001/jama.1992.03480100065032.

Hickson, G. B., and S. S. Entman. 2010. "Physicians Influence and the Malpractice Problem." *Obstetrics and Gynecology* 115 (4): 682–86. https://doi.org/10.1097/AOG.0b013e3181d732e9.

———. 2008. "Physician Practice Behavior and Litigation Risk: Evidence and Opportunity." *Clinical Obstetrics and Gynecology* 51 (4): 688–99. https://doi.org/10.1097/GRF.0b013e3181899c2c.

Hickson, G. B., C. F. Federspiel, J. W. Pichert, C. S. Miller, J. Gauld-Jaeger, and P. Bost. 2002. "Patient Complaints and Malpractice Risk." *JAMA* 287 (22): 2951–57. https://doi.org/10.1001/jama.287.22.2951.

Hunter, D. J. 1992. "Doctors as Managers: Poachers Turned Gamekeepers?" *Social Science & Medicine* 35 (4): 557–66. https://doi.org/10.1016/0277-9536(92)90349-U.

Institute of Medicine (IOM). 2015. *Measuring the Impact of Interprofessional Education on Collaborative Practice and Patient Outcomes.* Washington, DC: National Academies Press. https://doi.org/10.17226/21726.

Kaiser Family Foundation. 2018. "Total Health Care Employment." Published May. www.kff.org/other/state-indicator/total-health-care-employment/?current Timeframe=0&sortModel=%7B%22colId%22:%22Location%22,%22sort%22: %22asc%22%7D.

Kane, C. K. 2015. "Updated Data on Physician Practice Arrangements: Inching Toward Hospital Ownership." American Medical Association. Accessed November 5, 2019. www.m3globalresearch.com/img/resources/AMA_ PRP_Physician_Practice_Arrangements.pdf.

Kirkpatrick, I., E. Kuhlmann, K. Hartley, M. Dent, and F. Lega. 2016. "Medicine and Management in European Hospitals: A Comparative Overview." *BMC Health Services Research* 16 (Suppl. 2): 171. https://doi.org/10.1186/ s12913-016-1388-4.

Laugesen, M. 2016. *Fixing Medical Prices: How Physicians Are Paid.* Cambridge, MA: Harvard University Press.

Lee, J., and G. Anders. 2018. "In Some Cities, It's Too Expensive to Be a Nurse." LinkedIn. Published May 30. www.linkedin.com/pulse/some-cities-its-too-expensive-nurse-jaimy-lee/.

Maslach, C., S. E. Jackson, and M. Leiter. 2015. *The Maslach Burnout Inventory Manual.* Accessed October 5, 2019. www.researchgate.net/publication/ 277816643.

Meyer, R., I. Egger-Peitler, M. Holler, and G. Hammerschid. 2014. "Of Bureacrats and Passionate Public Managers: Institutional Logics, Executive Identities, and Public Service Motivation." *Public Administration* 92 (4): 861–85. https://doi.org/10.1111/j.1467-9299.2012.02105.x.

Moffa, C. 2010. "Is the Florence Nightingale Pledge in Need of a Makeover?" *Off the Charts.* Accessed October 5, 2019. https://ajnoffthecharts.com/ is-the-florence-nightingale-pledge-in-need-of-a-makeover/.

Munson, H. 1949. "Lystra E. Gretter." *American Journal of Nursing* 41 (6): 344–48.

Murray, G. D., and G. M. Teasdale. 2005. *The Relationship Between Volume and Health Outcomes.* Report of Volume/Outcome Sub-Group to Advisory Group to National Framework for Service Change NHS Scotland. Published February. www.sehd.scot.nhs.uk/nationalframework/Documents/ VolumeOutcomeReportWebsite.pdf.

National Association of Clinical Nurse Specialists (NACNS). 2019. "What Is a CNS?" Accessed October 5. https://nacns.org/about-us/what-is-a-cns/.

———. 2016. "CNS Scope of Practice and Prescriptive Authority." Accessed October 5, 2019. http://nacns.org/wp-content/uploads/2016/11/ PractPrescAuthority1605.pdf.

National Association of Long Term Care Administrator Boards. 2019. "National Association of Long Term Care Administrator Boards." Accessed October 5. www.nabweb.org.

National Council of State Boards of Nursing (NCSBN). 2019a. "NCLEX and Other Exams." Accessed October 5. www.ncsbn.org/nclex.htm.

———. 2019b. "The National Nursing Database." October 5. www.ncsbn.org/national-nursing-database.htm.

Numerato, D., D. Salvatore, and G. Fattore. 2012. "The Impact of Management on Medical Professionalism: A Review." *Sociology of Health & Illness* 34 (4): 626–44. https://doi.org/10.1111/j.1467-9566.2011.01393.x.

Nurse Journal. 2018. "100 Best Things to Do with a Nursing Degree." Accessed October 5, 2019. https://nursejournal.org/articles/100-things-you-can-do-with-a-nursing-degree/.

Oslund, C. 2016. "Which Industries Need Workers? Exploring Differences in Labor Market Activity." *Monthly Labor Review.* Published January. https://doi.org/10.21916/mlr.2016.1.

Penn Nursing. 2019. "American Nursing: An Introduction to the Past." Accessed October 5. www.nursing.upenn.edu/nhhc/american-nursing-an-introduction-to-the-past/.

Porter, M. E., and T. O. Teisberg. 2006. *Redefining Health Care: Creating Value-Based Competition on Results.* Boston: Harvard Business School Press.

Qureshi, M. O., and R. S. Syed. 2014. "The Impact of Robotics on Employment and Motivation of Employees in the Service Sector, with Special Reference to Health Care." *Safety and Health at Work* 5 (4): 198–202. https://doi.org/10.1016/J.SHAW.2014.07.003.

Rotenstein, L. S., M. Torre, M. A. Ramos, R. C. Rosales, C. Guille, S. Sen, and D. A. Mata. 2018. "Prevalence of Burnout Among Physicians: A Systematic Review." *JAMA* 320 (11): 1131–50. https://doi.org/10.1001/jama.2018.12777.

Schwenk, T. L., and K. J. Gold. 2018. "Physician Burnout—A Serious Symptom, but of What?" *JAMA* 320 (11): 1109–10. https://doi.org/10.1001/jama.2018.11703.

Seattle Children's Hospital. 2019. "Advanced Practice Provider (APP) Fellowship Program." Accessed October 5. www.seattlechildrens.org/healthcare-professionals/education/residency-fellowships/advanced-practice-provider-fellowship/.

Shwartz, N. D. 2017. "The Doctor Is In. Co-Pay? $40,000." *New York Times.* Published June 3. www.nytimes.com/2017/06/03/business/economy/high-end-medical-care.html.

Southwick, F. S., and S. M. Southwick. 2018. "The Loss of a Sense of Control as a Major Contributor to Physician Burnout." *JAMA Psychiatry* 75 (7): 665–66. https://doi.org/10.1001/jamapsychiatry.2018.0566.

Sowden, A., V. Aletras, M. Place, N. Rice, A. Eastwood, R. Grilli, B. Ferguson, J. Posnett, and T. Sheldon. 1997. "Volume of Clinical Activity in Hospitals and Healthcare Outcomes, Costs, and Patient Access." *Quality in Health Care* 6 (2): 109–14. www.ncbi.nlm.nih.gov/pubmed/10173253.

Thompson, D. 2018. "Health Care Just Became the U.S.'s Largest Employer." *Atlantic.* Published January 9. www.theatlantic.com/business/archive/2018/01/health-care-america-jobs/550079/.

Timmerman, L. 2013. "What's in a Name? A Lot, When It Comes to 'Precision Medicine.'" Xconomy. Published February 4. www.xconomy.com/national/2013/02/04/whats-in-a-name-a-lot-when-it-comes-to-precision-medicine/.

Torpey, E. 2014. "Healthcare: Millions of Jobs Now and in the Future." *Occupational Outlook Quarterly* 58 (1): 27–43. www.bls.gov/careeroutlook/2014/spring/art03.pdf.

Trapp, R. 2018. "What Do CEOs Do All Day?" *Forbes.* Published June 27. www.forbes.com/sites/rogertrapp/2018/06/27/what-do-ceos-do-all-day/#14313141653a.

University of Chicago School of Social Service Administration. 2019. "History." Accessed October 5. www.ssa.uchicago.edu/history.

———. 2018. "Who Was Michael M. Davis?" Published August 1. https://chas.uchicago.edu/2018/08/01/who-was-michael-m-davis/.

US Bureau of Labor Statistics (BLS). 2019. "Healthcare Occupations." *Occupational Outlook Handbook.* Updated September 4. www.bls.gov/ooh/healthcare/home.htm.

———. 2017a. "Employment Projections: 2016–26 ." Published October 27. www.bls.gov/news.release/archives/ecopro_10242017.pdf.

———. 2017b. "Occupational Employment Statistics." Accessed November 3, 2018. www.bls.gov/oes/tables.htm.

Vanderbilt Health. 2019. "Nurse Practitioner Fellowship Program." Accessed October 5. https://ww2.mc.vanderbilt.edu/nursingoap/50658.

Wagner, S. L. 1994. *Resource Allocation and Quality of Health Care Services: Implications for Policy in the Era of Healthcare Reform.* Louisville, KY: University of Louisville, Ektrom Library.

Warrington, J. 1839. *The Nurse's Guide: Containing a Series of Instructions to Females Who Wish to Engage in the Important Business of Nursing Mother and Child in the Lying-In Chamber.* Philadelphia, PA: Thomas, Cowperthwait and Co.

Windey, M., and K. Cullen. 2018. "Advanced Practice Registered Nurse Fellowships." *Journal for Nurses in Professional Development* 34 (1): 41–42. https://doi.org/10.1097/NND.0000000000000405.

World Health Organization (WHO). 2010. *Health Professions Networks Nursing and Midwifery Human Resources for Health: Framework for Action on Interprofessional Education and Collaborative Practice*. Accessed October 5, 2019. https://apps.who.int/iris/bitstream/handle/10665/70185/WHO_HRH_ HPN_10.3_eng.pdf;jsessio.

———. 2008. *The World Health Report 2008: Primary Health Care, Now More than Ever*. Accessed October 5, 2019. www.who.int/whr/2008/en/index.html.

PATIENT CARE: THE PURPOSE OF THE SYSTEM

Illness is the night-side of life, a more onerous citizenship. Everyone who is born holds dual citizenship, in the kingdom of the well and in the kingdom of the sick. Although we all prefer to use only the good passport, sooner or later each of us is obliged, at least for a spell, to identify ourselves as citizens of that other place. . . .

—Susan Sontag

Learning Objectives

- Understand models of health and well-being.
- Examine the importance of patient engagement.
- Evaluate the causes of health disparities.
- Develop a comparison of population health and public health.
- Recognize the impact of behavioral health on our healthcare system.
- Analyze the question "Do we overdiagnose and overtreat patients?"

Improving Health and Well-Being

The overall purpose of the healthcare system is to provide patient care with the aim of improving human health and well-being (see exhibit 7.1). This purpose may seem obvious, but it can easily become obscured as organizations attend to their day-to-day pursuits. Every component of the healthcare system has its own specific activities and concerns, yet success still depends on keeping ourselves and our organizations focused on the mission, vision, and values that support health and well-being.

The concepts of health and well-being are multidimensional and complex, but their most basic elements can be understood in the context of Blum's determinants of health. As shown in exhibit 7.2, Blum (1974) identified four major inputs that contribute to our health and well-being:

1. Environment (location and conditions)
2. Lifestyle (behavior and situation)

EXHIBIT 7.1
Area of Focus
for This Chapter

The Aim of the Healthcare System   Issues That Require Our Attention

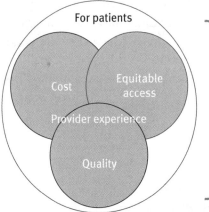

- Nature of our complex system
- Historical issues that have influenced the development of the system
- Beliefs and attitudes about health and healthcare
- Comparison with other developed countries
- Components of our healthcare system
- People and providers
- *Patient care—the purpose of the system*
- Financing a massive system
- Quality—easier said than done
- Medical and information technology
- The pharmaceutical industry
- Complementary and alternative medicine
- Politics/economics
- The future of the system

EXHIBIT 7.2
Blum's
Model of the
Determinants
of Health and
Well-Being

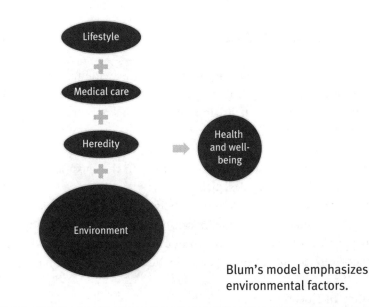

Blum's model emphasizes
environmental factors.

Source: Adapted from Blum (1974).

3. Heredity (genetic makeup)
4. Medical care (what we receive from the healthcare system)

Blum (1974) further theorized that none of these inputs could be considered in isolation; all four had to considered simultaneously for both individuals or groups. Given that the healthcare field had previously focused almost exclusively on medical care, Blum's attention to the other inputs was unusual and profound. Blum's ideas are sometimes referred to as the Force Field and Well-Being Paradigms of Health, reflecting their emphasis on environmental factors.

A similar model of health and well-being, shown in exhibit 7.3, is based on the approach of the Centers for Disease Control and Prevention (CDC 2019a, 2019b, 2018b, 2014). Like Blum's model, the CDC approach recognizes the need to consider all four inputs simultaneously. However, whereas the Blum model emphasizes the environment, the CDC places the greatest emphasis on lifestyle behaviors.

The difference in focus between the two models is likely due in part to the surrounding context. The CDC, as a government agency, has a responsibility to design and implement strategies to improve people's health and well-being. Within that area of accountability, an emphasis on lifestyle behaviors offers the greatest potential for the agency to gain traction. After all, people cannot always control their environment, but they can—with the support of CDC initiatives—make choices to support better health. In contrast, Blum's work was more theoretical in nature. He was able to think more broadly

EXHIBIT 7.3
The CDC Model of Health and Well-Being

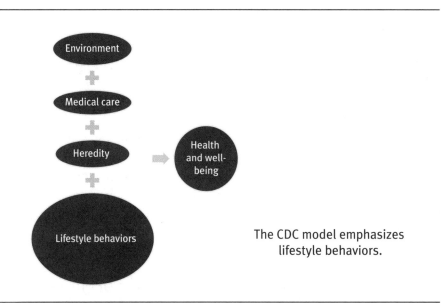

The CDC model emphasizes lifestyle behaviors.

Source: Adapted from CDC (2019a, 2019b, 2018b, 2014).

about the issues without the constraints of operational imperatives. Often in healthcare, when so many issues must be managed, the ideal and the doable are at odds. Nevertheless, all four inputs have significant impacts on health and well-being, and all should be addressed by healthcare organizations when planning and delivering care.

A number of questions should be asked when considering the role an organization plays in the health and well-being of patients. First, who is responsible for an individual's health and well-being? We might be able to agree that the individual, the healthcare system, and society as a whole all bear some responsibility—but, as the old saying goes, "When everybody is responsible, nobody is responsible."

Further questions explore the various dimensions. Are we here to simply provide medical care? Or should our purpose be bigger—to provide preventive services; to ensure safe places to live, work, and play; to see that individuals have proper nutrition; to promote healthy lifestyles; or to engage in advocacy for public policies that support health and well-being for all? The answers to these questions represent the organization's "macro" view of its role, and it is influenced by the way the organization is funded and the nature of its mission.

Often, people and organizations are so busily focused on their own aspects of the healthcare system that they ignore other aspects that might be equally important to health and well-being. As a result, the system misses opportunities for synergy and collaboration. For example, if a person is in repeated diabetic crisis and lacks access to medicine or proper nutrition, hospital staff might provide emergency medical services. However, continually providing emergency services is only a partial solution; it will never fully address the problem nor create an optimal outcome. To truly improve this person's health and well-being, the healthcare system must collaborate both with the individual and with society—just the kind of holistic thinking advanced by Blum.

What Is Health?

Health has been defined in a number of ways and from a variety of perspectives. The University of Ottawa (2019) has classified health definitions into three categories: those based on a holistic model, emphasizing "complete physical, mental and social well-being"; those based on a medical model, focusing on treating specific physical diseases; and those based on a wellness model, which treats health "as a process or force." Most views of health in the United States have centered on healthcare and physical wellness as primary factors.

According to the World Health Organization (WHO 1948), "Health is a state of complete physical, mental and social well-being and not merely the absence of disease or infirmity." In 1984, WHO further developed the idea of health in wellness terms, in part by adding the notion that health and well-being are not static but dynamic (WHO 1984).

Another definition, developed by Stokes, Noren, and Shindell (1982), states that health is "a state characterized by anatomic integrity; ability to perform personally valued family, work, and community roles; ability to deal with physical, biological, and social stress; a feeling of well-being; and freedom from the risk of disease and untimely death." The Stokes definition emphasizes the medical model of health, focusing on the absence of physical or mental impairment.

What Is Well-Being?

Well-being, to paraphrase many authors, is an outcome of all the aspects of life coming together in a meaningful way (Diener 2009; Huber et al. 2011; Schneiderman 2011; Scully 2004). It is the perception that life is going well. To measure well-being, we must take into account an overall judgment of life satisfaction and the whole gamut of human feeling (Blum 1974; Diener 2009; Diener, Napa Scollon, and Lucas 2009; Green and Elliott 2010; Dias and O'Donnell 2013). Well-being incorporates all the domains of life and the human condition—not just physical and mental health but also religion/spirituality, housing, food, environment, work, relationships, and so on. As a result, it is complex and ever-changing.

Of course, these definitions of *health* and *well-being* must be considered in the context of our country and our era. Is it even possible, in the United States, to separate health and well-being from economics, social services, healthcare delivery, and other social justice elements (e.g., race, gender, socioeconomic inequality)? It may not be. As professionals in the healthcare system, we must recognize that, even if we cannot find all the answers to these "big" questions, we still need to keep asking. Our field covers not just medicine but the whole scope of human experience.

Categories of Patient Care

Chapter 5 discussed the components of the US healthcare system across the broad categories of inpatient, outpatient, and long-term care. However, patient care can also be categorized in other ways, such as by duration, scope, and intensity of treatment. This section will identify and define several categories of care to provide background and insight for our discussion. The exact definitions of certain terms may vary from one place to another, but the overall meanings are generally consistent (McGill University Medical Centre 2014; Torrey 2019).

Care Services Defined by Duration of Treatment

The categories of acute and chronic care are based on duration of treatment. Acute care involves treatment for a short duration for an illness or injury that typically has a sudden onset. Acute care services are often intense, and they are frequently performed in hospital settings. Chronic care has a longer treatment duration—usually at least three months, though specific definitions vary. Chronic care typically addresses illnesses or injuries that may not be curable but that can be managed over time through proper medication and other forms of treatment. Examples may include hypertension, arthritis, diabetes, HIV, and Parkinson's disease. Such conditions can often be managed in the outpatient setting without the need for hospitalization, although there may be periods when acute care is needed. In some instances, acute care may evolve into chronic care. For example, a person might be treated on an acute basis for a hypertensive emergency (severely elevated blood pressure) and then require chronic care for the long-term treatment of the hypertensive condition. An additional category of subacute care includes services that go beyond nursing home care but are typically less complex than those received in acute care hospital settings.

Care Services Defined by Scope and Intensity of Treatment

Exhibit 7.4 provides a visual representation of the scope and intensity of inpatient and outpatient care. Primary care includes basic, routine services provided on an outpatient basis in a physician's office by various clinicians, such as physicians, advanced care professionals, nurses, and technicians. Primary care is often the first form of contact an individual has with the healthcare system, and it is critically important in the patient-centered medical home environment. Primary prevention is intended to prevent disease or injury before it occurs; examples include health education and immunizations.

EXHIBIT 7.4
Scope and
Intensity of Care

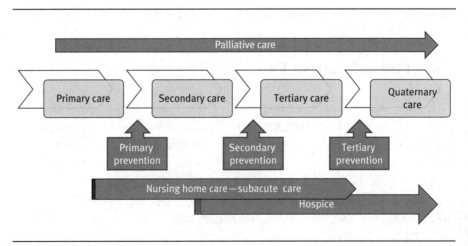

Secondary care services are typically acute in nature and are often per-formed in a hospital. They may also be performed on an outpatient basis by specialists who provide consults, complex diagnostic testing, or rehabilitative care. Examples of secondary services may include a routine appendectomy in a hospital or a nuclear stress test and cardiovascular lab on an outpatient basis. Secondary prevention includes screening services for early detec-tion of medical conditions; examples include regular physical exams and mammograms.

Tertiary care services involve complex levels of treatment. The treat-ment usually requires advanced technologies and is provided in an institu-tion such as a medical center. Examples may include coronary artery bypass, severe burn treatment, or bone marrow transplants. Tertiary prevention is the practice of providing interventions to prevent complications from chronic disease to avoid further medical consequences. Cardiac rehab programs, support groups, and chronic disease management programs are examples of tertiary prevention.

Quaternary care is best thought of as an extension of tertiary care, though the services are available from only a certain number of highly spe-cialized and skilled practitioners and a limited number of facilities. Examples may include experimental treatments or unusual surgical procedures such as limb reattachment.

Palliative care focuses on relieving symptoms and stresses associated with serious illness, with the aim of improving quality of life for the patient and family. Palliative care may be provided at any stage of life for any period of time, depending on need (WHO 2019). Palliative care differs from hos-pice care, which does not seek to cure the patient. Hospice care is typically provided to patients who are not expected to live longer than six months. The goal of hospice is to keep patients free from pain and in a comfortable environment, thereby supporting the highest quality of life level possible as they near the end of life. Hospice also works to support the dying patient's family. The setting for hospice may vary, ranging from the hospital to the home, depending on the level of medical support needed (National Hospice and Palliative Care Organization 2019).

The terms *upstreaming* and *downstreaming* are often applied in public health contexts. Upstreaming involves interventions to address underlying social or economic barriers to receiving health services and achieving better health outcomes. Preventive healthcare could be one example. Downstream-ing focuses on providing equitable access to care for disadvantaged popula-tions to reduce the negative health impacts of inequality. An example of downstreaming might involve providing free or low-cost prenatal services to disadvantaged mothers in an effort to reduce infant mortality (National Col-laborating Centre for Determinants of Health 2019).

What Constitutes Accountable Care?

Since the passage of the Affordable Care Act of 2010, many physicians have begun to focus on the concept of accountable care and the ways that concept can be expressed in practice. The Council of Accountable Physician Practices (CAPP), an affiliate of the American Medical Group Association Foundation, set out to explore these issues in detail. From the patient's point of view, what does physician practice accountability mean?

Based on its research, CAPP (2016a, 2016b) proposes that practices should strive to provide the following benefits of accountable care:

- Care team coordination
- Prevention
- 24/7 access
- Evidence-based medicine (treatments based on proof)
- Care enabled by robust technology

CAPP sponsored an online survey of 30,007 US consumers as well as an additional survey of 626 US physicians; both surveys were conducted by Nielsen's Strategic Health Perspectives. CAPP (2016a) describes the key findings as follows:

- Eighty-nine percent of primary care physicians say they often remind patients about preventive screenings, but only 14 percent of patients say they get these reminders. More than two-thirds of adult Americans are overweight or obese, yet only 5 percent of patients report that their physicians recommended a weight-loss program.
- Only half of patients are experiencing physicians who better know their history, primarily due to the ability to share information through electronic medical records. However, patients with multiple chronic illnesses, who would most benefit from care coordination, receive only slightly more follow-ups and care management than everyone else.
- Patients' electronic engagement with physicians is increasing but still low, with 20 to 30 percent of the total surveyed reporting that they have various forms of digital access. . . . Roughly 44 percent report access to online information, such as appointment scheduling, obtaining lab test results, or viewing information via portals. Older Americans are less likely to want to use digital technology for healthcare, which presents a challenge in fully leveraging this technology to improve care delivery to this population.

- Only about one-third have 24/7 access to care through their physician's office other than the emergency room.
- Sixty-five percent of physicians report using evidence-based guidelines to help determine treatment, with 39 percent of patients recalling discussions on new treatment options.

These findings suggested that a gap existed between what physicians believed and what patients believed was occurring in practice. CAPP concluded that the system needed to continue its efforts to educate and share information with patients to support quality care. It also encouraged payment reform to move toward value-based reimbursement; improved access to 24/7 care; greater "system-ness" and clinical integration; better technology for the sharing of information between providers, patients, and families; and the standardization of measures in language that patients and families can understand (CAPP 2016b).

Key Issues in Patient Care

Patient Engagement

As we look to reform the US healthcare system, one of the most important issues is patient engagement. Engaged patients take more responsibility for their own health and healthcare and are in greater compliance with medical instructions and medication use. Noncompliance can be a significant obstacle to optimal healthcare outcomes and a major source of waste in the system. Research suggests that patient engagement can be improved by promoting health literacy as well as by having patients and family play a greater role in the decision making about medical care (Glazier and Redelmeier 2010; Jackson and Williams 2015; Jaén et al. 2010). These findings support a general shift from provider-directed care toward more patient-centered or patient-directed care.

Health Disparities

Health disparities are the differences in health status that exist from one group to another. Some groups have significantly higher rates of certain diseases—as well as more deaths and suffering from those diseases—than other groups. Understanding the ways particular groups are affected by health issues, analyzing data about health disparities, and addressing preventable disparities are major concerns for the US healthcare system (National Institutes of Health [NIH] 2010).

Health disparities often affect members of minority groups. Approximately one-third of Americans identify themselves as being member of a minority group based on race or ethnicity (Office of Disease Prevention and Health Promotion 2019a; US Census Bureau 2019b). Minority groups may also be based on immigrant status, disability, biological sex or gender expression, sexual orientation, or other factors. Geography and income may also contribute to health disparities. If a person is unable to meet basic nutritional needs, lacks healthcare coverage, or is unable to access care because of transportation or other issues, health status will be affected (Kaiser Family Foundation [KFF] 2015; Lasser, Himmelstein, and Woolhandler 2006; Slade-Sawyer 2014; Williams, Walker, and Egede 2016).

Reducing disparities in healthcare not only will lead to better health for everyone; it will also reduce the cost of care. Failure to address healthcare needs at the proper time and with the proper services only serves to delay treatment, creating a need for more serious interventions later on. This delay leads to greater morbidity, suffering, and mortality, as well as higher costs for care that is needed after the condition has progressed to a more serious state or needs to be addressed on an emergency basis.

Some population groups are disproportionally affected by certain elements of the Blum model. In many instances, groups face bias and discrimination—whether willful or unconscious—on the basis of race or ethnicity, sexual orientation, gender expression, age, disability status, or immigration status. Biases can have a negative impact on patients' health, and people who act deliberately on such biases should not be working in the healthcare system (Barnes et al. 2004; CDC 2018a; Chen et al. 2005; Hafeez et al. 2017; Hausmann et al. 2008).

Some forms of bias are unintentional or unconscious, often stemming from erroneous beliefs that have been perpetuated over the years. One such example is the once-common belief that heart disease is a "male" condition. For many years, physicians treating women would often overlook heart disease because they erroneously believed that women were unlikely to suffer from it. This bias—sometimes known as "Yentl syndrome" (Healy 1991)—developed from the male-oriented study of heart disease predominant in many physicians' medical education. Heart disease expresses itself differently in men and women, so diagnosis requires attention to gender (Berger et al. 2008; Bugiardini and Bairey-Merz 2005; Merz 2011; Shaw, Bugiardini, and Merz 2009).

Often, healthcare systems categorize or stratify patients when considering the best way to provide services to them. Patients can be divided into groups based on gender, age, ethnicity, specific disease or disease category, patient vulnerability, or various other characteristics. The stratification of patients can often help the system to focus on patients' special needs, but sometimes patients will not fit neatly into any single group. For example, women's health is a common area of focus, but women often fit into other population categories, such as the homeless or frail elderly, at the same time.

The sections that follow will examine health disparities in greater detail. Additional information is available from the Centers for Medicare & Medicaid Services (CMS) Office of Minority Health in Collaboration with the RAND Corporation (2018) and the Office of Disease Prevention and Health Promotion (2019a).

Sex Differences

Clearly, men and women have different healthcare needs, not just in terms of reproductive health but also in the ways they respond to medications and other treatments and in the ways they the manifest disease (Eunice Kennedy Shriver National Institute of Children's Health and Human Development 2016). Sex and gender differences also influence people's perceptions of health and well-being (National Institutes of Health Office for Research on Women's Health [ORWH] 2019; Regitz-Zagrosek 2012). Healthcare organizations must be cognizant of these differences and make every effort to deliver treatment appropriate to each person's unique needs (Anderson 2008; Moran 2018). Organizations must also work to eliminate sex- and gender-based biases that may come about through societal perspectives, norms, and traditions, as well as biology (Matthews 2015). A wealth of information about biological sex and health disparities, women's health outcomes, and sex- and gender-related health concerns is available from such sources as the CDC, WHO, KFF, and the US Department of Health and Human Services (HHS).

Women in the United States, on average, live about five years longer than men. The figures vary somewhat by race and ethnicity, but the longevity difference appears to be lifelong and consistent within all groups (National Center for Health Statistics [NCHS] 2016). Exhibit 7.5 shows the gender differences in the leading causes of death in the United States. Heart disease and cancer are the leading causes of death for both men and women—representing more than 40 percent of all deaths—but the next three causes show variation. Women are significantly more likely to have stroke- or Alzheimer's-related deaths, whereas men are more likely to die from unintended injury. Chronic lower respiratory diseases are a major cause of death for both men and women (CDC 2019d, 2019e). The opioid crisis (discussed further in chapter 11) has also become an important cause of death for both men and women; in fact, it has led to a decrease in overall longevity in the United States (Sanger-Katz 2018). The leading type of cancer death in women is lung cancer. In a historical reversal, lung cancer is now

EXHIBIT 7.5
Gender
Differences in
Cause of Death

Men	Women
Heart disease (24.2%)	Heart disease (22.0%)
Cancer (22.5%)	Cancer (21.1%)
Unintended injuries (7.4%)	Stroke (6.2%)
Chronic lower respiratory diseases (5.2%)	Chronic lower respiratory diseases (6.1%)
Stroke (4.2%)	Alzheimer's disease (6.0%)

Source: CDC (2019d, 2019e).

more common among young women than young men, and the trend does not seem to be closely related to smoking behavior (Jemal et al. 2018).

Men have a higher incidence of heart disease than women do, and about 50 percent more men are affected by Parkinson's disease than women. Men also have higher risks of autism, kidney stones, and pancreatitis. These differences are likely related to genetics, hormones, metabolism, and social and behavioral factors (Harvard Medical School 2010).

Women tend to seek care more often than men, though they may face more barriers to receiving care because of economic status (NCHS 2001; Cameron et al. 2010; WHO 2007). Women often have a more difficult time quitting smoking than men, experience more depression, and are more likely to be on Medicaid. Frequently, women serve as caregivers and make healthcare decisions for others, often at the expense of their own care (ORWH 2018). Because women on average live longer than men, they are often without a spouse or significant other during their later years.

Violence and Domestic Violence

Without a doubt, violence is a serious public health and healthcare issue. The CDC (2017a) reports that one in seven children has experienced abuse or neglect in the past year, 20 people experience physical violence from an intimate partner every minute, half of all women experience sexual violence in their lifetime, and one in five men experiences sexual violence in their lifetime. As shown in exhibit 7.6, homicide ranks as one of the top five causes of death for several age groups; as shown in exhibit 7.7, suicide by firearm is a major cause of injury-related death (CDC 2017b, 2017c).

Many acts of violence fall disproportionately on women, children, and the disadvantaged. A study by Fox and Fridel (2017) reported that 44.8 percent of all homicides against women were committed by an intimate partner; the same was true for only 5 percent of homicides against men. These data were supported by a 2018 *Washington Post* investigative report about female

EXHIBIT 7.6
Leading Causes of Death by Age Group

10 Leading Causes of Death by Age Group, United States – 2016

Rank	<1	1–4	5–9	10–14	15–24	25–34	35–44	45–54	55–64	65+	Total
1	Congenital Anomalies 4,816	Unintentional Injury 1,261	Unintentional Injury 787	Unintentional Injury 847	Unintentional Injury 13,895	Unintentional Injury 23,984	Unintentional Injury 20,975	Malignant Neoplasms 41,291	Malignant Neoplasms 116,364	Heart Disease 507,118	Heart Disease 635,260
2	Short Gestation 3,927	Congenital Anomalies 433	Malignant Neoplasms 449	Suicide 436	Suicide 5,723	Suicide 7,366	Malignant Neoplasms 10,903	Heart Disease 34,027	Heart Disease 78,610	Malignant Neoplasms 422,927	Malignant Neoplasms 598,038
3	SIDS 1,500	Malignant Neoplasms 377	Congenital Anomalies 203	Malignant Neoplasms 431	Homicide 5,172	Homicide 5,376	Heart Disease 10,477	Unintentional Injury 23,377	Unintentional Injury 21,860	Chronic Low. Respiratory Disease 131,002	Unintentional Injury 161,374
4	Maternal Pregnancy Comp. 1,402	Homicide 339	Homicide 139	Homicide 147	Malignant Neoplasms 1,431	Malignant Neoplasms 3,791	Suicide 7,030	Suicide 8,437	Chronic Low. Respiratory Disease 17,810	Cerebro-vascular 121,630	Chronic Low. Respiratory Disease 154,596
5	Unintentional Injury 1,219	Heart Disease 118	Heart Disease 77	Congenital Anomalies 146	Heart Disease 949	Heart Disease 3,445	Homicide 3,369	Liver Disease 8,364	Diabetes Mellitus 14,251	Alzheimer's Disease 114,883	Cerebro-vascular 142,142
6	Placenta Cord. Membranes 841	Influenza & Pneumonia 103	Chronic Low. Respiratory Disease 68	Heart Disease 111	Congenital Anomalies 388	Liver Disease 925	Liver Disease 2,851	Diabetes Mellitus 6,267	Liver Disease 13,448	Diabetes Mellitus 56,452	Alzheimer's Disease 116,103
7	Bacterial Sepsis 583	Septicemia 70	Influenza & Pneumonia 48	Chronic Low. Respiratory Disease 75	Diabetes Mellitus 211	Diabetes Mellitus 792	Diabetes Mellitus 2,049	Cerebro-vascular 5,353	Cerebro-vascular 12,310	Unintentional Injury 53,141	Diabetes Mellitus 80,058
8	Respiratory Distress 488	Perinatal Period 60	Septicemia 40	Cerebro-vascular 50	Chronic Low. Respiratory Disease 206	Cerebro-vascular 575	Cerebro-vascular 1,851	Chronic Low. Respiratory Disease 4,307	Suicide 7,759	Influenza & Pneumonia 42,479	Influenza & Pneumonia 51,537
9	Circulatory System Disease 460	Cerebro-vascular 55	Cerebro-vascular 38	Influenza & Pneumonia 39	Influenza & Pneumonia 189	HIV 546	HIV 971	Septicemia 2,472	Septicemia 5,941	Nephritis 41,095	Nephritis 50,046
10	Neonatal Hemorrhage 398	Chronic Low Respiratory Disease 51	Benign Neoplasms 31	Septicemia 31	Complicated Pregnancy 184	Complicated Pregnancy 472	Septicemia 897	Homicide 2,152	Nephritis 5,650	Septicemia 30,405	Suicide 44,965

Source: Reprinted from CDC (2017b).

EXHIBIT 7.7
Leading Causes of Injury Deaths by Age Group

10 Leading Causes of Injury Deaths by Age Group Highlighting Violence-Related Injury Deaths, United States – 2016

Rank	<1	1–4	5–9	10–14	15–24	25–34	35–44	45–54	55–64	65+	Total
					Age Groups						
1	Unintentional Suffocation 1,023	Unintentional Drowning 425	Unintentional MV Traffic 384	Unintentional MV Traffic 455	Unintentional MV Traffic 7,037	Unintentional Poisoning 14,631	Unintentional Poisoning 13,278	Unintentional Poisoning 13,439	Unintentional Poisoning 9,438	Unintentional Fall 29,668	Unintentional Poisoning 58,335
2	Homicide Unspecified 132	Unintentional MV Traffic 334	Unintentional Drowning 147	Suicide Suffocation 247	Unintentional Poisoning 4,997	Unintentional MV Traffic 7,010	Unintentional MV Traffic 5,075	Unintentional MV Traffic 5,536	Unintentional MV Traffic 5,397	Unintentional MV Traffic 7,429	Unintentional MV Traffic 38,748
3	Unintentional MV Traffic 88	Unintentional Suffocation 118	Unintentional Fire/Burn 78	Suicide Firearm 160	Homicide Firearm 4,553	Homicide Firearm 4,510	Suicide Firearm 3,873	Suicide Firearm 3,882	Suicide Firearm 4,067	Suicide Firearm 5,756	Unintentional Fall 34,673
4	Homicide Other Spe.., Classifiable 63	Homicide Unspecified 134	Homicide Firearm 68	Unintentional Drowning 103	Suicide Firearm 2,683	Suicide Firearm 3,298	Homicide Firearm 2,555	Suicide Suffocation 2,112	Unintentional Fall 2,679	Unintentional Unspecified 5,021	Suicide Firearm 22,938
5	Unintentional Suffocation 60	Unintentional Fire/Burn 107	Unintentional Suffocation 35	Homicide Firearm 95	Suicide Suffocation 2,100	Suicide Suffocation 2,643	Suicide Suffocation 2,199	Suicide Poisoning 1,736	Suicide Poisoning 1,538	Unintentional Suffocation 3,631	Homicide Firearm 14,415
6	Undetermined Unspecified 38	Unintentional Pedestrian Other 82	Unintentional Other Land Transport 24	Unintentional Other Land Transport 64	Unintentional Drowning 530	Undetermined Poisoning 855	Suicide Poisoning 1,144	Homicide Firearm 1,420	Suicide Suffocation 1,474	Unintentional Poisoning 2,458	Suicide Suffocation 11,642
7	Unintentional Drowning 38	Homicide Firearm 64	Unintentional Pedestrian, Other 18	Unintentional Fire/Burn 52	Suicide Poisoning 426	Suicide Poisoning 767	Undetermined Poisoning 788	Unintentional Fall 1,238	Unintentional Suffocation 792	Adverse Effects 2,028	Suicide Poisoning 6,698
8	Homicide Suffocation 19	Homicide Other Spec., Classifiable 64	Unintentional Firearm 16	Unintentional Suffocation 39	Homicide Cut/Pierce 340	Homicide Cut/Pierce 420	Unintentional Fall 515	Undetermined Poisoning 929	Homicide Firearm 738	Unintentional Fire/Burn 1,150	Unintentional Suffocation 6,610
9	Adverse Effects 18	Unintentional Firearm 34	Unintentional Struck by or Against 15	Unintentional Poisoning 28	Undetermined Poisoning 289	Unintentional Drowning 463	Unintentional Drowning 396	Unintentional Drowning 478	Undetermined Poisoning 707	Suicide Poisoning 1,070	Unintentional Unspecified 6,507
10	Unintentional Natural/Environment 18	Unintentional Poisoning 34	Unintentional Other Transport 14	Unintentional Firearm 23	Unintentional Fall 199	Unintentional Fall 326	Homicide Cut/Pierce 350	Unintentional Suffocation 419	Undetermined Unspecified 625	Suicide Suffocation 859	Undetermined Poisoning 3,827

Note: MV = motor vehicle.

Source: Reprinted from CDC (2017c).

homicide deaths in 50 major US cities. Zezima and colleagues (2018) examined the deaths of approximately 7,000 women and were able to determine the relationship of the killer to the victim in 4,484 of those cases. They found that 46 percent of the killers were the intimate partner of the murdered woman. Many of these homicides were committed using a handgun. These distressing facts should serve as a call to action for people throughout the healthcare system to better understand, detect, and deter such incidents.

Lesbian, Gay, Bisexual, and Transgender Health

When addressing sex- and gender-related issues in healthcare, we need to consider not just matters of women's and men's health but also the needs of the lesbian, gay, bisexual, and transgender (LGBT) community. LGBT individuals have long been overlooked by the healthcare system and often face a significant amount of discrimination and bias (CDC 2018a; Hafeez et al. 2017).

The healthcare system and public health professionals should strive to provide culturally competent services for LGBT people, targeting the needs of the individual as well as the group. Healthcare for the LGBT community has been affected by a number of special circumstances and challenges, including lack of access to health insurance, a shortage of healthcare providers who are knowledgeable and culturally competent about LGBT health, and lack of access to necessary health services (CDC 2018a). The Office of Disease Prevention and Health Promotion (2019b) describes a number of alarming disparities facing the LGBT community:

- LGBT youth are two to three times more likely than others to attempt suicide.
- LGBT youth are more likely to be homeless.
- Lesbians are less likely to receive preventive services for cancer.
- Gay men have a higher risk of HIV and other sexually transmitted diseases (STDs), especially among communities of color.
- Transgender people have a high prevalence of HIV/STDs, victimization, mental health issues, and suicide; they are less likely to have health insurance than heterosexual or LGB individuals.
- Elderly LGBT individuals face additional barriers to health, often because of isolation or a lack of social services and culturally competent providers.
- LGBT populations have high rates of tobacco, alcohol, and other drug use.

These and other disparities have been documented by a variety of organizations and studies (CDC 2019c, 2018a; US Census Bureau 2019a, 2019c; HHS 2019a).

The attitudes of providers and other people in the healthcare system play an important role in the availability of services and manner of treatment for members of the LGBT community (Hafeez et al. 2017). People throughout healthcare must recognize the intersectionality of the LGBT community—it includes people of all genders, ages, races, socioeconomic statuses, and walks of life—and be cognizant of the harmful effects of homophobic or transphobic stereotypes and biases. To reduce disparities and ensure that everyone in the country receives the best possible care, the US healthcare system must be a welcoming place for LGBT people.

Race and Ethnicity

Racial and ethnic disparities in health have been a source of concern for many years. As of 2016, significant variations still exist in life expectancy and other health outcomes for African Americans and other ethnic and racial groups (Herman, Adkins, and Moon 2014; Williams, Walker, and Egede 2016). Life expectancy for African Americans, for instance, has long been significantly lower than for the white population. Maternal mortality also continues to be a disproportionate threat to African American women and other women of color (Flanders-Stephans 2000; Chalhoub and Rimar 2018).

A significant body of literature has set out to document these disparities and examine their causes. Signorello and colleagues (2014) found that socioeconomic factors were a strong predictor of mortality. A number of researchers have found that racism, stereotypes, and biases play an important role in the variation in health outcomes and decreased access to care (Dykes and White 2009; Hostetter and Klein 2018). Even patients with the same socioeconomic status and similar demographic information often see variations in care based on race or ethnicity.

Culturally competent care—care that emphasizes the patient–provider relationship and focuses on cultural sensitivity, responsiveness, effectiveness, and humility—is an imperative for improving health outcomes and addressing health disparities in the United States (Betancourt et al. 2003). The Institute for Healthcare Improvement (IHI) has published an excellent resource titled *Achieving Health Equity: A Guide for Healthcare Organizations* (Wyatt et al. 2016). In addition to providing valuable information about health disparities and the people affected, the guide offers healthcare organizations a framework for eliminating health inequities. The framework has five key components:

- Make health equity a strategic priority
- Develop structure and processes to support health equity work
- Deploy specific strategies to address the multiple determinants of health on which health care organizations can have a direct impact
- Decrease institutional racism within the organization
- Develop partnerships with community organizations to improve health and equity

Reducing health disparities is an ethical and moral imperative (Williams, Walker, and Egede 2016), but it also makes good business sense at a time when organizations are taking increased responsibility for the health and well-being of the patients they serve.

Age

When considering age as a factor in healthcare, we often think in terms of chronological milestones across the various segments of life: birth, childhood, adolescence, young adulthood, mature adulthood, and elderly adulthood. People in each of these segments have specific health needs and concerns, requiring special consideration from healthcare professionals. For example, differences in the ways children and elderly adults react to medication may require special dosing and attention to safety concerns (Yu et al. 2015).

People of the various age groups have differences in biology and are affected differently by social and environmental factors. Returning to exhibit 7.6, unintentional injury is the leading cause of death for children, adolescents, and people in early middle age. As people grow older, cancer and heart disease become the predominant causes of death. Nonetheless, unintentional injury remains an important concern for older people, and it has been a major focus for government policy and the healthcare professions (Mack et al. 2015).

A number of healthcare specialties specifically address the needs of certain age groups, including the following:

- Obstetrics, which focuses on prenatal care
- Neonatology, which focuses on the care of newborns, especially those with special medical concerns
- Pediatrics and pediatric subspecialties, which focus on the care of children
- Adolescent medicine, which focuses on the care of older children in their adolescent years prior to adulthood
- Family medicine, which provides care for all age groups with a typical focus on primary care
- Gerontology, which focuses on care for elderly adults

The Needs of Vulnerable Populations

At first glance, the term *vulnerable population* might seem simple. In some sense, anyone who has an illness has vulnerability. People who are ill may be confronted with devastating physical and mental effects, potentially including loss of life, and they often must navigate a healthcare world that feels complex, unfamiliar, and intimidating. The Cleveland Clinic (2013) produced a video titled "Empathy: Exploring the Human Connection" that characterizes this vulnerability in a moving and powerful way. The video begins with a quote from Thoreau: "Could a greater miracle take place than for us to look through each other's eyes for an instant?" It then presents the specific concerns of individuals throughout the healthcare setting: fearing the unknown, struggling to understand the complexities of care, receiving a devastating diagnosis, considering the effect of an illness on important life pursuits, and even seeing a loved one for the last time. The video highlights the need to cultivate not just sympathy but true empathy for every patient. Whereas sympathy indicates that we recognize and care about the suffering of others, empathy goes much further: It involves experiencing the feelings of another person.

The term *vulnerable population* can also be defined in a more specific sense to refer to a disadvantaged subsegment of the community likely to face significant health disparities. Vulnerable populations typically include people who lack the freedom, resources, or capability to protect themselves from risks, make informed choices, and access needed services (Shivayogi 2013). They may also be more susceptible to harmful environmental conditions such as air and water pollution.

Examples of vulnerable populations include the following (Bernal et al. 2017; Joszt 2018; Pauly and Pagán 2007; Ross et al. 2008; Waisel 2013):

- People with disabilities and chronic illnesses often have difficulty accessing the healthcare system—even though, in many cases, they need to access the healthcare system more frequently than most people do.
- Homeless people frequently experience adverse health outcomes and are often stigmatized based on their circumstances.
- People with certain mental conditions sometimes have a diminished capacity to make appropriate decisions for themselves; for instance, a person in a psychotic state might refuse necessary and vital treatment.
- People with low incomes often lack the economic resources to access the healthcare system and experience poor health outcomes as a result.
- People living in rural areas or inner-city areas often lack access to care and other resources that promote good health and well-being.
- LGBT people face significant discrimination, as well as higher rates of psychiatric disorders, substance abuse, and suicide.
- Both the very young and the very old may have difficulty receiving proper care because they often must depend on other people; because the medical research community has traditionally placed greater focus on other age groups (i.e., adults between the ages of 18 and 64); and because they often have lower immunity.

HIV/AIDS

One of the most devastating illnesses of the twentieth century was the human immunodeficiency virus (HIV), which causes acquired immunodeficiency syndrome (AIDS). In 1981, the CDC's *Morbidity and Mortality Weekly Report (MMWR)* described a strange syndrome that caused serious impairment of the immune system—the syndrome that would later be called AIDS (*MMWR* 1981). The emergence of HIV/AIDS caused a great deal of panic, and people who had the disease became the target of intense discrimination. Because many people who contracted HIV/AIDS were already part of a vulnerable population, the epidemic exacerbated these groups' disadvantaged status (CDC 2019c).

In 1992, AIDS was the leading cause of death for American men between the ages of 25 and 44; by 1995, it was the leading killer of all American adults in that age range (KFF 2018). That same year, a new class of drugs called protease inhibitors was applied to the treatment of HIV/AIDS, which would cause the death rate from the disease to decline significantly. Today, HIV/AIDS is considered a chronic disease if people are properly diagnosed and treated.

In 2016, approximately 1.1 million Americans were living with HIV; 15,807 people who had been diagnosed with HIV died (CDC 2019c). Of the newly acquired HIV infections in 2017, 66 percent of transmissions were through male-to-male sexual contact, 24 percent were through heterosexual contact, 6 percent were through intravenous drug use, and 3 percent were a combination of male-to-male sexual contact and intravenous drug use.

As part of the effort to completely conquer HIV/AIDS, programs have begun focusing on a "90–90–90" target, which consists of three goals: (1) 90 percent of people with HIV knowing their status, (2) 90 percent of people with HIV having access to treatment, and (3) 90 percent of people with HIV having a suppressed viral load (UNAIDS 2017). In 2016, Sweden became the first country to reach the 90–90–90 target.

A wealth of information is available—from the US government website www.hiv.gov, as well as myriad other sources—about the history of HIV/AIDS, the nature of the disease and treatment, and the programs and services to support providers and patients. People throughout the US healthcare system should be well acquainted with this information to ensure the delivery of effective, appropriate care.

A New Day for Ethical Healthcare and Research

Much of our thinking about the ethics of caring for vulnerable populations—and, specifically, any medical research involving those groups—has been influenced by two tragic events in human history: the Tuskegee Institute syphilis study and the World War II–era medical experiments conducted by Nazi Germany.

The Tuskegee Institute study was started by the US Public Health Service in 1932 and lasted until 1972. Its goal was to see how syphilis would progress when left untreated. The study included 600 black men—399 with syphilis and 201 who did not have the disease. The research was conducted without the patients' informed consent. In fact, researchers blatantly and knowingly lied to the patients, telling them that they were being treated for "bad blood" when, in fact, the program provided no treatment. The only compensation the participants received were medical exams, free meals, and burial insurance. The study, originally planned to go only six months, ran for more than 40 years, long after an effective treatment for the disease was available (CDC 2015a, 2015b). Today, we rightly recognize that the denial of much-needed treatment to participants in a research study is not only unethical but also criminal. Even at the time of the Tuskegee study, although regulations to protect participants were not yet formally in place, most people in the healthcare system—and likely the researchers themselves—understood the reprehensible wrongs that were being committed.

The second historic tragedy to shape our thinking about healthcare ethics and research took place during World War II, when Nazi Germany conducted a series of horrific medical experiments on prisoners. Following the end of the war, the Nuremberg trials on Nazi atrocities led to the development of the Nuremberg Code, shown in exhibit 7.8 (Nuremberg Military

EXHIBIT 7.8
The Nuremberg
Code

1. The voluntary consent of the human subject is absolutely essential.
      This means that the person involved should have legal capacity to give consent; should be so situated as to be able to exercise free power of choice, without the intervention of any element of force, fraud, deceit, duress, overreaching, or other ulterior form of constraint or coercion; and should have sufficient knowledge and comprehension of the elements of the subject matter involved, as to enable him to make an understanding and enlightened decision. This latter element requires that, before the acceptance of an affirmative decision by the experimental subject, there should be made known to him the nature, duration, and purpose of the experiment; the method and means by which it is to be conducted; all inconveniences and hazards reasonably to be expected; and the effects upon his health or person, which may possibly come from his participation in the experiment.
      The duty and responsibility for ascertaining the quality of the consent rests upon each individual who initiates, directs or engages in the experiment. It is a personal duty and responsibility which may not be delegated to another with impunity.

2. The experiment should be such as to yield fruitful results for the good of society, unprocurable by other methods or means of study, and not random and unnecessary in nature.

(continued)

EXHIBIT 7.8
The Nuremberg
Code
(continued)

3. The experiment should be so designed and based on the results of animal experimentation and a knowledge of the natural history of the disease or other problem under study, that the anticipated results will justify the performance of the experiment.

4. The experiment should be so conducted as to avoid all unnecessary physical and mental suffering and injury.

5. No experiment should be conducted, where there is an a priori reason to believe that death or disabling injury will occur; except, perhaps, in those experiments where the experimental physicians also serve as subjects.

6. The degree of risk to be taken should never exceed that determined by the humanitarian importance of the problem to be solved by the experiment.

7. Proper preparations should be made and adequate facilities provided to protect the experimental subject against even remote possibilities of injury, disability, or death.

8. The experiment should be conducted only by scientifically qualified persons. The highest degree of skill and care should be required through all stages of the experiment of those who conduct or engage in the experiment.

9. During the course of the experiment, the human subject should be at liberty to bring the experiment to an end, if he has reached the physical or mental state, where continuation of the experiment seemed to him to be impossible.

10. During the course of the experiment, the scientist in charge must be prepared to terminate the experiment at any stage, if he has probable cause to believe, in the exercise of the good faith, superior skill and careful judgement required of him, that a continuation of the experiment is likely to result in injury, disability, or death to the experimental subject.

["Trials of War Criminals before the Nuremberg Military Tribunals under Control Council Law No. 10," Vol. 2, pp. 181–182. Washington, D.C.: U.S. Government Printing Office, 1949.]

Source: Nuremberg Military Tribunal (1949).

Tribunal 1949). The document remains vital today, as it provides an ethical framework not just to guide medical research but also for addressing vulnerable populations. All who work in healthcare have a responsibility to protect vulnerable populations and work in the best interests of patients who are unable to advocate for themselves.

Anyone engaging in healthcare or medical research must ensure that proper protections are in place and that the benefits of the research or treatment outweigh the risks. To the greatest extent possible, patients and families must be fully informed of those risks and benefits (President's Council on Bioethics 1974). The foundation of ethical medical care and research is informed consent, which can be defined as "a process in which patients are given important information, including possible risks and benefits, about a medical procedure or treatment, genetic testing, or a clinical trial, . . . to help them decide if they want to be treated, tested, or take part in the trial" (National Cancer Institute 2018). Once treatment is underway, patients are expected to receive any new information that might affect their decision to continue.

Laws and regulations today apply strict ethical standards to healthcare and medical research, and these standards are monitored by provider groups, licensing boards, hospital committees, and institutional review boards (IRBs). IRBs monitor all research involving human subjects in hospitals, universities, and other facilities (US Food and Drug Administration 1998).

Transparency of Healthcare Information and Health Literacy

Most Americans have limited medical knowledge and limited ability to evaluate the quality of healthcare services provided. Furthermore, many Americans have traditionally paid little attention to the prices of healthcare services, given that third parties (e.g., insurance companies) pay most of the charges; in many instances, patients might not be aware of the price until after the service is performed. Healthcare consumers' relative lack of knowledge, in contrast to the expertise of providers, has created what economists would call an "information disequilibrium": Because providers know so much more about healthcare services than recipients do, they hold a more powerful position. For many years, consumers questioning providers about services and pricing was simply not part of the healthcare delivery culture; even those consumers who were inclined to do so would have difficulty accessing the necessary information (Mehrotra et al. 2017; Prager 2018; Whaley et al. 2014). Such conditions highlight the lack of transparency that has long surrounded healthcare information in the United States.

Most agree that increased use of healthcare information among the general public would have a positive impact on costs and quality in the US healthcare system, and steps have been taken to improve information transparency. For instance, a number of websites now allow users to compare price and quality data from one provider to another. The impact of these comparative tools on patients' choices is uncertain, however. Some studies have found that simply having the tools available does not significantly change patients' usage patterns or their selections based on price, suggesting that patients will need instruction about how to use the tools effectively (Desai et al. 2016; Mehrotra et al. 2016).

The generally low health literacy rate of the US population adds to the challenge of getting people to make better choices about maintaining their health and seeking appropriate care. *Health literacy* can be defined as "the degree to which individuals have the capacity to obtain, process, and understand basic health information and services needed to make appropriate health decisions" (Somers and Mahadevan 2010). Health literacy can be a problem of illiteracy in an absolute sense, as well as a problem pertaining specifically to information about health and healthcare.

Inadequate health literacy has been found to be an independent risk factor for hospital admission, based on a study of elderly managed care enrollees (Baker et al. 2002). It can also lead to an inefficient mix of services, increasing costs and producing suboptimal outcomes (Glanz, Rimer, and Viswanath 2008; Howard, Gazmararian, and Parker 2005). Overutilizing services and receiving unnecessary treatment can increase patient risk, given that no medical procedure is truly risk free. If we are to provide an optimal US healthcare system with lower costs, we will need a concerted effort to improve health literacy, especially among vulnerable populations (Adkins and Corus 2009; Somers and Mahadevan 2010; Vernon et al. 2003).

Several health literacy measurement tools are available from the Agency for Healthcare Research and Quality (AHRQ 2016). The Rapid Estimate of Adult Literacy in Medicine (REALM) test has been developed and validated to provide a quick assessment for patients (Arozullah et al. 2007). When providers are aware of a patient's level of health literacy, they are better able to present information in a way that the patient and the patient's family will be able to process and apply to their medical decision making.

Mental Health

Mental health includes psychological, emotional, and social well-being and affects how we feel, think, and act (HHS 2019b). It is as important as physical health. Without positive mental health, we cannot reach our full potential.

In 2017, more than 43 million adults had a mental health condition (Mental Health America 2017). Mental health conditions may arise for a number of reasons, including biological factors, such as genetics and brain chemistry; life experiences, such as trauma or abuse; and family history. Common mental health diagnoses include the following (National Institute of Mental Health 2019a):

- Anxiety disorders
- Attention deficit/hyperactivity disorder (ADHD)
- Bipolar disorders
- Borderline personality disorder (BPD)
- Depression
- Disruptive behavior disorders
- Eating disorders
- Insomnia disorders
- Obsessive-compulsive disorder (OCD)
- Post-traumatic stress disorder (PTSD)
- Schizophrenia

Like any other medical condition, an untreated mental health condition can lead to serious problems (National Institute of Mental Health 2019a). The risks associated with mental health are evident in the data concerning suicides, substance abuse, and major depressive episodes in younger people in the United States. In 2017, 47,000 people died by suicide, making it the tenth leading cause of death (National Institute of Mental Health 2019b).

According to the National Alliance on Mental Illness (2019), approximately 2 million people booked into jail each year have mental illness. This figure represents about 15 percent of all men and 30 percent of all women who are jailed in the United States. This association between mental illness and placement into the criminal justice system has been well documented for many years, and it is a source of great personal suffering for individuals and families, as well as significant costs for the criminal justice system (Swanson et al. 2013).

Patients with mental health conditions are typically treated on an outpatient basis, though they may receive treatment in hospitals for more acute and serious situations. A number of organizations provide services and advocate for people with mental health conditions, including the following:

- The Anxiety and Depression Association of America
- The Depression and Bipolar Support Alliance
- Mental Health America
- The National Alliance on Mental Illness

Grob (2011) provides an interesting, albeit tragic, history of the treatment of mental illness in the United States, from colonial times to the twentieth century. For many years, the mentally ill were misclassified, demonized, and subjected to countless horrific experiments in treatment, which did little more than produce further harm. Patients were warehoused and often abused throughout much of our nation's history. During the mid-1900s, the advent of psychotropic agents such as Thorazine (chlorpromazine) and lithium helped the treatment of mentally ill patients to progress in a more humane manner. The use of these drugs opened the possibility for many patients with mental illness to be deinstitutionalized and to live in the community; at the same time, however, overconfidence in the effectiveness of the drugs might have created misperceptions that other forms of care were no longer needed.

The realization that people with mental illness could live in their communities and pursue productive lives with the help of medication and other mental health support led to a significant demarcation point in the treatment of mental illness. The Community Mental Health Act of 1963—the last major bill signed by President John F. Kennedy before his assassination—provided $329 million in funding for the building of outpatient mental health centers (US Congress 1963). As a result, many inpatient psychiatric hospitals were closed. However, according to an extensive *Seattle Times* investigation on the fiftieth anniversary of the Community Mental Health Act, only about 50 percent of the proposed facilities were ever constructed (Smith 2013). Many communities were ill-equipped to deal with the large numbers of people with mental illness who were deinstitutionalized.

A 2017 assessment by the National Association of State Mental Health Program Directors provides a detailed analysis of the needs for psychiatric beds and other mental health services in the United States (Lutterman et al. 2017). In 2014, 170,000 patients were being treated in inpatient or 24-hour residential treatment beds on any given day, representing a 64 percent decrease since 1970. This decrease, however, does not reflect a decrease in serious mental illness overall; instead, it reflects an increase in outpatient treatment options as well as the failure to supply an adequate number of beds because of funding issues.

In many ways, treatment for mental health conditions in the United States has improved dramatically over the past several decades (Substance Abuse and Mental Health Services Administration 2019). Nonetheless, the need for mental health services remains largely unmet. About one-third of medically related disabilities are associated with mental or behavioral disorders (Anderson, Jané-llopis, and Hosman 2011), and the current US delivery system is unable to fully address these conditions (Lake and Turner 2017). As demand for services increases, many parts of the United States face a tremendous shortage of qualified professionals in mental health. In rural areas alone, an estimated 30,000 mental health professionals are needed (Johnson 2016; KFF 2017).

The United States has also seen a disturbing increase in violent incidents, such as mass shootings, that in some instances can be traced to untreated severe mental illness. Choe, Teplin, and Abram (2008) found that perpetration of violence and violent victimization were more common in cases of severe mental illness. However, most people with mental illness do not exhibit violence, and mental illness alone is not a strong predictor of such behavior (Stuart 2003; Varshney et al. 2016). People with mental illness are more likely to be victims of violence than to perpetrate such acts.

The National Council for Behavioral Health (2019) offers rigorous training in mental health first-aid, so that people are better able to recognize a mental health crisis, intervene safely to defuse the immediate situation, and get assistance for the person in need. Having a significant number of people trained in this area can serve as an important first line of mental health service in the community.

Public Health vs. Population Health

Patient care occurs not just within medical practices, hospitals, and long-term care facilities but also in the community at large (Weinstein et al. 2017). Public health is the science and practice of preventing disease, prolonging life, and promoting health efficiently through an organized community effort (CDC Foundation 2019). Whereas the practice of medicine typically focuses on individual care, public health seeks to have a maximum impact on the health status of a population. During the eighteenth and nineteenth centuries, much of the US healthcare system was devoted to public health. The emphasis at that time was largely on sanitation and other matters with a population focus; individual medical care was oftentimes reserved for the wealthy (Starr 2009).

Despite their differences in scope, public health and the practice of medicine do overlap, and they often draw from the same bases of knowledge and evidence (Chope 1956). An example of this overlap can be seen in our approach to influenza. Medicine primarily focuses on treating individuals who have been stricken with the disease, whereas public health professionals focus on immunizing as many people as possible to prevent the spread of disease (CDC 1999; Hacker 2008). However, medicine does contribute on the public health side by providing patients with vaccinations.

Efforts to address environmental health concerns—such as the need to monitor pollution, foodborne illness, airborne illness, and waterborne illness—have become increasingly important to US communities. Examples might include monitoring ozone levels and issuing alerts, monitoring foods and recalling contaminated items, monitoring air quality and issuing alerts about particulate matter that might cause lung or breathing issues, and monitoring water to protect against contamination (CDC 2019b).

A concept closely related to public health is population health, which Kindig and Stoddart (2003) define as "the health outcomes of a group of individuals, including the distribution of such outcomes within the group." Population health efforts will typically focus on a specific target population, or a patient group with similar conditions or characteristics—for instance, people with diabetes between the ages of 18 and 64.

At the risk of oversimplification, the distinction between medical care, population health, and public health revolves around scope: Medical care focuses on the individual, population health focuses on a targeted group, and public health focuses on the community at large. As illustrated in exhibit 7.9, all three concepts overlap and serve to improve health outcomes (Cohen et al. 2014; Falk 2014).

Population health takes into account the various determinants of health for a population as it considers policies and programs to improve health outcomes (Kindig 2019). The Institute for Healthcare Improvement

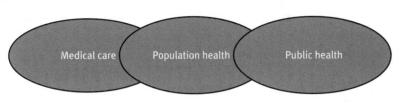

EXHIBIT 7.9
The Interlocking
Chain for Health
Outcomes

- Serves individuals
- Diagnosis
- Treatment
- Prevention
- Mostly private
- Collaboration across sectors

- Serves targeted populations
- Addresses determinants of health
- Applies interventions and strategies
- Data driven
- Government and private
- Collaboration across sectors

- Serves entire community
- Surveillance
- Identifies risk factors
- Interventions, policy, programs
- Community-based prevention
- Community-based promotion
- Mostly government
- Collaboration across sectors

(IHI) Triple Aim—which focuses on improving the patient experience of care (including quality and satisfaction), improving the health of populations, and reducing the per capita cost of healthcare (IHI 2018)—provides an excellent framework of population health. As the Triple Aim implies, population health seeks to balance greater value of care with improved equity and patient well-being (Kindig and Milstein 2018). Key population health activities include the following (Kindig 2019; Slabaugh et al. 2017):

- Developing educational approaches to improve clinical decision making and evidence-based practice
- Establishing practice guidelines
- Making policy to address health disparities
- Developing strategies to influence safety, cost, and clinical outcomes
- Implementing cost-effective strategies

Do We Overdiagnose and Overtreat Patients?

Clearly, advances in medical care have produced remarkable results, helping to minimize pain and suffering and significantly improving patients' quality of life. Concerns have been raised, however, about the possible overdiagnosis and overtreatment of patients, which would lead to unnecessary costs as well as unnecessary exposure to the risks of medical treatment.

Overdiagnosis occurs when an abnormality or disease is discovered through a diagnostic procedure or test but treating the condition would provide no real benefit to the patient. Overtreatment occurs when an abnormality or condition is treated even though it is self-limiting in nature or poses no harm to the patient (Berwick and Hackbarth 2012; Brownlee 2007; Coon et al. 2014; Lyu et al. 2017). Overdiagnosis and overtreatment should not be confused with misdiagnosis, which occurs when an incorrect diagnosis leads to patient harm through improper treatment or failure to treat. Overdiagnosis and overtreatment principally occur after screening procedures for various conditions create a need for further testing. This testing is often done out of providers' fear of omission, as well as an intolerance for uncertainty on the part of patients and physicians (Coon et al. 2014).

Overdiagnosis and overtreatment are closely related to the issue of medicalization, which occurs when medical diagnoses are applied to non-medical conditions. Medicalization is often a source of unnecessary or inappropriate care, though it is sometimes done out of legitimate necessity to obtain funding for a needed service. For example, a person might truly need counseling despite having no diagnosable mental illness; even if the counseling might actually prevent illness in the future, third parties will often refuse to pay for such services without a diagnosis (Parens 2011; Scull 2002).

Lyu and colleagues (2017) found that, from a physician's perspective, overdiagnosis and overtreatment are common. In a survey of more than 2,000 physicians, they found that 20.6 percent of overall medical care—including 22 percent of prescriptions, 24.9 percent of tests, and 11.1 percent of medical procedures—was regarded as unnecessary. The physicians cited fear of malpractice, patient requests and pressure, and difficulty in accessing records as primary reasons for unnecessary care. More than 70 percent of the respondents also believed that supplier-induced demand—which occurs when services are provided primarily to increase the income of the physician or other provider—was a factor. Respondents indicated that moving away from a fee-for-service compensation system for physicians would likely reduce the amount of unnecessary care.

The implications of these findings are clear. Beyond the risk to the patient, the additional worry, and the time wasted, the monetary cost of unnecessary care is enormous (Mercuri and Gafni 2018; Mulley 2009; van Dijk et al. 2013). Given that our healthcare system consumes more than $3 trillion in a year, 20 percent of that total is an astounding cost.

Patient Prejudice

As the healthcare staffs in the United States have grown more diverse, organizations have often encountered problems with prejudiced patients. For instance, some patients might not want to be treated by a physician who is a woman or a member of a different race or ethnicity. Modern healthcare administrators must be prepared to deal with this sensitive issue, and organizations must have policies and tools in place to ensure that providers, as well as patients, are protected against discrimination and abuse (Paul-Emile et al. 2016). Zero-tolerance policies, training for all staff, and the sharing of stories about the consequences of prejudice are essential.

Maldistribution of Services

Healthcare services in many areas of the United States are sparse, inadequate, or even nonexistent—to the point that zip code is often said to be more important than genetic code in determining a person's health (Slade-Sawyer 2014; Roeder 2015).

The Dartmouth Atlas Project (2019) provides resources on the distribution of hospital beds and physicians in various parts of the United States. Its data show a concentration of hospital beds in Appalachia, the Mid-South, and some Western states, partially a result of the Hill-Burton Act, which provided subsidies and encouraged the construction of hospitals. Interestingly, the density of physicians does not necessarily coincide with the density of hospital beds across the various regions. Significant gaps exist in the availability of important healthcare services from one region to another.

Various federal and state efforts have sought to alleviate these disparities, but attracting physicians and other healthcare professionals to certain areas can be difficult. Unlike buildings, of course, healthcare professionals have free will in deciding where to practice, and their decisions may take into account a variety of factors, including the cost of malpractice insurance (Chou and Lo Sasso 2009), income levels (Krist et al. 2005), family relationships, and quality of life. Many professionals undergo medical training in early adulthood at the same time that they are starting families; once those families have established roots in the community, relocation at the completion of training becomes more difficult (Ballance, Kornegay, and Evans 2009).

Two important federal programs have been established to address the maldistribution of services and the shortage of primary care physicians in certain areas: the National Health Service Corps (NHSC) and the Rural Health Clinic (RHC) program. The NHSC, founded in 1972, is a federal agency administered by the Health Resources and Services Administration (HRSA). Its mission is to build "healthy communities by supporting qualified health care providers dedicated to working in areas of the United States with limited access to care" (HRSA 2019). The NHSC uses scholarships and loan repayment to encourage primary care providers in eligible disciplines to work in designated health professional shortage areas (HPSAs). HPSAs are usually rural, tribal, or inner-city areas that have had difficulty attracting primary care physicians.

The Rural Health Clinic Services Act of 1977 sought to address the inadequate supply of physicians serving Medicare patients in rural areas and to increase the use of nonphysician practitioners, such as nurse practitioners (NPs) and physician assistants (PAs), in those areas (CMS 2019). The law represented the first major push for greater independence in the practice of NPs and PAs, who previously had worked almost entirely under the direct supervision of a physician (Silver and McAtee 1978); as a result, the law sparked significant controversy. Medicare pays RHCs an all-inclusive rate (AIR) for medically necessary primary health services and qualified preventive health services furnished by RHC practitioners (CMS 2019). About 4,500 RHCs operate in rural and other underserved areas of the United States. The clinics provide the following:

- Physician services
- Services and supplies "incident to" the services of a physician
- NP, PA, certified nurse-midwife (CNM), clinical psychologist (CP), and clinical social worker (CSW) services
- Medicare Part B–covered drugs furnished by and "incident to" services of an RHC practitioner
- Visiting nurse services to homebound patients in areas where CMS has certified a shortage of home health agencies

Efforts to address the maldistribution of services—as well as other conditions that contribute to health disparities—will require continued diligence and engagement on the part of the entire healthcare system, the government, and the patients being served.

Discussion Questions

1. What care services should be made available to every person in the United States?
2. What kind of balance exists between patient responsibility and the responsibility of the healthcare system?
3. What does the US healthcare system do to influence patient health behavior? In the future, how might the healthcare system do more to influence behavior?
4. Does our healthcare system have sufficient focus on preventive care? How might we increase the focus on prevention in the future?
5. How can the people working in the healthcare system help to reduce inequality and discrimination?

References

Adkins, N. R., and C. Corus. 2009. "Health Literacy for Improved Health Outcomes: Effective Capital in the Marketplace." *Journal of Consumer Affairs* 42 (3): 199–222. https://doi.org/10.1111/j.1745-6606.2009.01137.x.

Agency for Healthcare Research and Quality (AHRQ). 2016. "Health Literacy Measurement Tools (Revised)." Reviewed February. www.ahrq.gov/professionals/quality-patient-safety/quality-resources/tools/literacy/index.html.

Anderson, G. D. 2008. "Gender Differences in Pharmacological Response." *International Review of Neurobiology* 83: 1–10. https://doi.org/10.1016/S0074-7742(08)00001-9.

Anderson, P., E. Jané-Ilopis, and C. Hosman. 2011. "Reducing the Silent Burden of Impaired Mental Health." *Health Promotion International* 26 (Suppl. 1): i4–9. https://doi.org/10.1093/heapro/dar051.

Arozullah, A., P. Yarnold, C. Bennett, R. Soltysik, M. Wolf, R. Ferreira, S.-Y. Lee, S. Costello, A. Shakir, C. Denwood, F. Bryant, and T. Davis. 2007. "Development and Validation of a Short-Form, Rapid Estimate of Adult Literacy in Medicine." *Medical Care* 45 (11): 1026–33. https://doi.org/10.1097/MLR.0b013e3180616c1b.

Baker, D. W., J. A. Gazmararian, M. V. Williams, T. Scott, R. M. Parker, D. Green, J. Ren, and J. Peel. 2002. "Functional Health Literacy and the Risk of Hospital Admission Among Medicare Managed Care Enrollees." *American Journal of Public Health* 92 (8): 1278–83. www.ncbi.nlm.nih.gov/pubmed/12144984.

Ballance, D., D. Kornegay, and P. Evans. 2009. "Factors That Influence Physicians to Practice in Rural Locations: A Review and Commentary." *Journal of Rural Health* 25 (3): 276–81. https://doi.org/10.1111/j.1748-0361.2009.00230.x.

Barnes, L. L., C. F. M. De Leon, R. S. Wilson, J. L. Bienias, D. A. Bennett, and D. A. Evans. 2004. "Racial Differences in Perceived Discrimination in a Community Population of Older Blacks and Whites." *Journal of Aging and Health* 16 (3): 315–37. https://doi.org/10.1177/0898264304264202.

Berger, J. S., C. N. Bairey-Merz, R. F. Redberg, and P. S. Douglas. 2008. "Improving the Quality of Care for Women with Cardiovascular Disease." *American Heart Journal* 156 (5): 816–825.e1. https://doi.org/10.1016/j.ahj.2008.06.039.

Bernal, D. R., R. Becker Herbst, B. L. Lewis, and J. Feibelman. 2017. "Ethical Care for Vulnerable Populations Receiving Psychotropic Treatment." *Ethics & Behavior* 27 (7): 582–98. https://doi.org/10.1080/10508422.2016.1224187.

Berwick, D. M., and A. D. Hackbarth. 2012. "Eliminating Waste in US Health Care." *JAMA* 307 (14): 1513–16. https://doi.org/10.1001/jama.2012.362.

Betancourt, J. R., A. R. Green, J. E. Carrillo, and O. Ananeh-Firempong. 2003. "Defining Cultural Competence: A Practical Framework for Addressing Racial/Ethnic Disparities in Health and Health Care. Feature Article Public Health Reports." *Public Health Reports* 118 (4): 293–302. https://doi.org/10.1016/S0033-3549(04)50253-4.

Blum, H. L. 1974. *Planning for Health: Developing Application for Social Change Theory*. New York: Human Sciences Press.

Brownlee, S. 2007. *Overtreated: Why Too Much Medicine Is Making Us Sicker and Poorer*. New York: Bloomsbury Press.

Bugiardini, R., and C. N. Bairey-Merz. 2005. "Angina with 'Normal' Coronary Arteries: A Changing Philosophy." *JAMA* 293 (4): 477–84. https://doi.org/10.1001/jama.293.4.477.

Cameron, K. A., J. Song, L. M. Manheim, and D. D. Dunlop. 2010. "Gender Disparities in Health and Healthcare Use Among Older Adults." *Journal of Women's Health* 19 (9): 1643–50. https://doi.org/10.1089/jwh.2009.1701.

CDC Foundation. 2019. "What Is Public Health?" Accessed October 6. www.cdcfoundation.org/what-public-health.

Centers for Disease Control and Prevention (CDC). 2019a. "Behavioral Risk Factor Surveillance System." Reviewed August 27. www.cdc.gov/brfss/index.html.

———. 2019b. "Healthy Living." Accessed October 6. www.cdc.gov/healthyliving/index.html.

———. 2019c. "HIV Basics." Reviewed August 6. www.cdc.gov/hiv/basics/index.html.

———. 2019d. "Leading Causes of Death—Females—All Races and Origins—United States, 2016." Reviewed September 27. www.cdc.gov/women/lcod/2016/all-races-origins/index.htm.

———. 2019e. "Leading Causes of Death—Males—All Races and Origins—United States, 2016." Reviewed September 27. www.cdc.gov/healthequity/lcod/men/2016/all-races-origins/index.htm.

———. 2018a. "Lesbian, Gay, Bisexual, and Transgender Health." Reviewed March 28. www.cdc.gov/lgbthealth/index.htm.

———. 2018b. "Youth Risk Behavior Surveillance System." Reviewed August 22. www.cdc.gov/healthyyouth/data/yrbs/index.htm.

———. 2017a. "Key Injury and Violence Data." Reviewed May 8. www.cdc.gov/injury/wisqars/overview/key_data.html.

———. 2017b. "10 Leading Causes of Death by Age Group, United States—2016." Accessed November 18, 2019. www.cdc.gov/injury/wisqars/pdf/leading_causes_of_death_by_age_group_2016-508.pdf.

———. 2017c. "10 Leading Causes of Injury Deaths by Age Group Highlighting Violence-Related Injury Deaths, United States—2016." Accessed November 18, 2019. www.cdc.gov/injury/wisqars/pdf/leading_causes_of_injury_deaths_highlighting_violence_2016-508.pdf.

———. 2015a. "Research Implications: How Tuskegee Changed Research Practices." Reviewed December 14. www.cdc.gov/tuskegee/after.htm.

———. 2015b. "Tuskegee Study, 1932–1972." Reviewed December 14. www.cdc.gov/tuskegee/index.html.

———. 2014. "NCHHSTP Social Determinants of Health." Reviewed March 10. www.cdc.gov/nchhstp/socialdeterminants/definitions.html.

———. 1999. "Ten Great Public Health Achievements—United States, 1900–1999." *MMWR Weekly*. Published April 2. www.cdc.gov/mmwr/preview/mmwrhtml/00056796.htm.

Centers for Medicare & Medicaid Services (CMS). 2019. *Rural Health Clinic*. Published May. www.cms.gov/Outreach-and-Education/Medicare-Learning-Network-MLN/MLNProducts/downloads/ruralhlthclinfctsht.pdf.

Centers for Medicare & Medicaid Services Office of Minority Health in collaboration with the RAND Corporation. 2018. *Racial, Ethnic, and Gender Disparities in Health Care in Medicare Advantage*. Published April. www.cms.gov/About-CMS/Agency-Information/OMH/Downloads/2018-National-Level-Results-by-Race-Ethnicity-and-Gender.pdf.

Chalhoub, T., and K. Rimar. 2018. "The Health Care System and Racial Disparities in Maternal Mortality." Center for American Progress. Published May 10. www.americanprogress.org/issues/women/reports/2018/05/10/450577/health-care-system-racial-disparities-maternal-mortality/.

Chen, F. M., G. E. Fryer, R. L. Phillips, E. Wilson, and D. E. Pathman. 2005. "Patients' Beliefs About Racism, Preferences for Physician Race, and Satisfaction with Care." *Annals of Family Medicine* 3 (2): 138–43. https://doi.org/10.1370/afm.282.

Choe, J. Y., L. A. Teplin, and K. M. Abram. 2008. "Perpetration of Violence, Violent Victimization, and Severe Mental Illness: Balancing Public Health Concerns." *Psychiatric Services* 59 (2): 153–64. https://doi.org/10.1176/ps.2008.59.2.153.

Chope, H. D. 1956. "Public Health and Public Medical Care." *California Medicine* 85 (4): 220–25.

Chou, C.-F., and A. T. Lo Sasso. 2009. "Practice Location Choice by New Physicians: The Importance of Malpractice Premiums, Damage Caps, and Health Professional Shortage Area Designation." *Health Services Research* 44 (4): 1271–89. https://doi.org/10.1111/j.1475-6773.2009.00976.x.

Cleveland Clinic. 2013. "Empathy: Exploring the Human Connection." Published March 4. https://health.clevelandclinic.org/empathy-exploring-human-connection-video/.

Cohen, D., T. Huynh, A. Sebold, J. Harvey, C. Neudorf, and A. Brown. 2014. "The Population Health Approach: A Qualitative Study of Conceptual and Operational Definitions for Leaders in Canadian Healthcare." *SAGE Open Medicine* 2: 2050312114522618. https://doi.org/10.1177/2050312114522618.

Coon, E. R., R. A. Quinonez, V. A. Moyer, and A. R. Schroeder. 2014. "Overdiagnosis: How Our Compulsion for Diagnosis May Be Harming Children." *Pediatrics* 134 (5): 1013–23. https://doi.org/10.1542/peds.2014-1778.

Council of Accountable Physician Practices (CAPP). 2016a. "Nielsen Survey Shows Gaps in How Patients Are Experiencing Accountable Care." Published

June 15. http://accountablecaredoctors.org/integratedcoordinated-care/nielsen-survey-shows-gaps-patients-experiencing-accountable-care/.

———. 2016b. "Patient Expectations and the Accountability Gap: Consumer Healthcare Survey Results Press Conference." Published June 15. http://accountablecaredoctors.org/wp-content/uploads/2016/06/SHP-CAPP-2016-Consumer_Physician-Survey-FINAL.pdf.

Dartmouth Atlas Project. 2019. "Dartmouth Atlas of Health Care." Accessed October 6. www.dartmouthatlas.org.

Desai, S., L. A. Hatfield, A. L. Hicks, M. E. Chernew, and A. Mehrotra. 2016. "Association Between Availability of a Price Transparency Tool and Outpatient Spending." *JAMA* 315 (17): 1874–81. https://doi.org/10.1001/jama.2016.4288.

Dias, P., and O. O'Donnell (eds.). 2013. *Health and Inequality*. Bingley, UK: Emerald Insight.

Diener, E. (ed.). 2009. *The Science of Well-Being: The Collected Works of Ed Diener*. New York: Springer.

Diener, E., C. Napa Scollon, and R. E. Lucas. 2009. "The Evolving Concept of Subjective Well-Being: The Multifaceted Nature of Happiness." In *Assessing Well-Being*, edited by Ed Diener, 67–100. New York: Springer. https://doi.org/10.1007/978-90-481-2354-4_4.

Dykes, D. C., and A. A. White. 2009. "Getting to Equal: Strategies to Understand and Eliminate General and Orthopaedic Healthcare Disparities." *Clinical Orthopaedics and Related Research* 467 (10): 2598–2605. https://doi.org/10.1007/s11999-009-0993-5.

Eunice Kennedy Shriver National Institute of Children's Health and Human Development. 2016. "What Health Issues or Conditions Affect Women Differently than Men?" Reviewed December 1. www.nichd.nih.gov/health/topics/womenshealth/conditioninfo/howconditionsaffect.

Falk, L. H. 2014. "Population Health Versus Public Health: An Important Comparison." Health Catalyst. Published July 30. www.healthcatalyst.com/what-is-population-health/.

Flanders-Stephans, M. B. 2000. "Alarming Racial Differences in Maternal Mortality." *Journal of Perinatal Education* 9 (2): 50–51. https://doi.org/10.1624/105812400X87653.

Fox, J. A., and E. E. Fridel. 2017. "Gender Differences in Patterns and Trends in U.S. Homicide, 1976–2015." *Violence and Gender* 4 (2): 37–43. https://doi.org/10.1089/vio.2017.0016.

Glanz, K., B. K. Rimer, and K. Viswanath (eds.). 2008. *Health Behavior and Health Education: Theory, Research, and Practice*, 4th ed. San Francisco: Jossey-Bass.

Glazier, R. H., and D. A. Redelmeier. 2010. "Building the Patient-Centered Medical Home in Ontario." *JAMA* 303 (21): 2186–87. https://doi.org/10.1001/jama.2010.753.

Green, M., and M. Elliott. 2010. "Religion, Health, and Psychological Well-Being." *Journal of Religion and Health* 49 (2): 149–63. https://doi.org/10.1007/s10943-009-9242-1.

Grob, G. N. 2011. *The Mad Among Us: A History of the Care of America's Mentally Ill.* New York: Free Press.

Hacker, J. S. 2008. *The Case for Public Plan Choice in National Health Reform: Key to Cost Control and Quality Coverage.* Washington, DC: Institute for America's Future.

Hafeez, H., M. Zeshan, M. A. Tahir, N. Jahan, and S. Naveed. 2017. "Health Care Disparities Among Lesbian, Gay, Bisexual, and Transgender Youth: A Literature Review." *Cureus* 9 (4): e1184. https://doi.org/10.7759/cureus.1184.

Harvard Medical School. 2010. "Mars vs. Venus: The Gender Gap in Health." *Harvard Men's Health Watch.* Published January. www.health.harvard.edu/newsletter_article/mars-vs-venus-the-gender-gap-in-health.

Hausmann, L. R. M., K. Jeong, J. E. Bost, and S. A. Ibrahim. 2008. "Perceived Discrimination in Health Care and Health Status in a Racially Diverse Sample." *Medical Care* 46 (9): 905–14. https://doi.org/10.1097/MLR.0b013e3181792562.

Health Resources and Services Administration (HRSA). 2019. "National Health Service Corps." Reviewed July. https://bhw.hrsa.gov/loansscholarships/nhsc.

Healy, B. 1991. "The Yentl Syndrome." *New England Journal of Medicine* 325 (4): 274–76. https://doi.org/10.1056/NEJM199107253250408.

Herman, S., M. Adkins, and R. Y. Moon. 2014. "Knowledge and Beliefs of African-American and American Indian Parents and Supporters About Infant Safe Sleep." *Journal of Community Health* 40 (1): 12–19. https://doi.org/10.1007/s10900-014-9886-y.

Hostetter, M., and S. Klein. 2018. "In Focus: Reducing Racial Disparities in Health Care by Confronting Racism." Commonwealth Fund. Published September 27. www.commonwealthfund.org/publications/newsletter-article/2018/sep/focus-reducing-racial-disparities-health-care-confronting.

Howard, D. H., J. Gazmararian, and R. M. Parker. 2005. "The Impact of Low Health Literacy on the Medical Costs of Medicare Managed Care Enrollees." *American Journal of Medicine* 118 (4): 371–77. https://doi.org/10.1016/j.amjmed.2005.01.010.

Huber, M., J. A. Knottnerus, L. Green, H. Van Der Horst, A. R. Jadad, D. Kromhout, D., B. Leonard, K. Lorig, M. I. Loureiro, J. W. M. van der Meer, P. Schnabel, R. Smith, C. van Weel, and H. Smid. 2011. "How Should We Define Health?" *BMJ* 343: d4163. https://doi.org/10.1136/bmj.d4163.

Institute for Healthcare Improvement (IHI). 2018. "The IHI Triple Aim." Accessed December 12. www.ihi.org/Engage/Initiatives/TripleAim/Pages/default.aspx.

Jackson, G. L., and J. W. Williams. 2015. "Does PCMH 'Work'? The Need to Use Implementation Science to Make Sense of Conflicting Results." *JAMA Internal Medicine* 175 (8): 1369–70. https://doi.org/10.1001/jamainternmed.2015.2067.

Jaén, C. R., R. L. Ferrer, W. L. Miller, R. F. Palmer, R. Wood, M. Davila, E. E. Stewart, B. F. Crabtree, P. A. Nutting, and K. C. Stange. 2010. "Patient Outcomes at 26 Months in the Patient-Centered Medical Home National Demonstration Project." *Annals of Family Medicine* 8 (Suppl. 1): S57–67. https://doi.org/10.1370/afm.1121.

Jemal, A., K. D. Miller, J. Ma, R. L. Siegel, S. A. Fedewa, F. Islami, S. S. Devesa, and M. J. Thun. 2018. "Higher Lung Cancer Incidence in Young Women than Young Men in the United States." *New England Journal of Medicine* 378 (21): 1999–2009. https://doi.org/10.1056/NEJMoa1715907.

Johnson, S. 2016. "Demand for Mental Health Services Soars amid Provider Shortage." *Modern Healthcare*. Published December 31. www.modernhealthcare.com/article/20161231/TRANSFORMATION03/161229942.

Joszt, L. 2018. "5 Vulnerable Populations in Healthcare." *American Journal of Managed Care*. Published July 20. www.ajmc.com/newsroom/5-vulnerable-populations-in-healthcare.

Kaiser Family Foundation (KFF). 2018. "Global HIV/AIDS Timeline." Published July 20. www.kff.org/global-health-policy/timeline/global-hivaids-timeline/.

———. 2017. "Mental Health Care Health Professional Shortage Areas (HPSAs)." Accessed December 12, 2018. www.kff.org/other/state-indicator/mental-health-care-health-professional-shortage-areas-hpsas/?currentTimeframe=0&sortModel=%7B%22colId%22:%22Location%22,%22sort%22:%22asc%22%7D.

———. 2015. "Gender Differences in Health Care, Status, and Use: Spotlight on Men's Health." Published March 31. www.kff.org/womens-health-policy/fact-sheet/gender-differences-in-health-care-status-and-use-spotlight-on-mens-health/.

Kindig, D. 2019. "What Is Population Health?" University of Wisconsin Population Health Services. Accessed October 6. www.improvingpopulationhealth.org/blog/what-is-population-health.html.

Kindig, D. A., and B. Milstein. 2018. "A Balanced Investment Portfolio for Equitable Health and Well-Being Is an Imperative, and Within Reach." *Health Affairs* 37 (4): 579–84. https://doi.org/10.1377/hlthaff.2017.1463.

Kindig, D., and G. Stoddart. 2003. "What Is Population Health?" *American Journal of Public Health* 93 (3): 380–83. www.ncbi.nlm.nih.gov/pubmed/12604476.

Krist, A. H., R. E. Johnson, D. Callahan, S. H. Woolf, and D. Marsland. 2005. "Title VII Funding and Physician Practice in Rural or Low-Income Areas." *Journal of Rural Health* 21 (1): 3–11. www.ncbi.nlm.nih.gov/pubmed/15667004.

Lake, J., and M. S. Turner. 2017. "Urgent Need for Improved Mental Health Care and a More Collaborative Model of Care." *Permanente Journal* 21: 17–24. https://doi.org/10.7812/TPP/17-024.

Lasser, K. E., D. U. Himmelstein, and S. Woolhandler. 2006. "Access to Care, Health Status, and Health Disparities in the United States and Canada: Results of a Cross-National Population-Based Survey." *American Journal of Public Health* 96 (7): 1300–1307. https://doi.org/10.2105/AJPH.2004.059402.

Lutterman, T., R. Shaw, W. Fisher, and R. Manderscheid. 2017. *Trend in Psychiatric Inpatient Capacity, United States and Each State, 1970 to 2014.* National Association of State Mental Health Program Directors. Assessment No. 2. Published August. www.nasmhpd.org/sites/default/files/TACPaper.2.Psychiatric-Inpatient-Capacity_508C.pdf.

Lyu, H., T. Xu, D. Brotman, B. Mayer-Blackwell, M. Cooper, M. Daniel, E. C. Wick, V. Saini, S. Brownlee, and M. A. Makary. 2017. "Overtreatment in the United States." *PLOS ONE* 12 (9): e0181970. https://doi.org/10.1371/journal.pone.0181970.

Mack, K. A., K. D. Liller, G. Baldwin, and D. Sleet. 2015. "Preventing Unintentional Injuries in the Home Using the Health Impact Pyramid." *Health Education & Behavior* 42 (Suppl. 1), 115S–122S. https://doi.org/10.1177/1090198114568306.

Matthews, D. 2015. "How Gender Influences Health Inequalities." *Nursing Times* 111 (43): 21–23. www.ncbi.nlm.nih.gov/pubmed/26647615.

McGill University Medical Centre. 2014. "I Keep Hearing About 'Tertiary and Quaternary Care' at the MUHC. What Does This Mean?" Published June 4. https://muhc.ca/questions/article/question-sample-4.

Mehrotra, A., K. M. Dean, A. D. Sinaiko, and N. Sood. 2017. "Americans Support Price Shopping for Health Care, but Few Actually Seek Out Price Information." *Health Affairs* 36 (8): 1392–1400. https://doi.org/10.1377/hlthaff.2016.1471.

Mehrotra, A., P. J. Huckfeldt, A. M. Haviland, L. Gascue, and N. Sood. 2016. "Patients Who Choose Primary Care Physicians Based on Low Office Visit Price Can Realize Broader Savings." *Health Affairs* 35 (12): 2319–26. https://doi.org/10.1377/hlthaff.2016.0408.

Mental Health America. 2017. *The State of Mental Health in America 2018.* Accessed November 18, 2019. www.mhanational.org/sites/default/files/2018%20The%20State%20of%20MH%20in%20America%20-%20FINAL.pdf.

Mercuri, M., and A. Gafni. 2018. "Examining the Role of the Physician as a Source of Variation: Are Physician-Related Variations Necessarily Unwarranted?" *Journal of Evaluation in Clinical Practice* 24 (1): 145–51. https://doi.org/10.1111/jep.12770.

Merz, C. N. B. 2011. "The Yentl Syndrome Is Alive and Well." *European Heart Journal* 32 (11): 1313–15. https://doi.org/10.1093/eurheartj/ehr083.

Moran, M. 2018. "To What Extent Do Sex Differences Matter When Prescribing?" *Psychiatric News.* Published March 16. https://doi.org/10.1176/appi.pn.2018.pp3b2.

Morbidity and Mortality Weekly Report (MMWR). 1981. "Pneumocystis Pneumo-nia—Los Angeles." Centers for Disease Control and Prevention. Published June 5. www.cdc.gov/mmwr/preview/mmwrhtml/june_5.htm.

Mulley, A. G. 2009. "Inconvenient Truths About Supplier Induced Demand and Unwarranted Variation in Medical Practice." *BMJ* 339: b4073. https://doi.org/10.1136/bmj.b4073.

National Alliance on Mental Illness. 2019. "Jailing People with Mental Ill-ness." Accessed October 7. www.nami.org/Learn-More/Public-Policy/Jailing-People-with-Mental-Illness.

National Cancer Institute. 2018. "Informed Consent." Dictionary of Cancer Terms. Accessed October 7. www.cancer.gov/publications/dictionaries/cancer-terms/def/informed-consent.

National Center for Health Statistics (NCHS). 2016. "Deaths: Final Data for 2014." *National Vital Statistics Reports* 65 (4). Published June 30. www.cdc.gov/nchs/data/nvsr/nvsr65/nvsr65_04.pdf.

———. 2001. "New Study Profiles Women's Use of Health Care." Published July 26. www.cdc.gov/nchs/pressroom/01news/newstudy.htm.

National Collaborating Centre for Determinants of Health (NCCDH). 2019. "Upstream/Downstream." Accessed October 7. http://nccdh.ca/glossary/entry/upstream-downstream.

National Council for Behavioral Health. 2019. "Mental Health First Aid." Accessed October 7. www.mentalhealthfirstaid.org/.

National Hospice and Palliative Care Organization. 2019. "Hospice Care Overview for Professionals." Accessed October 7. www.nhpco.org/about/hospice-care.

National Institute of Mental Health. 2019a. "Health Topics." Accessed October 7. www.nimh.nih.gov/health/topics/index.shtml.

———. 2019b. "Suicide." Updated April. www.nimh.nih.gov/health/statistics/suicide.shtml.

National Institutes of Health (NIH). 2010. "Health Disparities." NIH Fact Sheet. Updated October. https://archives.nih.gov/asites/report/09-09-2019/report.nih.gov/nihfactsheets/Pdfs/HealthDisparities(NIMHD).pdf.

National Institutes of Health Office for Research on Women's Health (ORWH). 2019. "How Sex/Gender Influence Health & Disease." Accessed October 7. https://orwh.od.nih.gov/sex-gender/sexgender-influences-health-and-disease/infographic-how-sexgender-influence-health.

———. 2018. "National Women's Health Week: A Reminder that Putting Yourself First Doesn't Mean Putting Others Last." Published May 15. https://orwh.od.nih.gov/about/director/messages/national-womens-health-week-reminder-putting-yourself-first-doesnt-mean.

Nuremberg Military Tribunal. 1949. "The Nuremburg Code." In *Trials of War Criminals Before the Nuremberg Military Tribunals Under Control Council Law No. 10*, vol 2. Accessed October 7, 2019. https://history.nih.gov/research/downloads/nuremberg.pdf.

Office of Disease Prevention and Health Promotion. 2019a. "Disparities." US Department of Health and Human Services. Accessed October 7. www. healthypeople.gov/2020/about/foundation-health-measures/Disparities.

————. 2019b. "Lesbian, Gay, Bisexual, and Transgender Health." US Department of Health and Human Services. Accessed October 6. www. healthypeople.gov/2020/topics-objectives/topic/lesbian-gay-bisexual-and-transgender-health.

Parens, E. 2011. "On Good and Bad Forms of Medicalization." *Bioethics* 27 (1): 28–35. https://doi.org/10.1111/j.1467-8519.2011.01885.x.

Paul-Emile, K., A. K. Smith, B. Lo, and A. Fernández. 2016. "Dealing with Racist Patients." *New England Journal of Medicine* 374 (8): 708–11. https://doi. org/10.1056/NEJMp1514939.

Pauly, M. V., and J. A. Pagán. 2007. "Spillovers and Vulnerability: The Case of Community Uninsurance." *Health Affairs* 26 (5): 1304–14. https://doi. org/10.1377/hlthaff.26.5.1304.

Prager, E. 2018. "Will People Price Shop for Healthcare?" *Kellogg Insight.* Published January 4. https://insight.kellogg.northwestern.edu/article/will-people-price-shop-for-healthcare.

President's Council on Bioethics. 1974. "Former Bioethics Commissions." Accessed October 7, 2019. https://bioethicsarchive.georgetown.edu/pcbe/reports/past_commissions/.

Regitz-Zagrosek, V. 2012. "Sex and Gender Differences in Health." *EMBO Reports* 13 (7): 596–603. https://doi.org/10.1038/embor.2012.87.

Roeder, A. 2015. "Zip Code Better Predictor of Health than Genetic Code." Harvard T. H. Chan School of Public Health. Published August 4. www. hsph.harvard.edu/news/features/zip-code-better-predictor-of-health-than-genetic-code/.

Ross, D. M., B. Ramirez, T. Rotarius, and A. Liberman. 2008. "Healthcare Transitions and the Aging Population: A Framework to Measure the Value of Rapid Rehabilitation." *Health Care Manager* 30 (2): 96–117. https://doi. org/10.1097/HCM.0b013e318216ed89.

Sanger-Katz, M. 2018. "Bleak New Estimates in Drug Epidemic: A Record 72,000 Overdose Deaths in 2017." *New York Times.* Published August 15. www.nytimes. com/2018/08/15/upshot/opioids-overdose-deaths-rising-fentanyl.html.

Schneiderman, L. J. 2011. "Defining Medical Futility and Improving Medical Care." *Journal of Bioethical Inquiry* 8: 123. https://doi.org/10.1007/s11673-011-9293-3.

Scull, A. 2002. "The Antidepressant Era." *Journal of Health Politics, Policy and Law* 27 (1): 139–44. https://doi.org/10.1215/03616878-27-1-139.

Scully, J. L. 2004. "What Is a Disease?" *EMBO Reports* 5 (7): 650–53. https://doi. org/10.1038/sj.embor.7400195.

Shaw, L. J., R. Bugiardini, and C. N. B. Merz. 2009. "Women and Ischemic Heart Disease." *Journal of the American College of Cardiology* 54 (17): 1561–75. https://doi.org/10.1016/j.jacc.2009.04.098.

Shivayogi, P. 2013. "Vulnerable Population and Methods for Their Safeguard." *Perspectives in Clinical Research* 4 (1): 53–57. https://doi.org/10.4103/2229-3485.106389.

Signorello, L. B., S. S. Cohen, D. R. Williams, H. M. Munro, M. K. Hargreaves, and W. J. Blot. 2014. "Socioeconomic Status, Race, and Mortality: A Prospective Cohort Study." *American Journal of Public Health* 104 (12): e98–e107. https://doi.org/10.2105/AJPH.2014.302156.

Silver, H., and P. McAtee. 1978. "Rural Health Clinic Act of 1977." *Nurse Practitioner* 3 (5): 30–32.

Slabaugh, S. L., M. Shah, M. Zack, L. Happe, T. Cordier, E. Havens, E. Davidson, M. Miao, T. Prewitt, and H. Jia. 2017. "Leveraging Health-Related Quality of Life in Population Health Management: The Case for Healthy Days." *Population Health Management* 20 (1): 13–22. https://doi.org/10.1089/pop.2015.0162.

Slade-Sawyer, P. 2014. "Is Health Determined by Genetic Code or Zip Code? Measuring the Health of Groups and Improving Population Health." *North Carolina Medical Journal* 75 (6): 394–97. https://doi.org/10.18043/ncm.75.6.394.

Smith, M. 2013. "50 Years Later, Kennedy's Vision for Mental Health Not Realized." *Seattle Times*. Published October 20. www.seattletimes.com/nation-world/50-years-later-kennedyrsquos-vision-for-mental-health-not-realized/.

Somers, S. A., and R. Mahadevan. 2010. *Health Literacy Implications of the Affordable Care Act*. Center for Health Strategies, Inc. Published November. www.chcs.org/media/Health_Literacy_Implications_of_the_Affordable_Care_Act.pdf.

Starr, P. 2009. "Professionalization and Public Health: Historical Legacies, Continuing Dilemmas." *Journal of Public Health Management and Practice* 15 (6): S26–30. https://doi.org/10.1097/PHH.0b013e3181af0a95.

Stokes, J., J. Noren, and S. Shindell. 1982. "Definition of Terms and Concepts Applicable to Clinical Preventive Medicine." *Journal of Community Health* 8 (1): 33–41. www.ncbi.nlm.nih.gov/pubmed/6764783.

Stuart, H. 2003. "Violence and Mental Illness: An Overview." *World Psychiatry* 2 (2): 121–24. www.ncbi.nlm.nih.gov/pubmed/16946914.

Substance Abuse and Mental Health Services Administration. 2019. "Behavioral Health Treatments and Services." Updated January 30. www.samhsa.gov/treatment/mental-disorders.

Swanson, J. W., L. K. Frisman, A. G. Robertson, H.-J. Lin, R. L. Trestman, D. A. Shelton, K. Parr, E. Rodis, A. Buchanan, and M. S. Swartz. 2013. "Costs of Criminal Justice Involvement Among Persons with Serious Mental Illness in Connecticut." *Psychiatric Services* 64 (7): 630–37. https://doi.org/10.1176/appi.ps.002212012.

Torrey, T. 2019. "Primary, Secondary, Tertiary, and Quaternary Care." Verywell Health. Updated September 27. www.verywellhealth.com/primary-secondary-tertiary-and-quaternary-care-2615354.

UNAIDS. 2017. "Sweden—Championing Efforts to End AIDS." Published April 1. www.unaids.org/en/resources/presscentre/featurestories/2017/april/20170407_sweden.

University of Ottawa. 2019. "Definitions of Health." Accessed December 6. www.med.uottawa.ca/sim/data/health_definitions_e.htm.

US Census Bureau. 2019a. "American Community Survey (ACS)." Accessed October 7. www.census.gov/programs-surveys/acs/.

———. 2019b. "American FactFinder." Accessed October 7. https://factfinder.census.gov/faces/nav/jsf/pages/index.xhtml.

———. 2019c. "National Crime Victimization Survey (NCVS)." Accessed October 7. www.census.gov/programs-surveys/ncvs.html.

US Congress. 1963. "Mental Retardation Facilities and Community Mental Health Centers Construction Act of 1963." Public Law 88-164, October 31, 1963. www.govinfo.gov/content/pkg/STATUTE-77/pdf/STATUTE-77-Pg282.pdf.

US Department of Health and Human Services (HHS). 2019a. "National Survey on Drug Use and Health." Accessed October 7. https://nsduhweb.rti.org/respweb/homepage.cfm.

———. 2019b. "What Is Mental Health?" Updated April 5. www.mentalhealth.gov/basics/what-is-mental-health.

US Food and Drug Administration (FDA). 1998. "Guidance for Institutional Review Boards and Clinical Investigators." Published January. www.fda.gov/RegulatoryInformation/Guidances/ucm126420.htm.

van Dijk, C. E., B. van den Berg, R. A. Verheij, P. Spreeuwenberg, P. P. Groenewegen, and D. H. de Bakker. 2013. "Moral Hazard and Supplier-Induced Demand: Empirical Evidence in General Practice." *Health Economics* 22 (3): 340–52. https://doi.org/10.1002/hec.2801.

Varshney, M., A. Mahapatra, V. Krishnan, R. Gupta, and K. S. Deb. 2016. "Violence and Mental Illness: What Is the True Story?" *Journal of Epidemiology and Community Health* 70 (3): 223–25. https://doi.org/10.1136/jech-2015-205546.

Vernon, J. A., A. Trujillo, S. Rosenbaum, and B. Debuono. 2003. *Low Health Literacy: Implications for National Health Policy.* Accessed October 7, 2019. https://publichealth.gwu.edu/departments/healthpolicy/CHPR/downloads/LowHealthLiteracyReport10_4_07.pdf.

Waisel, D. B. 2013. "Vulnerable Populations in Healthcare." *Current Opinion in Anaesthesiology* 26 (2): 186–92. https://doi.org/10.1097/ACO.0b013e32835e8c17.

Weinstein, N. J., A. Geller, Y. Negussie, and A. Baciu (eds.). 2017. *Communities in Action: Pathways to Health Equity.* Washington, DC: National Academies Press.

Whaley, C., J. S. Chafen, S. Pinkard, G. Kellerman, D. Bravata, R. Kocher, and N. Sood. 2014. "Association Between Availability of Health Service Prices and Payments for These Services." *JAMA* 312 (16): 1670–76. https://doi.org/10.1001/jama.2014.13373.

Williams, J. S., R. J. Walker, and L. E. Egede. 2016. "Achieving Equity in an Evolving Healthcare System: Opportunities and Challenges." *American Journal of the Medical Sciences* 351 (1): 33–43. https://doi.org/10.1016/j.amjms.2015.10.012.

World Health Organization (WHO). 2019. "Palliative Care." Accessed October 7. www.who.int/palliativecare/en/.

———. 2007. *Women, Ageing and Health: A Framework for Action*. Accessed October 7, 2019. www.who.int/ageing/publications/Women-ageing-health-lowres.pdf.

———. 1984. *Health Promotion: A Discussion Document on the Concept and Principles*. Accessed October 7, 2019. http://apps.who.int/iris/bitstream/handle/10665/107835/E90607.pdf?sequence=1&isAllowed=y.

———. 1948. "Constitution of the World Health Organization." Adopted by the International Health Conference, June. http://apps.who.int/gb/bd/PDF/bd47/EN/constitution-en.pdf?ua=1.

Wyatt, R., M. Laderman, L. Botwinick, K. Mate, and J. Whittington. 2016. *Achieving Health Equity: A Guide for Healthcare Organizations*. Institute for Healthcare Improvement. Accessed November 18, 2019. www.ihi.org/resources/Pages/IHIWhitePapers/Achieving-Health-Equity.aspx.

Yu, Y. M., W. G. Shin, J.-Y. Lee, S. A. Choi, Y. H. Jo, S. J. Youn, M. S. Lee, and K. H. Choi. 2015. "Patterns of Adverse Drug Reactions in Different Age Groups: Analysis of Spontaneous Reports by Community Pharmacists." *PLOS ONE* 10 (7): e0132916. https://doi.org/10.1371/journal.pone.0132916.

Zezima, K., D. Paul, S. Rich, J. Tate, C. Ramirez, and A. A. Williams. 2018. "How Domestic Violence Leads to Murder." *Washington Post*. Published December 9. www.washingtonpost.com/graphics/2018/investigations/domestic-violence-murders/?utm_term=.25e0969cf1f4.

FINANCING A MASSIVE SYSTEM

> Usually people talk about healthcare costs in abstract terms, like they account for 18 percent of GDP. Most people know that's a problem, but no one goes to med school to change GDP.
> —Neel Shah, MD, Harvard Medical School and Ariadne Labs

Learning Objectives

- Understand the role of healthcare financing.
- Analyze and evaluate the various funding models for healthcare.
- Examine the fundamental principles of insurance.
- Review the characteristics of managed care.
- Evaluate the flaws of a fee-for-service healthcare system.
- Understand the various aspects of Medicare, Medicaid, and other US government programs.

Financing is a critical aspect of the US healthcare system (see exhibit 8.1). It enables patients to access services and supports the development of medical and other healthcare services by providing the economic resources needed. Third-party payment mechanisms are a key feature of healthcare financing. A third-party payer is an insurance company, government entity, or other party that provides the funding for medical care and health services for another person or group. Without third-party payers, patients' access to the healthcare system is reduced, and they experience suboptimal health outcomes (Freeman et al. 2008; Sommers, Gawande, and Baicker 2017).

Of all the countries of the world, the United States is the only developed economy that does not provide some form of universal third-party coverage to all of its citizens, and the country has been unable to implement such reforms despite several attempts over more than 100 years (Bump 2010; Reich et al. 2016). Many other countries have had less difficulty in balancing social and economic concerns because their societies are smaller, their populations are more homogeneous, and their cultures are more conducive to collective thought (Hoffman 2008; Iacobucci 2017; Reich et al. 2016). In some instances, countries also had to "start from scratch" after World War II.

EXHIBIT 8.1
Area of Focus
for This Chapter

The Aim of the Healthcare System

Issues That Require Our Attention

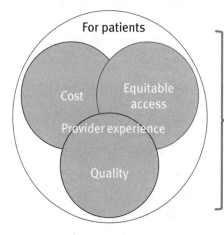

- Nature of our complex system
- Historical issues that have influenced the development of the system
- Beliefs and attitudes about health and healthcare
- Comparison with other developed countries
- Components of our healthcare system
- People and providers
- Patient care—the purpose of the system
- *Financing a massive system*
- Quality—easier said than done
- Medical and information technology
- The pharmaceutical industry
- Complementary and alternative medicine
- Politics/economics
- The future of the system

Five Main Funding Models

Exhibit 8.2 shows the five primary funding models currently found in the world's developed economies:

1. *The self-funded model* is an approach in which the individual or responsible party simply pays out-of-pocket for the cost of medical care or other health services. One might argue that this arrangement is not a funding model at all. Nonetheless, self-funding, or self-pay, contributes significant resources to many countries' healthcare systems for services not covered by insurance or government programs. Self-funding includes coinsurance and deductibles, as well as employees' portions of insurance premiums—all of which have risen sharply in the United States (Glied and Jackson 2018; Commonwealth Fund 2019).

2. *The Bismarck model,* named after Chancellor Otto von Bismarck, was created as part of the unification of Germany in the nineteenth century. Under a Bismarck plan, everyone in the country is covered

EXHIBIT 8.2
Healthcare
System
Financial
Models

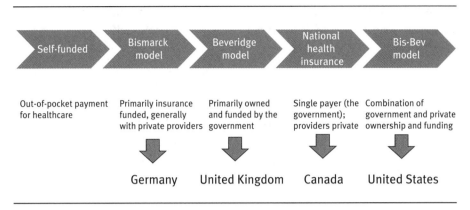

through an insurance-style, not-for-profit mechanism called a "sick fund," which is carefully regulated by the government. The Bismarck model is used in several European countries, including Germany, as well as in Japan (Lameire, Joffe, and Wiedemann 1999).

3. *The Beveridge model* is named after William Beveridge, the designer of the National Health System (NHS) in the United Kingdom. Under the Beveridge model, the government is the principal payer and owner of the healthcare system, and it tightly controls cost. In addition to the United Kingdom, some Scandinavian countries and New Zealand follow the Beveridge model (Fierlbeck 2011).

4. *The national health insurance model (NHI)* is a single-payer approach like that found in Canada. The government is the principal payer for care, but the providers are mostly private (Fierlbeck 2011).

5. *The hybrid model of Bismarck and Beveridge (Bis-Bev)*—as the name implies—has characteristics of the other models (Reid 2010). The United States is a prime example of this approach.

As noted earlier in the book, the US healthcare system—if it can be truly called a system—includes elements of all the world's funding models. If you receive services through the Veterans Health Administration, you are in a Beveridge system similar to that of the United Kingdom (government owned and operated, funded by taxes). If you have Medicare, you are participating in an NHI system similar to that of Canada (private care delivery, single government payer, funded by taxes and premiums). If you have Medicaid, your experience is determined by a combination of rules at the state and federal levels, funded by state and federal taxes. If you have employer-based group coverage—a category rather unique to the United States—your care is funded privately through self-insurance or insured mechanisms. Of course, your care may also be funded privately out of pocket (self-pay) or through charitable activities (no-pay).

People in the United States who are poor but do not qualify for Medicaid can go to a hospital emergency department (ED) as a last resort. The Emergency Medical Treatment and Active Labor Act (EMTALA), passed by the US Congress in 1986 as part of the Consolidated Omnibus Reconciliation Act (COBRA), seeks to ensure nondiscriminatory access to emergency medical care even when patients cannot afford to pay (Zibulewsky 2001). EMTALA was intended to prevent the "dumping" of patients for strictly financial reasons (Zuabi, Weiss, and Langdorf 2016). When uncompensated care is provided in an ED, the services are ultimately funded by everyone through subsidies and cost shifting (i.e., the practice of charging other payers more to recover the cost of care for people who cannot pay)—though the extent to which cost shifting occurs remains an area of controversy (Coughlin et al. 2014; Frakt 2011).

Exhibits 8.3 and 8.4 provide a breakdown of the sources of insurance coverage for the US population. Private insurance—primarily employer sponsored—covers most of the people in the United States. The use of private health insurance companies in the United States in some ways resembles other countries' Bismarck systems, which use insurance-style funds. However, those systems are almost universally not-for-profit and are much more heavily regulated by the government.

EXHIBIT 8.3
Insurance
Coverage in the
United States
(2017)

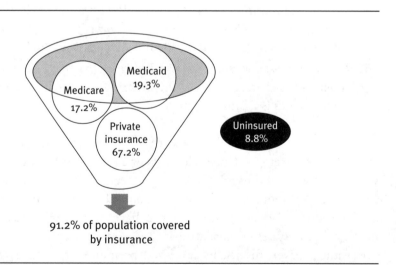

91.2% of population covered
by insurance

Note: Numbers do not add up to the total because some people have more than one source of coverage.
Source: Data from Berchick, Hood, and Barnett (2017).

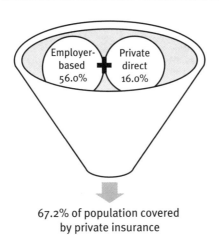

EXHIBIT 8.4
Private Sources
of Insurance
Coverage (2017)

67.2% of population covered
by private insurance

Note: Numbers do not add up to the total because some people have more than one source of coverage.
Source: Data from Berchick, Hood, and Barnett (2017).

Health Insurance in the United States

When discussing health insurance in the United States, we must distinguish between public or government-based insurance programs, such as Medicare and Medicaid, and private commercial health insurance, such as Blue Cross Blue Shield. Government-based insurance programs are sponsored by federal, state, or local government, or by some combination of government entities. The plans are funded through specific or indirect general taxes; premiums may be contributed as well, as in the case of Medicare. Private commercial insurance can be provided by for-profit or not-for-profit corporations. Plans are designed and sold to individuals and groups, often based on employers, and premiums are paid to the corporation in return for coverage (i.e., payment) for services designated by the plan (Morrisey 2013).

The United States has about 35 major health insurance carriers, each of which has a number of brands, subsidiaries, and policies. Major companies include the following (Insurance Providers 2019):

- AARP
- AETNA
- American National Insurance Company
- Assurant
- Blue Cross Blue Shield Association

- CIGNA
- Coventry Health Care
- Golden Rule Insurance Company
- Fortis
- Health Net
- Highmark
- Humana
- Kaiser Permanente
- Medical Mutual of Ohio
- Molina Healthcare
- UnitedHealth Group
- Unitrin
- WellPoint

Important Insurance Terms

A number of key insurance terms are used in everyday conversation, though their definitions are often misunderstood. The *insurer* is the insurance company or entity that is providing healthcare benefits. *Benefits* are the services covered by the plan and the amount the insurer will pay for those services. The *beneficiary* is the person insured by the health plan. The individual receiving benefits, or that individual's representative, may be called the *insured*. The *premium* is the amount of money paid either by the insured individual or the group sponsor (e.g., employer, association) for the insurance. Often, premiums are shared between the individual and the group sponsor.

Cost sharing occurs when the insured pays a portion of the costs out of pocket, and the various forms of cost sharing are often a source of confusion. Three common forms of cost sharing are deductibles, copayments, and coinsurance. The deductible is an amount of money that must be paid by the patient before any benefits are paid by the plan. A copayment is a flat amount that must be paid by the patient before benefits are paid by the plan. Coinsurance is a portion of the medical costs paid by the insured, typically as a percentage of the fee; it is distinct from a copayment (HealthCare.gov 2019a; RAND Corporation 2019). In some instances, a health plan will include all three of these forms of cost sharing.

Often, cost-sharing arrangements work independently of one another. For example, a plan might have an annual deductible of $1,000 that must be paid by the patient before any benefits are paid by the plan. In addition, each individual service the patient receives might have a coinsurance or a copayment. For example, even after the plan's deductible is met, the insured might still have to pay a $50 copayment each time they visit a physician; they might also have to pay a $100 copayment each time they visit the emergency department.

Cost sharing has been found to have a material impact on people's utilization of healthcare but, according to a study by the RAND Corporation (2016), no detrimental impact on health outcomes. However, if cost-sharing payments are too high, they can significantly detour access to care. This concern has taken on additional importance as high-deductible insurance plans (discussed later in the chapter) have become more commonplace (Agarwal, Mazurenko, and Menachemi 2017).

Four Principles of Insurance

Four principles are essential for a basic understanding of insurance:

1. *Risk is unpredictable for individuals.* For any individual, the likelihood of a healthcare event, such as a serious illness or injury, is difficult to predict. Insurance helps prepare for unpredictable, infrequent events that can have significant economic consequences when they occur.

2. *Risk is predictable in large groups.* Actuarial science has demonstrated that, within a large group, the probability of a particular healthcare event can be determined with great accuracy. For example, if we have data for a large enough sample, we approach what is known as a normal population—one that has a predictable, bell-shaped curve of probability for a particular event (National Institute of Standards and Technology 2012). These data can then be extrapolated to the group of individuals in a health plan. For instance, if we have a group of 20,000 people and know their demographic information (e.g., age, gender), we can predict that a certain number of people will have a cardiac event within a given year. We will not be able to predict who those individuals will be, but we will know the total number of occurrences. This knowledge of the number of occurrences—and the probable cost—enables insurance companies to determine how much of a premium will be needed to supply the benefits related to cardiac care. The healthcare field is increasingly using big data—vast quantities of information collected from diverse sources—to make better predictions (National Association of Insurance Commissioners 2019).

3. *Insurance plans allow risks to be pooled.* Continuing the example of the cardiac event, some individuals will have few or no healthcare events and will therefore require little, if any, of the pool or resources; other individuals will have serious events and will use a substantial amount.

4. *Losses are shared by all members.* Pooling of risk allows losses to be shared by all members of the group. On a more macro basis, losses can be shared by the entire population that is covered by the insurance provider (Relman 2012).

Moral Hazard and Adverse Selection

Two important concepts that have shaped health plan design and the very concept of health insurance are moral hazard and adverse selection (Nyman 2004). Simply put, moral hazard arises when people consume more medical services that necessary because they do not incur the full cost of those services (Sommers et al. 2016). Adverse selection occurs when the purchaser of a health plan has knowledge that the health plan does not have concerning future needs, creating what economists call information asymmetry.

Moral hazard and adverse selection affect the elasticity of demand for healthcare services. Elasticity is the degree to which demand for a service changes with price. With moral hazard and adverse selection, typical economic regulators are no longer in place on the part of the consumer of the care (Pauly 1968); many people believe that the resulting inelasticity is one of the reasons that healthcare in the United States is so expensive.

Intuitively, moral hazard and adverse selection both seem to make sense. Consider this example of moral hazard: If I told someone that they could pick out any car at a car dealership and that I would pay for it, is the person likely to pick the least expensive car? Will the person decline the offer? In most cases, the answer is probably no. A person who does not have a barrier of cost is going to make a choice based on other issues and preferences.

Consider a similar example for adverse selection: If two health plans are offered and one has a greater benefit level, an individual who anticipates significant healthcare needs in the near future is likely to choose the higher-benefit plan, even if the price is higher. Meanwhile, an individual with no anticipated health needs is likely to choose the lowest-cost plan, or even elect to have no plan at all. As a result of these choices, the higher-benefit plan is likely to contain a statistically skewed number of high utilizers of care, which significantly increases the cost to the plan; furthermore, that cost will not be offset by savings from low utilizers, because those individuals have mostly opted for a lower-cost plan or no plan at all.

Moral hazard and adverse selection continue to be a source of debate and controversy. If we make plans too generous, the greater utilization can lead to unnecessary increases in cost; however, if we include too many economic barriers (e.g., deductibles, coinsurances, copayments), we risk limiting people's ability to obtain necessary care (Maas 2016). A study by Powell and Goldman (2016) found that moral hazard and adverse selection contributed significantly to the cost of health plans. They compared low-benefit plans and high-benefit plans and concluded that 53 percent of the difference in spending between the two types was attributable to moral hazard and that 47 percent was a result of adverse selection (Powell and Goldman 2016).

Moral hazard can also influence the diffusion of technology. If a new technology is available in a community but no third parties are willing to pay for it, patients are likely to be unwilling or unable to pay for the service themselves; as a result, adoption of the technology will be limited. Providers often do not adopt technologies that are not covered by third-party payment (Cain and Mittman 2002).

Insurance Risk Rating and Pre-existing Conditions

A variety of methods have been used to assess people's level of risk for the purpose of determining insurance rates. Experience rating looks at the person's previous medical history, with consideration for any pre-existing conditions that might cause high utilization of healthcare. Another common practice is community rating, which rates individuals based on the experience of an entire designated community. Other forms of insurance rating include geographic rating, based on a person's physical location; duration rating, which accounts for the length of time a person has been in the health plan or has been covered by insurance; and industry rating, which accounts for the industry in which the person or group is employed, because some industries incur higher healthcare expenses than others (Kaiser Family Foundation [KFF] 2012). Of these methods, experience rating focused on pre-existing conditions has been the most problematic for people seeking health insurance in the United States. More than 52 million people are believed to have had declinable pre-existing conditions in 2015 (KFF 2015).

Methods of Paying for Services

Over the years, a variety of methodologies have been used to determine payment for medical services based on such units as episodes of care; a time frame such as a day (per diem), month, or year; a percentage of a fee schedule; or a fixed payment per person or recipient (Quinn 2015). Various authors have described these models differently (Goroll et al. 2007; Liu, Bozic, and Teisberg 2017; Mechanic and Altman 2009; Neprash et al. 2015; Shapiro 2016), but the central features of the most commonly used methodologies are as follows:

- *Fee-for-service.* As the name implies, this form of reimbursement provides payment for services on a per-unit basis. The rate of payment is sometimes based on the amount considered "usual and customary" for the service—that is, either the rate normally charged by the provider or the usual and customary rate for the community. More frequently, however, fee-for-service payments are based on a fee schedule (Quinn 2015).
- *Discounted fee-for-service.* Under this arrangement, payments are made based on a negotiated discount off the provider's fee schedule. In many instances, a provider will agree to a reduced fee schedule in return

for timely payment or improved access to patients. A discounted fee arrangement may also be done as a percentage of the Medicare fee schedule, which is widely available and often used as a benchmark for setting payments (Quinn 2015).

- *Indemnity plans.* These types of insurance policies have become virtually obsolete in healthcare with the advent of newer insurance models and the passage of the Affordable Care Act (ACA). Nonetheless, the basic payment methodology is to indemnify, or compensate, the insured against the cost of medical care up to certain policy limits. The policy limits are set in accordance with the insurance contract and may vary dramatically from company to company and policy to policy (Numbers 1979).

- *Prospective fee schedules.* Under this arrangement, payments are made based on a negotiated price, and the price does not necessarily have a relationship to an existing fee schedule of the provider. A prospective payment system, based on diagnosis-related groups (DRGs), was mandated by Congress in 1982 as a means of controlling escalating Medicare costs. Groups of conditions believed to have similar resource requirements are placed into DRGs, and a fixed payment is determined for treatment within each group. If the provider is efficient, the payment may exceed the cost of care, in which case the provider profits. If the cost exceeds the DRG payment, the provider takes a loss (Centers for Medicare & Medicaid Services [CMS] 2016).

- *Capitation.* Under capitation, payment is made on a per capita basis, based on a negotiated price. It is often expressed as a per-member per-month (PMPM) payment (Basu et al. 2017; Berwick 1996). To account for the wide variety of provider services, capitation rates are typically expressed in terms of a specific group or class of services. Rates may be expressed in a contract in terms of specific Current Procedural Terminology (CPT) codes. CPT is a nomenclature developed by the American Medical Association (AMA 2019) to describe various medical services. The AMA maintains the terminology for codes and updates it on an annual basis.

- *Bundled payments.* With this methodology, a single payment is made for an entire episode of an illness or treatment. For example, a single payment might be made to reimburse all the providers involved in a heart transplant, including the hospital, numerous physicians, laboratory and radiology, and ancillary services. One of the difficulties in the bundled payment approach is reaching agreement on the costs of all the component services needed for care, especially when some components are not integral parts of the same healthcare organization. In those instances, a separate agreement will need to be reached (Ginsburg 2011).

- *Value-based payment and pay for performance.* These approaches are often tied to a fee-for-service model, but payments are incentivized relative to performance metrics such as quality and efficiency (Ginsburg 2010; Kirkman-Liff 1990; Mandal et al. 2017).
- *Shared savings.* A shared savings model provides financial incentives when certain metrics and outcomes are achieved, usually tied to reduce cost. Shared savings is a central theme in the Affordable Care Act and its promotion of the accountable care organization model (Bennett 2012; Conrad 2015).

Payment models have the challenge of trying to balance the need to ensure fair and appropriate payment for services, the effort to reduce incentives to provide unnecessary care, the drive to reduce costs, and the interest of making sufficient resources available so that people can receive the care they need. To date, no perfect system has been found, but research and demonstration projects by governments and commercial payers continue, with the goal of finding the most appropriate structure of incentives to provide optimal care at reasonable cost (CMS 2018; Laugesen 2016). The Medicare Shared Savings Program is one such example.

The resource-based relative value scale (RBRVS), a system for determining payments for various medical services, has become a fundamental aspect of healthcare funding. Originally implemented in 1992 for the Medicare and Medicaid programs, it has since been widely adopted by virtually all payers. The RBRVS seeks to provide a consistent methodology for valuing medical services on a relative basis—expressed in terms of relative value units (RVUs)—taking into account the amount of work involved as well as the resources used. The formula for calculation of payment based on the RBRVS is shown in exhibit 8.5.

Types of Private Commercial Insurance

Private commercial insurance falls into four main categories: (1) fully insured group plans, (2) self-insured group plans, (3) individual plans, and (4) Medicare supplement and replacement plans.

Fully insured group plans are the traditional type of employer-sponsored health plan. Typically, a company purchases a plan from an insurance carrier for the benefit of employees and employees' families. The plans

---

$$\text{Payment} = \text{CF} \times [(\text{RVUw} \times \text{GPCIw}) + (\text{RVUp} \times \text{GPCIp}) + (\text{RVUm} \times \text{GPCIm})]$$

Note: CF= conversion factor; RVU = relative value unit; GPCI = Geographic Practice Cost Index; w = work; p = practice cost; m = malpractice.

Source: CMS (2017).

EXHIBIT 8.5
Resource-Based Relative Value Scale Formula

offer tax advantages because the premiums are tax-deductible by the company and the employee portion can be paid in pretax dollars. The Employee Retirement Income Security Act (ERISA) of 1974 established certain minimum standards for the protection of individuals in these plans, though its regulations do not apply to plans established or maintained by governmental entities; plans established by churches for their employees; plans that are maintained solely to comply with applicable workers' compensation, unemployment, or disability laws; or plans maintained outside the United States primarily for the benefit of nonresident aliens (US Department of Labor 2019a, 2019b; Polzer and Butler 1997). The 2013 court case *Larson v. United Healthcare Insurance Company* established a precedent that patients enrolled in a fully insured group plan have a right to sue the insurance company in an ERISA claim seeking the recovery of benefits (US Court of Appeals, Seventh Circuit 2013). For more information about ERISA and group health plans, see Hellinger and Young (2005).

Self-insured group plans are those in which the company assumes the responsibilities of the insurance company on behalf of its employees and beneficiaries. Self-insured group plans are not subject to ERISA or many state insurance regulations. Often, self-insured groups will purchase reinsurance, which limits their ultimate liability for losses due to extensive medical claims. Reinsurance policies establish deductible levels—usually on a per-individual basis as well as on an aggregate basis for the entire plan at a high level—that are known as risk corridors. Above those levels, the reinsurer pays the insured group for additional medical expenses. Reinsurance policies are offered by very large insurance companies and syndicates of insurance companies; examples include Zurich Insurance Group and Lloyd's of London (Becker 2018; Layton, McGuire, and Sinaiko 2016).

Individual insurance plans had been decreasing in popularity for many years, but they experienced a resurgence following the passage of the Affordable Care Act in 2010. The ACA sought to encourage the use of such policies for people who were not covered under a group plan or a government-sponsored plan, and it provided subsidies to make the plans more affordable for people with low to middle income. People primarily access individual plans through state or federally run websites known as healthcare marketplaces. Depending on the locality, individuals can select from a number of plans offered by different insurance companies (CMS 2019b; Obama 2016; Shartzer, Long, and Anderson 2016; US Department of Health and Human Services [HHS] 2017).

The fourth category of private insurance consists of Medicare supplement and replacement plans. Even when patients are covered by Medicare parts A (hospital insurance), B (medical insurance), and D (prescription drugs), their services will not be covered in full. Deductibles and coinsurances can be significant, and these patient responsibilities change each year (see exhibit 8.6 for the 2019 levels). Many Medicare recipients choose to purchase additional insurance, known as Medigap, to cover their Part A deductibles, the percentage of expenses not paid by Part B, and in some cases the Part D deductible as well. Medigap plans are standardized by law and are typically purchased from commercial insurance carriers or managed care companies; thus, Medigap is something of a hybrid program between government and commercial insurance.

Medicare Advantage plans, also known as Medicare Part C, are standardized managed care plans that replace traditional Medicare plans. These all-encompassing plans are sold by commercial insurance companies, and they often offer lower premiums and additional benefits for participants. In some cases, Part C plans are offered at no cost to the patient because of their

2019 Medicare Costs at a Glance	
Part A premium	Most people don't pay a monthly premium for Part A. If you buy Part A, you'll pay up to $437 each month. If you paid Medicare taxes for less than 30 quarters, the standard Part A premium is $437. If you paid Medicare taxes for 30–39 quarters, the standard Part A premium is $240.
Part A hospital inpatient deductible and coinsurance	You pay: • $1,364 deductible for each benefit period • Days 1–60: $0 coinsurance for each benefit period • Days 61–90: $341 coinsurance per day of each benefit period • Days 91 and beyond: $682 coinsurance per each "lifetime reserve day" after day 90 for each benefit period (up to 60 days over your lifetime) • Beyond lifetime reserve days: all costs
Part B premium	The standard Part B premium amount is $135.50 (or higher depending on your income).
Part B deductible and coinsurance	$185 per year. After your deductible is met, you typically pay 20% of the Medicare-approved amount for most doctor services (including most doctor services while you're a hospital inpatient), outpatient therapy, and durable medical equipment (dme).
Part C premium	The Part C monthly premium varies by plan.
Part D premium	The Part D monthly premium varies by plan (higher-income consumers may pay more).

EXHIBIT 8.6
Premium, Deductible, and Coinsurance Costs Under Medicare

Source: Reprinted from Medicare.gov (2018).

managed care features. These plans impose some restriction on choice, and they incorporate utilization review, precertification, and other features frequently found in commercial insurances and managed care plans outside of Medicare. They are required to cover all the services provided by traditional Medicare. Like other types of commercial insurance, Medicare Advantage plans can vary in design, so the insured can choose appropriate levels of deductible and benefits (HHS 2014). Medigap plans are not available to people who have Medicare Advantage plans (Medicare.gov 2019).

High-Deductible Plans, Health Savings Accounts, and Health Reimbursement Accounts

High-deductible plans, as the name implies, provide insurance protection to the insured but carry a significant deductible that must be funded by the patient or responsible party. They are often referred to as "consumer-directed plans" because, by design, they allow for greater choice on the part of patients or responsible parties on how to spend their healthcare dollars (Bundorf 2012). High-deductible plans have been around for many years, but their popularity has grown in recent years as the cost of insurance has escalated, as employers and patients alike have had to look for ways to reduce their insurance costs. High-deductible plans have been shown to reduce overall healthcare costs by imposing higher costs on individuals. If individuals feel that they are spending their own money for services, they are likely to be more careful with their consumption choices (Agarwal, Mazurenko, and Menachemi 2017; Global Burden of Disease 2015 Mortality and Causes of Death Collaborators 2016). The deductibles in high-deductible plans must be within limits established under the ACA (French et al. 2016).

Certain high-deductible plans have a health savings account (HSA) feature. An HSA is an account into which the patient can contribute money, tax free, for future medical expenses. The account is owned by the patient and portable, and it will never be taxed if the funds are used for medical or health services. Some employers may contribute to employee HSAs (Newhouse 2004). A health reimbursement account (HRA) is similar to an HSA, in that allowable medical and health services can be reimbursed using the funds allocated to it. However, the HRA is owned by an employer; thus, it does not belong to the patient and is not portable. Both HSAs and HRAs are allowed only with high-deductible plans, and both are regulated under the ACA (HealthCare.gov 2019b).

Exhibits 8.7 and 8.8 provide basic illustrations of the process of receiving and paying for care when patients are insured and when they are not. Despite their simplicity, the illustrations offer some clarification about the process and the potential influence of third-party payment on demand for service.

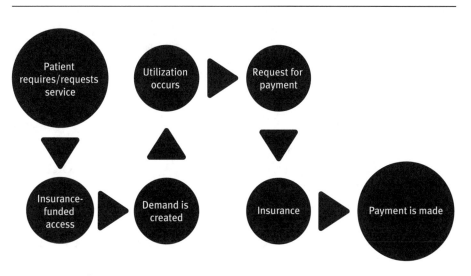

EXHIBIT 8.7
Healthcare
Financing Model
with Insurance

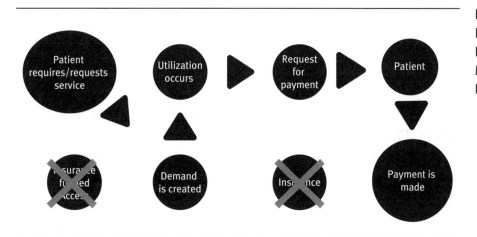

EXHIBIT 8.8
Healthcare
Financing
Model Without
Insurance

Managed Care

The rise of managed care in the United States has stemmed in part from a sense that fee-for-service arrangements have not served us well. Traditionally, the US healthcare system has focused on treating illness but not on creating wellness—a bias that has produced neither optimal outcomes nor low costs. Managed care offers a number of features that can help address past shortcomings and fundamentally transform our system.

Central features of managed care include the following (Kovner and Lemak 2015; Lee et al. 2018; Papanicolas, Woskie, and Jha 2018):

- Managed care organizations exercise formal control over patient utilization.

- The system seeks to streamline delivery and payment for care.
- Behavioral incentives are offered to providers and patients.
- An insurance mechanism is used.
- The functions of financing are integrated through information technology.

Flaws in Fee-for-Service

Fee-for-service plans, at least prior to passage of the ACA, did not cover wellness services to any great degree. Given the typically less-urgent nature of preventive services, they can be highly sensitive to price; if the services are not covered, patients will often avoid them (Ellis, Martins, and Zhu 2017). Today, the ACA requires that insurance plans cover preventive services 100 percent, yet the services remain underutilized—in part, because patients are not used to them being covered and not accustomed to a culture of prevention (Adepoju, Preston, and Gonzales 2015).

Given the focus of our policies and payment approaches, the US healthcare system has developed in such a way that sick care is more lucrative than well care. Services and procedures to treat illness simply cost more than those geared toward wellness, and they represent a greater economic gain for providers. Consider, for example, the difference between a 90-minute office visit for a cardiac patient and a 90-minute angioplasty (a common cardiovascular procedure). Although payment varies, the office visit might cost $350, but in the same amount of time a cardiologist could perform an angioplasty and receive more than $3,000 (American College of Cardiology 2018).

The traditional fee-for-service model offers no controls on utilization, which creates a moral hazard both on the provider side and on the patient side. Overutilization of specialty care is especially prevalent. As noted in chapter 6, the United States is unique in that it has more specialty physicians than it has primary physicians. Some providers overutilize out of fear of litigation. They might worry that they will be sued if they miss something, so they order tests that are not medically necessary. Patients often want more services, not less; some come to equate services with health (Hickson and Entman 2008; Sage 2006; Studdert et al. 2005).

Provider-induced demand (PID) occurs when a provider influences a patient's demand for care even though this demand goes against the provider's own interpretation of the patient's best interest (Ellis and McGuire 1986, 1993; McGuire 2000). Most medical providers are in a unique position to influence patient behavior, given the vast information disequilibrium between the patient and the provider. The provider must therefore act as an agent for the patient and take the utmost care to always work in the patient's best interest (McGuire 2000). Most providers will not intentionally overutilize services for their own financial gain; nonetheless, when a system lacks barriers or protections against overordering, PID becomes a risk (Mercuri and Gafni 2018).

Often, insurance companies actuarially determine what their costs are going to be, and then they pass those costs along to patients through the premium. However, simply passing along higher premiums only covers up the overutilization and other problems inherent in the fee-for-service system. Healthcare costs in the United States are increasing at a higher rate than inflation, but this trend is not so much due to increases in the true cost of care; rather, patients are paying the price for the system's inefficiencies (National Academy of Social Insurance 2015).

The Evolution of Managed Care

In 1929, Baylor University Hospital, led by Justin Kimball, was trying to find a way to pay for healthcare for its teaching staff. The hospital created a capitated contract with local providers, and the contract stated that patients would pay a certain sum (a capitation) each month in return for medical care. This contract is regarded as the precursor of the Blue Cross Blue Shield program (Block 1997). After Baylor University, other employers became active purchasers of health insurance using managed care mechanisms and managed care companies; as a result, employers began to wield enormous buying power.

Over time, different types of organizations emerged, and reformers sought ways to better control costs and provide better care. The Health Maintenance Organization (HMO) Act of 1973, which provided federal funds to start new HMOs, was somewhat like the ACA of its time. The law presented a new way of thinking about care delivery and got providers to focus increasingly on prevention (US Congress 1973).

Early on, the cost appeal of managed care was significant. Costs were lower because most of the contracts that were put in place provided deep discounts to billed charges and some restrictions on access. Restrictions on access proved problematic, however; as noted in chapter 3, Americans place a strong emphasis on personal freedom and do not like to have restrictions on the things they can and cannot do.

New systems and payment mechanisms continue to evolve. Accountable care organizations, defined in the ACA of 2010, provide a model for managed care organizations that assume greater financial risk for patient care. Organizations are now responsible for more of the cost of patient care and are also required to put greater focus on quality and outcome.

Today, almost all contracts are managed care contracts in some sense, and large provider panels may include practically every provider in the community. As a result, the economic position of providers has been weakened somewhat; they often need to compromise in negotiations to gain access to a large pool of patients enrolled with a major insurer, such as Blue Cross Blue Shield. The only large open-access insurance plan today is Medicare. If you have traditional Medicare, you can go to any provider you want—assuming they accept Medicare, which most do. Medicare will pay any enrolled provider the allowable fee-for-service amount.

Integration of the Quad Functions

A true managed care environment features an integration of the "quad functions" of healthcare:

- Delivery of healthcare service
- Financing
- Insurance
- Payment

Financing under managed care is determined through contract negotiation between employers and managed care organizations (MCOs). An MCO assumes risk like an insurance company would—to the point that the need for an insurance company, per se, is somewhat eliminated in a managed care system. Today, however, traditional insurance companies such as Blue Cross Blue Shield, UnitedHealth, and AETNA sell mostly managed care products; thus, MCOs and insurance companies are becoming largely indistinguishable. Most practice managers need not spend too much time worrying about the difference. Managed care often involves sharing risk with providers—a feature of earlier capitation arrangements.

On the delivery side, MCOs need to offer a comprehensive array of services. Most MCOs contract with their providers, though some large medical practices have managed to create a viable MCO through organic growth and acquisitions. Kaiser Permanente and Geisinger Health System, for instance, are large medical practices that are also MCOs, with the full array of medical services needed. In these cases, the organization serves as its own insurer and provides payment. It collects premiums from companies and individuals and, in return, delivers the care. Business divisions within the MCO perform the actuarial work and other administrative functions.

A managed care environment has supply-side regulators, in terms of having availability of service or restricting availability of service. Certificate of Need programs, for example, are one such example. Managed care has demand-side regulators as well—for instance, increasing the cost of a service or making a service less widely available, thereby reducing patient demand.

Efficiencies and Inefficiencies of Managed Care

Despite its promise, managed care has not worked quite as smoothly or as well as many hoped. In many instances, managed care quickly became "managed cost." Nonetheless, managed care has certainly brought some improvements in efficiency. It eliminated insurance and payer intermediaries and brought them together under one organization. It also implemented risk sharing with providers, which helped reduce provider-induced demand.

If a healthcare entity gets only a certain sum of money each month to provide care for a patient, it might think twice about ordering an unnecessary test. Of course, that same payment arrangement could potentially create an incentive to not provide a service that is truly needed. The goal must be prudent delivery of healthcare, which requires always thinking about what is truly best for the patient. Managed care produced the first real effort to collect data and manage the care of patients based on evidence; however, the available data and the systems to support analysis and decision making have had limitations in practice.

One major inefficiency of the current financing system is the complexity it causes for providers who must deal with numerous plans. Another inefficiency involves the potential for lengthy appeals and denials for services, which may occur when an MCO's medical policy is at odds with what the provider perceives to be best for the patient. These types of situations often arise with expensive imaging and laboratory tests. Over time, new organizational structures and payment mechanisms may help align services and payment systems in a way that minimizes complexity and maximizes efficiency.

Gatekeepers and Cost Control

Several mechanisms have been devised to lower costs in managed care systems. One common, yet controversial, cost-saving measure has involved reducing the number of choices available to patients and trying to steer patients toward healthcare entities that are more economically efficient. After all, when patients go to organizations that are less economically efficient, they are likely causing additional resources to be used. The more expensive healthcare entities are not necessarily the higher-quality ones.

The gatekeeper concept—in which a patient is required to go to a primary care doctor before going to a specialist—can help organizations prevent patients' self-referral to nonpreferred specialty providers. The concept is unpopular with many patients, but in many ways it makes sense from a patient care perspective. If patients do not fully understand their medical needs, why not go to a primary care doctor first to discuss the options for additional care? Most likely, dissatisfaction with the gatekeeper system is based less on the concept itself than on the way it has been carried out. Too often, the referral process comes across as disrespectful to the patients, as if they have no idea what they need for their own health.

The patient-centered medical home, a model that is considered highly respectful of patients' rights and autonomy, actually employs a gatekeeper concept: Patients go to the medical home first and then to appropriate specialists based on their contact with the medical home. The difference is that the medical home concept is based on a patient-first notion, and the gatekeeper concept is not simply employed as a mechanism to reduce referrals. Patients get to know the providers, and the providers get to know the patients. The patients come to see the medical home as the most appropriate place for any medical need, knowing that their best interest will be served in the long run.

Case Management

Case management is another managed care concept that, if properly executed, can provide a great benefit to patients—particularly those going through a complex series of medical treatments. Case managers help patients with their recovery and make sure they are in a safe and appropriate environment. Imagine, for example, that you have just received a hip replacement. A case manager can make sure your home is safe and ready to receive you after your procedure—removing any loose rugs or other tripping hazards from the floor, making sure someone will be there to provide assistance, making sure you can get to the bathroom, and taking care of any other necessary considerations. For many years, elderly people who have undergone procedures such as hip replacements have gone to nursing homes because they simply did not have home environments that could support them during recovery; newer approaches tend to place a greater emphasis on improving home-based services and monitoring patients in the home.

Chronic Disease Management

Chronic disease management is an extremely important process that, for many years, was only intermittently used. For a person with a chronic disease such as diabetes, for instance, disease management will involve monitoring the patient's health, overseeing treatment of the disease over time, and making sure the condition does not spiral out of control. Today, chronic disease management is an important feature of managed care that both improves outcomes and controls cost.

Utilization Review and Tiered Benefits

Clearly, some healthcare entities simply cost a lot more than others, and providers with higher costs often show no distinguishable improvements in quality of care. Utilization review helps MCOs assess providers and encourage the use of those that provide the highest quality at the lowest cost. Utilization review typically involves a retrospective look at what services have been provided and whether the use of various services has been appropriate based on trends, benchmarks, customary practices, and other metrics used in determining the quality of care.

MCOs often create payment tiers by ranking providers based on cost and quality and then providing payment according to the provider's rank. For example, providers in Tier 1, the highest tier, might be paid 100 percent of the allowable payment for the services they provide. Tier 2 providers, who have higher costs and lower quality, might be paid only 80 percent of the allowable payment. Tier 3 providers might be paid even less; in some plans, they might not receive any payment. This tier structure gives the patients an incentive to choose the provider that, at least according to the profile, provides higher quality at a lower cost. The practice is somewhat controversial, however, because its effectiveness depends on having an accurate profiling system, which may not always be the case.

Managed Competition

Managed competition is a strategy for efficiently buying health insurance, and it is a key concept used in the health insurance exchanges created under ACA. The central idea is that individuals should be able to choose from among insurance companies based on the premiums and the benefits provided. The effective use of managed competition requires that plans and benefits be standardized in such a way that reasonable comparisons can be made. Because insurance companies have traditionally offered multiple plans with varying benefit levels, the potential of managed competition has never been fully realized in the purchasing of health insurance.

The economist Alain Enthoven is sometimes referred to as the "father of managed competition." Originally, the concept applied to employers that offered several insurance options to employees, and it helped employees make selections on a cost–benefit basis (Enthoven 1989, 1993, 2009, 2011; Enthoven and Baker 2018; Enthoven and van de Ven 2007).

The Affordable Care Act and Commercial Insurance

The ACA has brought a number of important changes to the commercial healthcare insurance environment in the United States. The ACA required the creation of health insurance exchanges to enable people to more easily purchase coverage on the individual market. The ACA also defined specific services that must be covered in the commercial plans sold on the exchanges. Individual and small group plans must include items and services within the following ten categories:

1. Ambulatory patient services
2. Emergency services
3. Hospitalization
4. Maternity and newborn care
5. Mental health and substance use disorder services and behavioral health treatment
6. Prescription drugs
7. Rehabilitative and habilitative services and devices
8. Laboratory services
9. Preventive and wellness services and chronic disease management
10. Pediatric services, including oral and vision care

Plans in the exchanges belong to one of four "metal" categories—bronze, silver, gold, and platinum—based on how costs of care are split between the patient and the plan. The average medical deductibles for the four plan levels are shown in exhibit 8.9. The ACA did not affect Medicare, Medicaid, or other government payers, outside of its attempt to expand Medicaid coverage for the working poor who could not obtain coverage under the act's commercial provisions.

EXHIBIT 8.9

Average Medical Deductible in Bronze, Silver, Gold, and Platinum Plans

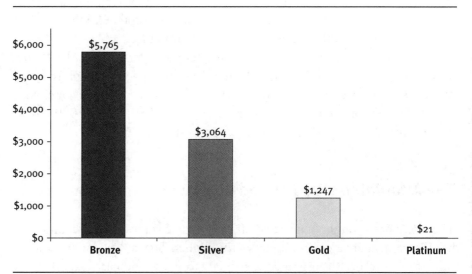

Source: Data from KFF (2014).

Government-Sponsored Insurance

Medicare and Medicaid

Medicare and Medicaid were created in 1965 through amendments to the Social Security Act. In general, Medicare is a program for people who are 65 or older or who have permanent disabilities, whereas Medicaid is a means-tested program intended to cover the poor. The two programs were established as part of the "Great Society" initiative under President Lyndon B. Johnson. Prior to 1965, private insurance was the only coverage available, except for a few targeted government programs that provided coverage for the poor or elderly. Some of the basic features of Medicare and Medicaid are shown in exhibit 8.10.

Medicare, established under Title XVIII of the Social Security Act, has four distinct components.

- Part A provides coverage for inpatient care and some skilled nursing and rehabilitation facility charges; however, it typically does not pay for medical practice services. Anyone who has worked for at least 40 quarters and paid payroll taxes into the health insurance trust automatically receives Medicare after reaching age 65. Part A is subject to an annual deductible.

- Part B provides coverage for outpatient services, including medical practice services. Coverage is voluntary and funded through Part B premiums, which are adjusted based on household income. Part B typically pays 80 percent of charges, leaving the other 20 percent to be paid by the patient.

- Part C, also known as Medicare Advantage, was brought into effect with the Balanced Budget Act of 1997. Part C does not add new benefits to parts A and B; rather, it packages them into a managed care

	Medicare	Medicaid
Eligibility	Over age 65 and the permanently disabled; no means testing	Means tested; varies by state
Funding	Payroll taxes and premiums	State and federal funding
Benefits	Standardized throughout the country	Varies by state with minimum federal standards; states may apply for waivers to create innovative programs

EXHIBIT 8.10
Important Features of Medicare and Medicaid

plan provided by several insurance companies. Part C often combines parts A, B, and D and the Medigap coverage under one umbrella policy.

- Part D, which provides coverage for prescription drugs, requires payment of a monthly premium, in addition to the Part B premium. This coverage is offered through stand-alone plans and through the Medicare Advantage program.

Medicaid, founded under Title XIX of the Social Security Act, is primarily intended to provide services to low-income Americans. A means-tested program operated jointly by the state and federal governments, Medicaid can vary significantly from one state to another, though all state programs are subject to a minimum threshold established by the federal government.

People who qualify for both Medicare and Medicaid are considered dual eligible. For this population, Medicare is typically the primary payer for medical services, and Medicaid pays the deductibles, coinsurance, and other medical expenses, much like a Medigap policy would.

The Medicare Access and CHIP Reauthorization Act (MACRA) of 2015 is an important law that established a new reimbursement and incentive structure for doctors treating Medicare patients. Information about the law and its impact on medical practice is available through CMS (2019c).

The Indian Health Service

The Indian Health Service (IHS) is an agency sponsored by the federal government that provides health services to American Indians and Alaska Natives (IHS 2019). One unique aspect of the services provided by this agency is the culturally competent integration of traditional Native American healthcare practices with modern Western medicine. Although Western medicine often focuses heavily on the physical manifestation of disease, Native American and other traditional cultures often focus more on the balance of spiritual and mental well-being (Bassett, Tsosie, and Nannauck 2012; Cohen 2006; Koithan and Farrell 2010).

The Veterans Health Administration

The Veterans Health Administration (VHA), within the US Department of Veterans Affairs (VA), is the largest integrated healthcare system in the United States. As of 2019, it had 1,255 healthcare facilities, including 170 medical centers and 1,074 outpatient sites of care, serving 9 million enrolled veterans each year (VA 2019c). Prior to 1981, the VHA had no eligibility requirements other than having served in the US armed services and receiving an honorable discharge. For people who entered active duty after 1981, the VHA, in most cases, requires 24 months of service, in addition to an honorable discharge (VA 2019b).

The VA provides comprehensive health benefits. Cost is determined at the time of enrollment using a financial assessment; often, services are provided at no cost. People who exceed an income threshold established by the VA may have to pay a copay for some services. If an applicant refuses to complete the financial assessment, copayments are required (VA 2019b).

In large part because of its size and complexity, the VHA has encountered a number of challenges. It has faced criticism for not always seeing patients in a timely manner, as well as for attempting to hide failures that have contributed to negative health outcomes. These issues have led to intense political pressure and continued calls for reform (Shane 2018).

TRICARE and CHAMPVA

TRICARE, a program sponsored by the federal government within the US Department of Defense (DoD), provides a wide range of services to active and retired members of the military and their families. It was formerly known as the Civilian Health and Medical Program of the Uniformed Services (CHAMPUS). Because private practitioners are often involved in the care of military personnel and their families, many practices need to bill and receive reimbursement from TRICARE for services provided. The system then provides a monetary conversion of the work and other identified factors to determine a fair price for each service (DoD 2019).

The Civilian Health and Medical Program of the Department of Veterans Affairs (CHAMPVA) is a comprehensive healthcare benefits program in which the VA shares the cost of covered services and supplies with eligible beneficiaries. The program is administered by the VHA Office of Community Care (VA 2019a).

Because of their similarities, CHAMPVA and TRICARE are often confused. A key difference is that CHAMPVA is a VA program, whereas TRICARE is a regionally managed DoD program. In some cases, a person might appear to be eligible for either program; however, anyone eligible for TRICARE is not eligible for CHAMPVA. In general, CHAMPVA covers most healthcare services and supplies that are medically and psychologically necessary (VA 2019a).

High-Risk Pools

High-risk pools are funding mechanisms used by state governments to provide insurance to individuals who have pre-existing conditions, do not qualify for government-sponsored insurance such as Medicare and Medicaid, do not have group coverage, and cannot purchase insurance in the private market.

At one time, prior to the implementation of ACA, high-risk pools operated in 35 states and enrolled about 226,000 people (Pollitz 2017)—a relatively small number, given that millions of people had deniable pre-existing conditions or were unable to afford insurance premiums. High-risk pools became unnecessary after the ACA prohibited private insurance carriers from denying insurance coverage because of pre-existing conditions. People with pre-existing conditions can now purchase insurance through the exchanges and receive subsidies based on their income. For the years between the ACA's passage in 2010 and the opening of the health insurance exchanges in 2014, a Pre-existing Condition Insurance Plan (PCIP) was established to help people with pre-existing conditions (HealthCare.gov 2019c).

Some people argue that high-risk pools are a reasonable alternative to the requirements under the ACA. The American Health Care Act (AHCA) of 2017 proposed allowing states to apply for a waiver of the ACA's pre-existing condition rule and instead offer a high-risk pool (American Medical Association 2017); the AHCA failed in the Senate, however, and did not become law. Much of the resistance to the idea is based on the fact that high-risk pools were not entirely successful when they were used in the past.

Prior to the ACA, many of the high-risk pools established on a state-by-state basis were not properly designed or funded, and the cost of the high-risk pool insurance remained too expensive. Richard Popper (2017), who oversaw the high-risk pool in the state of Maryland and helped with California's program, maintains that high-risk pools could work but only if properly structured and funded. California's program had problems because its benefits and subsidies were inadequate to keep premiums at a level that people interested in coverage could afford.

Federal Expenditures for Healthcare

The US federal government spends more than $1 trillion each year on healthcare. In addition, tax credits and tax exclusions for insurance premiums, health savings accounts, and deductibility of medical expenses by individuals amount to approximately $230 billion (Congressional Budget Office 2018a, 2018b). Medicare represents the largest portion of federal expenditures, totaling roughly $583 billion in 2018. Medicaid and the State Children's Health Insurance Program (SCHIP) account for another $399 billion, veterans' medical care accounts for $70.4 billion, and ACA subsidies account for $6 billion.

Federal healthcare expenditures continue to be a major political and economic issue in the United States, with sharp disagreement over potential solutions (Blancato 2017). Medicare is one of the most popular federal programs, and it is supported by a powerful lobby, AARP (formerly the American Association of Retired Persons), with 38 million members (AARP 2018a, 2018b).

Fraud and Abuse

The Centers for Medicare & Medicaid Services provides coverage for more than 145 million people who receive services and products from over a million providers (US Government Accountability Office [GAO] 2017). Given the massive amounts of money involved, as well as the size and complexity of the system, fraud and abuse are serious concerns for providers, administrators, and payers (Blumstein 1996). According to some estimates, as much as 10 percent of the money spent by Medicare is lost due to fraud and abuse (Greenberg 2013; GAO 2018). The Office of Inspector General of the US Department of Health and Human Services (HHS-OIG 2019) has a task force for the investigation and prosecution of fraud.

Common healthcare provider fraud schemes include the following (CMS 2019a, 2019d):

- Billing for services not rendered
- Incorrect reporting of diagnoses or procedures (includes unbundling)
- Overutilization of services
- Kickbacks and bribery
- False or unnecessary issuance of prescription drugs
- Misrepresenting provider of service
- Waiving of deductibles and/or copayments

Much fraud involves intentional criminal behavior, but other actions can be similarly destructive. For instance, enormous losses to federal programs may result from any of the following (CMS 2019d):

- Errors in the coding of services, resulting in overpayment (whether intentional or unintentional)
- Inefficiencies associated with the ordering of excessive tests or procedures
- Bending the rules by billing at a higher level than the services rendered would indicate (whether intentional or unintentional); commonly referred to as *upcoding*

All people responsible for the billing of healthcare services must be well trained, and they must maintain the highest ethical and professional standards to ensure compliance with all necessary rules and regulations. The rules concerning healthcare billing practices can be extremely complex; without special knowledge and expertise, a healthcare organization or provider can quickly find itself in serious trouble with OIG.

Federal laws dealing with Medicare fraud and abuse include the following:

- The False Claims Act aims to protect the government from being overcharged or sold substandard products and services; it imposes penalties for anyone who knowingly submits or causes the submission of a false claim to the federal government.

- The Anti-kickback Statute (AKS) prohibits people from offering, paying, soliciting, or receiving any remuneration directly or indirectly to induce or reward a referral of an item or service that is paid for by a federal healthcare program. In many instances, actions that might seem ordinary in other fields are illegal among healthcare providers. For example, a business in another field might pay for a referral that produces a sale or income; such an action among providers is strictly prohibited under the AKS. Some safe harbors do exist in the regulations for referral activity. For example, providers may invest in companies in which they do business, though that investment must be small relative to the size of the company and should not have a material impact on operations.
- The Physician Self-Referral Law, or Stark law, strictly prohibits physicians from referring certain designated health services to entities that are owned or controlled by the physician or immediate family members. Certain exceptions do apply, however. For example, physicians may refer to a laboratory contained within their practice.
- The Social Security Act includes broad prohibitions and penalties against making false claims or fraudulent statements to the Social Security Administration.
- The US Criminal Code has numerous statutes dealing with fraud and swindling that are generally applicable to healthcare fraud and abuse.

These laws specify criminal, civil, and administrative remedies that the government may impose on individuals or entities that commit fraud and abuse. Such penalties may include the following (CMS 2019d):

- Nonpayment of claims
- Civil monetary penalties
- Exclusion from all federal healthcare programs
- Civil and criminal liability, potentially including imprisonment

The largest healthcare fraud takedown in US history occurred in June 2018 (HHS-OIG 2018). More than 600 defendants in 58 federal districts were charged with participating in fraud schemes that caused about $2 billion in losses to Medicare and Medicaid. OIG also issued exclusion notices to 587 doctors, nurses, and other providers for conduct related to opioid diversion and abuse. The government's antifraud efforts have paid off: In 2018, OIG reported that, for every $1 spent on healthcare-related fraud and abuse investigations, more than $4 is recovered (HHS-OIG 2018).

Because most medical services today are billed electronically, data mining has become an important tool for the discovery and investigation of fraud. Investigators can now compare data across various providers of services and look for abnormal patterns that might suggest fraud or abuse (Koh and Tan 2005; Yang and Hwang 2006). In addition, Medicare actively solicits its beneficiaries for any information that they might have about suspected fraud (CMS 2019d).

Complexity of the Financing Function

Given the complexity and sheer number of health plans and financing arrangements in the United States, is it any wonder that the healthcare system has such incredible administrative costs (Fayomi-Olaleye 2017; Jiwani et al. 2014; Woolhandler, Campbell, and Himmelstein 2003)? Himmelstein and colleagues (2014) found that administrative costs accounted for 25.3 percent of all US hospital expenditures—by far the highest percentage of the nations included in the study. The countries with the next-highest levels of administrative costs were the Netherlands (19.8 percent) and England (15.5 percent) (Himmelstein et al. 2014).

If you were to ask virtually anyone in healthcare about the most difficult aspects of their work, they would almost certainly mention third-party payers and the revenue cycle. Medicare, Medicaid, other government payers, and commercial payers all have different rules and requirements for billing medical services (CMS 2019e); furthermore, new plan structures and payment mechanisms continue to emerge, adding additional levels of complexity.

Discussion Questions

1. Does the lack of an economic model that encourages change inhibit the development of the healthcare system and the medical profession?
2. Why does the United States not have a healthcare system that includes every person in the country? How can we make such a system a reality?
3. Can we simultaneously control cost and maintain innovation and quality in a free-enterprise system?

References

AARP. 2018a. "AARP Responds to 2018 Social Security and Medicare Trustees' Reports." News release. Published June 5. https://press.aarp.org/2018-6-5-AARP-Responds-2018-Social-Security-Medicare-Trustees-Report.

———. 2018b. "Inside the June/July Issue of *AARP The Magazine*." Published June 5. https://press.aarp.org/2018-6-5-Inside-the-June-July-Issue-of-AARP-The-Magazine.

Adepoju, O. E., M. A. Preston, and G. Gonzales. 2015. "Health Care Disparities in the Post–Affordable Care Act Era." *American Journal of Public Health* 105 (Suppl. 5): S665–67. https://doi.org/10.2105/AJPH.2015.302611.

Agarwal, R., O. Mazurenko, and N. Menachemi. 2017. "High-Deductible Health Plans Reduce Health Care Cost and Utilization, Including Use of Needed Preventive Services." *Health Affairs* 36 (10): 1762–68. https://doi.org/10.1377/hlthaff.2017.0610.

American College of Cardiology. 2018. "CMS Releases Final 2019 Physician Fee Schedule." Published November 1. www.acc.org/latest-in-cardiology/articles/2018/11/01/18/28/cms-releases-final-2019-physician-fee-schedule.

American Medical Association (AMA). 2019. "CPT (Current Procedural Terminology)." Accessed October 8. www.ama-assn.org/amaone/cpt-current-procedural-terminology.

———. 2017. "American Health Care Act Summary of Key Provisions, as Passed by the House of Representatives on May 4, 2017." Accessed October 8, 2019. www.ama-assn.org/sites/ama-assn.org/files/corp/media-browser/public/government/advocacy/ahca-top-line-summary.pdf.

Bassett, D., U. Tsosie, and S. Nannauck. 2012. "Our Culture Is Medicine: Perspectives of Native Healers on Posttrauma Recovery Among American Indian and Alaska Native Patients." *Permanente Journal* 16 (1): 19–27. https://doi.org/10.7812/tpp/11-123.

Basu, S., R. S. Phillips, Z. Song, A. Bitton, and B. E. Landon. 2017. "High Levels of Capitation Payments Needed to Shift Primary Care Toward Proactive Team and Nonvisit Care." *Health Affairs* 36 (9): 1599–605. https://doi.org/10.1377/hlthaff.2017.0367.

Becker, C. 2018. "Insuring the Health Insurers—Reinsurance Explained." National Conference of State Legislatures. Published May 7. www.ncsl.org/blog/2018/05/07/insuring-the-health-insurers-reinsurance-explained.aspx.

Bennett, A. R. 2012. "Accountable Care Organizations: Principles and Implications for Hospital Administrators." *Journal of Healthcare Management* 57 (4): 244–54. https://doi.org/10.1097/00115514-201207000-00005.

Berchick, E. R., E. Hood, and J. C. Barnett. 2017. *Health Insurance Coverage in the United States: 2017*. US Census Bureau. Published September 12. www.census.gov/library/publications/2018/demo/p60-264.html.

Berwick, D. M. 1996. "Payment by Capitation and the Quality of Care." *New England Journal of Medicine* 335 (16): 1227–31. https://doi.org/10.1056/NEJM199610173351611.

Blancato, B. 2017. "Why Big Medicare and Medicaid Cuts Are Likely." *Forbes*. Published December 12. www.forbes.com/sites/nextavenue/2017/12/12/ why-big-medicare-and-medicaid-cuts-are-likely/.

Block, L. E. 1997. "Evolution, Growth, and Status of Managed Care in the United States." *Public Health Reviews* 25 (3–4): 193–244. www.ncbi.nlm.nih.gov/ pubmed/9553445.

Blumstein, J. F. 1996. "The Fraud and Abuse Statute in an Evolving Health Care Marketplace: Life in the Health Care Speakeasy." *American Journal of Law & Medicine* 22 (2–3): 205–31.

Bump, J. B. 2010. "The Long Road to Universal Health Coverage: A Century of Lessons for Development Strategy." Center for Global Development. Presented March 2. www.cgdev.org/sites/default/files/archive/doc/events/3.02.10/ Jesse_Bump_Presentation.pdf.

Bundorf, M. K. 2012. *Consumer Directed Health Plans*. Robert Wood Johnson Foundation. Research Synthesis Report No. 24. Published October 1. www.rwjf. org/en/library/research/2012/10/consumer-directed-health-plans.html.

Cain, M., and R. Mittman. 2002. *Diffusion of Innovation in Health Care*. California Healthcare Foundation. Published May 16. www.chcf.org/wp-content/ uploads/2017/12/PDF-DiffusionofInnovation.pdf.

Centers for Medicare & Medicaid Services (CMS). 2019a. "Fraud & Abuse." Updated September 6. www.cms.gov/Outreach-and-Education/Look-Up-Topics/Fraud-and-Abuse/Fraud-page.html.

———. 2019b. "Health Insurance Marketplace." Accessed October 8. https:// marketplace.cms.gov/.

———. 2019c. "MACRA." Updated June 14. www.cms.gov/medicare/quality-initiatives-patient-assessment-instruments/value-based-programs/macra-mips-and-apms/macra-mips-and-apms.html.

———. 2019d. *Medicare Fraud & Abuse: Prevention, Detection, and Reporting*. Published February. www.cms.gov/Outreach-and-Education/Medicare-Learning-Network-MLN/MLNProducts/Downloads/Fraud-Abuse-MLN4649244.pdf.

———. 2019e. "Provider Compliance." Updated August 29. www.cms. gov/Outreach-and-Education/Medicare-Learning-Network-MLN/ MLNProducts/ProviderCompliance.html.

———. 2018. *Medicare Shared Savings Program Accountable Care Organization (ACO) 2018 Quality Measures: Narrative Specifications Document*. Published June 20. www.cms.gov/Medicare/Medicare-Fee-for-Service-Payment/sharedsavingsprogram/Downloads/2018-reporting-year-narrative-specifications.pdf.

———. 2017. *Medicare Physician Fee Schedule*. Published February. www. cms.gov/Outreach-and-Education/Medicare-Learning-Network-MLN/ MLNProducts/downloads/MedcrePhysFeeSchedfctsht.pdf.

———. 2016. "Design and Development of the Diagnosis Related Group (DRG)." Published October 1. www.cms.gov/icd10m/version37-fullcode-cms/full-code_cms/Design_and_development_of_the_Diagnosis_Related_Group_(DRGs).pdf.

Cohen, K. 2006. *Honoring the Medicine: An Essential Guide to Native American Healing.* New York: Ballantine.

Commonwealth Fund. 2019. "Out-of-Pocket Health Care Costs." Accessed October 8. www.commonwealthfund.org/trending/out-pocket-health-care-costs.

Congressional Budget Office. 2018a. *Federal Subsidies for Health Insurance Coverage for People Under Age 65: 2018 to 2028.* Published May. www.cbo.gov/system/files/2018-06/53826-healthinsurancecoverage.pdf.

———. 2018b. *The 2018 Long-Term Budget Outlook.* Published June. www.cbo.gov/system/files/2018-06/53919-2018ltbo.pdf.

Conrad, D. A. 2015. "The Theory of Value-Based Payment Incentives and Their Application to Health Care." *Health Services Research* 50 (Suppl. 2): 2057–89. https://doi.org/10.1111/1475-6773.12408.

Coughlin, T., J. Holahan, K. Caswell, and M. McGrath. 2014. "Uncompensated Care for the Uninsured in 2013: A Detailed Examination—Cost Shifting and Remaining Uncompensated Care Costs." Kaiser Family Foundation. Published May 30. www.kff.org/report-section/uncompensated-care-for-the-uninsured-in-2013-a-detailed-examination-cost-shifting-and-remaining-uncompensated-care-costs-8596/.

Ellis, R. P., B. Martins, and W. Zhu. 2017. "Health Care Demand Elasticities by Type of Service." *Journal of Health Economics* 55: 232–43. https://doi.org/10.1016/j.jhealeco.2017.07.007.

Ellis, R. P., and T. G. McGuire. 1993. "Supply-Side and Demand-Side Cost Sharing in Health Care." *Journal of Economic Perspectives* 7 (4): 135–51. https://pubs.aeaweb.org/doi/pdfplus/10.1257/jep.7.4.135.

———. 1986. "Provider Behavior Under Prospective Reimbursement Cost Sharing and Supply." *Journal of Health Economics* 5: 129–51. http://people.bu.edu/ellisrp/EllisPapers/1986_EllisMcGuire_JHE_MixedPayment.pdf.

Enthoven, A. C. 2011. "Reforming Medicare by Reforming Incentives." *New England Journal of Medicine* 364 (21): e44. https://doi.org/10.1056/NEJMp1104427.

———. 2009. "Integrated Delivery Systems: The Cure for Fragmentation." *American Journal of Managed Care* 15 (Suppl. 10): S284–90. www.ncbi.nlm.nih.gov/pubmed/20088632.

———. 1993. "The History and Principles of Managed Competition." *Health Affairs* 12 (Suppl. 1): 24–48. https://doi.org/10.1377/hlthaff.12.Suppl_1.24.

———. 1989. "Effective Management of Competition in the FEHBP." *Health Affairs* 8 (3): 33–50. https://doi.org/10.1377/hlthaff.8.3.33.

Enthoven, A. C., and L. C. Baker. 2018. "With Roots in California, Managed Competition Still Aims to Reform Health Care." *Health Affairs* 37 (9): 1425–30. https://doi.org/10.1377/hlthaff.2018.0433.

Enthoven, A. C., and W. P. M. M. van de Ven. 2007. "Going Dutch—Managed-Competition Health Insurance in the Netherlands." *New England Journal of Medicine* 357 (24): 2421–23. https://doi.org/10.1056/NEJMp078199.

Fayomi-Olaleye, S. 2017. "Collaborative Strategies Used to Reduce Billing Administrative Cost." PhD diss., Walden University. https://scholarworks.waldenu.edu/dissertations/4440/.

Fierlbeck, K. 2011. *Health Care in Canada: A Citizen's Guide to Policy and Politics.* Toronto: University of Toronto Press.

Frakt, A. B. 2011. "How Much Do Hospitals Cost Shift? A Review of the Evidence." *Milbank Quarterly* 89 (1): 90–130. https://doi.org/10.1111/j.1468-0009.2011.00621.x.

Freeman, J. D., S. Kadiyala, J. F. Bell, and D. P. Martin. 2008. "The Causal Effect of Health Insurance on Utilization and Outcomes in Adults." *Medical Care* 46 (10): 1023–32. https://doi.org/10.1097/MLR.0b013e318185c913.

French, M. T., J. Homer, G. Gumus, and L. Hickling. 2016. "Key Provisions of the Patient Protection and Affordable Care Act (ACA): A Systematic Review and Presentation of Early Research Findings." *Health Services Research* 51 (5): 1735–71. https://doi.org/10.1111/1475-6773.12511.

Ginsburg, M. 2010. "Value-Based Insurance Design: Consumers' Views on Paying More for High-Cost, Low-Value Care." *Health Affairs* 29 (11): 2022–26. https://doi.org/10.1377/hlthaff.2010.0808.

Ginsburg, P. B. 2011. "Reforming Provider Payment—The Price Side of the Equation." *New England Journal of Medicine* 365 (14): 1268–70. https://doi.org/10.1056/NEJMp1107019.

Glied, S. A., and A. Jackson. 2018. "How Would Americans' Out-of-Pocket Costs Change If Insurance Plans Were Allowed to Exclude Coverage of Preexisting Conditions?" Commonwealth Fund. Published November 1. www.commonwealthfund.org/publications/issue-briefs/2018/nov/excluding-preexisting-conditions-impact-on-out-of-pocket-costs.

Global Burden of Disease 2015 Mortality and Causes of Death Collaborators. 2016. "Global, Regional, and National Life Expectancy, All-Cause Mortality, and Cause-Specific Mortality for 249 Causes of Death, 1980–2015: A Systematic Analysis for the Global Burden of Disease Study 2015." *Lancet* 388 (10053): P1459–1544. https://doi.org/10.1016/S0140-6736(16)31012-1.

Goroll, A. H., R. A. Berenson, S. C. Schoenbaum, and L. B. Gardner. 2007. "Fundamental Reform of Payment for Adult Primary Care: Comprehensive Payment for Comprehensive Care." *Journal of General Internal Medicine* 22 (3): 410–15. https://doi.org/10.1007/s11606-006-0083-2.

Greenberg, J. 2013. "Medicare Fraud Rate Is 8 to 10 Percent, Says Roskam of Illinois." PolitiFact. Published June 17. www.politifact.com/truth-o-meter/statements/2013/jun/17/peter-roskam/rep-roskam-says-medicare-fraud-rate-8-10-percent/.

HealthCare.gov. 2019a. "Glossary." Accessed October 8. www.healthcare.gov/glossary/.

———. 2019b. "Health Savings Account (HSA)." Accessed December 5. www.healthcare.gov/glossary/health-savings-account-hsa/.

———. 2019c. "Pre-existing Condition Insurance Plan (PCIP)." Accessed October 8. www.healthcare.gov/glossary/pre-existing-condition-insurance-plan-pcip/.

Hellinger, F. J., and G. J. Young. 2005. "Health Plan Liability and ERISA: The Expanding Scope of State Legislation." *American Journal of Public Health* 95 (2): 217–23. https://doi.org/10.2105/AJPH.2004.037895.

Hickson, G. B., and S. S. Entman. 2008. "Physician Practice Behavior and Litigation Risk: Evidence and Opportunity." *Clinical Obstetrics and Gynecology* 51 (4): 688–99. https://doi.org/10.1097/GRF.0b013e3181899c2c.

Himmelstein, D. U., M. Jun, R. Busse, K. Chevreul, A. Geissler, P. Jeurissen, S. Thomson, M.-A. Vinet, and S. Woolhandler. 2014. "A Comparison of Hospital Administrative Costs in Eight Nations: US Costs Exceed All Others by Far." *Health Affairs* 33 (9): 1586–94. https://doi.org/10.1377/hlthaff.2013.1327.

Hoffman, B. 2008. "Health Care Reform and Social Movements in the United States." *American Journal of Public Health* 98 (Suppl. 1): S69–79. https://doi.org/10.2105/AJPH.98.Supplement_1.S69.

Iacobucci, G. 2017. "NHS in 2017: Keeping Pace with Society." *BMJ* 356: i6738. https://doi.org/10.1136/bmj.i6738.

Indian Health Service (IHS). 2019. "Agency Overview." Accessed December 3. www.ihs.gov/aboutihs/overview/.

Insurance Providers. 2019. "How Many Health Insurance Companies Are There in the United States?" Accessed October 8. www.insuranceproviders.com/how-many-health-insurance-companies-are-there-in-the-united-states/.

Jiwani, A., D. Himmelstein, S. Woolhandler, and J. G. Kahn. 2014. "Billing and Insurance-Related Administrative Costs in United States' Health Care: Synthesis of Micro-Costing Evidence." *BMC Health Services Research* 14: 556. https://doi.org/10.1186/s12913-014-0556-7.

Kaiser Family Foundation (KFF). 2015. "Estimated Number of Nonelderly Adults with Declinable Pre-existing Conditions under Pre-ACA Practices." Accessed October 8, 2019. www.kff.org/other/state-indicator/estimated-number-of-non-elderly-adults-with-declinable-pre-existing-conditions-under-pre-aca-practices/?currentTimeframe=0&sortModel=%7B%22colId%22:%22Location%22,%22sort%22:%22asc%22%7D.

————. 2014. "Medical and Prescription Drug Deductibles for Plans Offered in Federally Facilitated and Partnership Marketplaces for 2015." Published November 18. www.kff.org/health-reform/fact-sheet/medical-and-prescription-drug-deductibles-for-plans-offered-in-federally-facilitated-and-partnership-marketplaces-for-2015/.

————. 2012. *Insurance Market Reforms: Rate Restrictions.* Published June. www.kff.org/health-reform/fact-sheet/health-insurance-market-reforms-rate-restrictions/.

Kirkman-Liff, B. L. 1990. "Physician Payment and Cost-Containment Strategies in West Germany: Suggestions for Medicare Reform." *Journal of Health Politics, Policy and Law* 15 (1): 69–99. https://doi.org/10.1215/03616878-15-1-69.

Koh, H. C., and G. Tan. 2005. "Data Mining Applications in Healthcare." *Journal of Healthcare Information Management* 19 (2): 64–72. https://doi.org/10.1109/SCOPES.2016.7955586.

Koithan, M., and C. Farrell. 2010. "Indigenous Native American Healing Traditions." *Journal for Nurse Practitioners* 6 (6): 477–78. https://doi.org/10.1016/j.nurpra.2010.03.016.

Kovner, A. R., and C. H. Lemak. 2015. "Managing and Governing Health Care Organizations." In *Jonas and Kovner's Health Care Delivery in the United States*, 11th ed., edited by J. R. Knickman and A. R. Kovner, 297–310. New York: Springer.

Lameire, N., P. Joffe, and M. Wiedemann. 1999. "Healthcare Systems—An International Review: An Overview." *Nephrology Dialysis Transplantation* 14 (Suppl. 6): 3–9. https://doi.org/10.1093/ndt/14.suppl_6.3.

Laugesen, M. 2016. *Fixing Medical Prices: How Physicians Are Paid.* Cambridge, MA: Harvard University Press.

Layton, T. J., T. G. McGuire, and A. D. Sinaiko. 2016. "Risk Corridors and Reinsurance in Health Insurance Marketplaces: Insurance for Insurers." *American Journal of Health Economics* 2 (1): 66–95. https://doi.org/10.1162/ajhe_a_00034.

Lee, J. Y., S. Muratov, J. E. Tarride, and A. M. Holbrook. 2018. "Managing High-Cost Healthcare Users: The International Search for Effective Evidence-Supported Strategies." *Journal of the American Geriatrics Society* 66 (5): 1002–8. https://doi.org/10.1111/jgs.15257.

Liu, T. C., K. J. Bozic, and E. O. Teisberg. 2017. "Value-Based Healthcare: Person-Centered Measurement: Focusing on the Three C's." *Clinical Orthopaedics and Related Research* 475 (3): 315–17. https://doi.org/10.1007/s11999-016-5205-5.

Maas, S. 2016. "Moral Hazard and Adverse Selection in Health Insurance." National Bureau of Economic Research. *NBER Digest.* Published April. www.nber.org/digest/apr16/w21858.html.

Mandal, A. K., G. K. Tagomori, R. V. Felix, and S. C. Howell. 2017. "Value-Based Contracting Innovated Medicare Advantage Healthcare Delivery and Improved Survival." *American Journal of Managed Care* 23 (2): e41–49. https://ajmc.s3.amazonaws.com/_media/_pdf/AJMC_02_2017_Mandal%20(final).pdf.

McGuire, T. 2000. "Physician Agency." In *Handbook of Health Economics*, vol. 1, edited by A. J. Culyer and J. P. Newhouse, 461–536. New York: Elsevier.

Mechanic, R. E., and S. H. Altman. 2009. "Payment Reform Options: Episode Payment Is a Good Place to Start." *Health Affairs* 28 (2): w262–71. https://doi.org/10.1377/hlthaff.28.2.w262.

Medicare.gov. 2019. "What's Medicare Supplement Insurance (Medigap)?" Accessed October 8. www.medicare.gov/supplements-other-insurance/whats-medicare-supplement-insurance-medigap.

———. 2018. "Medicare Costs at a Glance." Accessed December 16. www.medicare.gov/your-medicare-costs/medicare-costs-at-a-glance.

Mercuri, M., and A. Gafni. 2018. "Examining the Role of the Physician as a Source of Variation: Are Physician-Related Variations Necessarily Unwarranted?" *Journal of Evaluation in Clinical Practice* 24 (1): 145–51. https://doi.org/10.1111/jep.12770.

Morrisey, M. A. 2013. "History of Health Insurance in the United States." In *Health Insurance*, by M. A. Morrisey, 3–25. Chicago: Health Administration Press.

National Academy of Social Insurance. 2015. *Addressing Pricing Power in Health Care Markets: Principles and Policy Options to Strengthen and Shape Markets*. Published April. www.urban.org/sites/default/files/publication/50116/2000212-Addressing-Pricing-Power-in-Health-Care-Markets.pdf.

National Association of Insurance Commissioners. 2019. "Big Data." Updated May 24. www.naic.org/cipr_topics/topic_big_data.htm.

National Institute of Standards and Technology (NIST). 2012. "What Do We Mean by 'Normal' Data?" *Engineering Statistics Handbook*. NIST/SEMATECH. Accessed October 13, 2019. www.itl.nist.gov/div898/handbook/pmc/section5/pmc51.htm.

Neprash, H. T., M. E. Chernew, A. L. Hicks, T. Gibson, and J. M. McWilliams. 2015. "Association of Financial Integration Between Physicians and Hospitals with Commercial Health Care Prices." *JAMA Internal Medicine* 175 (12): 1932–39. https://doi.org/10.1001/jamainternmed.2015.4610.

Newhouse, J. P. 2004. "Consumer-Directed Health Plans and the RAND Health Insurance Experiment." *Health Affairs* 23 (6): 107–13. https://doi.org/10.1377/hlthaff.23.6.107.

Numbers, R. L. 1979. "The Third-Party: Health Insurance in America." In *The Therapeutic Revolution: Essays in the History of Medicine*, edited by C. E. Vogal and H. J. Rosenberg, 177–200. Philadelphia, PA: University of Pennsylvania Press.

Nyman, J. A. 2004. "Is 'Moral Hazard' Inefficient? The Policy Implications of a New Theory." *Health Affairs* 23 (5): 194–99. https://doi.org/10.1377/hlthaff.23.5.194.

Obama, B. 2016. "United States Health Care Reform: Progress to Date and Next Steps." *JAMA* 316 (5): 525–32. https://doi.org/10.1001/jama.2016.9797.

Papanicolas, I., L. R. Woskie, and A. K. Jha. 2018. "Health Care Spending in the United States and Other High-Income Countries." *JAMA* 319 (10): 1024–39. https://doi.org/10.1001/jama.2018.1150.

Pauly, M. V. 1968. "The Economics of Moral Hazard: Comment." *American Economic Review* 58 (3, Pt. 1): 531–37. http://static.stevereads.com/papers_to_read/the_economics_of_moral_hazard.pdf.

Pollitz, K. 2017. "High-Risk Pools for Uninsurable Individuals." Kaiser Family Foundation. Published February 22. www.kff.org/health-reform/issue-brief/high-risk-pools-for-uninsurable-individuals/.

Polzer, K., and P. A. Butler. 1997. "Employee Health Plan Protections Under ERISA." *Health Affairs* 16 (5): 93–102. https://doi.org/10.1377/hlthaff.16.5.93.

Popper, R. 2017. "Do High-Risk Pools Work? It Depends." *Washington Post.* Published May 8. www.washingtonpost.com/opinions/do-high-risk-pools-work-it-depends/2017/05/08/586b95f4-319c-11e7-8674-437ddb6e813e_story.html?noredirect=on&utm_term=.84f0490d9c07.

Powell, D., and D. Goldman. 2016. "Disentangling Moral Hazard and Adverse Selection in Private Health Insurance." National Bureau of Economic Research. Working Paper 21858. Published January. www.nber.org/papers/w21858.ack.

Quinn, K. 2015. "The 8 Basic Payment Methods in Health Care." *Annals of Internal Medicine* 163 (4): 300–306. https://doi.org/10.7326/M14-2784.

RAND Corporation. 2019. "Health Insurance." Accessed October 8. www.rand.org/topics/health-insurance.html.

———. 2016. "40 Years of the RAND Health Insurance Experiment." Accessed October 8, 2019. www.rand.org/health-care/projects/HIE-40.html.

Reich, M. R., J. Harris, N. Ikegami, A. Maeda, C. Cashin, E. C. Araujo, K. Takemi, and T. G. Evans. 2016. "Moving Towards Universal Health Coverage: Lessons from 11 Country Studies." Lancet 387 (10020): 811–16. https://doi.org/10.1016/S0140-6736(15)60002-2.

Reid, T. R. 2010. *The Healing of America: A Global Quest for Better, Cheaper, and Fairer Health Care.* New York: Penguin.

Relman, A. 2012. "Why the US Healthcare System Is Failing, and What Might Rescue It." *BMJ* 344: e3052. https://doi.org/10.1136/BMJ.E3052.

Sage, W. M. 2006. "Malpractice Liability, Patient Safety, and the Personification of Medical Injury: Opportunities for Academic Medicine." *Academic Medicine* 81 (9): 823–26. https://doi.org/10.1097/00001888-200609000-00011.

Shane, L. 2018. "Controversies Mount as VA Officials Work to Stay Focused on Health Care Reforms." *Military Times*. Published February 13. www.militarytimes.com/veterans/2018/02/13/controveries-mount-as-va-officials-work-to-stay-focused-on-health-care-reforms/.

Shapiro, S. D. 2016. "Transformational Healthcare Models: Medical and Specialty Medical Homes." *Inflammatory Bowel Diseases* 22 (8): 1984–85. https://doi.org/10.1097/MIB.0000000000000866.

Shartzer, A., S. K. Long, and N. Anderson. 2016. "Access to Care and Affordability Have Improved Following Affordable Care Act Implementation; Problems Remain." *Health Affairs* 35 (1): 161–68. https://doi.org/10.1377/hlthaff.2015.0755.

Sommers, B. D., R. J. Blendon, E. J. Orav, and A. M. Epstein. 2016. "Changes in Utilization and Health Among Low-Income Adults After Medicaid Expansion or Expanded Private Insurance." *JAMA Internal Medicine* 176 (10): 1501–9. https://doi.org/10.1001/jamainternmed.2016.4419.

Sommers, B. D., A. A. Gawande, and K. Baicker. 2017. "Health Insurance Coverage and Health—What the Recent Evidence Tells Us." *New England Journal of Medicine* 377 (6): 586–93. https://doi.org/10.1056/NEJMsb1706645.

Studdert, D. M., M. M. Mello, W. M. Sage, C. M. DesRoches, J. Peugh, K. Zapert, and T. A. Brennan. 2005. "Defensive Medicine Among High-Risk Specialist Physicians in a Volatile Malpractice Environment." *Journal of the American Medical Association* 293 (21): 2609–17. https://doi.org/10.1001/jama.293.21.2609.

US Congress. 1973. "Health Maintenance Organization Act of 1973." Public Law 93-222. Accessed October 8, 2019. www.govinfo.gov/content/pkg/STATUTE-87/pdf/STATUTE-87-Pg914.pdf.

US Court of Appeals, Seventh Circuit. 2013. *Larson v. United Healthcare Insurance Company*. FindLaw. Accessed October 13, 2019. https://caselaw.findlaw.com/us-7th-circuit/1640194.html.

US Department of Defense (DoD). 2019. "TRICARE." Accessed October 8. www.tricare.mil/about/.

US Department of Health & Human Services (HHS). 2017. "What Is the Health Insurance Marketplace?" Reviewed August 4. www.hhs.gov/answers/affordable-care-act/what-is-the-health-insurance-marketplace/index.html.

———. 2014. "What Is Medicare Part C?" Reviewed August 11. www.hhs.gov/answers/medicare-and-medicaid/what-is-medicare-part-c/index.html.

US Department of Health & Human Services, Office of Inspector General (HHS-OIG). 2019. "Medicare Fraud Strike Force." Accessed October 8. https://oig.hhs.gov/fraud/strike-force/.

———. 2018. "2018 National Healthcare Fraud Takedown." Accessed October 8, 2019. https://oig.hhs.gov/newsroom/media-materials/2018/takedown/.

US Department of Labor. 2019a. "Employee Retirement Income Security Act (ERISA)." Accessed October 8. www.dol.gov/general/topic/retirement/erisa.

———. 2019b. "Health Plans & Benefits: ERISA." Accessed October 8. www.dol.gov/general/topic/health-plans/erisa.

US Department of Veterans Affairs (VA). 2019a. "CHAMPVA." Reviewed June 13. www.va.gov/COMMUNITYCARE/programs/dependents/champva/index.asp.

———. 2019b. "Eligibility for VA Health Care." Updated October 11. www.va.gov/health-care/eligibility/.

———. 2019c. "Veterans Health Administration." Accessed October 8. www.va.gov/health/.

US Government Accountability Office (GAO). 2018. *Medicare: Actions Needed to Better Manage Fraud Risks.* GAO-18-660T. Published July 17. www.gao.gov/products/GAO-18-660T.

———. 2017. *Medicare and Medicaid: CMS Needs to Fully Align Its Antifraud Efforts with the Fraud Risk Framework.* GAO-18-88. Published December 5. www.gao.gov/assets/690/688748.pdf.

Woolhandler, S., T. Campbell, and D. U. Himmelstein. 2003. "Costs of Health Care Administration in the United States and Canada." *New England Journal of Medicine* 349 (8): 768–75. https://doi.org/10.1056/NEJMsa022033.

Yang, W.-S., and S.-Y. Hwang. 2006. "A Process-Mining Framework for the Detection of Healthcare Fraud and Abuse." *Expert Systems with Applications* 31 (1): 56–58. https://doi.org/10.1016/j.eswa.2005.09.003.

Zibulewsky, J. 2001. "The Emergency Medical Treatment and Active Labor Act (EMTALA): What It Is and What It Means for Physicians." *Baylor University Medical Center Proceedings* 14 (4): 339–46. https://doi.org/10.1080/08998280.2001.11927785.

Zuabi, N., L. D. Weiss, and M. I. Langdorf. 2016. "Emergency Medical Treatment and Labor Act (EMTALA) 2002-15: Review of Office of Inspector General Patient Dumping Settlements." *Western Journal of Emergency Medicine* 17 (3): 245–51. https://doi.org/10.5811/westjem.2016.3.29705.

9

QUALITY AND SAFETY—EASIER SAID THAN DONE

> It is not enough to know, we must also apply; it is not enough to will, we also must do.
>
> —Johann Wolfgang von Goethe

Learning Objectives

- Understand the challenges of managing quality and safety.
- Assess the state of the art in process improvement.
- Consider the characteristics of a high reliability organization.
- Evaluate why healthcare is so "siloed."
- Understand the importance of leadership and governance in quality management.
- Explore the possibility of interprofessional education as a solution.

This chapter will examine the topics of quality and safety in healthcare (see exhibit 9.1). Of course, these two concepts are closely related, to the point that we cannot possibly discuss healthcare quality without considering safety as a foundational component. After all, if patients are not safe, it is difficult to imagine how quality care and quality outcomes can occur.

The Institute of Medicine (IOM 2001) defines *quality* as "the degree to which health services for individuals and populations increase the likelihood of desired health outcomes and are consistent with current professional knowledge." The IOM defines *safety*, in a healthcare context, as "the prevention of harm to patients." Expanding on these concepts, the Agency for Healthcare Research and Quality (AHRQ 2018) defines *patient safety* as "freedom from accidental or preventable injuries produced by medical care." To support quality and safety, a system of care delivery must focus on

- preventing errors;
- learning from the errors that do occur; and
- building on a culture of safety that involves healthcare professionals, organizations, and patients.

EXHIBIT 9.1
Area of Focus
for This Chapter

The Aim of the Healthcare System

Issues That Require Our Attention

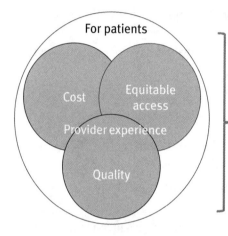

For patients

Cost

Equitable access

Provider experience

Quality

- Nature of our complex system
- Historical issues that have influenced the development of the system
- Beliefs and attitudes about health and healthcare
- Comparison with other developed countries
- Components of our healthcare system
- People and providers
- Patient care—the purpose of the system
- Financing a massive system
- *Quality—easier said than done*
- Medical and information technology
- The pharmaceutical industry
- Complementary and alternative medicine
- Politics/economics
- The future of the system

Quality and Safety: A Philosophical Background

Although quality in healthcare can be described, measured, and approached in a variety ways, it must start with a personal philosophy of excellence. More than 2,300 years ago, Aristotle (2009, 46) examined the topics of ethics and happiness, writing that "these virtues are formed in a man by his doing the actions." These ideas were echoed by Goethe (1906) 2,000 years later, with the statement that "It is not enough to know." Will Durant (1961, 98) sums up Aristotle's thoughts as follows: "We are what we repeatedly do. Excellence, then, is not an act but a habit." Quality and excellence are things we do automatically, not just because of rules, regulations, processes, or policies, but because quality and excellence are part of who we are. Great thought leaders on quality continue this line of thinking today.

Deming and the Red Bead Experiment

W. Edwards Deming, regarded as the father of the quality revolution, famously said, "We are here to make another world" (Deming Institute 2019a). Deming emphasized the importance of understanding the "why"—not simply the "what"—in achieving superior services and performance. He believed that people, for the most part, want to do their best, even when their working situation stands in the way, and that quality and high performance could not be achieved by inspection or coercion—a point illustrated by his famous red bead experiment (Deming 1986, 2000).

In the red bead experiment, a production line of unwitting participants is shown a box containing a mix of red and white beads (Hunter 2014a, 2014b). The participants are given a paddle that has 50 slots, which can accommodate 50 beads. An instructor, playing the role of a supervisor, tells the participants to dip the paddle into the box and pull out 50 beads, with the goal of pulling out only white beads. With each paddle of 50 beads drawn by the participants, the inspector counts and records the number of red beads. Of course, retrieving 50 white beads is almost statistically impossible, given the mix of beads in the box, so the participants fail to meet the goal.

Typically, the hapless production workers in the experiment will try in vain to convince the supervisor to alter the process. They might provide ideas for how to improve the process or even attempt to alter the process themselves, only to be chastised by the supervisor for deviating from the approved process. The supervisor might threaten, "If you don't improve your production, if you all don't work harder and do a better job making white beads, we will have to lay people off."

The point of the study is that the failure is not the result of the participants' performance, but rather a bad process. Adhering to an ineffective process does not produce better results, and when a supervisor refuses to listen to the production workers about how to improve the process, the situation will only get worse. Eventually, the company fails, and all the workers—as well as the supervisor—lose their jobs.

Earlier in my career, I had the good fortune to learn from Deming and experience the foundations of quality management firsthand; I even got to do the red bead experiment with him. The most interesting thing I have observed about the experiment is the incredible frustration it produces on the part of the participants. They want to do a good job, but they continually fail because the process is bad; when they attempt to alter the process, they are corrected and admonished, and their opinions are ignored. Even as part of a game, the situation is frustrating and demoralizing. Readers are encouraged to view some of the videos of the red bead experiment being conducted (see, for instance, Hunter 2014b).

Arguably, the teachings of Deming and the great thinkers before him are more relevant today than ever before, as so many of their ideas are repackaged into modern quality improvement tools. Often, however, this focus on tools can cause the true meaning and philosophy of quality and excellence to get lost. Tools do not replace wisdom, and a true appreciation for excellence should be guided by principles, not just targets. Applying a tool without an understanding of the "why" and without profound knowledge of what you are doing is not going to produce the desired results. If you do not truly understand the why, you might not even be working on the correct issue for improvement. Systems are complex, and the interactions of moving parts can often escape logic.

Applying Real Wisdom

Exhibit 9.2 emphasizes the idea that data are only a starting point; from there, we must understand the data and convert them into information, knowledge, and, finally, real wisdom or insight about what we do and why. Too often, we swim in a sea of data but have few insights as to the data's meaning. The old saying about "not seeing the forest for the trees" holds true. Clearly, a focus on process is important, but we also need an appreciation for the fundamental foundations of quality, as well as for the importance of the team and the value of each team member's knowledge and perspective.

Often, the established knowledge and principles that we honor as part of our profession can be counterproductive to innovation and problem solving; in other words, we can become hampered by what we know and believe (Isfahani et al. 2015; Robinson 2006). Cynthia Barton Rabe, in her book *The Innovation Killer*, describes the importance of "zero-gravity thinkers"—those people who might have little expertise about a particular problem or situation but who offer fresh ideas that are not bound by an existing knowledge base (Rabe 2006; Nayar 2012). Such individuals might be able to see solutions that others do not, especially if the solutions involve innovations that violate established teachings or professional discipline. Healthcare, in particular, has a great number of highly educated people who have been taught, for good reason, that deviation from the norm can be dangerous; thus, the field can be highly risk-averse with regard to changes in practices (Echazu and Nocetti 2013; Maggio et al. 2013; O'Brien 2008).

EXHIBIT 9.2
Use of Data to
Gain Insight

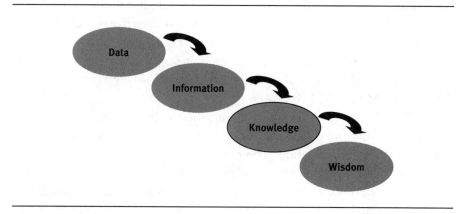

Sir Ken Robinson (2006) tells a story about a young girl who could not sit still in her chair at school. She was constantly moving about, and her behavior soon became a matter of concern. School officials and the girl's teacher encouraged the child's mother to take her to a specialist for evaluation of her "condition," and the mother complied. After examining the child, the specialist turned on the radio and asked the mother to accompany him out of the room. As the music played, he and the mother, observing from behind a two-way mirror, watched as the girl gracefully moved about the room. Finally, the doctor said, "Gillian isn't sick, she's a dancer." The prescription was not to put the child on medication so she could "calm down" but rather to enroll her in dance school. Robinson (2006) continues the story:

> She was eventually auditioned for the Royal Ballet School; she became a soloist; she had a wonderful career at the Royal Ballet. She eventually graduated from the Royal Ballet School; founded her own company, the Gillian Lynne Dance Company; and met Andrew Lloyd Webber. She's been responsible for some of the most successful musical theater productions in history, she's given pleasure to millions, and she's a multimillionaire. Somebody else might have put her on medication and told her to calm down.

These lessons are highly relevant to healthcare administration. Healthcare—as much as or more so than any other industry—needs creative people who can bring effective innovation to the delivery and financing of care; it also needs leaders who nurture the people around them and encourage them to bring new ideas to the table. Healthcare leaders must develop the talents of the people on their teams and recognize that the highest quality will be achieved by a variety of talents working in combination. Diversity is an asset, not a liability.

Why, Not Just What

Process without purpose is truly pointless. We cannot simply maintain a fastidious fixation on doing a discrete function without understanding the reasons behind it. To achieve our desired results, we need to incorporate a deep knowledge of healthcare delivery and its processes, as well as an appreciation for the need for change to provide the care that our patients need and deserve (Deming 1986). Knowing what to do is not enough; we must also know when to do it and why it must be done.

Deming spoke of a system of profound knowledge, which included four interrelated components: knowledge of the system, knowledge of psychology, the theory of knowledge, and knowledge of variation (Deming 2000; Deming Institute 2019b; Bedford 2012). Combining fundamental knowledge and wisdom of the past with new knowledge and a focus on the future prepares all stakeholders to deal effectively with the many changes in the years to come.

Above all else, we must first do the right thing and then do it correctly—which is not unlike the oft-repeated phrase attributed to Hippocrates: "First, do no harm" (Kleisiaris, Sfakianakis, and Papathanasiou 2014; North 2002; Nutton 2012). In the movie *Jurassic Park*, mathematician Ian Malcolm says to the park's creator, "Your scientists were so preoccupied with whether they *could* that they didn't stop to think if they *should*" (Spielberg 1993). In many ways, the same has happened in the US healthcare system. Too often, we have lost sight of purpose and pursued quick fixes to complex problems. Stakeholders have acted in their own best interests, responding to short-term incentives and fragmented laws, rules, programs, and policies without a clear, unified strategy and guiding principles (Heineman and Froemke 2012).

How does one balance the aim of emptying the hospital by improving people's health with the need to keep the beds full so the hospital can survive economically? People will often joke, "The healthcare system doesn't want you to die, but it really doesn't want you to be healthy either." That kind of thinking reflects the healthcare economic annuity: Keep the people coming as a base for more services (Lyu et al. 2017; Makary 2012). My own view is more hopeful, but serious change to our system's incentives will be necessary (Conrad 2015; Enthoven 2011; Friedberg et al. 2015; Ginsburg 2011; Heineman and Froemke 2012; Pracht, Langland-Orban, and Ryan 2018). We are living in a time when the "win–lose" game is delivering diminished returns, not just economically but emotionally and societally as well.

Change is essential to the future of healthcare, and meaningful change requires courage. Healthcare presents challenges at every turn, with constant temptations to take the easy road. To truly improve the system, however, leaders must have the courage to look beyond what is immediate and expedient and do what is necessary for long-term sustainable practice. To quote Deming, "A bad system will beat a good person every time" (Hunter 2015).

Deming (1986) often talked about his 14 points for management, one of which was to reduce or eliminate the use of slogans. Slogans, he believed, provide no clear understanding or direction for accomplishing the task at hand. In healthcare, a slogan might promise "excellent care" or "remarkable care" as part of an effort to differentiate an organization's services, but what do such slogans really mean? How would you operationalize such a slogan? Excellent or remarkable care to one person might be mediocre care to someone else. Rather than a simple declaration of intentions, organizations need to have goals and targets that are specific and based on measurement. When such goals are combined with an inculcated philosophy of quality and excellence in the organizational culture, improved outcomes will occur.

The State of the Art in Process Improvement

For many years, the US healthcare system placed a much greater emphasis on issues of access than it did on quality improvement (Kaiser Family Foundation 2011). That focus began to shift with the publication of two reports by the IOM—*To Err Is Human* in 1999 and *Crossing the Quality Chasm* in 2001—that raised serious concerns about quality and safety (IOM 1999, 2001). The reports estimated that as many as 98,000 people each year die as a result of medical errors in US hospitals and that preventable adverse events alone account for about $8.8 billion in healthcare spending—not to mention the pain, suffering, and disability they cause. The reports called for sweeping, immediate action to address the problem of medical errors and to create a culture of safety and quality in healthcare organizations. Everyone working in the healthcare field should be well versed in the issues addressed in these landmark reports.

Following the release of the IOM reports, efforts to improve quality and safety focused largely on standardization, with the aim of reducing variation. Soon, a variety of quality improvement tools and techniques were applied to healthcare management, including the following:

- Total quality management (TQM)
- Lean
- Six Sigma
- Lean Six Sigma
- Data analytics
- The Triple Aim

Total Quality Management

TQM, an early entrant into the quality improvement arena, is "a management approach to long-term success through customer satisfaction" in which "all members of an organization participate in improving processes, products, services, and the culture in which they work" (American Society for Quality [ASQ] 2019). TQM originated in the 1980s but still enjoys a following today; many of its features have provided a basis for other quality initiatives. The following elements are central to TQM, and they resemble strategies often seen today in Lean and Six Sigma (ASQ 2019):

- *Patient focus (or customer focus)*. Patients ultimately determine the level of quality. Of course, their assessment may be clouded by information disequilibrium. After all, how can a person who does not fully understand the situation or the complexities of healthcare know what quality looks like? Quality is truly in the eyes of the beholder.

- *Total employee involvement.* Everyone throughout the organization participates in working toward common goals.
- *Process-centered approach.* A focus on process thinking is a fundamental part of TQM. The process is the series of steps that takes inputs from suppliers (internal or external) and transforms them into outputs to be delivered to customers (internal or external). The necessary steps are defined, and performance measures are continuously monitored to detect unexpected variation.
- *Integrated system.* TQM focuses on the interconnecting processes across the various departments and functional areas of an organization. Patients should interact with the organization's functions as a single experience, not as a series of functions or separately managed processes. The individual functions add up to the larger patient treatment or procedure, and the aggregate of all patient care reflects the performance of the organization.
- *Strategic and systematic approach.* Everyone must understand the organization's vision, mission, and values. Organizational performance must be monitored and communicated continuously. Strategic management involves the formulation of a strategic plan that integrates quality as a core component.
- *Continual improvement.* The organization should be both analytical and creative in meeting patient needs on an ongoing basis.
- *Fact-based decisions.* TQM requires that the organization continually collect and analyze data to inform decision making. As a popular quote sometimes attributed to Peter Drucker says, "If you can't measure it, you can't manage it."
- *Communication.* Effective communication is critical for maintaining morale and motivating employees at every level. Communications must be relevant, frequent, fact based, transparent, and timely.

Implementation of TQM and other quality improvement methodologies often encounters roadblocks. Exhibit 9.3 presents a list of factors, developed by the AHRQ, that can inhibit the success of Lean implementation; these same observations can be applied to other quality improvement strategies as well (Aij and Teunissen 2017).

Japanese Management Concepts

Virtually all of today's quality models have been shaped by ideas put forth by Deming, Philip B. Crosby, Armand V. Feigenbaum, Joseph Juran, and others from the early years of the quality revolution (Crosby 1979; Deming 1986; Feigenbaum 1951; Juran and De Feo 2016; Juran and Gryna 1993; Neyestani 2017). In addition, Kaoru Ishikawa brought a number of Japanese

Factor	Lessons Learned
Leadership	• Loss of a process owner following an RCE led to poor follow through in implementing and revising process changes. • Lack of staff accountability by the process owner and leadership for changes made by the RCEs and for completing activities on the action plan can derail RCE success. • Lack of outward support from all senior executives creates a climate where lack of adherence to process changes by all staff is tolerated.
Scope	• Failure to review the medical evidence base may lead to a focus on improving processes that are unrelated to reducing UTI rates. • Attempting to improve too many processes can overwhelm staff. • Failure to complete all steps of the improvement process can derail the effort.
Resources	• Without resources being allocated for data collection, it is difficult to determine the impact of Lean on efficiency, clinical outcomes, patient experience, and patient safety or to revise processes that are not working. • Lean events are time consuming for staff. • Staff turnover might make it difficult to make and sustain process changes and to develop a Lean culture.
Communication about Lean	• There is not always effective communication about events and solutions to the staff who do not participate in the event.
Lean team composition and size	• Using the same staff repeatedly on Lean events might lead to burnout.

EXHIBIT 9.3
Major Factors
That Inhibit
Lean Success

Note: RCE = rapid cycle event; UTI = urinary tract infection.
Source: Reprinted from Agency for Healthcare Research and Quality (2014b).

management concepts to Americans, including the famous Ishikawa diagram, or fishbone chart. A valuable tool for root cause analysis, the chart is useful for diagramming the various components of a larger process (Ishikawa 1986).

Another important Japanese concept is *nemawashi*. The term has no direct English translation, but it refers to an informal process of quietly laying the foundation for a proposed change or project by talking to the people involved and gathering support and feedback. The term reflects the collective mentality commonly emphasized in Japanese culture. English phrases that convey similar meaning might include "consensus building," "sending up trial balloons," "getting on board," and "getting on the same page" (Kopp 2012). I first became familiar with the word through Deming, and I attempted to research the concept while working on my master's thesis. Of course, literature searches were more difficult then, but my exhaustive search produced just a single reference to the word (in Japanese). If you Google the term today, you will find more than 100,000 hits.

The Baldrige Award

One of the most noteworthy initiatives to grow out of the quality movement is the Baldrige Performance Excellence Program, under the auspices of the National Institute of Standards and Technology (NIST). Established by the Malcolm Baldrige National Quality Improvement Act of 1987, the program seeks to recognize and improve the performance of the nation's businesses, hospitals, schools, nonprofit organizations, and government agencies. To be recognized with the Baldrige Award, organizations must undergo a rigorous process to demonstrate their adherence to exceptional levels of quality management (Baldrige Foundation 2019; NIST 2019). Some hospitals and healthcare organizations have begun modeling their systems around the Baldrige guidelines and using the International Organization for Standardization (ISO) 9000 family of standards. The ISO 9000 family provides tools and guidance to support quality improvement and to help organizations meet the requirements of patients and other stakeholders (ISO 2019).

The Leapfrog Group

The Leapfrog Group, founded in 2000, is an organization of large employers and other healthcare purchasers brought together by the goal to drive "giant leaps forward" in the quality and safety of US healthcare (Leapfrog Group 2019). Its members include Fortune 100 companies, consumer advocacy groups, and approximately 30 regional business coalitions on health. The business coalitions consist of employers who work together to provide high-quality healthcare for their employees at a lower cost. Coalition members leverage their purchasing power to negotiate reduced rates and premiums for benefits programs (Lehigh Valley Business Coalition on Healthcare 2019).

Lean in Healthcare

The application of Lean in healthcare is primarily a process improvement approach that focuses on the following (Drotz and Poksinska 2014; Poksinska 2010; Toussaint and Berry 2013):

- Defining value from the patient point of view
- Mapping value streams
- Eliminating waste to create continuous flow

EXHIBIT 9.4
The Plan-Do-
Study-Act Cycle

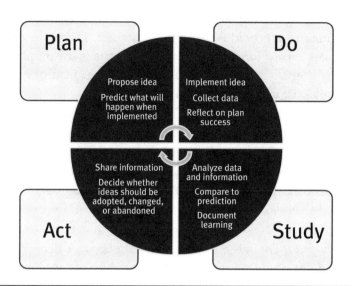

The PDSA Cycle

Plan
Propose idea
Predict what will happen when implemented

Do
Implement idea
Collect data
Reflect on plan success

Share information
Decide whether ideas should be adopted, changed, or abandoned

Analyze data and information
Compare to prediction
Document learning

Act

Study

Lean is often coupled with the plan-do-study-act (PDSA) cycle, also known as the Deming cycle (see exhibit 9.4). The PDSA cycle offers a stepwise framework for incorporating incremental change into a process and measuring the results. As the name implies, the steps of PDSA are done repeatedly in a cycle to bring about continuous quality improvement (Berwick 1998; Institute for Healthcare Improvement [IHI] 2019). The steps can be completed any number of times for any specific process.

Another important focus of Lean is the elimination of waste. In healthcare, *waste* can be defined as anything that does not add value for the patient. Lean strives to eliminate eight types of waste (Skhmot 2017):

1. *Defects.* Waste associated with defects reflects time spent doing something wrong, finding errors, and correcting errors. In healthcare, defects can lead not only to waste and additional costs but also to pain, suffering, disability, and even death to patients.

2. *Overproduction.* This type of waste involves doing more than is needed or requested by the patient. Unnecessary diagnostic tests are the most common example.

3. *Transportation.* Transportation waste occurs whenever unnecessary movement of people or items is required—for instance, when a poor hospital layout requires patients or specimens to be transported over long distances.

4. *Waiting.* Many of the most common complaints in healthcare involve patients waiting unnecessarily for a doctor's appointment or for some other healthcare event. Waste associated with waiting produces uneven patient flow and causes stress to patients and staff. Even the existence of a waiting room could be regarded as a waste: In an efficient system, a designated space for waiting would serve little if any purpose; thus, the costs, construction, maintenance, and management of a waiting area could be considered wasteful.

5. *Inventory.* Having excessive inventory leads to unnecessary financial costs associated with storage and maintenance. It also creates the potential for expiration of dated supplies and medications.

6. *Motion.* This type of waste occurs when employees, because of poor layout or work flow, move more than should be necessary during the course of their work. Waste of motion might occur, for instance, if nursing stations are located long distances from patient care areas.

7. *Overprocessing.* The waste of overprocessing occurs when work is done that does not produce value for the patient—for instance, when an organization collects information that is never used.

8. *Skills, or human potential.* This type of waste—one of the greatest wastes of all—occurs when employees are not engaged and listened to, when ideas are not considered, and when career aspirations are not supported and nurtured. Such waste often results in burnout, turnover, and the loss of valuable intellectual capital.

High Reliability Organizations

The concept of the high reliability organization is extremely important when discussing quality and safety in healthcare. According to Weick and Sutcliffe (2015), high reliability organizations function under difficult and demanding conditions yet have fewer problems than one might expect, because they have learned to "manage the unexpected" and use fragments of past experiences to optimize outcomes. Some of the key attributes of high reliability organizations are shown in exhibit 9.5. Unsurprisingly, each characteristic centers on the people and management elements of the system. As I have told my students, if you do not wish to become obsolete, you should learn to do what machines cannot—and that is to deal effectively with people.

This emphasis on the human element requires an understanding of when and how people succeed and fail. James Reason (1990), in his book *Human Error*, notes that the human mind is only capable of about a 90 percent rate of accuracy; thus, systems that rely on human performance alone will have high rates of failure. Atul Gawande (2009), in his book *The Checklist Manifesto*, states that medical errors can be reduced dramatically simply by requiring the people who perform procedures to follow a detailed checklist to ensure that all the proper steps are completed in the correct order.

Characteristic	Description
Preoccupation with Failure	Everyone is aware of and thinking about the potential for failure. People understand that new threats emerge regularly from situations that no one imagined could occur, so all personnel actively think about what could go wrong and are alert to small signs of potential problems. The absence of errors or accidents leads not to complacency but to a heightened sense of vigilance for the next possible failure. Near misses are viewed as opportunities to learn about systems issues and potential improvements, rather than as evidence of safety.
Reluctance to Simplify	People resist simplifying their understanding of work processes and how and why things succeed or fail in their environment. People in HROs understand that the work is complex and dynamic. They seek underlying rather than surface explanations. While HROs recognize the value of standardization of workflows to reduce variation, they also appreciate the complexity inherent in the number of teams, processes, and relationships involved in conducting daily operations.
Sensitivity to Operations	Based on their understanding of operational complexity, people in HROs strive to maintain a high awareness of operational conditions. This sensitivity is often referred to as "big picture understanding" or "situation awareness." It means that people cultivate an understanding of the context of the current state of their work in relation to the unit or organizational state—i.e., what is going on around them—and how the current state might support or threaten safety.
Deference to Expertise	People in HROs appreciate that the people closest to the work are the most knowledgeable about the work. Thus, people in HROs know that in a crisis or emergency the person with greatest knowledge of the situation might not be the person with the highest status and seniority. Deference to local and situation expertise results in a spirit of inquiry and de-emphasis on hierarchy in favor of learning as much as possible about potential safety threats. In an HRO, everyone is expected to share concerns with others and the organizational climate is such that all staff members are comfortable speaking up about potential safety problems.
Commitment to Resilience	Commitment to resilience is rooted in the fundamental understanding of the frequently unpredictable nature of system failures. People in HROs assume the system is at risk for failure, and they practice performing rapid assessments of and responses to challenging situations. Teams cultivate situation assessment and cross monitoring so they may identify potential safety threats quickly and either respond before safety problems cause harm or mitigate the seriousness of the safety event.

EXHIBIT 9.5
Characteristics of High Reliability

Note: HRO = high reliability organization.
Source: Reprinted from AHRQ (2019).

Consider, for the sake of comparison, pilots preparing to take off in an aircraft. As a matter of routine, they carefully run through a rigorous checklist of all the important actions required before departure, ensuring to a high degree of reliability that the aircraft will perform correctly. Certainly, experienced pilots are aware of all these elements, and in most cases they could run the steps purely by memory. However, because of the high stakes of aircraft safety and the ever-present risk of distraction or other human failure, pilots use the checklist every time.

Healthcare was late in accepting this principle. Why should practitioners have to spend their time and effort running through a checklist if they have already performed the procedure hundreds of times in the past? The answer is human error. When failures have serious consequences—as in the case of wrong-site surgery, failure to administer a preoperative antibiotic, or even doing the wrong procedure—relying on the human mind as our only safeguard is insufficient (Donaldson 2009). We simply are not capable of absolute perfection.

Importance of a Safety Culture

In *Crossing the Quality Chasm*, the IOM (2001) stressed the importance of a safety culture: "The biggest challenge to moving toward a safer health system is changing the culture from one of blaming individuals for errors to one in which errors are treated not as personal failures, but as opportunities to improve the system and prevent harm." Machines and processes do not create culture—people do (Joosten, Bongers, and Janssen 2009).

Continued Quality Concerns

Despite the widespread use of quality improvement methodologies and the billions of dollars spent on quality and safety efforts, the data on medical errors and patient outcomes continue to raise concerns. A 2013 study in the *Journal of Patient Safety* estimated that between 210,000 and 440,000 preventable hospital deaths occur in the United States each year (James 2013); the Leapfrog Group (2016) estimated that 206,201 avoidable deaths occur in hospitals annually; and Makary and Daniel (2016) estimated that the number of deaths resulting from medical errors was as high as 250,000. The Centers for Disease Control and Prevention (CDC) does not report medical errors as a cause of death, but if medical errors were recorded in this manner, they would rank as the country's third leading cause of death, after heart disease and cancer (Kavanagh et al. 2017; Allen and Pierce 2016; Shanafelt, Sinsky, and Swensen 2017).

Comparison with Other Countries

Schneider and colleagues (2017) at the Commonwealth Fund analyzed 11 healthcare systems in countries with similarities to the United States, using 72 indicators across five areas: (1) care process, (2) access, (3) administrative efficiency, (4) equity, and (5) healthcare outcomes. The United States ranked last in overall performance (see exhibit 9.6) and was last or near last in four of the five areas (all except care process). The United States ranked especially poorly in system performance relative to spending (see exhibit 9.7).

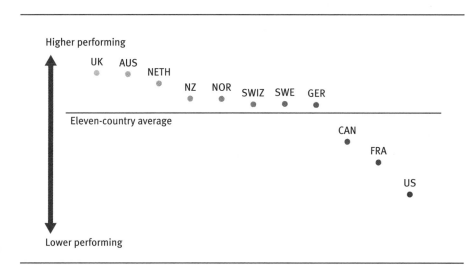

EXHIBIT 9.6

Healthcare System Performance Scores

Source: Reprinted with permission from Schneider et al. (2017).

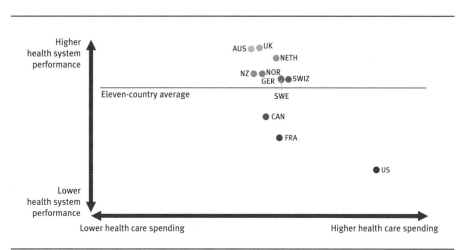

EXHIBIT 9.7

Healthcare System Performance Scores Relative to Spending

Note: Health care spending as a percent of GDP.
Source: Reprinted with permission from Schneider et al. (2017).

Clearly, the United States has much to learn from other countries that produce superior results, and exposure to healthcare systems around the world should be part of the education process for all future healthcare leaders, policymakers, and providers. Given its wealth and resources, the United States has the potential to develop the best healthcare system in the world; doing so, however, will require substantial change (Schneider and Squires 2017).

Failed Strategies?

Why have the improvement methods developed and implemented thus far failed to produce measurable leaps forward in quality, safety, and performance? It is certainly not from a lack of trying or good intentions. The answer could be that process-oriented improvements are insufficient for a system in need of more fundamental change; it could also be that financial and business pressures limit the level of change organizations are willing to accept. Florida Power and Light (FPL), for instance, was one of the first users and advocates of TQM, even winning Japan's Deming Prize for quality management (Gitlow, Loredo, and Dekker 1992; Niven 1993). Ultimately, however, it abandoned its program because of worker complaints about excessive "red tape" and its inability to demonstrate the cost benefit (Mathews 1993).

Most of the quality improvement tools being used in healthcare have been borrowed from the manufacturing industry, which, of course, primarily deals with inanimate objects. Questions remain about how effectively such tools can be applied to healthcare, given the nature of the field and the unpredictability of the human element. For instance, Virginia Mason Medical Center was one of the first healthcare organizations to embrace Lean as a quality improvement methodology. However, in 2016, it was denied full accreditation from The Joint Commission after failing to meet a number of quality and safety standards; instead, it received only "contingent accreditation" (Aleccia 2016). Virginia Mason's diligent work on improvement has clearly provided benefits to the organization, but many of the benefits have been associated with cost cutting as opposed to quality.

Moraros, Lemstra, and Nwankwo (2016) conducted an extensive review of the use of Lean in healthcare and concluded: "While some may strongly believe that Lean interventions lead to quality improvements in healthcare, the evidence to date simply does not support this claim. More rigorous, higher quality and better conducted scientific research is required to definitively ascertain the impact and effectiveness of Lean in healthcare settings." Other writers have similarly stressed the need for more and better research on quality improvement strategies such as Lean and Six Sigma in healthcare (AHRQ 2014a; Amaratunga and Dobranowski 2016; DelliFraine, Langabeer, and Nembhard 2010).

Patient Experience and Satisfaction

Patient experience and patient satisfaction reflect the full range of interactions the patient has with all components of the healthcare system. Although the terms are sometimes used interchangeably, they are not the same. Patient experience relies on an objective evaluation of whether something did or did not occur in the healthcare setting. Patient satisfaction, on the other hand, is subjective, relying on the perspective of the individual patient. Two people, for instance, might experience the exact same treatment but have very different levels of satisfaction (AHRQ 2017).

Attention to both experience and satisfaction is essential for healthcare quality and a key aspect of patient-centered care. Patients who have positive experiences tend to be more compliant with care instructions, which can have a significant impact on healthcare outcomes (Brown and Bussell 2011; Hodari et al. 2006; Levinson, Lesser, and Epstein 2010; Thom, Hall, and Pawlson 2004).

Surveys and Metrics

Several tools have been developed to measure patient experience and satisfaction. The Hospital Consumer Assessment of Healthcare Providers and Systems (HCAHPS) survey, for instance, is a government-sponsored tool that is administered to patients within 42 days of discharge from a hospital. The survey contains 19 core questions about important aspects of the patient's hospital experience, including the following (Centers for Medicare & Medicaid Services [CMS] 2019b):

- Communication with nurses and doctors
- Responsiveness of hospital staff
- Cleanliness and quietness of the hospital environment
- Pain management
- Communication about medicines
- Discharge information
- Overall rating of the hospital, and whether they would recommend it

HCAHPS also includes additional items intended to direct patients to relevant questions, to adjust for the mix of patients across hospitals, and to support congressionally mandated reports. The survey is often used for comparing hospitals and is increasingly being incorporated into payment models. Hospitals that are paid under the government's Inpatient Prospective Payment System are required to report HCAHPS data.

Similar surveys have been developed for the ambulatory care environment. The Consumer Assessment of Healthcare Providers and Systems

Outpatient and Ambulatory Surgery (OAS CAHPS) survey includes questions about the patient's experiences with the following (CMS 2019a):

- Preparation for a surgery or procedure
- Check-in processes
- Cleanliness of the facility
- Communications with the facility staff
- Discharge from the facility
- Preparation for recovering at home

The survey also includes questions about whether the patients received information and instructions concerning possible side effects during recovery. The survey can be administered by mail, by phone, or by mail with a follow-up phone call. The OAS CAHPS survey was implemented on a voluntary basis in 2016, with the first reported results in 2018. It is expected to be used, much as HCAHPS is, for the comparison of facilities and in payment models (CMS 2019a).

Research findings on the relationship between HCAHPS results, patient experience, patient satisfaction, and healthcare quality have thus far been inconclusive (Bendapudi et al. 2006; Manary et al. 2013; Pérotin et al. 2013; White and Griffith 2019). Some researchers see no relationship between care quality and survey results, whereas others have found an association (Kennedy, Tevis, and Kent 2014). At this point, the survey results are best viewed as tools to support the improvement of experience and satisfaction, as opposed to measures of actual healthcare outcomes. The growing interest in patient satisfaction and experience has spawned a new industry that works to develop, administer, and analyze appropriate metrics (*Modern Healthcare* 2017).

Healthcare Is "Siloed"

Exhibit 9.8 points to an important problem with patient experience in the United States. The various departments and functions of our healthcare system are too often presented as a series of separate "silos" with which patients interact. Such an arrangement enables organizations to more easily assign accountability, define scope of responsibility, and measure individual functions, but it does not reflect the way patients actually experience healthcare. Patients typically view their interaction with the healthcare delivery system as a single experience; thus, a problem in any part of that experience (i.e., in any silo) can make the overall experience unsatisfactory. As the old saying goes, "the chain is only as strong as its weakest link."

Surely, many of us have experienced delays and inefficiencies while receiving services from different parts of a healthcare organization—for

EXHIBIT 9.8
How a Patient
Experiences
Healthcare

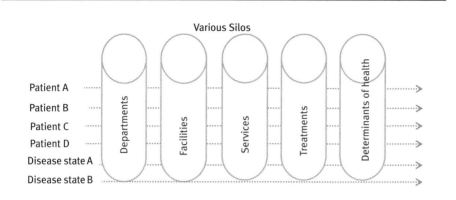

Various Silos

Patient A
Patient B
Patient C
Patient D
Disease state A
Disease state B

Departments   Facilities   Services   Treatments   Determinants of health

The patient sees care in a longitudinal fashion.

instance, having to reregister because systems are completely independent of one another. Many organizations have sought to address this issue by focusing on the Lean principle of "flow"—the smooth transition from one stage of a process to the next, without delay, unnecessary complexity, or other barriers to a seamless process (Andersen, Røvik, and Ingebrigtsen 2014; Moraros, Lemstra, and Nwankwo 2016). Better coordination and collaboration among health professionals can have a significant impact on patient experience, quality, and safety (Cunningham et al. 2012).

A Focus on People

By now, it has probably become evident that quality improvement centers around affecting people and their behavior. Behavior is really the only thing we can see and evaluate; we cannot know what a person is truly thinking or feeling, but we can know that person's actions. People in every segment of the healthcare workforce need to be trained, educated, motivated, and engaged to generate the desired outcomes (Barnett et al. 2011; Fulford, Peile, and Carroll 2012; Weick and Sutcliffe 2015). Resistance to change and other obstacles to improvement need to be addressed and overcome (AHRQ 2014b; Kaplan et al. 2014; Waring and Bishop 2010).

Behavioral Economics
Smoking and obesity are leading causes of illness and disability in the United States, and both issues are largely behavioral in nature. Everyone knows that eating too much fast food is unhealthy, yet the US fast-food industry generated $198 billion in revenue in 2018—and that number is expected to grow

to $223 billion by 2020 (Statista 2019). A study by Moriarty and colleagues (2012) found that the annual incremental mean costs of smoking by age group ranged from $1,274 to $1,401 and that the costs associated with a designated level of morbid obesity ranged from $5,467 to $5,530. Smoking and obesity are primary risk factors for diabetes, a disease that affected an estimated 30.3 million people—or 9.4 percent of the US population—in 2015 (CDC 2017). The prevalence of diabetes is expected to increase by 54 percent to more than 54.9 million Americans between 2015 and 2030 (Rowley et al. 2017). Over the same period, annual deaths attributed to diabetes will climb by 38 percent to 385,800, and total annual medical and societal costs related to diabetes will increase 53 percent to more than $622 billion.

Why do we as a population so often engage in unhealthy behaviors against the advice of healthcare professionals, public service announcements, and general common knowledge? Part of the answer lies in behavioral economics. The field of behavioral economics applies insights from the study of psychology to analyze human behavior and to explain economic decision making (Heshmat 2017; Thaler 2015). Behavioral economics has contributed many of the techniques by which the fast-food industry and other businesses influence people's behavior and encourage unhealthy choices. However, the field also holds great promise in the areas of quality and safety (Rabin 2016; *Economist* 2018). Human beings often act irrationally and make decisions that are not in their own best interest. By gaining a better understanding of the reasons behind such behavior, we can work toward improvements that will have a positive impact on health.

Key Principles

Certain principles of behavioral economics are particularly relevant to health behaviors. First, human beings tend to be strongly motivated by meaning, as opposed to simple reward. Therefore, an attempt to influence people's behavior will be most effective if it includes not just a basic instruction but also a clear explanation of the action and its implications (Pink 2011). Second, people, by nature, tend to favor immediate reward over future value or benefit. Dan Ariely (2010), in his book *Predictably Irrational*, uses the example of a box of chocolates. If a person is offered a choice between receiving one box of chocolates immediately and receiving a box and a half of chocolates sometime in the future, people will overwhelmingly choose the immediate reward, even though that option has fewer chocolates.

This latter principle was the focus of the famous "Stanford marshmallow experiment" conducted by Mischel, Ebbesen, and Zeiss (1972). The researchers would place children in a room with a marshmallow on a plate. Each child could choose to eat the single marshmallow immediately, or they could choose to wait ten minutes and receive an additional marshmallow.

Follow-up studies of the children who participated in the experiment found that those who were able to delay eating the marshmallow showed greater competence and higher test scores in the years ahead. The findings of the marshmallow study have at times been called into question, but they nonetheless suggest that delayed gratification and consideration for one's "future self" may be important contributors to future success. For example, a person might achieve greater success in the long term by delaying an immediate income to receive an education to secure a higher income in the future.

The marshmallow experiment incorporated various techniques that helped distract the children from the marshmallow and delay their desire to eat it. Often, children who were able to delay their gratification did so by singing, by sitting on their hands, or by looking away and concentrating on something other than the marshmallow (Mischel, Ebbesen, and Zeiss 1972). This aspect of the study has significant implications for healthcare. Attempts to influence people to change their negative health behaviors are more likely to be effective when they incorporate techniques and devices to help people overcome their natural tendencies to favor immediate gratification over future value. Awareness and knowledge are not enough.

Another important psychological element in behavioral economics is choice. Is choice always a good idea? How much choice is too much? Choice relates to the phenomenon of rational optimization, which involves trying to decide which option in a set of options is the best. Sometimes, offering people too many options can make their decision making more difficult or cause them to regret whatever choice they ultimately make. Often, a discrepancy exists between people's stated preference for increased choice and their actual reaction to the provision of choice (Botti and Iyengar 2006).

Iyengar and Lepper (2000) conducted a simple experiment involving two tables with samples of jam—one with 6 samples and another with 24 samples. Surprisingly, people who were confronted with the larger number of samples purchased less jam and were less satisfied with their purchases than the people who were presented with fewer choices. The retailer Costco fully subscribes to the findings of Iyengar and Lepper. The firm has studied the impact of the number of choices on purchasing behavior and concluded that offering limited choice is beneficial (Quintanilla 2012).

Consider all the choices people make with their healthcare. They have insurance choices, provider choices, treatment choices, and lifestyle choices (e.g., diet, exercise). Obviously, we want to make the best choice, but in some instances the variety of options can become too much for the human mind to process. Sometimes, a trade-off exists between making the best choice and limiting the amount of effort involved in making the choice; often, people will use simplifying heuristic strategies to help narrow a choice based on limited information (Payne, Bettman, and Johnson 1993). Difficulty in choosing from among options can sometimes cause people to defer to the easiest solution, which is to do nothing.

The concept of "libertarian paternalism," developed by Thaler and Sunstein (2008), posits that people should be given choices (a feature of libertarianism) but that the decisions should be guided by experts (a feature of paternalism). For instance, patients can be given a set of options, but physicians can "nudge" them toward decisions that are in their best interest.

Further research on the psychological aspects of healthcare decision making will be essential in the years ahead, particularly as the system increasingly emphasizes patient engagement, patient-centered care, and end-of-life decision making (Doonan and Katz 2015; Herzlinger and Parsa-Parsi 2004; Steer 2006; Thaler and Sunstein 2008; Drought and Koenig 2002; Zolkefli 2017). Students are encouraged to review Thomas Rice's (2013) article "The Behavioral Economics of Health and Health Care" for more information on this important concept.

Examples of Behavioral Economic Interventions

Behavioral economics offers a variety of tools and strategies that can help improve the health of our communities (Ariely 2010; Rabin 2016; Thaler 2015; Heather and Vuchinich 2003; Loewenstein et al. 2012).

The "Ulysses contract," for instance, is a kind of contract in which a person agrees to be bound by another person's decision in the future. The Ulysses contract is named after the hero of Homer's *Odyssey*. In the story, Ulysses asks his men to tie him to the mast of the ship so he can experience the Sirens' song, and he gives them instructions not to release him under any circumstances (Homer 1999). Ulysses contracts have sometimes been used in mental health situations, where a patient empowers a provider to override the patient's later objection to treatment. The ethics and legality of Ulysses contracts in healthcare have been called into question, and such contracts often are not enforced (Davis 2008; Walker 2012). In some instances, people can effectively form Ulysses contracts with themselves by making it impossible for them to engage in certain behaviors. For instance, by putting your smart phone in the trunk of your car before departing, you can make it impossible to use the phone while driving.

Another behavioral economics tool is a simple agreement between the patient and the provider—for instance, the patient might agree to follow a prescribed course of treatment or lifestyle change. Often the agreement will carry no penalties, but the mere act of committing the agreement to writing and having the parties sign it increases the probability that the actions will be completed.

Simple reminders and the power of suggestion can also be excellent behavioral economic tools (Payne et al. 2015). In one study, customers were given shopping baskets with a yellow line across the middle, and a sign instructed shoppers to use one side of the basket for fruits and vegetables and the other side for everything else. Average produce sales more than doubled (Moss 2013).

The behavioral economic technique of "opting out" has proved highly effective in organ donation. If a country's organ donation program is designed in a way that assumes people's participation and requires them to opt out if they do not wish to donate, it will likely have nearly universal participation; on the other hand, if a program requires people to "opt in" to become a donor, it will likely have a low participation rate. Simply put, people are more likely to not act than act (Johnson and Goldstein 2004).

Interprofessional Education

Education will be a key element in our effort to improve the outcomes produced by the healthcare system (Birk 2017; Buring et al. 2009; Guraya and Barr 2018). Interprofessional education (IPE) is an educational approach that seeks to prepare students in the health professions to provide patient care in a collaborative team environment (Alston et al. 2012; Asch and Weinstein 2014; Brashers, Owen, and Haizlip 2015; IOM 2015; World Health Organization [WHO] 2010). IPE has three main goals (Parsell and Bligh 1998):

1. To enhance understanding of other professional roles and responsibilities
2. To help to develop skills needed for effective teamwork
3. To increase knowledge of clinical skills or topics

IPE occurs when students from two or more healthcare professional groups (e.g., physicians, nurses, social workers, physical therapists, physician assistants, administrative professionals) learn together and gain an appreciation for what each group does as part of the patient care system (Barr et al. 2005; Patrician et al. 2012; Reeves et al. 2013). IPE seeks to address the siloed nature of US healthcare, which contributes to many of the challenges we face.

The reason IPE has such great promise is that healthcare professionals who learn to work in a collaborative manner produce better patient outcomes, higher quality of care, and better working environments. When professionals know one another better, they are more likely to communicate effectively and develop mutual respect (IOM 2015; Shrader et al. 2018). IPE has also demonstrated the potential to reduce medical errors and lower costs, though further research is needed to fully understand this impact (Hammick et al. 2007).

Negative communication, poor working relationships, and disruptive behavior in healthcare settings can have tragic consequences (Hickson et al. 1994; Hickson and Entman 2008). Gerald B. Hickson of the Vanderbilt Center for Patient and Professional Advocacy, along with his colleagues, has done extensive research on ways of reducing disruptive behavior and negative interactions, thereby improving patient care and lowering cost (Hickson et al. 1992; Hickson et al. 2007).

Leadership and Governance for Quality

A number of problems with healthcare quality and safety are associated with matters of leadership and governance. Sometimes, when leaders feel secure in their positions, they become less willing to take appropriate risk and commit to innovation and improvement (Hlavacek 2018). In some instances, healthcare boards are under too much influence by top leaders in the organization; thus, the leaders take on the position of governing themselves, which may not be in the best interest of the organization or its mission (Wagner 2017).

Effective leadership and governance, including clinical governance, are essential for healthcare quality. Leadership for quality in healthcare settings can come from a variety sources, including managers, boards, and physician leaders (Lee et al. 2013; Weiner 2009; Weiner, Shortell, and Alexander 1997). Strong leadership from the top promotes clinical involvement at all levels.

Veenstra and colleagues (2017) write:

> . . . clinical governance is a practice-based, value-driven approach that has the goal of delivering the highest possible quality care and ensuring the safety of patients. Bottom-up approaches and effective teamwork are crucial for high quality and safe healthcare. Striving for high quality and safe healthcare is underpinned by continuous learning, shared responsibility and good relationships and collaboration between healthcare professionals, managers and patients.

In a WHO report, Kickbusch and Gleicher (2012) further emphasize collaboration:

> Collaboration is the new imperative. . . . Lessons can be learned from the rich literature on collaborative governance, including considering the process and design of collaboration; the virtuous circle of communication, trust, commitment and understanding; the choice of tools and mechanisms; and transparency and accountability.

The IHI has developed an excellent framework for governance of health system quality. The framework involves the following components (Daley Ullem et al. 2018):

- Simplify concepts: Use simple, trustee-friendly language that defines actionable processes and activities for trustees and those who support them to oversee quality.
- Incorporate all six STEEEP dimensions of quality: Understand quality as care that is safe, timely, effective, efficient, equitable, and patient centered (STEEEP), as defined by the Institute of Medicine.
- Include community health and value: Ensure that population health and health care value are critical elements of quality oversight.
- Govern quality in and out of the hospital setting: Advance quality governance throughout the health system, not solely in the hospital setting.
- Advance organizational improvement knowledge: Support trustees in understanding the ways to evaluate, prioritize, and improve performance on dimensions of quality.
- Identify the key attributes of a governance culture of quality: Describe the elements of a board culture and commitment to high-quality, patient-centered, equitable care.

Exhibits 9.9, 9.10, and 9.11 provide insights into governance and leadership for quality improvement. The exhibits show the components of quality from the patient's perspective, a vision of effective board governance, and the framework by which knowledge areas and processes can be implemented to achieve that vision.

When considering quality and safety, healthcare leaders, managers, board members, and others can start by reflecting on some rather straightforward questions:

- What is quality and safety in the healthcare environment? What does it mean?
- What is a culture of safety and quality?
- What are the benefits?
- What is the cost of poor quality and safety lapses?
- What is harm, and how do we prevent it?
- How does the lack of timely attention to quality and safety affect our finances and our reputation?
- What are our vulnerabilities related to quality and safety?
- Who is responsible for and who will manage and oversee the elements of quality and safety in the organization?

- How do we monitor quality and safety in the organization?
- How do we ensure that we have the proper training (with regard to knowledge, skills, and practices) to support a culture of quality and safety?

EXHIBIT 9.9
Core Components
of Quality from
the Patient's
Perspective

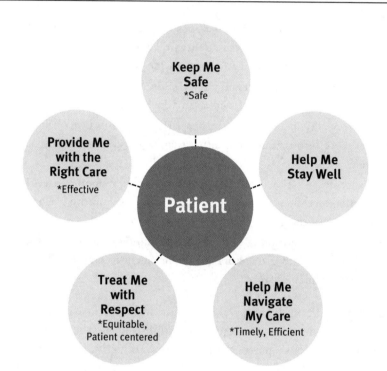

*IOM STEEEP dimensions of quality: Safe, Timely, Effective, Efficient, Equitable, and Patient Centered

Source: Daley Ullem E, Gandhi TK, Mate K, Whittington J, Renton M, Huebner J. *Framework for Effective Board Governance of Health System Quality*. IHI White Paper. Boston, MA: Institute for Healthcare Improvement; 2018. (Available on ihi.org.)

EXHIBIT 9.10
Vision of
Effective Board
Governance of
Health System
Quality

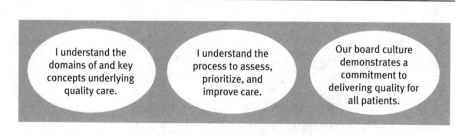

Source: Daley Ullem E, Gandhi TK, Mate K, Whittington J, Renton M, Huebner J. *Framework for Effective Board Governance of Health System Quality*. IHI White Paper. Boston, MA: Institute for Healthcare Improvement; 2018. (Available on ihi.org.)

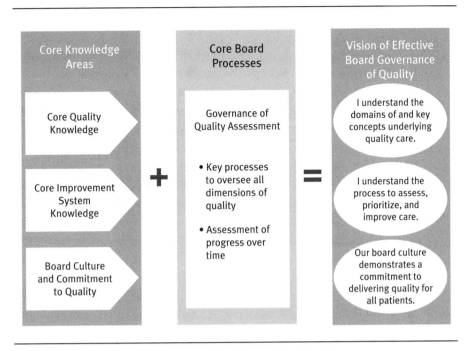

EXHIBIT 9.11
Framework for
Governance of
Health System
Quality

Source: Daley Ullem E, Gandhi TK, Mate K, Whittington J, Renton M, Huebner J. *Framework for Effective Board Governance of Health System Quality.* IHI White Paper. Boston, MA: Institute for Healthcare Improvement; 2018. (Available on ihi.org.)

The Need for a Balanced Approach

Clearly, improving quality and safety in healthcare will require constant diligence and absolute commitment from people at every level of the organization. As we seek to improve, we often have a tendency to direct our focus on one particular idea or strategy, or to shift from one extreme to the other; such an approach, however, is not well suited for the movement toward quality. Many strategies have shown promise and demonstrated beneficial results, yet no single strategy alone seems to be the answer for sustained transformative improvement. A balanced approach of proven strategies coupled with newer initiatives is likely a more productive path to lasting change and a healthier America.

Discussion Questions

1. How do you define *quality* and *safety*? What role does perspective play in your definitions?
2. Are service, experience, and outcome equally important?
3. Can we manage quality in healthcare in the same way that we manage quality in other industries?

References

Agency for Healthcare Research and Quality (AHRQ). 2019. "High Reliability."
Updated September. https://psnet.ahrq.gov/primer/high-reliability.

———. 2018. "Environmental Scan of Patient Safety Education and Training Programs." Reviewed April. www.ahrq.gov/research/findings/final-reports/environmental-scan-programs/envscan-program1.html.

———. 2017. "What Is Patient Experience?" Reviewed March. www.ahrq.gov/cahps/about-cahps/patient-experience/index.html.

———. 2014a. *Improving Care Delivery Through Lean: Implementation Case Studies.* AHRQ Publication No. 13(15)-0056. Published November. www.ahrq.gov/sites/default/files/publications/files/leancasestudies.pdf.

———. 2014b. "Major Factors That Inhibit Lean Success." Reviewed November. www.ahrq.gov/professionals/systems/system/systemdesign/leancasestudies/lean-exhibit4-19.html.

Aij, K. H., and M. Teunissen. 2017. "Lean Leadership Attributes: A Systematic Review of the Literature." *Journal of Health Organization and Management* 31 (7–8): 713–29. https://doi.org/10.1108/JHOM-12-2016-0245.

Aleccia, J. 2016. "Virginia Mason Is Denied Full Accreditation After Lapses." *Seattle Times.* Published June 21. www.seattletimes.com/seattle-news/virginia-mason-is-denied-full-accreditation-after-lapses/.

Allen, M., and O. Pierce. 2016. "Only Heart Disease and Cancer Exceed Medical Errors as Causes of Death." National Public Radio. Published May 3. www.npr.org/sections/health-shots/2016/05/03/476636183/death-certificates-undercount-toll-of-medical-errors.

Alston, C., L. Paget, G. Halvorson, B. Novelli, J. Guest, P. McCabe, K. Hoffman, C. Koepke, M. Simon, S. Sutton, S. Okun, P. Wicks, T. Undem, V. Rohrbach, and I. Von Kohorn. 2012. *Communicating with Patients on Health Care Evidence.* Institute of Medicine Discussion Paper. Published September. https://nam.edu/wp-content/uploads/2015/06/VSRT-Evidence.pdf.

Amaratunga, T., and J. Dobranowski. 2016. "Systematic Review of the Application of Lean and Six Sigma Quality Improvement Methodologies in Radiology." *Journal of the American College of Radiology* 13 (9): 1088–1095.e7. https://doi.org/10.1016/j.jacr.2016.02.033.

American Society for Quality (ASQ). 2019. "What Is Total Quality Management (TQM)?" Accessed October 13. https://asq.org/quality-resources/total-quality-management.

Andersen, H., K. A. Røvik, and T. Ingebrigtsen. 2014. "Lean Thinking in Hospitals: Is There a Cure for the Absence of Evidence? A Systematic Review of Reviews." *BMJ Open* 4 (1): e003873. https://doi.org/10.1136/bmjopen-2013-003873.

Ariely, D. 2010. *Predictably Irrational: The Hidden Forces That Shape Our Decisions.* New York: Harper Perennial.

Aristotle. 2009. *Selections from Nicomachean Ethics and Politics*. London: CRW Publishing.

Asch, D. A., and D. F. Weinstein. 2014. "Innovation in Medical Education." *New England Journal of Medicine* 371 (9): 794–95. https://doi.org/10.1056/NEJMp1407463.

Baldrige Foundation. 2019. "The Foundation for the Malcolm Baldrige National Quality Award." Accessed October 13. https://baldrigefoundation.org.

Barnett, J., K. Vasileiou, F. Djemil, L. Brooks, and T. Young. 2011. "Understanding Innovators' Experiences of Barriers and Facilitators in Implementation and Diffusion of Healthcare Service Innovations: A Qualitative Study." *BMC Health Services Research* 11: 342. https://doi.org/10.1186/1472-6963-11-342.

Barr, H., I. Koppel, S. Reeves, M. Hammick, and D. Freeth. 2005. *Effective Interprofessional Education: Argument, Assumption and Evidence*. Oxford, UK: Blackwell.

Bedford, D. A. D. 2012. "The Role of Knowledge Management in Creating Transformational Organizations and Transformational Leaders." *Journal of Knowledge Management Practice* 13 (4): 32–44.

Bendapudi, N. M., L. L. Berry, K. A. Frey, J. T. Parish, and W. L. Rayburn. 2006. "Patients' Perspectives on Ideal Physician Behaviors." *Mayo Clinic Proceedings* 81 (3): 338–44. https://doi.org/10.4065/81.3.338.

Berwick, D. M. 1998. "Developing and Testing Changes in Delivery of Care." *Annals of Internal Medicine* 128 (8): 651–56. https://doi.org/10.7326/0003-4819-128-8-199804150-00009.

Birk, T. J. 2017. "Principles for Developing an Interprofessional Education Curriculum in a Healthcare Program." *Journal of Healthcare Communications* 2 (1). https://doi.org/10.4172/2472-1654.100049.

Botti, S., and S. S. Iyengar. 2006. "The Dark Side of Choice: When Choice Impairs Social Welfare." *Journal of Public Policy & Marketing* 25 (1): 24–38. https://doi.org/10.1509/jppm.25.1.24.

Brashers, V., J. Owen, and J. Haizlip. 2015. "Interprofessional Education and Practice Guide No. 2: Developing and Implementing a Center for Interprofessional Education." *Journal of Interprofessional Care* 29 (2): 95–99. https://doi.org/10.3109/13561820.2014.962130.

Brown, M. T., and J. K. Bussell. 2011. "Medication Adherence: WHO Cares?" *Mayo Clinic Proceedings* 86 (4): 304–14. https://doi.org/10.4065/mcp.2010.0575.

Buring, S. M., A. Bhushan, A. Broeseker, S. Conway, W. Duncan-Hewitt, L. Hansen, and S. Westberg. 2009. "Interprofessional Education: Definitions, Student Competencies, and Guidelines for Implementation." *American Journal of Pharmaceutical Education* 73 (4): 59. https://doi.org/10.5688/aj730459.

Centers for Disease Control and Prevention (CDC). 2017. *National Diabetes Statistics Report, 2017: Estimates of Diabetes and Its Burden in the United States*

Background. Accessed October 13, 2019. www.cdc.gov/diabetes/pdfs/data/statistics/national-diabetes-statistics-report.pdf.

Centers for Medicare & Medicaid Services (CMS). 2019a. "Consumer Assessment of Healthcare Providers & Systems (CAHPS)." Updated September 16. www.cms.gov/Research-Statistics-Data-and-Systems/Research/CAHPS/index.html.

———. 2019b. "HCAHPS: Patients' Perspectives of Care Survey." Updated October 9. www.cms.gov/Medicare/Quality-Initiatives-Patient-Assessment-instruments/hospitalqualityinits/hospitalHCAHPS.html.

Conrad, D. A. 2015. "The Theory of Value-Based Payment Incentives and Their Application to Health Care." *Health Services Research* 50: 2057–89. https://doi.org/10.1111/1475-6773.12408.

Crosby, P. B. 1979. *Quality Is Free: The Art of Making Quality Certain.* New York: McGraw-Hill.

Cunningham, F. C., G. Ranmuthugala, J. Plumb, A. Georgiou, J. I. Westbrook, and J. Braithwaite. 2012. "Health Professional Networks as a Vector for Improving Healthcare Quality and Safety: A Systematic Review." *BMJ Quality & Safety* 21 (3): 239–49. https://doi.org/10.1136/BMJQS-2011-000187.

Daley Ullem, E., T. Ganhdi, K. Mate, J. Whittington, M. Renton, and H. Joellen. 2018. *Framework for Effective Board Governance of Health System Quality.* Institute for Healthcare Improvement. Accessed October 13, 2019. www.ihi.org/resources/Pages/IHIWhitePapers/Framework-Effective-Board-Governance-Health-System-Quality.aspx.

Davis, J. K. 2008. "How to Justify Enforcing a Ulysses Contract When Ulysses Is Competent to Refuse." *Kennedy Institute of Ethics Journal* 18 (1): 87–106. www.ncbi.nlm.nih.gov/pubmed/18561579.

DelliFraine, J. L., J. R. Langabeer, and I. M. Nembhard. 2010. "Assessing the Evidence of Six Sigma and Lean in the Health Care Industry." *Quality Management in Health Care* 19 (3): 211–25. https://doi.org/10.1097/QMH.0b013e3181eb140e.

Deming, E. 2000. *The New Economics: For Industry, Government, Education,* 2nd ed. Cambridge, MA: MIT Press.

———. 1986. *Out of the Crisis.* Cambridge, MA: MIT Center for Advanced Engineering Study.

Deming Institute. 2019a. "Large List of Quotes by W. Edwards Deming." Accessed December 19. https://blog.deming.org/w-edwards-deming-quotes/large-list-of-quotes-by-w-edwards-deming/.

———. 2019b. "The Deming System of Profound Knowledge." Accessed October 13. https://deming.org/explore/so-p-k.

Donaldson, M. S. 2009. "An Overview of *To Err is Human*: Re-emphasizing the Message of Patient Safety." In *Patient Safety and Quality: An Evidence-Based Handbook for Nurses,* 2nd ed., vol. 1, edited by R. G. Hughes, 37–45. Rockville, MD: Agency for Healthcare Research and Quality. www.ncbi.nlm.nih.gov/books/NBK2673/.

Doonan, M., and G. Katz. 2015. "Choice in the American Healthcare System: Changing Dynamics Under the Affordable Care Act." *Current Sociology* 63 (5): 746–62. https://doi.org/10.1177/0011392115590092.

Drotz, E., and B. Poksinska. 2014. "Lean in Healthcare from Employees' Perspectives." *Journal of Health Organization and Management* 28 (2): 177–95. https://doi.org/10.1108/JHOM-03-2013-0066.

Drought, T. S., and B. A. Koenig. 2002. "'Choice' in End-of-Life Decision-Making: Researching Fact or Fiction?" *Gerontologist* 42 (Spec. No. 3): 114–28. https://doi.org/10.1093/geront/42.suppl_3.114.

Durant, W. 1961. *The Story of Philosophy: The Lives and Opinions of the Great Philosophers of the Western World.* New York: Simon & Schuster.

Echazu, L., and D. Nocetti. 2013. "Priority Setting in Health Care: Disentangling Risk Aversion from Inequality Aversion." *Health Economics* 22 (6): 730–40. https://doi.org/10.1002/hec.2858.

Economist. 2018. "Hospitals Are Learning from Industry How to Cut Medical Errors." Published June 28. www.economist.com/international/2018/06/28/hospitals-are-learning-from-industry-how-to-cut-medical-errors.

Enthoven, A. C. 2011. "Reforming Medicare by Reforming Incentives." *New England Journal of Medicine* 364 (21): e44. https://doi.org/10.1056/NEJMp1104427.

Feigenbaum, A. 1951. *Quality Control: Principles, Practice and Administration.* New York: McGraw-Hill.

Friedberg, M. W., M. B. Rosenthal, R. M. Werner, K. G. Volpp, and E. C. Schneider. 2015. "Effects of a Medical Home and Shared Savings Intervention on Quality and Utilization of Care." *JAMA Internal Medicine* 175 (8): 1362–68. https://doi.org/10.1001/jamainternmed.2015.2047.

Fulford, K. W. M., E. Peile, and H. Carroll. 2012. *Essential Values-Based Practice: Clinical Stories Linking Science with People.* New York: Cambridge University Press.

Gawande, A. 2009. *The Checklist Manifesto: How to Get Things Right.* New York: Henry Holt.

Ginsburg, P. B. 2011. "Reforming Provider Payment—The Price Side of the Equation." *New England Journal of Medicine* 365 (14): 1268–70. https://doi.org/10.1056/NEJMp1107019.

Gitlow, H., E. Loredo, and M. Dekker. 1992. "Total Quality Management at Florida Power & Light Company: A Case Study." *Quality Engineering* 5 (1): 123–58.

Goethe, J. W. von. 1906. *The Maxims and Reflections of Goethe.* Project Gutenberg. Accessed December 10, 2019. www.gutenberg.org/files/33670/33670-h/33670-h.htm.

Guraya, S. Y., and H. Barr. 2018. "The Effectiveness of Interprofessional Education in Healthcare: A Systematic Review and Meta-Analysis. *Kaohsiung Journal of Medical Sciences* 34 (3): 160–65. https://doi.org/10.1016/j.kjms.2017.12.009.

Hammick, M., D. Freeth, I. Koppel, S. Reeves, and H. Barr. 2007. "A Best Evidence Systematic Review of Interprofessional Education: BEME Guide No. 9." *Medical Teacher* 29 (8): 735–51. https://doi.org/10.1080/01421590701682576.

Heather, N., and R. Vuchinich. 2003. *Choice, Behavioral Economics, and Addiction.* New York: Pergamon Press.

Heineman, M., and S. Froemke (dirs.). 2012. *Escape Fire: The Fight to Rescue American Healthcare.* Aisle C Production and Our Time Projects. www.escapefiremovie.com.

Herzlinger, R. E., and R. Parsa-Parsi. 2004. "Consumer-Driven Health Care: Lessons from Switzerland." *JAMA* 292 (10): 1213–20. https://doi.org/10.1001/jama.292.10.1213.

Heshmat, S. 2017. "What Is Behavioral Economics?" *Psychology Today.* Published May 3. www.psychologytoday.com/us/blog/science-choice/201705/what-is-behavioral-economics.

Hickson, G. B., E. W. Clayton, S. S. Entman, C. S. Miller, P. B. Githens, K. Whetten-Goldstein, and F. A. Sloan. 1994. "Obstetricians' Prior Malpractice Experience and Patients' Satisfaction with Care." *JAMA* 272 (20): 1583–87. https://doi.org/10.1001/jama.1994.03520200039032.

Hickson, G. B., E. W. Clayton, P. B. Githens, and F. A. Sloan. 1992. "Factors That Prompted Families to File Medical Malpractice Claims Following Perinatal Injuries." *JAMA* 267 (10): 1359–63. https://doi.org/10.1001/jama.1992.03480100065032.

Hickson, G. B., and S. S. Entman. 2008. "Physician Practice Behavior and Litigation Risk: Evidence and Opportunity." *Clinical Obstetrics and Gynecology* 51 (4): 688–99. https://doi.org/10.1097/GRF.0b013e3181899c2c.

Hickson, G. B., J. W. Pichert, L. E. Webb, and S. G. Gabbe. 2007. "A Complementary Approach to Promoting Professionalism: Identifying, Measuring, and Addressing Unprofessional Behaviors." *Academic Medicine* 82 (11): 1040–48. https://doi.org/10.1097/ACM.0b013e31815761ee.

Hlavacek, J. 2018. *Fat Cats Don't Hunt: Implanting the Right Leadership and Culture to Accelerate Innovation and Organic Growth.* Asheville, NC: United Business Press.

Hodari, K. T., J. R. Nanton, C. L. Carroll, S. R. Feldman, and R. Balkrishnan. 2006. "Adherence in Dermatology: A Review of the Last 20 Years." *Journal of Dermatological Treatment* 17 (3): 136–42. https://doi.org/10.1080/09546630600688515.

Homer. 1999. *The Odyssey.* Edited by R. Fagles and B. H. Langiana. New York: Penguin Classics.

Hunter, J. 2015. "A Bad System Will Beat a Good Person Every Time." W. Edwards Deming Institute. Published February 26. https://blog.deming.org/2015/02/a-bad-system-will-beat-a-good-person-every-time/.

————. 2014a. "Lessons From the Red Bead Experiment with Dr. Deming." W. Edwards Deming Institute. Published March 10. https://blog.deming. org/2014/03/lessons-from-the-red-bead-experiment-with-dr-deming/.

————. 2014b. "The Red Bead Experiment with Dr. W. Edwards Deming." W. Edwards Deming Institute. Published February 25. https://blog.deming. org/2014/02/deming-red-bead-experiment/.

Institute for Healthcare Improvement (IHI). 2019. "Triple Aim for Populations." Accessed October 13. www.ihi.org/Topics/TripleAim/Pages/default.aspx.

Institute of Medicine (IOM). 2015. *Measuring the Impact of Interprofessional Education on Collaborative Practice and Patient Outcomes*. Washington, DC: National Academies Press.

————. 2001. *Crossing the Quality Chasm: A New Health System for the 21st Century*. Washington, DC: National Academies Press. www.ncbi.nlm.nih.gov/ pubmed/25057539.

————. 1999. *To Err Is Human: Building a Safer Health System*. Washington, DC: National Academies Press. www.ncbi.nlm.nih.gov/pubmed/25077248.

International Organization for Standardization (ISO). 2019. "ISO 9001 Quality Management." Accessed October 13. www.iso.org/iso-9001-quality-management.html.

Isfahani, S. S., M. A. Hosseini, M. F. Khoshknab, H. Peyrovi, and H. R. Khanke. 2015. "Nurses' Creativity: Advantage or Disadvantage." *Iranian Red Crescent Medical Journal* 17 (2): e20895. https://doi.org/10.5812/ircmj.20895.

Ishikawa, K. 1986. *Guide to Quality Control*, 2nd ed. Tokyo: Asian Productivity Organization.

Iyengar, S. S., and M. R. Lepper. 2000. "When Choice Is Demotivating: Can One Desire Too Much of a Good Thing?" *Journal of Personality and Social Psychology* 79 (6): 995–1006. www.ncbi.nlm.nih.gov/pubmed/11138768.

James, J. 2013. "A New, Evidence Based Estimate of Patient Harms Associated with Hospital Care." *Journal of Patient Safety* 9 (3): 122–28. https://doi. org/10.1097/PTS.0b013e3182948a69.

Johnson, E. J., and D. G. Goldstein. 2004. "Defaults and Donation Decisions." *Transplantation* 78 (12): 1713–16. https://10.1097/01.TP.0000149788.10382.B2.

Joosten, T., I. Bongers, and R. Janssen. 2009. "Application of Lean Thinking to Health Care: Issues and Observations." *International Journal for Quality in Health Care* 21 (5): 341–47. https://doi.org/10.1093/intqhc/mzp036.

Juran, J. M., and J. A. De Feo (eds.). 2016. *Juran's Quality Handbook: The Complete Guide to Performance Excellence*, 7th ed. New York: McGraw-Hill Education.

Juran, J. M., and F. M. Gryna. 1993. *Quality Planning and Analysis: From Product Development Through Use*, 3rd ed. New York: McGraw-Hill.

Kaiser Family Foundation. 2011. "Timeline: History of Health Reform in the U.S." Published March 25. www.kff.org/wp-content/uploads/2011/03/5-02-13-history-of-health-reform.pdf.

Kaplan, G. S., S. H. Patterson, J. M. Ching, and C. C. Blackmore. 2014. "Why Lean Doesn't Work for Everyone." *BMJ Quality & Safety* 23 (12): 970–73. https://doi.org/10.1136/bmjqs-2014-003248.

Kavanagh, K. T., D. M. Saman, R. Bartel, and K. Westerman. 2017. "Estimating Hospital-Related Deaths Due to Medical Error." *Journal of Patient Safety* 13 (1): 1–5. https://doi.org/10.1097/PTS.0000000000000364.

Kennedy, G. D., S. E. Tevis, and K. C. Kent. 2014. "Is There a Relationship Between Patient Satisfaction and Favorable Outcomes?" *Annals of Surgery* 260 (4): 592–598, 598–600. https://doi.org/10.1097/SLA.0000000000000932.

Kickbusch, I., and D. Gleicher. 2012. *Governance in Health for the 21st Century*. Geneva, Switzerland: World Health Organization. www.euro.who.int/__data/assets/pdf_file/0019/171334/RC62BD01-Governance-for-Health-Web.pdf.

Kleisiaris, C. F., C. Sfakianakis, and I. V. Papathanasiou. 2014. "Health Care Practices in Ancient Greece: The Hippocratic Ideal." *Journal of Medical Ethics and History of Medicine* 7: 6. www.ncbi.nlm.nih.gov/pmc/articles/PMC4263393/.

Kopp, R. 2012. "Defining Nemawashi." Japan Intercultural Consulting. Published December 20. www.japanintercultural.com/en/news/default.aspx?newsID=234.

Leapfrog Group. 2019. "Raising the Bar for Safer Health Care." Accessed October 13. www.leapfroggroup.org/about.

———. 2016. "Selecting the Right Hospital Can Reduce Your Risk of Avoidable Death by 50%, According to Analysis of Newly Updated Hospital Safety Score Grades." Published April 25. www.hospitalsafetygrade.org/about-us/newsroom/display/442022.

Lee, S.-Y. D., B. J. Weiner, M. I. Harrison, and C. M. Belden. 2013. "Organizational Transformation." *Medical Care Research and Review* 70 (2): 115–42. https://doi.org/10.1177/1077558712458539.

Lehigh Valley Business Coalition on Healthcare. 2019. "About Us." Accessed December 10. www.lvbch.com/lvbch_4_1_2_0_about.html.

Levinson, W., C. S. Lesser, and R. M. Epstein. 2010. "Developing Physician Communication Skills for Patient-Centered Care." *Health Affairs* 29 (7): 1310–18. https://doi.org/10.1377/hlthaff.2009.0450.

Loewenstein, G., D. A. Asch, J. Y. Friedman, L. A. Melichar, and K. G. Volpp. 2012. "Can Behavioural Economics Make Us Healthier?" *BMJ* 344 (7863): 1–3. https://doi.org/10.1136/bmj.e3482.

Lyu, H., T. Xu, D. Brotman, B. Mayer-Blackwell, M. Cooper, M. Daniel, E. C. Wick, V. Saini, S. Brownlee, and M. A. Makary. 2017. "Overtreatment in the United States." *PLOS ONE* 12 (9): e0181970. https://doi.org/10.1371/journal.pone.0181970.

Maggio, L., N. Tannery, H. Chen, O. Cate, and B. O'Brien. 2013. "Evidence-Based Medicine Training in Undergraduate Medical Education: A Review and Critique of the Literature Published 2006–2011." *Academic Medicine* 88 (7): 1022–28. https://doi.org/10.1097/ACM.0b013e3182951959.

Makary, M. 2012. *Unaccountable: What Hospitals Won't Tell You and How Transparency Can Revolutionize Health Care*. New York: Bloomsbury Press.

Makary, M. A., and M. Daniel. 2016. "Medical Error—The Third Leading Cause of Death in the US." *BMJ* 353: i2139. https://doi.org/10.1136/BMJ.I2139.

Manary, M. P., W. Boulding, R. Staelin, and S. W. Glickman. 2013. "The Patient Experience and Health Outcomes." *New England Journal of Medicine* 368 (3): 201–3. https://doi.org/10.1056/NEJMp1211775.

Mathews, J. 1993. "Totaled Quality Management." *Washington Post*. Published June 6. www.washingtonpost.com/archive/business/1993/06/06/totaled-quality-management/c0ca5500-bbed-40f9-9bc8-a6e4704b20cf/?utm_term=.35f7fb964afe.

Mischel, W., E. B. Ebbesen, and A. R. Zeiss. 1972. "Cognitive and Attentional Mechanisms in Delay of Gratification." *Journal of Personality and Social Psychology* 21 (2): 204–18. www.ncbi.nlm.nih.gov/pubmed/5010404.

Modern Healthcare. 2017. "2017 Largest Patient Satisfaction Measurement Firms Respondents." Published October 25. www.modernhealthcare.com/article/20171025/INFO/310259999.

Moraros, J., M. Lemstra, and C. Nwankwo. 2016. "Lean Interventions in Healthcare: Do They Actually Work? A Systematic Literature Review." *International Journal for Quality in Health Care* 28 (2): 150–65. https://doi.org/10.1093/intqhc/mzv123.

Moriarty, J., M. Branda, K. Olsen, N. Shah, B. Borah, A. Wagie, J. Egginton, and J. Naessens. 2012. "The Effects of Incremental Costs of Smoking and Obesity on Health Care Costs Among Adults." *Journal of Occupational and Environmental Medicine* 54 (3): 286–91. https://doi.org/10.1097/JOM.0b013e318246f1f4.

Moss, M. 2013. "Nudged to the Produce Aisle by a Look in the Mirror." *New York Times*. Published August 27. www.nytimes.com/2013/08/28/dining/wooing-us-down-the-produce aisle.html.

National Institute of Standards and Technology (NIST). 2019. "Baldrige Performance Excellence Program." Accessed December 12. www.nist.gov/baldrige.

Nayar, V. 2012. "'Zero Gravity Thinkers' Are the Key to Innovation." *Business Insider*. Published July 31. www.businessinsider.com/this-one-thing-could-single-handedly-transform-your-business-into-an-innovative-sustainable-enterprise-2012-7.

Neyestani, B. 2017. *Principles and Contributions of Total Quality Mangement (TQM) Gurus on Business Quality Improvement*. De La Salle University. Published February. https://doi.org/10.5281/zenodo.345428.

Niven, D. 1993. "When Times Get Tough, What Happens to TQM?" *Harvard Business Review* 71 (3): 2–11. https://hbr.org/1993/05/when-times-get-tough-what-happens-to-tqm.

North, M. (trans.) 2002. "The Hippocratic Oath." National Library of Medicine. Accessed October 13, 2019. www.nlm.nih.gov/hmd/greek/greek_oath.html.

Nutton, V. 2012. *Ancient Medicine.* New York: Routledge.

O'Brien, M. 2008. "Leading Innovation in a Risk-Averse Healthcare Environment." *Healthcare Financial Management* 62 (8): 112–14. Retrieved from www.ncbi.nlm.nih.gov/pubmed/18709873.

Parsell, G., and J. Bligh. 1998. "Interprofessional Learning." *Postgraduate Medical Journal* 74: 89–95. www.ncbi.nlm.nih.gov/pmc/articles/PMC2360816/pdf/postmedj00086-0027.pdf.

Patrician, P. A., M. Dolansky, C. Estrada, C. Brennan, R. Miltner, J. Newsom, D. Olds, M. Splaine, and S. Moore. 2012. "Interprofessional Education in Action." *Nursing Clinics of North America* 47 (3): 347–54. https://doi.org/10.1016/j.cnur.2012.05.006.

Payne, C., M. Niculescu, D. Just, and M. Kelly. 2015. "Shopper Marketing Nutrition Interventions: Social Norms on Grocery Carts Increase Produce Spending Without Increasing Shopper Budgets." *Preventive Medicine Reports* 2: 287–91. https://doi.org/10.1016/j.pmedr.2015.04.007.

Payne, J. W., J. R. Bettman, and E. J. Johnson. 1993. *The Adaptive Decision Maker.* New York: Cambridge University Press.

Pérotin, V., B. Zamora, R. Reeves, W. Bartlett, and P. Allen. 2013. "Does Hospital Ownership Affect Patient Experience? An Investigation into Public-Private Sector Differences in England." *Journal of Health Economics* 32 (3): 633–46. https://doi.org/10.1016/j.jhealeco.2013.03.003.

Pink, D. H. 2011. *Drive: The Surprising Truth About What Motivates Us.* New York: Riverhead Books.

Poksinska, B. 2010. "The Current State of Lean Implementation in Health Care: Literature Review." *Quality Management in Healthcare* 19 (4): 319–29. https://doi.org/10.1097/QMH.0b013e3181fa07bb.

Pracht, E. E., B. Langland-Orban, and J. L. Ryan. 2018. "The Probability of Hospitalizations for Mild-to-Moderate Injuries by Trauma Center Ownership Type." *Health Services Research* 53 (1): 35–48. https://doi.org/10.1111/1475-6773.12646.

Quintanilla, C. 2012. "The Costco Craze: Inside the Warehouse Giant." CNBC. Published April 9. www.cnbc.com/the-costco-craze-inside-the-warehouse-giant/.

Rabe, C. B. 2006. *The Innovation Killer: How What We Know Limits What We Can Imagine—And What Smart Companies Are Doing About It.* New York: Amacom.

Rabin, M. 2016. "Psychology and Economic Theory." Harvard University. Accessed October 13, 2019. https://scholar.harvard.edu/files/rabin/files/2035syllabus2016.pdf.

Reason, J. 1990. *Human Error*. New York: Cambridge University Press.

Reeves, S., L. Perrier, J. Goldman, D. Freeth, and M. Zwarenstein. 2013. "Inter-professional Education: Effects on Professional Practice and Healthcare Outcomes." *Cochrane Database of Systematic Reviews*, no. 3: CD002213. https://doi.org/10.1002/14651858.CD002213.pub3.

Rice, T. 2013. "The Behavioral Economics of Health and Health Care." *Annual Review of Public Health* 34 (1): 431–47. https://doi.org/10.1146/annurev-publhealth-031912-114353.

Robinson, K. 2006. "Do Schools Kill Creativity?" TED Talk. Published February. www.ted.com/talks/ken_robinson_says_schools_kill_creativity?language=en.

Rowley, W. R., C. Bezold, Y. Arikan, E. Byrne, and S. Krohe. 2017. "Diabetes 2030: Insights from Yesterday, Today, and Future Trends." *Population Health Management* 20 (1): 6–12. https://doi.org/10.1089/pop.2015.0181.

Schneider, E. C., D. O. Sarnak, D. Squires, A. Shah, and M. M. Doty. 2017. "Mirror, Mirror 2017: International Comparison Reflects Flaws and Opportunities for Better U.S. Health Care." Commonwealth Fund. Published July 14. www.commonwealthfund.org/publications/fund-reports/2017/jul/mirror-mirror-2017-international-comparison-reflects-flaws-and.

Schneider, E. C., and D. Squires. 2017. "From Last to First—Could the U.S. Health Care System Become the Best in the World?" *New England Journal of Medicine* 377 (10): 901–3. https://doi.org/10.1056/NEJMp1708704.

Shanafelt, T., C. A. Sinsky, and S. Swensen. 2017. "Medical Errors and Preventable Deaths in U.S. Hospitals." *NEJM Catalyst*. Published January 23. https://catalyst.nejm.org/medical-errors-preventable-deaths/.

Shrader, S., S. Jernigan, N. Nazir, and J. Zaudke. 2018. "Determining the Impact of an Interprofessional Learning in Practice Model on Learners and Patients." *Journal of Interprofessional Care*. Published September 13. https://doi.org/10.1080/13561820.2018.1513465.

Skhmot, N. 2017. "The 8 Wastes of Lean." *The Lean Way*. Published August 5. https://theleanway.net/The-8-Wastes-of-Lean.

Spielberg, S. (dir.). 1993. *Jurassic Park*. Universal Studios.

Statista. 2019. "Quick Service Restaurants: Revenue US 2002–2018." Accessed October 13. www.statista.com/statistics/196614/revenue-of-the-us-fast-food-restaurant-industry-since-2002/.

Steer, P. J. 2006. "So What's So New About Patient Choice?" *BMJ* 332 (7547): 981.1. https://doi.org/10.1136/bmj.332.7547.981.

Thaler, R. H. 2015. *Misbehaving: The Making of Behavioral Economics*. New York: W. W. Norton.

Thaler, R. H., and C. R. Sunstein. 2008. *Nudge: Improving Decisions About Health, Wealth, and Happiness*. New Haven, CT: Yale University Press.

Thom, D. H., M. A. Hall, and L. G. Pawlson. 2004. "Measuring Patients' Trust in Physicians When Assessing Quality of Care." *Health Affairs* 23 (4): 124–32. https://doi.org/10.1377/hlthaff.23.4.124.

Toussaint, J. S., and L. L. Berry. 2013. "The Promise of Lean in Health Care." *Mayo Clinic Proceedings* 88 (1): 74–82. https://doi.org/10.1016/j.mayocp.2012.07.025.

Veenstra, G. L., K. Ahaus, G. A. Welker, E. Heineman, M. J. van der Laan, and F. L. H. Muntinghe. 2017. "Rethinking Clinical Governance: Healthcare Professionals' Views: A Delphi Study." *BMJ Open* 7 (1): e012591. https://doi.org/10.1136/bmjopen-2016-012591.

Wagner, S. L. 2017. *Fundamentals of Medical Practice Management.* Chicago: Health Administration Press.

Walker, T. 2012. "Ulysses Contracts in Medicine." *Law and Philosophy* 31 (1): 77–98. https://doi.org/10.1007/s10982-011-9116-z.

Waring, J. J., and S. Bishop. 2010. "Lean Healthcare: Rhetoric, Ritual and Resistance." *Social Science & Medicine* 71 (7): 1332–40. https://doi.org/10.1016/j.socscimed.2010.06.028.

Weick, K. E., and K. M. Sutcliffe. 2015. *Managing the Unexpected: Sustained Performance in a Complex World.* New York: John Wiley & Sons.

Weiner, B. J. 2009. "A Theory of Organizational Readiness for Change." *Implementation Science* 4 (1): 67–76. https://doi.org/10.1186/1748-5908-4-67.

Weiner, B. J., S. M. Shortell, and A. Alexander. 1997. "Promoting Clinical Involvement in Hospital Quality Improvement Efforts: The Effects of Top Management, Board, and Physician Leadership." *Health Services Research* 32 (4): 491–510. www.ncbi.nlm.nih.gov/pmc/articles/PMC1070207/pdf/hsresearch00036-0116.pdf.

White, K. R., and J. R. Griffith. 2019. *The Well-Managed Healthcare Organization,* 9th ed. Chicago: Health Administration Press.

World Health Organization (WHO). 2010. *Framework for Action on Interprofessional Education and Collaborative.* Accessed October 13, 2019. www.who.int/hrh/resources/framework_action/en/.

Zolkefli, Y. 2017. "Evaluating the Concept of Choice in Healthcare." *Malaysian Journal of Medical Sciences* 24 (6): 92–96. https://doi.org/10.21315/mjms2017.24.6.11.

10

THE IMPACT OF TECHNOLOGY ON US HEALTHCARE

> Healthcare is the only civil system where new technology makes prices go up instead of down.
>
> —Jaan Tallinn

Learning Objectives

- Analyze the relationship between healthcare costs and the constant development of new medical technologies.
- Gain familiarity with a variety of emerging medical technologies.
- Evaluate the impact of e-therapy, telemedicine, e-health, and telehealth on the US healthcare system.
- Recognize the pros and cons of electronic health records and electronic medical records.
- Understand how information technology and value-based care are interdependent.
- Apply key principles of cybersecurity to the workings of a healthcare organization.

Medical and Information Technology

This chapter will focus on the impact of technology on the US healthcare system (see exhibit 10.1). Deciding where to start a discussion of this topic is difficult, because we will be studying emerging technologies and their impact on healthcare in perpetuity! Technological advances and innovations occur at a rapid pace, almost beyond our system's ability to manage the change. Evolving technologies can help expand the capabilities of our healthcare system, improve quality, and increase access, although—as stated in Tallinn's quote at the start of the chapter—they can also be a major driver of costs.

Technology in healthcare largely falls into one of three categories: (1) medical technology, (2) information technology, and (3) data analytics and knowledge management. The additional area of pharmaceutical technology will be addressed in chapter 11.

The Aim of the Healthcare System

Issues That Require Our Attention

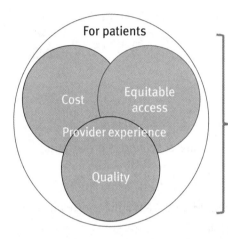

For patients

Cost

Equitable access

Provider experience

Quality

- Nature of our complex system
- Historical issues that have influenced the development of the system
- Beliefs and attitudes about health and healthcare
- Comparison with other developed countries
- Components of our healthcare system
- People and providers
- Patient care—the purpose of the system
- Financing a massive system
- Quality—easier said than done
- *Medical and information technology*
- The pharmaceutical industry
- Complementary and alternative medicine
- Politics/economics
- The future of the system

Medical technology involves the application of science and technical knowledge for the improvement of medical care and the health of society (Cohen et al. 2004). The phrase is often used to refer specifically to technologies involved in direct patient care. Examples may include the following:

- Telemedicine
- Implantable devices
- Robotically assisted surgical devices
- Genomics
- Precision medicine
- Diagnostics
- Radiology and imagining
- Laboratory services
- Tissue engineering/replacement and artificial organs

Medical technology has brought about tremendous improvement in our ability to diagnose and treat various conditions, yet it has also contributed to skyrocketing costs and an increased dependency on technology and the healthcare system for our well-being (Kamra, Singh, and De 2016; Kumar 2011).

The terms *information technology* (IT) and *health information technology* (HIT), for the purposes of this discussion, are interchangeable, though specific definitions may vary. The North Dakota Information Technology Department (2019) defines *information technology* broadly as "the use of hardware, software, services and supporting infrastructure to manage and deliver information using voice, data, and video." The definition further states that IT encompasses all of the following:

- All computers with a human interface
- All computer peripherals that will not operate unless connected to a computer or network
- All voice, video, and data networks and the equipment, staff, and purchased services needed to operate them
- All technology services provided by vendors or contractors
- All functions associated with developing, purchasing, licensing, or maintaining software

The definition of IT in healthcare can be further refined to refer to the electronic systems that healthcare professionals—and, increasingly, patients—use to store, share, and analyze health information.

Key concerns of HIT include the following (Office of the National Coordinator for Health Information Technology [ONC] 2018a):

- Electronic health records (EHRs), which help providers record, store, access, and share patient information digitally
- Personal health records (PHRs), which can be used to track information about the care a patient receives and various other health issues outside the formal care environment (e.g., eating behavior, exercise, blood pressure readings)
- Electronic prescribing (e-prescribing), which allows for direct, paperless communication with a pharmacy (minimizing risk of lost prescriptions or problems with legibility)
- Privacy and security (i.e., cybersecurity) initiatives to protect personal health information (PHI)—for example, by encryption that allows only authorized people to read it.

The category of data analytics and knowledge management includes technologies that support effective decision making in healthcare. Examples include the following:

- Analytical systems that draw vast amounts of data from diverse sources, sometimes known as "big data" (*NEJM Catalyst* 2018; Dinov et al. 2016)

- Evidence-based practice-support systems (Kathol, deGruy, and Rollman 2014)
- Medical decision-support systems incorporating artificial intelligence (Eckerson 2007; Schiff 2012)
- Other decision-making technologies (Alliance of Advanced BioMedical Engineering 2019; Feldman, Martin, and Skotnes 2012; Taylor 2017; Siegel 2013; Medical Futurist 2016; Zimmer 2011).

Medical Technologies in Constant Development

Our use of technology in healthcare is vast, and new developments continually emerge, bringing both opportunities and challenges (Ashrafian et al. 2017; Westgate 2017). Exhibit 10.2 provides just a small sampling of the important technologies we see in healthcare today. Many technologies are brand new or still in development, whereas others are well established. Echocardiogram (EKG) machines, for instance, have been around for

EXHIBIT 10.2

Healthcare Technology Examples

Imaging
Ultrasound devices
Positron emission tomography (PET scan)
Teleradiology
Nuclear imaging
Magnetic resonance imaging (MRI)
Intraoperative MRI

Diagnostic Testing
Monoclonal antibodies to detect pathogens and evidence of infection (e.g., HIV)
Genetic testing for gene mutations that cause disease (e.g., amyotrophic lateral sclerosis)
Advanced laboratory services to detect early-stage disease (e.g., Alzheimer's disease, Parkinson's disease)
Noninvasive testing of cognitive decline

Surgical Treatments and Technologies
Artificial joints (e.g., hips, knees, shoulders)
Implantable cardiac devices for monitoring heart function
Implantable cardiac devices for treatment (e.g., defibrillators, pacemakers, stents)
Minimally invasive surgical techniques such as those using a laparoscope (e.g., appendectomy, cholecystectomy, hysterectomy)
Reconstructive surgery using donor- or patient-derived tissues (e.g., coronary bypass, skin graft, corneal transplant)

more than 100 years; the Dutch physiologist Wilhelm Einthoven developed the machine in the late 1800s, eventually earning a Nobel Prize (Rubin 2017).

Numerous technologies have been refined and improved over the course of many years, to the point that procedures that once were largely unknown—hip replacements and back surgeries, for instance—are now commonplace (Anderson, Neary, and Pickstone 2007; Wolford, Palso, and Bercovitz 2015). Our future technologies continually evolve from the technologies that exist in the present, becoming much more advanced with the passage of time. Today, cameras small enough be swallowed have transformed traditional procedures such as colonoscopies.

Many of the wearable or implantable technologies in use today (e.g., smart watches) developed from the miniaturization of devices that were previously too large or too heavy for that kind of use (Kirby 2016; Medtech Plus 2019). Wearable monitoring technologies are a major area of development for healthcare, given their ability to collect continuous data and provide snapshots of a patient's health status at any given time. Modern material science, biomedical research, and bioengineering have made these devices a reality, and their uses, applications, and possibilities continue to be explored (Marakhimov and Joo 2017). Chapter 14 will examine the future implications of these and other technological advances in greater detail.

Telemedicine, E-health, and Telehealth

Telemedicine, e-health (sometimes written as *eHealth*), and telehealth represent exciting new areas of service delivery, with the potential to be among the biggest disruptors ever seen in healthcare. The terms are closely related—in that they all involve the delivery of health-related information and services electronically via the internet—yet they have subtle distinctions. *Telemedicine* refers to the electronic delivery of treatment to patients, as an alternative to face-to-face care. *E-health* and *telehealth*, on the other hand, are more general terms that can refer to a variety of health-related services, including patient education. An important component of e-health is mHealth, which pertains specifically to the use of mobile technologies (Otto et al. 2018).

Telemedicine and e-health activities may be either synchronous or asynchronous in nature. Synchronous activities are those that occur in real time—for instance, face-to-face videoconferencing. Asynchronous activities do not occur in real time but rather involve the storage and forwarding of information; use of an online educational module would be one such example (Ruiz, Mintzer, and Leipzig 2006; Verhoeven et al. 2010).

Overcoming Limitations of Geography

As noted in previous chapters, healthcare delivery, access, costs, and quality can vary widely from one location to another, and such discrepancies have long been a concern for people living in remote or underserved areas. If a patient lives 200 miles away from the nearest specialist, accessing needed services can be difficult. And when the travel is too demanding, the patient might choose to simply not keep regular appointments, which then becomes a compliance issue.

For many years, healthcare has been regarded as a "local matter," and in some respects it still is: If you are having a heart attack, you will need immediate service at the local emergency room. In many other situations, however, telemedicine and e-health offer solutions that can minimize the need for travel and provide access to important services regardless of geography; in many cases, they can reduce costs as well.

As patients gain access to providers beyond their local areas, options for acute, chronic, and preventive services multiply, and competition increases. With the speed and ubiquitous nature of the internet, patients today can see a doctor across the continent or even in another country if they prefer (Miyazaki et al. 2012; American Hospital Association 2017; Bipartisan Policy Center 2018; Knickman and Kovner 2015; Varghese and Phillips 2009). Some barriers still exist, such as regulation and licensing issues, but continued technological advances and regulatory changes are expected to further expand the availability of services in the years ahead (Weiss and Pollack 2017; Dinesen et al. 2016; Dinesen and Toft 2009). Forward-thinking scholars have written extensively about this reality for many years (Heinzelmann, Lugn, and Kvedar 2005; Huston and Huston 2000; LaMay 1997).

Implications for Mental and Behavioral Health

The expansion of services through digital modalities is having a major impact in the areas of mental and behavioral health. For many years, shortages of qualified professionals, maldistribution of services, and issues of patient compliance have hindered the effective treatment of people with mental and behavioral health needs (Lake and Turner 2017). As many as 25 percent of patients who visit a primary care office have diagnosable mental illnesses, yet the conditions have often gone untreated because of the limited availability of personnel and resources. With telemedicine, however, mental and behavioral health services can be provided remotely with little delay, embedded in primary care processes, and made more readily available to people in rural and underserved areas (Townley and Yalowich 2015; Mace, Boccanelli, and Dormond 2018).

Mace, Boccanelli, and Dormond (2018) conducted a study of 329 behavioral health provider organizations representing all 50 states, plus additional informants, and they found that 48 percent of respondents used telehealth for behavioral health services. Direct videoconferencing was the most commonly used modality, most frequently used by psychiatrists and mental health counselors. The study also identified several barriers to implementation, most notably reimbursement issues, cost of implementation, lack of organizational and political leadership, workforce shortages, the need for staff education and training, and reluctance on the part of clients. A number of legal and ethical issues still need to be resolved concerning telemedicine for mental and behavioral health, and a consensus on best practices for these areas remains to be developed (Kavalaris et al. 2015; Novotney 2011; Donkin et al. 2011; Lutterman et al. 2017).

Overcoming Barriers to Change

Resistance to change—from both patients and providers—can be a serious barrier to telemedicine initiatives and other innovations (Linkous 2012). People often have a tendency to resist change, whether out of fear, uncertainty, or the idea that "if it ain't broke, don't fix it" (Gorman 2015; Kumar and Khiljee 2016). Gilley, Godek, and Gilley (2009) describe such resistance within organizations as "organizational immunity to change."

Additional barriers and complications come into play when technologies cross multiple governmental jurisdictions. For instance, if videoconferencing is used across state lines, the psychiatrist might need to obtain a license in the state in which the services are received. Questions of liability and ethics may also arise. If somebody from India, for example, is delivering healthcare via the internet to a patient in the United States, who is liable when a problem occurs? The law is still developing in this area (American Medical Association [AMA] 2015; Parimbelli et al. 2018; Stanberry 2006).

Morris, Wooding, and Grant (2011) found that, on average, newly developed health interventions needed 17 years before they were fully accepted by healthcare providers. Everett Rogers (2003), who wrote extensively on the diffusion of innovation and the barriers to that diffusion, identified five groups based on the speed with which they adopt new technology:

- Innovators (representing about 2.5 percent of the population)
- Early adopters (13.5 percent of the population)
- Early majority (34 percent of the population)
- Late majority (34 percent of the population)
- Laggards (16 percent of the population)

This distribution roughly translates to a bell-shaped curve.

The AMA (2014) has developed a framework for telemedicine to help guide its development and implementation. Key elements include the following:

- Developing a solid evidence base
- Promoting the patient–physician relationship and care coordination
- Ensuring that physicians are able practice in the patient's state
- Identifying technical solutions and requirements
- Enabling appropriate reporting, payment, and coverage
- Providing education and tools for physicians

Information Management

The field of information management encompasses a large array of technological, managerial, and analytical processes. Organizations often produce a vast quantity of data yet have difficulty using it, because it is not in the form of usable information. It is sometimes said that "we are drowning in a sea of data, but starving for information." Information management seeks to address that concern.

Healthcare organizations collect information from a wide variety of sources, including the following:

- Medical records from all sources available
- Demographic information about the patient
- Treatment plans
- Identification of the patient within the last provider organization
- Details of the admitting/receiving clerk
- Insurance/health plan information
- Relevant appointments
- Diagnoses
- Allergies
- Medication lists
- Physician orders
- Anticipated goals (care plan), including rehabilitation plans
- Home health/hospice information
- Follow-up notes and plans
- Nursing details
- Self-care status
- Disabilities and impairments

- Nutrition details
- Therapist details
- Social service details
- Laboratory systems information
- Imaging systems, or picture archiving and communication (PAC) systems
- Human resource systems
- Accounting systems
- Financial management systems

Data collected from these sources are then organized, collated, and analyzed to produce usable information that can be applied in the healthcare setting or for administrative purposes. Organizations often use systems called data warehouses to manage this abundance of information. Data warehouses are not the same as databases. Whereas a database is "any collection of data organized for storage, accessibility, and retrieval," a data warehouse is a specific type of database that "integrates copies of transaction data from disparate source systems and provisions them for analytical use" (Cardon 2018).

Health informatics uses these stored data and goes beyond the emphasis on transactions to provide insights for healthcare improvement. Specific applications may address such areas as treatments for cancer, nursing care, images and diagnostics, consumer health, public health, or clinical research.

Electronic Health Records and Electronic Medical Records

The terms *electronic health record* (EHR) and *electronic medical record* (EMR) are often used interchangeably, but they are not the same. Technically, an EMR is simply an electronic version of the kind of paper chart traditionally used by a healthcare organization. It has the extra capabilities that digital technology provides—such as the ability to track data over time and screen records easily for the purposes of improving care—but it is still a single-facility system. The EHR, on the other hand, goes beyond the clinical record of a single facility and includes information from all the providers treating the patient—potentially including hospitals, nursing homes, and laboratories, as well as all physicians and clinical specialists.

The EHR provides a longitudinal record with a broad view of the patient's treatment and health status over time. When physicians lack complete information about a patient's hospitalizations or other provider visits, they are more likely to duplicate procedures, perform unnecessary tests, or recommend treatment that is suboptimal or inappropriate. Relying on patients to provide this information is not always effective: Patients are often poor historians about the course of their treatment, particularly when that treatment is complex and multifaceted. A true EHR system ensures that the necessary information is available to support better coordination of care, better measurement of quality, and reduced risk of medical error.

As organizations merge, are acquired, or band together through affiliation agreements, the interoperability of EHR systems—that is, the ability of the systems to talk to one another—is extremely important. Many electronic systems were built on proprietary technologies, making interoperability and the creation of longitudinal records difficult. In many cases, the only solution has been to replace the old legacy systems with more modern longitudinal EHRs (Chapple 2018).

Personal Health Records and Patient Portals

A personal health record (PHR) is "an electronic application through which patients can maintain and manage their health information (and that of others for whom they are authorized) in a private, secure, and confidential environment" (ONC 2016). The PHR contains similar information to the EHR and EMR, but it is intended to be used and managed by the patient or responsible party. It helps keep patients informed and engaged in the management of their care and health status.

PHRs are individually managed, and so their effectiveness may vary depending on how well they have been maintained. The public has become increasingly computer savvy, yet the skills, access, and attention to detail necessary to maintain a PHR are not universal. When a PHR has an incomplete accounting of services received by the patient, its benefit as a system for provider use is diminished. In some ways, the PHR has the same potential flaws as the EMR.

Discussion continues about how PHRs best fit into the healthcare environment, and more research is needed to fully understand how they might be used to benefit patients and providers (Irizarry, DeVito Dabbs, and Curran 2015; Kaelber et al. 2008; Kaelber and Pan 2008). A report by the Markle Foundation (2006) provides a wealth of information on this topic.

A patient portal is a secure website through which patients can conveniently access their personal health information at any time, using a user name and password. Patient portals differ from PHRs in that they are typically provided by providers of healthcare services. Patients can use patient portals to access such health information as the following (ONC 2019b):

- Recent doctor visits
- Discharge summaries
- Medications

- Immunizations
- Allergies
- Lab results

Some patient portals also allow patients to do the following:

- Securely message their doctor
- Request prescription refills
- Schedule nonurgent appointments
- Check benefits and coverage
- Update contact information
- Make payments
- Download and complete forms
- View educational materials

Patients generally have limited ability to add or change information in the portal records (Mayo Clinic 2017; Xtelligent Healthcare Media 2017).

Incentives for EHR Adoption

Even though early electronic records for healthcare existed more than 40 years ago, we still must do more to integrate these innovations into regular patient care (Shortliffe 2005). A number of US laws and policies have sought to encourage the adoption of EHRs. The American Recovery and Reinvestment Act of 2009 provided $27 billion in incentive payments to hospitals and physicians who adopted electronic record systems in line with certain criteria (Schilling 2018; Worzala 2009). One of the most important of these criteria involved demonstrating "meaningful use"—that is, use of the information system in a meaningful way to provide care and improve engagement. Key elements of meaningful use include the following:

- Patient access to the system
- Patient–provider messaging, educational resources, and information gathering (e.g., uploading data from home monitoring devices)
- Self-management tools and electronic reporting on the patient care experience

Meaningful use criteria were implemented in three stages between 2011 and 2016, as shown in exhibit 10.3. Stage 1 began with a focus on capturing and sharing data, stage 2 focused on advanced clinical processes, and stage 3 focused on improving outcomes. Stage 3 required the meaningful interaction of patients with providers using electronic means, and it

EXHIBIT 10.3
Stages of
Meaningful Use

Stage 1: Meaningful use criteria focus on data capture and sharing	Stage 2: Meaningful use criteria focus on advanced clinical processes	Stage 3: Meaningful use criteria focus on improved outcomes
Electronic capture of health information in a standardized format	More rigorous health information exchange (HIE)	Improvement in quality, safety, and efficiency, leading to better health outcomes
Use of that information to track key clinical conditions	Increased requirements for e-prescribing and incorporating lab results	Decision support for national high-priority conditions
Communication of that information for care coordination processes	Electronic transmission of patient care summaries across multiple settings	Patient access to self-management tools
Initiation of the reporting of clinical quality measures and public health information	More patient-controlled data	Access to comprehensive patient data through patient-centered HIE
Use of information to engage patients and their families in care		Improved population health
Time line: 2011–2012	Time line: 2014	Time line: 2016

Source: Adapted from ONC (2013).

encouraged a focus on improving population health. In 2017, the meaningful use criteria were incorporated into the new Merit-Based Incentive Payment System (ONC 2019a).

Confidentiality Concerns in EHR

Every healthcare professional should be well versed in the healthcare privacy protections under the Health Insurance Portability and Accountability Act (HIPAA) of 1996 (US Department of Health and Human Services [HHS] 2019b, 2017a, 2017b). HIPAA allows for the legal use of personal health information strictly for the purposes of healthcare delivery operations and reimbursement. Another party has no reason to access or review a person's medical records unless it is involved in the delivery of care or related operations (e.g., billing activity that requires specific information). Access should be on a need-to-know basis. The party does not have an unequivocal right to peruse the record and "read all about it." One should go to the record and get the information specifically needed—"no more, no less," as they say.

I recall, in the early years of HIPAA, leading student discussions about the need for the law. I would ask, "How many of you would want to have a sensitive medical procedure done or a sensitive medical condition treated at the healthcare organization where you work?" Most indicated that they would not, feeling that their privacy would undoubtedly be compromised.

Healthcare organizations must spend a great deal of energy and resources making sure their records are safeguarded, or else they could face severe penalties. The number of complaints related to HIPAA has increased as new technologies have enabled easier access to electronic records. HIPAA complaints are investigated by the US Department of Health and Human Services Office of Civil Rights (OCR). Near the end of 2019, the office reported: "Since the compliance date of the Privacy Rule in April 2003, OCR has received over 223,135 HIPAA complaints and has initiated over 987 compliance reviews. We have resolved ninety-nine percent of these cases (219,964)" (HHS 2019a).

Health Information Exchange

Longitudinal views provided by patient records are often incomplete because of a lack of integration of clinical content from the various providers the patient has seen. To address this issue, many healthcare systems are working to better integrate with affiliated practices and providing them with access to critical patient information.

Health information exchange (HIE) refers to the organization and sharing of electronic health-related information in a manner that protects the confidentiality, privacy, and security of the information. Organizations can participate in large HIE organizations or regional health information organizations (RHIOs) to gain better access to patient data as well as population health information. HIEs enable the sharing of health information among providers and, as appropriate, with individuals on a local, regional, and national basis (see exhibit 10.4). They support better integration of patient information while employing nationally recognized standards for interoperability and security (ONC 2017). The interplay of EHRs and HIEs is an important aspect of the infrastructure to create the Nationwide Health Information Network (NHIN), now called the eHealth Exchange (ONC 2018b; Sequoia Project 2019).

The Wisconsin Statewide Health Information Network (WISHIN) provides an example of how an HIE can be organized to work for the benefit of health organizations and their patients. The exchange connects more than 1,000 providers and enables the widespread, timely, and secure sharing of health information to support patients and caregivers throughout the state (WISHIN 2013).

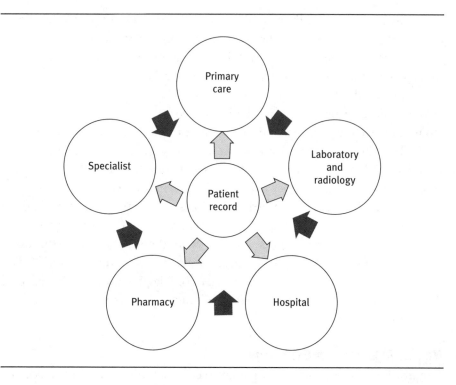

Information Technology and Value-Based Care

As the US healthcare system seeks to transition toward value-based care, a modern IT system is essential. The delivery of value-based care depends heavily on the availability of contemporaneous data on the care provided, the outcomes associated with that care, the patient base of the practice, and the costs of the practice's operations. It simply is not possible with manual systems, where data capture is difficult, costly, time consuming, and often inaccurate (Ebbevi et al. 2016; *NEJM Catalyst* 2017; Tinetti, Naik, and Dodson 2016; Veenstra et al. 2017).

Collection of Metrics for Population Health

For most of our nation's history, healthcare has focused on care for individual patients. Today, however, taking good care of individual patients is no longer sufficient; we must also focus on the health of the entire population being served. Population health management is a key element of what has been called the "second curve" of medicine (Health Research and Education Trust 2013), and it requires well-developed IT systems to support the collection of various data and metrics. If we cannot measure the population health outcomes we seek, we cannot measure the improvements our innovations create. To paraphrase Peter Drucker, if you can't measure it, you can't manage it (Prusak 2010).

Cloud Computing

Another IT topic that has become highly relevant to health practice managers is cloud computing, which enables users to access data, resources, and computing power through a network of remote servers, rather than having to maintain the hardware and software themselves. Cloud computing incorporates the concept of "software as a service" (SaaS), which allows for software to be accessed via the internet rather than installed locally. Essentially, cloud computing allows virtually every aspect of health IT service to be done "on the cloud."

Cloud computing can offer many potential advantages to a health practice, including the following (Carnevale et al. 2017; Taneja and Maney 2018):

- *Cost*. The cost of cloud computing can be significantly less than the cost of maintaining the software, hardware, and services within the practice. Cloud services often have the latest hardware and software available, which many small and medium-sized practices would be unable to afford.
- *Security*. The physical security and cybersecurity of IT systems are growing areas of concern for most practices. Moving the practice's IT functions to the cloud reduces the likelihood of a physical loss of IT assets and may reduce the probability of cyber threats.
- *24/7 services*. Most cloud computing services operate on a 24/7 basis.
- *Backup*. Reputable cloud service companies offer sophisticated backup services to prevent catastrophic IT failures.
- *Scalability*. Cloud services tend to be much more scalable than traditional IT systems—in other words, the systems can more easily be enlarged to accommodate more work.
- *Expertise*. Most small and medium-sized practices do not have the same level of IT expertise that is available from a cloud computing service.
- *Flexibility*. Although most cloud services require a service contract of a specified length, the commitment is likely less than the commitment the organization would make when buying the necessary equipment and software and hiring the appropriate expertise.

Of course, cloud computing may also present some disadvantages:

- *Reliance on the internet*. Cloud services depend on a working internet connection, and problems with that connection can cause IT systems to fail. Organizations must consider the reliability of their internet service provider as well as their routers when making the decision to use such services.

- *Lost data.* Providers are not perfect. Data may be lost if a company goes out of business or performs at a lower level of quality than expected.
- *Compatibility.* If an organization does not switch all of its IT services to the cloud-based service, the functions may encounter compatibility issues. Such issues will need to be addressed before moving forward to the cloud.
- *Stakeholder temperament.* Some people simply are not comfortable with the idea of their data and important business functions being handled remotely by a cloud service. Discussions with stakeholders throughout the practice should occur before moving forward.

Cybersecurity

The increasing connectedness and digitization of the healthcare world have contributed to new a type of risk, as security breaches and other computer-based crimes have become commonplace. Cyber criminals have discovered that healthcare facilities are rich sources of personal information that can be used for identity theft and even blackmail. Unfortunately, many health-care organizations are easy targets. According to a Bloomberg report, cyber attacks cost healthcare facilities more than $6 billion per year (Pettypiece 2015).

The *HIPAA Journal* (2018) states that the top 10 security breaches in 2017 exposed nearly 3 million patient records, through either hacking or other IT events (e.g., accidental or unintended release of records). In 2018, Atrium Health, headquartered in Charlotte, North Carolina, had a beach that potentially exposed 2.65 million patient records (Arndt 2018). The breach was carried out through an outside billing agent—highlight-ing the fact that patient information may be exposed not only by the organization itself but also by entities working on behalf of the healthcare organization.

Healthcare's cybersecurity problem is massive; however, no one really knows the true extent of the problem because organizations are often unaware of the events or are reluctant to report them when they occur (Lau-ritsen and Cork 2017). Cyber risk has become so widespread that organiza-tions can now buy insurance to pay damages in the event of a breach (PWC Netherlands 2019).

Common Cyber Risks

Common cyber risks include the following (Center for Internet Security 2019; Landi 2018):

- Phishing attacks typically involve emails that are disguised so that they appear to be from a trusted party. The messages usually ask the recipient to click on a link and enter personal information (e.g., name, passwords), thus enabling the sender to access accounts or systems.
- Trojans and malware are special programs designed by hackers. The programs enable the hacker to access information in systems on the affected computer and on the networks to which the computer is connected.
- Ransomware and advertising scams are also programs designed by hackers. If downloaded by a user, the programs cause the computer to be infected by various viruses. In the case of ransomware, data in the system become unavailable to the user unless a ransom is paid to the hacker, at which point a code is provided to unlock the data. Ransomware has become a real and growing threat.
- Password theft is simply the stealing of a password from a person who has access to the system.
- Third-party access can be a threat if vendors and other parties that deal with the organization and have access to its IT systems steal data directly or allow computers to become infected with malicious software.

What Is the Healthcare Organization's Responsibility?

Data breaches often occur despite the best efforts of the organization to prevent them. Nevertheless, one of the most important things an organization can do is to make sure that clear policies and procedures are in place for the use of all electronic communication devices. Policies should address such issues as the following (Center for Internet Security 2019; Harrison and Pagliery 2015; Landi 2018; Pettypiece 2015; Wagner 2017):

- Proper access of information
- Password security
- Appropriate management and surveillance of security policies
- Appropriate electronic safeguards in the form of firewalls, web and email encryption, and malware protection

The organization must also make sure that all staff members receive sufficient training on these policies and procedures.

Technology and Cost

Thanks to its commitment to the advancement of science, its entrepreneurial spirit, and its overall economic environment, the United States has become a powerhouse in the development of new medical technologies (Ferguson 2017; Medical Futurist 2016)—with both positive and negative effects (Berwick 2008). Technological advances have greatly expanded the capabilities of healthcare, bringing numerous benefits to patients; yet, at the same time, these advances have led to significantly higher costs (Cohen et al. 2004; Callahan and Baily 2008). At the risk of making light of the topic, one might say that "death is cheap." Prior to the development of our current technologies, providers were much more limited in what they could do to cure illnesses, alleviate suffering and disability, and extend life—and costs were lower as a result. Today, we have become much more dependent on the use of expensive, technologically advanced treatments (Kumar 2011). Furthermore, patients who have their medical conditions mitigated through technology often require expensive care for the rest of their lives. Many people would argue that technology is the single most significant factor in the dramatic increase of overall healthcare costs in the United States.

In most industries—electronics, for instance—technology leads to improvement in productivity, which reduces pressure on wages and ultimately reduces the cost of the product or service (Nordhaus 2006). Healthcare is different, however, in that technology often does not lead to improvement in productivity; rather, it typically leads to the accretion of more services to the overall continuum and armamentarium of healthcare. At the same time, healthcare must compete with other industries to attract the best and brightest talent, which puts an upward pressure on wages. The effect of having increased wages without a proportional increase in productivity is known as Baumol's Cost Disease, after the economist William Baumol (Baumol 2012; Bailey, Anttiroiko, and Valkama 2016; Maiello 2017). When providers take care of unique patient care needs in a one-on-one setting, their ability to increase productivity is limited. And when providers do attempt to improve productivity—for instance, by increasing the number of patients seen in a given period—the efforts have often led to dissatisfaction on the part of both patients and providers (Bodenheimer and Sinsky 2014). Some scholars do point out, however, that this relationship is far from conclusive and that increased productivity and satisfaction can exist together (Boffeli et al. 2012; Wood et al. 2009).

Organizations must commit significant resources to absorbing and managing the abundance of new technologies, processes, and knowledge that continue to emerge. PubMed (2019), a service of the US National Library of Medicine, currently has more than 30 million citations, and Jinha (2010) estimates that more than 50 million scholarly articles have been published since medical publishing began in 1665. What person can read them all? Of course, no one. Managing the influx of information, medical technologies, and drugs and devices will be a major challenge in the years ahead (Taneja and Maney 2018).

Innovation and Leadership

The effective management and application of technology in healthcare requires strong leadership, with an openness to new ideas and ways of thinking. Leaders must avoid being "held hostage" by their own insights and successes, and thus locked in their ways. As the saying goes, "the true definition of insanity is doing the same thing over and over again and expecting different results." Leaders also must not allow allegiance to their own group to create a "tribal" environment that hampers cooperation across organizational lines (Costich, Scutchfield, and Ingram 2015). Many of the challenges associated with technology will require the cooperation of multiple organizations and professional groups (Porter-O'Grady and Malloch 2017). A study by Paulus, Davis, and Steele (2008) of the Geisinger Health System found that "Clinician leadership at all levels, when paired with business partners and engaged clinical champions, supports progress in clinical transformation."

Often in healthcare, we seem to invent things faster than we can effectively use them. Looking ahead, we will need a new system architecture and a new paradigm of leadership, because the old paradigms are becoming obsolete. Tim Porter-O'Grady and colleagues have written extensively on the topic of "quantum leadership," which seems particularly well suited for our current environment (Porter-O'Grady and Malloch 2017, 2011). Quantum leadership is a process of "leading from the future," whereby a high-performing organization projects a mind-set that helps pull it toward a desired future state. On the surface, quantum leadership might seem like a "far-out" concept, but it really just involves placing creativity and innovation on a higher level. In contrast to traditional linear thinking, quantum leadership focuses its vision on the next generation of services and the next modes of operation.

A fundamental concept of quantum physics is the idea that everything is connected—an idea that is highly applicable to modern healthcare. Other fundamental concepts include having a moral purpose and acting to make a difference in the lives of people in the organization, as well as the community in general; relationship building; and making informed decisions by acquiring knowledge, listening, and empowering (Porter-O'Grady 1999). Thomas Kilmann (1989, 2009) espouses similar ideas about the quantum organization and its potential for resolving conflict and organizing for creativity and innovation. Judging from a review of the literature, quantum leadership appears to have been more readily accepted in nursing than in other disciplines (*American Nurse Today* 2013; Porter-O'Grady and Malloch 2011; Porter-O'Grady 1999; Watson et al. 2018).

Innovation can be risky, and adoption of innovations often moves slowly in a cautious, risk-averse field such as healthcare (Berwick 2003). Clayton Christensen (1997), in his book *The Innovator's Dilemma*, discusses two factors that often interfere with large organizations' ability to innovate and cause them to lose ground to competitors. First, because innovation often does not produce immediate value in the early stages, it may be less meaningful to large organizations that are primarily focused on current operational results. Second, large organizations tend to have high expectations for sales, whereas smaller organizations are often less concerned with immediate returns and more willing to innovate. Thus, smaller organizations are often better able to focus on niche markets and improve their products and services exponentially over time, eventually pushing into larger areas of the industry and ultimately displacing the technologies of the larger organizations. Christensen and Raynor (2003) stress the importance of having leaders committed to change and disruptive growth.

A key aspect of leadership is the development of followers. In today's digital age, the development of effective knowledge workers requires special emphasis on the following:

- Conceptual thinking versus functional analysis
- Multiple intelligences, including emotional intelligence
- Outcome-based practice, as opposed to process-focused activities
- Team performance, as opposed to individual performance
- Integration and a focus on the whole organization and its mission

These ideas, which are core elements of quantum leadership, suggest a substantial leap toward the creation of environments capable of dealing with rapid change, uncertainty, ethical demands, and interconnectedness.

The Technological Imperative

More than 50 years ago, the noted healthcare economist Victor Fuchs (1968) introduced the idea of the technological imperative. He wrote: "Medical tradition emphasizes giving the best care that is technically possible; the only legitimate and explicitly recognized constraint is the state of the art." Because of this imperative, physicians are "usually under considerable pressure to use the latest procedures and the most elaborate treatment."

The United States is foremost among the countries of the world in terms of medical innovation. Technology has been a wonderful asset for our healthcare system, and our society seems to have a constant desire for advanced medical technology at any cost. We should pause, however, to ask: To what extent does our push for innovation help us accomplish the goals of the healthcare system, and to what extent might it be counterproductive? How might we develop smarter ways to use this technology to achieve its fullest potential? The degree to which technology dominates our healthcare system can at times become a burden (Collier 2018; Rutten and Bonsel 1992); it may raise ethical concerns as well. Ultimately, healthcare is more than a technology. Technology cannot replace care and comparison, nor should it lessen our personal responsibility to care for patients (Barger-Lux and Heaney 1986; Hofmann 2002).

Advancement of health IT and continued integration of our IT systems will be essential in the years ahead (see exhibit 10.5). As we move along this path, we must ensure that our efforts are grounded in the fundamentals of who our IT systems should serve, for what purpose, and in what manner, to better serve our patients and our communities (see exhibit 10.6).

EXHIBIT 10.5
Continuum
of IT System
Integration

For whom?	Patients
	Providers
	Support staff
For what purpose?	Patient care
	Documentation
	Research
	Imaging
	Other ancillaries
	Communication
	Decision support
What characteristics?	Usable
	Specific
	Secure
	Smooth flowing
	Implementable
	Scalable

EXHIBIT 10.6
What IT
Systems
Should Do

Discussion Questions

1. What are the main categories of technology use in healthcare?
2. Are there limits to the value of technological advances?
3. In what ways does medical technology drive healthcare cost?
4. Do we overuse medical technology in the United States?

References

Alliance of Advanced BioMedical Engineering. 2019. "Monitoring." Accessed October 13. https://aabme.asme.org/categories/monitoring.

American Hospital Association (AHA). 2017. "Emerging Strategies to Ensure Access to Health Care Services." Published November 16. www.aha.org/system/files/2018-06/task-force-emergency-medical-center.pdf.

American Medical Association (AMA). 2015. "What Physicians Need to Know About Telemedical Liability." Published February 11. www.ama-assn.org/practice-management/sustainability/what-physicians-need-know-about-telemedical-liability.

———. 2014. "Physicians Take On Telemedicine to Bolster Care Delivery." Published July 3. www.ama-assn.org/practice-management/digital/physicians-take-telemedicine-bolster-care-delivery.

American Nurse Today. 2013. "Quantum Leadership: Upside Down." Published March 11. www.americannursetoday.com/quantum-leadership-upside-down/.

Anderson, J., F. Neary, and J. Pickstone. 2007. *Surgeons, Manufacturers, and Patients: A Transatlantic History of Total Hip Replacement.* New York: Palgrave Macmillan.

Arndt, R. 2018. "Atrium Health Data Breach Exposes up to 2.65 Million Patients' Data." *Modern Healthcare.* Published November 28. www.modernhealthcare.com/article/20181128/NEWS/181129940.

Ashrafian, H., O. Clancy, V. Grover, and A. Darzi. 2017. "The Evolution of Robotic Surgery: Surgical and Anaesthetic Aspects." *British Journal of Anaesthesia* 119 (Suppl. 1): i72–84. https://doi.org/10.1093/bja/aex383.

Bailey, S. J., A.-V. Anttiroiko, and P. Valkama. 2016. "Application of Baumol's Cost Disease to Public Sector Services: Conceptual, Theoretical and Empirical Falsities." *Public Management Review* 18 (1): 91–109. https://doi.org/10.1080/14719037.2014.958092.

Barger-Lux, M. J., and R. P. Heaney. 1986. "For Better and Worse: The Technological Imperative in Health Care." *Social Science & Medicine* 22 (12): 1313–20. https://doi.org/10.1016/0277-9536(86)90094-8.

Baumol, W. J. 2012. *The Cost Disease: Why Computers Get Cheaper and Health Care Doesn't.* New Haven, CT: Yale University Press.

Berwick, D. M. 2008. "Taming the Technology Beast." *JAMA* 299 (24): 2898–99. https://doi.org/10.1001/jama.299.24.2898.

———. 2003. "Disseminating Innovations in Health Care." *JAMA* 290 (15): 1969–75. https://doi.org/10.1001/jama.289.15.1969.

Bipartisan Policy Center. 2018. *Reinventing Rural Health Care: A Case Study of Seven Upper Midwest States.* Published January. https://bipartisanpolicy.org/wp-content/uploads/2018/01/BPC-Health-Reinventing-Rural-Health-Care-1.pdf.

Bodenheimer, T., and C. Sinsky. 2014. "From Triple to Quadruple Aim: Care of the Patient Requires Care of the Provider." *Annals of Family Medicine* 12 (6): 573–76. https://doi.org/10.1370/afm.1713.

Boffeli, T. J., K. L. Thongvanh, S. J. H. Evans, and C. R. Ahrens. 2012. "Patient Experience and Physician Productivity: Debunking the Mythical Divide at HealthPartners Clinics." *Permanente Journal* 16 (4): 19–25. https://doi.org/10.7812/tpp/12-049.

Callahan, D., and M. Baily. 2008. "Health Care Costs and Medical Technology." In *From Birth to Death and Bench to Clinic: The Hastings Center Bioethics Briefing Book for Journalists, Policymakers, and Campaigns,* edited by Mary Crowley, 79–82. Garrison, NY: Hastings Center. www.thehastingscenter.org/wp-content/uploads/Health-Care-Costs-BB17.pdf.

Cardon, D. 2018. *Database vs. Data Warehouse: A Comparative Review.* Health Catalyst. Accessed October 13, 2019. www.healthcatalyst.com/wp-content/uploads/2014/05/Database-vs-Data-Warehouse-A-Comparative-Review.pdf.

Carnevale, L., A. Celesti, M. Fazio, P. Bramanti, and M. Villari. 2017. "How to Enable Clinical Workflows to Integrate Big Healthcare Data." In *Proceedings of the 2017 IEEE Symposium on Computers and Communications.* Accessed October 13, 2019. https://doi.org/10.1109/ISCC.2017.8024634.

Center for Internet Security. 2019. "Cyber Attacks: In the Healthcare Sector." Accessed October 13. www.cisecurity.org/blog/cyber-attacks-in-the-healthcare-sector/.

Chapple, M. 2018. "What Is Your Hospital's Strategy for Sunsetting Legacy Systems?" *HealthTech.* Published August 2. https://healthtechmagazine.net/article/2018/08/what-your-hospitals-strategy-sunsetting-legacy-systems.

Christensen, C. M. 1997. *The Innovator's Dilemma: The Revolutionary Book That Will Change the Way You Do Business.* Boston: Harvard Business School Press.

Christensen, C. M., and M. E. Raynor. 2003. *The Innovator's Solution: Creating and Sustaining Successful Growth.* Boston: Harvard Business School Press.

Cohen, A. B, R. S. Hanft, W. E. Encinosa, S. M. Spernak, S. A. Stewart, and C. C White. 2004. *Technology in American Health Care.* Ann Arbor, MI: University of Michigan Press.

Collier, R. 2018. "Medical Technology Often a Burden If Designed Without Physician Input." *Canadian Medical Association Journal/Journal de l'Association Medicale Canadienne* 190 (36): E1091–92. https://doi.org/10.1503/cmaj.109-5656.

Costich, J. F., F. D. Scutchfield, and R. C. Ingram. 2015. "Population Health, Public Health, and Accountable Care: Emerging Roles and Relationships." *American Journal of Public Health* 105 (5): 846–50. https://doi.org/10.2105/AJPH.2014.302484.

Dinesen, B., B. Nonnecke, D. Lindeman, E. Toft, K. Kidholm, K. Jethwani, H. M. Young, H. Spindler, C. U. Oestergaard, J. A. Southard, M. Gutierrez, N. Anderson, N. M. Albert, J. J. Han, and T. Nesbitt. 2016. "Personalized Telehealth in the Future: A Global Research Agenda." *Journal of Medical Internet Research* 18 (3): e53. https://doi.org/10.2196/jmir.5257.

Dinesen, B., and E. Toft. 2009. "Telehomecare Challenge Collaboration Among Healthcare Professionals." *Wireless Personal Communications* 51 (4): 711–24. https://doi.org/10.1007/s11277-009-9767-3.

Dinov, I. D., B. Heavner, M. Tang, G. Glusman, K. Chard, M. Darcy, R. Madduri, J. Pa, C. Spino, C. Kesselman, I. Foster, E. W. Deutsch, N. D. Price, J. D. Van Horn, J. Ames, K. Clark, L. Hood, B. M. Hampstead, W. Dauer, and A. W. Toga. 2016. "Predictive Big Data Analytics: A Study of Parkinson's Disease Using Large, Complex, Heterogeneous, Incongruent, Multi-Source and Incomplete Observations." *PLOS ONE* 11 (8): e0157077. https://doi.org/10.1371/journal.pone.0157077.

Donkin, L., H. Christensen, S. L. Naismith, B. Neal, I. B. Hickie, and N. Glozier. 2011. "A Systematic Review of the Impact of Adherence on the Effectiveness of e-Therapies." *Journal of Medical Internet Research* 13 (3): e52. https://doi.org/10.2196/jmir.1772.

Ebbevi, D., H. H. Forsberg, A. Essén, and S. Ernestam. 2016. "Value-Based Health Care for Chronic Care." *Quality Management in Health Care* 25 (4): 203–12. https://doi.org/10.1097/QMH.0000000000000115.

Eckerson, W. 2007. "Extending the Value of Your Data Warehousing Investment." Data Warehouse Institute. Published May 10. http://tdwi.org/articles/2007/05/10/predictive-analytics.aspx?sc_lang=en.

Feldman, B., E. M. Martin, and T. Skotnes. 2012. "Big Data in Healthcare: Hype and Hope." Published October. www.scribd.com/document/107279699/Big-Data-in-Healthcare-Hype-and-Hope.

Ferguson, M. 2017. "Health Economics Outcomes: Research and Evidence Strategies." In *Managing Medical Devices Within a Regulatory Framework*, edited by B. A. Fiedler, 277–95. Waltham, MA: Elsevier. https://doi.org/10.1016/B978-0-12-804179-6.00016-2.

Fuchs, V. R. 1968. "The Growing Demand for Medical Care." *New England Journal of Medicine* 279 (4): 190–95. https://doi.org/10.1056/NEJM196807252790405.

Gilley, A., M. Godek, and J. W. Gilley. 2009. "Change, Resistance, and the Organizational Immune System." *SAM Advanced Management Journal* 74 (4): 4–10.

Gorman, D. 2015. "On the Barriers to Significant Innovation in and Reform of Healthcare." *Internal Medicine Journal* 45 (6): 597–99. https://doi.org/10.1111/imj.12775.

Harrison, V., and J. Pagliery. 2015. "Nearly 1 Million New Malware Threats Released Every Day." CNN. Published April 14. https://money.cnn.com/2015/04/14/technology/security/cyber-attack-hacks-security/index.html.

Health Research and Education Trust. 2013. *Metrics for the Second Curve of Health Care.* Published April. www.hpoe.org/Reports-HPOE/Metrics_Second_Curve_4_13.pdf.

Heinzelmann, P. J., N. E. Lugn, and J. C. Kvedar. 2005. "Telemedicine in the Future." *Journal of Telemedicine and Telecare* 11 (8): 384–90. https://doi.org/10.1177/1357633X0501100802.

HIPAA Journal. 2018. "Largest Healthcare Data Breaches of 2017." Published January 4. www.hipaajournal.com/largest-healthcare-data-breaches-2017/.

Hofmann, B. 2002. "Is There a Technological Imperative in Health Care?" *International Journal of Technology Assessment in Health Care* 18 (3): 675–89. https://doi.org/10.1017/S0266462302000491.

Huston, T. L., and J. L. Huston. 2000. "Is Telemedicine a Practical Reality?" *Communications of the ACM* 43 (6): 91–95. https://doi.org/10.1145/336460.336481.

Irizarry, T., A. DeVito Dabbs, and C. R. Curran. 2015. "Patient Portals and Patient Engagement: A State of the Science Review." *Journal of Medical Internet Research* 17 (6): e148. https://doi.org/10.2196/jmir.4255.

Jinha, A. E. 2010. "50 Million: An Estimate of the Number of Scholarly Articles in Existence." *Learned Publishing* 23 (3): 258–63. https://doi.org/10.1087/20100308.

Kaelber, D. C., A. K. Jha, D. Johnston, B. Middleton, and D. W. Bates. 2008. "A Research Agenda for Personal Health Records (PHRs)." *Journal of the American Medical Informatics Association* 15 (6): 729–36. https://doi.org/10.1197/jamia.M2547.

Kaelber, D., and E. C. Pan. 2008. "The Value of Personal Health Record (PHR) Systems." In *AMIA Annual Symposium Proceedings, 2008,* 343–47. www.ncbi.nlm.nih.gov/pubmed/18999276.

Kamra, V., H. Singh, and K. K. De. 2016. "Factors Affecting Patient Satisfaction: An Exploratory Study for Quality Management in the Health-Care Sector." *Total Quality Management & Business Excellence* 27 (9–10): 1013–27. https://doi.org/10.1080/14783363.2015.1057488.

Kathol, R. G., F. deGruy, and B. L. Rollman. 2014. "Value-Based Financially Sustainable Behavioral Health Components in Patient-Centered Medical Homes." *Annals of Family Medicine* 12 (2): 172–75. https://doi.org/10.1370/afm.1619.

Kavalaris, S., F.-E. Kioupakis, K. Kaltsas, and E. Serrelis. 2015. "ScienceDirect Development of a Multi-Vector Information Security Rating Scale for Smart Devices as a Means for Raising Public InfoSec Awareness." *Procedia Computer Science* 65: 500–509. https://doi.org/10.1016/j.procs.2015.09.122.

Kilmann, R. H. 2009. "A Completely Integrated Program for Creating and Maintaining Organizational Success." Killman Diagnostics. Accessed October 14, 2019. https://kilmanndiagnostics.com/a-completely-integrated-program-for-creating-and-maintaining-organizational-success/.

———. 1989. "A Completely Integrated Program for Creating and Maintaining Organizational Success." *Organizational Dynamics* 18 (1): 4–19. https://doi.org/10.1016/0090-2616(89)90028-4.

Kirby, C. 2016. "How Miniaturized Electronic Devices Can Be Used as Medical Therapeutics." Stanford Engineering. Published April 12. https://engineering.stanford.edu/magazine/article/how-miniaturized-electronic-devices-can-be-used-medical-therapeutics.

Knickman, J. R., and A. R. Kovner. 2015. "The Future of Health Care Delivery and Health Policy." In *Jonas and Kovner's Health Care Delivery in the United States*, 11th ed., edited by J. R. Knickman and A. R. Kovner, 333–42. New York: Springer.

Kumar, R. D. C., and N. Khiljee. 2016. "Leadership in Healthcare." *Anaesthesia and Intensive Care Medicine* 17 (1): 63–65. https://doi.org/10.1016/j.mpaic.2015.10.012.

Kumar, R. K. 2011. "Technology and Healthcare Costs." *Annals of Pediatric Cardiology* 4 (1): 84–86. https://doi.org/10.4103/0974-2069.79634.

Lake, J., and M. S. Turner. 2017. "Urgent Need for Improved Mental Health Care and a More Collaborative Model of Care." *Permanente Journal* 21: 17-024. https://doi.org/10.7812/TPP/17-024.

LaMay, C. L. 1997. "Telemedicine and Competitive Change in Health Care." *SPINE* 22 (1): 88–97.

Landi, H. 2018. "What Can the Industry Learn from Recent High-Profile Healthcare Cyber Attacks?" Healthcare Innovation. Published July 26. www.hcinnovationgroup.com/cybersecurity/article/13030570/what-can-the-industry-learn-from-recent-highprofile-healthcare-cyber-attacks.

Lauritsen, J. L., and D. L. Cork. 2017. "Expanding Our Understanding of Crime." *Criminology & Public Policy* 16 (4): 1075–98. https://doi.org/10.1111/1745-9133.12332.

Linkous, J. 2012. *The Role of Telehealth in an Evolving Health Care Environment.* Washington, DC: National Academies Press.

Lutterman, T., R. Shaw, W. Fisher, and R. Manderscheid. 2017. *Trend in Psychiatric Inpatient Capacity, United States and Each State, 1970 to 2014.* National Association of State Mental Health Program Directors. Assessment No. 2. Published August. www.nasmhpd.org/sites/default/files/TACPaper.2.Psychiatric-Inpatient-Capacity_508C.pdf.

Mace, S., A. Boccanelli, and M. Dormond. 2018. *The Use of Telehealth Within Behavioral Health Settings: Utilization, Opportunities, and Challenges.* University of Michigan, School of Public Health, Behavioral Health Workforce Research Center. Published March. www.behavioralhealthworkforce. org/wp-content/uploads/2018/05/Telehealth-Full-Paper_5.17.18-clean.pdf.

Maiello, M. 2017. "Diagnosing William Baumol's Cost Disease." *Chicago Booth Review.* Published May 18. http://review.chicagobooth.edu/ economics/2017/article/diagnosing-william-baumol-s-cost-disease.

Marakhimov, A., and J. Joo. 2017. "Consumer Adaptation and Infusion of Wearable Devices for Healthcare." *Computers in Human Behavior* 76: 135–48. https://doi.org/10.1016/j.chb.2017.07.016.

Markle Foundation. 2006. *Connecting Americans to Their Health Care: A Common Framework for Networked Personal Health Information.* Published December 7. http://library.ahima.org/PdfView?oid=74759.

Mayo Clinic. 2017. "Personal Health Records and Patient Portals." Published July 6. www.mayoclinic.org/healthy-lifestyle/consumer-health/in-depth/ personal-health-record/art-20047273.

Medical Futurist. 2016. "Top 20 Medical Technology Advances: Medicine in the Future—Part I." Published July 14. https://medicalfuturist.com/20-potential-technological-advances-in-the-future-of-medicine-part-i.

Medtech Plus. 2019. "Digitization and Miniaturization." Accessed October 14. www.medtech.plus/en/trend-topics/digitization-and-miniaturization.

Miyazaki, M., E. Igras, L. Liu, and T. Ohyanagi. 2012. "Global Health Through EHealth/Telehealth." In *eHealth and Remote Monitoring*, edited by A. H. El Hassani. https://doi.org/10.5772/47922.

Morris, Z. S., S. Wooding, and J. Grant. 2011. "The Answer Is 17 Years, What Is the Question: Understanding Time Lags in Translational Research." *Journal of the Royal Society of Medicine* 104 (12): 510–20. https://doi.org/10.1258/ jrsm.2011.110180.

NEJM Catalyst. 2018. "Healthcare Big Data and the Promise of Value-Based Care." Published January 1. https://catalyst.nejm.org/big-data-healthcare/.

———. 2017. "What Is Value-Based Healthcare?" Published January 1. https:// catalyst.nejm.org/what-is-value-based-healthcare/.

Nordhaus, W. D. 2006. *Baumol's Diseases: A Macroeconomic Perspective.* National Bureau of Economic Research. Working Paper 12218. Published May. www. nber.org/papers/w12218.

North Dakota Information Technology Department. 2019. "Definition of Information Technology." Accessed October 14. www.nd.gov/itd/about-us/ definition-information-technology.

Novotney, A. 2011. "A New Emphasis on Telehealth." *Journal of the American Psychological Association* 42 (6): 40. www.apa.org/monitor/2011/06/ telehealth.aspx.

Office of the National Coordinator for Health Information Technology (ONC). 2019a. "Meaningful Use." Reviewed October 22. www.healthit.gov/topic/meaningful-use-and-macra/meaningful-use.

———. 2019b. "What Is a Patient Portal?" Accessed December 18. www.healthit.gov/faq/what-patient-portal.

———. 2018a. *Health IT: Advancing America's Health Care.* Accessed October 14, 2019. www.healthit.gov/sites/default/files/pdf/health-information-technology-fact-sheet.pdf.

———. 2018b. *What Is the NHIN?* Accessed October 14, 2019. www.healthit.gov/sites/default/files/what-Is-the-nhin--2.pdf.

———. 2017. "Health Information Exchange." Reviewed October 12. www.healthit.gov/topic/health-it-basics/health-information-exchange.

———. 2016. "What Is a Personal Health Record?" Reviewed May 2. www.healthit.gov/faq/what-personal-health-record-0.

———. 2013. "What Is Meaningful Use?" Reviewed June 1. www.healthit.gov/faq/what-meaningful-use.

Otto, L., L. Harst, H. Schlieter, B. Wollschlaeger, P. Richter, and P. Timpel. 2018. "Towards a Unified Understanding of eHealth and Related Terms—Proposal of a Consolidated Terminological Basis." In *Proceedings of the 11th International Joint Conference on Biomedical Engineering Systems and Technologies*, vol. 5, 533–39. https://doi.org/10.5220/0006651005330539.

Parimbelli, E., B. Bottalico, E. Losiouk, M. Tomasi, A. Santosuosso, G. Lanzola, S. Quaglini, and R. Bellazzi. 2018. "Trusting Telemedicine: A Discussion on Risks, Safety, Legal Implications and Liability of Involved Stakeholders." *International Journal of Medical Informatics* 112: 90–98. https://doi.org/10.1016/j.ijmedinf.2018.01.012.

Paulus, R. A., K. Davis, and G. D. Steele. 2008. "Continuous Innovation in Health Care: Implications of the Geisinger Experience." *Health Affairs* 27 (5): 1235–45. https://doi.org/10.1377/hlthaff.27.5.1235.

Pettypiece, S. 2015. "Rising Cyber Attacks Costing Health System $6 Billion Annually." Bloomberg. Published May 7. www.bloomberg.com/news/articles/2015-05-07/rising-cyber-attacks-costing-health-system-6-billion-annually.

Porter-O'Grady, T. 1999. "Quantum Leadership: New Roles for a New Age." *Journal of Nursing Administration* 29 (10): 37–42. https://doi.org/10.1097/00005110-199910000-00008.

Porter-O'Grady, T., and K. Malloch. 2017. *Quantum Leadership: Creating Sustainable Value in Health Care*, 5th ed. New York: Jones & Bartlett.

———. 2011. *Quantum Leadership: Advancing Innovation, Transforming Health Care*, 3rd ed. New York: Jones & Bartlett.

Prusak, L. 2010. "What Can't Be Measured." *Harvard Business Review.* Published October 7. https://hbr.org/2010/10/what-cant-be-measured.

PubMed. 2019. "PubMed FAQs." Updated July 25. www.ncbi.nlm.nih.gov/books/
    NBK3827/#pubmedhelp.FAQs.

PWC Netherlands. 2019. "Cybercrime in Insurance." Accessed October 14. www.
    pwc.nl/en/industries/insurers/cybercrime-in-insurance.html.

Rogers, E. M. 2003. *Diffusion of Innovations*, 5th ed. New York: Free Press.

Rubin, A. 2017. "History of the EKG Machine." Jamaica Hospital Medical Center.
    Published August 24. https://jamaicahospital.org/newsletter/?p=4528.

Ruiz, J. G., M J. Mintzer, and R. M. Leipzig. 2006. "The Impact of E-Learning
    in Medical Education." *Academic Medicine* 81 (3): 207–12. https://doi.
    org/10.1097/00001888-200603000-00002.

Rutten, F. F., and G. J. Bonsel. 1992. "High Cost Technology in Health Care: A
    Benefit or a Burden?" *Social Science & Medicine* 35 (4): 567–77. https://doi.
    org/10.1016/0277-9536(92)90350-Y.

Schiff, M. 2012. "BI Experts: Why Predictive Analytics Will Continue to Grow."
    Data Warehouse Institute. Published March 6. http://tdwi.org/Articles/
    2012/03/06/Predictive-Analytics-Growth.aspx?Page=1.

Schilling, B. 2018. "The Federal Government Has Put Billions into Promoting
    Electronic Health Record Use: How Is It Going?" Commonwealth
    Fund. Accessed October 14, 2019. www.commonwealthfund.org/
    publications/newsletter-article/federal-government-has-put-billions-
    promoting-electronic-health.

Sequoia Project. 2019. "About the Sequoia Project." Accessed December 20.
    https://sequoiaproject.org/about-us/.

Shortliffe, E. H. 2005. "Strategic Action in Health Information Technology: Why
    the Obvious Has Taken So Long." *Health Affairs* 24 (5): 1222–33. https://
    doi.org/10.1377/hlthaff.24.5.1222.

Siegel, E. 2013. *Predictive Analytics: The Power to Predict Who Will Click, Buy, Lie,
    or Die*. Hoboken, NJ: John Wiley & Sons.

Stanberry, B. 2006. "Legal and Ethical Aspects of Telemedicine." *Journal of
    Telemedicine and Telecare* 12 (4): 166–75. https://doi.org/10.1258/
    135763306777488825.

Taneja, H., and K. Maney. 2018. "The End of Scale." *MIT Sloan Management Review*
    59 (3): 67–72. https://sloanreview.mit.edu/article/the-end-of-scale/.

Taylor, K. 2017. "12 Medical Technology Innovations Likely to Transform Health
    Care in 2017." Deloitte Center for Health Solutions. Published January
    17. http://blogs.deloitte.com/centerforhealthsolutions/12-medical-
    technology-innovations-likely-transform-health-care-2017/.

Tinetti, M. E., A. D. Naik, and J. A. Dodson. 2016. "Moving from Disease-Centered
    to Patient Goals–Directed Care for Patients with Multiple Chronic Conditions."
    JAMA Cardiology 1 (1): 9–10. https://doi.org/10.1001/jamacardio.2015.0248.

Townley, C., and R. Yalowich. 2015. *Improving Behavioral Health Access & Integra-
    tion Using Telehealth & Teleconsultation: A Health Care System for the 21st*

Century. National Academy for State Health Policy. Published November. https://nashp.org/wp-content/uploads/2015/11/Telemedicine1.pdf.

US Department of Health and Human Services (HHS). 2019a. "Enforcement Highlights." Reviewed December 10. www.hhs.gov/hipaa/for-professionals/compliance-enforcement/data/enforcement-highlights/index.html.

———. 2019b. "Health Information Privacy." Accessed October 14. www.hhs.gov/hipaa/index.html.

———. 2017a. "HIPAA Case Examples." Reviewed June 7. www.hhs.gov/hipaa/for-professionals/compliance-enforcement/examples/index.html.

———. 2017b. "HIPAA for Professionals." Reviewed June 16. www.hhs.gov/hipaa/for-professionals/index.html.

Varghese, S. B., and C. A. Phillips. 2009. "Caring in Telehealth." *Telemedicine and e-Health* 15 (10): 1005–9. https://doi.org/10.1089/tmj.2009.0070.

Veenstra, G. L., K. Ahaus, G. A. Welker, E. Heineman, M. J. van der Laan, and F. L. H. Muntinghe. 2017. "Rethinking Clinical Governance: Healthcare Professionals' Views: A Delphi Study." *BMJ Open* 7 (1): e012591. https://doi.org/10.1136/bmjopen-2016-012591.

Verhoeven, F., K. Tanja-Dijkstra, N. Nijland, G. Eysenbach, and L. van Gemert-Pijnen. 2010. "Asynchronous and Synchronous Teleconsultation for Diabetes Care: A Systematic Literature Review." *Journal of Diabetes Science and Technology* 4 (3): 666–84. https://doi.org/10.1177/193229681000400323.

Wagner, S. L. 2017. *Fundamentals of Medical Practice Management.* Chicago: Health Administration Press.

Watson, J., T. Porter-O'Grady, S. Horton-Deutsch, and K. Malloch. 2018. "Quantum Caring Leadership: Integrating Quantum Leadership with Caring Science." *Nursing Science Quarterly* 31 (3): 253–58. https://doi.org/10.1177/0894318418774893.

Weiss, B., and A. A. Pollack. 2017. "Barriers to Global Health Development: An International Quantitative Survey." *PLOS ONE* 12 (10): e0184846. https://doi.org/10.1371/journal.pone.0184846.

Westgate, A. 2017. "Top Five Most Disruptive Technologies on the Healthcare Horizon." *Managed Healthcare Executive.* Published September 11. www.managedhealthcareexecutive.com/business-strategy/top-five-most-disruptive-technologies-healthcare-horizon.

Wisconsin Statewide Health Information Network (WISHIN). 2013. "Who Is WISHIN?" Accessed October 14, 2019. www.wishin.org/AboutWISHIN.aspx.

Wolford, M. L., K. Palso, and A. Bercovitz. 2015. "Hospitalization for Total Hip Replacement Among Inpatients Aged 45 and Over: United States, 2000–2010." *NCHS Data Brief* 186: 1–8. www.ncbi.nlm.nih.gov/pubmed/26375255.

Wood, G. C., R. Spahr, J. Gerdes, Z. S. Daar, R. Hutchison, and W. F. Stewart. 2009. "Patient Satisfaction and Physician Productivity: Complementary or Mutually

Exclusive?" *American Journal of Medical Quality* 24 (6): 498–504. https://doi.org/10.1177/1062860609338869.

Worzala, C. 2009. "Policy Update: Federal Incentives for the Adoption of Electronic Health Records." *Journal of Oncology Practice* 5 (5): 262–63. https://doi.org/10.1200/JOP.091034.

Xtelligent Healthcare Media. 2017. "How Do Patient Portals and Personal Health Records Differ?" Published February 17. https://patientengagementhit.com/features/how-do-patient-portals-and-personal-health-records-differ.

Zimmer, B. 2011. "Is It Time to Welcome Our New Computer Overlords?" *Atlantic*. Published February 17. www.theatlantic.com/technology/archive/2011/02/is-it-time-to-welcome-our-new-computer-overlords/71388/.

11

THE PHARMACEUTICAL INDUSTRY IN THE UNITED STATES

We try to remember that medicine is for the patient. We try never to forget that medicine is for the people. It is not for the profits. The profits follow, and if we have remembered that, they have never failed to appear. The better we have remembered it, the larger they have been.
—George Merck

Pharmaceutical costs are the single fastest-growing part of our health care budget.
—John Kitzhaber

Learning Objectives

- Review the origins of the pharmaceutical industry.
- Understand the role of the Food and Drug Administration in the US healthcare system.
- Evaluate pharmaceutical cost and pricing and their impact on the healthcare system.
- Create an impact narrative regarding science and industry's influence on medicine.
- Understand the origins and importance of the opioid crisis and the lesson it provides for the healthcare system.
- Consider precision medicine and the future of drug development.

Few would doubt the impact that the pharmaceutical industry has had—and will continue to have—on healthcare in the United States. In this chapter, we will examine the important contributions that modern medicines have made to human health, the relationship of the pharmaceutical industry to the US healthcare system, and key issues and challenges that leaders in healthcare will need to address (see exhibit 11.1).

Pharmaceutical and biological science has had a tremendous influence on the practice of medicine and our approaches to the treatment of disease. Before the discovery and development of antibiotics such as penicillin, a simple infection could be life threatening (American Chemical Society 2019);

EXHIBIT 11.1
Area of Focus
for This Chapter

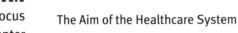

The Aim of the Healthcare System

Issues That Require Our Attention

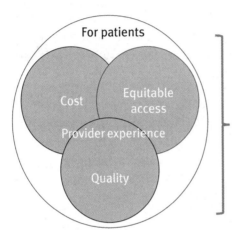

For patients

Cost

Equitable access

Provider experience

Quality

- Nature of our complex system
- Historical issues that have influenced the development of the system
- Beliefs and attitudes about health and healthcare
- Comparison with other developed countries
- Components of our healthcare system
- People and providers
- Patient care—the purpose of the system
- Financing a massive system
- Quality—easier said than done
- Medical and information technology
- *The pharmaceutical industry*
- Complementary and alternative medicine
- Politics/economics
- The future of the system

today, many such ailments are barely noticed. Not long ago, physicians would perform surgical interventions for common stomach ulcers; today, such ulcers can be prevented and treated with medications that reduce the formation of stomach acid. Some of these sophisticated medications can be purchased over the counter without a prescription.

The opening quote by George Merck reminds me of something a physician said to me many years ago, when I was a young administrator: "If we take care of the patients, they will take care of us." This proposition seems reasonable. The problem, however, is that the connections between patient care, the source of payment for services, and the suppliers of services have become increasingly distant and complex, particularly with regard to pharmaceuticals. When that statement was made to me years ago, it was hardly in the context of a multibillion dollar industry.

Origins and Growth of the US Pharmaceutical Industry

Historically, most agents that were used to treat illness were derived from natural sources—primarily plants—and practitioners who were skilled in the use of plant material for such purposes were highly valued in the community.

Today, natural products continue to be used to preserve health and treat certain medical conditions (Johnson 2018). However, the development of the pharmaceutical industry as we know it today stemmed largely from advances in the field of organic chemistry during the eighteenth century, which produced the knowledge and methods needed to synthesize and extract pharmaceutical agents.

The German chemist Friedrich Wilhelm Adam Sertürner was the first to create a drug using his knowledge of organic chemistry. Looking for a drug that could control pain and pleasure, he extracted and isolated morphine—named after Morpheus, the Roman god of sleep—between 1803 and 1817 (Krishnamurti and Rao 2016). This development opened the door for countless further discoveries and creations, up to the complex biological agents in use today. Some of the significant pharmaceuticals manufactured in the industry's early history included epinephrine, barbiturates, insulin, and penicillin and other antibiotics. Local apothecary shops that began in the mid-1800s would eventually develop into major pharmaceutical companies such as GlaxoSmithKline, Abbott Laboratories, Eli Lilly, and Pfizer (Pharmaphorum 2010).

The success of many of these companies has been driven by biomedical advances that have helped treat, or even cure, serious diseases. For instance, Gilead Sciences has developed drugs that cure hepatitis C and enable HIV/AIDS patients to live nearly normal lives—the kind of drugs that are often regarded as "game changers" (Doheney 2013). However, as these and other drugs have been developed, high prices have often diminished the ability of patients to access the drugs they need (Henry 2018). Issues related to pharmaceutical costs will be further discussed later in the chapter.

Today, according to the Pharmaceutical Research and Manufacturers of America (2016), the US biopharmaceutical industry directly employs 854,000 people and supports an additional 3.5 million jobs in related areas. According to the US Bureau of Labor Statistics (2017), pharmaceutical and medical manufacturing accounted for 287,550 US jobs in 2017. The world's ten largest pharmaceutical companies are shown in exhibit 11.2.

EXHIBIT 11.2
The Ten Largest Pharmaceutical Companies

Company	Annual Revenue
Pfizer	$53.7 billion
Roche	$45.6 billion
Johnson & Johnson	$40.7 billion
Sanofi	$39.3 billion
Merck & Co.	$37.7 billion

(continued)

EXHIBIT 11.2
The Ten Largest
Pharmaceutical
Companies
(continued)

Company	Annual Revenue
Novartis	$34.9 billion
AbbVie	$32.8 billion
Amgen	$23.7 billion
GlaxoSmithKline	$23 billion
Bristol-Myers Squibb	$22.6 billion

Source: Data from Ellis (2019); Vara (2019).

As the pharmaceutical industry has continued to grow and evolve, journalism and investigative reporting have helped shed light on what has often been described as a secretive industry (Grosse 2008; Hirschler 2018; Johnson 2016; Kacik and Bannow 2018; Kounang 2015; LaMattina 2016; Woodruff 2019).

The Food and Drug Administration

All pharmaceuticals and medical devices that are produced and sold in the United States must be approved by the US Food and Drug Administration (FDA). The FDA has its origins in the Agricultural Division of the Patent Office, which was established in 1848 (FDA 2018g). During the early 1900s, Harvey Washington Wiley, the chief chemist of the Bureau of Chemistry of the US Department of Agriculture, advocated vigorously for federal public health protection. Around the same time, the public became outraged by the cruel and unhygienic conditions in the Chicago stockyards, as described in Upton Sinclair's (1906) book *The Jungle.*

The Pure Food and Drug Act of 1906 represented the culmination of more than a quarter-century of efforts to address long-running abuses in the consumer product marketplace (US House of Representatives 2019). Passed in large part because of Wiley's efforts, the law established the federal consumer protection agency that would eventually become known as the FDA. The position of chief chemist of the Bureau of Chemistry evolved into the role of commissioner of the FDA.

The FDA's Mission

The FDA is responsible for "protecting the public health by ensuring the safety, efficacy, and security of human and veterinary drugs, biological products, and medical devices"; "ensuring the safety of the nation's food supply, cosmetics, and products that emit radiation"; and "regulating the manufacturing, marketing, and distribution of tobacco products" (FDA 2018f).

The agency also works to "speed innovations that make medical products more effective, safer, and more affordable" and to help Americans "get the accurate, science-based information they need to use medical products and foods to maintain and improve their health." The FDA also plays a role in counterterrorism efforts by "ensuring the security of the food supply and by fostering development of medical products to respond to deliberate and naturally emerging public health threats."

As we consider this mission in the context of the issues facing the pharmaceutical industry today, two details are worth pointing out: First, the mission does not mention the pricing of pharmaceuticals. Second, the mission does not require that new pharmaceutical products perform better than those already on the market; the drugs simply must be "safe and effective" (FDA 2019b).

The Drug Approval Process

The FDA's Center for Drug Evaluation and Research (CDER) is the federal "watchdog" group responsible for carefully evaluating new pharmaceuticals, both generic and brand name, before they can be sold in the United States (Berry and Martin 2008; Kashyap, Gupta, and Raghunandan 2013; FDA 2016a). This activity aims to prevent quackery and provides doctors as well as patients with important information about the safe and effective use of medications.

A drug's suitability for sale depends largely on CDER's determination that its health benefits outweigh its known risks. The drug approval process involves several steps, as illustrated in exhibit 11.3. First, during the preclinical research phase, the active molecules are synthesized and purified, and animal testing is conducted under the guidance of the institutional review board. The drug then enters three clinical study phases (FDA 2016b):

- Phase 1 studies the potential side effects and toxicity of the medication in healthy volunteers.
- Phase 2 helps determine the effectiveness and appropriate dosing for the medication.
- Phase 3 involves larger-scale studies of the safety and efficacy of the drug in the target population.

After these phases have been satisfactorily completed, a new drug application (NDA) is submitted to the FDA, and the FDA reviews the data and decides whether to grant approval.

A fourth phase of study involves postmarket surveillance of the medication to ensure that the drug is indeed safe and effective. Even large clinical

EXHIBIT 11.3
The Drug Approval Process

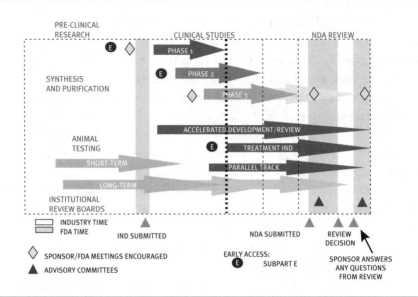

Note: IND = investigational new drug.
Source: Adapted from FDA (2016b).

trials may be unable to completely predict a drug's effects on a population; phase 4 can help identify rare potential side effects that might have gone undiscovered during phase 3 (Pocock, Clayton, and Stone 2015).

The FDA offers special classifications for accelerated review of medications that show significant promise in treating serious illnesses that have few if any alternative treatments. The accelerated process was included in the FDA Modernization Act of 1997, and further applications for fast tracking were allowed under the Food and Drug Administration Safety and Innovation Act (FDASIA) of 2012 (FDA 2012, 2014, 2018a). According to the FDA (2012), FDASIA strengthens the agency's ability to safeguard and advance public health in the following ways:

- Giving the authority to collect user fees from industry to fund reviews of innovator drugs, medical devices, generic drugs and biosimilar biological products;
- Promoting innovation to speed patient access to safe and effective products;
- Increasing stakeholder involvement in FDA processes; and
- Enhancing the safety of the drug supply chain.

The number of fast-track applications submitted to the FDA between 1998 and 2018 is shown in exhibit 11.4. Only 2 percent did not meet the goal for adjudication (FDA 2019c).

Fast-Track Requests Received (March 1, 1998, through September 30, 2018)							
Number Submitted	Goal	Within Goal					
		Granted	Denied	Pending	Total	%	
486	60 days	321	149	8	478	98	

Source: FDA (2019c).

EXHIBIT 11.4
Center for Drug Evaluation and Research "Fast-Track" Designation Request Performance Report

Over-the-Counter Drugs

The FDA is also responsible for approving over-the-counter (OTC) medicine, or medicine that can be purchased without a prescription. Nonprescription drugs are safe and effective when used in accordance with the instructions on the label and as directed by a healthcare professional (FDA 2018d). Common examples of OTC drugs include pain and fever medication; aspirin, acetaminophen, and ibuprofen; and antihistamines and decongestants for allergies. OTC drugs are sold by many companies under a variety of brand names. All must be standardized, labeled, and produced in safe and effective doses as required by the FDA.

Sometimes, proven prescription drugs (known by the abbreviation *Rx*) may be switched to nonprescription status (FDA 2018c). The primary benefit of such a switch is to increase consumers' access to the medication; often, the switch will also have the added benefit of reducing cost (Gertner and Horowitz 2018). Before an Rx-to-OTC switch can occur, the FDA conducts a careful analysis of the possible issues related to the change. For a medicine to be granted OTC status, it must be effective, have a wide safety margin, and have understandable labeling to ensure proper use. Consumers must be able to self-diagnose, self-select, and self-medicate.

According to the Consumer Health Care Products Association (2019), more than 100 OTC medicines on the market today were available only by prescription less than 40 years ago. Manufacturers usually see an Rx-to-OTC switch as a significant market opportunity, because OTC status often leads to an increase in sales (Jaap 2019). The FDA regards the switch as a potential way to reduce healthcare costs without compromising safety (Gertner and Horowitz 2018).

Orphan Drugs

"Orphan diseases" are conditions that affect only a relatively small number of patients—typically, fewer than 200,000 people in the United States, or no more than 6 to 8 percent of the world population (Sharma et al. 2010). The United States has an estimated 6,000 to 8,000 rare genetic diseases that collectively affect 30 million individuals (Shen et al. 2015). Some diseases are ultra-rare, potentially with only tens of cases. When a particular disease affects such a limited number of people, drug development is often regarded as impractical or too costly for the limited benefit it will produce. Nonetheless, pharmaceutical development focused on rare diseases has advanced rapidly as genetics and technology have improved.

The field of genetic disease, or Mendelian disease, has great promise for drug development because such diseases can in some cases be treated or cured by editing a single gene (Gupta and Musunuru 2014; Hsu, Lander, and Zhang 2014; Komor, Badran, and Liu 2017; Tran et al. 2016). Advances in genome editing, a form of genetic engineering, have made such treatments possible. The two main types of genome editing are germline therapy and somatic therapy. Germline therapies change DNA in reproductive cells (e.g., sperm, eggs), causing the modification to be passed down from one generation to the next. Somatic therapies, on the other hand, target nonreproductive cells, meaning that the changes made affect only the person who receives the gene therapy (National Human Genome Research Institute 2019).

A technology known as CRISPR (which stands for *clustered regularly interspaced short palindromic repeats*) has significantly improved our ability to edit DNA (Hsu, Lander, and Zhang 2014). An enzyme called Cas9 (also called CRISPR-associated protein 9) works like a pair of "molecular scissors" to cut strands of DNA for the purpose of changing or repairing aspects of the genetic code (US National Library of Medicine 2019). By cutting and replacing genes, the function of the DNA can be changed and, in some cases, disease-causing functions can be altered. The sophistication of these new gene therapies is remarkable, albeit expensive. One gene therapy with the possibility of curing hemophilia has an estimated price tag of over $1 million (Gold 2018; *PBS NewsHour* 2017).

Traditionally, pharmaceutical companies have tended to focus on what has been called the "long-tail"—the 20 percent of gene mutations that produce 80 percent of disease; this tendency, however, would leave the remaining 20 percent of genetic disease treatment largely unexplored (Crowe 2018b; Ekins 2017; Shen et al. 2015). To address this concern, special rules have been put in place—through the Orphan Drug Act of 1983 and other initiatives—to incentivize the development of rare-disease treatments that might otherwise bring limited financial benefits to pharmaceutical companies (FDA 2018b; Herder 2017).

The FDA's Office of Orphan Products Development (OOPD) supports potential sponsors of orphan products through the following programs (FDA 2011):

- The Orphan Drug Designation Program qualifies certain products for special financial incentives.

- The Orphan Products Grant Program provides funding for certain clinical investigations.
- The Pediatric Device Consortia Grant Program facilitates the development of pediatric medical devices.
- The Humanitarian Use Device Program motivates businesses to develop medical devices for rare diseases and conditions.

Sponsors of OOPD-designated orphan drugs can receive the following benefits:

- *Exclusivity.* The first sponsor to obtain FDA marketing approval for a designated rare disease or condition receives seven years of marketing exclusivity.
- *Tax credit.* A sponsor may claim half the costs of qualified clinical research as tax credits.
- *Waiver of fees.* The sponsor's fee (under the Prescription Drug User Fee Act) when the marketing application is submitted to the FDA is waived.

OOPD also administers grants to defray the costs of clinical research needed to investigate orphan products.

The FDA Safety and Innovation Act provided for an expedited review process for drugs believed to represent a potential "breakthrough" in the treatment of serious disease. It also gave the FDA authority to "collect user fees from the industry to fund reviews of innovator drugs, medical devices, generic drugs and biosimilar biological products" (FDA 2012).

Risk Evaluation and Mitigation Strategies

The FDA can use Risk Evaluation and Mitigation Strategies (REMS) to help protect consumers from adverse drug events. The FDA might require a manufacturer to carry out a REMS if a medication has particular risks that, on average, outweigh its benefits or if additional interventions beyond FDA-approved labeling are needed to minimize those risks. REMS are designed to reinforce actions that support the safe use of the medication. An example of a REMS might be a requirement that all patients receive special monitoring during the period in which a side effect is most likely to occur, so that the side effect can be detected and treated (FDA 2019d). The FDA website provides a list of medications that have currently active REMS.

Off-Label Use of Medicines

Approval of a drug by the FDA indicates that the scientific evidence has been evaluated and that the drug's benefits have been found to outweigh its risks. Once a drug has been approved, drug companies are largely prohibited from promoting the drug for uses other than those approved by the agency. The same restrictions, however, generally do not apply to physicians. The FDA allows physicians to prescribe many drugs "off label"—in other words, for indications that have not been approved by the agency.

The drug quetiapine, for instance, is commonly used to treat schizophrenia, but it is also used off-label to treat bipolar disorder. Similarly, lisinopril is used to treat hypertension, but it is frequently given off-label to treat coronary artery disease (Ipaktchin 2008). Other examples involve the use of cancer agents approved for one type of cancer to treat other cancerous conditions. Changes in dosage or mode of administration may be done off-label as well (FDA 2018e).

Much debate has centered on whether and how the FDA should regulate the pharmaceutical industry's communications to physicians about off-label uses (FDA 2018e). Efforts by pharmaceutical companies to encourage off-label use have sparked concern and criticism (Hey and Kesselheim 2016; Richardson 2016), though some courts have ruled that off-label promotion of drugs constitutes protected speech (Vivian 2013).

When physicians recommend off-label drug use, they may be entering a relatively unknown area of medicine (Richardson 2016). Difficult ethical issues may arise when a physician has to weigh the limited scientific support for an off-label use with the lack of other available treatment options. Furey and Wilkins (2016) suggest that a shared decision model be employed, making sure the patient has clear and complete information about the possible benefits and risks. This area of regulation and practice is far from settled; research and examination are ongoing (Avorn, Sarpatwari, and Kesselheim 2015; Wittich, Burkle, and Lanier 2012).

The Role of the Federal Trade Commission

Another government agency that plays an important role in regulating the pharmaceutical industry for the purpose of consumer protection is the Federal Trade Commission (FTC). The mission of the FTC (2019) is "protecting consumers and competition by preventing anticompetitive, deceptive, and unfair business practices through law enforcement, advocacy, and education without unduly burdening legitimate business activity." Two of the FTC's strategic goals bring the agency into direct involvement with the pharmaceutical industry (FTC 2019):

1. Protect consumers from unfair and deceptive practices in the marketplace
2. Maintain competition to promote a marketplace free from anticompetitive mergers, business practices, or public policy outcomes

A chief responsibility of the FTC is protecting against monopolistic behavior, which occurs when a company, group, or individual has exclusive control over a commercial activity. The FTC also guards against collusive agreements and behaviors between companies (Fox 2011; Friedman and Friedman 1982).

The FTC supports lower drug costs, yet it has taken a decidedly market-oriented approach to its regulatory role. In response to a US Department of Health and Human Services (HHS 2018a) proposal titled "Blueprint to Lower Drug Prices and Reduce Out-of-Pocket Costs," the FTC chairman Joe Simons stated (FTC 2018):

> The Federal Trade Commission is committed to maintaining competition in the pharmaceutical industry. The pharmaceutical industry provides American consumers with access to life-saving medicines and significantly affects our economy. Regulatory barriers and abuse of government processes that delay and constrain competition can lead to higher prices and reduce access to those medicines—all to the detriment of consumers. The FTC firmly believes that a vibrant, competitive marketplace offers the greatest benefits to consumers. The Commission's comments are directed toward that goal.

Pharmaceutical Industry Associations

The biopharmaceutical industry is represented by a number of important groups. Three of the most important are the Pharmaceutical Research and Manufacturers of America (PhRMA), the International Federation of Pharmaceutical Manufacturers and Associations (IFPMA), and the International Pharmaceutical Federation (FIP).

The Pharmaceutical Research and Manufacturers of America

PhRMA's (2019b) mission is "to conduct effective advocacy for public policies that encourage the discovery of important, new medicines for patients by biopharmaceutical research companies." The organization describes its advocacy as follows (PhRMA 2019a):

> PhRMA is committed to advocating for public policies that encourage the discovery and delivery of innovative treatments to patients. From access to medicines and programs like Medicare and Medicaid to intellectual property to drug safety, we work to ensure patient needs and preferences are central.

A potent political force, PhRMA works to achieve this aim in Washington, DC, and across the United States.

The International Federation of Pharmaceutical Manufacturers and Associations

IFPMA is an advocacy organization consisting of more than 140 pharmaceutical manufacturers and related associations throughout the world. The organization's website explains (IFPMA 2016):

> We facilitate collaboration, dialogue, and understanding within our industry and with other global players in the health community. . . . We bring the industry and broader health community together to foster innovation, promote resilient regulatory systems and high standards of quality, uphold ethical practices, and advocate sustainable health policies to meet global needs.

IFPMA offers a wealth of information about the pharmaceutical industry, as shown in exhibit 11.5.

EXHIBIT 11.5
Industry Information Compiled by the International Federation of Pharmaceutical Manufacturers and Associations

Research and Development (R&D)

- Developing a medicine or vaccine generally takes 10–15 years.
- The research-based pharmaceutical industry spent about $149.8 billion on R&D in 2015.
- In 2015, 56 new pharmaceuticals were launched, out of more than 7,000 compounds in development.
- From 2011 to 2015, the number of new chemical or biological entities launched on the world market was 226—a significant increase from 146 a decade earlier.
- In 2014, 5 of the 11 leading global R&D firms were pharmaceutical companies.

Contribution to Diseases That Disproportionately Affect the Developing World

- Drugs and vaccines against malaria are estimated to have saved 1.14 million African children's lives between 2011 and 2015.
- Between 2000 and 2014, immunization campaigns helped reduce the number of deaths from measles in Africa by 79 percent.
- In 2014, 401 drugs were in the pipeline for diabetes, and 208 were in development for HIV/AIDS.
- In 2014, the industry was the third-largest funder of neglected diseases research, investing more than $534 million.

(continued)

Contribution to a Healthy Society

- In 2014, the numbers of drugs in development for various diseases were as follows:
  - Cancer: 1,919
  - Cardiovascular diseases: 563
  - Neurology: 1,308
  - Infectious diseases: 1,261
- For every $1 spent on new medicines for hypertension in the United States, $10.11 in medical spending is saved.

The Pharmaceutical Market

- The global pharmaceutical market was expected to reach nearly $1,430 billion (in US dollars) by 2020.
- "Pharmerging" countries—that is, countries just beginning to use more modern pharmaceuticals—were expected to account for 25 percent of global spending on pharmaceuticals by 2020, compared to 23 percent in 2015.
- The US share of the global market was expected to increase from 40.3 percent in 2015 to 41 percent in 2020; Europe's share was expected to fall from 13.5 percent in 2015 to 13.1 percent in 2020.

Source: Adapted from IFPMA (2017).

EXHIBIT 11.5
Industry Information Compiled by the International Federation of Pharmaceutical Manufacturers and Associations *(continued)*

The International Pharmaceutical Federation

FIP is the global advocacy organization for pharmacy, pharmaceutical sciences, and pharmaceutical education (FIP 2019b). Representing more than 150 organizations and 4 million practitioners and scientists, its stated mission is "to support global health by enabling the advancement of pharmaceutical practice, sciences and education" (FIP 2019a).

Pharmaceutical Pricing and Cost

The pricing and cost of pharmaceuticals are among the most contentious and politically charged issues in all of US healthcare. Many emerging drugs offer new hope for previously untreatable diseases, yet they do so at a tremendous cost. The IQVIA Institute for Human Data Science (2018) projects that prescription drug prices will continue to grow by 2 to 5 percent through 2022, with the increase largely driven by the development of new medicines, especially in the orphan drug class.

The United States in Comparison with Other Countries

The United States spends less of its total healthcare spending on pharmaceuticals than many other countries do. In 2017, pharmaceutical spending in the United States accounted for 11.96 percent of the nation's total health spending, which is lower than the numbers for Germany (14.07 percent), Japan (18.57 percent), and Russia (28.99), among others (Organisation for Economic Co-operation and Development [OECD] 2019). Nonetheless, prescription drug costs per person in the United States are nearly double the level of other high-income countries (Bishop 2018).

Schumock and colleagues (2018) compiled the following data on pharmaceutical costs in the United States:

- Total prescription sales in the United States for 2017 were $455.9 billion, 1.7 percent higher than in 2016.
- Prescription expenditures in nonfederal hospitals totaled $34.2 billion in 2017, a 0.7 percent decrease from 2016; clinic expenditures, however, rose to $70.8 billion, an increase of 10.9 percent.

Americans pay the highest pharmaceutical costs in the world, and numerous examples exist of drugs in the United States that cost significantly more than identical medications sold in other countries (Giuliani, Selke, and Garattini 1998; Kaló et al. 2007; Mak 2018; Menon 2001; Miraldo 2009; Rémuzat et al. 2015; Shafrin 2014). Much has been written in the scholarly literature, as well as in the popular press, about these price discrepancies and the reasons behind them (Bishop 2018; Hirschler 2018; Papanicolas, Woskie, and Jha 2018). Unlike many countries, the United States does not regulate drug prices directly (von der Schulenburg, Vandoros, and Kanavos 2011). In the United States, prices for hospital and physician services and most other segments of the healthcare system are set by Medicare (through regulation) and by third-party payers (through negotiation). However, the Medicare Modernization Act of 2003 prohibited Medicare from negotiating prices with pharmaceutical manufacturers (Cubanski et al. 2018; Oliver, Lee, and Lipton 2004). This approach has begun to change somewhat, with HHS now allowing more negotiation on behalf of Medicare Part D by pharmacy benefit managers (PBMs) and Medicare Advantage plans being able to negotiate for physician-administered drugs the way private-sector insurers do (HHS 2018a, 2018b). Still, critics argue that these changes are not enough. Many people believe that Medicare needs to have greater flexibility to negotiate prices, much as health plans in other countries do (Oliver, Lee, and Lipton 2004).

Several other factors have been identified as contributors to high drug costs, including the following (Feldman 2016, 2018a, 2018b, 2019; Feldman et al. 2017; Frakt, Pizer, and Feldman 2012; Collier 2013):

- Monopoly power of manufacturers, including "evergreening" (i.e., a strategy whereby drug companies extend the patent on a drug by making small changes in the product)

- The profit motive of companies that produce or provide drugs or drug benefits
- Rebates that reward the use of a specific drug by patients covered by the services of a PBM or health insurer
- Direct-to-consumer marketing
- Generic drug price increases without new development

Furthermore, Young and colleagues have found that a relationship often exists between a country's GDP and what it pays for drugs (Young et al. 2017; Young, Soussi, and Toumi 2017).

Examples of alarming drug prices are commonplace. In one infamous case, Turing Pharmaceuticals purchased the rights to a drug used to treat parasitic infections, and it raised the price to $750 per dose—50 times the drug's previous price—even though it had done no additional research or innovation (LaMattina 2016). The price of lomustine, a drug used to treat brain tumors and Hodgkin's lymphoma, increased by 1,400 percent between 2013 and 2018, and the price of the antipsychotic drug fluphenazine increased by 1,900 percent in 2016 (Cohen et al. 2019). Drugs for treating serious illnesses such as hepatitis C or cancer frequently cost $10,000 or more per month.

Monopoly Power

Kesselheim, Avorn, and Sarpatwari (2016) attribute the high drug prices in the United States to the "government-protected monopolies" provided to drug companies through patents and FDA-granted exclusivity rights. If an essential drug is available from only one source, prices will increase. Stanbrook (2013) posits that limiting the practice of evergreening would help lower drug costs.

The Profit Motive

The way in which drug prices are determined is controversial and often lacks transparency. The initial pricing of a drug is set by the pharmaceutical company that develops and manufactures it, and the drug companies, of course, are in business to make a profit. Prices are also influenced by health insurance companies and pharmacy benefit managers, which work on behalf of insurance companies to negotiate with pharmaceutical companies for discounts on drug prices. Health insurance companies establish the medical policy and parameters, provide approval for treatments, and establish copays and deductibles, and the PBMs determine the structure of the prescription drug benefit and how much the patient will pay. For-profit drug and health benefit companies have a fiduciary obligation to benefit the organization and its shareholders, even though this motive may seem at odds with the humanitarian nature of healthcare (Sandel 1998).

Pharmaceutical companies often argue that the price of a drug is related to its cost of development, as well as the need to fund future research and development. Critics, however, contend that pricing is largely based on what the market will bear—in other words, companies will charge as much as possible. Companies will sometimes relate the pricing of a new drug to the cost of other treatment options, seeking to create a value proposition in which the new drug is less costly than the alternatives that had been used previously (Berndt and Newhouse 2012; Bishop 2018; Institute for Clinical and Economic Review 2019; Kesselheim, Avorn, and Sarpatwari 2016; *PBS News Hour* 2011).

Much of the debate over the cost of drugs revolves around the cost of development. The complexities of the science, compliance with regulations, and the expense of developmental work can pose challenges for drugs emerging from the pipeline (Morrison 2017). Grabowski, Vernon, and DiMasi (2002) found that only three in ten pharmaceuticals ever generate enough returns to equal their cost of development.

Rebates and the 340B Program

Drug manufacturers often use rebate agreements with PBMs or insurers to encourage the use of certain products. Such agreements are often kept secret, and they are often a source of controversy because their benefit to patients is unclear, if not unknown. The biggest criticism of rebates is that they can be used to incentivize the use of specific drugs that may or may not be in the best interest of the patient. Whether rebates do anything more than increase profits to the organization receiving the rebate is a matter of debate.

Feldman (2018b, 2019) has posited the idea that the rebate mechanism also allows manufacturers to raise the price of drugs and then provide a greater rebate to PBMs, thereby allowing the PBMs to claim more success in their negotiations with the manufacturers to their clients. Although this theory is difficult to prove, examples have been found where consumers can purchase a prescription drug at a pharmacy out-of-pocket for less than if they used an insurance plan administered by a PBM (Aitken et al. 2016; Dusetzina et al. 2017; Herper 2012).

The 340B Drug Pricing Program is a federal government program that entitles qualifying hospitals to receive discounts on outpatient drugs, thereby increasing the profitability of drug administration (Health Resources and Services Administration [HRSA] 2019). The 340B program is linked to the Disproportionate Share Hospital (DSH) designation, with a requirement for participating hospitals to have a DSH adjustment percentage greater than 11.75 percent. The HRSA (2018) writes:

> Disproportionate Share Hospitals serve a significantly disproportionate number of low-income patients and receive payments from the Centers

for Medicaid and Medicare Services to cover the costs of providing care to uninsured patients. Disproportionate share hospitals are defined in Section 1886(d)(1)(B) of the Social Security Act.

Because DSHs treat significantly more patients funded by federal tax dollars, the 340B program aims to help those entities "stretch scarce federal resources as far as possible, reaching more eligible patients and providing more comprehensive services" (HRSA 2019).

A study by Castellon and colleagues (2014) found that the 340B program did indeed decrease medication costs to the uninsured. Conti and Bach (2014) found that the program contributed to an expansion of hospital-affiliated outpatient clinics but that many of the expansions were focused on wealthier communities, thereby providing financial gains to the organizations but diverging from the program's stated purpose. Findings by Desai and McWilliams (2018) supported the conclusions of Conti and Bach:

> The 340B Program has been associated with hospital–physician consolidation in hematology–oncology and with more hospital-based administration of parenteral drugs in hematology–oncology and ophthalmology. Financial gains for hospitals have not been associated with clear evidence of expanded care or lower mortality among low-income patients.

Often, programs that are designed with the best intentions for a specific purpose change over time as organizations learn to use them creatively. Hence, any such incentive program needs to be carefully planned and implemented to ensure that it ultimately serves the need for which it was created and truly adds value to the delivery of care. The complexity of 340B and other pricing programs makes cost-effectiveness evaluation and the determination of high-value care difficult (Whittington, Campbell, and McQueen 2018).

Direct-to-Consumer Marketing

For many years, drug manufacturers primarily marketed their products directly to providers. In the 1980s, however, direct-to-consumer (DTC) advertising of drugs became legal in the United States, and the field has since grown dramatically (World Health Organization 2011). Today, it is nearly impossible to watch television or go on the internet without encountering DTC advertisements for pharmaceuticals. According to a report by *USA Today* and *Kaiser Health News*, DTC advertising by pharmaceutical manufacturers increased by 62 percent from 2012 until 2016, ultimately exceeding $6 billion (Horovitz and Appleby 2017). Obviously, manufacturers would not spend this kind of money if they did not receive a positive return on their investment (Tibble 2017).

The FDA regulates pharmaceutical advertising and seeks to ensure that the information contained in it is truthful, balanced, and accurately communicated. One of the FDA's specific concerns is the "lowballing," or intentional understating, of risk—which helps explain why drug ads typically contain copious amounts of information about potential side effects (FDA 2016a). In 2018, HHS proposed a requirement that television ads for prescription medication also include the drug's list price (Sullivan 2018).

DTC marketing of drugs has been a controversial health issue for many years (World Health Organization 2011). The United States and New Zealand are the only two countries that allow it, and physicians in New Zealand have begun calling for a ban (Bulik 2017). The American Medical Association (2019) published a medical ethics opinion on DTC marketing, with the following guidance for physicians:

- Physicians should remain objective about advertised drugs, services, and treatments, avoiding any bias for or against the advertised products.
- Physicians should engage in dialogue with patients who request advertised drugs or services.
- Physicians should resist commercially induced pressure to use drugs or services unnecessarily.
- Physicians should report instances in which DTC advertising promotes false expectations, fails to enhance consumer education, conveys unclear or misleading health claims, fails to refer patients to their physicians for additional information, does not identify the target population at risk, or encourages consumers to self-diagnose and treat themselves.

In 2004, the FDA conducted a survey of 500 physicians in an attempt to better understand the issue of DTC marketing. Key findings included the following (FDA 2015):

- Most physicians felt that DTC ads led patients to ask more questions during their visits and made them more aware of possible treatments.
- Many physicians thought that the ads made patients more involved in their healthcare.
- Physicians were concerned that the ads did not convey the risks as well as they convey the benefits. 78 percent of physicians believed that their patients understood the possible benefits of the drug well; only 40 percent believed that their patients understood the risks.

- Many physicians felt pressured to prescribe specific brand-name drugs when asked; at the same time, the questions engendered better discussions between patients and physicians about treatments.
- 80 percent of physicians believed that patients knew what condition a specific drug treated; 82 percent felt that patients understood that only a doctor could decide whether a drug is right for them.

DTC marketing can also make it more difficult for physicians to convince patients to use older treatments that are equally effective but less expensive. Such difficulty can lead not only to higher overall healthcare costs but also to a waste of time that could be better spent on other issues (Lazarus 2017; Patsner 2009; Ventola 2011).

Generic Drugs

Once brand-name drugs are no longer protected by patents and exclusivities, generic drugs—offering the exact same benefits—can be approved and sold. Generic drugs generally cost less than brand-name drugs, yet the prices of generics have begun to rise—in some cases, quite substantially (Edlin 2018; Court 2017). This trend appears to be a result of simple price increases imposed by manufacturers as well as the role of industry "middlemen" involved in negotiating prices and distributing drugs. The exact causes are difficult to pinpoint, and each of the parties involved tends to blame the other.

Greater competition among generic drug makers leads to lower prices; the more companies produce a drug, the less it will cost (Dave, Hartzema, and Kesselheim 2017; Kesselheim, Avorn, and Sarpatwari 2016). Cohen and colleagues (2019) have argued for FDA rule changes on generics and greater importation of generic drugs.

Biosimilars

A biosimilar is a drug that is highly similar to an existing FDA-approved product (FDA 2019a). Biosimilars are not generic drugs, because the molecules are slightly different, but they can have a similar effect on the body to produce a desired therapeutic response (Choy and Jacobs 2014; Zheng, Shih, and Chen 2017). A number of orphan drug subgroups that had previously targeted only a small number of people have become more widely practical because of the capability to make small modifications targeting different mutations within the same gene. The FDA requires biosimilar and interchangeable biological products to meet approval standards set by the agency.

Biosimilars can potentially serve a similar purpose in the marketplace to that of generic drugs in the past, and they offer hope for reducing the costs of expensive biological drugs. However, biosimilars will need to gain broader acceptance and better methods for reaching providers and the public. The Biologics Price Competition and Innovation Act of 2009 aimed to allow for faster approval of these medications (FDA 2016c).

Key issues that will affect the ability of biosimilars to become mainstream therapy include the following (Buske et al. 2017; Choy and Jacobs 2014; Patel 2017; van de Vooren, Curto, and Garattini 2015; Zelenetz et al. 2011; Zheng, Shih, and Chen 2017):

- Regulation will be a challenge, as the FDA approval process is rigorous, costly, and time consuming. In addition, most of these drugs are intended for worldwide distribution; thus, manufacturers will have to manage the varying approval processes from country to country.
- Biosimilars will need to be priced competitively to convince providers and payers to prefer them over currently available reference products; in most cases thus far, the drugs have not shown a significant decrease in cost.
- Confusion and lack of awareness remain a problem for this class of medications. All the various stakeholders involved in decision making will need to be educated.
- The nomenclature for complex biological molecules often leads to confusion for providers, payers, and patients; a clear methodology for naming the drugs is essential.
- Biosimilars often target small groups of patients; thus, recruiting suitable clinical trial sites and investigators can be a problem.
- Providers may be concerned about the interchangeability of the drug with the reference product, and safety concerns have not yet been fully resolved.

Actions to Mitigate Pharmaceutical Cost

Several ideas have been proposed to lower pharmaceutical costs—or at least slow the pace of increases—and to expand availability. The proposals generally fall into two categories:

1. Increase regulation, and allow for more importation of drugs from other countries, such as Canada.
2. Increase competition by removing certain incentives and enhancing regulatory restrictions on monopoly power.

The United States has primarily used market mechanisms, with a focus on ending rebates and increasing the use of negotiation (Cubanski et al. 2018; HHS 2018b; Woodruff 2019).

Many countries have systems for regulating drug prices and placing caps on price increases. Canada has a Patented Medicine Prices Review Board (PMPRB) that limits price increases on all patented medicines and requires greater transparency and disclosure of dealings between manufacturers and PBMs (Crowe 2018a; Government of Canada 2019; Lo 2018). The United Kingdom uses a strict cost-effectiveness analysis to determine what drugs it will use in its healthcare system and how much it will pay for those drugs (Ewbank et al. 2018; Lo 2018). The UK's cost-effectiveness analysis uses the quality-adjusted life year (QALY) as its metric for determining a drug's value. The QALY is a measure of a person or group's state of health in which the benefits, expressed in terms of length of life, are adjusted to reflect the quality of life (National Institute for Health and Care Excellence 2019). One QALY is equal to one year of life in perfect health. QALYs are calculated by estimating the years of life remaining for a patient following an intervention and weighting each year with a quality-of-life score (ranging from 0 to 1). The level of quality reflects such factors as the person's ability to carry out the activities of daily life, freedom from pain, and freedom from mental disturbance.

Some countries use reference pricing as a method to control costs. Reference pricing compares a drug with existing equivalent drugs on the market (i.e., the reference group) and then sets reimbursement based on the group of drugs considered to be interchangeable. Without reference pricing, drugs that treat hypertension, for instance, might belong to a common class (e.g., ace inhibitors) and function essentially the same way, yet have vastly different costs. Under a reference pricing schema, all the drugs in that class would be required to have a similar price, and new drugs that were not substantially different from or better than older drugs could not be introduced into the market at a much higher cost. Reference pricing can be used either within a country or between countries, and it has been proposed as a mechanism to reduce costs in the United States (Brown and Robinson 2016; Kaiser et al. 2014; Kanavos and Reinhardt 2003).

Another approach to cost containment involves the creation of a new company to provide products directly to its founders. In 2018, Intermountain Healthcare, along with Mayo Clinic and HCA (a for-profit hospital company), decided to form an independent company, called Civica Rx, to market 14 commonly used generic drugs that had been in short supply or faced rising prices (Kodjak 2018; Ramsey 2018). In another example, Intermountain Healthcare, Ascension, SSM Health, and Trinity Health, working with the US Department of Veterans Affairs, pooled their capital and expertise to form a not-for-profit generic drug company, creating a more reliable source of supplies and making the organizations less vulnerable to unexpected cost increases (Intermountain Healthcare 2018). These new organizations represent a significant innovation in the way health systems can organize and obtain supplies, adding an additional dimension to their horizontal integration (Kacik and Bannow 2018).

Undue Influence of Industry on Science and Medicine

One of the enduring concerns in US healthcare is the potential for conflicts of interest and undue influence by the pharmaceutical industry on healthcare providers and scientists (DeAngelis and Fontanarosa 2008; Hyder et al. 2007; Haque et al. 2013; Rhee 2012; Tungaraza and Poole 2007). Reports of such influence and potential lapses in judgment are commonplace.

One key area of concern surrounds the practice of providing meals and other *de minimis* benefits to physicians who listen to pharmaceutical industry representatives or attend industry events; even relatively modest benefits pose a risk of influencing physicians' prescribing behavior. DeJong and colleagues (2016) conducted a study of 279,669 physicians and found that 63,524 of them had received payments associated with four target drugs. Of those payments, 95 percent were meals, with a mean value of less than $20. The researchers found a positive association between receipt of the meals and rates of prescribing the targeted drugs. Many people believe that the opioid crisis—which is the subject of the next section—is in part a result of the pharmaceutical industry's powerful role in the research, marketing, and acceptance of medications (Manchikanti et al. 2009; Sanger-Katz 2018; Throckmorton, Gottlieb, and Woodcock 2018; Hadland et al. 2019).

The Opioid Crisis

We cannot possibly talk about the pharmaceutical industry today without addressing the opioid epidemic. Opioid addiction—reflected in both the inappropriate use of prescribed medications and the illegal use of heroin—has risen dramatically since the 1990s, and it now constitutes a severe biopsychosocial crisis throughout the United States and elsewhere (Berezow 2018; Scholl et al. 2018). Opioid overdose is now a leading cause of accidental death (Kolodny et al. 2015; Sanger-Katz 2018), and it has contributed to an overall decline in the average life expectancy of people in the United States (Saiidi 2019).

The current crisis is not the first time opioids have been recognized as a major health threat. More than 100 years ago, a dramatic rise in heroin use led to the passage of the Harrison Narcotic Control Act of 1914, which caused patients and physicians alike to become more wary of the opioid threat (Meldrum 2016; Terry 1915). However, as George Santayana (1905) wrote, "Those who cannot remember the past are condemned to repeat it."

When considering our present crisis and its origins, people frequently point to the overmarketing and overutilization of opioid medications and the lack of sufficient knowledge about the medications' addictive properties. However, such an assessment risks oversimplifying a complex medical and social problem with myriad causes (Jones, Viswanath, et al. 2018).

In 1995, the American Pain Society embarked on a campaign to recognize pain as the "fifth vital sign," seeking to raise awareness of under-treated pain and urging physicians to assess patients' pain regularly (Mandell 2016). That same year, the powerful opioid OxyContin was approved by the FDA (2019f). The Veterans Health Administration (VHA) supported the "fifth vital sign" campaign in 1999 (VHA 2000; Mularski et al. 2006). In 2000, The Joint Commission published standards for pain management that were in some ways consistent with the American Pain Society's position, although the commission denies ever having endorsed the idea of pain as a vital sign (Baker 2017; The Joint Commission 2018). These recommendations have since been revised (Baker 2017).

The new pain management standards of the late 1990s and early 2000s provided a new mandate for physicians to better control pain (Morone and Weiner 2013). Around the same time, regulators promised less scrutiny on opioid prescribers, to help alleviate physician concerns (Jones, Viswanath, et al. 2018; Joranson et al. 2002). Use of the Hospital Consumer Assessment of Healthcare Providers and Systems (HCAHPS) survey may have further contributed to the overprescribing of opioids by using "pain management" as a key indicator in the assessment of hospitals (Mahoney 2017); the survey has since been revised to remove this emphasis (HCAHPS 2019).

Many of the factors that contributed to the increased use of opioids were well-intended efforts to provide better care for patients; all is not so innocent, however. Pharmaceutical companies heavily promoted the use of opioids, and some evidence suggests that the dangers associated with the drugs were underestimated or deliberately concealed (Van Zee 2009). The state attorneys general of Nevada, Texas, Florida, North Carolina, North Dakota, and Tennessee said that OxyContin maker Purdue Pharma had "violated state consumer protection laws by falsely denying or downplaying the addiction risk while overstating the benefits of opioids" (Bellon 2018). From 1997 to 2002, the number of OxyContin prescriptions increased from 670,000 to more than 6 million (Hwang, Chang, and Alexander 2015).

Another potential contributor to the opioid crisis was a label change made by the FDA in 2001, shifting the approval from "short-term" use to "long-term" use for chronic pain (Whitaker 2019). The change made the drug much more widely available and prescribed. Former FDA commissioner David Kessler, who left the position prior to the labeling change, states that no studies had been done to demonstrate the safety or effectiveness of opioids for long-term use. In 2019, FDA commissioner Scott Gottlieb issued a statement in response to the deepening crisis, indicating that opioid manufacturers will be required to research and demonstrate the safety and effectiveness of these medications for long-term use (FDA 2019e).

The Centers for Disease Control and Prevention (CDC 2018) describes the progression of the opioid crisis in three waves (see exhibit 11.6).

- The first wave began with the increased prescribing of opioids during the 1990s.
- The second wave began in 2010, with rapid increases in overdose deaths involving heroin.
- The third wave began in 2013, with significant increases in overdose deaths involving synthetic opioids, such as fentanyl. These drugs are often mixed with other illicit drugs (e.g., cocaine).

The third wave, driven by synthetic drugs, has been the most deadly. In 2016, 46 percent of all opioid deaths were related to fentanyl or other synthetic opioids (see exhibit 11.7). Fentanyl is often mixed with other opioids, and people sometimes ingest the substance without knowing the quantity. The primary source of illegal fentanyl is importation from China (Cass 2017; Knierim 2018).

EXHIBIT 11.6
Three Waves of the Rise in Opioid Overdose Deaths

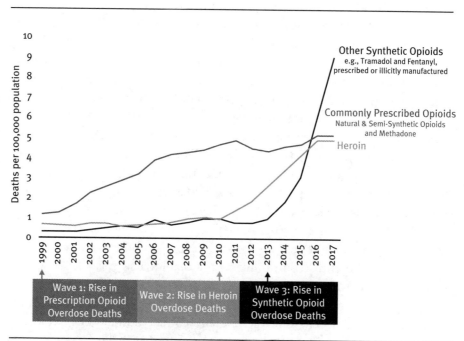

Source: Reprinted from CDC (2018).

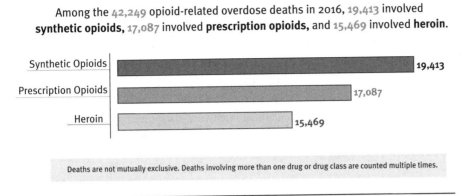

Among the 42,249 opioid-related overdose deaths in 2016, 19,413 involved **synthetic opioids,** 17,087 involved **prescription opioids,** and 15,469 involved **heroin.**

Synthetic Opioids	19,413
Prescription Opioids	17,087
Heroin	15,469

Deaths are not mutually exclusive. Deaths involving more than one drug or drug class are counted multiple times.

EXHIBIT 11.7
Synthetic Opioids and Overdose Deaths

Source: Reprinted from National Institute on Drug Abuse (2018); data from Jones, Einstein, and Compton (2018).

In 2018, the FDA approved a new drug, Dsuvia, over the objections and concerns of many in the addiction and medical communities (Krans 2018; Silverman 2018). The drug is reported to be ten times stronger than fentanyl and 1,000 times stronger than morphine. Officially, the drug will only be available in hospitals, but experts fear that it will be illegally manufactured in other countries and become available through illicit sources.

Addressing the opioid crisis in the United States will require a multifaceted approach, incorporating regulation of drug manufacturing and prescription practices, better treatment for addiction, controls on the illegal importation of drugs, and a prolonged education campaign for both physicians and the public (Volkow et al. 2018; Manchikanti et al. 2018).

The Future of Pharmaceuticals

Like so much in our healthcare system, the pharmaceutical industry is complex and rapidly changing. New technologies continue to emerge, enabling new therapies for diseases that were once thought to be untreatable. The field of precision medicine, in conjunction with our improved understanding of human genomics, offers the promise of specific, targeted treatments that take into account individual differences in people's genes, microbiomes, environments, and lifestyles (Holst 2015). Scientific innovations are also allowing for pharmaceuticals to be used and administered in novel ways. Many drugs that were once delivered only via injection or infusion are now available in oral forms or through inhalers.

The rapid pace of change will present challenges for regulation and approval. Many new drugs being developed today will be provided to patients in other countries, making international regulation a growing area of concern. Efforts are currently underway to establish a more uniform approach to regulation across countries, to minimize the repetitive and cumbersome nature of the process, to accelerate the availability of important treatment options internationally, and to take into account issues of language and culture.

In the years ahead, patients will benefit from new lifesaving and life-changing therapies, yet the costs of those therapies will be significant. The way we pay for pharmaceuticals will continue to be a source of controversy and debate among regulators, industry participants, patients, and other payers well into the future.

Discussion Questions

1. Describe the origins and development of the pharmaceutical industry in the United States.
2. What is the role of the Food and Drug Administration?
3. Why has the opioid crisis become so severe? What can it teach us about the US healthcare system?
4. How much does the United States annually spend on pharmaceuticals?
5. What are some of the reasons that drug prices are so high in the United States?
6. In what areas should future drug development focus?

References

Aitken, M., E. R. Berndt, D. Cutler, M. Kleinrock, and L. Maini. 2016. "Has the Era of Slow Growth for Prescription Drug Spending Ended?" *Health Affairs* 35 (9): 1595–1603. https://doi.org/10.1377/hlthaff.2015.1636.

American Chemical Society. 2019. "Discovery and Development of Penicillin." Accessed October 14. www.acs.org/content/acs/en/education/whatis chemistry/landmarks/flemingpenicillin.html.

American Medical Association (AMA). 2019. "Direct-to-Consumer Advertisement of Prescription Drugs." Accessed October 14. www.ama-assn.org/delivering-care/ethics/direct-consumer-advertisement-prescription-drugs.

American Pain Society. 1995. *Assessment of Pain*. Glenview, IL: American Pain Society.

Avorn, J., A. Sarpatwari, and A. S. Kesselheim. 2015. "Forbidden and Permitted Statements About Medications—Loosening the Rules." *New England Journal of Medicine* 373 (10): 967–73. https://doi.org/10.1056/NEJMhle1506365.

Baker, D. 2017. *The Joint Commission's Pain Standards: Origins and Evolution.* Published May 5. www.jointcommission.org/assets/1/6/Pain_Std_History_ Web_Version_05122017.pdf.

Bellon, T. 2018. "U.S. State Lawsuits Against Purdue Pharma over Opioid Epidemic Mount." Reuters. Published May 15. www.reuters.com/article/us-usa-opioids-litigation/u-s-state-lawsuits-against-purdue-pharma-over-opioid-epidemic-mount-idUSKCN1IG2WU.

Berezow, A. 2018. "A Brief History of the Opioid Epidemic." American Council on Science and Health. Published August 22. www.acsh.org/news/ 2018/08/22/brief-history-opioid-epidemic-13346.

Berndt, E. R., and J. P. Newhouse. 2012. "Pricing and Reimbursement in US Pharmaceutical Markets." In *The Oxford Handbook on the Economics of the Biopharmaceutical Industry*, edited by P. M. Danzon and S. Nicholson, 201–65. New York: Oxford University Press.

Berry, I., and R. Martin. 2008. *The Pharmaceutical Regulatory Process.* Boca Raton, FL: CRC Press.

Bishop, S. 2018. "Policy Prescriptions for High Drug Costs: Experts Weigh In." Commonwealth Fund. Published April 3. www.commonwealthfund.org/ publications/blog/2018/mar/policy-prescriptions-for-high-drug-costs.

Brown, T. T., and J. C. Robinson. 2016. "Reference Pricing with Endogenous or Exogenous Payment Limits: Impacts on Insurer and Consumer Spending." *Health Economics* 25 (6): 740–49. https://doi.org/10.1002/ hec.3181.

Bulik, B. 2017. "Doctors in New Zealand—the Only Non-U.S. Country That Allows DTC Advertising—Call for Bans." Fierce Pharma. Published March 20. www.fiercepharma.com/marketing/doctors-new-zealand-only-other-country-allows-dtc-advertising-hate-it-too.

Buske, C., M. Ogura, H.-C. Kwon, and S. W. Yoon. 2017. "An Introduction to Biosimilar Cancer Therapeutics: Definitions, Rationale for Development and Regulatory Requirements." *Future Oncology* 13 (15S): 5–16. https://doi. org/10.2217/fon-2017-0153.

Cass, A. 2017. "Where Does Fentanyl Come From? China Is Primary Source in U.S., and Much Is Ending Up in Ohio." *News-Herald* (Willoughby, OH). Published February 7. www.news-herald.com/news/ohio/where-does-fentanyl-come-from-china-is-primary-source-in/article_333c7750-17c3-57b2-bbc2-f8a57599081b.html.

Castellon, Y. M., S. Bazargan-Hejazi, M. Masatsugu, and R. Contreras. 2014. "The Impact of Patient Assistance Programs and the 340B Drug Pricing Program on Medication Cost." *American Journal of Managed Care* 20 (2): 146–50. www.ncbi.nlm.nih.gov/pubmed/24738532.

Centers for Disease Control and Prevention (CDC). 2018. "Opioid Overdose: Understanding the Epidemic." Reviewed December 19. www.cdc.gov/ drugoverdose/epidemic/index.html.

Choy, E., and I. A. Jacobs. 2014. "Biosimilar Safety Considerations in Clinical Practice." *Seminars in Oncology* 41 (Suppl. 1): S3–S14. https://doi.org/10.1053/J.SEMINONCOL.2013.12.001.

Cohen., R., T. Gupta, T. Bollyky, J. Ross, and A. Kesselhiem. 2019. "Policy Options for Increasing Generic Drug Competition Through Importation." *Health Affairs Blog.* Published January 7. www.healthaffairs.org/do/10.1377/hblog20190103.333047/full/.

Collier, R. 2013. "Drug Patents: The Evergreening Problem." *Canadian Medical Association Journal/Journal de l'Association Medicale Canadienne* 185 (9): E385-6. https://doi.org/10.1503/cmaj.109-4466.

Consumer Healthcare Products Association. 2019. "Rx-to-OTC Switch." Accessed October 14. www.chpa.org/switch.aspx.

Conti, R. M., and P. B. Bach. 2014. "The 340B Drug Discount Program: Hospitals Generate Profits by Expanding to Reach More Affluent Communities." *Health Affairs* 33 (10): 1786–92. https://doi.org/10.1377/hlthaff.2014.0540.

Court, E. 2017. "Why Did These Generic Drugs' Prices Jump as Much as 85%?" MarketWatch. Published June 29. www.marketwatch.com/story/on-the-very-day-of-a-senate-hearing-on-drug-costs-the-prices-of-these-common-generics-were-raised-as-much-as-85-2017-06-21.

Crowe, K. 2018a. "Canada Has Found the Key to Lowering Drug Prices, but It Won't Be Used Any Time Soon." CBC. Published November 24. www.cbc.ca/news/health/canada-drug-price-patented-medicine-pharmaceutical-industry-pmprb-1.4919200.

———. 2018b. "The Million-Dollar Drug." CBC. Published November 17. https://newsinteractives.cbc.ca/longform/glybera.

Cubanski, J., T. Neuman, S. True, and M. Freed. 2018. "Searching for Savings in Medicare Drug Price Negotiations." Kaiser Family Foundation. Published July. www.kff.org/medicare/issue-brief/searching-for-savings-in-medicare-drug-price-negotiations/.

Dave, C. V., A. Hartzema, and A. S. Kesselheim. 2017. "Prices of Generic Drugs Associated with Numbers of Manufacturers." *New England Journal of Medicine* 377 (26): 2597–98. https://doi.org/10.1056/NEJMc1711899.

DeAngelis, C. D., and P. B. Fontanarosa. 2008. "Impugning the Integrity of Medical Science: The Adverse Effects of Industry Influence. *JAMA* 299 (15): 1833–35. https://doi.org/10.1001/jama.299.15.1833.

DeJong, C., T. Aguilar, C.-W. Tseng, G. A. Lin, W. J. Boscardin, and R. A. Dudley. 2016. "Pharmaceutical Industry–Sponsored Meals and Physician Prescribing Patterns for Medicare Beneficiaries." *JAMA Internal Medicine* 176 (8): 1114–22. https://doi.org/10.1001/jamainternmed.2016.2765.

Desai, S., and J. M. McWilliams. 2018. "Consequences of the 340B Drug Pricing Program." *New England Journal of Medicine* 378 (6): 539–48. https://doi.org/10.1056/NEJMsa1706475.

Doheney, K. 2013. "New Oral Hepatitis C Drugs: FAQ." WebMD. Published December 9. www.webmd.com/hepatitis/news/20131126/new-hepatitis-c-drugs#1.

Dusetzina, S. B., R. M. Conti, N. L. Yu, and P. B. Bach. 2017. "Association of Prescription Drug Price Rebates in Medicare Part D with Patient Out-of-Pocket and Federal Spending." *JAMA Internal Medicine* 177 (8): 1185–88. https://doi.org/10.1001/jamainternmed.2017.1885.

Edlin, M. 2018. "How New Initiatives Could Affect Generic Drug Costs." *Managed Healthcare Executive*. Published July 4. www.managedhealthcareexecutive.com/biosimilars/how-new-initiatives-could-affect-generic-drug-costs.

Ekins, S. 2017. "Industrializing Rare Disease Therapy Discovery and Development." *Nature Biotechnology* 35 (2): 117–18. https://doi.org/10.1038/nbt.3787.

Ellis, M. 2019. "Who Are the Top 10 Pharmaceutical Companies in the World?" ProClinical. Published March 20. www.proclinical.com/blogs/2019-3/the-top-10-pharmaceutical-companies-in-the-world-2019.

Ewbank, L., D. Omojomolo, K. Sullivan, and H. McKenna. 2018. *The Rising Cost of Medicines to the NHS: What's the Story?* King's Fund. Published April. www.kingsfund.org.uk/sites/default/files/2018-04/Rising-cost-of-medicines.pdf.

Federal Trade Commission (FTC). 2019. "About the FTC." Accessed October 14. www.ftc.gov/about-ftc.

———. 2018. "FTC Submits Statement to HHS on Its Blueprint to Lower Drug Prices." Published July 17. www.ftc.gov/news-events/press-releases/2018/07/ftc-submits-statement-hhs-its-blueprint-lower-drug-prices.

Feldman, R. 2019. *Drugs, Money, and Secret Handshakes: The Unstoppable Growth of Prescription Drug Prices.* New York: Cambridge University Press.

———. 2018a. "May Your Drug Price Be Ever Green." *Journal of Law and the Biosciences* 5 (3): 590–647 https://doi.org/10.1093/jlb/lsy022.

———. 2018b. "Why Prescription Drug Prices Have Skyrocketed." *Washington Post*. Published November 26. www.washingtonpost.com/outlook/2018/11/26/why-prescription-drug-prices-have-skyrocketed/?utm_term=.514aec248cf7.

———. 2016. "Regulatory Property: The New IP." *Columbia Journal of Law & the Arts* 40 (1): 53–103.

Feldman, R., E. Frondorf, A. K. Cordova, and C. Wang. 2017. "Empirical Evidence of Drug Pricing Games: A Citizen's Pathway Gone Astray." *Stanford Technology Law Review* 20 (1): 39–91.

Fox, J. 2011. *The Myth of the Rational Market: A History of Risk, Reward, and Delusion on Wall Street*, reprint ed. New York: Harper Business.

Frakt, A. B., S. D. Pizer, and R. Feldman. 2012. "Should Medicare Adopt the Veterans Health Administration Formulary?" *Health Economics* 21 (5): 485–95. https://doi.org/10.1002/hec.1733.

Friedman, M., and R. D. Friedman. 1982. *Capitalism and Freedom*. Chicago: University of Chicago Press.

Furey, K., and K. Wilkins. 2016. "Prescribing 'Off-Label': What Should a Physician Disclose?" *AMA Journal of Ethics* 18 (6): 587–593. https://doi.org/10.1001/journalofethics.2016.18.6.ecas3-1606.

Gertner, H., and D. Horowitz. 2018. "FDA Proposes New Ways for Drugs to Become Available Over-the-Counter." Hogan Lovells. *Focus on Regulation*. Published July 19. www.hlregulation.com/2018/07/19/fda-proposes-new-ways-for-prescription-drugs-to-become-available-over-the-counter/.

Giuliani, G., G. Selke, and L. Garattini. 1998. "The German Experience in Reference Pricing." *Health Policy* 44 (1): 73–85. https://doi.org/10.1016/S0168-8510(98)00012-8.

Gold, J. 2018. "Hemophilia Factors Remain Costly Despite Choices." National Public Radio. Published March 5. www.npr.org/sections/health-shots/2018/03/05/589469361/miracle-of-hemophilia-drugs-comes-at-a-steep-price.

Government of Canada. 2019. "Patented Medicine Prices Review Board." Updated February 19. http://pmprb-cepmb.gc.ca/home.

Grabowski, H., J. Vernon, and J. A. DiMasi. 2002. "Returns on Research and Development for 1990s New Drug Introductions." *PharmacoEconomics* 20 (Suppl. 3): 11–29. https://doi.org/10.2165/00019053-200220003-00002.

Grosse, S. D. 2008. "Assessing Cost-Effectiveness in Healthcare: History of the $50,000 per QALY Threshold." *Expert Review of Pharmacoeconomics & Outcomes Research* 8 (2): 165–78. https://doi.org/10.1586/14737167.8.2.165.

Gupta, R. M., and K. Musunuru. 2014. "Expanding the Genetic Editing Tool Kit: ZFNs, TALENS, and CRISPR-Cas9." *Journal of Clinical Investigation* 124 (10): 4154–61. https://doi.org/10.1172/JCI72992.

Hadland, S. E., A. Rivera-Aguirre, B. D. L. Marshall, and M. Cerdá. 2019. "Association of Pharmaceutical Industry Marketing of Opioid Products with Mortality from Opioid-Related Overdoses." *JAMA Network Open* 2 (1): e186007. https://doi.org/10.1001/jamanetworkopen.2018.6007.

Haque, O. S., J. De Freitas, H. J. Bursztajn, L. Cosgrove, A. A. Gopal, R. Paul, I. Shuv-Ami, and S. Wolfman. 2013. *The Ethics of Pharmaceutical Industry Influence in Medicine*. UNESCO Chair in Bioethics. Published May. www.unesco-chair-bioethics.org/wp-content/uploads/2015/09/The-Ethics-of-Pharmaceutical-Industry-Influence-in-Medicine.pdf.

Health Resources and Services Administration (HRSA). 2019. "340B Drug Pricing Program." Reviewed December. www.hrsa.gov/opa/index.html.

———. 2018. "Disproportionate Share Hospitals." Reviewed May. www.hrsa.gov/opa/eligibility-and-registration/hospitals/disproportionate-share-hospitals/index.html.

Henry, B. 2018. "Drug Pricing; Challenges to Hepatitis C Treatment Access." *Journal of Health & Biomedical Law* 14: 265–83. www.ncbi.nlm.nih.gov/pubmed/30258323.

Herder, M. 2017. "What Is the Purpose of the Orphan Drug Act?" *PLOS Medicine* 14 (1): e1002191. https://doi.org/10.1371/journal.pmed.1002191.

Herper, M. 2012. "Inside the Secret World of Drug Company Rebates." *Forbes.* Published May 10. www.forbes.com/sites/matthewherper/2012/05/10/why-astrazeneca-gives-insurers-60-discounts-on-nexiums-list-price/#37e0d15b2b25.

Hey, S. P., and A. S. Kesselheim. 2016. "An Uninformative Truth: The Logic of Amarin's Off-Label Promotion." *PLOS Medicine* 13 (3): e1001978. https://doi.org/10.1371/journal.pmed.1001978.

Hirschler, B. 2018. "How the U.S. Pays 3 Times More for Drugs." *Scientific American.* Published October 13. www.scientificamerican.com/article/how-the-u-s-pays-3-times-more-for-drugs/.

Holst, L. 2015. "The Precision Medicine Initiative: Data-Driven Treatments as Unique as Your Own Body." *White House Blog.* Published January 30. https://obamawhitehouse.archives.gov/blog/2015/01/30/precision-medicine-initiative-data-driven-treatments-unique-your-own-body.

Horovitz, B., and J. Appleby. 2017. "Prescription Drug Costs Are Up; So Are TV Ads Promoting Them." *USA Today.* Published March 16. www.usatoday.com/story/money/2017/03/16/prescription-drug-costs-up-tv-ads/99203878/.

Hospital Consumer Assessment of Healthcare Providers and Systems (HCAHPS). 2019. "CAHPS Hospital Survey." Updated October 9. www.hcahpsonline.org.

Hsu, P. D., E. S. Lander, and F. Zhang. 2014. "Development and Applications of CRISPR-Cas9 for Genome Engineering." *Cell* 157 (6): 1262–78. https://doi.org/10.1016/j.cell.2014.05.010.

Hwang, C. S., H.-Y. Chang, and G. C. Alexander. 2015. "Impact of Abuse-Deterrent OxyContin on Prescription Opioid Utilization." *Pharmacoepidemiology and Drug Safety* 24 (2): 197–204. https://doi.org/10.1002/pds.3723.

Hyder, A. A., G. Bloom, M. Leach, S. B. Syed, D. H. Peters, and Future Health Systems: Innovations for Equity. 2007. "Exploring Health Systems Research and Its Influence on Policy Processes in Low Income Countries." *BMC Public Health* 7: 309. https://doi.org/10.1186/1471-2458-7-309.

Institute for Clinical and Economic Review (ICER). 2019. "About ICER." Accessed October 14. https://icer-review.org/about/.

Intermountain Healthcare. 2018. "Leading U.S. Health Systems Announce Plans to Develop a Not-for-Profit Generic Drug Company." Published January 18. https://intermountainhealthcare.org/news/2018/01/leading-us-health-systems-announce-plans-to-develop-a-not-for-profit-generic-drug-company/.

International Federation of Pharmaceutical Manufacturers and Associations (IFPMA). 2017. The *Pharmaceutical Industry and Global Health: Facts and Figures 2017.* Accessed October 14, 2019. www.ifpma.org/wp-content/uploads/2017/02/IFPMA-Facts-And-Figures-2017.pdf.

————. 2016. *Committed to a Healthier Future.* Published November. www.ifpma.org/wp-content/uploads/2016/01/IFPMA-Brochure.pdf.

International Pharmaceutical Federation (FIP). 2019a. "What We Do." Accessed December 26. www.fip.org/vision-mission.

————. 2019b. "Who We Are." Accessed October 14. https://fip.org/about.

Ipaktchin, S. 2008. "14 Drugs Identified as Most Urgently Needing Study for Off-Label Use, Stanford Professor Says." Stanford Medicine. Published November 24. https://med.stanford.edu/news/all-news/2008/11/14-drugs-identified-as-most-urgently-needing-study-for-off-label-use-stanford-professor-says.html.

IQVIA Institute for Human Data Science. 2018. *Medicine Use and Spending in the U.S.: A Review of 2017 and Outlook to 2022.* Published April 19. www.iqvia.com/insights/the-iqvia-institute/reports/medicine-use-and-spending-in-the-us-review-of-2017-outlook-to-2022.

Jaap, C. 2019. "Rx-to-OTC Switches Represent Huge Market Potential." Pharmaceutical Development Group. Accessed October 14. https://pharmdevgroup.com/rx-to-otc-switches-represent-huge-market-potential/.

Johnson, C. 2016. "Drug Companies Are Sharing Their Data—But Few Are Looking." *Washington Post.* Published March 29. www.washingtonpost.com/news/wonk/wp/2016/03/29/pharma-companies-are-sharing-their-data-but-few-are-looking/?utm_term=.cfd4c8c24080.

Johnson, V. 2018. *American Eden: David Hosack, Botany, and Medicine in the Garden of the Early Republic.* New York: Liveright.

The Joint Commission. 2018. "Common Myths About The Joint Commission Pain Standards." Accessed October 15, 2019. www.jointcommission.org/assets/1/18/Pain-Myths-poster11x17.pdf.

Jones, C. M., E. B. Einstein, and W. M. Compton. 2018. "Changes in Synthetic Opioid Involvement in Drug Overdose Deaths in the United States." *JAMA* 319 (17): 1819–21. https://doi.org/10.1001/jama.2018.2844.

Jones, M. R., O. Viswanath, J. Peck, A. D. Kaye, J. S. Gill, and T. T. Simopoulos. 2018. "A Brief History of the Opioid Epidemic and Strategies for Pain Medicine." *Pain and Therapy* 7 (1): 13–21. https://doi.org/10.1007/s40122-018-0097-6.

Joranson, D. E., A. M. Gilson, J. L. Dahl, and J. D. Haddox. 2002. "Pain Management, Controlled Substances, and State Medical Board Policy: A Decade of Change." *Journal of Pain and Symptom Management* 23 (2): 138–47. https://doi.org/10.1016/s0885-3924(01)00403-1.

Kacik, A., and T. Bannow. 2018. "Providers' Solution for High Drug Prices: Make Them Ourselves." *Modern Healthcare.* Published January 20. www.modernhealthcare.com/article/20180120/NEWS/180129989.

Kaiser, U., S. J. Mendez, T. Rønde, and H. Ullrich. 2014. "Regulation of Pharmaceutical Prices: Evidence from a Reference Price Reform in Denmark." *Journal of Health Economics* 36: 174–87. https://doi.org/10.1016/j.jhealeco.2014.04.003.

Kaló, Z., N. Muszbek, J. Bodrogi, and J. Bidló. 2007. "Does Therapeutic Reference Pricing Always Result in Cost-Containment?" *Health Policy* 80 (3): 402–12. https://doi.org/10.1016/j.healthpol.2006.04.002.

Kanavos, P., and U. Reinhardt. 2003. "Reference Pricing for Drugs: Is It Compatible with U.S. Health Care?" *Health Affairs* 22 (3): 16–30. https://doi.org/10.1377/hlthaff.22.3.16.

Kashyap, U. N., V. Gupta, and H. Raghunandan. 2013. "Comparison of Drug Approval Process in United States & Europe." *Journal of Pharmaceutical Sciences and Research* 5 (6): 131–36. http://citeseerx.ist.psu.edu/viewdoc/download?doi=10.1.1.375.519&rep=rep1&type=pdf.

Kesselheim, A. S., J. Avorn, and A. Sarpatwari. 2016. "The High Cost of Prescription Drugs in the United States." *JAMA* 316 (8): 858–71. https://doi.org/10.1001/jama.2016.11237.

Knierim, P. 2018. "Statement of Paul E. Knierim, Deputy Chief of Operations, Office of Global Enforcement Drug Enforcement Administration Before the Subcommittee on Africa, Global Health, Global Human Rights and International Organizations, Committee on Foreign Affairs U.S. House of Representatives for a Hearing Entitled 'Tackling Fentanyl: The China Connection.'" Presented September 6. www.dea.gov/sites/default/files/2018-09/DEA%20Testimony%20-%20China%20and%20Fentanyl%20HFAC_0.pdf.

Kodjak, A. 2018. "Civica Rx Formed by Hospitals to Make Drugs at Predictable Prices." National Public Radio. Published September 6. www.npr.org/sections/health-shots/2018/09/06/644935958/hospitals-prepare-to-launch-their-own-drug-company-to-fight-high-prices-and-shor?utm_source=npr_newsletter&utm_medium=email&utm_content=20180906&utm_campaign=npr_email_a_friend&utm_term=storys.

Kolodny, A., D. Courtwright, C. S. Hwang, P. Kreiner, J. L. Eadie, T. Clark, and G. Alexander. 2015. "The Prescription Opioid and Heroin Crisis: A Public Health Approach to an Epidemic of Addiction." *Annual Review of Public Health* 36: 559–74. https://doi.org/10.1146/annurev-publhealth-031914-122957.

Komor, A. C., A. H. Badran, and D. R. Liu. 2017. "CRISPR-Based Technologies for the Manipulation of Eukaryotic Genomes." *Cell* 169 (3): 559. https://doi.org/10.1016/j.cell.2017.04.005.

Kounang, N. 2015. "Pharmaceuticals Cheaper Abroad Because of Regulation." CNN. Published September 28. www.cnn.com/2015/09/28/health/us-pays-more-for-drugs/index.html.

Krans, B. 2018. "Super Opioid, FDA Approval and Addiction Concerns." *Healthline*. Published November 1. www.healthline.com/health-news/should-fda-approve-super-opioid-thats-stronger-than-fentanyl.

Krishnamurti, C., and S. C. Rao. 2016. "The Isolation of Morphine by Serturner." *Indian Journal of Anaesthesia* 60 (11): 861–62. https://doi.org/10.4103/0019-5049.193696.

LaMattina, J. 2016. "Life After Martin Shkreli: A Conversation with Turing Pharmaceuticals' R & D Head." *Forbes*. Published August 24. www.forbes.com/sites/johnlamattina/2016/08/24/life-after-martin-shkreli-a-conversation-with-turing-pharmaceuticals-rd-head/#6d80d72d5216.

Lazarus, D. 2017. "Direct-to-Consumer Drug Ads: A Bad Idea That's About to Get Worse." *Los Angeles Times*. Published February 15. www.latimes.com/business/la-fi-lazarus-drugadvertising-20170215-story.html.

Lo, C. 2018. "Cost Control: Drug Pricing Policies Around the World." *Pharmaceutical Technology*. Published February 12. www.pharmaceutical-technology.com/features/cost-control-drug-pricing-policies-around-world/.

Mahoney, D. 2017. "Revised HCAHPS Pain Management Questions: What You Need to Know." *Industry Edge*. Published May. www.pressganey.com/docs/default-source/industry-edge/issue-16---may/revised-hcahps-pain-management-questions__what-you-need-to-know.pdf?sfvrsn=2.

Mak, H. Y. 2018. "Managing Imperfect Competition by Pay for Performance and Reference Pricing." *Journal of Health Economics* 57: 131–46. https://doi.org/10.1016/j.jhealeco.2017.11.002.

Manchikanti, L., J. Sanapati, R. M. Benyamin, S. Atluri, A. D. Kaye, and J. A. Hirsch. 2018. "Reframing the Prevention Strategies of the Opioid Crisis: Focusing on Prescription Opioids, Fentanyl, and Heroin Epidemic." *Pain Physician* 21 (4): 309–26. www.ncbi.nlm.nih.gov/pubmed/30045589.

Manchikanti, L., V. Singh, S. Datta, S. P. Cohen, and J. A. Hirsch. 2009. "Comprehensive Review of Epidemiology, Scope, and Impact of Spinal Pain." *Pain Physician* 12 (4): E35–70. www.ncbi.nlm.nih.gov/pubmed/19668291.

Mandell, B. F. 2016. "The Fifth Vital Sign: A Complex Story of Politics and Patient Care." *Cleveland Clinic Journal of Medicine* 83 (6): 400–1. www.mdedge.com/ccjm/article/109138/drug-therapy/fifth-vital-sign-complex-story-politics-and-patient-care.

Meldrum, M. L. 2016. "The Ongoing Opioid Prescription Epidemic: Historical Context." *American Journal of Public Health* 106 (8): 1365–66. https://doi.org/10.2105/AJPH.2016.303297.

Menon, D. 2001. "Pharmaceutical Cost Control in Canada: Does It Work?" *Health Affairs* 20 (3): 92–103. https://doi.org/10.1377/hlthaff.20.3.92.

Miraldo, M. 2009. "Reference Pricing and Firms' Pricing Strategies." *Journal of Health Economics* 28 (1): 176–197. https://doi.org/10.1016/j.jhealeco.2008.09.006.

Morone, N. E., and D. K. Weiner. 2013. "Pain as the Fifth Vital Sign: Exposing the Vital Need for Pain Education." *Clinical Therapeutics* 35 (11): 1728–32. https://doi.org/10.1016/j.clinthera.2013.10.001.

Morrison, C. 2017. "Fresh from the Biotech Pipeline—2016." *Nature Biotechnology* 35: 108–12. https://doi.org/10.1038/nbt.3783.

Mularski, R. A., F. White-Chu, D. Overbay, L. Miller, S. M. Asch, and L. Ganzini. 2006. "Measuring Pain as the 5th Vital Sign Does Not Improve Quality of Pain Management." *Journal of General Internal Medicine* 21 (6): 607–12. https://doi.org/10.1111/j.1525-1497.2006.00415.x.

National Human Genome Research Institute (NHGRI). 2019. "What Is Genome Editing?" Updated August 15. www.genome.gov/27569222/genome-editing/.

National Institute for Health and Care Excellence (NICE). 2019. "Quality-Adjusted Life Year (QALYs)." Glossary. Accessed October 15. www.nice.org.uk/Glossary?letter=Q.

National Institute on Drug Abuse (NIDA). 2018. "Fentanyl and Other Synthetic Opioids Drug Overdose Deaths." Updated May. www.drugabuse.gov/related-topics/trends-statistics/infographics/fentanyl-other-synthetic-opioids-drug-overdose-deaths.

Oliver, T., T. Lee, and H. Lipton. 2004. "A Political History of Medicare and Prescription Drug Coverage." *Milbank Quarterly* 82 (2): 283–354. https://doi.org/10.1111/j.0887-378X.2004.00311.x.

Organisation for Economic Co-operation and Development (OECD). 2019. "Pharmaceutical Spending (Indicator)." Accessed October 15. https://doi.org/10.1787/998febf6-en.

Papanicolas, I., L. R. Woskie, and A. K. Jha. 2018. "Health Care Spending in the United States and Other High-Income Countries." *JAMA* 319 (10): 1024–39. https://doi.org/10.1001/jama.2018.1150.

Patel, K. 2017. "Biosimilars: Issues, Challenges, and Strategy for Success." Center for Biosimilars. Published September 12. www.centerforbiosimilars.com/contributor/kashyap-patel/2017/10/biosimilars-issues-challenges-and-strategy-for-success.

Patsner, B. 2009. "Problems Associated with Direct-to-Consumer Advertising (DTC) of Restricted, Implantable Medical Devices: Should the Current Regulatory Approaches Be Changed?" *Food and Drug Law Journal* 64 (1): 1–41. www.ncbi.nlm.nih.gov/pubmed/19998571.

PBS NewsHour. 2017. "We May Soon Have Our First $1 Million Drug. Who Will Pay for It? And How?" Published October 15. www.pbs.org/newshour/health/may-soon-first-1-million-drug-will-pay.

———. 2011. "Why Does Health Care Cost So Much in the United States?" Published November 25. www.pbs.org/newshour/health/why-does-healthcare-cost-so-much.

Pharmaceutical Research and Manufacturers of America (PhRMA). 2019a. "Advocacy." Accessed December 26. www.phrma.org/Advocacy.

———. 2019b. "Our Mission." Accessed October 15. www.phrma.org/en/About/Our-Mission. www.phrma.org/industryprofile/2018/.

———. 2016. *The Economic Impact of the U.S. Biopharmaceutical Industry.* Published May. http://phrma-docs.phrma.org/sites/default/files/pdf/biopharmaceuticaul-industry-economic-impact.pdf.

Pharmaphorum. 2010. "A History of the Pharmaceutical Industry." Published October 1. https://pharmaphorum.com/articles/a_history_of_the_pharmaceutical_industry/.

Pocock, S. J., T. C. Clayton, and G. W. Stone. 2015. "Challenging Issues in Clinical Trial Design: Part 4 of a 4-Part Series on Statistics for Clinical Trials." *Journal of the American College of Cardiology* 66 (25): 2886–98. https://doi.org/10.1016/j.jacc.2015.10.051.

Ramsey, L. 2018. "Civica Rx Generic Drug Company Started by Hospitals Picked Martin VanTrieste as CEO." *Business Insider.* Published January 8. www.businessinsider.com/civica-rx-generic-drug-company-started-by-hospitals-picked-martin-vantrieste-as-ceo-2018-9.

Rémuzat, C., D. Urbinati, O. Mzoughi, E. El Hammi, W. Belgaied, and M. Toumi. 2015. "Overview of External Reference Pricing Systems in Europe." *Journal of Market Access & Health Policy* 3 (1): 27675. https://doi.org/10.3402/jmahp.v3.27675.

Rhee, J. 2012. "The Influence of the Pharmaceutical Industry on Healthcare Practitioners' Prescribing." *Internet Journal of Academic Physician Assistants* 7 (1): 6–9. https://doi.org/10.5580/1c4f.

Richardson, E. 2016. "Off-Label Drug Promotion." *Health Affairs* and Robert Wood Johnson Foundation. Health Policy Brief. Published June 30. https://doi.org/10.1377/hpb20160630.920075.

Saiidi, U. 2019. "US Life Expectancy Has Been Declining. Here's Why." Published July 9. www.cnbc.com/2019/07/09/us-life-expectancy-has-been-declining-heres-why.html.

Sandel, M. J. 1998. "What Money Can't Buy: The Moral Limits of Markets." In *Tanner Lectures on Human Values.* Delivered May 11–12, Oxford University. https://doi.org/10.1007/s10677-012-9385-0.

Sanger-Katz, M. 2018. "Bleak New Estimates in Drug Epidemic: A Record 72,000 Overdose Deaths in 2017." *New York Times.* Published August 15. www.nytimes.com/2018/08/15/upshot/opioids-overdose-deaths-rising-fentanyl.html.

Santayana, G. 1905. *The Life of Reason.* Project Gutenberg. Accessed December 31, 2019. www.gutenberg.org/files/15000/15000-h/15000-h.htm.

Scholl, L., P. Seth, M. Kariisa, N. Wilson, and G. Baldwin. 2018. "Drug and Opioid-Involved Overdose Deaths—United States, 2013–2017." *MMWR Weekly Report* 67 (5152): 1419–27. https://doi.org/10.15585/mmwr.mm6751521e1.

Schumock, G. T., J. Stubbings, M. D. Wiest, E. C. Li, K. J. Suda, L. M. Matusiak, R. J. Hunkler, and L. C. Vermeulen. 2018. "National Trends in Prescription Drug Expenditures and Projections for 2018." *American Journal of*

Health-System Pharmacy 75 (14): 1023–38. https://doi.org/10.2146/ajhp180138.

Shafrin, J. 2014. "What Is Reference Pricing?" *Healthcare Economist.* Published July 28. www.healthcare-economist.com/2014/07/28/what-is-reference-pricing/.

Sharma, A., A. Jacob, M. Tandon, and D. Kumar. 2010. "Orphan Drug: Development Trends and Strategies." *Journal of Pharmacy & Bioallied Sciences* 2 (4): 290–99. https://doi.org/10.4103/0975-7406.72128.

Shen, T., A. Lee, C. Shen, and C. Lin. 2015. "The Long Tail and Rare Disease Research: The Impact of Next-Generation Sequencing for Rare Mendelian Disorders." *Genetics Research* 97: e15. https://doi.org/10.1017/S0016672315000166.

Silverman, E. 2018. "Despite Criticism, FDA Approves an Opioid 10 Times More Powerful than Fentanyl." STAT. Published November 2. www.statnews.com/pharmalot/2018/11/02/fda-dsuvia-fentanyl-approval/.

Sinclair, U. 1906. *The Jungle.* New York: Grosset & Dunlap.

Stanbrook, M. B. 2013. "Limiting Evergreening for a Better Balance of Drug Innovation Incentives." *Canadian Medical Association Journal/Journal de l'Association Medicale Canadienne* 185 (11): 939. https://doi.org/10.1503/cmaj.130992.

Sullivan, T. 2018. "HHS Proposes New DTC Advertising Requirement." Policy & Medicine. Published October 18. www.policymed.com/2018/10/hhs-proposes-new-dtc-advertising-requirement.html.

Terry, C. E. 1915. "The Harrison Anti-Narcotics Act." *American Journal of Public Health* 5 (6): 518. www.ncbi.nlm.nih.gov/pmc/articles/PMC1286619/.

Throckmorton, D. C., S. Gottlieb, and J. Woodcock. 2018. "The FDA and the Next Wave of Drug Abuse—Proactive Pharmacovigilance." *New England Journal of Medicine* 379 (3): 205–7. https://doi.org/10.1056/NEJMp1806486.

Tibble, S. 2017. "Experts Tell Congress How to Cut Drug Prices. We Give You Some Odds." *Kaiser Health News.* Published September 12. https://khn.org/news/experts-tell-congress-how-to-cut-drug-prices/view/republish/.

Tran, E., P. F. Robbins, Y.-C. Lu, T. D. Prickett, J. J. Gartner, L. Jia, A. Pasetto, Z. Zheng, S. Ray, E. M. Groh, I. R. Kriley, and S. A. Rosenberg. 2016. "T-Cell Transfer Therapy Targeting Mutant KRAS in Cancer." *New England Journal of Medicine* 375 (23): 2255–62. https://doi.org/10.1056/NEJMoa1609279.

Tungaraza, T., and R. Poole. 2007. "Influence of Drug Company Authorship and Sponsorship on Drug Trial Outcomes." *British Journal of Psychiatry* 191 (1): 82–83. https://doi.org/10.1192/bjp.bp.106.024547.

US Bureau of Labor Statistics. 2017. "May 2017 OES Industry-Specific Occupational Employment and Wage Estimates: Pharmaceutical and Medicine Manufacturing." Accessed October 14, 2019. www.bls.gov/oes/2017/may/naics4_325400.htm.

US Department of Health and Human Services (HHS). 2018a. "HHS Blueprint to Lower Drug Prices and Reduce Out-of-Pocket Costs." *Federal Register* 83 (95): 22692–700. www.federalregister.gov/ documents/2018/05/16/2018-10435/hhs-blueprint-to-lower-drug-prices-and-reduce-out-of-pocket-costs.

———. 2018b. "Trump Administration Gives Medicare New Tools to Negotiate Lower Drug Prices for Patients." News release. Published August 7. www. hhs.gov/about/news/2018/08/07/trump-administration-gives-medicare-new-tools-to-negotiate-lower-drug-prices-for-patients.html.

US Food and Drug Administration (FDA). 2019a. "Biosimilars." Updated September 23. www.fda.gov/drugs/developmentapprovalprocess/howdrugsaredevelopedandapproved/approvalapplications/therapeuticbiologicapplications/ biosimilars/default.htm.

———. 2019b. "Drug vs. New Drug." Accessed October 14. www.accessdata.fda. gov/scripts/cder/training/otc/topic3/topic3/da_01_03_0030.htm.

———. 2019c. "Fast Track Designation Request Performance." Updated September 9. www.fda.gov/aboutfda/centersoffices/officeofmedicalproductsand tobacco/cber/ucm122932.htm.

———. 2019d. "Risk Evaluation and Mitigation Strategies (REMS)." Updated August 8. www.fda.gov/Drugs/DrugSafety/REMS/default.htm.

———. 2019e. "Statement from FDA Commissioner Scott Gottlieb, M.D. on the Agency's 2019 Policy and Regulatory Agenda for Continued Action to Forcefully Address the Tragic Epidemic of Opioid Abuse." News release. Published February 26. www.fda.gov/NewsEvents/Newsroom/PressAnnouncements/ ucm632067.htm.

———. 2019f. "Timeline of Selected FDA Activities and Significant Events Addressing Opioid Misuse and Abuse." Updated December 20. www. fda.gov/drugs/information-drug-class/timeline-selected-fda-activities-and-significant-events-addressing-opioid-misuse-and-abuse.

———. 2018a. "Fact Sheet: Medical Device User Fee Amendments of 2012." Updated March 28. www.fda.gov/RegulatoryInformation/LawsEnforced-byFDA/SignificantAmendmentstotheFDCAct/FDASIA/ucm313695. htm.

———. 2018b. "Orphan Drug Act—Relevant Excerpts." Updated March 9. www.fda. gov/forindustry/developingproductsforrarediseasesconditions/howtoapply fororphanproductdesignation/ucm364750.htm.

———. 2018c. "Prescription to Over-the-Counter (OTC) Switch List." Updated September 20. www.fda.gov/AboutFDA/CentersOffices/OfficeofMedical ProductsandTobacco/CDER/ucm106378.htm.

———. 2018d. "Understanding Over-the-Counter Medicines." Updated May 16. www.fda.gov/Drugs/ResourcesForYou/Consumers/BuyingUsingMedicine Safely/UnderstandingOver-the-CounterMedicines/default.htm.

———. 2018e. "Understanding Unapproved Use of Approved Drugs." Updated February 5. www.fda.gov/forpatients/other/offlabel/default.htm.

———. 2018f. "What We Do." Updated March 28. www.fda.gov/AboutFDA/WhatWeDo/default.htm#mission.

———. 2018g. "When and Why Was FDA Formed?" Updated Mach 28. www.fda.gov/about-fda/fda-basics/when-and-why-was-fda-formed.

———. 2016a. "CDER: The Consumer Watchdog for Safe and Effective Drugs." Updated May 4. www.fda.gov/Drugs/ResourcesForYou/Consumers/ucm143462.htm.

———. 2016b. "FDA Drug Approval Process Infographic." Updated February 26. www.fda.gov/drugs/drug-information-consumers/fda-drug-approval-process-infographic-vertical.

———. 2016c. "Implementation of the Biologics Price Competition and Innovation Act of 2009." Updated February 12. www.fda.gov/drugs/guidancecomplianceregulatoryinformation/ucm215089.htm.

———. 2015. "The Impact of Direct-to-Consumer Advertising." Updated October 23. www.fda.gov/Drugs/ResourcesForYou/Consumers/ucm143562.htm.

———. 2014. "Guidance for Industry: Expedited Programs for Serious Conditions—Drugs and Biologics." Published May. www.fda.gov/media/86377/download.

———. 2012. "Food and Drug Administration Safety and Innovation Act (FDASIA)." Reviewed March 28, 2018. www.fda.gov/RegulatoryInformation/LawsEnforcedbyFDA/SignificantAmendmentstotheFDCAct/FDASIA/default.htm.

———. 2011. "FDA at Rare Disease Day, February 28, 2011." Published February 28. www.fda.gov/forindustry/developingproductsforrarediseasesconditions/ucm239698.htm.

US House of Representatives. 2019. "Historical Highlights: The Pure Food and Drug Act." Accessed October 15. http://history.house.gov/Historical-Highlights/1901-1950/Pure-Food-and-Drug-Act/.

US National Library of Medicine. 2019. "What Are Genome Editing and CRISPR-Cas9?" Published October 15. https://ghr.nlm.nih.gov/primer/genomicresearch/genomeediting.

van de Vooren, K., A. Curto, and L. Garattini. 2015. "Biosimilar Versus Generic Drugs: Same But Different?" *Applied Health Economics and Health Policy* 13 (2): 125–27. https://doi.org/10.1007/s40258-015-0154-9.

Van Zee, A. 2009. "The Promotion and Marketing of OxyContin: Commercial Triumph, Public Health Tragedy." *American Journal of Public Health* 99 (2): 221–27. https://doi.org/10.2105/AJPH.2007.131714.

Vara, V. 2019. "The Top Ten Pharmaceutical Companies by Market Share in 2018." *Pharmaceutical Technology.* Published March 7. www.pharmaceutical-technology.com/features/top-pharmaceutical-companies/.

Ventola, C. L. 2011. "Direct-to-Consumer Pharmaceutical Advertising: Therapeutic or Toxic?" *P&T: A Peer-Reviewed Journal for Formulary Management* 36 (10): 669–84. www.ncbi.nlm.nih.gov/pubmed/22346300.

Veterans Health Administration (VHA). 2000. *Pain as the 5th Vital Sign Toolkit.* Published October. www.va.gov/PAINMANAGEMENT/docs/Pain_As_the_5th_Vital_Sign_Toolkit.pdf.

Vivian, J. 2013. "Off-Label Promotion Is Free Speech." *US Pharmacist* 38 (1): 40–42. www.uspharmacist.com/article/off-label-promotion-is-free-speech.

Volkow, N. D., E. B. Jones, E. B. Einstein, and E. M. Wargo. 2018. "Prevention and Treatment of Opioid Misuse and Addiction." *JAMA Psychiatry* 76 (2): 208–16. https://doi.org/10.1001/jamapsychiatry.2018.3126.

von der Schulenburg, F., S. Vandoros, and P. Kanavos. 2011. "The Effects of Drug Market Regulation on Pharmaceutical Prices in Europe: Overview and Evidence from the Market of ACE Inhibitors." *Health Economics Review* 1: 18. https://doi.org/10.1186/2191-1991-1-18.

Whitaker, B. 2019. "Opioid Epidemic: Did the FDA Ignite the Crisis?" CBS. *60 Minutes.* Published February 24. www.cbsnews.com/news/opioid-epidemic-did-the-fda-ignite-the-crisis-60-minutes/.

Whittington, M. D., J. D. Campbell, and R. B. McQueen. 2018. "Achieving High Value Care for All and the Perverse Incentives of 340B Price Agreements." *Neurology. Clinical Practice* 8 (2): 148–52. https://doi.org/10.1212/CPJ.0000000000000437.

Wittich, C. M., C. M. Burkle, and W. L. Lanier. 2012. "Ten Common Questions (and Their Answers) About Off-Label Drug Use." *Mayo Clinic Proceedings* 87 (10): 982–90. https://doi.org/10.1016/j.mayocp.2012.04.017.

Woodruff, J. 2019. "Sec. Azar on How New Proposal 'Brings Transparency' to Drug Pricing." *PBS NewsHour.* Published February 1.www.pbs.org/newshour/show/sec-azar-on-how-new-proposal-brings-transparency-to-drug-pricing.

World Health Organization (WHO). 2011. "Direct-to-Consumer Advertising Under Fire." *Bulletin of the World Health Organization* 87 (8): 565–644. www.who.int/bulletin/volumes/87/8/09-040809/en/.

Young, K. E., I. Soussi, M. Hemels, and M. Toumi. 2017. "A Comparative Study of Orphan Drug Prices in Europe." *Journal of Market Access & Health Policy* 5 (1): 1297886. https://doi.org/10.1080/20016689.2017.1297886.

Young, K. E., I. Soussi, and M. Toumi. 2017. "The Perverse Impact of External Reference Pricing (ERP): A Comparison of Orphan Drugs Affordability in 12 European Countries. A Call for Policy Change." *Journal of Market Access & Health Policy* 5 (1): 1369817. https://doi.org/10.1080/20016689.2017.1369817.

Zelenetz, A. D., I. Ahmed, E. L. Braud, J. D. Cross, N. Davenport-Ennis, B. D. Dickinson, S. E. Goldberg, S. Gottlieb, P. E. Johnson, G. H. Lyman, R. Markus, U. A. Matulonis, D. Reinke, E. C. Li, J. DeMartino, J. K. Larsen, and J. M. Hoffman. 2011. "NCCN Biosimilars White Paper: Regulatory, Scientific, and Patient Safety Perspectives." *Journal of the National Comprehensive Cancer Network* 9 (Suppl. 4): S1–22. https://doi.org/10.6004/jnccn.2011.0136.

Zheng, M. K., D. Q. Shih, and G. C. Chen. 2017. "Insights on the Use of Biosimilars in the Treatment of Inflammatory Bowel Disease." *World Journal of Gastroenterology* 23 (11): 1932–43. https://doi.org/10.3748/wjg.v23.i11.1932.

COMPLEMENTARY AND ALTERNATIVE MEDICINE

By Charles Stephen Wagner

There's a popular saying among doctors: There's no such thing as alternative medicine; if it works, it's just called medicine.

—Ed Yong

Learning Objectives

- Recognize the contribution of natural products to medicine.
- Understand the role of complementary and alternative medicine (CAM) in modern healthcare.
- Possess basic knowledge of common CAM treatments.
- Consider why CAM is more widely accepted in Europe and other parts of the world than in the United States.
- Evaluate ways in which integrating CAM into conventional healthcare might be possible and beneficial.
- Assess our current evidence-based approach to CAM.

Introduction

This chapter will examine the role of complementary and alternative medicine in the US healthcare system (see exhibit 12.1). *Complementary and alternative medicine* is a nonspecific term that refers to various therapies that are not considered part of conventional medicine. Major areas within the CAM designation include biological therapies (e.g., natural products, dietary supplements, probiotics, diet-based therapies, vitamins and minerals), mind–body therapies (e.g., meditation, deep breathing, tai chi, yoga), and body manipulation (e.g., osteopathic medicine, acupuncture, chiropractic, massage). Often, these practices fit into a larger traditional or nonconventional medical system, such as traditional Chinese medicine (TCM), Ayurveda, homeopathy, or naturopathy. *Complementary* therapies are used in conjunction with

EXHIBIT 12.1
Area of Focus
for This Chapter

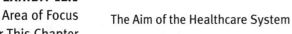

The Aim of the Healthcare System

Issues That Require Our Attention

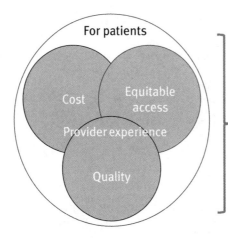

- Nature of our complex system
- Historical issues that have influenced the development of the system
- Beliefs and attitudes about health and healthcare
- Comparison with other developed countries
- Components of our healthcare system
- People and providers
- Patient care—the purpose of the system
- Financing a massive system
- Quality—easier said than done
- Medical and information technology
- The pharmaceutical industry
- **Complementary and alternative medicine**
- Politics/economics
- The future of the system

conventional medicine, whereas *alternative* therapies are used instead of conventional medicine.

The efficacy and safety of many CAM therapies have not been properly evaluated, especially with regard to pediatric care. However, a number of therapies have been supported by clinical evidence, and many of those have been slowly incorporated into conventional medicine. The resulting combination of therapies has created the field of integrative medicine (IM), through which a full range of biological, emotional, social, and spiritual health needs can be addressed. When properly integrated, CAM therapies—especially the use of natural products and diet-based therapies—have great potential for preventing chronic disease, managing symptoms and side effects, and enhancing patient health and quality of life. However, medical practitioners must be able to direct patients toward safe and effective therapies that are supported by scientific evidence.

A survey by the National Center for Complementary and Integrative Health (NCCIH 2017) found that about one-third of all US adults use complementary health approaches of various types (see exhibit 12.2). About 59 million Americans spend money out-of-pocket for complementary health approaches, with a total expense of more than $30 billion a year. Natural products constitute the most widely used category of CAM therapies in the

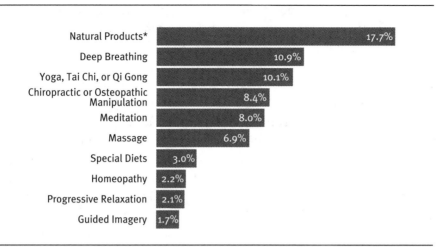

EXHIBIT 12.2
Ten Most
Common
Complementary
Health
Approaches
Among Adults
(2012)

*Dietary supplements other than vitamins and minerals.
Source: Reprinted from NCCIH (2019a).

United States, accounting for $12.8 billion in out-of-pocket spending in 2012. Much of this natural product use is for overall wellness, rather than for treatment of a specific disease.

The history and prevalence of CAM therapies vary throughout the world. In countries where such therapies represent the primary care method for most of the people, the terms *complementary* and *alternative* do not truly apply; terms such as *ethnomedicine, indigenous medicine,* or *traditional medicine* may be more appropriate. Countries also differ in their regulation of CAM therapies. Many countries in Europe and Asia, for instance, have special regulatory categories for natural products, whereas the United States has generally regulated them as food items (World Health Organization [WHO] 1998).

Over the years, modern medicine has replaced a number of traditional therapies with more technologically advanced treatments. CAM therapies remain popular, however, and many are receiving a second look, with a greater emphasis on clinical evidence. This chapter will present a discussion of the history, utility, and integration of CAM therapies, with a focus on natural products, in hopes of cautiously inching toward wider acceptance of well-substantiated approaches.

Natural Products

As humankind has coevolved with other life forms, the human body has developed biological targets that can be manipulated by natural products. A natural product, in the broadest sense, is any substance derived from an organism. Most often within the context of medicinal chemistry, however, the term refers to a secondary metabolite of a plant or fungus. The history of medicinal plant and fungi use among humans dates back to prehistoric times (Shipley and Kindscher 2016).

Exhibit 12.3 lists some of the most widely used natural products in the United States today, along with the percentages of US adults using them in 2012 (NCCIH 2017). A sampling of reasons why patients might wish to use natural products is provided in exhibit 12.4. Searches on databases such as Science Direct, the National Center for Biotechnology Information, Google Scholar, and PubMed show that natural products have been the subject of substantially more preclinical and clinical studies than other CAM therapies. Nonetheless, use of the products by conventional medical doctors in the United States has been limited in part because of a lack of standardized, regulated, high-quality processing and a shortage of rigorous clinical trials.

Natural products represent the sector of CAM therapies with the greatest potential for integration into conventional medicine, and they have historically been the pharmaceutical industry's most successful source of drug leads. During the 1990s and 2000s, however, the industry's focus on natural product discovery, with the exception of cannabidiol, declined (Dias, Urban, and Roessner 2012). Experts believe that less than 10 percent of the world's biodiversity has been screened for medicinal properties (Veeresham 2012). Medicines continually evolve, as diseases do, and natural products, in part because of their chemical diversity, continue to offer great potential for drug discovery, nutritional and lifestyle improvements, and preventive measures.

EXHIBIT 12.3
Most Widely
Used Natural
Products by US
Adults

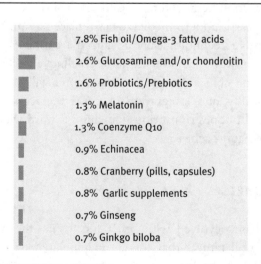

Source: Reprinted from NCCIH (2017).

Category of Use	Reason for Use	Example of Natural Product
Responding to health claims or endorsements	Family/friend anecdotes, scientific research, advertising, trends	Taking ginkgo biloba to increase memory after seeing news reports
Conscious of health, overall wellness	Preventive measures, anti-aging, energy, beauty, stress reduction	Taking ginseng as a natural stimulant to have an "edge"
Seeking new cure for pre-existing illness or disease	Conventional medicine has not worked to satisfaction; avoiding side effects of pharmaceuticals	Taking melatonin to avoid side effects of sleeping pills
Improving management of chronic disease	Increasing quality of life, alleviating side effects, managing pain	Taking cinnamon supplements to help control blood sugar
Cynic/mistrustful of conventional medicine	Dissatisfaction with conventional medical system, treatments, personnel; sociological barriers	Relying on traditional Chinese herbs for acute and chronic illnesses
Limited access to conventional medicine	Affordability, access	Taking garlic to treat a respiratory infection inexpensively
Miscellaneous	Unaware of use, statement of identity/ personal philosophy, experimentation	Taking probiotics to see if they will improve digestion

EXHIBIT 12.4
Reasons for the Use of Natural Products

History and Development of Natural Products and CAM

Human beings' use of natural products for health purposes dates back to prehistoric times. Archaeological evidence suggests that the Neanderthals used more than 60 taxa of plants for food, medicine, and ritual uses (Shipley and Kindscher 2016). Despite tremendous advances in science and technology over the years, our reliance on plants and fungi has remained. The story of modern pharmaceutical drug development begins with morphine, the first natural product isolated from a plant. The drug was first isolated by Friedrich Serturner during the early 1800s; however, some 5,000 years earlier, the opium poppy, the source of morphine, was mentioned on a Sumerian clay tablet (Norn, Kruse, and Kruse 2005). Up to 50 percent of the drugs approved by the FDA between 1981 and 2000 were derived in some way from natural products (Newman and Cragg 2012). This section will review several of the earliest and most important drugs to be isolated from natural sources.

The World Health Organization's (2019) list of essential medicines compiles the drugs that experts deem to be the most cost-effective options for key health problems globally. About 10 percent of the drugs on the list are derived exclusively from flowering plants (Veeresham 2012). Morphine and its derivatives—extracted from *Papaver somniferum*—constitute the strongest class of analgesics and are included on the WHO's list. More classical analgesics—including nonsteroidal anti-inflammatory drugs (NSAIDs) such as aspirin, ibuprofen, and naproxen, as well as paracetamol (Tylenol)—also have their origins in plants. Even though aspirin is on the WHO's list, its use has declined since the arrival of paracetamol and ibuprofen—likely in part because of aspirin's association with gastrointestinal damage and reduced blood clotting. Interestingly, one clinical study found that a natural willow bark mixture (containing 240 milligrams of salicin) provided broad-spectrum analgesic and anti-inflammatory activity with no adverse effects on blood clotting or the gastrointestinal mucosa (Vlachojannis, Magora, and Chrubasik 2011).

Many early medical traditions used fungi and mold to treat infections. Across ancient and medieval Europe and Asia, moldy bread and other items were often placed on wounds to help with healing (Wainwright 1989). Penicillin, the first modern antibiotic, was discovered and isolated from *Penicillium* mold by Alexander Fleming in 1928. Penicillin was mass produced by the 1940s, and total synthesis was completed by 1957. However, even at the time of discovery, researchers noted the potential for pathogens to display antibiotic resistance to penicillin. Antibiotic-resistant pathogens are a growing public health concern, especially in the context of nosocomial infections and healthcare in the developing world.

Paclitaxel (Taxol), the best-selling cancer drug ever manufactured, was isolated from *Taxus brevifolia*, the Pacific yew tree, by Monroe E. Wall, Mansukh C. Wani, and their colleagues, who published their findings in 1971 (Wani and Horwitz 2014). The drug is the standard treatment for ovarian, breast, lung, bladder, prostate, melanoma, esophageal, and pancreatic cancers, as well as Kaposi's sarcoma. It is now produced by cell culture.

The first chemical isolation of quinine from the bark of the *Cinchona* tree occurred in 1820, and it became widely used for the treatment of malaria. However, the WHO no longer recommends it for that purpose, having replaced it with another natural product, artemisinin, from the *Artemisia annua*, or sweet wormwood plant. The use of artemisinin for malaria treatment came about as a result of a Chinese government screening effort known as Project 523 (Neill 2011). Tu Youyou, a researcher associated with the project, would eventually win a Nobel Prize for her discovery and isolation of artemisinin, as well as for the synthesis of more effective derivatives. Tu's discovery, however, actually had roots in ancient Chinese methods. The qinghao (*Artemisia* extract) recipe for malaria had appeared as far back as Ge Hong's *Handbook of Prescriptions for Emergencies* in 340 C.E., and it had been mentioned by Li Shizhen in the *Bencao Gangmu*, or the *Compendium of Materia Medica*, written in 1578 (Hsu 2006). Artemisinin derivatives, when used in combination, are the most effective treatment for malaria.

Many other historical examples exist of natural products being used both as raw ingredients and as purified single-ingredient pharmaceuticals. An ongoing effort is underway to further characterize these substances on the preclinical level in hopes of developing new drugs to be approved by the US Food and Drug Administration (FDA). However, even once a preclinical lead is established, the fate of such a drug depends on costly clinical trials, which can take decades and billions of dollars. As a result, most natural products are labeled as CAM therapies and remain virtually unregulated in the United States.

The Current Regulatory Situation

In the United States, natural products with health-related claims may be marketed as conventional foods, as dietary supplements, or as drugs, depending on the nature of the claim (Palatini and Komarnytsky 2019). These distinctions were set forth in the Dietary Supplement Health and Education Act (DSHEA) of 1994 and further explained in FDA industry guidelines of 2004 and 2015 (FDA 2016). The US approach differs from the practices of European and Canadian regulatory authorities, which put natural remedies in their own category with unique standards.

Under the DSHEA, a natural product is only considered a drug if it bears a disease claim (Palatini and Komarnytsky 2019). Manufacturers of natural products cannot legally make disease claims without an approved new drug application (NDA), but disease claims may be spread by sources other than the manufacturers, often via the internet. Thus, many natural products have well-known but unsubstantiated medical uses, and many self-medicating consumers use them without regulatory assurance of efficacy and safety (Palatini and Komarnytsky 2019).

For many years, natural products were well-established medicines that were included in the US Pharmacopeia and prescribed by physicians (Palatini and Komarnytsky 2019). In 1962, however, the FDA issued strict new guidelines concerning drug safety and efficacy, and only a few natural medicines were allowed to remain on the market unchanged (e.g., Lydia E. Pinkham's

Vegetable Compound, first marketed in 1875). Many of the other products shifted to the over-the-counter (OTC) drug market under Category II, signifying "not generally recognized as safe or effective," or Category III, signifying "insufficient data available to permit final classification" (FDA 2015). Because many of the products lack sufficient safety and efficiency data to satisfy the FDA's drug standards, much of today's natural product industry has chosen to market its products as foods, or dietary supplements (Palatini and Komarnytsky 2019). Thus, many such products have been met with general mistrust from the scientific and medical communities.

Botanical drugs are a category of natural product that requires approval by the FDA. Because they are subject to more rigorous standards and testing than other natural remedies, botanical drugs represent one of the most promising options for integrating CAM into conventional medical practice (Palatini and Komarnytsky 2019).

Botanical Drugs: A Potential Integrative Breakthrough

The FDA's Center for Drug Evaluation and Research (CDER) has developed specific regulatory guidelines for products intended to be developed and used as "botanical drugs" (Palatini and Komarnytsky 2019; FDA 2016). This category includes products derived from "plant materials, algae, macroscopic fungi, and combinations thereof" that are "intended for use in the diagnosis, cure, mitigation, treatment or prevention of disease in humans" (FDA 2017). Often, botanical drug products will rely on unique characteristics and mixtures, as opposed to a single active ingredient, and they may be delivered in a variety of forms, including teas, powders, tablets, and topical gels (Palatini and Komarnytsky 2019; FDA 2017). The CDER guidelines for botanical drugs take into account the complex nature of these therapies.

Before an investigational drug can be administered to human volunteers, an investigational new drug (IND) application must be filed with the FDA. The IND application includes chemical and manufacturing data, animal test results, and all pharmacology and safety data gathered during the preclinical stage (FDA 2018). The same FDA staff that oversees approvals of conventional drugs reviews the applications for botanical drugs (Palatini and Komarnytsky 2019). However, an additional Botanical Review Team (BRT), established in 2003, provides scientific expertise and historical background on botanical issues, ensures consistent interpretation and implementation of the botanical drug guidelines, compiles information on botanical drug submissions, and helps sponsors of botanical applications to interpret the regulations and interact with the FDA (Chen et al. 2008).

The biology of medicinal plants, the pharmacology of botanical products, and prior human experiences with such products can introduce significant complexities, making conventional clinical trials difficult and expensive (Palatini and Komarnytsky 2019). To address this concern, the FDA has developed a "totality of evidence" approach based on the full range of knowledge and expertise gained through the review of botanical IND and NDA submissions (FDA 2016). In addition to the conventional chemistry, manufacturing, and controls (CMC) data, this integrated approach considers such evidence as raw material control, clinically relevant bioassays, and other data deemed necessary by the BRT. The degree to which these other data are used depends on the extent to which the botanical mixture can be characterized and quantified (FDA 2016).

Capitalizing on the knowledge of botanical products may allow for cheaper alternatives to the costly process of conventional drug approval. A key advantage of botanical drugs lies in their ability to be directly evaluated for clinical efficacy first, as opposed to being subjected to preclinical testing. Once efficacy has been proved, the products can be developed either as standardized heterogeneous mixtures or as purified single-chemical drugs (Palatini and Komarnytsky 2019). Essentially, prior history of human use offers the capability to "jump-start" the development process. However, the degree to which findings from past experiences can substitute for conventional studies is often unclear.

Past human experiences may provide some degree of comfort in a botanical product's safety, but such experiences are often informal, anecdotal, or rooted in theory rather than rigorous science. Many botanical products have been traditionally used to treat a variety of seemingly unrelated symptoms, without a clear explanation of the substances' effects on the underlying diseases. Traditional definitions of diagnoses, symptoms, and treatment-related adverse events may be vague, hard to understand, or difficult to correlate with medical terminology (Palatini and Komarnytsky 2019; Chen et al. 2008).

Botanical drugs are complex mixtures of chemical entities, potentially consisting of a single part of one plant, multiple parts of the same plant, or various parts from many plants (Palatini and Komarnytsky 2019; Mishra and Tiwari 2011). FDA (2016) regulations require that the contribution of each component of the fixed combination be shown, which is a daunting task. Even for plants that have been studied extensively, only a small number of the constituent elements have been isolated and identified. When the chemical composition of botanicals is only partially defined, determining the strength and potency of the products is difficult, adding to the challenge of CMC and clinical pharmacology studies (Chen et al. 2008; Mishra and Tiwari 2011).

Another issue that complicates the approval of botanical drugs is the possibility of batch-to-batch variation—in other words, the likelihood that future marketed batches will not have the same therapeutic effect as the batches used in clinical trials (Palatini and Komarnytsky 2019). Plant growth and composition can be significantly affected by soil, weather, seasons, geography, agricultural practices, and other factors, and further inconsistencies may stem from variations in processing methods. Thus, tight controls must be imposed to ensure the presence of the active compounds and to minimize the likelihood of contamination (Chen et al. 2008; Mishra and Tiwari 2011). A detailed description of the raw materials and processes—not just of the drug substances and final product—is required for all botanical products.

Integrating CAM into Conventional Healthcare: Evidence-Based Preventive Medicine

The underlying tenet of integrative medicine is that evidence-based interventions from across appropriate disciplines should focus on the whole person, including a range of influences affecting health, while facilitating a relationship between practitioners and patients. In this manner, CAM therapies can help fill in the gaps that conventional medicine sometimes glosses over. Use of such practices should be guided by clinical trials (with proper blinding, randomization, and controls) and meta-analyses of those trials, as they represent the highest level of evidence. Accounting for dosage and preparation of natural products is critical for finding the most efficacious form of a therapy.

Exhibit 12.5 shows the leading causes of death in the United States in 2017, as reported by the Centers for Disease Control and Prevention (CDC). The majority of US deaths today are caused by complex, multifactorial diseases that correlate highly with lifestyle risk factors such as tobacco use, physical inactivity, poor diet, and alcohol and illicit drug consumption. Whereas conventional medicine excels in treating acute and infectious diseases, CAM therapies can be especially useful for mitigating lifestyle risk

EXHIBIT 12.5
Number of Deaths for Leading Causes (2017)

Heart disease: 647,457

Cancer: 599,108

Accidents (unintentional injuries): 169,936

Chronic lower respiratory diseases: 160,201

Stroke (cerebrovascular diseases): 146,383

Alzheimer's disease: 121,404

Diabetes: 83,564

Influenza and pneumonia: 55,672

Nephritis, nephrotic syndrome, and nephrosis: 50,633

Intentional self-harm (suicide): 47,173

Source: Data from CDC (2017a).

factors and encouraging healthy behavior. Many CAM approaches center around a healthy diet, adequate physical activity, good digestion, stress reduction, and restful sleep. When evidence-backed CAM therapies are integrated into conventional practice by healthcare providers, patients can benefit from the "best of both worlds."

CAM therapies tend to emphasize preventive care for patients more than conventional medicine does. The use of natural products, as well as diet-based therapies, has shown a marked potential to contribute to primary, secondary, and tertiary preventive measures. Katz and colleagues (2014, 175) explain:

> Primary prevention keeps the disease process from becoming established by eliminating causes of disease or by increasing resistance to disease. Secondary prevention interrupts the disease process before it becomes symptomatic. Tertiary prevention limits the physical and social consequences of symptomatic disease.

The following sections will examine a number of important health concerns for which CAM therapies have shown promise.

Reducing Inflammation

Inflammation is a complex biological response to harmful stimuli, and it relates directly—whether as a cause or a symptom—to a wide range of health conditions. Although acute inflammation can be beneficial for the isolation and elimination of a pathogen or injury, chronic inflammation underpins many major diseases. In general, chronic inflammation results in the localized overproduction of certain molecular mediators delivered by the blood, ultimately creating and maintaining a toxic environment favorable for the development of disease. Essentially, the body attacks itself continuously (Middleton, Kandaswami, and Theoharides 2000). Major diseases that involve chronic inflammation include heart disease, stroke, cancers, diabetes, gastrointestinal disorders, autoimmune disorders, and many skin disorders.

Atherosclerosis, the main cause of coronary heart disease, occurs when plaque builds up in a person's arteries. Such plaque formation is dramatically increased through the combination of cigarette smoke and low-density lipoprotein (LDL) cholesterol (i.e., "bad" cholesterol). In response to this buildup, the body initiates an inflammatory response, ultimately causing blood clots (Harvard Medical School 2017). Atherosclerosis is highly preventable through antioxidative CAM-based therapies, mainly diet-based therapies and natural product use (Shu 1998; Willcox, Ash, and Catignani 2004).

Inflammation is postulated to contribute to approximately 15 to 25 percent of human cancers, and at least 30 percent of cancers are thought to be preventable (Lashinger, Ford, and Hursting 2014; WHO 2007).

Although natural products may at times be effective cancer treatments (e.g., taxol, *Vinca* alkaloids), they offer their greatest benefit through their role in prevention. Many avoidable cancers are associated with oxidative damage, and plants have great therapeutic potential as antioxidants (Middleton, Kandaswami, and Theoharides 2000). Plants mainly use antioxidants as protection against ultraviolet damage, given that they are often exposed to more intense light than is necessary for photosynthesis.

Antioxidants neutralize free radicals (unpaired electrons) and prevent the propagation of highly damaging reactive oxygen species (ROS) molecules. They function based on the presence of hydroxyl ion ($OH-$) groups, which "scavenge" free radicals via H atom donation. The antioxidant takes on the extra electron after donation. Antioxidants also rely on conjugated (overlapping) pi orbitals to disperse electrons. Most ROS are negatively charged, and many antioxidants are neutral or positive. Often, the term *polyphenol* is used to describe healthful compounds in plants and natural products, and it refers to the presence of multiple phenolic rings, and thus hydroxyl groups. Polyphenols encompass such compounds as flavonoids, flavanols, flavones, and anthocyanins. They are found in large quantities in red and blue berries, red wine, and green and black tea. The safety record of plant antioxidants is impeccable, yet use of purified and concentrated plant forms (other than vitamins) is rarely seen (Middleton, Kandaswami, and Theoharides 2000; Willcox, Ash, and Catignani 2004).

Lowering Blood Pressure

High blood pressure, or hypertension, is a chronic condition in which arterial blood pressure is persistently elevated. It is the main risk factor associated with cardiovascular mortality—and thus is the most common risk factor for premature death worldwide. Hypertension affects roughly a quarter of the world's population, and many more likely go undiagnosed (CDC 2019).

An estimated 90 percent of cardiovascular disease is preventable (McGill, McMahan, and Gidding 2008), and a number of CAM approaches, including diet-based therapies and natural products, are useful for controlling hypertension (Tabassum and Ahmad 2011). According to the British Hypertension Society, effective lifestyle modification may lower blood pressure as much as individual antihypertensive medication can (Williams et al. 2004). Here again, natural products and diets that lower inflammation can be of great use, because of their ability to prevent oxidation and production of pro-inflammatory molecules such as nitric oxide (a blood vessel dilator). Many of the same natural products can also act more directly on cardiovascular homeostasis by improving lipid profiles, improving vascular reactivity, and reducing undesirable immune response (Rouhi-Boroujeni et al. 2017).

Clinical evidence supports the use of diet-based therapies for the prevention and control of hypertension (Appel et al. 1997; Blumenthal et al.

2010; Hever 2016). The DASH (Dietary Approaches to Stop Hypertension) diet, which is promoted by the National Institutes of Health (2018), emphasizes salt reduction, whole grains, fruits and vegetables, and legumes, as well as low-fat dairy foods. Vegetarian and plant-based diets in general are useful for reducing dietary cholesterol and saturated fats (Hever 2016). Plant-based diets also help boost consumption of fiber, potassium, zinc, selenium, magnesium, iron, folate, and vitamins A and C—nutrients that often run low in the US population. Adequate potassium uptake has been linked to significant reductions in blood pressure and stroke (Aburto et al. 2013). The ratio of potassium to sodium in a person's diet is highly indicative of cardiovascular disease risk, and it is a practical metric for self-monitoring. Ideally, the potassium–sodium ratio should be around 16:1; for most modern Americans, however, it is closer to 1:1 (Harvard Medical School 2011).

Physicians should engage patients in conversations about diet, with questions aimed at addressing legume, leafy green, and whole grain consumption in relation to red meat, refined sugar, and fried food consumption. Diet should be regarded as a cornerstone of preventive medicine and, at least in part, as a viable treatment for gastrointestinal and other chronic diseases (Hever 2016). Exhibit 12.6 lists a number of natural products useful for the prevention of cardiovascular disease.

EXHIBIT 12.6
Natural Products for Preventing Cardiovascular Disease

Natural Product	Mechanism	Clinical Effect	Notes on Use
Green tea	Antioxidant, antimutagenic, anticarcinogenic	Reduced risk of CVD; lowers blood pressure	Must be properly sourced; high levels of lead in some
Red wine	Antioxidant, antithrombotic; increases HDL-C	Reduced risk of CVD	Drink no more than two glasses per day
Curcumin (turmeric)	Antioxidant; increases HDL-C	Reduced atherosclerosis, acute coronary syndrome	Must be properly sourced; high levels of lead in some
Garlic	Antioxidant	Lowers blood pressure	Must be taken raw
Olive oil	Lowers malondialdehyde, LDL, HDL, total cholesterol; antioxidant	Reduced risk of CVD, lowers blood pressure	High polyphenol olive oil used in studies

Note: CVD = cardiovascular disease; HDL = high-density lipoproteins; HDL-C = high-density lipoprotein cholesterol; LDL = low-density lipoproteins.

Controlling Blood Glucose

Chronic hyperglycemia is a condition in which an excessive amount of glucose circulates in the blood plasma. This highly inflammatory condition contributes to a number of complications over time, including obesity; kidney damage; neurological damage; cardiovascular damage; and damage to the retinas, feet, and legs. Diabetes is one of the many causes of hyperglycemia, and diabetic neuropathy may be a consequence of long-term hyperglycemia. Hyperglycemia is associated with poor wound healing and susceptibility to infections, as well as insulin resistance. As the body becomes overrun and is less able to transport the excess glucose, it stops responding to the increased presence of insulin (the transporter) (American Diabetes Association 2014).

Natural products and diet-based therapies are highly useful in preventing hyperglycemic states in both diabetic and nondiabetic patients. The patient may use natural products in conjunction with meals or as meal replacements, to help decrease the reliance on metformin or exogenous insulin. Preclinical and even clinical studies have suggested modest beneficial glycemic effects for many plant extracts, though strong, conclusive clinical effects have been attributed to only a few (Mentreddy, Mohamed, and Rimando 2005). The natural products and dietary interventions found to be most effective revolve around the addition of soluble plant fibers and resistant starches to the diet (although some natural products contain other molecules with uncertain effects). These substances delay glucose absorption and act as a prebiotic to the gut microbiome, which will in turn help digest dietary sugars (Deng 2012; Kim et al. 2009; Mentreddy, Mohamed, and Rimando 2005; Yagi et al. 2009). Exhibit 12.7 lists a number of plant compounds that can help control blood glucose.

Improving Sleep

Insufficient sleep has been linked to the development, worsening, and increased risk of major diseases such as diabetes, cardiovascular disease, obesity, and depression (CDC 2018). According to the CDC (2017b), about 35 percent of US adults get less than the recommended seven hours of sleep per 24-hour period, and 68 percent of high school students get less than the recommended eight hours for adolescents. People who sleep less are more likely to smoke, drink excessively, and be physically inactive. Sleeping pills such as benzodiazepines, barbiturates, and other hypnotics show a high potential for dependency and abuse, are unsafe to mix with alcohol, and can have numerous side effects, including impairment the following day.

Research suggests that melatonin supplementation is safe and effective for treating sleep disorders related to a disrupted circadian rhythm (e.g., jet lag, delayed sleep phase syndrome, sleep deterioration associated with aging); results have generally been clinically insignificant for the treatment of

Compound	Plant	Clinical Effect	Notes on Use
Mannan, glucomannan, galactomannan, arboran A and B	Aloe, fenugreek	Hypoglycemic; reduces triglycerides	Aloe gel and fenugreek seed were used in trials
B-glucan	Oats	Hypoglycemic; reduces triglycerides	
Inulin	Jerusalem artichoke, chicory	Hypoglycemic; reduces triglycerides; improves antioxidant status	
Resistant starch (RS)	Green banana, oats, legumes	Hypoglycemic; reduces triglycerides; increases insulin sensitivity	Green banana flour has highest level of RS
Polyphenols	Olive oil	Hypoglycemic; reduces postprandial oxidative stress	High-polyphenol olive oils or extracts

EXHIBIT 12.7

Plant Compounds for Controlling Blood Glucose

insomnia or other sleep disorders (Buscemi et al. 2004; Montes et al. 2003; NCCIH 2019b; Sánchez-Barceló et al. 2010). These findings may suggest that melatonin supplementation will provide the greatest benefit for people who have had their sleep temporarily disrupted but who otherwise sleep normally.

The human body gradually produces less and less endogenous melatonin after childhood, so sustaining melatonin levels through diet may be a better option than short-term supplementation. Oral melatonin tablets generally show a low bioavailability, though studies still show a marked increase in serum melatonin for 20 minutes after dose, with levels remaining elevated for four hours after ingestion. Increasing dietary sources of melatonin could help gradually elevate and sustain serum levels more effectively over the long term, while also providing other benefits.

Melatonin is found widely in the plant and fungi kingdoms. Natural sources high in melatonin include the medicinal herbs *Scutellaria baicalensis* and St. John's wort flowers. Foods high in melatonin include Basidiomycota mushrooms (*Boletus edulis, Lactarius deliciosus*), sprouted legumes, cereal grains, tropical fruits (e.g., bananas, pineapples, oranges), tart cherries, grapes, and nuts. These foods not only add melatonin to the diet but also improve antioxidant status and can have general chemoprotective effects. Melatonin itself is an antioxidant and anti-inflammatory agent with beneficial effects on blood pressure, lipids, and glucose metabolism demonstrated in vitro (Meng et al. 2017; Peuhkuri, Sihvola, and Korpela 2012; Sánchez-Barceló et al. 2010).

In two double-blind, randomized, placebo-controlled trials, magnesium supplementation has been found to improve primary insomnia of older adults (Abbasi et al. 2012; Rondanelli et al. 2011). Both studies showed improvement in the subjective measure of sleep, as well as in objective measures such as increased sleep time, sleep efficiency, concentration of serum melatonin, and decrease in sleep onset latency and serum cortisol levels. Magnesium combined with melatonin and zinc appears to improve sleep, as magnesium may enhance the effects of melatonin. Significant clinical data on humans is generally limited to elderly populations, but studies on animals abound.

Increasing Adherence to Conventional Therapies

Although modern pharmaceuticals can be superior to natural products in a variety of ways, often they come with adverse effects that detract from the patient's quality of life and negatively affect adherence to treatment. Some natural products have been shown to be clinically effective in reducing or preventing side effects from major conventional treatments such as chemotherapy, radiation, antibiotics, and other toxicities. Exhibit 12.8, for instance, lists a number of natural products that may be highly useful in oncology by reducing or preventing side effects of chemotherapy and radiation (Simone et al. 2007; Zhang et al. 2018). Integration of the proper forms and doses of such products can help improve patients' adherence to conventional therapies.

The gut microbiome plays a major role in regulating most human physiological functions, including gastrointestinal health, immunity, metabolism (weight control), cognition, and mood (Galland 2014; Shreiner, Kao, and Young 2015). Antibiotics, although essential to modern medical practice, take a toll on the gut flora, with potential side effects such as diarrhea, nausea, vomiting, stomach pain, headache, and even cognitive issues such as confusion and delirium (Warstler and Bean 2016). Evidence suggests that probiotics may help reduce antibiotic-associated diarrhea, as well as such conditions as infectious diarrhea and irritable bowel syndrome (Penner, Fedorak, and Madsen 2005). One meta-analysis showed that, across 881 patients receiving various antibiotics (beta-lactams, clindamycin, cephalosporins) for 7 to 14 days, *Lactobacillus* and *Saccharomyces boulardii* showed overall strong positive effects on diarrhea, though the study found little agreement on dosage (Cremonini et al. 2002).

Side Effect	Natural Product (clinical trials)	Effect/Mechanism
Oral mucositis	*Plantago major* Hangeshashinto Chamomile *Aloe vera* Turmeric Ginger Tocotrienol Quercetin Honey Black mulberry molasses Propolis Glutamine	Anti-inflammation, antioxidation, antimicrobial
Gastrointestinal toxicity	Red ginseng 6-ginggerol Persumac Zhu-Ye-Shi-Gao *Aloe vera* Green tea Glutamine	Anti-inflammation, antioxidation, antiemetic, reduced gut permeability (glutamine)
Hepatotoxicity	Milk thistle Active hexose correlated compound	Antioxidation, anti-inflammation, antifibrosis
Nephrotoxicity	Lycopene Honey / royal jelly	Antioxidation, anti-inflammation, hypoglycemic
Hematopoietic injury	Shuang-Huang-Sheng-Bai Sheng-Mai Ginsenoside Rg3 Dang-Gui-Bu-Xue	Immunomodulatory, inhibition of tumor growth and proliferation

EXHIBIT 12.8
Natural Products with Potential to Treat Side Effects of Chemotherapy and Radiation

Conclusion

The greatest limitations affecting the integration of CAM therapies with conventional medicine lie in the lack of high-quality clinical trials and standardized, well-sourced ingredients. Based on the high-quality clinical evidence that does exist, a number of CAM practices—especially the use of natural products and diet-based therapies—show promise as complementary therapies. Healthcare leaders and practitioners should possess sufficient knowledge of proven CAM therapies to guide their proper and effective integration into the modern healthcare delivery system.

Discussion Questions

1. Can CAM therapies be integrated into standard medical practice? Should they be?
2. Why do healthcare administrators need to understand CAM?
3. Why are CAM therapies so popular?
4. Should CAM therapies be included as a standard part of healthcare coverage?

References

Abbasi, B., M. Kimiagar, K. Sadeghniiat, M. M. Shirazi, M. Hedayati, and B. Rashid-khani. 2012. "The Effect of Magnesium Supplementation on Primary Insomnia in Elderly: A Double-Blind Placebo-Controlled Clinical Trial." *Journal of Research in Medical Sciences* 17 (12): 1161–69. www.ncbi.nlm.nih.gov/pubmed/23853635.

Aburto, N. J., S. Hanson, H. Gutierrez, L. Hooper, P. Elliott, and F. P. Cappuccio. 2013. "Effect of Increased Potassium Intake on Cardiovascular Risk Factors and Disease: Systematic Review and Meta-Analyses." *BMJ* 346: f1378. https://doi.org/10.1136/bmj.f1378.

American Diabetes Association. 2014. "Diagnosis and Classification of Diabetes Mellitus." *Diabetes Care* 37 (Suppl. 1): S81–90. https://doi.org/10.2337/dc14-S081.

Appel, L. J., T. J. Moore, E. Obarzanek, W. M. Vollmer, L. P. Svetkey, F. M. Sacks, G. A. Bray, T. M. Vogt, J. A. Cutler, M. M. Windhauser, P.-H. Lin, N. Karanja, D. Simons-Morton, M. McCullough, J. Swain, P. Steele, M. A. Evans, E. R. Miller, and D. W. Harsha. 1997. "A Clinical Trial of the Effects of Dietary Patterns on Blood Pressure." *New England Journal of Medicine* 336 (16): 1117–24. https://doi.org/10.1056/NEJM199704173361601.

Blumenthal, J. A., M. A. Babyak, A. Hinderliter, L. L. Watkins, L. Craighead, P.-H. Lin, C. Caccia, J. Johnson, R. Waugh, and A. Sherwood. 2010. "Effects of the DASH Diet Alone and in Combination with Exercise and Weight Loss on Blood Pressure and Cardiovascular Biomarkers in Men and Women with High Blood Pressure: The ENCORE Study." *Archives of Internal Medicine* 170 (2): 126–35. https://doi.org/10.1001/archinternmed.2009.470.

Buscemi, N., B. Vandermeer, R. Pandya, N. Hooton, L. Tjosvold, L. Hartling, G. Baker, S. Vohra, and T. Klassen. 2004. "Melatonin for Treatment of Sleep Disorders: Summary." Agency for Healthcare Research and Quality. AHRQ Evidence Report Summaries. Published November. www.ncbi.nlm.nih.gov/books/NBK11941/.

Centers for Disease Control and Prevention (CDC). 2019. "High Blood Pressure (Hypertension) Information." Reviewed October 2. www.cdc.gov/blood pressure/index.htm.

———. 2018. "Sleep and Sleep Disorders: Sleep and Chronic Disease." Reviewed August 8. www.cdc.gov/sleep/about_sleep/chronic_disease.html.

———. 2017a. "Leading Causes of Death." Reviewed March 17. www.cdc.gov/nchs/fastats/leading-causes-of-death.htm.

———. 2017b. "Sleep and Sleep Disorders: Data and Statistics." Reviewed May 2. www.cdc.gov/sleep/data_statistics.html.

Chen, S. T., J. Dou, R. Temple, R. Agarwal, K.-M. Wu, and S. Walker. 2008. "New Therapies from Old Medicines." *Nature Biotechnology* 26 (10): 1077–83. https://doi.org/10.1038/nbt1008-1077.

Cremonini, F., S. D. Caro, E. C. Nista, F. Bartolozzi, G. Capelli, G. Gasbarrini, and A. Gasbarrini. 2002. "Meta-analysis: The Effect of Probiotic Administration on Antibiotic-Associated Diarrhoea." *Alimentary Pharmacology & Therapeutics* 16 (8): 1461–67. https://doi.org/10.1046/j.1365-2036.2002.01318.x.

Deng, R. 2012. "A Review of the Hypoglycemic Effects of Five Commonly Used Herbal Food Supplements." *Recent Patents on Food, Nutrition & Agriculture* 4 (1): 50–60. www.ncbi.nlm.nih.gov/pubmed/22329631.

Dias, D. A., S. Urban, and U. Roessner. 2012. "A Historical Overview of Natural Products in Drug Discovery." *Metabolites* 2 (2): 303–36. https://doi.org/10.3390/metabo2020303.

Galland, L. 2014. "The Gut Microbiome and the Brain." *Journal of Medicinal Food* 17 (12): 1261–72. https://doi.org/10.1089/jmf.2014.7000.

Harvard Medical School. 2017. "Targeting Inflammation: A Missing Link in Heart Treatments." Harvard Heart Letter. Published December. www.health.harvard.edu/heart-health/targeting-inflammation-a-missing-link-in-heart-treatments.

———. 2011. "Sodium/Potassium Ratio Important for health." Harvard Heart Letter. Published September. www.health.harvard.edu/heart-health/sodiumpotassium-ratio-important-for-health.

Hever, J. 2016. "Plant-Based Diets: A Physician's Guide." *Permanente Journal* 20 (3): 93–101. https://doi.org/10.7812/TPP/15-082.

Hsu, E. 2006. "Reflections on the 'Discovery' of the Antimalarial Qinghao." *British Journal of Clinical Pharmacology* 61 (6): 666–70. https://dx.doi.org/10.1111%2Fj.1365-2125.2006.02673.x.

Katz, D. L., J. G. Elmore, D. M. G. Wild, and S. C. Lucan. 2014. *Jekel's Epidemiology, Biostatistics, Preventive Medicine, and Public Health*, 4th ed. Philadelphia, PA: Saunders/Elsevier.

Kim, K., H. Kim, J. Kwon, S. Lee, H. Kong, S.-A. Im, Y.-H. Lee, Y.-R. Lee, S.-T. Oh, T. H. Jo, Y. I. Park, C.-K. Lee, and K. Kim. 2009. "Hypoglycemic and Hypolipidemic Effects of Processed *Aloe vera* Gel in a Mouse Model of

Non-Insulin-Dependent Diabetes Mellitus." *Phytomedicine* 16 (9): 856–63. https://doi.org/10.1016/j.phymed.2009.02.014.

Lashinger, L. M., N. A. Ford, and S. D. Hursting. 2014. "Interacting Inflammatory and Growth Factor Signals Underlie the Obesity–Cancer Link." *Journal of Nutrition* 144 (2): 109–13. https://doi.org/10.3945/jn.113.178533.

McGill, H. C. Jr., C. A. McMahan, and S. S. Gidding. 2008. "Preventing Heart Disease in the 21st Century." *Circulation* 117 (9): 1216–27. https://doi.org/10.1161/CIRCULATIONAHA.107.717033.

Meng, X., Y. Li, S. Li, Y. Zhou, R. Y. Gan, D. P. Xu, and H. B. Li. 2017. "Dietary Sources and Bioactivities of Melatonin." *Nutrients* 9 (4): E367. https://doi.org/10.3390/nu9040367.

Mentreddy, R., A. I. Mohamed, and A. M. Rimando. 2005. "Medicinal Plants with Hypoglycemic/Anti-Hyperglycemic Properties: A Review." In *Industrial Crops and Rural Development: Proceedings of 2005 Annual Meeting of the Association for the Advancement of Industrial Crops: International Conference on Industrial Crops and Rural Development*. Accessed October 15, 2019. https://naldc.nal.usda.gov/download/45708/PDF.

Middleton, E., C. Kandaswami, and T. C. Theoharides. 2000. "The Effects of Plant Flavonoids on Mammalian Cells: Implications for Inflammation, Heart Disease, and Cancer." *Pharmacological Reviews* 52 (4): 673–751. www.ncbi.nlm.nih.gov/pubmed/11121513.

Mishra, B. B., and V. K. Tiwari. 2011. "Natural Products: An Evolving Role in Future Drug Discovery." *European Journal of Medicinal Chemistry* 46 (10): 4769–4807. https://doi.org/10.1016/j.ejmech.2011.07.057.

Montes, L. G. A., M. P. O. Uribe, J. C. Sotres, and G. H. Martin. 2003. "Treatment of Primary Insomnia with Melatonin: A Double-Blind, Placebo-Controlled, Crossover Study." *Journal of Psychiatry and Neuroscience* 28 (3): 191–96. www.ncbi.nlm.nih.gov/pmc/articles/PMC161743/.

National Center for Complementary and Integrative Health (NCCIH). 2019a. "Complementary, Alternative, or Integrative Health: What's in a Name?" National Institutes of Health. Updated April 2. https://nccih.nih.gov/health/integrative-health.

———. 2019b. "Melatonin: What You Need to Know." National Institutes of Health. Updated October 15. https://nccih.nih.gov/health/melatonin.

———. 2017. "What Complementary and Integrative Approaches Do Americans Use?" National Institutes of Health. Updated September 27. https://nccih.nih.gov/research/statistics/NHIS/2012/key-findings.

National Institutes of Health. 2018. "DASH Ranked Best Diet Overall for Eighth Year in a Row by U.S. News and World Report." Published January 3. www.nih.gov/news-events/news-releases/dash-ranked-best-diet-overall-eighth-year-row-us-news-world-report.

Neill, U. S. 2011. "From Branch to Bedside: Youyou Tu Is Awarded the 2011 Lasker-DeBakey Clinical Medical Research Award for Discovering

Artemisinin as a Treatment for Malaria." *Journal of Clinical Investigation* 121 (10): 3768–73. https://dx.doi.org/10.1172%2FJCI60887.

Newman, D. J., and G. M. Cragg. 2012. "Natural Products as Sources of New Drugs over the 30 Years from 1981 to 2010." *Journal of Natural Products* 75 (3): 311–35. https://doi.org/10.1021/np200906s.

Norn, S., P. R. Kruse, and E. Kruse. 2005. "History of Opium Poppy and Morphine." *Dansk Medicinhistorisk Arbog* 33: 171–84. www.ncbi.nlm.nih.gov/pubmed/17152761.

Palatini, K., and S. Komarnytsky. 2019. "The Quality, Safety, and Efficacy of Botanical Drugs." In *Botanical Drug Products: Recent Developments and Market Trends*, edited by J. N. Lokhande and Y. V. Pathak, 159–86. Boca Raton, FL: CRC Press.

Penner, R., R. N. Fedorak, and K. L. Madsen. 2005. "Probiotics and Nutraceuticals: Non-medicinal Treatments of Gastrointestinal Diseases." *Current Opinion in Pharmacology* 5 (6): 596–603. https://doi.org/10.1016/j.coph.2005.06.009.

Peuhkuri, K., N. Sihvola, and R. Korpela. 2012. "Diet Promotes Sleep Duration and Quality." *Nutrition Research* 32 (5): 309–19. https://doi.org/10.1016/j.nutres.2012.03.009.

Rondanelli, M., A. Opizzi, F. Monteferrario, N. Antoniello, R. Manni, and C. Klersy. 2011. "The Effect of Melatonin, Magnesium, and Zinc on Primary Insomnia in Long-Term Care Facility Residents in Italy: A Double-Blind, Placebo-Controlled Clinical Trial." *Journal of the American Geriatrics Society* 59 (1): 82–90. https://doi.org/10.1111/j.1532-5415.2010.03232.x.

Rouhi-Boroujeni, H., E. Heidarian, H. Rouhi-Boroujeni, F. Deris, and M. Rafieian-Kopaei. 2017. "Medicinal Plants with Multiple Effects on Cardiovascular Diseases: A Systematic Review." *Current Pharmaceutical Design* 23 (7): 999–1015. https://doi.org/10.2174/1381612822666161021160524.

Sánchez-Barceló, E. J., M. D. Mediavilla, D. X. Tan, and R. J. Reiter. 2010. "Clinical Uses of Melatonin: Evaluation of Human Trials." *Current Medicinal Chemistry* 17 (19): 2070–95. https://doi.org/10.2174/092986710791233689.

Shipley, G. P., and K. Kindscher. 2016. "Evidence for the Paleoethnobotany of the Neanderthal: A Review of the Literature." *Scientifica* 2016: 8927654. https://doi.org/10.1155/2016/8927654.

Shreiner, A. B., J. Y. Kao, and V. B. Young. 2015. "The Gut Microbiome in Health and in Disease." *Current Opinion in Gastroenterology* 31 (1): 69–75. https://doi.org/10.1097/MOG.0000000000000139.

Shu, Y. Z. 1998. "Recent Natural Products Based Drug Development: A Pharmaceutical Industry Perspective." *Journal of Natural Products* 61 (8): 1053–71. https://doi.org/10.1021/np9800102.

Simone, C. B. II, N. L. Simone, V. Simone, and C. B. Simone. 2007. "Antioxidants and Other Nutrients Do Not Interfere with Chemotherapy or Radiation

Therapy and Can Increase Kill and Increase Survival, Part 1." *Alternative Therapies in Health and Medicine* 13 (1): 22–28. www.ivcinfusions.com/articles/Antioxidants_Nutrients_Chemotherapy_part_1.pdf.

Tabassum, N., and F. Ahmad. 2011. "Role of Natural Herbs in the Treatment of Hypertension." *Pharmacognosy Reviews* 5 (9): 30–40. https://doi.org/10.4103/0973-7847.79097.

US Food and Drug Administration (FDA). 2018. "The Drug Development Process—Step 3: Clinical Research." Reviewed January 4. www.fda.gov/forpatients/approvals/drugs/ucm405622.htm.

———. 2017. "What Is a Botanical Drug?" Reviewed August 11. www.fda.gov/about-fda/center-drug-evaluation-and-research-cder/what-botanical-drug.

———. 2016. *Botanical Drug Development Guidance for Industry.* Published December. www.fda.gov/media/93113/download.

———. 2015. "Over-the-Counter (OTC) Drug Monograph Process." Reviewed January 7. www.fda.gov/drugs/current-good-manufacturing-practices-cgmp-drugs-reports-guidances-and-additional-information/over-counter-otc-drug-monograph-process.

Veeresham, C. 2012. "Natural Products Derived from Plants as a Source of Drugs." *Journal of Advanced Pharmaceutical Technology and Research* 3 (4): 200–1. https://dx.doi.org/10.4103%2F2231-4040.104709.

Vlachojannis, J., F. Magora, and S. Chrubasik. 2011. "Willow Species and Aspirin: Different Mechanism of Actions." *Phytotherapy Research* 25 (7): 1102–04. https://doi.org/10.1002/ptr.3386.

Wainwright, M. 1989. "Moulds in Folk Medicine." *Folklore* 100 (2): 162–66.

Wani, M. C., and S. B. Horwitz. 2014. "Nature as a Remarkable Chemist: A Personal Story of the Discovery and Development of Taxol." *Anticancer Drugs* 25 (5): 482–87. www.ncbi.nlm.nih.gov/pmc/articles/PMC3980006/.

Warstler, A., and J. Bean. 2016. "Antimicrobial-Induced Cognitive Side Effects." *Mental Health Clinician* 6 (4): 207–14. https://doi.org/10.9740/mhc.2016.07.207.

Willcox, J., S. Ash, and F. Catignani. 2004. "Antioxidants and Prevention of Chronic Disease." *Critical Reviews in Food Science and Nutrition* 44 (4): 275–95. https://doi.org/10.1080/10408690490468489.

Williams, B., N. R. Poulter, M. J. Brown, M. Davis, G. T. McInnes, J. F. Potter, S. M. Thom, and P. S. Sever. 2004. "British Hypertension Society Guidelines for Hypertension Management 2004 (BHS-IV): Summary." *BMJ* 328 (7440): 634–40. https://doi.org/10.1136/bmj.328.7440.634.

World Health Organization (WHO). 2019. *World Health Organization Model List of Essential Medicines.* Published June. https://apps.who.int/iris/bitstream/handle/10665/325771/WHO-MVP-EMP-IAU-2019.06-eng.pdf.

———. 2007. *Cancer Control: Prevention.* Accessed October 15, 2019. www.who.int/cancer/publications/cancer_control_prevention/en/.

———. 1998. *Regulatory Situation of Herbal Medicines: A Worldwide Review.* Accessed October 15, 2019. http://apps.who.int/iris/handle/10665/63801.

Yagi, A., S. Hegazy, A. Kabbash, and E. A.-E. Wahab. 2009. "Possible Hypoglycemic Effect of *Aloe vera* L. High Molecular Weight Fractions on Type 2 Diabetic Patients. *Saudi Pharmaceutical Journal* 17 (3): 209–15. https://doi.org/10.1016/j.jsps.2009.08.007.

Zhang, Q.-Y., F.-X. Wang, K.-K. Jia, and L.-D. Kong. 2018. "Natural Product Interventions for Chemotherapy and Radiotherapy-Induced Side Effects." *Frontiers in Pharmacology* 9. https://doi.org/10.3389/fphar.2018.01253.

HEALTH POLICY AND ECONOMICS

> I have no idea what's awaiting me, or what will happen when this all ends. For the moment I know this: there are sick people and they need curing.
>
> —Albert Camus, *The Plague*

Learning Objectives

- Analyze the role of government in healthcare.
- Recognize the significance of voter interest in healthcare issues.
- Understand the policy cycle and the way health policy is made.
- Review some of the most significant federal regulations concerning health.
- Apply current public information to future health reform.
- Assess the difference between universal coverage and national health insurance.

This chapter will examine key political and economic concerns of US healthcare (see exhibit 13.1). In chapter 2, we discussed the distinction between the concepts of social justice and market justice. Market justice favors individualism, self-interest, personal effort, and voluntary behavior, whereas social justice supports the fair allocation of healthcare based on individual need. Throughout our history, health policy in the United States has been fraught with tension between these two concepts. A fundamental divide exists between the idea that healthcare is a right to which all people are entitled and the idea that healthcare is just another good or service that should be subject to the market forces of our economy (Gawande 2017).

Some people feel that the market should determine the way healthcare services are provided, with minimal involvement of the government. Others, however, feel that the government should play a more active role in managing key aspects of the system and ensuring equal access to care for all people, regardless of their ability to pay. As healthcare has become costlier and more intensive, and as economic disparities have grown across the population, the opposing sides of this debate have become increasingly divided and entrenched.

EXHIBIT 13.1
Area of Focus
for This Chapter

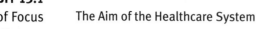

The Aim of the Healthcare System

Issues That Require Our Attention

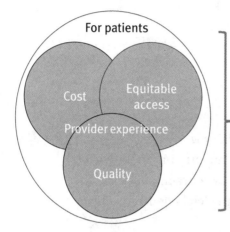

For patients

Cost

Equitable access

Provider experience

Quality

- Nature of our complex system
- Historical issues that have influenced the development of the system
- Beliefs and attitudes about health and healthcare
- Comparison with other developed countries
- Components of our healthcare system
- People and providers
- Patient care—the purpose of the system
- Financing a massive system
- Quality—easier said than done
- Medical and information technology
- The pharmaceutical industry
- Complementary and alternative medicine
- *Politics/economics*
- The future of the system

The purpose of this chapter is not to "answer" this long-standing debate but rather to focus readers on the complicated issues that must be addressed and to challenge readers to think critically about potential solutions. The future of healthcare delivery will offer countless possibilities for better health and better treatment of disease, yet it will also bring new questions and challenges—particularly with regard to regulation and funding.

Health policy serves not only to regulate healthcare but also to allocate resources to various groups, including patients, the providers of services, and other entities across the healthcare landscape. To a large extent, health policy in the United States has been fragmented and piecemeal, and many players in the policy arena have lacked a firm understanding of the healthcare field.

Despite the noble mission of healthcare, politics and money drive the system, and to deny this reality is to simply be naïve (Gusmano 2012; Marmor 2000, 2013). Demonstrations of this influence are easy to find. One analysis, for instance, linked political donations from insurance companies to senators' opposition to a single-payer "Medicare for All" proposal. Between 2010 and 2016, senators who did not support the proposal received nearly twice as much money from the insurance industry as those who did (Diep 2017).

The Role of Government in Healthcare

Health policy occurs at every level of government and affects virtually every aspect of healthcare. Typically, the most important health policy decisions surround issues of access, cost, and quality. Policies that define provider payment schemes, licensing, and funding for training programs all affect provider availability and patient access to care. A number of policy initiatives have sought to specifically address access for elderly adults, minority groups, inhabitants of rural communities, low-income patients, and people with HIV/AIDS.

Some policies have targeted the costs associated with healthcare. A number of policymakers have sought to address prescription drug prices, though government actions have generally not managed to prevent price increases. For Medicare and Medicaid, reimbursement to providers is set by the Centers for Medicare & Medicaid Services (CMS), but CMS regulations have had limited effect on overall healthcare cost increases.

Quality improvement policies generally focus on six qualities that were originally espoused in the Institute of Medicine's (IOM 2001) *Crossing the Quality Chasm* report. The IOM states:

Health care should be:

- *Safe*—avoiding injuries to patients from the care that is intended to help them.
- *Effective*—providing services based on scientific knowledge to all who could benefit and refraining from providing services to those not likely to benefit (avoiding underuse and overuse, respectively).
- *Patient-centered*—providing care that is respectful of and responsive to individual patient preferences, needs, and values, and ensuring that patient values guide all clinical decisions.
- *Timely*—reducing waits and sometimes harmful delays for both those who receive and those who give care.
- *Efficient*—avoiding waste, including waste of equipment, supplies, ideas, and energy.
- *Equitable*—providing care that does not vary in quality because of personal characteristics such as gender, ethnicity, geographic location, and socioeconomic status.

The report also sets forth a number of healthcare system goals that are useful in policymaking (IOM 2001; Berwick 2002).

1. Care based on continuous healing relationships
2. Customization based on patient needs and values

3. The patient as the source of control

4. Shared knowledge and the free flow of information

5. Evidence-based decision making

6. Safety as a system property

7. The need for transparency

8. Anticipation of needs

9. Continuous decrease in waste

10. Cooperation among clinicians

Research in these areas of quality is ongoing and will inform future efforts and policy development.

Levels of Government

Health policy is constantly developing at the federal, state, and local levels, and the actions of the various government agencies are not always aligned as well as one might hope. To paraphrase Morton Grodzins (1960), US health policy is not a layer cake, with clearly delineated sections, but rather a marble cake, with an irregular mingling of colors and ingredients.

Indeed, the laws and regulations concerning US healthcare tend to be confusing, frustrating, and imperfect. Nonetheless, they have also done a great deal of good in certain areas. For instance, regulatory processes that guard against unprofessional and dangerous practices have helped weed out quackery, thereby elevating the overall caliber of healthcare in the United States (Duffy 2011; Field 2007; Starr 1982).

For many years, government involvement in healthcare occurred principally at the local level, dealing with such matters as sanitation and epidemics. Over time, however, healthcare policymaking has become increasingly centralized at the federal level (Daniel 2006; Granshaw and Porter 1989; Rosenberg and Golden 1992; Siraisi 2012; Starr 1982; Wear 1992). Tensions are ongoing between groups that favor more federal intervention and those that prefer greater control at the state and local level.

With varying levels of success, the federal, state, and local levels of government coordinate essential responsibilities for our healthcare system, including the following (American Public Health Association 1995, 2019; Costich, Scutchfield, and Ingram 2015):

- Creation of laws, regulations, and policies to promote health, safety, and public well-being
- Surveillance, planning, and program development
- Promotion of local health coverage

- Development and enforcement of standards
- Provision of health services

Key healthcare responsibilities of the federal government include the following (Altman and Morgan 1983; IOM 2003, 2015; Knickman and Kovner 2015; McDaid, Sassi, and Merkur 2015; Murawski 2018):

- Development of laws and regulations related to health and safety
- Operation of national healthcare programs and distribution of funding based on legislation (e.g., Medicare, Medicaid, the Affordable Care Act)
- Support for healthcare workforce education
- Operation of the Centers for Disease Control and Prevention (CDC) to focus national attention to public health concerns
- Major research funding and initiatives through the National Institutes of Health

State and local governments have health departments that engage in a combination of functions, including the following:

- Development of policies and policy recommendations for maintaining and protecting the public's health
- Collection and analysis of data on the health status of the community for the purpose of informing policymakers
- Provision of important public health and health services (e.g., vaccinations, prenatal care, patient education, emergency preparedness) for the community
- Implementation of federal programs and allocation of funds from government sources
- Supplementation of funding for targeted programs specific to the community

The states license healthcare professionals and healthcare facilities and enforce the standards for licensure. They also administer their Medicaid programs, within federal guidelines, and share in the cost of Medicaid according to a formula (Kaiser Family Foundation [KFF] 2019). Subsidies by the states support medical schools and other institutions of higher education.

Voters Care About Healthcare

Prior to the US midterm elections of 2018, the Kaiser Family Foundation conducted an extensive study of voter attitudes concerning healthcare and the federal government's involvement. KFF's polling, as shown in

Health Care Is Top Issue For Voters In The Midterm Elections

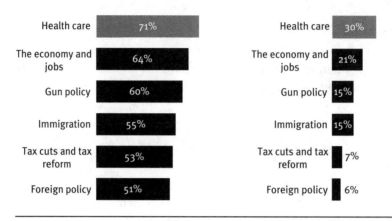

Percent who say each of the following issues is "very important" in making their decision about who to vote for Congress this year:

When asked to choose one, percent who say each of the following is the "most important" issue in making their decision about who to vote for Congress this year:

Issue	Very important	Issue	Most important
Health care	71%	Health care	30%
The economy and jobs	64%	The economy and jobs	21%
Gun policy	60%	Gun policy	15%
Immigration	55%	Immigration	15%
Tax cuts and tax reform	53%	Tax cuts and tax reform	7%
Foreign policy	51%	Foreign policy	6%

Note: Questions asked of and reported among total registered voters.

Source: Reprinted from Kirzinger and colleagues (2018) with permission from Kaiser Family Foundation.

exhibit 13.2, found that 71 percent of registered voters considered healthcare a top issue in that year's election (Kirzinger et al. 2018). As shown in exhibit 13.3, costs ranked as the most important healthcare issue—by a wide margin—for Democrats, Republicans, and independents alike. Other issues raised by respondents included access, universal coverage, and Medicare.

The Pew Research Center, which also conducted extensive survey work prior to the 2018 elections, found that 60 percent of respondents felt that the federal government was responsible for ensuring health coverage for its citizens, as shown in exhibit 13.4 (Kiley 2018). Researchers also found that Americans had serious concerns about healthcare costs (Milanez and Strauss 2018).

In addition, researchers asked respondents whether they thought the Affordable Care Act (ACA) had a mostly positive or mostly negative effect on the United States as a whole. As shown in exhibit 13.5, 44 percent of respondents in 2017 believed that the ACA's effects were mostly positive (up from 24 percent in 2013), and 35 percent felt the effects were mostly negative (down slightly from 38 percent in 2013). The percentage of people who felt the law had "not much effect" on the country dropped significantly, from 31 percent in 2013 to just 14 percent in 2017 (Fingerhut 2017).

Another question asked about the personal effect the ACA had on the respondent and the respondent's family. The percentage of respondents

EXHIBIT 13.3
Voter Concerns
over Healthcare
Costs

Health Care Costs Are Top Health Care Issue For Voters

<u>REGISTERED VOTERS:</u> When you say health care is an important issue for 2018 candidates to talk about, what health care issue are you mainly talking about? (open-end)

	DEMOCRATS:	INDEPENDENTS:	REPUBLICANS:	TOTAL:
Health care costs	29%	29%	25%	27%
Increasing access to health care	13%	9%	4%	9%
Universal coverage	13%	8%	3%	8%
Medicare/senior concerns	10%	7%	5%	7%
Prescription drug costs	6%	7%	7%	7%

Note: Question asked of those who say health care is an important issue for 2018 candidates to talk about and reported among all voters. Only top five responses shown.

Source: Reprinted from Kirzinger and colleagues (2018) with permission from Kaiser Family Foundation.

EXHIBIT 13.4
Opinions About
Government
Responsibility
for Healthcare
Coverage

More Americans say federal govt has responsibility to ensure health coverage

Is it the responsibility of the federal government to make sure that all Americans have health care coverage? (%)

Yes, govt responsibility
No, not govt responsibility

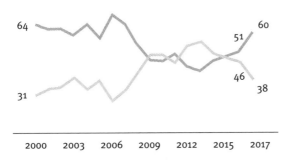

2000 2003 2006 2009 2012 2015 2017

Notes: 2000–2013 data from Gallup. "Don't know" response not shown.

Source: Reprinted from Kiley (2018) with permission from Pew Research Center.

EXHIBIT 13.5
Opinions About
the Affordable
Care Act

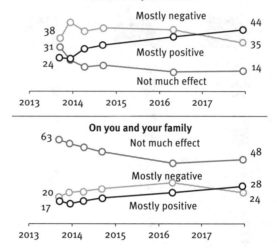

More say the health care law has had a positive than negative effect on nation

% who say the 2010 health care law has had a ____ effect so far...

On the country as a whole

Mostly negative — 44

38

31 — 35

24 — Mostly positive

Not much effect — 14

2013 2014 2015 2016 2017

On you and your family

63 — Not much effect — 48

Mostly negative — 28

20 — 24

17 — Mostly positive

2013 2014 2015 2016 2017

Note: "Don't know" responses not shown.

Source: Reprinted from Fingerhut (2017) with permission from Pew Research Center.

saying the effect was mostly positive rose from 17 percent in 2013 to 28 percent in 2017 (Fingerhut 2017). The percentage saying the effect was mostly negative also increased, from 20 percent to 24 percent. The percentage saying the law had "not much effect" declined from 63 percent to 48 percent.

These data show that Americans are both highly interested in and deeply divided over matters of health policy. Favorable opinions about the ACA have grown somewhat, but the law still does not enjoy a wide majority of support. People tend to view the ACA—like so much of health policy—through their own lens. Policy today seems to be more heavily dominated by ideology than it has in the past (Greene 2013; Schwartzmantel 2008).

Making Health Policy

Various writers have offered colorful descriptions of the way laws and regulations are made. Godfrey Saxe once remarked, "Laws, like sausages, cease to inspire respect in proportion as we know how they are made" (*University Chronicle* 1863). Equally insightful, Uwe Reinhardt (2019, 152) states, "Politically, you cannot legislate what rationally makes perfect sense."

Healthcare is a heavily regulated field, both because of the life-and-death nature of its services and because of its history of quackery (American

Medical Association [AMA] 2012; Budetti 2008; Field 2008; Friedman and Friedman 1982; Gadbois et al. 2015; Gorman 2015; Young 1967). Many of the complexities of healthcare regulation and policymaking date from the origins of the federalist structure of American governance. Health policy is set primarily at the state and federal levels, with some influence by local government (Feldstein 2015); however, the state and federal governments often have competing interests in healthcare, and the boundaries between the portions of the regulatory process that each entity directs are often in dispute. Further adding to the complexity are the variations in regulation that exist from one state to another, which are difficult for multistate organizations to navigate. Modern healthcare administrators must ensure that adequate resources are devoted to understanding and complying with all federal, state, and local regulations (Field 2007). Exhibit 13.6 presents a condensed list of many of the government entities that create and implement health-related policies and regulations in the United States.

EXHIBIT 13.6
A Condensed List of Government Players in Healthcare

Federal Government

- The public and interest groups
- Congress and committees
- Executive branch
  - US Department of Health and Human Services
    Agency for Healthcare Research and Quality
    Agency for Toxic Substances and Disease Registry
    Centers for Disease Control and Prevention (CDC)
    Food and Drug Administration
    Health Resources and Services Administration
    Centers for Medicare & Medicaid Services (CMS)
    Indian Health Service
    National Institutes of Health
    Office of the Assistant Secretary of Health
    Office of the Secretary
    Program Support Center
    Substance Abuse and Mental Health Services Administration
    Office of the Assistant Secretary for Preparedness and Response
  - CMS departments
    Office of Strategic Operations and Regulatory Affairs
    Office of Minority Health
    Office of Equal Opportunity and Civil Rights
    Center for Clinical Standards and Quality
    Office of Clinician Engagement
    Center for Medicare
    Center for Program Integrity
    Center for Medicare and Medicaid Innovation

(continued)

EXHIBIT 13.6
A Condensed
List of
Government
Players in
Healthcare
(continued)

Center for Consumer Information and Insurance Oversight
Center for Medicaid and CHIP Services
Offices of Hearings and Inquiries
Digital services
Medicare health plan operations
Quality improvement and survey and certification operations
o CDC Washington Office
Center for Global Health
National Institute for Occupational Safety and Health
Office for State, Tribal, Local, and Territorial Support
Office of Equal Employment Opportunity
Office of Infectious Diseases
National Center for Emerging and Zoonotic Infectious Diseases
National Center for HIV/AIDS, Viral Hepatitis, STD, and TB Prevention
National Center for Immunization and Respiratory Diseases
Office of Minority Health and Health Equity
Office of Noncommunicable Diseases, Injury, and Environmental Health
National Center for Chronic Disease Prevention and Health Promotion
National Center for Environmental Health / Agency for Toxic Substances
   and Disease Registry
National Center for Injury Prevention and Control
National Center on Birth Defects and Developmental Disabilities
Office of Public Health Preparedness and Response
Office of Public Health Scientific Service
Center for Surveillance, Epidemiology, and Laboratory Services
National Center for Health Statistics
Office of the Associate Director for Communication
Office of the Associate Director for Laboratory Science and Safety
Office of the Associate Director for Policy
Office of the Associate Director for Science
Office of the Chief of Staff
Office of the Chief Operating Officer
The Office of Public Health Preparedness
o Military healthcare
Defense Health Agency
Force Health Protection and Readiness
Uniformed Services University of the Health Sciences
Defense Centers of Excellence for Psychological Health and Traumatic
   Brain Injury
o Veterans Health Administration

State and Local Government

- State legislatures and their committees on health
- State departments of health and human services
- County and municipal departments of health and human services

Note: State and local entities will vary throughout the country.

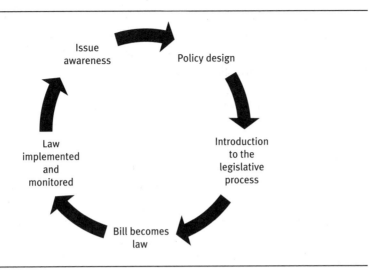

EXHIBIT 13.7
Healthcare
Policy Cycle

The development of US health policy occurs in a cycle, as pictured in exhibit 13.7. The cycle begins when a health-related issue gains the attention of political leaders. Such issues are often brought to the leaders' attention by individual constituents or special interest groups. Special interest groups in healthcare may include employers, patients and their advocates, insurance companies, practitioners and provider organizations, or producers of products and services—virtually anyone concerned with the cost, quality, and accessibility of the system.

Once an issue is considered for legislative action, a policy is designed, and legislation is drafted. The draft legislation, before it becomes law, is called a bill. The policy design process involves several important components:

- Gathering information
- Identifying and considering stakeholders and their level of involvement
- Understanding the power structure that supports or does not support the policy, and understanding stakeholders' interests and priorities
- Consideration of any existing policies
- A cost–benefit analysis
- A description of the plan for implementation
- Continued defining and redefining throughout the process

Once the policy has been designed, a political strategy for moving the policy forward must be developed, building both public support and legislative support. In the case of the US Congress, both the House of Representatives and the Senate have committees that will determine whether the bill will be taken to the full body for a final vote. In the House, committees likely to be involved in health policy include the Ways and Means Committee, the Commerce Committee, and the Committee on Appropriations. In the Senate, the committees most responsible for healthcare issues include the Committee on Health, Education, Labor, and Pensions and the Committee on Finance.

Both houses of Congress must approve the bill before the president can sign it into law. In many instances, the two houses will pass slightly different versions of the same law, in which case the two sides will need to work out the differences and create a mutually agreeable final version of the bill. Once the bill is passed by both houses of Congress, it is sent to the president for signature.

Once the bill becomes law, it often must be interpreted by the agency in the executive branch that will be responsible for its implementation. These interpretations are considered regulations and published in the *Federal Register*. Sometimes, if serious disagreement surrounds the law's implementation, the matter will be referred to the courts.

The policy cycle continues with evaluation of the law after it has been implemented (de Leeuw, Clavier, and Breton 2014). The specific outcomes the program is looking to produce should be defined at the outset, so that progress can be monitored and measured. Is the policy working to address the needs that were identified at the start of the process? Has the law been effectively implemented? Are any adjustments or new strategies needed?

An additional question involves when the program should be discontinued. How do we know when the mission has been accomplished? Sometimes, inertia takes over, and policymakers find that letting a program continue is easier than taking action to end it. In some instances, vested interests in the program might advocate for its continuation, regardless of evidence. To minimize these risks, clear end points for the program should be established as part of the policymaking process (Curran et al. 2012; Landsverk et al. 2011).

Significant Federal Regulations

The US healthcare system has been shaped by numerous federal laws and regulations across a wide range of concerns. This section does not aim to provide a full accounting of these regulations, but it will highlight some of those that have had the greatest impact.

The Hill-Burton Act

The Hospital Survey and Construction Act of 1946, commonly known as the Hill-Burton Act, significantly increased the number of hospital beds, improved the distribution of those beds, and improved the quality of hospital facilities across the United States (Schumann 2016). Clark and colleagues (1980) summarize the act's impact as follows:

1. Hill-Burton had a major redistributive impact on state bed supplies;
2. physician redistribution lagged far behind progress in bed redistribution; and
3. interstate distribution of physicians appears to have been unaffected by Hill-Burton–associated bed redistribution.

Medicare and Medicaid

The Medicare and Medicaid programs were established in 1965 under Title XVIII and Title XIX of the Social Security Act. The programs have been discussed in earlier chapters but merit additional mention here, given that their impact on the US healthcare delivery system has been enormous. Today, more than 60 million people are enrolled in Medicare, and more than 75 million are enrolled in a Medicaid program for at least part of the year (CMS 2019b). CMS administers Medicare and works with the states to administer Medicaid. It also maintains national quality measures and implements reforms to support better patient care (CMS 2018b).

Medicare and Medicaid have been a driving force behind the tremendous growth in US medical spending since the mid-1900s (CMS 2018a, 2019c). In 1960, five years before the programs were established, national health expenditures amounted to 27.2 million; by 1970, they had grown to 76.6 million.

The National Environmental Policy Act of 1969

The National Environmental Policy Act (NEPA) of 1969 led to the creation of the US Environmental Protection Agency (EPA) and established a national framework "to promote efforts which will prevent or eliminate damage to the environment and biosphere and stimulate the health and welfare of man" (EPA 2019).

The EPA does not deal directly in healthcare policy, but its environmental protection efforts have a major impact on health and well-being. The effects of pollution on human health are well known, and the cost estimates of environmental disease are staggering (Hollenbach and Cloutier 2015; Knol et al. 2009; Remoundou and Koundouri 2009). Trasande and Liu (2011) estimated that the total cost of environmental disease in children was $76.6 billion in 2008. Equally troubling is the effect of pollutants such as hydrocarbons and lead on children's ability to learn (Grandjean and Bellanger 2017; Landrigan and Goldman 2011).

The Health Maintenance Organization Act of 1973

The Health Maintenance Organization (HMO) Act of 1973 provided federal financial assistance for the development of HMOs and helped individual HMOs meet federal qualification requirements (Dorsey 1975; US Congress 1973). It also included a "dual choice" mandate that required employers to offer coverage from at least one federally qualified HMO to all employees (Rosoff 1975).

The Health Care Quality Improvement Act of 1986

The Health Care Quality Improvement Act (HCQIA) of 1986 encouraged the use of peer review for the purpose of weeding out bad providers (Heffernan 1996). The law granted immunity to people who reported certain events—such as actions against one's license, malpractice settlements, and negative determinations of hospital privileges—to the National Practitioner Data Bank (NPDB) as part of the peer review process (NPDB 2019). Some people have argued, however, that the law fails to provide the intended safeguards. Van Geertruyden (2001) points out that immunity under the HCQIA may protect people who engage in bad-faith peer review, creating a scenario analogous to a "fox guarding the henhouse."

The Health Insurance Portability and Accountability Act of 1996

The Health Insurance Portability and Accountability Act (HIPAA) of 1996 is well known to most people in healthcare. One of the law's primary purposes is to ensure the privacy of people's protected health information (PHI). Under HIPAA, PHI includes any "individually identifiable health information" that is held or transmitted orally, on paper, or electronically by the health organization (US Department of Health and Human Services [HHS] 2013). It may include demographic information; past, present; or future physical or mental health status; or any other information that could be reasonably used to identify a person (e.g., birth date, Social Security number, home address). The rule applies to health plans, healthcare providers, and business associates that might work with plans and providers (HHS 2016, 2017b, 2019b).

Because the privacy of one's PHI is considered a civil right in the United States, the HHS Office of Civil Rights is charged with enforcing HIPAA. The number of HIPAA complaints has risen dramatically in the years since the law was passed, in part because the use of the internet and social media has created a heightened risk of data breaches, whether inadvertent or with criminal intent (Arndt 2018; HHS 2017a, 2019a; *HIPAA Journal* 2018).

The Balanced Budget Act of 1997

The Balanced Budget Act of 1997 created Medicare Part C, also known as Medicare Advantage, as well as the Children's Health Insurance Program

(CHIP) (US Congress 1997). CHIP was established to provide coverage for uninsured low-income children.

In 2018, CHIP covered about 9.6 million children for at least part of the year (CMS 2019a). The impact of CHIP is most commonly reported in three main areas (Bisgaier and Rhodes 2011; Howell et al. 2010):

- *Coverage.* Medicaid and CHIP have significantly expanded health coverage. Together, the programs cover as many as one in every three US children (Paradise 2014). From 1997 to 2012, the uninsured rate for children fell by half, from 14 percent to 7 percent (American Academy of Pediatrics, Committee on Child Health Financing 2014). All CHIP programs cover dental, physical, occupational, and speech and language therapies, often without limits (Strauss 2017).
- *Access to care.* Children with Medicaid and CHIP have better access to primary and preventive care than uninsured children do. They also have significantly better access to specialist and dental care (Paradise 2014).
- *Outcomes.* Some studies have indicated that Medicaid and CHIP expansions have had a positive impact in terms of reducing child mortality and preventing avoidable hospitalizations (Howell et al. 2010); other studies, however, have not established such a clear link (Rosenbach et al. 2007).

The Medicare Prescription Drug, Improvement, and Modernization Act of 2003

The Medicare Prescription Drug, Improvement, and Modernization Act of 2003, also called the Medicare Modernization Act (MMA), created Medicare Part D, a prescription drug benefit (KFF 2004). The act also provided subsidies for low-income individuals. Like Medicare Part B, Part D is a voluntary benefit and requires the beneficiary to pay a premium for the plan selected (Havrda et al. 2005; Jennings 2004; Seay 2005).

The Patient Safety and Quality Improvement Act of 2005

The Patient Safety and Quality Improvement Act (PSQIA) of 2005 sought to promote a culture of safety and encouraged the development of quality improvement strategies (Agency for Healthcare Research and Quality [AHRQ] 2014, 2019). The law created patient safety organizations (PSOs), made up of external experts, to collect, aggregate, and analyze safety information reported by providers (HHS 2017c). The law included confidentiality protections for the information reported. The PSQIA was the first major regulatory action to use data analysis to look for patterns to identify safety concerns and suggest remedies.

The Affordable Care Act of 2010

The Affordable Care Act (ACA) of 2010 represented the most ambitious effort to reform our healthcare system since the passage of Medicare and Medicaid. One of its central goals was to move the US system in the direction of universal coverage (US House of Representatives 2010). Key provisions of the ACA expanded Medicaid and CHIP, established requirements for individuals and businesses to buy and provide coverage, provided government subsidies to assist with those requirements, introduced health insurance exchanges to help consumers compare and purchase insurance plans, and supported innovative approaches to healthcare delivery and payment. See chapter 2 for a more detailed summary of the law's provisions.

The Hospital Readmissions Reduction Program

The Hospital Readmissions Reduction Program (HRRP), established under the ACA in 2012, financially penalizes hospitals that have higher-than-expected 30-day readmission rates for certain conditions (e.g., acute myocardial infarction, heart failure, pneumonia) (McIlvennan, Eapen, and Allen 2015). The 30-day readmission rate is the percentage of patients discharged from the hospital who are readmitted with 30 days.

The goal of the HRRP is to encourage more careful follow-up with patients following discharge. Effective follow-up can help catch potential problems early on and allow the issues to be managed on an outpatient basis before they become more serious. In the past, hospitals had little incentive to engage in follow-up activities, and they generally were unable to provide such services without compensation.

One example of effective follow-up involves patients with heart failure. Complications associated with heart failure can often be detected when the patient begins to retain water, causing rapid weight gain, because the heart is not functioning properly. By calling patients daily and checking on their weight, medical professionals can quickly detect potential changes in their condition. If a problem is detected, a medical intervention can be done on an outpatient basis, before a crisis occurs—potentially avoiding an emergency room visit and subsequent hospitalization (AHRQ 2013). Even if the early intervention ultimately does not prevent an admission, the patient's condition will likely not be as serious and the hospitalization will not be as complicated.

Overcoming Fragmentation

Elsewhere in the book, we have spoken of the fragmented, or "siloed," nature of US healthcare. This fragmentation exists not only within the healthcare system but also across other segments of life, often with serious

EXHIBIT 13.8
The Pillars of
Well-Being and
the Healthcare
System

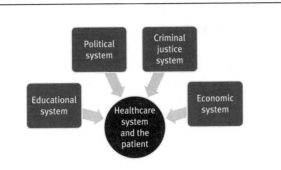

policy implications. Education, the political system, criminal justice, and the economy function as pillars of well-being in our society, and failures in any of those areas can result in social dysfunction that finds its way into the healthcare system (see exhibit 13.8). Violence, addiction, unhealthy lifestyles, poor education, and poverty are all contributors to escalating healthcare needs, yet their solutions fall in large part outside of the healthcare pillar. Such complex problems cannot be solved by any one segment of society on its own, even with the best intentions or heroic effort.

Leonardo da Vinci used the term *collegamento*, meaning *connection*, to describe his insights in the areas of art, science, and engineering (Isaacson 2018; da Vinci 2013). He saw the relationships across these disparate fields, linked by the beauty of nature in science, design, and art. Too often, policymakers overlook such connections, and interactions across the pillars of well-being go unnoticed. The resulting fragmentation hampers our efforts to address complex societal problems.

Consider, for instance, the opioid crisis, which was discussed at length in chapter 11. Understandably, many efforts to address the crisis have focused on prescription practices and the production of opioids; however, a comprehensive approach also must address the root causes of addiction. Similarly, when an outbreak of communicable disease occurs, we must, of course, focus on treating the people who are ill; at the same time, however, we must work to identify and eliminate the source of the infection. In public health, efforts that prioritize eliminating the root cause of a problem, as opposed to merely treating the symptoms, are known as *upstreaming*, and effective upstreaming often requires reaching across sectors.

The siloed nature of our educational, political, criminal justice, and economic systems inherently prevents collaboration and impedes the development of systematic solutions to complex problems. At times, the incentives are perverse. Traditionally, the US healthcare system has paid for the volume of services provided but largely neglected to allocate sufficient resources for prevention (Lyu et al. 2017; Makary 2012)—with that framework, how can we be surprised that the system is so money driven? Likewise, the other pillars have had their own incentives to perpetuate the current approach. In the documentary *Escape Fire*, Donald Berwick, former CMS administrator and founder of the Institute for Healthcare Improvement, says that "everybody in the system is doing exactly what they should, from their own point of view" (Heineman and Froemke 2012). In many instances, addressing our most urgent and complex health challenges will require the various pillars to expand their points of view.

Another obstacle to proper collaboration across the pillars is the lack of a common pool of meaning. In other words, the various parties do not have a common base of facts and a shared understanding of those facts. Often, ideological divisions take hold—between advocates of social justice and market justice, between supporters and opponents of government intervention, between people who raise concerns about climate change and those who deny its existence. The list could go on. When such divisions drive people away from a common pool of meaning, we lose the potential for collaboration, upstreaming, and true solutions to our problems (Adams et al. 2003; Blendon and Benson 2001; Marcus, Dorn, and McNulty 2012; Shonk 2019).

The Outlook for US Health Policy

The future of healthcare policy in the United States is difficult to envision. Much will depend on political matters and which party or "moral tribe" is in control of the process (Greene 2013). So often, the argument returns to the most fundamental question: Does everyone in the United States have a right to healthcare? The country has thus far been unable to agree on an answer to that question.

People who favor the social justice approach will continue to seek greater government involvement and funding to serve more of the country's people. People in the market justice camp, meanwhile, will advocate for more market-based solutions that place greater emphasis on individual choice of plans and funding options.

Political Rhetoric

Attempts to move the country toward universal coverage have been further clouded by vague or deceptive language. The term *universal coverage*—meaning that everyone is covered by some mechanism, whether public or private—is often used interchangeably with *national health insurance* or *socialized medicine*, both of which imply much greater government involvement. This lack of specificity may at times be intentional, for political effect, or it might occur out of genuine misunderstanding. Regardless, it has the effect of deepening divisions and heightening confusion.

Much of the political rhetoric that focuses on people's ability to purchase their own care seems out of step with the realities of our system. Because a majority of Americans have third-party coverage, only a small percentage of people—typically, the wealthy and the uninsured—directly pay for their healthcare. I recall a conversation I had years ago with Uwe Reinhardt, the late Princeton healthcare economist. He said, "Why do we care so much about what the rich do? They will always do what they want, because they can afford to do so. We need to design a system that is suited to most of us."

Part of the problem continues to stem from our system's incredible maze of laws, rules, and regulations. When policymakers are unable to grasp the intricacies of the healthcare system, they are more likely to be swayed by a political argument than a pragmatic one. Ideology takes over, making compromise difficult and ensuring that the political back-and-forth continues.

The Future of the Affordable Care Act

Nothing exemplifies the country's deep political divisions and divergent attitudes toward healthcare more than ongoing debate over the ACA. The law was passed by Democrats, without a single Republican vote, during the presidency of Barack Obama. Republicans subsequently challenged the law in the courts and attempted—more than 50 times—to repeal it (Reuters 2018; Berensen 2017). During the presidency of Donald Trump, the Republican approach shifted away from full repeal of the ACA and toward dismantling the law one piece at a time, undercutting key elements necessary for the law to function as intended. The Trump administration also made decisions to relax enforcement of certain ACA provisions (Vogenberg and Smart 2018).

Initially, the ACA's individual and employer mandates promised that everyone would be covered by insurance in some fashion. The mandates were intended to ensure that insurance companies would have more potentially healthy enrollees to offset those with more serious medical conditions, thereby creating an actuarially normal distribution that insurance companies could price accordingly (French et al. 2016). Insurance companies agreed to support the ACA based on these provisions. In January 2019, however, the individual mandate was repealed, effectively eliminating this important strategy within the law (Jost 2018).

Other efforts have focused on eliminating some of the required coverage elements for insurance plans. These elements had been included in the ACA for the purpose of standardizing plans, ensuring that all plans meet a specified level of coverage, and creating a less complicated environment for the purchase of health insurance (Morrisey 2013). However, if a plan covers more services, it will have a higher cost; hence, standardized coverage requirements have the effect of removing many lower-cost options from the market. Consider, for instance, a couple in their sixties who have no intention of having children. Should they be allowed to buy a cheaper policy that does not include maternity benefits, or should their choice be restricted to more expensive options that meet that requirement?

Despite the various modifications, the ACA remains the law of the land as of 2020. Just as conservatives were quick to weaken the ACA's provisions when they gained control of Congress, liberal politicians would likely push a more progressive approach if the political winds shifted in their favor. Given our country's political divide, the long-term future of the ACA is difficult to predict.

The law could remain in effect, likely with further modifications; it could be repealed without replacement; or it could be repealed and replaced. If it were to be repealed without a replacement, roughly 20 million people would be expected to lose coverage, either by choice or because they could no longer afford a plan (Ku et al. 2017; Obama 2017; Oberlander 2018). The impact would depend largely on whether provisions that prevent underwriting based on pre-existing conditions were allowed to return. Some people have proposed replacing the ACA with a single-payer system or through efforts to expand coverage through Medicaid, Medicare, and the various individual markets (Friedmann, Andrews, and Humphreys 2017; Glied and Jackson 2017; Jost 2018; Jost and Lazarus 2017; Long et al. 2017; RAND Corporation 2018).

In the meantime, patients, providers, employers, and virtually all stakeholders in the healthcare system must live with the uncertainty. How can we approach our planning when the laws might change with the next political cycle?

To a large extent, the current debate over healthcare reform seems to lack a political center. Perhaps, in time, a reasonable compromise can be reached to better align our laws, incentives, and objectives and to ensure some basic level of care to all citizens—not a conservative, liberal, or progressive approach but a pragmatic one (Anderson 2006; Inskeep, Greene, and Martin 2011; Starr 1982, 2011, 2018).

A Moral Dilemma

At the root of our national debate over healthcare reform is the moral dilemma of what actions we are willing to take to advance the health and well-being of the nation's people.

The English philosopher Phillipa Foot (2001) designed a classic thought experiment that sheds light on the ways people approach moral dilemmas and decide between right and wrong. In Foot's scenario, five people are tied to a railroad track as a runaway trolley approaches. You are at the switch that could divert the trolley to a different track, where only one person is tied. The scenario has two possible outcomes: If you do nothing, five people are killed; if you engage the switch to divert the train, only one person is killed. When various versions of this scenario have been tested, as many as 90 percent of respondents choose not to engage the switch. The body of knowledge associated with this experiment has come to be known as "trolleyology" (Altschuler 2014; Conover 2013).

Similar tendencies for weighing the well-being of an individual versus that of a group have been examined by Ariely (2010), who points to the fact that fundraising campaigns for humanitarian relief often focus on a single person rather than on the masses of people affected by a crisis. Evidence suggests that potential donors are more likely to give when they see the effects on an individual.

Rosenbaum (2018) describes a trolleylike scenario involving driverless cars. Should the cars' autonomous driving systems be programmed to protect the passenger at all cost or to do the least harm? Should the system be set so that it swerves the car into a wall to avoid a group of pedestrians, even if the action causes the death of the passenger?

Greene (2013) conducted an experiment to test the practical validity of trolleyology and to further examine moral decision making. He recruited a group of medical doctors and public health professionals—all of whom managed health resources or public health programs—and presented them with a scenario in which a hospital had a limited number of life-support machines. The dilemma was whether to save the lives of several patients who needed brief access to life-support equipment by sacrificing a gravely ill patient who needed access to the same equipment. The clear majority of respondents were unwilling to sacrifice the individual, although responses varied somewhat depending on the respondent's field. Only 12 percent of physicians said they would allow the more gravely ill patient to die, whereas 21 percent of public health professionals were willing to do so.

Similar decision scenarios can be extended to any number of healthcare examples—for instance, allocating funds toward prevention rather than intensive treatment. As healthcare continues to consume more resources with ever-expanding options for care, these types of moral dilemmas will undoubtedly increase.

Greene (2013) suggests that our approach to moral dilemmas is rooted in the way our brains function, noting that our society has evolved faster than our neurobiology:

> Our brains were designed for tribal life, for getting along with a select group of others (Us) and for fighting off everyone else (Them). But

modern times have forced the world's tribes into a shared space, resulting in epic clashes of values along with unprecedented opportunities. As the world shrinks, the moral lines that divide us become more salient and more puzzling.

Given the nature of these moral dilemmas, it is unsurprising that the political process is so challenging. Ultimately, we are talking about the rationing of healthcare. The concept of rationing is highly unpopular in the United States, but we have been rationing care all along, whether by price, by access, by literacy, or by choice. The need to balance competing priorities in the face of scarce resources is an unpleasant reality across our healthcare system (Knoepffler, Zerth, and O'Malley 2019).

More than 100,000 people in the United States are currently waiting for kidney transplants (National Kidney Foundation 2020). People often must wait several years for a transplant, and many people die before receiving one. In 2013, Nobel Prize–winning economist Alvin Roth (2016) devised a concept known as a "kidney donor chain" to match living donors with recipients. The central idea is for a living donor to agree to donate a kidney to another person, whom they likely do not know, with no expectation of receiving anything in return. The idea has been further developed so that a person can agree to donate a kidney to an unknown recipient at the same time that a friend or loved one receives a kidney from another willing unknown donor (Melcher et al. 2013; Rees et al. 2009; Solman 2019; Seaborg 2018). In either case, the concept represents a heightened level of altruism that cannot be easily explained in simple economic terms. Would you volunteer to participate in such a program?

Working Toward a New Approach

Given the complexity of our healthcare challenges and the shortcomings of our political discourse, perhaps we need a new approach.

John Merrow's (2017) *Addicted to Reform* provides an interesting look at educational reform, with implications that are highly applicable to US healthcare. He describes the US "addiction" to school reform as follows (Merrow 2017, 2):

> Here's how school reform typically works. A specific educational problem is attacked vigorously until victory can be declared. Then we move on to a new problem and a new reform strategy. But after a decade or so, that first problem reemerges, leading to another reform strategy. It's a never-ending cycle, one that keeps us from confronting and addressing public education's real problem: an outmoded system of schooling that is harming many children and our nation's future.

Merrow then offers a 12-step program for improving public education.

By borrowing some of the most relevant points from Merrow's (2017) program and adding a healthcare twist, we arrive at the following seven-step process for improving healthcare reform:

1. *Own the problem.* Too often, we seem to want to blame everyone else for the complexities and high costs of our healthcare system.
2. *Ask the right questions.* To paraphrase Albert Einstein, to get the correct answer to a problem, you first need to ask the right question.
3. *Make connections.* We need to address our "silo" problem, look at our issues in a broader context, and be willing to work together.
4. *Embrace technology carefully.* Certainly, we have a tremendous amount of new and emerging technology at our disposal—but are we carefully applying it in a way that optimizes the desired results?
5. *Embrace providers in a respectful manner.* The people who work in healthcare are experiencing burnout at an unprecedented rate, in large part because we are pushing the existing system beyond its capabilities without fundamentally reforming the system itself. Our incentives are incorrect.
6. *Measure what matters.* The various metrics we have in healthcare can be bewildering, and often we focus so much on the numbers that we lose sight of what we are actually trying to accomplish. Healthcare leaders should think carefully about what really represents healthcare productivity and value. Is it dollars or is it health?
7. *Choose a new path.* This point might be the most difficult of all, because of all the entrenched vested interests and the inherent divisiveness of people's views on health policy. Finding reasonable compromise might seem impossible, but we must try.

Health policymakers in the United States must contend with a wide variety of influences, but their ultimate purpose is to serve the public's interest. The future of US health policy will need to address the country's own ever-expanding health needs while also determining the country's role in global initiatives. Many of our most important policy issues remain unresolved, and failure to move past our ideological differences will have serious consequences for years to come.

Discussion Questions

1. Why has universal coverage been so hard to achieve?
2. What are some of the moral dilemmas facing health policymakers?

3. What impact does the high cost of drugs and other healthcare services have on the possibility of universal coverage?

4. What are the differences between universal coverage, national health insurance, and a government-owned healthcare system?

5. How can we possibly reach consensus on health in such a diverse and pluralist society?

References

Adams, W. M., D. Brockington, J. Dyson, and B. Vira. 2003. "Managing Tragedies: Understanding Conflict over Common Pool Resources." *Science* 302 (5652): 1915–16. https://doi.org/10.1126/science.1087771.

Agency for Healthcare Research and Quality (AHRQ). 2019. "Culture of Safety." Updated September. https://psnet.ahrq.gov/primer/culture-safety.

———. 2014. "The Patient Safety and Quality Improvement Act of 2005." Reviewed October. www.ahrq.gov/policymakers/psoact.html.

———. 2013. "Re-Engineered Discharge (RED) Toolkit—Tool 5: How to Conduct a Postdischarge Followup Phone Call." Reviewed March. www.ahrq.gov/professionals/systems/hospital/red/toolkit/redtool5.html.

Altman, D. E., and D. H. Morgan. 1983. "The Role of State and Local Government in Health." *Health Affairs* 2 (4): 7–31. https://doi.org/10.1377/hlthaff.2.4.7.

Altschuler, G. C. 2014. "Trolleyology: A History of the 'Trolley Problem' Thought Experiment." *Psychology Today*. Published January 23. www.psychologytoday.com/us/blog/is-america/201401/trolleyology.

American Academy of Pediatrics, Committee on Child Health Financing. 2014. "Children's Health Insurance Program (CHIP): Accomplishments, Challenges, and Policy Recommendations." *Pediatrics* 133 (3): e784–93. https://doi.org/10.1542/peds.2013-4059.

American Medical Association (AMA). 2012. "Quackery Abroad." *JAMA* 307 (21): 2236. https://doi.org/10.1001/jama.2012.3015.

American Public Health Association. 2019. "What Is Public Health?" Accessed October 15. www.apha.org/what-is-public-health.

———. 1995. "The Role of Public Health in Ensuring Healthy Communities." Policy No. 9521(PP). Published January 1. www.apha.org/policies-and-advocacy/public-health-policy-statements/policy-database/2014/07/30/10/48/the-role-of-public-health-in-ensuring-healthy-communities.

Anderson, G. 2006. "The Health Care Mess: How We Got into It and What It Will Take to Get Out." *JAMA* 295 (3): 331–31. https://doi.org/10.1001/jama.295.3.331-b.

Ariely, D. 2010. *Predictably Irrational: The Hidden Forces That Shape Our Decisions.* New York: Harper Perennial.

Arndt, R. 2018. "Atrium Health Data Breach Exposes Up to 2.65 Million Patients' Data." *Modern Healthcare*. Published November 28. www.modernhealthcare. com/article/20181128/NEWS/181129940.

Berensen, T. 2017. "Reminder: The House Voted to Repeal Obamacare More than 50 Times." *Time*. Published March 24. http://time.com/4712725/ ahca-house-repeal-votes-obamacare/.

Berwick, D. M. 2002. "A User's Manual for the IOM's 'Quality Chasm' Report." *Health Affairs* 21 (3): 80–90. https://doi.org/10.1377/hlthaff.21.3.80.

Bisgaier, J., and K. V. Rhodes. 2011. "Auditing Access to Specialty Care for Children with Public Insurance." *New England Journal of Medicine* 364 (24): 2324–33. https://doi.org/10.1056/NEJMsa1013285.

Blendon, R. J., and J. M. Benson. 2001. "Americans' Views on Health Policy: A Fifty-Year Historical Perspective." *Health Affairs* 20 (2): 33–46. https://doi. org/10.1377/hlthaff.20.2.33.

Budetti, P. P. 2008. "Market Justice and US Health Care." *JAMA* 299 (1): 92–94. https://doi.org/10.1001/jama.2007.27.

Centers for Medicare & Medicaid Services (CMS). 2019a. "Children's Health Insurance Program (CHIP)." Accessed October 15. www.medicaid.gov/chip/ index.html.

———. 2019b. "CMS Fast Facts." Updated July 11. www.cms.gov/research-statistics-data-and-systems/statistics-trends-and-reports/cms-fast-facts/ index.html.

———. 2019c. "NHE Fact Sheet." Updated April 26. www.cms.gov/research-statistics-data-and-systems/statistics-trends-and-reports/nationalhealth expenddata/nhe-fact-sheet.html.

———. 2018a. "National Health Expenditure Projections 2017–2026." www.cms. gov/Research-Statistics-Data-and-Systems/Statistics-Trends-and-Reports/ NationalHealthExpendData/Downloads/ForecastSummary.pdf.

———. 2018b. "National Impact Assessment of the Centers for Medicare and Medicaid Services (CMS) Quality Measures Reports." Updated May 8. www. cms.gov/Medicare/Quality-Initiatives-Patient-Assessment-Instruments/ QualityMeasures/National-Impact-Assessment-of-the-Centers-for-Medicare-and-Medicaid-Services-CMS-Quality-Measures-Reports.html.

Clark, L. J., M. J. Field, T. L. Koontz, and V. L. Koontz. 1980. "The Impact of Hill-Burton: An Analysis of Hospital Bed and Physician Distribution in the United States, 1950–1970." *Medical Care* 18 (5): 532–50. https://doi. org/10.1097/00005650-198005000-00006.

Conover, C. 2013. "'Trolleyology' Shows Why Up to 90% of Americans Should Oppose Obamacare." *Forbes*. Published November 25. www.forbes.com/ sites/theapothecary/2013/11/25/trolleyology-shows-why-up-to-90-of-americans-should-oppose-obamacare/#2536b2217328.

Costich, J. F., F. D. Scutchfield, and R. C. Ingram. 2015. "Population Health, Public Health, and Accountable Care: Emerging Roles and Relationships." *American Journal of Public Health* 105 (5): 846–50. https://doi.org/10.2105/AJPH.2014.302484.

Curran, G. M., M. Bauer, B. Mittman, J. M. Pyne, and C. Stetler. 2012. "Effectiveness-Implementation Hybrid Designs: Combining Elements of Clinical Effectiveness and Implementation Research to Enhance Public Health Impact." *Medical Care* 50 (3): 217–26. https://doi.org/10.1097/MLR.0b013e3182408812.

Daniel, T. M. 2006. "The History of Tuberculosis." *Respiratory Medicine* 100 (11): 1862–70. https://doi.org/10.1016/j.rmed.2006.08.006.

da Vinci, Leonardo. 2013. *Leonardo's Notebooks: Writing and Art of the Great Master.* Edited by H. A. Suh. New York: Black Dog & Leventhal.

de Leeuw, E., C. Clavier, and E. Breton. 2014. "Health Policy—Why Research It and How: Health Political Science." *Health Research Policy and Systems* 12: 55. https://doi.org/10.1186/1478-4505-12-55.

Diep, F. 2017. "Here's How Much Money Every Senator Received from Health-Insurance Companies in the Last Election Cycle." *Pacific Standard.* Published September 19. https://psmag.com/news/health-insurance-senate-money-connections.

Dorsey, J. L. 1975. "The Health Maintenance Organization Act of 1973 (P.L. 93-222) and Prepaid Group Practice Plans." *Medical Care* 13 (1): 1–9. https://doi.org/10.1097/00005650-197501000-00001.

Duffy, T. P. 2011. "The Flexner Report—100 Years Later." *Yale Journal of Biology and Medicine* 84 (3): 269–76. www.ncbi.nlm.nih.gov/pmc/articles/PMC3178858/.

Feldstein, P. J. 2015. *Health Policy Issues: An Economic Perspective,* 6th ed. Chicago: Health Administration Press.

Field, R. I. 2008. "Why Is Health Care Regulation So Complex?" *P&T: A Peer-Reviewed Journal for Managed Care and Hospital Formulary Management* 33 (10): 607–8. www.ncbi.nlm.nih.gov/pmc/articles/PMC2730786/.

———. 2007. *Health Care Regulation in America: Complexity, Confrontation, and Compromise.* New York: Oxford University Press.

Fingerhut, H. 2017. "For the First Time, More Americans Say 2010 Health Care Law Has Had a Positive than Negative Effect on U.S." Pew Research Center. Published December 11. www.pewresearch.org/fact-tank/2017/12/11/for-the-first-time-more-americans-say-2010-health-care-law-has-had-a-positive-than-negative-impact-on-u-s/.

Foot, P. 2001. *Natural Goodness.* Oxford, UK: Clarendon Press.

French, M. T., J. Homer, G. Gumus, and L. Hickling. 2016. "Key Provisions of the Patient Protection and Affordable Care Act (ACA): A Systematic Review and Presentation of Early Research Findings." *Health Services Research* 51 (5): 1735–71. https://doi.org/10.1111/1475-6773.12511.

Friedman, M., and R. D. Friedman. 1982. *Capitalism and Freedom.* Chicago: University of Chicago Press.

Friedmann, P. D., C. M. Andrews, and K. Humphreys. 2017. "How ACA Repeal Would Worsen the Opioid Epidemic." *New England Journal of Medicine* 376: e16. https://doi.org/10.1056/NEJMp1700834.

Gadbois, E. A., E. A. Miller, D. Tyler, and O. Intrator. 2015. "Trends in State Regulation of Nurse Practitioners and Physician Assistants, 2001 to 2010." *Medical Care Research and Review* 72 (2): 200–219. https://doi.org/10.1177/1077558714563763.

Gawande, A. 2017. "Is Health Care a Right?" *New Yorker.* Published October 2. www.newyorker.com/magazine/2017/10/02/is-health-care-a-right.

Glied, S., and A. Jackson. 2017. "The Future of the Affordable Care Act and Insurance Coverage." *American Journal of Public Health* 107 (4): 538–40. https://doi.org/10.2105/AJPH.2017.303665.

Gorman, D. 2015. "On the Barriers to Significant Innovation in and Reform of Healthcare." *Internal Medicine Journal* 45 (6): 597–99. https://doi.org/10.1111/imj.12775.

Grandjean, P., and M. Bellanger. 2017. "Calculation of the Disease Burden Associated with Environmental Chemical Exposures: Application of Toxicological Information in Health Economic Estimation." *Environmental Health* 16 (1): 123. https://doi.org/10.1186/s12940-017-0340-3.

Granshaw, L. P., and R. Porter. 1989. *The Hospital in History.* New York: Routledge.

Greene, J. D. 2013. *Moral Tribes: Emotion, Reason, and the Gap Between Us and Them.* New York: Penguin. www.penguinrandomhouse.com/books/299057/moral-tribes-by-joshua-greene/.

Grodzins, M. 1960. "The Federal System." In *Goals for Americans: The Report of the President's Commission on National Goals,* 265–82. Englewood Cliffs, NJ: Prentice Hall. https://archive.org/stream/goalsforamerican00unitrich/goalsforamerican00unitrich_djvu.txt.

Gusmano, M. K. 2012. "Power, Politics, and Health Spending Priorities." *Virtual Mentor* 14 (11): 885–89. https://doi.org/10.1001/virtualmentor.2012.14.11.msoc1-1211.

Havrda, D. E., B. A. Omundsen, W. Bender, and M. A. Kirkpatrick. 2005. "Impact of the Medicare Modernization Act on Low-Income Persons." *Annals of Internal Medicine* 143 (8): 600–608. https://doi.org/10.7326/0003-4819-143-8-200510180-00011.

Heffernan, M. 1996. "The Health Care Quality Improvement Act of 1986 and the National Practitioner Data Bank: The Controversy over Practitioner Privacy Versus Public Access." *Bulletin of the Medical Library Association* 84 (2): 263–69. www.ncbi.nlm.nih.gov/pubmed/8826636.

Heineman, M., and S. Froemke (dirs.). 2012. *Escape Fire: The Fight to Rescue American Healthcare.* Aisle C Production and Our Time Projects. www.escapefiremovie.com.

HIPAA Journal. 2018. "Largest Healthcare Data Breaches of 2017." Published January 4. www.hipaajournal.com/largest-healthcare-data-breaches-2017/.

Hollenbach, J. P., and M. M. Cloutier. 2015. "Childhood Asthma Management and Environmental Triggers." *Pediatric Clinics of North America* 62 (5): 1199–1214. https://doi.org/10.1016/j.pcl.2015.05.011.

Howell, E., S. Decker, S. Hogan, A. Yemane, and J. Foster. 2010. "Declining Child Mortality and Continuing Racial Disparities in the Era of the Medicaid and SCHIP Insurance Coverage Expansions." *American Journal of Public Health* 100 (12): 2500–2506. https://doi.org/10.2105/AJPH.2009.184622.

Inskeep, S., D. Greene, and R. Martin. 2011. "Paul Starr: Will the Healthcare War Ever End?" KCRW. Published December 14. www.kcrw.com/news-culture/shows/kcrw-presents-zocalo-public-square/paul-starr-will-the-healthcare-war-ever-end.

Institute of Medicine (IOM). 2015. *Measuring the Impact of Interprofessional Education on Collaborative Practice and Patient Outcomes.* Washington, DC: National Academies Press.

———. 2003. *The Future of the Public's Health in the 21st Century.* Washington, DC: National Academies Press.

———. 2001. *Crossing the Quality Chasm: A New Health System for the 21st Century.* Washington, DC: National Academies Press.

Isaacson, W. 2018. *Leonardo da Vinci.* New York: Simon & Schuster.

Jennings, C. P. 2004. "The Medicare Prescription Drug, Improvement, and Modernization Act of 2003." *Policy, Politics, & Nursing Practice* 5 (1): 57–58. https://doi.org/10.1177/1527154403262104.

Jost, T. S. 2018. "Mandate Repeal Provision Ends Health Care Calm." *Health Affairs* 37 (1): 13–14. https://doi.org/10.1377/hlthaff.2017.1551.

Jost, T. S., and S. Lazarus. 2017. "Trump's Executive Order on Health Care—Can It Undermine the ACA if Congress Fails to Act?" *New England Journal of Medicine* 376 (13): 1201–3. https://doi.org/10.1056/NEJMp1701340.

Kaiser Family Foundation (KFF). 2019. "Federal Medical Assistance Percentage (FMAP) for Medicaid and Multiplier." Accessed October 15. www.kff.org/medicaid/state-indicator/federal-matching-rate-and-multiplier/?currentTimeframe=0&sortModel=%7B%22colId%22:%22Location%22,%22sort%22:%22asc%22%7D.

———. 2004. *Prescription Drug Coverage for Medicare Beneficiaries: An Overview of the Medicare Prescription Drug, Improvement, and Modernization Act of 2003.* Published January 14. www.kff.org/wp-content/uploads/2013/01/prescription-drug-coverage-for-medicare-beneficiares-an-overview-of-the-medicare-prescription-drug-improvement-act-2003.pdf.

Kiley, J. 2018. "60% in US Say Health Care Coverage Is Government's Responsibility." Pew Research Center. Published October 3. www.pewresearch.org/fact-tank/2018/10/03/most-continue-to-say-ensuring-health-care-coverage-is-governments-responsibility/.

Kirzinger, A., L. Hamel, B. DiJulio, C. Munana, and M. Brodie. 2018. "KFF Election Tracking Poll: Health Care in the 2018 Midterms." Kaiser Family Foundation. Published October 18. www.kff.org/health-reform/poll-finding/kff-election-tracking-poll-health-care-in-the-2018-midterms/.

Knickman, J. R., and A. R. Kovner. 2015. "The Future of Health Care Delivery and Health Policy." In *Jonas and Kovner's Health Care Delivery in the United States*, 11th ed., edited by J. R. Knickman and A. R. Kovner, 333–42. New York: Springer.

Knoepffler, N., J. Zerth, and M. O'Malley. 2019. "Prioritization Not Rationing in Cancer Care." In *Regulatory and Economic Aspects in Oncology*, edited by E. Walter, 189–205. New York: Springer. https://doi.org/10.1007/978-3-030-01207-6_12.

Knol, A. B., A. C. Petersen, J. P. Van Der Sluijs, and E. Lebret. 2009. "Dealing with Uncertainties in Environmental Burden of Disease Assessment." *Environmental Health* 8: 21. https://doi.org/10.1186/1476-069X-8-21.

Ku, L., E. Steinmetz, E. Brantley, N. Holla, and B. Bruen. 2017. "The American Health Care Act: Economic and Employment Consequences for States." Commonwealth Fund. Published June 14. www.commonwealthfund.org/publications/issue-briefs/2017/jun/ahca-economic-and-employment-consequences.

Landrigan, P. J., and L. R. Goldman. 2011. "Children's Vulnerability to Toxic Chemicals: A Challenge and Opportunity to Strengthen Health and Environmental Policy." *Health Affairs* 30 (5): 842–50. https://doi.org/10.1377/hlthaff.2011.0151.

Landsverk, J., C. H. Brown, J. Rolls Reutz, L. Palinkas, and S. M. Horwitz. 2011. "Design Elements in Implementation Research: A Structured Review of Child Welfare and Child Mental Health Studies." *Administration and Policy in Mental Health* 38 (1): 54–63. https://doi.org/10.1007/s10488-010-0315-y.

Long, S. K., L. Bart, M. Karpman, A. Shartzer, and S. Zuckerman. 2017. "Sustained Gains in Coverage, Access, and Affordability Under the ACA: A 2017 Update." *Health Affairs* 36 (9): 1656–62. https://doi.org/10.1377/hlthaff.2017.0798.

Lyu, H., T. Xu, D. Brotman, B. Mayer-Blackwell, M. Cooper, M. Daniel, E. C. Wick, V. Saini, S. Brownlee, and M. A. Makary. 2017. "Overtreatment in the United States." *PLOS ONE* 12 (9): e0181970. https://doi.org/10.1371/journal.pone.0181970.

Makary, M. 2012. *Unaccountable: What Hospitals Won't Tell You and How Transparency Can Revolutionize Health Care*. New York: Bloomsbury Press.

Marcus, L. J., B. C. Dorn, and E. J. McNulty. 2012. "The Walk in the Woods: A Step-by-Step Method for Facilitating Interest-Based Negotiation and Conflict Resolution." *Negotiation Journal* 28 (3): 337–49. https://doi.org/10.1111/j.1571-9979.2012.00343.x.

Marmor, T. R. 2013. "Health Care Politics and Policy: The Business of Medicine: A Course for Physician Leaders." *Yale Journal of Biology and Medicine* 86 (3): 407–411. www.ncbi.nlm.nih.gov/pubmed/24058315.

———. 2000. *The Politics of Medicare*, 2nd ed. New York: Aldine de Gruyter.

McDaid, D., F. Sassi, and S. Merkur (eds.). 2015. *Promoting Health, Preventing Disease: The Economic Case*. Berkshire: Open University Press.

McIlvennan, C. K., Z. J. Eapen, and L. A. Allen. 2015. "Hospital Readmissions Reduction Program." *Circulation* 131 (20): 1796–1803. https://doi.org/10.1161/CIRCULATIONAHA.114.010270.

Melcher, M. L., J. L. Veale, B. Javaid, D. B. Leeser, C. L. Davis, G. Hil, and J. E. Milner. 2013. "Kidney Transplant Chains Amplify Benefit of Nondirected Donors." *JAMA Surgery* 148 (2): 165–69. https://doi.org/10.1001/2013.jamasurg.25.

Merrow, J. 2017. *Addicted to Reform: A 12-Step Program to Rescue Public Education*. New York: New Press.

Milanez, I., and M. Strauss. 2018. "Most in US Say High Costs of Medical Treatments Are a Big Problem." Pew Research Center. Published July 9. www.pewresearch.org/fact-tank/2018/07/09/americans-are-closely-divided-over-value-of-medical-treatments-but-most-agree-costs-are-a-big-problem/.

Morrisey, M. A. 2013. "History of Health Insurance in the United States." In *Health Insurance*, by M. A. Morrisey, 3–25. Chicago: Health Administration Press.

Murawski, J. 2018. "Calling Health Care a Right, Most NC Influencers Say Expand Medicaid, Keep Obamacare." *Charlotte Observer*. Published August 11. www.charlotteobserver.com/news/politics-government/influencers/article216448620.html.

National Kidney Foundation. 2020. "Organ Donation and Transplantation Statistics." Accessed January 16. www.kidney.org/news/newsroom/factsheets/Organ-Donation-and-Transplantation-Stats.

National Practitioner Data Bank (NPDB). 2019. "Title IV of P.L. 99-660." Accessed October 16, 2019. www.npdb.hrsa.gov/resources/titleIv.jsp.

Obama, B. H. 2017. "Repealing the ACA Without a Replacement—The Risks to American Health Care." *New England Journal of Medicine* 376 (4): 297–99. https://doi.org/10.1056/NEJMp1616577.

Oberlander, J. 2018. "The Republican War on Obamacare—What Has It Achieved?" *New England Journal of Medicine* 379 (8): 703–5. https://doi.org/10.1056/NEJMp1806798.

Paradise, J. 2014. "The Impact of the Children's Health Insurance Program (CHIP): What Does the Research Tell Us?" Kaiser Family Foundation. Published July. www.kff.org/medicaid/issue-brief/the-impact-of-the-childrens-health-insurance-program-chip-what-does-the-research-tell-us/.

RAND Corporation. 2018. "The Future of U.S. Health Care: Replace or Revise the Affordable Care Act?" Accessed October 16. www.rand.org/health-care/key-topics/health-policy/in-depth.html.

Rees, M. A., J. E. Kopke, R. P. Pelletier, D. L. Segev, M. E. Rutter, A. J. Fabrega, J. Rogers, O. G. Pankewycz, J. Hiller, A. E. Roth, T. Sandholm, U. Unver, and R. A. Montgomery. 2009. "A Nonsimultaneous, Extended, Altruistic-Donor

Chain." *New England Journal of Medicine* 360 (11): 1096–1101. https://doi.org/10.1056/NEJMoa0803645.

Reinhardt, U. E. 2019. *Priced Out: The Economic and Ethical Costs of American Health Care*. Princeton, NJ: Princeton University Press.

Remoundou, K., and P. Koundouri. 2009. "Environmental Effects on Public Health: An Economic Perspective." *International Journal of Environmental Research and Public Health* 6 (8): 2160–78. https://doi.org/10.3390/ijerph6082160.

Reuters. 2018. "Federal Judge Rules Obamacare Unconstitutional." Published December 14. www.reuters.com/article/us-usa-healthcare-court/u-s-federal-judge-rules-obamacare-unconstitutional-idUSKBN1OE01Y.

Rosenbach, M., C. Irvin, A. Merrill, S. Shulman, J. Czajka, C. Trenholm, S. Williams, S. S. Limpa-Amara, and A. Katz. 2007. *National Evaluation of the State Children's Health Insurance Program: A Decade of Expanding Coverage and Improving Access: Final Report*. Mathematica Policy Research. Published September. www.cms.gov/Research-Statistics-Data-and-Systems/Statistics-Trends-and-Reports/Reports/downloads/rosenbach9-19-07.pdf.

Rosenbaum, L. 2018. "Trolleyology and the Dengue Vaccine Dilemma." *New England Journal of Medicine* 379 (4): 305–7. https://doi.org/10.1056/NEJMp1804094.

Rosenberg, C. E., and J. L. Golden (eds.). 1992. *Framing Disease: Studies in Cultural History*. New Brunswick, NJ: Rutgers University Press.

Rosoff, A. 1975. "The Federal HMO Assistance Act: Helping Hand or Hurdle." *American Business Law Journal* 13 (2): 137–69. https://doi.org/10.1111/j.1744-1714.1975.tb00971.x.

Roth, A. E. 2016. *Who Gets What—And Why: The New Economics of Matchmaking and Market Design*, reprint ed. New York: Eamon Dolan/Mariner Books.

Schwartzmantel, J. 2008. *Ideology and Politics*. Washington, DC: Sage.

Schumann, J. H. 2016. "Hill-Burton Act: A Health Care Milestone Worth Remembering." National Public Radio. Published October 2. www.npr.org/sections/health-shots/2016/10/02/495775518/a-bygone-era-when-bipartisanship-led-to-health-care-transformation.

Seaborg, E. 2018. "New Donor Chains Could Change Approach to Paired Donation." *Kidney News*. Accessed October 16, 2019. www.kidneynews.org/kidney-news/cover-story/new-donor-chains-could-change-approach-to-paired-donation.

Seay, M. 2005. "Pharmaceuticals: Medicare Modernization Act—2005. End of Year Issue Brief." Health Policy Tracking Service. Issue Brief. Published December 31.

Shonk, K. 2019. "5 Conflict Resolution Strategies." Program on Negotiation, Harvard Law School. Published October 7. www.pon.harvard.edu/daily/conflict-resolution/conflict-resolution-strategies/.

Siraisi, N. G. 2012. "Medicine, 1450–1620, and the History of Science." *Isis: An International Review Devoted to the History of Science and Its Cultural Influences* 103 (3): 491–514. https://doi.org/10.1086/667970.

Solman, P. 2019. "How an Economist's Idea to Create Kidney Transplant Chains Has Saved Lives." *PBS NewsHour.* Published February 7. www.pbs.org/newshour/show/how-an-economists-idea-to-create-kidney-transplant-chains-has-saved-lives.

Starr, P. 2018. "A New Strategy for Health Care: Looking Beyond Trump, Democrats Ought to Focus on Opening Medicare to People at Age 50 and Capping Excessive Health-Care Prices." *American Prospect.* Published January 4. prospect.org/health/new-strategy-health-care/.

———. 2011. *Remedy and Reaction: The Peculiar American Struggle over Health Care Reform.* New Haven, CT: Yale University Press.

———. 1982. *The Social Transformation of American Medicine.* New York: Basic Books.

Strauss, V. 2017. "9 Million Kids Get Health Insurance Under CHIP. Congress Just Let It Expire." *Washington Post.* Published October 1. www.washingtonpost.com/news/answer-sheet/wp/2017/10/01/9-million-kids-get-health-insurance-under-chip-congress-just-let-it-expire/.

Trasande, L., and Y. Liu. 2011. "Reducing the Staggering Costs of Environmental Disease in Children, Estimated at $76.6 Billion in 2008." *Health Affairs* 30 (5): 863–70. https://doi.org/10.1377/hlthaff.2010.1239.

University Chronicle. 1863. "An Impeachment Trial." October 3. https://books.google.de/books?id=cEHiAAAAMAAJ&pg=PA164#v=onepage&q&f=false.

US Congress. 1997. "H.R. 2015—Balanced Budget Act of 1997." Accessed October 16, 2019. www.congress.gov/bill/105th-congress/house-bill/2015.

———. 1973. "Health Maintenance Organization Act of 1973." Pubic Law 93-222. www.govinfo.gov/content/pkg/STATUTE-87/pdf/STATUTE-87-Pg914.pdf.

US Department of Health and Human Services (HHS). 2019a. "Enforcement Highlights." Reviewed September 13. www.hhs.gov/hipaa/for-professionals/compliance-enforcement/data/enforcement-highlights/index.html.

———. 2019b. "Health Information Privacy." Accessed October 15. www.hhs.gov/hipaa/index.html.

———. 2017a. "Civil Money Penalty." Reviewed June 7. www.hhs.gov/hipaa/for-professionals/compliance-enforcement/examples/cignet-health/index.html.

———. 2017b. "HIPAA for Professionals." Reviewed June 16. www.hhs.gov/hipaa/for-professionals/index.html.

———. 2017c. "Patient Safety and Quality Improvement Act of 2005 Statute and Rule." Reviewed June 16. www.hhs.gov/hipaa/for-professionals/patient-safety/statute-and-rule/index.html.

———. 2016. "Individuals' Right Under HIPAA to Access Their Health Information." Reviewed February 25. www.hhs.gov/hipaa/for-professionals/privacy/guidance/access/index.html.

———. 2013. "Summary of the HIPAA Privacy Rule." Reviewed July 26. www.hhs. gov/hipaa/for-professionals/privacy/laws-regulations/index.html.

US Environmental Protection Agency (EPA). 2019. "Summary of the National Environmental Policy Act." Accessed October 15. www.epa.gov/laws-regulations/ summary-national-environmental-policy-act.

US House of Representatives. 2010. *Compilation of Patient Protection and Affordability Care Act Including Patient Protection and Affordability Care Act Related Portions of Health Care and Education Reconciliation Act of 2010.* Accessed October 16, 2019. http://housedocs.house.gov/energycommerce/ ppacacon.pdf.

van Geertruyden, Y. H. 2001. "The Fox Guarding the Henhouse: How the Health Care Quality Improvement Act of 1986 and State Peer Review Protection Statutes Have Helped Protect Bad Faith Peer Review in the Medical Community." *Journal of Contemporary Health Law and Policy* 18 (1). http:// scholarship.law.edu/jchlp/vol18/iss1/8.

Vogenberg, F. R., and M. Smart. 2018. "Regulatory Change Versus Legislation Impacting Health Care Decisions and Delivery." *P&T: A Peer-Reviewed Journal for Hospital and Formulary Management* 43 (1): 34–38. www.ncbi. nlm.nih.gov/pubmed/29290674.

Wear, A. (ed.). 1992. *Medicine in Society: Historical Essays.* Cambridge: Cambridge University Press.

Young, J. H. 1967. *The Medical Messiahs: A Social History of Health Quackery in Twentieth-Century America.* Princeton, NJ: Princeton University Press.

14

THE FUTURE OF HEALTHCARE IN THE UNITED STATES

Even more than what you think, how you think matters. The stakes for understanding this could not be higher than they are today, because we are not just battling for what it means to be scientists. We are battling for what it means to be citizens.

—Atul Gawande

Learning Objectives

- Understand the rapidly changing nature of the US healthcare system.
- Analyze some of "the good, the bad, and the ugly" about current and future developments in healthcare.
- Evaluate some of the critical questions that need to be addressed regarding the US healthcare system.
- Assess the challenges associated with controlling costs and ensuring the fair distribution of care.
- Recognize the potential impact of artificial intelligence, big data, genomics, precision medicine, and robotics on the healthcare system.
- Consider the potential impact of new care models and processes on the healthcare system.

The Good, the Bad, and the Ugly

The Good, the Bad, and the Ugly is the title of a classic western movie, but the phrase can just as easily describe the future of healthcare in the United States (see exhibit 14.1). Certainly, the US healthcare system has a lot of good: Our ability to improve the health of our citizens is expanding, and our research, contributed knowledge, and specialized skills provide benefits throughout the world. Science and technology continue to open countless new avenues in medicine, and data analytics provides an unprecedented opportunity to apply massive amounts of information to support better delivery of care. Of course, along with the good comes the bad: Healthcare costs are high and

EXHIBIT 14.1
Area of Focus
for This Chapter

The Aim of the Healthcare System

Issues That Require Our Attention

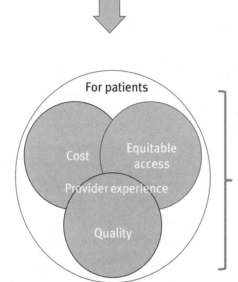

For patients

- Cost
- Equitable access
- Provider experience
- Quality

- Nature of our complex system
- Historical issues that have influenced the development of the system
- Beliefs and attitudes about health and healthcare
- Comparison with other developed countries
- Components of our healthcare system
- People and providers
- Patient care—the purpose of the system
- Financing a massive system
- Quality—easier said than done
- Medical and information technology
- The pharmaceutical industry
- Complementary and alternative medicine
- Politics/economics
- *The future of the system*

will continue to rise. The healthcare needs of the population are expanding in both scope and complexity, and many of the services and treatment options that can best meet those needs are extremely expensive. Finally, we have the ugly. The United States has thus far been unable to equitably distribute healthcare and provide universal access for its people.

The future direction of US healthcare will be shaped by many forces. Certainly, the ongoing debate over the Affordable Care Act (ACA) and healthcare reform, as discussed in the previous chapter, will have far-reaching consequences. However, numerous other forces—scientific advances, societal values, evolving healthcare needs, changes in infrastructure, and so on—will have a major impact as well (Fingerhut and Abdou 2017; Hignett, Albolino, and Catchpole 2018; Kickbusch and Gleicher 2012; King 2009; Pesec and Shererz 2015). Healthcare, like most industries, has become increasingly reliant on technology. Learning to take full advantage of emerging technological opportunities will be essential for our system's future (Ashrafian et al. 2017; Wu et al. 2016; Y Media Labs 2019).

In this time of change, we need to ask ourselves: What skills will be most essential for the people working in healthcare in the years ahead? Surely, the future leaders of US healthcare will need to possess a wide variety of qualities and capabilities, but perhaps the most important is that they be critical and creative thinkers. They must be perpetual students, always learning and digging for the most accurate and most unbiased information to support their decisions. This chapter will touch on numerous topics, any of which could easily have merited a full volume of its own. These brief discussions are intended to serve only as a starting point from which to launch your own more detailed explorations.

Fundamental Questions

Collectively, the United States needs to ask itself three fundamental questions about the future of its healthcare system:

1. How will patients and providers in the system interface with technology?
2. How will society pay for the ever-increasing cost of our healthcare system?
3. How will we provide equitable access to and distribution of healthcare services?

In many respects, these questions have not changed over the past 100 years; they have only become more difficult and complex.

The US healthcare system has structural limits, yet people's need for healthcare seems limitless (Callahan 2011). Confronting our problems with cost and access will likely require some form of rationing. In general, the United States has not explicitly rationed care as many other countries have done, but rationing has occurred nonetheless (Hoffman 2012). Care may be rationed, for instance, through limits on access associated with insurance status, through policies that set limits on certain care options (e.g., maximum number of mental health visits allowed, eligibility requirements for certain services), and through complex precertification rules that often discourage patients from seeking needed services (Scheunemann and White 2011; Pearl 2017).

The most straightforward example of rationing in the US healthcare system involves organ donation. The United Network for Organ Sharing (UNOS) is a private nonprofit organization that manages the organ transplant system under contract with the federal government (UNOS 2019). Donated organs are a scarce lifesaving resource, and UNOS adheres to carefully crafted policies when allocating them. In the case of kidney transplants, for instance, each potential recipient is given an Estimated Post-Transplant Survival (EPTS) score. The people with the highest EPTS scores are the ones who would be expected to benefit the most from a transplant; hence, they receive priority (Callahan 2011; Dalal 2015).

Any discussion of healthcare rationing introduces questions of its own: Is it possible to ration care in a fair manner across the population, given the complexities of our system? Can we even agree on a definition of the word *fair*?

In debates over how the US healthcare system might best deliver its services, much political rhetoric has focused on the extremes—either a government-funded "Medicare for All" approach or a market-based solution that leaves numerous people uncovered or underinsured. Some people have advocated more centrist solutions, though the rancorous political environment has made compromise difficult. I would argue, based on a review of the literature, that no one has yet found the optimal solution.

The Future Is Change

Some people might be overly pessimistic about the future of the US healthcare system, whereas others might be overly optimistic. A better course is to be realistic about our need for change.

Our understanding of human health and its determinants offers great promise for enhancing the lives of all Americans. However, many of the factors that influence our health go beyond the boundaries of our healthcare system, into such areas as politics, economics, the environment, lifestyle behaviors, and societal trends (Iacobucci 2017). The only way we can achieve true reform is to abandon the philosophy of incrementalism and attack the root causes of the system's failures. Meaningful change will require a new mind-set—one that focuses not just on the volume of healthcare services provided but on the degree of value that is achieved.

Exhibit 14.2 shows some key distinctions between our volume-based "first curve" and a value-based "second curve," and it illustrates the difficult transformation that our system needs to achieve. Across the center of the exhibit is an "acid river." This phrase comes from a popular team-building exercise in which a group must build a "bridge" across an imaginary river of acid and get each member safely across. The group is given a limited amount of material with which to build the bridge, and participants must work collaboratively, repeatedly remove and replace segments, and experiment with what will work. Ultimately, the group uses innovation to overcome its limited resources—much as we will need to do in healthcare.

Achieving this transition across the US healthcare system will require universal adoption of certain necessary changes, such as the use of electronic records and adherence to standards of care. As illustrated in exhibit 14.3, the rate of change in any system is related to the rate of adoption by the various stakeholders.

Everett Rogers (2003) wrote extensively about the adoption of innovation, identifying various types of adopters and stages of adoption. The

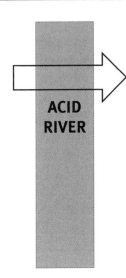

First Curve: Volume
- Fee for service
- Quality indifference
- Regulations impeding collaboration (hospitals/physicians)
- Acute care focus
- IT investment variable
- Little or no financial risk
- Scale not very important

ACID RIVER

Second Curve: Value
- Incentives for outcomes, focused on Triple Aim
- Quality metrics important for determining payment
- Integration, coordination, and alignment of providers (clinical integration)
- Outpatient focus (inpatient care reserved for the sickest of the sick)
- IT investment essential
- Shared risk
- Scale important

EXHIBIT 14.2
Transition to a Value-Based System

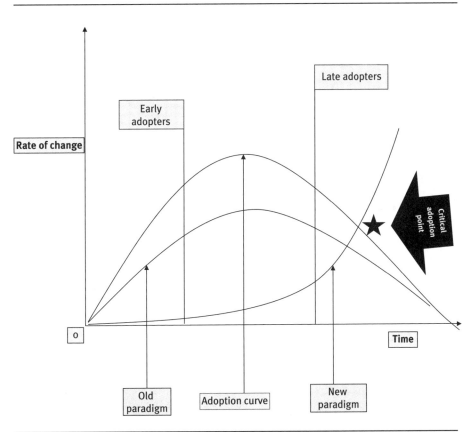

EXHIBIT 14.3
The Second Curve and the Adoption of Innovation

first people to adopt a new innovation or paradigm are the early adopters. Other stakeholders will usually wait and observe the early adopters until they see sufficient evidence that the new paradigm is the proper way to go. Late adopters are slower to change but ultimately will. However, late adoption can have significant implications for healthcare: If adoption is spread over too long a period, the organization may need to operate multiple systems simultaneously, increasing cost, adding complexity, creating system fatigue, and reducing effectiveness. Some stakeholders will never adopt change and will not challenge the old paradigm. In fact, they may hinder adoption by actively working against change.

Healthcare generates a staggering amount of new information and is constantly subject to changes in systems and management practices; hence, the rapid pace of change has become increasingly difficult to absorb. In 2010, for instance, 75 trials and 11 systematic reviews were being published each day, and few of them were reviewed or processed in a way that would help practitioners incorporate the findings into practice (Bastian, Glasziou, and Chalmers 2010). Even more telling is the growing number of trials registered with the US National Library of Medicine, as shown in exhibit 14.4.

EXHIBIT 14.4
Number of
Registered
Studies

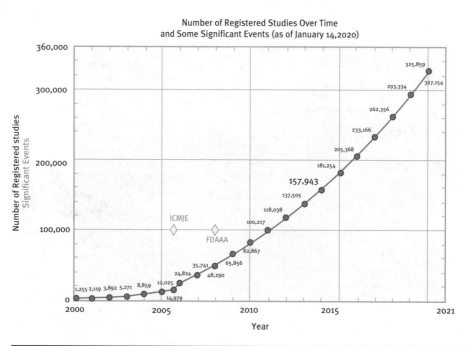

Note: ICMJE indicates the point when the International Committee of Medical Journal Editors (ICMJE) began requiring trial registration as a condition of publication; FDAAA indicates the point when the registration requirements of the Food and Drug Administration Amendments Act (FDAAA) of 2007 began and were implemented on clinicaltrials.gov.

Source: Reprinted from US National Library of Medicine (2020).

As of early 2020, 327,154 studies had been registered with locations in all 50 states and in 209 countries. These studies may have great potential value to healthcare, but making the information accessible and usable to stakeholders throughout the system is nearly impossible without the assistance of data management technology.

Given this influx of new information, widespread adoption of innovations into clinical practice has been found to take as long as 17 years (Hodgkins et al. 2018). By contrast, the iPhone was first introduced in 2007 and was widely considered indispensable less than ten years later (Jackson 2018). The future of our healthcare transition will depend not only on the availability of new technologies and care alternatives but also on which ones are adopted and how quickly we adopt them. Both promoters and skeptics of adoption have often been wrong in their predictions of how change will occur.

Approaching New Technologies

Advances in technology are happening at an almost unfathomable pace. Virtual reality for medical experiences, wireless brain sensors, 3D-printed body parts, and naturally moving prosthetic limbs are just a sampling of the breakthroughs that are here or on the horizon.

On November 25, 1962, an episode of *The Jetsons* showed young Elroy Jetson seeing his doctor over a video screen (Blitzer and Benedict 1962)—probably the first known example of a virtual physician visit. Decades later, that experience is a reality for many patients. Groundbreaking ideas can come from unconventional sources, including Saturday morning cartoons! Similarly, the "tricorder" device that appeared in *Star Trek* episodes during the 1960s prompted engineers to develop more sophisticated scanners for use in patient examination (Best 2019; Gross and Altman 2016).

Technological innovations hold incredible potential, yet they should still be approached with caution. One of the world's earliest technologies, fire, can provide warmth and comfort, but it can also cause destruction. As Darth Vader says in the original *Star Wars* movie, "Don't be too proud of this technological terror you've constructed" (Lucas 1977). Vader, of course, was speaking of the Death Star, but even innovations that were developed with the best intentions can have harmful effects.

If the cost of a new technology goes beyond society's ability to pay, or if the cost is too high relative to the benefit, the technology might not be worth pursuing. In addition, technologies that take too much of the humanity out of patient care should be approached with caution. Overreliance on technology and overconfidence in computerized systems can have detrimental effects (Campbell et al. 2007; Institute for Safe Medication Practices

2016; Parasuraman and Manzey 2010). As we employ new technological innovations, we must still remember that well-trained human caregivers are in the best position to help patients ensure good health.

Telemedicine and Related Modalities

Telemedicine, telehealth, e-health, and mHealth will play an increasingly important role in the future of US healthcare. All of these terms refer to applications of information and communication technology in healthcare, yet they have notable distinctions in meaning. Whereas the term *telemedicine* refers specifically to medical treatment, *telehealth* has a broader meaning, encompassing education and other aspects of health and health-related services. The term *e-health* is typically applied to the use of electronic records, administrative systems, lab services, and other functions in modern healthcare delivery. Within the general concept of e-health is *mHealth*, which deals specifically with the use of mobile devices (Bashshur et al. 2009, 2011, 2014). This section will review some of the most important functions of telemedicine and its related modalities.

Patient Portals

Patient portals are websites that offer the patient and the provider a convenient way to communicate, share test results or other information, request services such as a prescription refill, and schedule appointments. The more robust patient portals often include embedded email or messaging services.

Virtual Appointments

The use of virtual telemedicine appointments originally helped improve access to high-quality care for individuals in remote regions. However, such appointments are now offered locally as well, especially for more routine services. Various applications can allow information about the patient's condition to be uploaded to the provider, allowing for quick intervention when warranted.

Remote Monitoring

A variety of technological tools are useful for monitoring patients remotely, especially in the case of a chronic illness such as diabetes, hypertension, or heart failure. The use of remote monitoring through mobile devices and home systems is likely to expand.

Personal Health Records

An electronic personal health record is maintained and controlled by a patient or guardian and allows for quick access to information about diagnoses, medications, drug allergies, emergency procedures, or other aspects of health-care. The records can typically be accessed via a mobile device or computer.

Electronic Consultation

Electronic technologies enable providers and patients to more effectively communicate about health concerns and conveniently share X-rays, test results, exam records, and other information. Electronic consultations may also occur between providers.

Personal Health Applications on Mobile Devices

As of 2020, the world had roughly 8 billion mobile subscriptions (Ericsson 2018), and use of mobile devices was common across all age groups (Carroll et al. 2017). The use of health-related mobile applications is widespread, and it is likely to expand further as technology improves and programs become more accessible and easier to use (Price et al. 2014; Al Rawajbeh and Haboush 2015). Mobile apps can be used to record vital health information such as heart rate, body temperature, and respiration; remind patients to take their medicine; track physical activity (e.g., the number of steps taken daily); assist with food and nutrition (e.g., through food logs and calorie counters); and store important health information that could easily be shared with a provider if desired. With the rise of mHealth, technology companies are becoming healthcare companies, and many are seeking Food and Drug Administration (FDA) approval for their applications to be considered medical devices (FDA 2019).

Evidence and Concerns Related to Telemedicine

A survey published by *Becker's Hospital Review* (2015) found that physicians consider the following ten uses of telemedicine the most important:

1. Concierge services for fee-paying patients
2. Medication management and prescription renewal
3. Minor urgent care (e.g., colds, fevers, minor injuries)
4. Birth control counseling
5. Home health care
6. Chronic condition management
7. Pediatric after-hours needs
8. Behavioral health
9. Posthospital discharge
10. Postsurgical follow-up

A number of researchers have sought to examine the effects of telemedicine on health outcomes. Kruse and colleagues (2017) reviewed numerous studies on the use of telemedicine in the treatment of chronic heart disease, and they found that it was generally associated with improvements in hospital admissions, mortality, cost-effectiveness, and overall health measures. Other reported benefits included decreased travel time, higher patient satisfaction, and better quality of life. Russo, McCool, and Davies (2016) found that use of telemedicine at the US Department of Veterans Affairs helped reduce the amount of patient travel and increase the number of visits for needed services.

Some studies have highlighted limitations or concerns associated with the use of telemedicine. Like other components of healthcare, telemedicine may contribute to confusion and fragmentation, allowing for gaps in care or the delivery of inappropriate or overlapping care. Even though telemedicine services are often less costly than other forms of care, they still are not free, and reimbursement by third-party payers can vary significantly. Furthermore, in some remote areas, internet services are not sufficiently robust to support telemedicine applications (de Souza et al. 2017; Kruse et al. 2018). The regulation of telemedicine services and the protection of patient privacy are additional areas of concern; oversight and jurisdiction of many of these areas remain to be determined (Hale and Kvedar 2014; Hall and McGraw 2014; Stanberry 2006).

When used correctly, telemedicine and its related modalities can support a productive partnership between patients and providers—one in which patients have greater control over their care and are more actively engaged in monitoring and improving their own health. The potential for these tools to improve the healthcare quality and accessibility and to reduce costs is considerable (American Hospital Association 2015; Dorsey and Topol 2016; PR Newswire 2014; Otto et al. 2018).

Artificial Intelligence and Big Data

The theoretical physicist Michio Kaku (2011) has pointed out that a modern smart phone has greater computing power than the computer that was used to land the first man on the moon. As computing capabilities continue to increase, the implications for our healthcare system are enormous. One of the most important implications involves the use of "big data"—the vast quantities of data accumulated from healthcare entities and other sources.

The field of data analytics focuses on converting large quantities of unstructured data into information that organizations can use. As shown in exhibit 14.5, unstructured data are of little use if we are not able to create information from them to support new applications. First, the data must be collected; then the data must be analyzed and formatted in a way that creates information, which can be turned into new knowledge about patients and

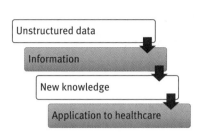

EXHIBIT 14.5
Transforming
Data to
Application

the population the organization serves. Only then can the data be put into action. With advances in computer technology and data analytics, we are now able to use big data more effectively than ever before.

Imagine if a person were asked to comb through 50,000 patient records, collect information of a particular category, and organize that information in a way that would be useful for the organization; the task would take weeks, months, or even years, depending on the amount of data available. With a modern supercomputer such as IBM's Watson, such tasks can be completed instantaneously.

IBM's Watson is able to do several things that, until recently, would be nearly unimaginable. Watson can read the entirety of existing medical literature—more than any human being could read in a lifetime—in a matter of seconds. Watson can then turn that enormous mass of unstructured data into usable information, enabling it to respond to specific issues. Watson can also understand human speech. Questions can be posed to Watson, and the machine can use information acquired through a search of all available data and present appropriate answers and solutions. Because it can iterate with each nuance provided by the user and because it goes through its various algorithms so quickly each time, it is able to mimic human intelligence.

So how can Watson and artificial intelligence be applied in our healthcare system? How might such a machine assist providers in treating complex medical conditions? Will supercomputers be the physicians of our future? An application of Watson to US healthcare might go as follows:

1. A connection is made to Watson on the cloud.
2. Watson is given basic information about a patient, probably via upload of the patient record.
3. Watson is asked a question about the patient.
4. Watson reviews all medical literature and the clinical information provided.
5. Watson provides structured responses to the question in the form of possible diagnoses, treatments, and their probability of success.

6. Watson requests new information—for example, the results of a test.

7. Watson is given this new information and, after a further iteration, provides an additional response.

8. Based on patient specifics, Watson ultimately provides a complete set of facts on the patient's case, diagnosis, treatment options, and prognosis.

Given the supercomputer's access to all known information about the patient's diagnosis, it is able to give the provider the best possible responses to any clinical issues presented.

Clearly, use of such a platform could be a great benefit to patients, assist with the increasing complexity of care, and help manage the massive volumes of data being produced. Also, because the technology is instantaneously updated for new developments and findings in the medical field, practitioners would always have access to the latest information (Ferrucci et al. 2013; Leske 2013; Siegel 2013). Nonetheless, we still must ask ourselves whether today's healthcare organizations are prepared to effectively use technologies such as Watson. Do they fully understand the implications, and can they practically apply the technology?

Genomics and Precision Medicine

The combination of advanced analytics with genetic testing opens up a whole new dimension of healthcare. Genomics enables clinicians to tailor treatment for each person's genetic profile, rather than simply treating patients based on more general criteria.

A provider can use an advanced technological platform, with access to a patient's genetic information, to support the delivery of precision medicine, as shown in exhibit 14.6. President Barack Obama introduced a Precision Medicine Initiative in his 2015 State of the Union address. The initiative defines *precision medicine* as "an emerging approach for disease treatment and prevention that takes into account individual variability in genes, environment, and lifestyle for each person" (National Institutes of Health [NIH] 2020). The initiative is a long-term research endeavor, involving the NIH and other research centers, with the vision of using individual genetics, environmental conditions, and lifestyle factors to determine the best possible approaches for preventing or treating disease (Ashley 2015; Dvorsky 2015; Holst 2015; Neergard 2015; Porche 2015; White House 2015).

The first sequencing of the human genome, completed in 2003, took more than 13 years and cost $2.7 billion (National Human Genome Research

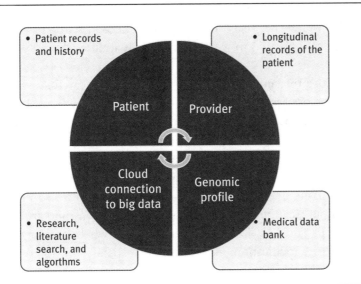

EXHIBIT 14.6
Precision
Medicine

Institute [NHGRI] 2019). Soon, the cost came down to $100,000. Today, companies can do a human gene sequence in a matter of days or even hours, at a cost of less than $1,000 (US National Library of Medicine 2019). Partial analysis can cost even less. Exhibit 14.7 illustrates this incredible reduction in cost over time.

We can now envision the day when patients will enter the healthcare system, present the clinician with an electronic file containing their genome, and simply say, "Treat me." The key word in this statement is *me*—meaning

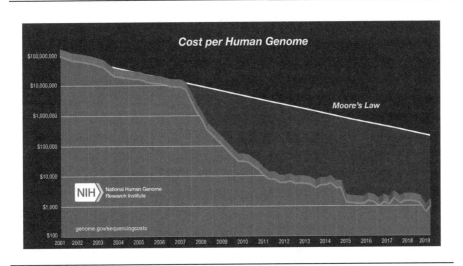

EXHIBIT 14.7
Cost of
Sequencing a
Genome

Source: Reprinted from NHGRI (2019).

specifically *me*, not an imaginary "average" person between the ages of 18 and 64 who weighs between 100 and 250 pounds. Treatment will take into account the various ways in which the individual differs from others (Dvorsky 2015).

As with other innovations, we still must think carefully about how to accommodate precision medicine in our healthcare system. Are practitioners ready to adopt practices that will fundamentally change the way they approach their work? Exhibit 14.8 presents one model for how precision medicine might function in day-to-day healthcare delivery. The patient and the patient's genetic profile interact with the provider and a data analytics platform with a connection to the cloud. Once a specific diagnosis has been determined, all treatment options known at any given time are assessed for the specific patient. As databases grow and knowledge of specific genetic interactions with medications and treatments expands, the ability to pinpoint treatments will likely improve.

The NIH (2020) has launched a cohort initiative in which approximately 1 million people will share biological samples, genetic data, and diet and lifestyle information, all linked to electronic health records, for the purpose of determining how such information can best be brought to clinical practice (see exhibit 14.9). Every leader and practitioner in the US healthcare system should be cognizant of this emerging field.

EXHIBIT 14.8
Technology-
Assisted
Diagnosis

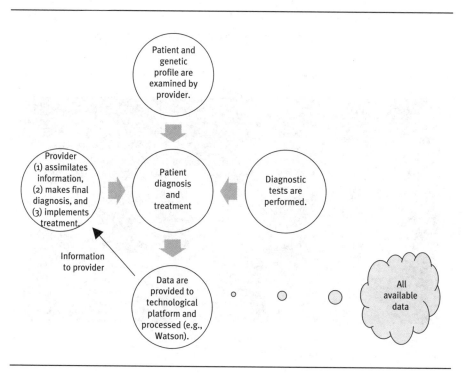

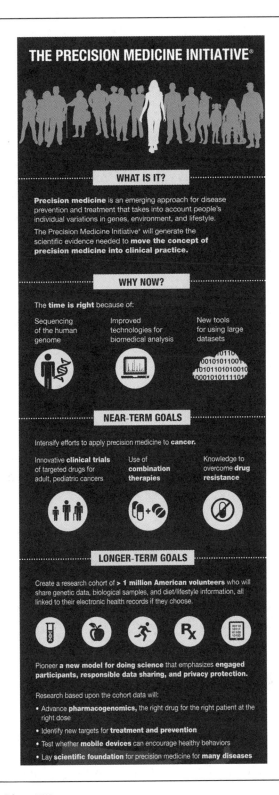

Source: Reprinted from NIH.

EXHIBIT 14.9
Precision
Medicine
Initiative Cohort
Program

Robotics

Like other industries, healthcare has been significantly affected by advances in robotics (Calo 2016). Robots can provide support to caregivers, perform certain physician tasks, provide assistance to older adults and people with physical and cognitive disabilities, and even serve as a source of companionship (Riek 2017; Vandemeulebroucke, Dierckx de Casterlé, and Gastmans 2018). Artificial limbs function with robotic technology (Knickman and Kovner 2015), and tiny robots called "microbots" can even be used inside a person's body (Umay, Fidan, and Barshan 2017). In addition, robots are often used in simulation labs to enhance the education of health workers. The Cleveland Clinic named robotic surgery one of the top ten healthcare innovations of 2019, because "continued advancement in the field has led to more precise and effective surgeries with improved surgical outcomes" (Consult QD 2018).

Another prospect for robotics—albeit a more distant one—will involve the integration of humans and machines. The Defense Advanced Research Projects Agency (DARPA) is developing semiautonomous ground robots to carry out complex tasks in dangerous, human-engineered environments, and such advances will likely have major implications for healthcare (DARPA 2019; Gaudin 2017). Innovations that sound like science fiction may at some point become reality, such as artificial limbs that can be controlled by the patient's brain and the enhancement of brain function through networking with computers (Abiri et al. 2017; Flemisch et al. 2019; Huang, Tu, and He 2016; Shafei, Rastad, and Kamangar 2016; Umay, Fidan, and Barshan 2017; Zaiba 2018).

Manual repetitive jobs have long been at risk of being replaced by robots; with the use of artificial intelligence, however, more jobs relying on analytical skills and judgment are likely to face the same risk. Nonetheless, many valuable human functions—such as working well with people and collaborating in team settings—will be extremely difficult to replace with robots or AI alone (Korzep 2010; Patino, Mestre, and Sánchez 2016; Rabbitt, Kazdin, and Scassellati 2015; Randell et al. 2014; Browne 2018).

Cybersecurity Threats

The expanding use of digital technologies in healthcare presents numerous potential benefits, but it also carries risks. As a growing number of electronic systems and devices become involved in the delivery and management of care, opportunities open up for criminal elements to exploit vulnerabilities. Cybersecurity efforts are therefore essential—not only to protect patients' personal privacy but also to maintain the integrity of the organization and its services.

Healthcare records offer a rich treasure trove of personal information that hackers and thieves may seek to use for a variety of purposes. Identity theft, from either patients or employees, is a constant concern. Although few cases have been documented, the theft of personal health information could potentially be used for blackmail and extortion from patients who wish to keep sensitive information from becoming known.

In some instances, hackers choose to infect systems, destroy hard drives, or delete information for purposes of revenge on an organization; in other instances, the hackers seemingly have no motive other than sheer malevolence. Ransomware is a type of computer attack in which an organization's vital records are made inaccessible unless it pays money to the hacker to restore access. In many cases, access is never restored even after the ransom has been paid (Pot 2016). Restoration of a compromised system can cost organizations substantial resources.

Often, hackers use social engineering techniques to exploit the human element of an organization. Social engineering relies on human interaction, and it generally seeks to manipulate or deceive people into breaking normal security procedures. For instance, a phishing email might ask the recipient to click on a deceptive link and enter a password. By tricking or convincing a vulnerable employee to abandon best practices, a hacker can gain entry—electronically or even physically—to the organization's systems (TechTarget 2014).

Social Media

The heightened connectedness that we have through social media has had a significant impact on healthcare, and that impact is likely to grow in the coming years. Imagine the following scenario: Your five-year-old son, who has had a touch of the flu, seems unusually quiet, has a minor rash, and has a slight fever. You take him to the urgent care center, and the provider recommends Tylenol and says the boy will be fine in a day or two. Feeling relieved, you log on to Facebook and post a picture of yourself and your son, with an account of the day's events. A few moments later, a pediatrician friend calls, saying that your son likely has Reye's syndrome and needs to go immediately to the hospital. Though certainly not the preferred method of diagnosis, this social media interaction might have saved your child's life.

From the patient perspective, social media are commonly used for the following purposes (Hayon, Goldsmith, and Garito 2014; Hung et al. 2013; Jaganath et al. 2012; Sarasohn-Kahn et al. 2008):

- To find consumer recommendations about practitioners
- To develop a sense of belonging to a group or community of people who share similar interests or ailments

- To learn about others' experiences regarding medications or treatment options
- To find emotional support
- To learn more about a condition and how to manage it
- To share knowledge about a disease or health-related issue

From the perspective of a healthcare organization, common uses of social media include the following:

- To communicate with patients and remind them about needed medical services or healthcare compliance issues
- To establish an online presence to enhance the organization's perceived authority and to augment the patient's experience
- To communicate with colleagues within and outside the organization

Healthcare organizations must also be aware, however, of the potential for negative exposure via social media. For instance, a patient who has had an unpleasant experience with the organization can quickly tweet or post an unfavorable review, which may then have an influence on existing or potential patients (Hayon, Goldsmith, and Garito 2014).

The internet and social media can provide a valuable service by helping to "democratize" healthcare and improving the public's access to health-related knowledge. At the same time, however, they can contribute to the spread of incorrect or misleading information, with potentially harmful effects. According to surveys, 80 percent of American adults use online searches when considering medical treatment (Fox 2003), and 35 percent have gone online to figure out a medical condition (Fox and Duggan 2013). Regardless of the risk of misinformation, Americans are clearly inclined to use the internet for health information. Organizations should therefore be prepared to provide guidance to patients and families about the proper use of internet resources.

Organizations considering social media use should have carefully crafted policies and procedures, and they should exercise caution about what information they share. Furthermore, all members of the organization should be well-versed in the proper use of social media. Privacy violations associated with social media have become commonplace (Advisory Board 2017).

Ever-Larger Systems of Providers

In the past, healthcare organizations generally served limited geographic areas. Over time, however, organizations have become larger—both by organic growth and through mergers and acquisitions—and expanded the reach of their operations. Many large healthcare systems today are national, or at least multistate, in scope (Rothacker and Murawski 2018). This trend is apparent not only in the amount of merger activity but also in the ways organizations brand themselves. In 2018, for example, Carolinas HealthCare System rebranded itself as Atrium Health, so that its name would no longer limit the organization to a specific geographic area (Kacik 2018).

Medical and surgical specialty practices, in particular, are increasingly becoming part of larger healthcare systems, though the rates vary by specialty. Nikpay, Richards, and Penson (2018) found that the consolidation rate for cardiology and oncology practices from 2007 to 2017 was 34 percent, whereas it was only 4 percent for dermatology practices—likely a result of the greater capital intensity of cardiology and oncology practices. Primary care practices tend to find fewer benefits from alignment with larger health systems. In some cases, primary practices have left larger organizations to gain greater control over their practices (Roberts 2018).

New Organizational Structures and Care Models

Another evolving trend in US healthcare involves the development of new organizational structures and care models. Because hospital care represents a large part of the nation's healthcare expenditures, one approach to controlling costs has focused on developing smaller facilities.

Minihospitals

Minihospitals, or microhospitals, are small-scale inpatient facilities that provide community-based services in efficient and modern settings. They are typically 15,000 to 50,000 square feet in size and have eight to ten inpatient beds for observation and short-stay use (Saulsberry 2016). Minihospitals are not intended to be full-service hospitals. They are often affiliated with larger medical centers that can receive more seriously ill or injured patients (transported from the minihospital via helicopter or ambulance) when necessary. In many instances, minihospitals have replaced larger, older hospitals that had become inefficient or obsolete (Giancotti, Guglielmo, and Mauro 2017; Lovelace 2018).

Services offered by minihospitals may include the following:

- Emergency room (ER) services (some may be freestanding ERs)
- Imaging services
- Pharmacy services
- Laboratory services
- Physician services
- Outpatient surgery services

Some minihospitals have additional health and wellness features or community meeting areas.

Virtual Hospitals

Another new facility innovation is the virtual hospital, or the "hospital without patients" (Allen 2017). These facilities have no hospital beds but are staffed with physicians, nurses, technicians, and other care providers who connect with patients and provide services remotely via advanced technology. The concept takes telehealth to the next level.

Virtual hospitals provide care oversight for patients at other locations—often, at facilities where the expertise needed for more complex care is lacking. Virtual hospital care allows for video consultation, collaboration with local medical staff, and the close monitoring of patients. A virtual intensive care unit enables virtual hospital staff to track a patient's vital signs in real time to ensure that any developments can be quickly addressed by local staff, under the virtual provider's guidance. Virtual hospitals have helped provide care for people with chronic obstructive pulmonary disease, heart failure, and other chronic conditions. Virtual services are especially important in rural areas where provider shortages are common.

The first virtual hospital to become fully operational was Mercy Virtual in Chesterfield, Missouri (Mercy Virtual 2019). The hospital opened in 2015, after having been in development since 2006 (Allen 2017). Medicare payment reforms enabled the hospital to receive the necessary reimbursement for services to allow it to operate profitably (American Hospital Association 2015).

A New Joint Venture

In January 2018, Berkshire Hathaway, JP Morgan Chase, and Amazon announced a new joint venture for the purpose of improving healthcare services and lowering healthcare costs for the companies' employees. The new entity, which has been named Haven, will take a more outcomes-based approach to healthcare, under the leadership of prominent surgeon and writer Atul Gawande (Tozzi 2019; Hunnicut and Hunter 2018; Hensley 2018; Rege 2018; Silver and Votruba 2018).

Given the technological prowess of Amazon and the management and financial expertise of Berkshire Hathaway and JP Morgan Chase—along with the extraordinary financial resources of all three—Haven will likely be a formidable effort to improve delivery and cost. The three companies combined have more than a million employees, meaning that as many as 3 million lives could be covered under the auspices of their healthcare plans. The firms have stated that the venture will be free of the need to produce profit or surpluses; its primary focus will be on its employee health mission and development of a better care model. Gawande (2019) has stated that Haven wants "to share our innovations and solutions to help others."

The idea of an "Amazon-like" approach to healthcare has been contemplated for some time (Alsop 1999). In some ways, the Haven model seems like an extension of the business coalitions of the 1970s and 1980s, when businesses banded together to engage in discussions with providers and insurance companies in hopes of better pricing.

Relatively little is known about the plan at this point, but two significant points distinguish it from the ventures that have been pursued in the past. First, the venture does not rely on the government to serve as an intermediary or to lead change in healthcare delivery. Thus, the effort will likely not be met with the same political divisiveness that has hampered past reform efforts. Second, rather than focusing on providers and payers, the Haven strategy seems to focus primarily on the patient. One of the key aims is expected to be increasing the transparency of the healthcare system and providing more complete information to the people being served. The choice of Gawande as the leader for this venture is significant. He is one of the most prominent thought leaders in healthcare today and has written extensively on many of the issues that need to be addressed (Gawande 1999, 2004, 2012, 2015, 2016; Bates and Gawande 2003; Morse 2018; Pearl 2018; Silver and Votruba 2018).

Nobody knows how the Haven experiment will go, but few would argue that providing greater transparency, streamlining services, and improving efficiency would be a bad thing. I suspect that the companies will focus on the quality of outcomes more than the expense, knowing that, ultimately, the focus on outcomes will improve the value proposition. If we hope to develop a system that truly prioritizes the health of all patients, then we need to move away from the emphasis on how we get paid for services. Perhaps this new venture will create a model for doing just that.

Wellness and an Aging Population

The US population is getting older, and with age often comes the need for additional medical services. However, the idea that aging inevitably involves a general deterioration in health might be something that we too readily accept. Andrew Weil (2008), in his book *Healthy Aging*, points out that our later years do not have to be a period of continuous slow decline. Instead, we can strive to live long, healthy lives, without extended periods of debilitation in old age. Much of what happens in our later years depends on how we have cared for ourselves over the course of our lives, encompassing a wide variety of determinants of health. Looking forward, our healthcare system should encourage patients to take charge of their health and their aging process.

The Blue Zones Project

A number of insights into healthy aging have come from the Blue Zones Project, a research effort sponsored by the National Geographic Society. The purpose of the project is to identify and learn from "blue zones"—that is, areas where people tended to live exceptionally long and healthy lives—throughout the world. Blue zones were found in Europe, Asia, and North America, so geography did not seem to be a determining factor. Research on blue zones, regardless of location, suggests that the following behaviors and values are likely to contribute to healthy aging and long lives (Blue Zones Project 2019; Buettner 2017):

- *A healthy plant-based diet.* The diet is not necessarily vegetarian, but it has relatively little red meat.
- *Daily activity incorporated into lifestyle.* Researchers found that the blue zone communities did not engage in large amounts of intentional exercise (e.g., going to the gym, running on a treadmill) but that people walked daily and incorporated significant amounts of physical activity into their daily lives.
- *Healthy social relationships.* Maintaining healthy relationships with family, friends, and other community members was found to be highly important. Even in the age of smart phones and social media, face-to-face personal interactions are an important aspect of good health.
- *Restricted caloric intake.* Blue zone communities have found ways to minimize overeating—for instance, by not serving food family style, or by making it less convenient to take additional portions.
- *Outlook and sense of purpose.* The Japanese term *ikigai* roughly translates to "reason for living," or "reason I get up in the morning." We all need purpose, and we all need to feel important. We need to feel that our lives have value to ourselves and to those around us. This outlook is not just a feel-good platitude; it is a key aspect of healthy living. Healthcare professionals should take seriously the need to cultivate ikigai and prioritize strong friendships and communities.

These and other evidence-based wellness practices can have a major impact on our future health, and they should be emphasized throughout our organizations—not only for patients but also for employees and ourselves.

Addressing Alzheimer's Disease

Care for people with Alzheimer's disease is a serious healthcare and societal concern, and it is likely to command even greater attention as the US population grows older (Fineberg 2013; Kelley et al. 2013; Murray and US Burden of Disease Collaborators 2013; GBD 2015 Mortality and Causes of Death

EXHIBIT 14.10
Alzheimer's Disease Facts and Figures

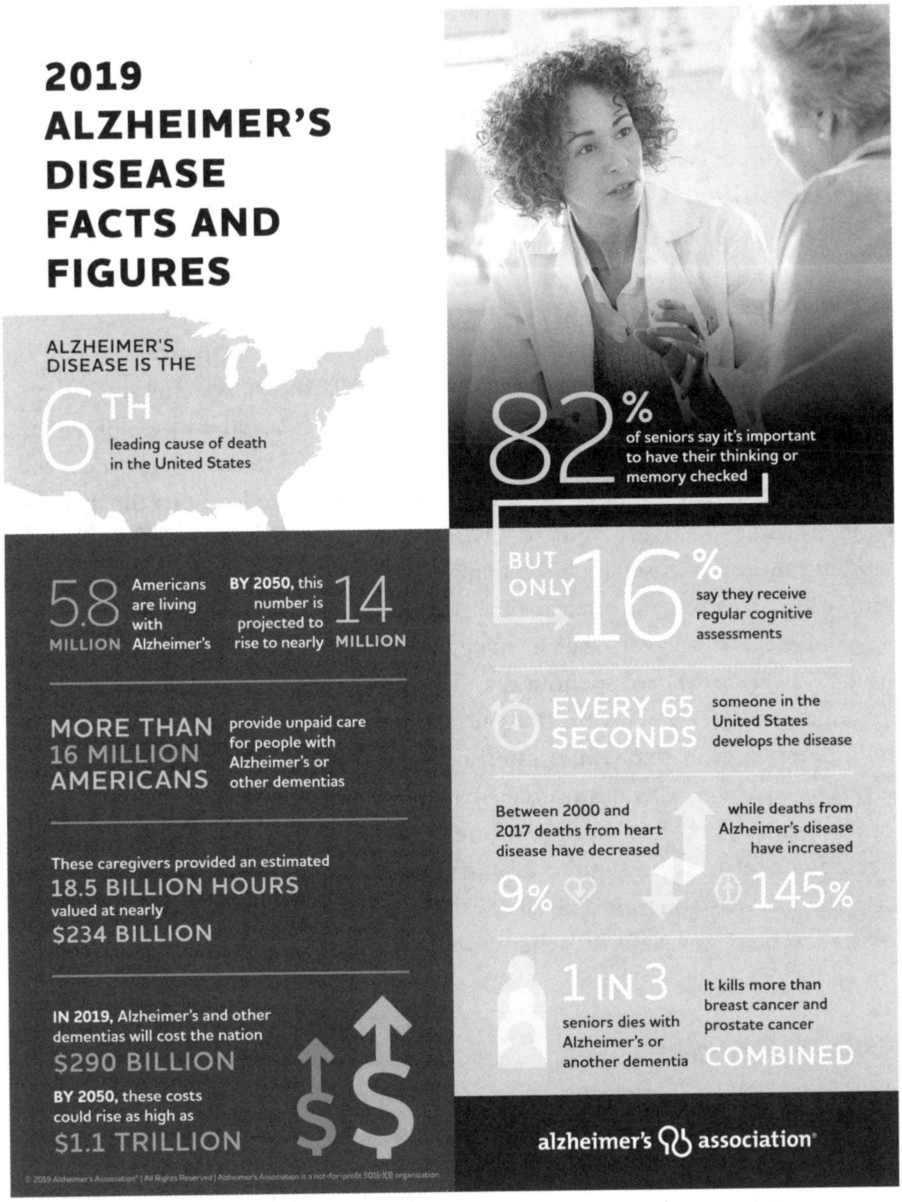
2019 ALZHEIMER'S DISEASE FACTS AND FIGURES
ALZHEIMER'S DISEASE IS THE
6TH
leading cause of death in the United States
82%
of seniors say it's important to have their thinking or memory checked
BUT ONLY
16%
say they receive regular cognitive assessments
5.8 MILLION
Americans are living with Alzheimer's
BY 2050, this number is projected to rise to nearly
14 MILLION
MORE THAN 16 MILLION AMERICANS
provide unpaid care for people with Alzheimer's or other dementias
These caregivers provided an estimated
18.5 BILLION HOURS
valued at nearly
$234 BILLION
IN 2019, Alzheimer's and other dementias will cost the nation
$290 BILLION
BY 2050, these costs could rise as high as
$1.1 TRILLION
EVERY 65 SECONDS
someone in the United States develops the disease
Between 2000 and 2017 deaths from heart disease have decreased
9%
while deaths from Alzheimer's disease have increased
145%
1 IN 3
seniors dies with Alzheimer's or another dementia
It kills more than breast cancer and prostate cancer
COMBINED
alzheimer's association
© 2019 Alzheimer's Association® | All Rights Reserved | Alzheimer's Association is a not-for-profit 501(c)(3) organization

Source: Reprinted with permission from the Alzheimer's Association (2019).

Collaborators 2016). According to the Alzheimer's Association (2019), the disease is now the sixth leading cause of death in the United States. More than 5.8 million people are currently diagnosed with Alzheimer's disease, and the number is expected to rise to more than 14 million by 2050. From 2000 to 2017, the number of deaths from heart disease decreased by 9 percent; over the same period, deaths from Alzheimer's disease increased by 145 percent (Alzheimer's Association 2019).

In addition to its effects on patients, Alzheimer's disease places a tremendous burden on caregivers, many of whom are unpaid family members or friends. The Alzheimer's Association (2019) estimates that caregivers for people with Alzheimer's or other dementias provided 18.5 billion hours of informal (i.e., unpaid) care in 2018, with a value of roughly $234 billion. In addition, direct care costs and payments for other services amounted to $290 billion in 2019 and are expected to exceed $1.1 trillion by 2050. Much of this cost is paid out of pocket (see exhibit 14.10).

Improving End-of-Life Care

Years ago, I delivered a presentation for the Western Historical Society on the differences between the Japanese and US healthcare systems since World War II. One of the most interesting distinctions involved end-of-life (EOL) care. I found that relatively few Japanese people died in hospitals unless they experienced an acute injury or illness; they were more likely to die at home or in a hospice or palliative care environment. The United States has begun working more seriously on EOL issues, but many aspects of the delivery system in this area remain unclear or unresolved.

Research suggests that hospice and palliative care can improve quality of life, lower healthcare spending, and help people live longer (Rowland and Schumann 2010). Such care does not have a curative focus, but it tends to be a better option than futile intensive care. Futile care is any curative care given to a patient who has no reasonable hope of recovery (Kasman 2004).

High levels of medical spending in the final years of one's life have long been a concern in the United States (Emanuel and Emanuel 1994; French et al. 2017). A stronger emphasis on hospice, palliative care, and other EOL issues can help control costs while also truly improving the healthcare system for all people.

Culinary Medicine

The Blue Zones Project and other research efforts have demonstrated the benefits of wellness practices that encourage and empower patients to make lifestyle and diet decisions that help improve and maintain good health. Culinary medicine is a wellness approach that incorporates nutrition and cooking habits into the pursuit of health goals (La Puma 2016). Healthcare practitioners should be cognizant of the various obstacles that may prevent patients from accessing nutritious food (e.g., financial insecurity, time stress). Areas where affordable, high-quality foods are difficult to find are sometimes known as food deserts.

Narrative Medicine

Narrative medicine is an approach that emphasizes getting to know the patient's "story" for the purpose of better understanding the sources, nature, and context of the patient's condition. Providing care in this manner requires strong communication skills and a willingness to consider the psychosocial aspects of health and disease, but the experience can be transformative for both the patient and the provider (Fioretti et al. 2016; Krisberg 2017; Muneeb et al. 2017). Typically, time constraints have limited the degree to which busy practitioners can incorporate narrative medicine, as well as other innovative approaches, into their daily work. However, as we shift to a value-based model of care, such strategies may prove to be worthwhile.

Comparative Effectiveness Research

Extensive clinical research is constantly adding to the already numerous treatment options available for many conditions. As a result, comparative effectiveness research (CER) has become increasingly important. CER compares various medical treatment options based on the degree to which they improve health outcomes. The American Recovery and Reinvestment Act of 2009 authorized the expenditure of $1.1 billion to conduct research that compares "clinical outcomes, effectiveness, and appropriateness of items, services, and procedures that are used to prevent, diagnose, or treat diseases, disorders, and other health conditions" (Congress.gov 2020). This area of research will likely be a mainstay of healthcare administration and policymaking in the future, especially as cost pressures continue and healthcare choices become more diverse (DeMaria 2009).

Climate Change and Health

Regardless of the political rhetoric over the topic, anthropomorphic climate change represents a serious threat to human health and well-being. Determining how this phenomenon will affect health and the need for healthcare services in the future is one of the most pressing—and uncertain—issues facing the US healthcare system today.

The impact of climate change is likely to be felt in a variety of ways, whether through extreme weather events and wildfires, reduced air quality, or the spread of disease. The climate affects a wide variety of health issues and disease processes, including the following (Luber et al. 2014):

- Asthma, respiratory allergies, and airway diseases
- Cancer
- Cardiovascular disease and stroke
- Effects of heat
- Human developmental effects

- Mental health and stress-related disorders
- Neurological diseases and disorders
- Nutrition and foodborne diseases
- Vector-borne and zoonotic diseases
- Waterborne diseases
- Weather-related morbidity and mortality

Climate change has the potential to significantly alter the health needs of specific geographic areas. For instance, Crimmins and colleagues (2016) project that, by 2080, a much larger portion of the United States will support disease-carrying ticks, which will affect the occurrence of Lyme's disease and other serious ailments. Some of these health impacts are already occurring. Cases of Zika, spread primarily by mosquitoes, have appeared in areas beyond those regions where "tropical" diseases would typically be expected (Centers for Disease Control and Prevention [CDC] 2019b). Certain people and communities are especially vulnerable to threats of this nature, including children, the elderly, the sick, and the poor (Berman et al. 2017; Dennekamp and Carey 2010; McKee, Greer, and Stuckler 2017; Patz and Kovats 2002; Semenza et al. 2012). These threats will increase, and the time to prepare for the future changes may be finite (Akerlof et al. 2015; Fann et al. 2015; Interagency Working Group on Climate Change 2010).

Members of the healthcare community should support responsible government policy on climate change. The US response must go beyond the healthcare sector to include issues of energy, agriculture, transportation, and other fields. Many of the actions to address climate change will offer additional societal benefits as well. For example, reducing the consumption of meat not only can help reduce global emissions and therefore slow global warming (Springmann et al. 2018); it can also benefit the physical health of the population. Similarly, promoting the development and use of public transportation not only can help cut emissions; it also can improve air quality and encourage more physical activity and community interaction in people's daily lives. If we do the right thing on climate change, the positive effects are likely to spread (Hess, Schramm, and Luber 2014; Kaku 2018; McKee, Greer, and Stuckler 2017; Organisation for Economic Co-operation and Development 2013; *Lancet* 2009; Westerling and Bryant 2008).

New and Evolving Disease Threats

Imagine that a patient in the emergency room is extremely ill, with an illness that the attending physicians find puzzling. They begin to run a series of diagnostic studies when a young physician comes on duty. After being brought up to speed on the unusual case, she comments: "I know what this is. During my fellowship at the Center for Tropical Medicine in London, we saw a lot of these cases. It's a parasite." The young physician interviews the patient and learns that—just as suspected—the patient had been in a tropical region where the parasitic disease was endemic. After further study, the diagnosis was confirmed, and the patient was properly treated. In a city of more than 1 million people, this disease had never before been seen.

The occurrence of infectious diseases in areas where they had never occurred previously has become increasingly common. Now more than ever, health is a global phenomenon—in large part because of the degree of global travel and connectedness, as well as far-reaching concerns such as climate change. Patients today are often asked during routine medical exams whether they have recently traveled outside the country.

The threat of new and unfamiliar disease creates serious challenges for the healthcare system. Administrators and clinicians must remain constantly vigilant for new ailments, and they must be prepared to respond accordingly. Such efforts require an understanding of demographics and population trends, knowledge of cultural shifts and migration patterns, careful disease surveillance, and continuous training on emerging threats.

Zoonoses

As the world's population has grown in size and come into closer contact with wildlife, often for extended periods, zoonoses, or zoonotic diseases, have become an increasing concern. A zoonosis is any disease that can be transmitted from animals (whether domestic or wild) to humans. Zoonotic pathogens can become especially dangerous when they mutate and spread from human to human or through vectors such as mosquitos. Notable examples of zoonoses include swine flu; bird (avian) flu; Nipah virus, from pigs; Ebola, from monkeys, gorillas, and chimpanzees; and Zika, which is mosquito-borne but originally from monkeys (Ahmad and Tan 2014; Bengis et al. 2004; Boseret et al. 2013; Broder et al. 2013; Cauchemez et al. 2016; CDC 2014, 2019b; Chomel and Osburn 2006; Field 2009; Groopman and Hartzband 2017; Hahn et al. 2014; Hastwell 2014; Hepojoki et al. 2017; Himsworth et al. 2013; Kruse, Kirkemo, and Handeland 2004; Lindblad, El Fiky, and Zajdowicz 2015; Luby 2013; Meaney-Delman et al. 2016; Meslin, Stöhr, and Heymann 2000; Miller, Farnsworth, and Malmberg 2013; O'Shea et al. 2014; Singh et al. 2017; Spickler 2018; Tomley and Shirley 2009; Wang 2016).

The spread of zoonoses, including serious parasitic diseases, is exacerbated by climate change (Short, Caminade, and Thomas 2017). As changing conditions cause species—along with their pathogens—to move into new territories, human and domestic animal infections become more likely. Warmer environments may also enable pathogens to thrive in places where their host (e.g., the mosquito) previously would not have been able to survive.

Pandemics

A pandemic is a widespread occurrence of infectious disease that affects a large population or region. Coronavirus disease 2019 (COVID-19), for instance, created a global crisis as it spread rapidly from country to country; the World Health Organization (2020) declared it a pandemic in March 2020, just a few months after the first cases appeared. The role of a healthcare organization in responding to a pandemic may vary depending on the circumstances. However, the organization, at a minimum, needs to be prepared to deal with significant numbers of patients who are affected, while simultaneously ensuring the protection of staff and other patients (CDC 2019a). The American Nurses Association (2010) offers an excellent guide for adapting standards of care under pandemic circumstances. Organizations may also look to cooperate with local community hospitals and health departments as part of an overall National Incident Management System.

Antibiotic-Resistant Infections

Alexander Fleming discovered penicillin in 1928, which led to the proliferation of new antibiotic categories during the 1950s, in the "Golden Age of Antibiotics" (Aminov 2010). Antibiotics have been hailed as "miracle drugs," and, indeed, they have enabled us to save countless lives. Unfortunately, this sense of "miracle" effectiveness has also led to their overuse, with serious consequences. Because of the adaptability of pathogens, more infections have become resistant to antibiotic treatment (Gould 2016; Schwartz 2004).

Each year in the United States, at least 2 million people become infected with bacteria that are resistant to antibiotics (Frieden 2013). This threat is not new, but the response of the US healthcare system has been dangerously slow (Laxminarayan et al. 2013; Neu 1992). Some people are even wondering if we are entering a "post-antibiotic era" of healthcare (Alanis 2005). Infections that now have limited ability to be treated with antibiotics—or, in some cases, have no effective antibiotic—include the following (National Institute of Allergy and Infectious Diseases 2016):

- Antibiotic-resistant Mycobacterium tuberculosis (TB)
- Methicillin-resistant Staphylococcus aureus (MRSA)
- Vancomycin-resistant *Enterococci* (VRE)
- Neisseria gonorrhoeae (gonorrhea)
- *Clostridium difficile*
- Gram-negative bacteria

The development of new antibiotics has been slow for several decades. Finding agents that kill pathogens is not difficult; however, many of these compounds are highly toxic to humans as well. Developing a new antibiotic often takes 10 to 20 years, and the financial returns are often insufficient. As a result, many commercial enterprises are hesitant to engage in antibiotic development activities (Conly and Johnston 2005; Hughes and Karlén 2014; World Health Organization 2011).

In addition to trying to find new antibiotics, researchers are also working on nonantibiotic approaches, including the following:

- Bacteriophages and phase therapy, which target the infecting bacterial cells
- Use of vaccines to prevent the spread of multidrug-resistant pathogens
- Microbiota modulation, which takes advantage of the natural immune system of the body

All of these areas need additional research, but they show promise for helping to control bacterial infections while combating the overuse of antibiotics (Ruiz et al. 2017).

The US healthcare system should take a lesson from the antibiotic resistance crisis: Everything we do has unintended consequences—sometimes good, sometimes bad. We need to think critically about our choices. We should not simply default to the easiest path or blindly adopt new technologies across the board. An additional lesson from this crisis is that patient education efforts are worth the time. Many patients did not understand how antibiotics worked and were not made aware of the dangers of overuse. Now we are all paying the price.

Bioterrorism

Bioterrorism is the intentional use of a biological agent, such as a virus or bacteria, to harm a human population. Acts of bioterrorism could involve direct infections to people, the contamination of water or food supplies, or the infection of animal populations. Bioterrorism is an ever-present threat, and we must remain vigilant to its possibilities through surveillance and preparedness (Zarcadoolas, Pleasant, and Greer 2005).

The CDC (2018) classifies bioterrorism agents into three primary categories. Category A consists of high-priority agents that pose the greatest risk to the public and to national security. The following factors distinguish the agents of this category:

- They can be easily spread or transmitted from person to person.
- They result in high death rates and may have a major public health impact.
- They might cause public panic and social disruption.
- They require special actions for public health preparedness.

Category B agents are the next highest priority because they are moderately easy to spread, result in moderate illness rates and low death rates, and require enhancements to the CDC's laboratory capacity and disease monitoring. Category C agents include emerging pathogens that could be engineered for mass spread in the future. Such agents are readily available, can be produced and disseminated easily, and have potential for high morbidity and mortality.

Mental and Behavioral Health

The need for mental and behavioral health services in the United States is overwhelming. As many as one in five people in the country has a diagnosable mental health condition (National Institute of Mental Health [NIMH] 2019a), yet serious treatment gaps continue to exist. Many patients who need treatment are unable to receive it, whether because of cost, shortages of professionals and facilities, the fragmentation of care, or the stigma often associated with mental health services (Kazdin 2017; Wainberg et al. 2017). The number of psychiatric beds in the United States has decreased by more than 500,000 since the 1950s (Lutterman et al. 2017).

The societal cost of mental illness is significant. Mental illness accounts for about one-third of all adult health-related disability, and it can be the source of tremendous personal suffering (Lake and Turner 2017). Suicide is the second leading cause of death in the United States for people between the ages of 10 and 34 (NIMH 2019b). If our healthcare system is to truly support people's health and well-being, mental and behavioral health issues demand immediate attention.

Behavioral Economics

Americans today are bombarded with advertisements for fast food, soft drinks, and other products detrimental to their health, all while computer screens, smart phones, and social media alerts keep them increasingly sedentary and distracted. In his book *The Hacking of the American Mind*, Robert Lustig (2017) examines the various ways in which corporations have been able to influence people's thinking and drive them toward unhealthy choices. If we are to counteract this influence and encourage people to adopt healthier lifestyles, the field of behavioral economics will play a pivotal role.

Fundamentally, behavioral economics works by providing an emotional hook to an activity that is being encouraged. Advertisers employ such techniques when they, for instance, create flashy commercials of attractive people enjoying fast food. The foods themselves might be extremely high in calories, but the people in the commercials are lively and beautiful—the picture of health. The ads are designed and carefully tested to get consumers to take action—specifically, to buy the food items featured in the commercials. In healthcare, we sometimes present patients with brochures full of facts and figures, but how well can such materials stand up against skillfully produced ad campaigns? Generally, not very well.

The healthcare sector needs to more effectively use behavioral economics to make healthy choices easier and more appealing. We also need to help people recognize the mechanisms that keep them stuck in cycles of unhealthy behavior. Research at the University of Massachusetts Medical School has found that simple mindfulness training, along with teaching the basic neuroscience of habit loops (i.e., the interplay of trigger, behavior, and reward), can help people realize that certain behaviors are not as rewarding as they might have seemed (Brewer 2017). Brewer (2017, 10) defines mindfulness as "paying attention to our moment-to-moment experience in a particular way."

Eating a piece of cheesecake, for instance, might be less enticing when we pay closer attention to the full experience—including the heartburn and sluggishness that often comes afterward. Similarly, a heavy social media habit might seem less enjoyable when we take into account the crick in our neck and the sense of guilt we feel over all that wasted time every day. What good are we really getting out of eating a piece of cheesecake, or obsessively checking our phones? Not much. When we pay close attention to our direct experience, we allow our brains to make new habit loops based on what *is* truly rewarding: being healthy and engaging with people in real life.

Brewer's (2017) mindfulness methods have proved highly effective in helping people to quit smoking, reduce anxiety, and avoid unhealthy eating. Brewer's team at MindSciences (2020) has developed a series of mobile applications—titled Craving to Quit, Unwinding Anxiety, and Eat Right Now—that seek to enhance mindfulness for specific purposes. The apps include training videos, provider interaction through optional group video meetings, and access to support through an online community. They stand as an excellent example of how behavioral economics techniques can be harnessed in a positive way to make us healthier.

A number of other behavioral techniques—several of which were described in chapter 9—can help bring about positive changes in patient behavior. Simple contracts or agreements between patients and providers, in which the patient commits to complying with certain instructions, can be highly effective, even if violating the agreement carries no penalties (Ariely 2010). Gamification, or the use of gaming to influence behavior, is also on the rise. Important information and lessons can be incorporated into the games themselves (King et al. 2013).

Other techniques may involve small gifts and reminders. For instance, Sooner Care (2017), the Oklahoma Medicaid Program, ran a pilot program in which small "behavioral nudges" and financial incentives were given to patient groups to encourage them to fill their statin prescriptions. The nudges consisted of letters and personalized reminders, and the financial incentives were five-dollar gift cards; a control group received neither. The study found that patients who received a nudge were significantly more likely to have their prescriptions filled; gift card recipients did not show the same level of improvement.

Too often, people fall into the psychological trap of focusing on immediate rewards while discounting future rewards, and this tendency can present a serious obstacle to efforts to influence healthy behavior (Ariely 2010; Thaler 2015). When attempting to break an unhealthy habit, a person might say, "I'll only do this one more time, and then I'll never do it again"—only to eventually break the promise and repeat the undesired action. Relying on willpower to resist temptation is not always sufficient; better results are likely with planned behaviors that take into account the future implications of our actions. For instance, if we are trying not to eat a particular food, we should start by not buying that food, thereby removing the temptation.

A Post-ACA Healthcare Insurance World

As discussed in the previous chapter, the outlook for the ACA is uncertain, and nobody truly knows what the future of healthcare reform will be. The ACA sought to increase healthcare coverage through Medicaid expansions and the individual and employer mandates, but political differences have limited the law's effectiveness. Only about half of the states expanded Medicaid under the ACA, and the individual mandate has been repealed (French et al. 2016; Glied and Jackson 2017; Griffith, Evans, and Bor 2017). Some people favor further rollbacks or a complete repeal of the ACA, whereas others are calling for a universal coverage plan with a single-payer approach (Blahous et al. 2018; Fuchs 2018; Gaffney et al. 2016).

Most polling has shown that Americans generally favor the idea of universal coverage. In a 2019 poll by the Kaiser Family Foundation, 56 percent of respondents were in favor of a "Medicare for All" type of plan that would cover all Americans (Singh and Palosky 2019). In the same poll, 77 percent of respondents felt that people between the ages of 50 and 64 should be able to buy health insurance through Medicare, and 75 percent thought that people who did not get insurance through their employer or their state Medicaid program should be able to buy into Medicare. Roughly the same percentage indicated that they would support a national government-administered health plan like Medicare that was open to anyone if people also had the

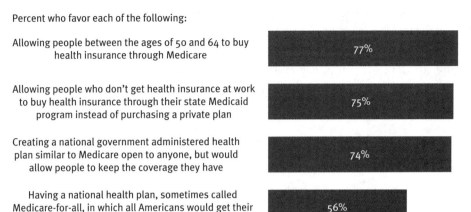

Percent who favor each of the following:

Allowing people between the ages of 50 and 64 to buy health insurance through Medicare — 77%

Allowing people who don't get health insurance at work to buy health insurance through their state Medicaid program instead of purchasing a private plan — 75%

Creating a national government administered health plan similar to Medicare open to anyone, but would allow people to keep the coverage they have — 74%

Having a national health plan, sometimes called Medicare-for-all, in which all Americans would get their insurance from a single government plan — 56%

EXHIBIT 14.11
Public Attitudes Toward Expansion of Medicare and Medicaid

Source: Reprinted with permission from R. Singh and C. Palosky, "Poll: Majorities Favor a Range of Options to Expand Public Coverage, Including Medicare-for-All," Kaiser Family Foundation, published January 23, 2019, www.kff.org/health-reform/press-release/poll-majorities-favor-a-range-of-options-to-expand-public-coverage-including-medicare-for-all/.

option of keeping their current coverage (see exhibit 14.11). The difficulty, however, lies in the details. The more specific the proposals become, the less favorably they tend to be viewed (Keller 2018).

Most "Medicare for All" proposals do not place all citizens into the current Medicare program but rather provide a public option similar to Medicare that would be available alongside other commercial insurance products (Neuman, Pollitz, and Tolbert 2018). Other proposals, however, represent a complete change to a single-payer system, with everyone covered under the same Medicare-style plan. Many people who are opposed to a single-payer system fear that a public option—even if only offered as an option—would make the health insurance market less attractive to commercial insurance payers, leading to fewer options being available (Obama 2016; Singh and Palosky 2019).

An important twist in many of the reform proposals is a global budgeting approach to healthcare payments, in which a lump sum is provided for covered individuals (Woodruff 2019). This approach provides incentives for healthcare systems to focus less on production of services and more on health outcomes and reductions in cost (Feldstein 2019; Himmelstein et al. 2014; Sharfstein et al. 2017; Song et al. 2014). Global budgeting is somewhat like the ultimate capitation system, where all services are included in a single per-person payment on a monthly or yearly basis.

New York Times columnist David Brooks (2019) has called "Medicare for All" an "impossible dream," saying that "there's no plausible route from here to there." He argues that the transition would be incredibly difficult because of the dramatic change it would require from numerous elements of society, including patients, insurance companies, employers, hospitals, doctors, and the government. Americans' suspicions of higher taxes and government oversight pose yet another barrier. Whereas other countries have been able to develop single-payer systems from a clean slate, the United States must work with a massive, complex system that has taken shape over the course of many years. So much would need to be undone that large-scale change seems virtually impossible. Regardless of one's position on "Medicare for All," Brooks makes a compelling argument about the difficulty of the path before us.

Closing Thoughts

When we compare the healthcare challenges of the United States with those seen elsewhere in the world, a common reaction is to simply say, "Well, Americans are just different." To some extent, the statement is true. The United States *is* very different from other countries, given our history, our values, our geography, our diverse population, and numerous other factors. As a result, the solutions we need may well be different from—and potentially more complex than—those that have been employed in other countries.

The United States has been trying to achieve universal healthcare for more than a century, but progress has been hampered by deeply held differences in beliefs. Many Americans believe healthcare is a right for all people, whereas others feel it is a privilege that should be subject to market forces like any other good or service. The country's political divisions have further complicated the debate and made compromise difficult. Still, given the massive amounts of money spent on healthcare in the United States, is it really not possible to provide care to everyone?

Our lack of universal coverage has contributed to the development of a cumbersome patchwork of healthcare entities and regulations, with additional services provided through humanitarian activities. Many patients seek emergency room care as a last resort—an expensive and inefficient option that leads to suboptimal health outcomes. Healthcare organizations provide significant amounts of uncompensated care, although those costs eventually accrue to other payers. More and more often, we see people essentially begging for help when expensive medical services are needed.

Efforts to address these and other problems have been impeded by inertia throughout the system. Many Americans who have healthcare coverage are satisfied with their current care and see no need for change; furthermore, many are nervous about the disruption that universal healthcare could bring. Similarly, many healthcare providers, as well as organizations that supply goods and services to the healthcare system, are concerned that single-payer coverage would reduce their leverage in the marketplace. Despite the noble intentions of patient care, the US healthcare system is driven by economic gain.

At times, the obstacles to effective healthcare reform seem insurmountable. Nonetheless, the US healthcare system is undergoing dramatic change, and the rate of that change is likely to increase in the years ahead. If we remain attached to the old paradigms of healthcare delivery, we will run into unimaginable difficulties. The realignment of incentives and the development of new systems will be essential for comprehensive reform. Our current and future healthcare leaders must always be willing to carefully examine new information, consider emerging ideas and concepts, and incorporate effective strategies to maximize value and navigate tomorrow's challenges.

Discussion Questions

1. How does technology influence the cost and equitable distribution of healthcare?
2. What will the funding mechanisms of the future look like?
3. How will the lack of equitable mental health care affect the country's healthcare system and society?
4. How does climate change affect health in the United States, and in what ways might the US healthcare system address its impact?
5. What would be the implications of a "post-antibiotic era" for the US healthcare system?

References

Abiri, R., G. Heise, X. Zhao, Y. Jiang, and F. Abiri. 2017. "Brain Computer Interface for Gesture Control of a Social Robot: An Offline Study." Published July 22. http://arxiv.org/abs/1707.07233.

Advisory Board. 2017. "Think Before You Tweet: The Potential Legal Pitfalls of Hospitals' Social Media Use." Advisory Board Daily Briefing. Published October 13. www.advisory.com/daily-briefing/2017/10/13/think-before-you-tweet.

Ahmad, S. B., and C. T. Tan. 2014. "Nipah Encephalitis—An Update. *Medical Journal of Malaysia* 69 (Suppl. A): 103–11. www.ncbi.nlm.nih.gov/pubmed/25417957.

Akerlof, K. L., P. L. Delamater, C. R. Boules, C. R. Upperman, and C. S. Mitchell. 2015. "Vulnerable Populations Perceive Their Health as at Risk from Climate Change." *International Journal of Environmental Research and Public Health* 12 (12): 15419–33. https://doi.org/10.3390/ijerph121214994.

Alanis, A. J. 2005. "Resistance to Antibiotics: Are We in the Post-antibiotic Era?" *Archives of Medical Research* 36 (6): 697–705. https://doi.org/10.1016/j.arcmed.2005.06.009.

Allen, A. 2017. "A Hospital Without Patients." *Politico.* Published November 8. www.politico.com/agenda/story/2017/11/08/virtual-hospital-mercy-st-louis-000573.

Al Rawajbeh, M., and A. Haboush. 2015. "Advanced Object Monitoring Using Wireless Sensors Network." *Procedia Computer Science* 65: 17–24. https://doi.org/10.1016/j.procs.2015.09.071.

Alsop, S. 1999. "Is There an Amazon.com for Every Industry?" *Fortune,* January 11, 159–60. https://archive.fortune.com/magazines/fortune/fortune_archive/1999/01/11/253770/index.htm.

Alzheimer's Association. 2019. "Facts and Figures." Accessed January 29, 2020. www.alz.org/alzheimers-dementia/facts-figures.

American Hospital Association (AHA). 2015. *The Promise of Telehealth for Hospitals, Health Systems and Their Communities.* Published January. www.aha.org/system/files/research/reports/tw/15jan-tw-telehealth.pdf.

American Nurses Association (ANA). 2010. *ANA's Principles for Nursing Documentation Guidance for Registered Nurses.* Accessed October 16, 2019. www.nursingworld.org/~4af4f2/globalassets/docs/ana/ethics/principles-of-nursing-documentation.pdf.

Aminov, R. I. 2010. "A Brief History of the Antibiotic Era: Lessons Learned and Challenges for the Future." *Frontiers in Microbiology* 1: 134. https://doi.org/10.3389/fmicb.2010.00134.

Ariely, D. 2010. *Predictably Irrational: The Hidden Forces That Shape Our Decisions.* New York: Harper Perennial.

Ashley, E. A. 2015. "The Precision Medicine Initiative: A New National Effort." *JAMA* 313 (21): 2119–20. https://doi.org/10.1001/jama.2015.3595.

Ashrafian, H., O. Clancy, V. Grover, and A. Darzi. 2017. "The Evolution of Robotic Surgery: Surgical and Anaesthetic Aspects." *British Journal of Anaesthesia* 119 (Suppl. 1): i72–84. https://doi.org/10.1093/bja/aex383.

Bashshur, R., G. W. Shannon, E. A. Krupinski, and J. Grigsby. 2011. "The Taxonomy of Telemedicine." *Telemedicine and e-Health* 17 (6): 484–94. https://doi.org/10.1089/tmj.2011.0103.

Bashshur, R. L., G. W. Shannon, E. A. Krupinski, J. Grigsby, J. C. Kvedar, R. S. Weinstein, J. H. Sanders, K. S. Rheuban, T. S. Nesbitt, D. C. Alverson, R. C. Merrell, J. D. Linkous, A. S. Ferguson, R. J. Waters, M. E. Stachura, D. G. Ellis, N. M. Antoniotti, B. Johnston, C. R. Doarn, P. Yellowlees, S. Normandin, and J. Tracy. 2009. "National Telemedicine Initiatives: Essential to Healthcare Reform." *Telemedicine and e-Health* 15 (6): 600–610. https://doi.org/10.1089/tmj.2009.9960.

Bashshur, R. L., G. W. Shannon, B. R. Smith, D. C. Alverson, N. Antoniotti, W. G. Barsan, N. Bashshur, E. M. Brown, M. J. Coye, C. R. Doarn, S. Ferguson, J. Grigsby, E. A. Krupinski, J. C. Kvedar, J. Linkous, R. C. Merrell, T. Nesbitt,

R. Poropatich, K. S. Rheuban, J. H. Sanders, A. R. Watson, R. S. Weinstein, and P. Yellowlees. 2014. "The Empirical Foundations of Telemedicine Interventions for Chronic Disease Management." *Telemedicine and e-Health* 20 (9): 769–800. www.ncbi.nlm.nih.gov/pubmed/24968105.

Bastian, H., P. Glasziou, and I. Chalmers. 2010. "Seventy-Five Trials and Eleven Systematic Reviews a Day: How Will We Ever Keep Up?" *PLOS Medicine* 7 (9): e1000326. https://doi.org/10.1371/journal.pmed.1000326.

Bates, D. W., and A. A. Gawande. 2003. "Improving Safety with Information Technology." *New England Journal of Medicine* 348: 2526–34. https://doi.org/10.1056/NEJMsa020847.

Becker's Hospital Review. 2015. "10 Top Uses for Telemedicine, According to Physicians." *Health IT & CIO Report.* Published June 23. www.beckershospitalreview.com/healthcare-information-technology/10-top-uses-for-telemedicine-according-to-physicians.html.

Bengis, R. G., F. A. Leighton, J. R. Fischer, M. Artois, T. Mörner, and C. M. Tate. 2004. "The Role of Wildlife in Emerging and Re-emerging Zoonoses." *Revue Scientifique et Technique* 23 (2): 497–511. www.ncbi.nlm.nih.gov/pubmed/15702716.

Berman, J. D., K. Ebisu, R. D. Peng, F. Dominici, and M. L. Bell. 2017. "Drought and the Risk of Hospital Admissions and Mortality in Older Adults in Western USA from 2000 to 2013: A Retrospective Study." *Lancet Planetary Health* 1 (1): e17–25. https://doi.org/10.1016/S2542-5196(17)30002-5.

Best, J. 2019. "Building the Tricorder: The Race to Create a Real-Life Star Trek Medical Scanner." ZD Net. Published April 5. www.zdnet.com/article/building-the-tricorder-the-race-to-create-a-real-life-star-trek-medical-scanner/.

Blahous, C., J. Fish, L. F. Smith, and S. R. Strategist. 2018. "The Costs of a National Single-Payer Healthcare System." Mercatus Center, George Mason University. Working paper. Published July. www.mercatus.org/system/files/blahous-costs-medicare-mercatus-working-paper-v1_1.pdf.

Blitzer, B., and T. Benedict. 1962. *The Jetsons.* Episode 10, "Uniblab." Aired November 25. Screen Gems–Hanna Barbera Cartoons.

Blue Zones Project. 2019. "Blue Zones Project." Accessed October 16. www.bluezonesproject.com.

Boseret, G., B. Losson, J. G. Mainil, E. Thiry, and C. Saegerman. 2013. "Zoonoses in Pet Birds: Review and Perspectives." *Veterinary Research* 44 (1): 36–53. https://doi.org/10.1186/1297-9716-44-36.

Brewer, J. 2017. *The Craving Mind.* New Haven, CT: Yale University Press.

Broder, C. C., K. Xu, D. B. Nikolov, Z. Zhu, D. S. Dimitrov, D. Middleton, J. Pallister, T. W. Geisbert, K. N. Bossart, and L.-F. Wang. 2013. "A Treatment for and Vaccine Against the Deadly Hendra and Nipah Viruses." *Antiviral Research* 100 (1): 8–13. https://doi.org/10.1016/j.antiviral.2013.06.012.

Brooks, D. 2019. "'Medicare for All': The Impossible Dream." *New York Times.* March 4. www.nytimes.com/2019/03/04/opinion/medicare-for-all.html.

Browne, R. 2018. "Healthcare and AI: Doctors Warn on the Pace of Technological Change." CNBC. Published August 17. www.cnbc.com/2018/08/17/healthcare-and-ai-doctors-warn-on-the-pace-of-technological-change.html.

Buettner, D. 2017. "9 Lessons from the World's Blue Zones on Living a Long, Healthy Life." World Economic Forum. Published June 26. www.weforum.org/agenda/2017/06/changing-the-way-america-eats-moves-and-connects-one-town-at-a-time/.

Callahan, D. 2011. "Rationing: Theory, Politics, and Passions." *Hastings Center Report* 41 (2): 23–27. https://doi.org/10.1353/hcr.2011.0031.

Calo, R. (ed.). 2016. *A Roadmap for US Robotics: From Internet to Robotics 2016 Edition.* Published November 7. http://jacobsschool.ucsd.edu/uploads/docs/2016/roadmap3-final-2b.pdf.

Campbell, E. M., D. F. Sittig, K. P. Guappone, R. H. Dykstra, and J. S. Ash. 2007. "Overdependence on Technology: An Unintended Adverse Consequence of Computerized Provider Order Entry." In *AMIA Annual Symposium Proceedings, 2007*, 94–98. www.ncbi.nlm.nih.gov/pubmed/18693805.

Carroll, J. K., A. Moorhead, R. Bond, W. G. LeBlanc, R. J. Petrella, and K. Fiscella. 2017. "Who Uses Mobile Phone Health Apps and Does Use Matter? A Secondary Data Analytics Approach." *Journal of Medical Internet Research* 19 (4): e125. https://doi.org/10.2196/jmir.5604.

Cauchemez, S., M. Besnard, P. Bompard, T. Dub, P. Guillemette-Artur, D. Eyrolle-Guignot, H. Salje, M. D. Van Kerkhove, V. Abadie, C. Garel, A. Fontanet, and H.-P. Mallet. 2016. "Association Between Zika Virus and Microcephaly in French Polynesia, 2013–15: A Retrospective Study." *Lancet* 387 (10033): 2125–32. https://doi.org/10.1016/S0140-6736(16)00651-6.

Centers for Disease Control and Prevention (CDC). 2019a. "Pandemic Influenza." Reviewed January 24. www.cdc.gov/flu/pandemic-resources/index.htm.

———. 2019b. "Zika Virus." Reviewed June 4. www.cdc.gov/zika/index.html.

———. 2018. "Bioterrorism Agents/Diseases." Reviewed April 4. https://emergency.cdc.gov/agent/agentlist-category.asp.

———. 2014. "Ebola Virus Disease Outbreak—West Africa, September 2014." *MMWR Weekly Report* 63 (39): 865–66. www.cdc.gov/mmwr/preview/mmwrhtml/mm6339a4.htm.

Chomel, B. B., and B. I. Osburn. 2006. "Zoological Medicine and Public Health." *Journal of Veterinary Medical Education* 33 (3): 346–51. www.ncbi.nlm.nih.gov/pubmed/17035205.

Congress.gov. 2020. "H.R.1—American Recovery and Reinvestment Act of 2009." Accessed January 21. www.congress.gov/bill/111th-congress/house-bill/1/text.

Conly, J., and B. Johnston. 2005. "Where Are All the New Antibiotics? The New Antibiotic Paradox." *Canadian Journal of Infectious Diseases & Medical Microbiology/Journal Canadien Des Maladies Infectieuses et de La Microbiologie Medicale* 16 (3): 159–60. https://doi.org/10.1155/2005/892058.

Consult QD. 2018. "Cleveland Clinic Unveils Top 10 Medical Innovations for 2019." Published October 24. https://consultqd.clevelandclinic.org/cleveland-clinic-unveils-top-10-medical-innovations-for-2019/.

Crimmins, A., J. Balbus, J. L. Gamble, C. B. Beard, J. E. Bell, D. Dodgen, R. J. Eisen, N. Fann, M. Hawkins, S. C. Herring, L. Jantarasami, D. M. Mills, S. Saha, M. C. Sarofim, J. Trtanj, and L. Ziska. 2016. *The Impacts of Climate Change on Human Health in the United States: A Scientific Assessment.* US Global Change Research Program. Published April. https://doi.org/10.7930/J0R49NQX.

Dalal, A. R. 2015. "Philosophy of Organ Donation: Review of Ethical Facets." *World Journal of Transplantation* 5 (2): 44–51. https://doi.org/10.5500/wjt.v5.i2.44.

Defense Advanced Research Projects Agency (DARPA). 2019. "Defense Advanced Research Projects Agency." Accessed October 16, 2019. www.darpa.mil.

DeMaria, A. N. 2009. "Comparative Effectiveness Research." *Journal of the American College of Cardiology* 53 (11): 973–75. https://doi.org/10.1016/j.jacc.2009.02.010.

Dennekamp, M., and M. Carey. 2010. "Air Quality and Chronic Disease: Why Action on Climate Change Is Also Good for Health." *New South Wales Public Health Bulletin* 21 (6): 115–21. https://doi.org/10.1071/NB10026.

de Souza, C. H. A., R. A. Morbeck, M. Steinman, C. P. Hors, M. M. Bracco, E. H. Kozasa, and E. R. Leão. 2017. "Barriers and Benefits in Telemedicine Arising Between a High-Technology Hospital Service Provider and Remote Public Healthcare Units: A Qualitative Study in Brazil." *Telemedicine and e-Health* 23 (6): 527–32. https://doi.org/10.1089/tmj.2016.0158.

Dorsey, E. R., and E. J. Topol. 2016. "State of Telehealth." *New England Journal of Medicine* 375 (2): 154–61. https://doi.org/10.1056/NEJMra1601705.

Dvorsky, G. 2015. "How Obama's Precision Medicine Initiative Will Revolutionize Healthcare." IO9. Published January 21. http://io9.com/how-obamas-precision-medicine-initiative-will-revolutio-1680866890.

Emanuel, E. J., and L. L. Emanuel. 1994. "The Economics of Dying—The Illusion of Cost Savings at the End of Life." *New England Journal of Medicine* 330 (8): 540–44. https://doi.org/10.1056/NEJM199402243300806.

Ericsson. 2018. "Ericsson Mobility Report November 2018." Published November. www.ericsson.com/en/mobility-report/reports/november-2018.

Fann, N., C. G. Nolte, P. Dolwick, T. L. Spero, A. C. Brown, S. Phillips, and S. Anenberg. 2015. "The Geographic Distribution and Economic Value of Climate Change-Related Ozone Health Impacts in the United States in 2030." *Journal of the Air & Waste Management Association* 65 (5): 570–80. https://doi.org/10.1080/10962247.2014.996270.

Feldstein, P. J. 2019. *Health Policy Issues: An Economic Perspective*, 7th ed. Chicago: Health Administration Press.

Ferrucci, D., A. Levas, S. Bagchi, D. Gondek, and E. T. Mueller. 2013. "Watson: Beyond Jeopardy!" *Artificial Intelligence* 199–200: 93–105. https://doi.org/10.1016/j.artint.2012.06.009.

Field, H. E. 2009. "Bats and Emerging Zoonoses: Henipaviruses and SARS." *Zoonoses and Public Health* 56 (6–7): 278–84. https://doi.org/10.1111/j.1863-2378.2008.01218.x.

Fineberg, H. V. 2013. "The State of Health in the United States." *JAMA* 310 (6): 585–86. https://doi.org/10.1001/jama.2013.13805.

Fingerhut, A. W., and C. M. Abdou. 2017. "The Role of Healthcare Stereotype Threat and Social Identity Threat in LGB Health Disparities." *Journal of Social Issues* 73 (3): 493–507. https://doi.org/10.1111/josi.12228.

Fioretti, C., K. Mazzocco, S. Riva, S. Oliveri, M. Masiero, and G. Pravettoni. 2016. "Research Studies on Patients' Illness Experience Using the Narrative Medicine Approach: A Systematic Review." *BMJ Open* 6 (7): e011220. https://doi.org/10.1136/bmjopen-2016-011220.

Flemisch, F., M. C. A. Baltzer, S. Sadeghian, R. Meyer, D. L. Hernández, and R. Baier. 2019. "Making HSI More Intelligent: Human Systems Exploration Versus Experiment for the Integration of Humans and Artificial Cognitive Systems." In *Intelligent Human Systems Integration 2019*, edited by W. Karwowski and T. Ahram, 563–69. Cham, Switzerland: Springer. https://doi.org/10.1007/978-3-030-11051-2_85.

Fox, S., and M. Duggan. 2013. "One in Three American Adults Have Gone Online to Figure Out a Medical Condition." Pew Research Center. Published January 15. www.pewinternet.org/2013/01/15/health-online-2013/.

Fox, S. 2003. "Internet Health Resources: Health Searches and Email Have Become More Commonplace, but There Is Room for Improvement in Searches and Overall Internet Access." Pew Research Center. Published July 16. www.pewinternet.org/2003/07/16/internet-health-resources/.

French, E. B., J. McCauley, M. Aragon, P. Bakx, M. Chalkley, S. H. Chen, B. J. Christensen, H. Chuang, A. Côté-Sergent, M. De Nardi, E. Fan, D. Echevin, P.-Y. Geoffard, C. Gastaldi-Ménager, M. Gortz, Y. Ibuka, J. B. Jones, M. Kallestrup-Lamb, M. Karlsson, T. J. Klein, G. de Lagasnerie, P.-C. Michaud, O. O'Donnell, N. Rice, J. S. Skinner, E. van Doorslaer, N. R. Ziebarth, and E. Kelly. 2017. "End-of-Life Medical Spending in Last Twelve Months of Life Is Lower than Previously Reported." *Health Affairs* 36 (7): 1211–17. https://doi.org/10.1377/hlthaff.2017.0174.

French, M. T., J. Homer, G. Gumus, and L. Hickling. 2016. "Key Provisions of the Patient Protection and Affordable Care Act (ACA): A Systematic Review and Presentation of Early Research Findings." *Health Services Research* 51 (5): 1735–71. https://doi.org/10.1111/1475-6773.12511.

Frieden, T. 2013. *Antibiotic Resistance Threats in the United States.* Centers for Disease Control and Prevention. Accessed October 16, 2019. www.cdc.gov/drugresistance/pdf/ar-threats-2013-508.pdf.

Fuchs, V. R. 2018. "Is Single Payer the Answer for the US Health Care System?" *JAMA* 319 (1): 15–16. https://doi.org/10.1001/jama.2017.18739.

Gaffney, A., S. Woolhandler, M. Angell, and D. U. Himmelstein. 2016. "Moving Forward from the Affordable Care Act to a Single-Payer System." *American Journal of Public Health* 106 (6): 987–88. https://doi.org/10.2105/AJPH.2015.303157.

Gaudin, S. 2017. "DARPA: We're on Cusp of Merging Human and Machine." Computerworld. Published February 13. www.computerworld.com/article/3168840/darpa-we-re-on-cusp-of-merging-human-and-machine.html.

Gawande, A. 2019. "Haven." Accessed October 16, 2019. https://havenhealthcare.com/.

———. 2016. "Quantity and Quality of Life: Duties of Care in Life-Limiting Illness." *JAMA* 315 (3): 267–69. https://doi.org/10.1001/jama.2015.19206.

———. 2015. "Overkill: An Avalanche of Unnecessary Medical Care Is Harming Patients Physically and Financially. What Can We Do About It?" *New Yorker*. Published May 11. www.newyorker.com/magazine/2015/05/11/overkill-atul-gawande.

———. 2012. "Big Med." *New Yorker*. Published August 6. www.newyorker.com/magazine/2012/08/13/big-med.

———. 2004. "On Washing Hands." *New England Journal of Medicine* 350 (13): 1283–86. https://doi.org/10.1056/NEJMp048025.

———. 1999. "The Cancer-Cluster Myth." *New Yorker*. Published January 31. www.newyorker.com/magazine/1999/02/08/the-cancer-cluster-myth.

GBD 2015 Mortality and Causes of Death Collaborators. 2016. "Global, Regional, and National Life Expectancy, All-Cause Mortality, and Cause-Specific Mortality for 249 Causes of Death, 1980–2015: A Systematic Analysis for the Global Burden of Disease Study 2015." *Lancet* 388 (10053): P1459–44. https://doi.org/10.1016/S0140-6736(16)31012-1.

Giancotti, M., A. Guglielmo, and M. Mauro. 2017. "Efficiency and Optimal Size of Hospitals: Results of a Systematic Search." *PLOS ONE* 12 (3): e0174533. https://doi.org/10.1371/journal.pone.0174533.

Glied, S., and A. Jackson. 2017. "The Future of the Affordable Care Act and Insurance Coverage." *American Journal of Public Health* 107 (4): 538–40. https://doi.org/10.2105/AJPH.2017.303665.

Gould, K. 2016. "Antibiotics: From Prehistory to the Present Day." *Journal of Antimicrobial Chemotherapy* 71 (3): 572–75. https://doi.org/10.1093/jac/dkv484.

Griffith, K., L. Evans, and J. Bor. 2017. "The Affordable Care Act Reduced Socioeconomic Disparities in Health Care Access." *Health Affairs* 36 (8): 1503–10. https://doi.org/10.1377/hlthaff.2017.0083.

Groopman, J., and P. Hartzband. 2017. "The Power of Regret." *New England Journal of Medicine* 377 (16): 1507–9. https://doi.org/10.1056/NEJMp1709917.

Gross, E., and M. Altman. 2016. "An Oral History of Star Trek." *Smithsonian*. Published May. www.smithsonianmag.com/arts-culture/oral-history-star-trek-180958779/.

Hahn, M. B., J. A. Patz, E. S. Gurley, J. H. Epstein, P. Daszak, M. S. Islam, and S. P. Luby. 2014. "The Role of Landscape Composition and Configuration on Pteropus Giganteus Roosting Ecology and Nipah Virus Spillover Risk in Bangladesh." *American Journal of Tropical Medicine and Hygiene* 90 (2): 247–55. https://doi.org/10.4269/ajtmh.13-0256.

Hale, T. M., and J. C. Kvedar. 2014. "Privacy and Security Concerns in Telehealth." *Virtual Mentor* 16 (12): 981–85. https://doi.org/10.1001/virtualmentor.2014.16.12.jdsc1-1412.

Hall, J. L., and D. McGraw. 2014. "For Telehealth to Succeed, Privacy and Security Risks Must Be Identified and Addressed." *Health Affairs* 33 (2): 216–21. https://doi.org/10.1377/hlthaff.2013.0997.

Hastwell, A. 2014. "How Often Do Deadly Diseases Jump from Animals to Humans?" ABC Science. Published July 30. www.abc.net.au/science/articles/2014/07/30/4056579.htm.

Hayon, K., T. Goldsmith, and L. Garito. 2014. *A Guide to Social Media for Physician Practices*. Boston: Massachusetts Medical Society.

Hensley, S. 2018. "Atul Gawande: CEO of Health Venture by Amazon, JPMorgan and Berkshire Hathaway." National Public Radio. Published June 20. www.npr.org/sections/health-shots/2018/06/20/621808003/atul-gawande-named-ceo-of-health-venture-by-amazon-berkshire-hathaway-and-jpmorg.

Hepojoki, S., E. Lindh, O. Vapalahti, and A. Huovilainen. 2017. "Prevalence and Genetic Diversity of Coronaviruses in Wild Birds, Finland." *Infection Ecology & Epidemiology* 7 (1): 1408360. https://doi.org/10.1080/20008686.2017.1408360.

Hess, J. J., P. J. Schramm, and G. Luber. 2014. "Public Health and Climate Change Adaptation at the Federal Level: One Agency's Response to Executive Order 13514." *American Journal of Public Health* 104 (3): e22–30. https://doi.org/10.2105/AJPH.2013.301796.

Hignett, S., S. Albolino, and K. Catchpole. 2018. "Health and Social Care Ergonomics: Patient Safety in Practice." *Ergonomics* 61 (1): 1–4. https://doi.org/10.1080/00140139.2017.1386454.

Himmelstein, D. U., M. Jun, R. Busse, K. Chevreul, A. Geissler, P. Jeurissen, S. Thomson, M.-A. Vinet, and S. Woolhandler. 2014. "A Comparison of Hospital Administrative Costs in Eight Nations: US Costs Exceed All Others by Far." *Health Affairs* 33 (9): 1586–94. https://doi.org/10.1377/hlthaff.2013.1327.

Himsworth, C. G., K. L. Parsons, C. Jardine, and D. M. Patrick. 2013. "Rats, Cities, People, and Pathogens: A Systematic Review and Narrative Synthesis of Literature Regarding the Ecology of Rat-Associated Zoonoses in Urban Centers."

Vector-Borne and Zoonotic Diseases 13 (6): 349–59. https://doi.org/10.1089/vbz.2012.1195.

Hodgkins, M. L., C. Khoury, C. Katz, S. Lloyd, and M. Barron. 2018. "Health Care Industry Requires a Roadmap to Accelerate the Impact of Digital Health Innovations." *Health Affairs*. Published June 8. www.healthaffairs.org/do/10.1377/hblog20180606.523635/full/.

Hoffman, B. R. 2012. *Health Care for Some: Rights and Rationing in the United States Since 1930*. Chicago: University of Chicago Press.

Holst, L. 2015. "The Precision Medicine Initiative: Data-Driven Treatments as Unique as Your Own Body." *White House Blog*. Published January 30. https://obamawhitehouse.archives.gov/blog/2015/01/30/precision-medicine-initiative-data-driven-treatments-unique-your-own-body.

Huang, J., X. Tu, and J. He. 2016. "Design and Evaluation of the RUPERT Wearable Upper Extremity Exoskeleton Robot for Clinical and In-Home Therapies." *IEEE Transactions on Systems, Man, and Cybernetics: Systems* 46 (7): 926–35. https://doi.org/10.1109/TSMC.2015.2497205.

Hughes, D., and A. Karlén. 2014. "Discovery and Preclinical Development of New Antibiotics." *Upsala Journal of Medical Sciences* 119 (2): 162–69. https://doi.org/10.3109/03009734.2014.896437.

Hung, M., J. Conrad, S. D. Hon, C. Cheng, J. D. Franklin, and P. Tang. 2013. "Uncovering Patterns of Technology Use in Consumer Health Informatics." *Wiley Interdisciplinary Reviews: Computational Statistics* 5 (6): 432–47. https://doi.org/10.1002/wics.1276.

Hunnicut, T., and C. Hunter. 2018. "Amazon, Berkshire, JPMorgan Name Atul Gawande CEO of Healthcare Venture." Reuters. Published June 20. www.reuters.com/article/us-berkshire-buffett-healthcare/amazon-berkshire-jpmorgan-name-atul-gawande-ceo-of-healthcare-venture-idUSKBN1JG1WZ.

Iacobucci, G. 2017. "NHS in 2017: Keeping Pace with Society." *BMJ* 356: i6738. https://doi.org/10.1136/bmj.i6738.

Institute for Safe Medication Practices. 2016. "Understanding Human Over-Reliance on Technology." Published September 8. www.ismp.org/resources/understanding-human-over-reliance-technology.

Interagency Working Group on Climate Change. 2010. *A Human Health Perspective on Climate Change: A Report Outlining the Research Needs on the Human Health Effects of Climate Change*. Published April 22. https://doi.org/10.1289/ehp.1002272.

Jackson, K. 2018. "A Brief History of the Smartphone." Science Node. Published July 25. https://sciencenode.org/feature/How%20did%20smartphones%20evolve.php.

Jaganath, D., H. K. Gill, A. C. Cohen, and S. D. Young. 2012. "Harnessing Online Peer Education (HOPE): Integrating C-POL and Social Media to Train Peer Leaders in HIV Prevention." *AIDS Care: Psychological and Socio-Medical*

Aspects of AIDS/HIV 24 (5): 593–600. https://doi.org/10.1080/09540121. 2011.630355.

Kacik, A. 2018. "Carolinas HealthCare Changes Its Name to Atrium Health." *Modern Healthcare.* Published February 7. www.modernhealthcare.com/ article/20180207/NEWS/180209925.

Kaku, M. 2018. *The Future of Humanity: Terraforming Mars, Interstellar Travel, Immortality, and Our Destiny Beyond Earth.* New York: Doubleday.

———. 2011. *Physics of the Future: How Science Will Shape Human Destiny and Our Daily Lives by the Year 2100.* New York: Doubleday.

Kasman, D. L. 2004. "When Is Medical Treatment Futile? A Guide for Students, Residents, and Physicians." *Journal of General Internal Medicine* 19 (10): 1053–56. https://doi.org/10.1111/j.1525-1497.2004.40134.x.

Kazdin, A. E. 2017. "Addressing the Treatment Gap: A Key Challenge for Extending Evidence-Based Psychosocial Interventions." *Behaviour Research and Therapy* 88: 7–18. https://doi.org/10.1016/j.brat.2016.06.004.

Keller, M. 2018. "Seventy Percent of Americans Support 'Medicare for All' in New Poll." The Hill. Published August 23. https://thehill.com/policy/ healthcare/403248-poll-seventy-percent-of-americans-support-medicare-for-all.

Kelley, A. S., K. McGarry, S. Fahle, S. M. Marshall, Q. Du, and J. S. Skinner. 2013. "Out-of-Pocket Spending in the Last Five Years of Life." *Journal of General Internal Medicine* 28 (2): 304–9. https://doi.org/10.1007/ s11606-012-2199-x.

Kickbusch, I., and D. Gleicher. 2012. *Governance in Health for the 21st Century.* World Health Organization. Accessed October 16, 2019. www.euro.who. int/__data/assets/pdf_file/0019/171334/RC62BD01-Governance-for-Health-Web.pdf.

King, D., F. Greaves, C. Exeter, and A. Darzi. 2013. "'Gamification': Influencing Health Behaviours with Games." *Journal of the Royal Society of Medicine* 106 (3): 76–78. https://doi.org/10.1177/0141076813480996.

King, N. 2009. "Health Inequalities and Health Inequities." In *Health Care Ethics: Critical Issues for the 21st Century,* 2nd ed., edited by E. E. Morrison and B. Furlong, 339–54. Sudbury, MA: Jones & Bartlett Learning.

Knickman, J. R., and A. R. Kovner. 2015. "The Future of Health Care Delivery and Health Policy." In *Jonas and Kovner's Health Care Delivery in the United States,* 11th ed., edited by J. R. Knickman and A. R. Kovner, 333–42. New York: Springer.

Korzep, K. 2010. "The Future of Technology and the Effect It May Have on Replacing Human Jobs." *Technology and Health Care* 18 (4–5): 353–58. https:// doi.org/10.3233/THC-2010-0592.

Krisberg, K. 2017. "Narrative Medicine: Every Patient Has a Story." Association of American Medical Colleges. Published March 28. https://news.aamc.org/ medical-education/article/narrative-medicine-every-patient-has-story/.

Kruse, C. S., P. Karem, K. Shifflett, L. Vegi, K. Ravi, and M. Brooks. 2018. "Evaluating Barriers to Adopting Telemedicine Worldwide: A Systematic Review." *Journal of Telemedicine and Telecare* 24 (1): 4–12. https://doi.org/10.1177/1357633X16674087.

Kruse, C. S., M. Soma, D. Pulluri, N. T. Nemali, and M. Brooks. 2017. "The Effectiveness of Telemedicine in the Management of Chronic Heart Disease—A Systematic Review." *JRSM Open* 8 (3): 205427041668174. https://doi.org/10.1177/2054270416681747.

Kruse, H., A. M. Kirkemo, and K. Handeland. 2004. "Wildlife as Source of Zoonotic Infections." *Emerging Infectious Diseases* 10 (12): 2067–72. https://doi.org/10.3201/eid1012.040707.

Lake, J., and M. S. Turner. 2017. "Urgent Need for Improved Mental Health Care and a More Collaborative Model of Care." *Permanente Journal* 21: 17-024. https://doi.org/10.7812/TPP/17-024.

Lancet. 2009. "What Is Health? The Ability to Adapt." 373 (9666): P781. https://doi.org/10.1016/S0140-6736(09)60456-6.

La Puma, J. 2016. "What Is Culinary Medicine and What Does It Do?" *Population Health Management* 19 (1): 1–3. https://doi.org/10.1089/pop.2015.0003.

Laxminarayan, R., A. Duse, C. Wattal, A. K. M. Zaidi, H. F. L. Wertheim, N. Sumpradit, E. Vlieghe, G. L. Hara, I. M. Gould, H. Goosens, C. Greko, A. D. So, M. Bigdeli, G. Tomson, W. Woodhouse, E. Ombaka, A. Quizhpe Peralta, F. N. Qamar, F. Mir, S. Kariuki, Z. A. Bhutta, A. Coates, R. Bergstrom, G. D. Wright, E. D. Brown, and O. Cars. 2013. "Antibiotic Resistance—The Need for Global Solutions." *Lancet Infectious Diseases* 13 (12): P1057–98. https://doi.org/10.1016/S1473-3099(13)70318-9.

Leske, N. 2013. "Doctors Seek Help on Cancer Treatment from IBM Supercomputer." Reuters. Published February 8. http://in.reuters.com/article/2013/02/08/ibm-watson-cancer-idINDEE9170G120130208.

Lindblad, R., A. El Fiky, and T. Zajdowicz. 2015. "Ebola in the United States." *Journal of Allergy and Clinical Immunology* 135 (4): 868–71. https://doi.org/10.1016/j.jaci.2014.12.012.

Lovelace, B. 2018. "No-Frills Micro Hospitals Emerge as a New Way to Cut Health-Care Costs." CNBC. Published March 2. www.cnbc.com/2018/03/02/no-frills-micro-hospitals-emerge-as-a-new-way-to-cut-health-care-costs.html.

Luber, G., K. Knowlton, J. Balbus, H. Frumkin, M. Hayden, J. Hess, M. McGeehin, N. Sheats, L. Backer, C. B. Beard, K. L. Ebi, E. Maibach, R. S. Ostfeld, C. Wiedinmyer, E. Zielinski-Gutiérrez, and L. Ziska. 2014. "Human Health." In *Climate Change Impacts in the United States*, edited by J. M. Melillo, T. C. Richmond, and G. W. Yohe, 220–56. Washington, DC: US Global Research Program. https://doi.org/10.7930/J0PN93H5.

Luby, S. P. 2013. "The Pandemic Potential of Nipah Virus." *Antiviral Research* 100 (1): 38–43. https://doi.org/10.1016/j.antiviral.2013.07.011.

Lucas, G. (dir.). 1977. *Star Wars: Episode IV—A New Hope.* Lucasfilm.

Lustig, R. H. 2017. *The Hacking of the American Mind: The Science Behind the Corporate Takeover of Our Bodies and Brains.* New York: Avery.

Lutterman, T., R. Shaw, W. Fisher, and R. Manderscheid. 2017. *Trend in Psychiatric Inpatient Capacity, United States and Each State, 1970 to 2014.* National Association of State Mental Health Program Directors. Assessment No. 2. Published August. www.nasmhpd.org/sites/default/files/TACPaper.2.Psychiatric-Inpatient-Capacity_508C.pdf.

McKee, M., S. L. Greer, and D. Stuckler. 2017. "What Will Donald Trump's Presidency Mean for Health? A Scorecard." *Lancet* 389 (10070): P748–54. https://doi.org/10.1016/S0140-6736(17)30122-8.

Meaney-Delman, D., S. L. Hills, C. Williams, R. R. Galang, P. Iyengar, A. K. Hennenfent, I. B. Rabe, A. Panella, T. Oduyebo, M. A. Honein, S. Zaki, N. Lindsey, J. A. Lehman, N. Kwit, J. Bertolli, S. Ellington, I. Igbinosa, A. A. Minta, E. E. Petersen, P. Mead, S. A. Rasmussen, and D. J. Jamieson. 2016. "Zika Virus Infection Among U.S. Pregnant Travelers—August 2015–February 2016." *MMWR Weekly Report* 65 (8): 211–14. https://doi.org/10.15585/mmwr.mm6508e1.

Mercy Virtual. 2019. "About." Accessed October 16. www.mercyvirtual.net/about/.

Meslin, F. X., K. Stöhr, and D. Heymann. 2000. "Public Health Implications of Emerging Zoonoses." *Revue Scientifique et Technique* 19 (1): 310–17. www.ncbi.nlm.nih.gov/pubmed/11189723.

Miller, R. S., M. L. Farnsworth, and J. L. Malmberg. 2013. "Diseases at the Livestock-Wildlife Interface: Status, Challenges, and Opportunities in the United States." *Preventive Veterinary Medicine* 110 (2): 119–32. https://doi.org/10.1016/j.prevetmed.2012.11.021.

MindSciences. 2020. "Our Programs." Accessed January 28. www.mindsciences.com/#ern.

Morse, S. 2018. "Atul Gawande Says Amazon, Berkshire, JPMorgan Healthcare Venture Will Take Gradual Progress." *Healthcare IT News.* Published June 21. www.healthcareitnews.com/news/atul-gawande-says-amazon-berkshire-jpmorgan-healthcare-venture-will-take-gradual-progress.

Muneeb, A., H. Jawaid, N. Khalid, and A. Mian. 2017. "The Art of Healing through Narrative Medicine in Clinical Practice: A Reflection." *Permanente Journal* 21: 17-013. https://doi.org/10.7812/TPP/17-013.

Murray, C. J. L., and US Burden of Disease Collaborators. 2013. "The State of US Health, 1990–2010: Burden of Diseases, Injuries, and Risk Factors." *JAMA* 310 (6): 591–608. https://doi.org/10.1001/jama.2013.13805.

National Human Genome Research Institute (NHGRI). 2019. "The Cost of Sequencing a Human Genome." Updated July 10. www.genome.gov/27565109/the-cost-of-sequencing-a-human-genome/.

National Institute of Allergy and Infectious Diseases. 2016. "Examples of Antimicrobial Resistance." Reviewed March 17. www.niaid.nih.gov/research/antimicrobial-resistance-examples.

National Institute of Mental Health (NIMH). 2019a. "Mental Illness." Updated February. www.nimh.nih.gov/health/statistics/mental-illness.shtml.

———. 2019b. "Suicide." Updated April. www.nimh.nih.gov/health/statistics/suicide.shtml.

National Institutes of Health. 2020. "The Precision Medicine Initiative." Accessed January 17. https://syndication.nih.gov/multimedia/pmi/infographics/pmi-infographic.pdf.

Neergard, L. 2015. "Obama Proposes 'Precision Medicine' to End One-Size-Fits-All." AP News. Published January 30. https://apnews.com/b6d25f42f3394bcd801dd8a0cf137898.

Neu, H. C. 1992. "The Crisis in Antibiotic Resistance." *Science* 257 (5073): 1064–73. https://doi.org/10.1126/science.257.5073.1064.

Neuman, T., K. Pollitz, and J. Tolbert. 2018. "Medicare-for-All and Public Plan Buy-In Proposals: Overview and Key Issues." Kaiser Family Foundation. Published October 9. www.kff.org/medicare/issue-brief/medicare-for-all-and-public-plan-buy-in-proposals-overview-and-key-issues/.

Nikpay, S. S., M. R. Richards, and D. Penson. 2018. "Hospital-Physician Consolidation Accelerated in the Past Decade in Cardiology, Oncology." *Health Affairs* 37 (7): 1123–27. https://doi.org/10.1377/hlthaff.2017.1520.

Obama, B. 2016. "United States Health Care Reform: Progress to Date and Next Steps." *JAMA* 316 (5): 525–32. https://doi.org/10.1001/jama.2016.9797.

Organisation for Economic Co-operation and Development (OECD). 2013. *Health at a Glance 2013: OECD Indicators.* Accessed October 16, 2019. https://doi.org/10.1787/health_glance-2013-en.

O'Shea, T. J., P. M. Cryan, A. A. Cunningham, A. R. Fooks, D. T. S. Hayman, A. D. Luis, A. J. Peel, R. K. Plowright, and J. L. N. Wood. 2014. "Bat Flight and Zoonotic Viruses." *Emerging Infectious Diseases* 20 (5):741–45. https://doi.org/10.3201/eid2005.130539.

Otto, L., L. Harst, H. Schlieter, B. Wollschlaeger, P. Richter, and P. Timpel. 2018. "Towards a Unified Understanding of eHealth and Related Terms—Proposal of a Consolidated Terminological Basis." In *Proceedings of the 11th International Joint Conference on Biomedical Engineering Systems and Technologies*, vol. 5, 533–39. https://doi.org/10.5220/0006651005330539.

Parasuraman, R., and D. H. Manzey. 2010. "Complacency and Bias in Human Use of Automation: An Attentional Integration." *Human Factors* 52 (3): 381–410. https://doi.org/10.1177/0018720810376055.

Patino, T., R. Mestre, and S. Sánchez. 2016. "Miniaturized Soft Bio-Hybrid Robotics: A Step Forward into Healthcare Applications." *Lab on a Chip* 16: 3626–30. https://doi.org/10.1039/c6lc90088g.

Patz, J. A., and R. S. Kovats. 2002. "Hotspots in Climate Change and Human Health." *BMJ* 325: 1094. https://doi.org/10.1136/bmj.325.7372.1094.

Pearl, R. 2018. "Why Atul Gawande Will Soon Be the Most Feared CEO in Healthcare." *Forbes.* Published June 25. www.forbes.com/sites/robertpearl/2018/06/25/atul-gawande-ceo/#366d413c369b.

———. 2017. "Why Healthcare Rationing Is a Growing Reality for Americans." *Forbes.* Published February 2. www.forbes.com/sites/robertpearl/2017/02/02/why-healthcare-rationing-is-a-growing-reality-for-americans/#1c3522e92dba.

Pesec, M., and T. Sherertz. 2015. "Global Health from a Cancer Care Perspective." *Future Oncology* 11 (15): 2235–45. https://doi.org/10.2217/fon.15.142.

Porche, D. J. 2015. "Precision Medicine Initiative." *American Journal of Men's Health* 9 (3): 177. https://doi.org/10.1177/1557988315574512.

Pot, J. 2016. "Kansas Hospital Pays Off Ransomware, Doesn't Get Files Back." Digital Trends. Published May 24. www.digitaltrends.com/computing/ransomware-hospital-hackers-demand-more-money/.

Price, M., E. K. Yuen, E. M. Goetter, J. D. Herbert, E. M. Forman, R. Acierno, and K. J. Ruggiero. 2014. "mHealth: A Mechanism to Deliver More Accessible, More Effective Mental Health Care." *Clinical Psychology & Psychotherapy* 21 (5): 427–36. https://doi.org/10.1002/cpp.1855.

PR Newswire. 2014. "Wearable Technology Ecosystem: 2014–2020—Opportunities, Challenges, Strategies, Industry Verticals & Forecasts." Published August 19. www.prnewswire.com/news-releases/wearable-technology-ecosystem-2014---2020---opportunities-challenges-strategies-industry-verticals--forecasts-271867511.html.

Rabbitt, S. M., A. E. Kazdin, and B. Scassellati. 2015. "Integrating Socially Assistive Robotics into Mental Healthcare Interventions: Applications and Recommendations for Expanded Use." *Clinical Psychology Review* 35: 35–46. https://doi.org/10.1016/J.CPR.2014.07.001.

Randell, R., J. Greenhalgh, J. Hindmarsh, D. Dowding, D. Jayne, A. Pearman, P. Gardner, J. Croft, and A. Kotze. 2014. "Integration of Robotic Surgery into Routine Practice and Impacts on Communication, Collaboration, and Decision Making: A Realist Process Evaluation Protocol." *Implementation Science* 9:52. https://doi.org/10.1186/1748-5908-9-52.

Rege, A. 2018. "Dr. Atul Gawande: Amazon-Berkshire-JPMorgan Venture Will Tackle 3 Types of Healthcare Waste." *Becker's Hospital Review.* Published June 25. www.beckershospitalreview.com/hospital-management-administration/dr-atul-gawande-amazon-berkshire-jpmorgan-venture-will-tackle-3-types-of-healthcare-waste.html.

Riek, L. D. 2017. "Healthcare Robotics." *Communications of the ACM* 60 (11): 68–78. http://dx.doi.org/10.1145/0000000.0000000.

Roberts, D. 2018. "More Atrium Health Doctors May Leave the System, Experts Say." *Charlotte Observer*. Published May 17. www.charlotteobserver.com/news/business/article211322889.html.

Rogers, E. M. 2003. *Diffusion of Innovations*, 5th ed. New York: Free Press.

Rothacker, R., and J. Murawski. 2018. "Carolinas HealthCare System Changes Name to Atrium Health." *Charlotte Observer*. Published February 7. www.charlotteobserver.com/news/business/article198815854.html.

Rowland, K., and S.-A. Schumann. 2010. "Palliative Care: Earlier Is Better." *Journal of Family Practice* 59 (12): 695–98. www.ncbi.nlm.nih.gov/pmc/articles/PMC3183935/.

Ruiz, J., I. Castro, E. Calabuig, and M. Salavert. 2017. "Non-antibiotic Treatment for Infectious Diseases." *Revista Espanola de Quimioterapia* 30 (Suppl. 1): 66–71. www.ncbi.nlm.nih.gov/pubmed/28882020.

Russo, J. E., R. R. McCool, and L. Davies. 2016. "VA Telemedicine: An Analysis of Cost and Time Savings." *Telemedicine and e-Health* 22 (3): 209–15. https://doi.org/10.1089/tmj.2015.0055.

Sarasohn-Kahn, S., J. Barrette, E. Barsky, B. Heywood, D. Hoch, and D. Kibbe. 2008. *The Wisdom of Patients: Health Care Meets Online Social Media*. California HealthCare Foundation. Published April. www.chcf.org/wp-content/uploads/2017/12/PDF-HealthCareSocialMedia.pdf.

Saulsberry, K. 2016. "To Grow Your Hospital, Think Micro." Advisory Board. Published May 20. www.advisory.com/research/Revenue-Cycle-Advancement-Center/at-the-margins/2016/05/micro-hospitals.

Scheunemann, L. P., and D. B. White. 2011. "The Ethics and Reality of Rationing in Medicine." *Chest* 140 (6): 1625–32. https://doi.org/10.1378/chest.11-0622.

Schwartz, R. S. 2004. "Paul Ehrlich's Magic Bullets." *New England Journal of Medicine* 350 (11): 1079–80. https://doi.org/10.1056/NEJMp048021.

Semenza, J. C., J. E. Suk, V. Estevez, K. L. Ebi, and E. Lindgren. 2012. "Mapping Climate Change Vulnerabilities to Infectious Diseases in Europe." *Environmental Health Perspectives* 120 (3): 385–92. https://doi.org/10.1289/ehp.1103805.

Shafei, R., S. A. Rastad, and A. Kamangar. 2016. "Effecting of Electronic-Tablet-Based Menu and Its Impact on Consumer Choice Behavior (An Empirical Study in Iranian Restaurant)." In *2016 10th International Conference on e-Commerce in Developing Countries: With Focus on e-Tourism*, 1–8. https://doi.org/10.1109/ECDC.2016.7492987.

Sharfstein, J., S. Gerovich, E. Moriarty, and D. Chin. 2017. *An Emerging Approach to Payment Reform: All-Payer Global Budgets for Large Safety-Net Hospital Systems*. Commonwealth Fund. Published August. www.commonwealthfund.org/sites/default/files/documents/___media_files_publications_fund_report_2017_aug_sharfstein_all_payer_global_budgets_safety_net_hospitals.pdf.

Short, E. E., C. Caminade, and B. N. Thomas. 2017. "Climate Change Contribution to the Emergence or Re-Emergence of Parasitic Diseases." *Infectious Diseases* 10: 1178633617732296. https://doi.org/10.1177/1178633617732296.

Siegel, E. 2013. *Predictive Analytics: The Power to Predict Who Will Click, Buy, Lie, or Die.* Hoboken, NJ: John Wiley & Sons.

Silver, J., and M. Votruba. 2018. "Here's How Atul Gawande and the Amazon-Berkshire-JPMorgan Health-Care Venture Could Slash Costs 15%–20%." MarketWatch. Published June 26. www.marketwatch.com/story/heres-how-atul-gawande-and-the-amazon-berkshire-jpmorgan-health-care-venture-could-slash-costs-15-20-2018-06-22.

Singh, R., and C. Palosky. 2019. "Poll: Majorities Favor a Range of Options to Expand Public Coverage, Including Medicare-for-All." Kaiser Family Foundation. Published January 23. www.kff.org/health-reform/press-release/poll-majorities-favor-a-range-of-options-to-expand-public-coverage-including-medicare-for-all/.

Singh, R. K., K. Dhama, Y. S. Malik, M. A. Ramakrishnan, K. Karthik, R. Khandia, R. Tiwari, A. Munjal, M. Saminathan, S. Sachan, P. A. Desingu, J. J. Kattoor, H. M. N. Iqbal, and S. K. Joshi. 2017. "Ebola Virus—Epidemiology, Diagnosis, and Control: Threat to Humans, Lessons Learnt, and Preparedness Plans—An Update on Its 40 Year's Journey." *Veterinary Quarterly* 36 (1): 98–135. https://doi.org/10.1080/01652176.2017.1309474.

Song, Z., S. Rose, D. G. Safran, B. E. Landon, M. P. Day, and M. E. Chernew. 2014. "Changes in Health Care Spending and Quality 4 Years into Global Payment." *New England Journal of Medicine* 371 (18): 1704–14. https://doi.org/10.1056/NEJMsa1404026.

Sooner Care. 2017. *Encouraging Diabetics to Use Statins: Nudging for Long-Term Health.* Ideas 42. Published February. www.ideas42.org/wp-content/uploads/2015/08/Project-Brief_Statins.pdf.

Spickler, A. R. 2018. "Zoonotic Diseases." *Merck Veterinary Manual.* Accessed October 16, 2019. www.merckvetmanual.com/public-health/zoonoses/zoonotic-diseases.

Springmann, M., M. Clark, D. M. D'Croz, K. Wiebe, B. L. Bodirsky, L. Lassaletta, W. de Vries, S. J. Vermeulen, M. Herrero, K. M. Carlson, M. Jonell, M. Troell, F. DeClerck, L. J. Gordon, R. Zurayk, P. Scarborough, M. Rayner, B. Loken, J. Fanzo, H. C. J. Godfray, D. Tilman, J. Rockström, and W. Willett. 2018. "Options for Keeping the Food System Within Environmental Limits." *Nature* 562 (7728): 519–25. https://doi.org/10.1038/s41586-018-0594-0.

Stanberry, B. 2006. "Legal and Ethical Aspects of Telemedicine." *Journal of Telemedicine and Telecare* 12 (4): 166–75. https://doi.org/10.1258/135763306777488825.

TechTarget. 2014. "How to Hone an Effective Vulnerability Management Program." Updated June. https://searchsecurity.techtarget.com/essentialguide/How-to-hone-an-effective-vulnerability-management-program.

Thaler, R. H. 2015. *Misbehaving: The Making of Behavioral Economics.* New York: W. W. Norton.

Tomley, F. M., and M. W. Shirley. 2009. "Livestock Infectious Diseases and Zoonoses." *Philosophical Transactions of the Royal Society B: Biological Sciences* 364 (1530): 2637–42. https://doi.org/10.1098/rstb.2009.0133.

Tozzi, J. 2019. "Amazon-JPMorgan-Berkshire Health-Care Venture to Be Called Haven." Bloomberg. Published March 6. www.bloomberg.com/news/articles/2019-03-06/amazon-jpmorgan-berkshire-health-care-venture-to-be-called-haven.

Umay, I., B. Fidan, and B. Barshan. 2017. "Localization and Tracking of Implantable Biomedical Sensors." *Sensors* 17 (3): 583. https://doi.org/10.3390/s17030583.

United Network for Organ Sharing (UNOS). 2019. "About UNOS." Accessed October 16. https://unos.org/about/.

US Food and Drug Administration (FDA). 2019. "Device Software Functions Including Mobile Medical Applications." Updated September 26. www.fda.gov/MedicalDevices/DigitalHealth/MobileMedicalApplications/default.htm.

US National Library of Medicine. 2020. "Trends, Charts, and Maps." Accessed January 17. https://clinicaltrials.gov/ct2/resources/trends.

———. 2019. "What Is the Cost of Genetic Testing, and How Long Does It Take to Get the Results?" Accessed October 16. https://ghr.nlm.nih.gov/primer/testing/costresults.

Vandemeulebroucke, T., B. Dierckx de Casterlé, and C. Gastmans. 2018. "The Use of Care Robots in Aged Care: A Systematic Review of Argument-Based Ethics Literature." *Archives of Gerontology and Geriatrics* 74: 15–25. https://doi.org/10.1016/j.archger.2017.08.014.

Wainberg, M. L., P. Scorza, J. M. Shultz, L. Helpman, J. J. Mootz, K. A. Johnson, Y. Neria, J.-M. E. Bradford, M. A. Oquendo, and M. R. Arbuckle. 2017. "Challenges and Opportunities in Global Mental Health: A Research-to-Practice Perspective." *Current Psychiatry Reports* 19 (5): 28. https://doi.org/10.1007/s11920-017-0780-z.

Wang, B. 2016. "Zika Virus." *New England Journal of Medicine* 375: 293–95. https://doi.org/10.1056/NEJMc1606769.

Weil, A. 2008. *Healthy Aging: A Lifelong Guide to Your Well-Being*. New York: Random House.

Westerling, A. L., and B. P. Bryant. 2008. "Climate Change and Wildfire in California." *Climatic Change* 87 (Suppl. 1): 231–49. https://doi.org/10.1007/s10584-007-9363-z.

White House. 2015. "Fact Sheet: President Obama's Precision Medicine Initiative." Published January 30. https://obamawhitehouse.archives.gov/the-press-office/2015/01/30/fact-sheet-president-obama-s-precision-medicine-initiative.

Woodruff, J. 2019. "Why These House Democrats Think Medicare for All Is the Best Path for U.S. Health Care." *PBS NewsHour.* Published February 28. www.pbs.org/newshour/show/why-these-house-democrats-say-medicare-for-all-is-americans-best-health-option.

World Health Organization (WHO). 2020. "Coronavirus Disease (COVID-19) Outbreak." Accessed March 25. www.who.int/westernpacific/emergencies/covid-19.

———. 2011. "Race Against Time to Develop New Antibiotics." *Bulletin of the World Health Organization* 89 (2): 88–89. https://doi.org/10.2471/BLT.11.030211.

Wu, J., H. Li, S. Cheng, and Z. Lin. 2016. "The Promising Future of Healthcare Services: When Big Data Analytics Meets Wearable Technology." *Information & Management* 53 (8): 1020–33. https://doi.org/10.1016/j.im.2016.07.003.

Y Media Labs. 2019. "The Future of Healthcare: How Mobile Medical Apps Give Us Control Back." Accessed October 16, 2019. https://ymedialabs.com/future-of-healthcare.

Zaiba, A. 2018. "Human Robot Interface and Visual Compressive Detecting on Robot Arm." *Current Trends in Information Technology* 8 (3): 5–12. http://computerjournals.stmjournals.in/index.php/CTIT/article/view/199.

Zarcadoolas, C., A. Pleasant, and D. S. Greer. 2005. "Understanding Health Literacy: An Expanded Model." *Health Promotion International* 20 (2): 195–203. https://doi.org/10.1093/heapro/dah609.

APPENDIX A

Organizations and Websites

American Association for Physician Leadership (www.physicianleaders.org)

American Association of Integrated Healthcare Delivery Systems (www.aaihds. org)

American College of Healthcare Executives (www.ache.org)

American Health Care Association (www.ahca.org)

American Health Information Management Association (www.ahima.org)

American Medical Association (www.ama-assn.org)

American Medical Group Association (www.amga.org)

American Organization for Nursing Leadership (www.aonl.org)

American Public Health Association (www.apha.org)

American Society for Health Care Human Resources Administration (www. ashhra.org)

American Society for Health Care Risk Management (www.ashrm.org)

America's Health Insurance Plans (www.ahip.org)

Association of University Programs in Health Administration (www.aupha.org)

Blue Cross Blue Shield Association (www.bluecares.com)

Bridges to Excellence (www.bridgestoexcellence.org)

Center for Health Care Strategies (www.chcs.org)

Center for Studying Health System Change (www.hschange.org)

Centers for Disease Control and Prevention (www.cdc.gov)

Centers for Medicare & Medicaid Services (www.cms.gov)

Commission on Accreditation of Rehabilitation Facilities (www.carf.org)

Commonwealth Fund (www.commonwealthfund.org)

Council of Teaching Hospitals and Health Systems (www.aamc.org/coth)

Dartmouth Atlas Project (www.dartmouthatlas.org)

Healthcare Financial Management Association (www.hfma.org)

Healthcare Information and Management Systems Society (www.himss.org)

Healthgrades (www.healthgrades.com)

The Joint Commission (www.jointcommission.org)

Leapfrog Group (www.leapfroggroup.org)

Medical Group Management Association (www.mgma.com)

Medical Outcomes Trust (www.outcomes-trust.org)

National Association for Home Care and Hospice (www.nahc.org)

National Association of Managed Care Physicians (www.accme.org/find-cme-provider/national-association-managed-care-physicians)

National Institute for Health and Care Excellence (www.nice.org.uk)

National Institutes of Health (www.nih.gov)

National Library of Medicine (www.nlm.nih.gov)
Robert Wood Johnson Foundation (www.rwjf.org)
Society for Health Care Strategy and Market Development (www.shsmd.org)
US Department of Health and Human Services (www.hhs.gov)

APPENDIX B

Recommended Publications Relating to Healthcare Administration

American Journal of Health Behavior
American Journal of Health Promotion
American Journal of Health Studies
American Journal of Preventive Medicine
American Journal of Public Health
Australian and New Zealand Journal of Public Health
Frontiers of Health Services Management
Health Affairs
Healthcare Executive
Health Care Management Review
Health Care Supervisor
Health Education and Behavior
Health Education Research
Health Policy
Health Promotion International
Health Psychology
Health Services Management Research
Health Values
Hospitals and Health Services Administration
Journal of Behavioral Medicine
Journal of Disaster Studies, Policy and Management
Journal of Emergency Management
Journal of Family and Community Health
Journal of Healthcare Management
Journal of Homeland Security and Emergency Management
Journal of Public Health Management and Practice
Journal of School Health
Journal of the American Medical Association
MGMA Connection
Milbank Quarterly
Modern Healthcare
New England Journal of Medicine
Public Health Reports
Social Science & Medicine

GLOSSARY

accountable care organization (ACO): A group of providers who share responsibility for a population of patients with regard to the quality, cost, and coordination of their care.

advanced practice professional (APP): A category of medical service provider that includes nurse practitioners, physician assistants, and clinical nurse specialists; sometimes called "physician extenders."

adverse selection: An issue that arises in health insurance when the purchaser has knowledge that the health plan does not have concerning future needs, creating information asymmetry.

allied health professional (AHP): An individual trained to support, complement, or supplement the professional functions of physicians, dentists, and other health professionals; AHPs include physician assistants, dental hygienists, medical technicians, nurse midwives, nurse practitioners, physical therapists, psychologists, and nurse anesthetists.

allopathic training: Conventional physician training, typically leading to a doctor of medicine (MD) degree.

almshouse: A type of institution used for the housing of the poor; sometimes known as a poorhouse.

ambulatory care: Healthcare services provided on an outpatient basis, rather than by admission to a hospital or other facility.

American exceptionalism: The idea that the United States is unique in its ideals of personal freedom and democracy.

artificial intelligence: The mimicking of human intelligence by machines.

average daily census: The average number of hospital beds occupied daily over a specified period.

average length of stay: A utilization metric that is calculated by dividing the total days of care by the total number of discharges.

behavioral economics: A field that applies insights from the study of psychology to analyze human behavior and to explain economic decision making.

Beveridge model: A healthcare funding model, named after William Beveridge of the United Kingdom, in which the government is the principal payer and owner of the healthcare system and tightly controls cost.

big data: Vast quantities of structured and unstructured data from a variety of sources that may be analyzed and formatted to produce meaningful information.

biomedical model: An approach to health and healthcare that focuses on clinical diagnosis and the use of medical interventions to cure and relieve symptoms of disease and discomfort.

biosimilar: A drug that is highly similar to an existing approved product.

bioterrorism: The intentional use of a biological agent, such as a virus or bacteria, to harm a human population.

Bismarck model: A healthcare funding model, named after German Chancellor Otto von Bismarck, in which everyone in the country is covered through an insurance-style, not-for-profit mechanism that is carefully regulated by the government.

blue zone: An area where people tend to live exceptionally long and healthy lives.

bundled payments: A payment methodology in which a single payment is made for an entire episode of an illness or treatment.

burnout: A problem associated with high stress and physical or emotional exhaustion in the work setting.

capitation: An approach by which payment is made on a per capita basis with a negotiated price; often expressed as a per-member per-month (PMPM) payment.

case management: A range of activities aimed at helping patients (particularly those undergoing a complex series of treatments) with their recovery and making sure they are in a safe and appropriate environment.

Certificate of Need (CON): A certificate issued by a governmental body to an individual or organization proposing to construct or modify a health facility, or to offer a new or different service.

certification: A voluntary system of standards that practitioners can choose to meet to demonstrate accomplishment or ability in their profession.

chronic disease: A condition that lasts for one year or longer and requires ongoing medical attention or limits activities of daily living.

clinical nurse specialist (CNS): A clinician with advanced training in a specialized area of nursing.

cloud computing: The use of a network of remote servers to access data, resources, and computing power.

coinsurance: A portion of medical costs paid by an insured individual, typically as a percentage of the fee.

community health center (CHC): A type of neighborhood-based primary care setting that receives federal and state support.

comparative effectiveness research (CER): Research that compares various medical treatment options based on the degree to which they improve health outcomes.

complementary and alternative medicine (CAM): Various therapies that are not considered part of conventional medicine.

computerized physician order entry (CPOE): An electronic prescribing system in which the physician enters orders into a computer, orders are integrated with patient information, and orders are automatically checked for potential errors or problems.

continuing care retirement community (CCRC): A type of long-term care facility that offers a continuum of services that can be varied to match each individual's present stage.

copayment: A flat amount that must be paid by the patient before benefits are paid by the insurance plan.

cost sharing: An arrangement in which an insured individual pays a portion of healthcare costs out of pocket; common forms include deductibles, copayments, and coinsurance.

culinary medicine: A wellness approach that incorporates nutrition and cooking habits into the pursuit of health goals.

cultural authority: A level of public trust for a professional group that warrants the granting of relative autonomy and ability to self-regulate.

cultural competence: A set of behaviors, attitudes, and policies that enable effective work in cross-cultural situations.

culture: Integrated patterns of human behavior, including language, thoughts, communications, actions, customs, beliefs, values, and institutions.

data analytics: The field concerned with converting unstructured data into information that can be used by organizations.

database: A collection of information organized for accessibility and retrieval.

data warehouse: A type of database that integrates transaction data from multiple sources and facilitates analytical use.

decision paralysis: The inability to make decisions in a timely manner.

decision rules: Explicit or implicit statements, procedures, and ways of thinking that determine how decisions are made by individuals and organizations.

deductible: An amount of money that must be paid by the patient before any benefits are paid by the insurance plan.

determinant of health: A condition or factor that has a direct or indirect impact on a person's health.

discounted fee-for-service: An arrangement in which payments are made based on a negotiated discount off the provider's fee schedule.

downstreaming: A public health intervention that seeks to provide equitable access to care for disadvantaged populations to reduce the negative health impacts of inequality.

e-health: The electronic delivery of health-related services, including patient education; a more general term than *telemedicine*.

elasticity: The degree to which demand for a service changes with price.

electronic health record (EHR): An electronic record that helps providers record, store, access, and share patient information digitally; usually includes information from all providers treating the patient.

electronic medical record (EMR): The electronic version of a traditional medical chart; patient information is typically limited to a single facility.

fee-for-service (FFS): An approach to reimbursement in which payment for services is provided on a per-unit basis.

flow: The smooth transition from one stage of a process to the next, without delay, unnecessary complexity, or other barriers; a key Lean principle.

food desert: An area where affordable, high-quality foods are difficult to find.

formulary: A list of approved drugs for treatment of various diseases and conditions.

for-profit hospital: A hospital that is primarily owned by shareholders, with the goal of making a profit from the facility's operations.

futile care: Any curative care given to a patient who has no reasonable hope of recovery.

gamification: The use of games for the purpose of educating or influencing behavior.

genomics: A branch of science that focuses on the structure, function, and mapping of an organism's genetic material.

global budgeting: An approach to healthcare payments in which a lump sum is provided for covered individuals; global budgeting provides incentives to focus less on production of services and more on health outcomes and reductions in cost.

governance: A system of policies and procedures designed to oversee the management of the enterprise.

health disparity: A difference in health status from one group to another.

health information exchange (HIE): The organization and sharing of electronic health-related information in a manner that protects confidentiality, privacy, and security.

health information technology (HIT): The use of hardware, software, services, and infrastructure for the management and delivery of information in healthcare.

health literacy: The degree to which people are able to obtain, process, and understand basic health information and make informed health decisions.

health system: The various organizations, people, and activities that have the primary purpose of promoting, restoring, or maintaining health.

high reliability organization: An organization that operates under challenging conditions but experiences fewer problems than would be expected, because of its ability to "manage the unexpected."

high-risk pool: A funding mechanisms used by state governments to provide insurance to individuals who have pre-existing conditions, do not qualify for government-sponsored insurance such as Medicare and Medicaid, do not have group coverage, and cannot purchase insurance in the private market.

home health care: The delivery of health-related services to patients within their own homes.

hospice: Care that seeks to address the physical, emotional, social, and spiritual needs of patients who are not expected to survive for more than six months.

independent practice association (IPA): A network of independent physicians that contracts with managed care organizations and employers.

informational disequilibrium: A situation in which one party to an exchange has significantly more information about the subject matter than the other party.

information technology (IT): The use of hardware, software, services, and infrastructure for the management and delivery of information.

inpatient services: Healthcare services that require admission to a hospital.

insurance risk rating: The assessment of people's level of risk for the purpose of determining insurance rates.

integrated delivery system (IDS): A network of healthcare facilities linked under a parent holding company to provide a coordinated continuum of services.

intermediate care facility for individuals with intellectual disability (ICF/ID): A specialized long-term care facility that provides comprehensive, individualized, and rehabilitative services to individuals with developmental disabilities.

interprofessional education and interprofessional practice (IPE/IPP): A framework to enable clinical and administrative staff to work together in a more collaborative fashion to meet the goals of the organization and provide better care for patients.

inventory: The supply or stock of goods and products that a practice has for sale.

Lean: A process improvement approach, derived from the Toyota Production System, that emphasizes the mapping of value streams and the elimination of waste.

licensure: A mandatory system of state-imposed standards that people must meet to practice a given profession.

long-term acute care hospital (LTACH): A highly specialized hospital for the treatment of patients needing extended hospitalization.

managed care: An approach by which organizations seek to manage costs, control patient utilization, and streamline delivery and payment for care.

managed care organization (MCO): An organization that offers managed care health plans.

managed competition: A strategy for the efficient purchasing of health insurance, in which individuals are able to make comparisons among insurance companies of premiums and benefits provided.

manifest destiny: The idea that American people and institutions have special qualities that can benefit all people and therefore have a destiny to spread their influence.

market justice theory: The idea that healthcare is a product for purchase and therefore, like all other goods and services, is subject to the principles of economic theory.

meaningful use: A set of standards for the use of electronic health record systems to provide care and improve patient engagement.

Medicaid: A means-tested program operated jointly by the state and federal governments to provide healthcare coverage for low-income Americans.

medicalization: The act of defining a nonmedical problem in medical terms and using a medical intervention to treat it.

medical technology: The application of science and technical knowledge for the improvement of medical care and the health of society.

Medicare: A US government program that provides healthcare coverage for people age 65 or older, as well as certain people with disabilities or end-stage renal disease.

Medigap: A supplemental health insurance policy sold by private insurance companies that is designed to cover healthcare costs not paid for by Medicare.

mHealth: The delivery of health-related services via mobile technologies.

mindfulness: Close attention to the various aspects of one's moment-to-moment experience.

minihospital: A small-scale inpatient facility that provides community-based services in an efficient and modern setting; also called a microhospital.

mission: An organization's purpose or reason for existing.

moral hazard: A tendency for people to consume more medical services than necessary when they do not incur the full cost of those services.

narrative medicine: An approach to medicine that emphasizes looking beyond the symptoms and getting to know the patient's "story."

national health insurance (NHI): A single-payer funding approach in which the government is the principal payer for care but the providers are mostly private.

nemawashi: A Japanese term referring to an informal process of quietly laying the foundation for a proposed change or project by talking to the people involved and gathering support and feedback.

not-for-profit hospital: A hospital that does not seek to make a profit for the benefit of its owners; it serves a charitable role in the community and receives tax benefits in return.

nurse practitioner (NP): A category of medical service provider licensed to diagnose and treat illness and disease in collaboration with a licensed physician.

occupancy rate: The percentage of a hospital's capacity that is being used.

off-label use: The use of a medicine for indications other than those approved by a regulatory body.

operational knowledge: The body of information necessary to effectively understand how an organization works and what drives success.

orphan disease: A condition that affects only a relatively small number of patients.

osteopathic training: A branch of medical training that emphasizes holistic care and the use of spinal and other manual adjustments more than conventional allopathic training does; training typically leads to a doctor of osteopathic medicine (DO) degree.

outpatient services: Healthcare services that do not involve an overnight stay in a hospital or other institution; sometimes called *ambulatory care.*

overdiagnosis: A form of waste that occurs when an abnormality or disease is discovered through a diagnostic procedure or test but treating the condition would provide no real benefit to the patient.

over-the-counter (OTC) medicine: Medicine that can be purchased without a prescription.

overtreatment: A form of waste that occurs when an abnormality or condition is treated even though it is self-limiting in nature or poses no harm to the patient.

palliative care: Care delivered to a person with a life-limiting illness or condition for the primary purpose of making the patient feel better; it often involves pain management, cognitive behavioral therapy, and spiritual counseling.

pandemic: A widespread occurrence of infectious disease that affects a large population or region.

patient-centered medical home (PCMH): A model that provides patients with a single location that serves as a starting point for all medical concerns, thereby offering greater continuity of care and expert guidance to the healthcare delivery system.

patient safety: Freedom from accidental or preventable harm associated with medical care.

pay for performance: An approach in which payments to providers are tied to specific performance metrics, to create incentives for better performance.

personal health record (PHR): An electronic record through which patients can track and manage information about their health and the care they receive.

pharmacy benefit manager (PBM): A company that manages prescription drug benefits under contract with a managed care organization, self-insured company, government program, or other payer.

physician assistant (PA): A category of medical provider licensed to diagnose and treat illness and disease in collaboration with a licensed physician.

physician–hospital organization (PHO): A joint venture between a hospital and some or all of the physicians who have admitting privileges at the hospital.

plan-do-study-act (PDSA) cycle: A stepwise framework for incorporating incremental change into a process and measuring the results; also known as the Deming cycle.

population health: An approach to health that focuses on the health outcomes of a group of people within a population, as well as the distribution of outcomes within the group.

precision medicine: An emerging approach to medicine that takes into account each individual's genetic profile, environment, and lifestyle.

preferred provider organization (PPO): A health insurance plan with an established provider network; members receive maximum benefits when they use a preferred provider.

premium: The amount of money paid either by the insured individual or the group sponsor for insurance.

primary care: Services provided by clinicians who address a majority of a patient's personal healthcare needs and serve as the patient's first point of contact with the medical system.

primary prevention: Actions intended to prevent disease or injury before it occurs.

provider-induced demand (PID): A problem that occurs when a provider influences a patient's demand for care without regard for the patient's best interests.

psychosocial model of health: An approach that considers community and population well-being in the context of positive relationships, support networks, self-esteem, and responsibility.

public health: The practice of preventing disease, prolonging life, and promoting health through organized community effort.

quality: The degree to which services improve the likelihood of desired health outcomes and are in keeping with current professional knowledge.

quantum leadership: A concept that emphasizes "leading from the future" by projecting a mind-set that helps pull an organization toward a desired future state.

ransomware: A type of computer attack in which an organization's vital records are made inaccessible unless it pays money to a hacker to restore access.

rationing: Using a process to allocate scarce or expensive resources.

resource-based relative value scale (RBRVS): A system for determining payments for various medical services; the scale determines the rate at which Medicare will reimburse physicians.

sentinel event: An unexpected event that causes mortality or serious harm to a patient.

sick fund: A fund established to provide compensation to workers who became ill or injured on the job.

single-specialty hospital (SSH): A hospital that provides treatment relating to a single specialty (e.g., cardiac services).

skilled nursing facility (SNF): A long-term care facility that offers 24-hour comprehensive care to chronically ill and elderly people who are no longer able to live at home; commonly called a *nursing home*.

social engineering: An information security threat based on exploiting human interactions; such techniques generally try to manipulate or deceive people into breaking normal security procedures.

social justice theory: The idea that healthcare is a social good that should not be subject to strict economic principles.

stakeholders: All the individuals and groups that have a vested interest in an organization.

STEEEP: An acronym for six dimensions of quality, emphasizing that care should be safe, timely, effective, efficient, equitable, and patient centered.

SWOT analysis: A strategic planning technique that systematically looks at an organization's strengths, weaknesses, opportunities, and threats.

teaching hospital: A hospital that provides American Medical Association–approved graduate medical education for physicians and education for other medical professionals.

telehealth: The electronic delivery of health-related services, including patient education.

telemedicine: The electronic delivery of treatment to patients, as an alternative to face-to-face care.

total quality management (TQM): An approach to quality improvement that emphasizes long-term success through customer satisfaction and the participation of all members of the organization in improving processes, products, services, and the culture.

tripartite model of disease: An approach to disease that focuses on three components: agent, host, and environment.

Triple Aim: A concept, developed by the Institute for Healthcare Improvement, that emphasizes the pursuit of lower per capita costs, better experience of care, and improved health of populations.

universal coverage: A system in which every person has healthcare coverage via some mechanism, whether public or private.

upstreaming: Public health interventions that seek to address underlying social or economic barriers to receiving health services and achieving better health outcomes.

urgent care center: An outpatient facility that provides services to patients who have illnesses or injuries that are not life-threatening but that require immediate attention.

utilization review: An organized process by which to review admissions, duration of stay, services furnished, medical necessity of services, and efficiency of services at a healthcare organization.

ABOUT THE AUTHOR

Stephen L. Wagner, PhD, FACHE, LFACMPE, FAcEM, has been active in the healthcare field for more than 45 years, focusing on the US system and its ongoing transformation. Dr. Wagner has extensive experience as a healthcare executive and is devoted to educating future leaders in the field. He is an assistant professor and the executive in residence for the Master of Health Administration program in the School of Health and Medical Sciences at Seton Hall University. He has taught there for the past 23 years, since the beginning of the program.